MACROECONOMICS

ROGER A. ARNOLD
CALIFORNIA STATE UNIVERSITY
SAN MARCOS

9E

SOUTH-WESTERN
CENGAGE Learning™

Australia • Brazil • Japan • Korea • Mexico • Singapore • Spain • United Kingdom • United States

SOUTH-WESTERN
CENGAGE Learning™

Macroeconomics, 9E
Roger A. Arnold

Vice President of Editorial, Business: Jack W. Calhoun
Vice President/Editor-in-Chief: Alex von Rosenberg
Senior Acquisitions Editor: Michael W. Worls
Senior Developmental Editors: Jennifer E. Thomas, Laura Bofinger
Editorial Assistant: Lena Mortis
Marketing Manager: John Carey
Marketing Communications Manager: Sarah Greber
Senior Content Project Manager: Kim Kusnerak
Media Editor: Deepak Kumar
Senior Manufacturing Buyer: Sandee Milewski
Production Service: Macmillan Publishing Solutions
Compositor: Macmillan Publishing Solutions
Senior Art Director: Michelle Kunkler
Cover/Internal Designer: Ke Design/Mason, Ohio
Cover Image: © Digital Vision Photography
Rights Account Manager—Text: Mollika Basu
Photography Manager: Deanna Ettinger
Photo Researcher: Susan Van Etten

Library of Congress Control Number: 2008938432
ISBN-13: 978-0-324-78550-0
ISBN-10: 0-324-78550-X
Instructor's Edition ISBN 13: 978-0-324-78565-4
Instructor's Edition ISBN 10: 0-324-78565-8

South-Western Cengage Learning
5191 Natorp Boulevard
Mason, OH 45040
USA

Cengage Learning products are represented in Canada by Nelson Education, Ltd.

For your course and learning solutions, visit www.cengage.com
Purchase any of our products at your local college store or at our preferred online store **www.ichapters.com**

Printed in the United States of America
1 2 3 4 5 6 7 12 11 10 09 08

To
Sheila, Daniel,
and David

Brief Contents

Contents

CHAPTER 8 THE SELF-REGULATING ECONOMY 184

ECONOMICS 24/7

Natural Disasters and the Economy **194**

The Story Behind the Curves on the Blackboard **198**

OFFICE HOURS

"Do Economists Really Know What the Natural Unemployment Rate Equals?" **199**

CHAPTER 9 ECONOMIC INSTABILITY: A CRITIQUE OF THE SELF-REGULATING ECONOMY 203

ECONOMICS 24/7

Negative Savings and House Wealth **212**

The Multiplier on Spring Break **214**

Why Economists Might Disagree **224**

OFFICE HOURS

"Does a Lot Depend on Whether Wages Are Flexible or Inflexible?" **225**

CHAPTER 14 MONETARY POLICY 311

PART 5 EXPECTATIONS AND GROWTH

CHAPTER 15 EXPECTATIONS THEORY AND THE ECONOMY 333

CHAPTER 18 INTERNATIONAL FINANCE 394

ECONOMICS 24/7

OFFICE HOURS

CHAPTER 19 GLOBALIZATION AND INTERNATIONAL IMPACTS ON THE ECONOMY 423

ECONOMICS 24/7

OFFICE HOURS

Roger Arnold

Your Partner for Success

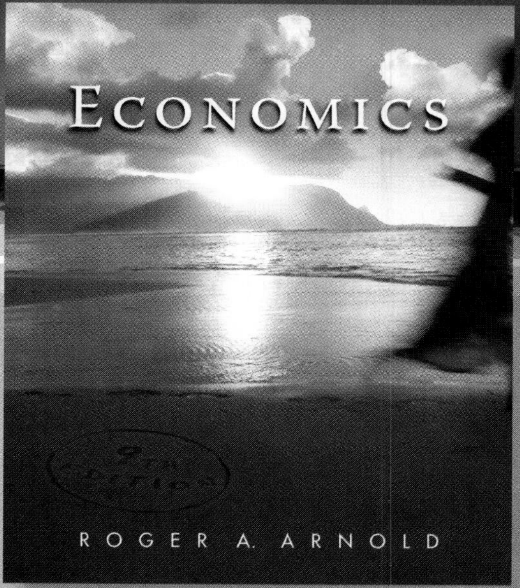

Let Roger Arnold's ***Economics*** be your partner for success. With innovative new pedagogical features, increased coverage of globalization, easy customization, and fully integrated digital and course management options, ***Economics*** may be the perfect solution for your classroom. Packed with intriguing pop culture examples, the text bolsters student interest by illustrating that economics is both a huge factor in how the world works, and an integral part of the day-to-day experiences of the average college student.

What's new in the 9th Edition?

Office Hours

This new feature seeks to emulate the kinds of questions students bring to Economics instructors after class. *Office Hours* explores key concepts such as how the money supply works; the purpose of the PPF; marginal revenue and marginal costs; and the purpose of the *AD/AS* framework.

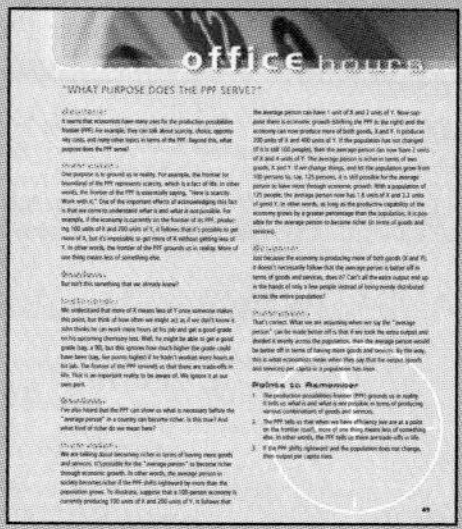

Enhanced "Thinking Like an Economist"

This classic feature now rotates through the narrative along with two new features: *Finding Economics* and *Common Misconceptions.* Incorporating *Thinking Like an Economist* into the narrative of each chapter helps to better emphasize the importance of developing this skill – to view the world through the lens of economic analysis.

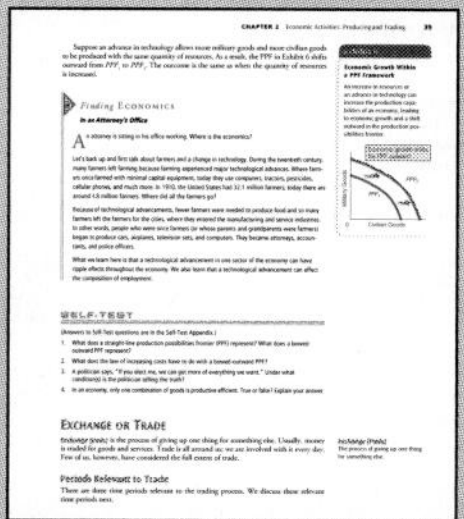

- ***Finding Economics*** illustrates the economics around us, such as how a technological advance in farming may end up resulting in more attorneys, accountants, or teachers.
- ***Common Misconceptions*** illuminates murky questions like whether one person's profit is another person's loss, and whether the wealthy really pay a lower percentage of taxes than others.

Enhanced Globalization Coverage

This chapter has been significantly expanded, revised and updated. It now offers a total picture of how globalization affects the U.S., and how economies interact throughout the world.

Many new applications

The Ninth Edition of *Economics* includes many new applications in the proven student favorite – Economics 24/7 features. Here are just a few of the applications that are new to the Ninth Edition, demonstrating Arnold's empahsis on current events that are relevant to students' lives:

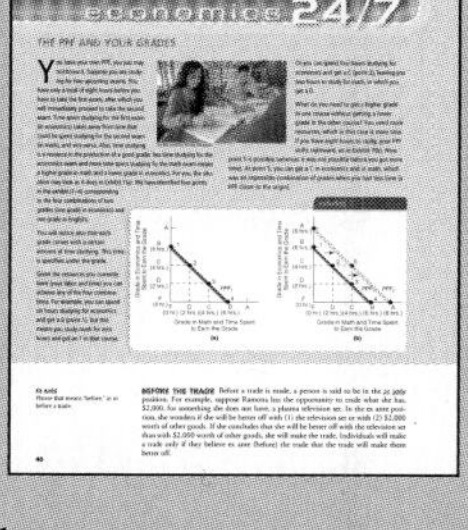

- Which is better, a tax rebate, or a tax bonus?
- Is economics at work in the plastic surgeon's office?
- What economic concepts are illustrated in the popular ABC television series, LOST?
- Is the law of demand at work for iPods?
- How can we accurately compare GDP between different countries?
- How does the government spend taxpayers' money?
- Why is it so hard to eat only one potato chip?

www.cengage.com/economics/arnold

Arnold's Study Solutions – Your Partner

With EconCentral and Tomlinson Videos, students waste no time reinforcing chapter concepts and sharpening their skills with interactive, hands-on applications.

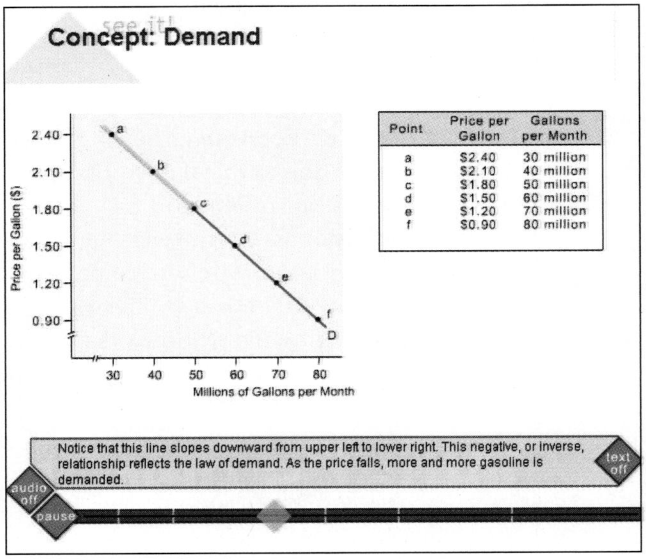

EconCentral

Multiple resources for learning and reinforcing principles concepts are now available in one place!

EconCentral is your one-stop shop for the learning tools and activities to help students succeed. Available for an additional price, EconCentral equips learners with a portal to a wealth of resources that help them both study and apply economic concepts. As they read and study the chapters, students can access video tutorials with *Ask the Instructor Videos.* They can review with *Flash Cards* and the *Graphing Workshop* as well as check their understanding of the chapter with *interactive quizzing.*

Ready to help students apply chapter concepts to the real world? EconCentral gives you ABC News videos, EconNews articles, Economic debates, Links to Economic Data, and more. All the study and application resources in EconCentral are organized by chapter to help your students get the most from *Economics, 9e* and from your lectures.

Visit **www.cengage.com/economics/arnold/9e/econcentral** to see the study options available!

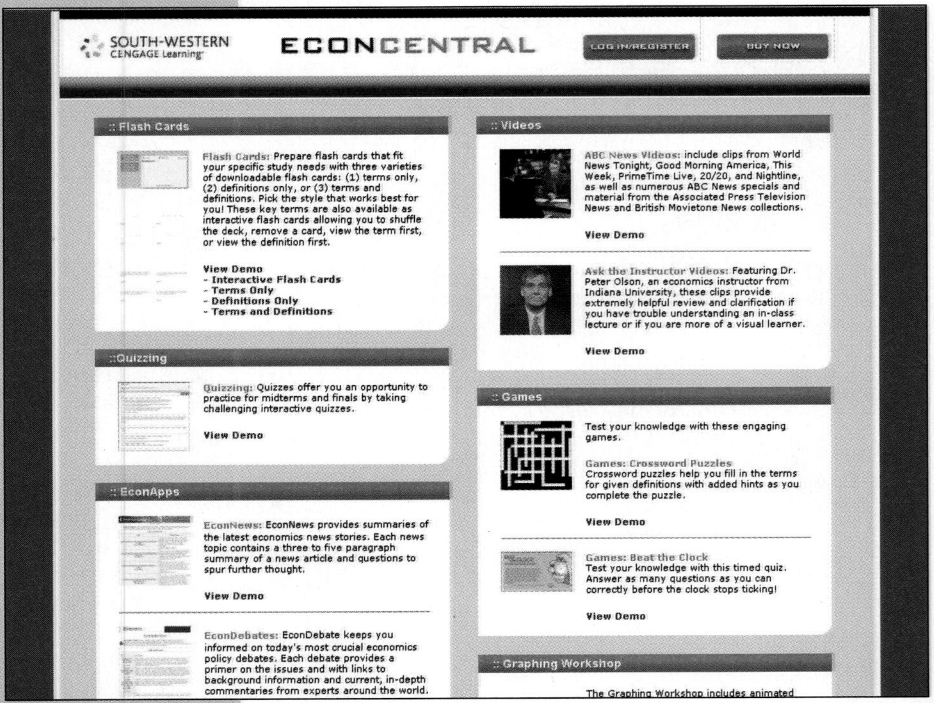

for Success

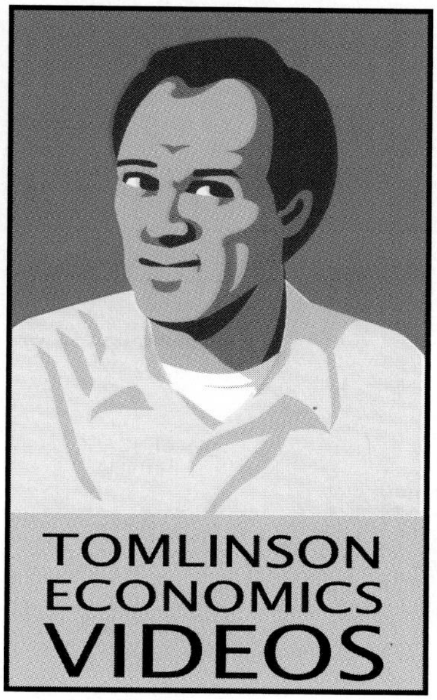

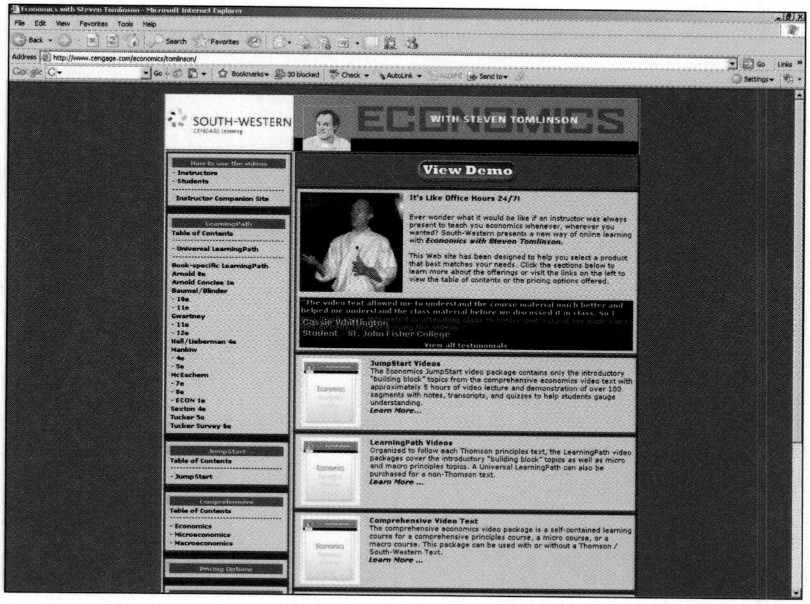

Tomlinson Economics Videos

Award winning teacher, actor and professional communicator, Steven Tomlinson (Ph.D. Economics, Stanford) walks students through all of the topics covered in principles of economics in an online video format. Segments are organized to follow the organization of the Arnold text and most videos include class notes that students can download and quizzes for students to test their understanding.

Find out more at **www.cengage.com/economics/tomlinson.**

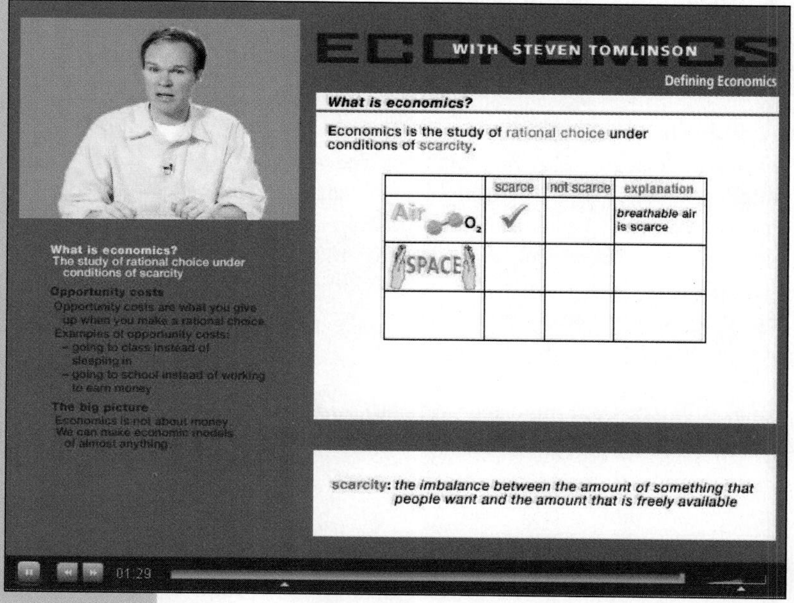

Arnold and Aplia™ – Your Partners for Success

Aplia

Founded in 2000 by economist and Stanford Professor Paul Romer, Aplia™ is dedicated to improving learning by increasing student effort and engagement. The most successful online product in Economics by far, Aplia has been used by more than 800,000 students at over 850 institutions.

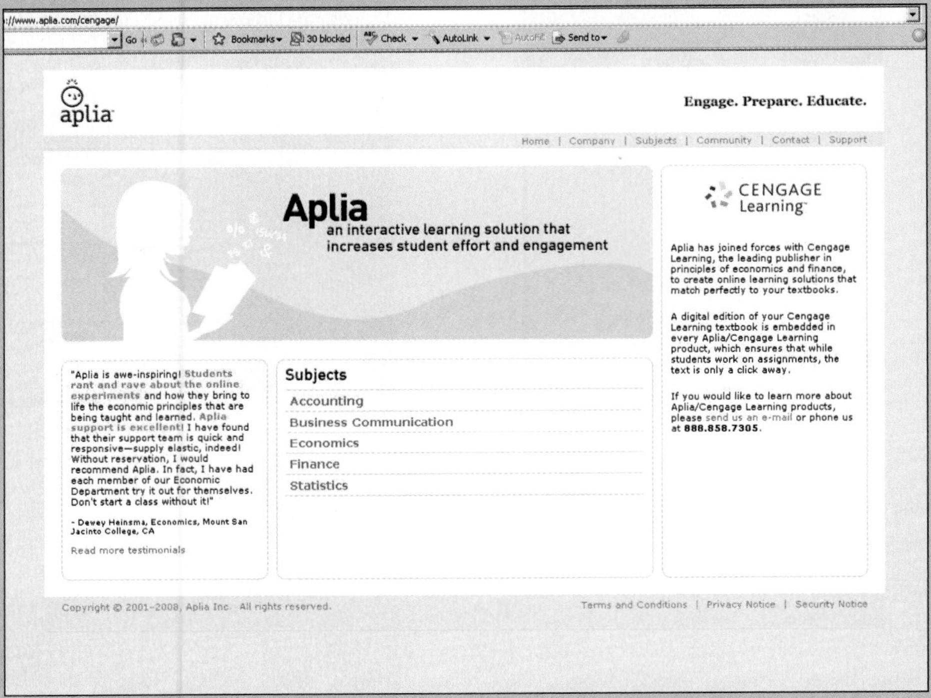

Visit **www.aplia.com/cengage** for more details. For help, questions, or a live demonstration, please contact Aplia at **support@aplia.com.**

Grade It Now by Aplia™

Good news! In response to student and professor feedback and research, Aplia Economics is moving to a new format called ***Grade It Now.***

What is ***Grade It Now?*** Looking into student behavior while using Aplia, we found that students were spending much more time using graded problem sets than practice problem sets, and that many students were not reading the available feedback. We wanted to give students more incentive to learn from their mistakes. ***Grade It Now*** provides that incentive by giving students immediate, comprehensive feedback and allowing multiple attempts at each question.

Do you have questions or want more details about ***Grade It Now?*** Send an e-mail to **info@aplia.com** or call 888.858.7305.

In Appreciation

This book could not have been written and published without the generous expert assistance of many people. A deep debt of gratitude is owed to the reviewers of the first through eighth editions and to the reviewers of this edition, the ninth.

First Edition Reviewers

Jack Adams
University of Arkansas, Little Rock

William Askwig
University of Southern Colorado

Michael Babcock
Kansas State University

Dan Barszcz
College of DuPage, Illinois

Robert Berry
Miami University, Ohio

George Bohler
Florida Junior College

Tom Bonsor
Eastern Washington University

Michael D. Brendler
Louisiana State University

Baird Brock
Central Missouri State University

Kathleen Bromley
Monroe Community College, New York

Douglas Brown
Georgetown University

Ernest Buchholz
Santa Monica Community College, California

Gary Burbridge
Grand Rapids Junior College, Michigan

Maureen Burton
California Polytechnic University, Pomona

Carol Carnes
Kansas State University

Paul Coomes
University of Louisville, Kentucky

Eleanor Craig
University of Delaware

Wilford Cummings
Grosmont College, California

Diane Cunningham
Glendale Community College, California

Douglas C. Darran
University of South Carolina

Edward Day
University of Southern Florida

Johan Deprez
University of Tennessee

James Dietz
California State University, Fullerton

Stuart Dorsey
University of West Virginia

Natalia Drury
Northern Virginia Community College

Lu Ann Duffus
California State University, Hayward

John Eckalbar
California State University, Chico

John Elliot
University of Southern California

Charles Fischer
Pittsburg State University, Kansas

John Gemello
San Francisco State University

Carl Guelzo
Cantonsville Community College, Maryland

Jan Hansen
University of Wisconsin, Eau Claire

John Henderson
Georgia State University

Ken Howard
East Texas Baptist University

Mark Karscig
Central Missouri State University

Stanley Keil
Ball State University, Indiana

Richard Kieffer
State University of New York, Buffalo

Gene Kimmett
William Rainey Harper College, Illinois

Luther Lawson
University of North Carolina

Frank Leori
College of San Mateo, California

Kenneth Long
New River Community College, Virginia

Michael Magura
University of Toledo, Ohio

Bruce McCrea
Lansing Community College, Michigan

Gerald McDougall
Wichita State University, Kansas

Kevin McGee
University of Wisconsin, Oshkosh

Francois Melese
Auburn University, Alabama

Herbert Miliken
American River College, California

Richard Miller
Pennsylvania State University

Ernest Moser
Northeast Louisiana University

Farhang Niroomand
University of Southern Mississippi

Eliot Orton
New Mexico State University

Marty Perline
Wichita State University, Kansas

Harold Petersen
Boston College

Douglas Poe
University of Texas, Austin

Joseph Rezney
St. Louis Community College, Missouri

Terry Ridgway
University of Nevada, Las Vegas

Thomas Romans
State University of New York, Buffalo

Robert Ross
Bloomsburg State College, Pennsylvania

Keith A. Rowley
Baylor University, Texas

Anandi Sahu
Oakland University, Michigan

Richard Scoggins
California State University, Long Beach

Paul Seidenstat
Temple University, Pennsylvania

Shahram Shafiee
North Harris County College, Texas

Alan Sleeman
Western Washington University

John Sondey
University of Idaho

Robert W. Thomas
Iowa State University

Richard L. Tontz
California State University, Northridge

Roger Trenary
Kansas State University

Bruce Vanderporten
Loyola University, Illinois

Thomas Weiss
University of Kansas

Richard O. Welch
University of Texas at San Antonio

Donald A. Wells
University of Arizona

John Wight
University of Richmond, Virginia

Thomas Wyrick
Southwest Missouri State University

Second Edition Reviewers

Scott Bloom
North Dakota State University

Thomas Carroll
University of Nevada, Las Vegas

Larry Cox
Southwest Missouri State University

Diane Cunningham
Los Angeles Valley College

Emit Deal
Macon College

Michael Fabritius
University of Mary Hardin Baylor

Frederick Fagal
Marywood College

Ralph Fowler
Diablo Valley College

Bob Gilette
Texas A&M University

Lynn Gillette
Indiana University, Indianapolis

Simon Hakim
Temple University

Lewis Karstensson
University of Nevada, Las Vegas

Abraham Kidane
California State University, Dominguez Hills

W. Barbara Killen
University of Minnesota

J. David Lages
Southwest Missouri State University

Anthony Lee
Austin Community College

Marjory Mabery
Delaware County Community College

Bernard Malamud
University of Nevada, Las Vegas

Michael Marlow
California Polytechnic State University, San Luis Obispo

Phil J. McLewin
Ramapo College of New Jersey

Tina Quinn
Arkansas State University

Terry Ridgway
University of Nevada, Las Vegas

Paul Snoonian
University of Lowell

Paul Taube
Pan American University

Roger Trenary
Kansas State University

Charles Van Eaton
Hillsdale College

Mark Wheeler
Bowling Green State University

Thomas Wyrick
Southwest Missouri State University

Third Edition Reviewers

Carlos Aguilar
University of Texas, El Paso

Rebecca Ann Benakis
New Mexico State University

Scott Bloom
North Dakota State University

Howard Erdman
Southwest Texas Junior College

Arthur Friedberg
Mohawk Valley Community College

Nancy A. Jianakoplos
Colorado State University

Lewis Karstensson
University of Nevada, Las Vegas

Rose Kilburn
Modesto Junior College

Ruby P. Kishan
Southeastern Community College

Duane Kline
Southeastern Community College

Charles A. Roberts
Western Kentucky University

Bill Robinson
University of Nevada, Las Vegas

Susan C. Stephenson
Drake University

Charles Van Eaton
Hillsdale College

Richard O. Welch
The University of Texas at San Antonio

Calla Wiemer
University of Hawaii at Manoa

Fourth Edition Reviewers

Uzo Agulefo
North Lake College

Kari Battaglia
University of North Texas

Scott Bloom
North Dakota State University

Harry Ellis, Jr.
University of North Texas

Mary Ann Hendryson
Western Washington University

Eugene Jones
Ohio State University

Ki Hoon Him
Central Connecticut State University

James McBrearty
University of Arizona

John A. Panagakis
Onondaga Community College

Bill Robinson
University of Nevada, Las Vegas

George E. Samuels
Sam Houston State University

Ed Scahill
University of Scranton

Charles Van Eaton
Hillsdale College

Thomas Wyrick
Southwest Missouri State University

Fifth Edition Reviewers

Kari Battaglia
University of North Texas

Douglas A. Conway
Mesa Community College

Lee A. Craig
North Carolina State University

Harry Ellis, Jr.
University of North Texas

Joe W. Essuman
University of Wisconsin, Waukesha

Dipak Ghosh
Emporia State University

Shirley J. Gideon
The University of Vermont

Mary Ann Hendryson
Western Washington University

Calvin A. Hoerneman
Delta College

George H. Jones
University of Wisconsin, Rock County

Donald R. Morgan
Monterey Peninsula College

John A. Panagakis
Onondaga Community College

Bill Robinson
University of Nevada, Las Vegas

Steve Robinson
The University of North Carolina at Wilmington

David W. Yoskowitz
Texas Tech University

Sixth Edition Reviewers

Hendrikus J.E.M. Brand
Albion College

Curtis Clarke
Dallas County Community College

Andrea Gorospe
Kent State University, Trumbull

Mehrdad Madresehee
Lycoming College

L. Wayne Plumly
Valdosta State University

Craig Rogers
Canisius College

Uri Simonsohn
Carnegie Mellon University

Philip Sprunger
Lycoming College

Lea Templer
College of the Canyons

Soumya Tohamy
Berry College

Lee Van Scyoc
University of Wisconsin, Oshkosh

Seventh Edition Reviewers

Pam Coates
San Diego Mesa College

Peggy F. Crane
Southwestern College

Richard Croxdale
Austin Community College

Harry Ellis, Jr.
University of North Texas

Craig Gallet
California State University, Sacramento

Kelly George
Embry-Riddle Aeronautical University

Anne-Marie Gilliam
Central Piedmont Community College

Richard C. Schiming
Minnesota State University, Mankato

Lea Templer
College of the Canyons

Jennifer VanGilder
California State University, Bakersfield

William W. Wilkes
Athens State University

Janice Yee
Wartburg College

Eighth Edition Reviewers

Dr. Clive R. Belfied
Queens College, City University of New York

Barry Bomboy
J. Sargeant Reynolds Community College

James Bryan
North Harris Montgomery Community College

Peggy F. Crane
Southwestern College

Richard Croxdale
Austin Community College

Harry Ellis, Jr.
University of North Texas

Kelly George
Embry Riddle Aeronautical University

Alan Kessler
Providence College

Denny Myers
Oklahoma City Community College

Charles Newton
Houston Community College

Ahmad Saranjam
Northeastern University

Jennifer VanGilder, PhD
California State University Bakersfield

Janice Yee
Wartburg College

Ninth Edition Reviewers

Bart Allen
Northern Oklahoma College

Nand Arora
Cleary University

Fathollah Bagheri
University of North Dakota

Mohammad Bajwa
Northampton Community College

Atin Basuchoudhary
Virginia Military Institute

Susan Bell
Seminole Community College

Douglas Campbell
University of Memphis

Franny Chan
Mt. San Antonio College

Stephen B. Davis
Southwest Minnesota State University

William L. Davis
University of Tennessee, Martin

James Dulgeroff
California State University, San Bernandino

Dr. J. Pat Fuller
Brevard Community College

Dr. Robert Garnett
Texas Christian University

Lynde Gilliam
Metropolitan State College of Denver

Judith A. Grenkowicz
Kirtland Community College

Pablo Hernandez
Hollins University

Philip L. Hersch
Wichita State University

Michael Heslop
Northern Virginia Community College (NOVA)

Chandrea Hopkins
College of Lake County

Brian K. Jackson
Oklahoma Wesleyan University

Bun Song Lee
Northwestern State University

Joanne Leoni
Johnson & Wales University

Michael L. Marlow
California Polytechnic State University

Peter Mavrokordatos
Tarrant County Community College

Dominic F. Minadeo
Troy University

Dr. Barbara B. Murray
Baltimore City Community College

Bernard J. Sharkey, Jr.
Louisiana State University

Joe Silverman
MiraCosta College

Martha Stuffler
Irvine Valley College

Vicky Tucker
Lewis University

Mary Louis White
Albright University

I would like to thank Peggy Crane of Southwestern College, who revised the Test Bank, and Jane Himarios of the University of Texas at Arlington, who revised the Instructor's Manual. I owe a dept of gratitude to all the fine and creative people I worked with at South-Western/Cengage Learning. These persons include Jack Calhoun; Alex von Rosenberg; Michael Worls, Executive Editor for Economics; Jennifer Thomas, Senior Developmental Editor; Kim Kusnerak, Senior Content Project Manager; John Carey, Senior Marketing Manager; Michelle Kunkler, Senior Art Director; and Sandee Milewski, Senior Frontlist Buyer.

My deepest debt of gratitude goes to my wife, Sheila, and to my two sons, David, eighteen years old, and Daniel, twenty one years old. They continue to make all my days happy ones.

Roger A. Arnold

CHAPTER 1

WHAT ECONOMICS IS ABOUT

Introduction You are about to begin your study of economics. Before we start discussing particular topics in economics, we think it best to give you an overview of *what economics is* and of some of the *key concepts* in economics. These key concepts can be compared to musical notes: just as musical notes repeat themselves in any song (you hear the musical note G over and over again), so do the key concepts in economics repeat themselves. Some of the key concepts we discuss include scarcity, opportunity cost, efficiency, marginal decision making, and exchange.

A DEFINITION OF ECONOMICS

In this section, we discuss a few key economic concepts; then we incorporate knowledge of these concepts into a definition of economics.

Goods and Bads

Economists talk about *goods* and *bads*. A **good** is anything that gives a person **utility** or satisfaction. Here is a partial list of some goods: a computer, a car, a watch, a television set, friendship, and love. You will notice from our list that a good can be either tangible or intangible. A computer is a tangible good; friendship is an intangible good. Simply put, for something to be a good (whether tangible or intangible), it simply has to give you utility or satisfaction.

A **bad** is something that gives a person **disutility** or dissatisfaction. If the flu gives you disutility or dissatisfaction, then it is a bad. If the constant nagging of an acquaintance is something that gives you disutility or dissatisfaction, then it is a bad.

People want goods and they do not want bads. In fact, they will pay to get goods ("Here is $1,000 for the computer"), and they will pay to get rid of bads they currently have ("I'd be willing to pay you, doctor, if you can prescribe something that will shorten the time I have the flu").

Good
Anything from which individuals receive utility or satisfaction.

Utility
The satisfaction one receives from a good.

Bad
Anything from which individuals receive disutility or dissatisfaction.

Disutility
The dissatisfaction one receives from a bad.

Can something be a *good* for one person and a *bad* for another person? Well, because a good is something that gives one utility and a bad is something that gives one disutility, this question is simply asking whether something can give utility to one person and disutility to another. Can you identify such a thing? What about cigarette smoking? For some people, smoking cigarettes gives them utility; for other people, it gives them disutility. We conclude that smoking cigarettes can be a good for some people and a bad for others. This must be why the wife tells her husband, "If you want to smoke, you should do it outside." In other words, get those *bads* away from me.

Resources

Goods do not just appear before us when we snap our fingers. It takes resources to produce goods. (Sometimes *resources* are referred to as *inputs* or *factors of production.*)

Generally, economists divide resources into four broad categories: *land, labor, capital,* and *entrepreneurship.* **Land** includes natural resources, such as minerals, forests, water, and unimproved land. For example, oil, wood, and animals fall into this category. (Sometimes economists refer to this category simply as *natural resources.*)

Labor consists of the physical and mental talents people contribute to the production process. For example, a person building a house is using his or her own labor.

Capital consists of produced goods that can be used as inputs for further production. Factories, machinery, tools, computers, and buildings are examples of capital. One country might have more capital than another. This means that it has more factories, machinery, tools, and so on.

Entrepreneurship refers to the particular talent that some people have for organizing the resources of land, labor, and capital to produce goods, seek new business opportunities, and develop new ways of doing things.

Land
All natural resources, such as minerals, forests, water, and unimproved land.

Labor
The physical and mental talents people contribute to the production process.

Capital
Produced goods that can be used as inputs for further production, such as factories, machinery, tools, computers, and buildings.

Entrepreneurship
The particular talent that some people have for organizing the resources of land, labor, and capital to produce goods, seek new business opportunities, and develop new ways of doing things.

Scarcity and a Definition of Economics

We are now ready to define a key concept in economics: *scarcity.* **Scarcity** is the condition in which our wants (for goods) are greater than the limited resources (land, labor, capital, and entrepreneurship) available to satisfy those wants. In other words, we want goods, but there are just not enough resources available to provide us with all the goods we want.

Look at it this way: Our wants (for goods) are infinite, but our resources (which we need to produce the goods) are finite. Scarcity is our infinite wants hitting up against finite resources.

Many economists say that if scarcity didn't exist, neither would economics. In other words, if our wants weren't greater than the limited resources available to satisfy them, there would be no field of study called economics. This is similar to saying that if matter and motion didn't exist, neither would physics or that if living things didn't exist, neither would biology. For this reason, we define **economics** in this text as the science of scarcity. More completely, *economics is the science of how individuals and societies deal with the fact that wants are greater than the limited resources available to satisfy those wants.*

Scarcity
The condition in which our wants are greater than the limited resources available to satisfy those wants.

Economics
The science of scarcity; the science of how individuals and societies deal with the fact that wants are greater than the limited resources available to satisfy those wants.

Thinking like AN ECONOMIST

Scarcity Affects Everyone

Everyone in the world has to face scarcity, even billionaires. Take, for example, Bill Gates, the cofounder of Microsoft and one of the richest people in the world. He may be able to satisfy more of his wants for tangible goods (houses, cars) than most people, but this doesn't mean he has the resources to satisfy all his wants. His wants might include more time with his children, more friendship, no disease in the world, peace on earth, and a hundred other things that he does not have the resources to "produce."

economics 24/7

LOST

Lost is an ABC television series; the pilot for the show aired on September 22, 2004. The show is about people who have survived a plane crash (Oceanic flight 815) and now inhabit a mysterious tropical island.

© 2007 AMERICAN BROADCASTING COMPANY, INC.

The tropical island is unlike any island anyone has ever seen or visited before. We'll show you just how later, but before we do, let's return to our discussion of scarcity, goods, and resources. We know that scarcity is a condition where our wants for goods are greater than the resources available to satisfy those wants.

Now ask: If you didn't need resources to produce goods—if you didn't need *anything* to produce goods—would you have overcome scarcity? Would you have defeated scarcity?

The answer is yes. Obviously the only reason you cannot have all the goods you want is because resources are needed to produce goods, and there are a finite number of resources in the world. Wood is needed to produce a chair, labor is needed to produce a computer, and capital is needed to produce a car. If you didn't need wood, labor, or capital to produce any good—if you didn't need *anything* to produce goods—then you could have all the goods you desire. And if you could have all the goods you desire, you would have defeated or overcome scarcity. Make sense?

With this as background, listen to the words of Ben, one of the characters on *Lost*. In the third season of *Lost*, Episode 13 ("The Man from Tallahassee"), he speaks the following words to John Locke, one of the survivors of the plane crash.

I can show you things. Things I know you want to see very badly. Let me put it so you'll understand. Picture a box. You know something about boxes, don't you John? What if I told you that somewhere on this island there's a very large box . . . and whatever you imagined . . . whatever you wanted to be in it . . . when you opened that box, there it would be. What would you say about that, John?

They key words are, "there's a very large box . . . and whatever you imagined . . . whatever you wanted to be in it . . . when you opened that box, there it would be." In other words, if you wish for a good—any good—there it will be. You do not have to produce the good, you do not need any resources before you can produce the good. All you have to do is wish for it and "there it would be."

In other words, the box on the *Lost* island is all anyone needs, and then with that box, anything you wish for will be yours. That is a setting in which scarcity is no more. And because scarcity is no more, neither is choice, which is one of the effects of scarcity. There is no need to decide between good X and Y, you can have both. And what about the cost of these goods? Is there a cost to them? Certainly not, for if you don't have to give up one thing to get something else (which is the case in real life), the opportunity cost of what you get is zero. Wishing for X at 10:05 doesn't mean you have given up the chance to get Y, because with a magic box, you can wish for Y at 10:05 and one second.

In conclusion, the *Lost* island is truly an unusual and very different island. It is an island where for some people scarcity, choices, and costs are no more. You just might say that it is a make-believe island.

THINKING IN TERMS OF SCARCITY'S EFFECTS Scarcity has effects. Here are three: (1) the need to make choices, (2) the need for a rationing device, and (3) competition. We describe each.

Choices People have to make choices because of scarcity. Because our unlimited wants are greater than our limited resources, some wants must go unsatisfied. We must choose which wants we will satisfy and which we will not. Jeremy asks: Do I go to Hawaii or do I pay off my car loan earlier? Ellen asks: Do I buy the new sweater or two new shirts?

Rationing Device
A means for deciding who gets what of available resources and goods.

Need for a Rationing Device A **rationing device** is a means of deciding who gets what. It is scarcity that implies the need for a rationing device. If people have infinite wants for goods and there are only limited resources to produce the goods, then a rationing device must be used to decide who gets the available quantity of goods. Dollar price is a rationing device. For example, there are 100 cars on the lot and everyone wants a new car. How do we decide who gets what quantity of the new cars? The answer is "use the rationing device dollar price." Those people who pay the dollar price for the new car end up with a new car.

Is dollar price a fair rationing device? Doesn't it discriminate against the poor? After all, the poor have fewer dollars than the rich, so the rich can get more of what they want than can the poor. True, dollar price does discriminate against the poor. But then, as the economist knows, every rationing device discriminates against someone.

Suppose that dollar price could not be used as a rationing device tomorrow. Some rationing device would still be necessary because scarcity would still exist. How would we ration gas at the gasoline station, food in the grocery store, or tickets for the Super Bowl? Let's consider some alternatives to dollar price as a rationing device.

Suppose first come, first served is the rationing device. For example, suppose there are only 40,000 Super Bowl tickets. If you are one of the first 40,000 in line for a Super Bowl ticket, then you get a ticket. If you are person number 40,001 in line, you don't. Such a method discriminates against those who can't get in line quickly. What about slow walkers or people with a disability? What about people without cars who can't drive to where the tickets are distributed?

Or suppose brute force is the rationing device. For example, if there are 40,000 Super Bowl tickets, then as long as you can take a ticket away from someone who has a ticket, the ticket is yours. Who does this rationing method discriminate against? Obviously, it discriminates against the weak and non-aggressive.

Or suppose beauty is the rationing device. The more beautiful you are, the better your chance of getting a Super Bowl ticket. Again, the rationing device discriminates against someone.

These and many other alternatives to dollar price could be used as a rationing device. However, each discriminates against someone, and none is clearly superior to dollar price.

In addition, if first come, first served, brute force, beauty, or another alternative to dollar price is the rationing device, what incentive would the producer of a good have to produce the good? With dollar price as a rationing device, a person produces computers and sells them for money. He then takes the money and buys what he wants. But if the rationing device were, say, brute force, he would not have an incentive to produce. Why produce anything when someone will end up taking it away from you? In short, in a world where dollar price isn't the rationing device, people are likely to produce much less than in a world where dollar price is the rationing device.

Scarcity and Competition Do you see much competition in the world today? Are people competing for jobs? Are states and cities competing for businesses? Are students competing for grades? The answer to all these questions is yes. The economist wants to know why this competition exists and what form it takes. First, the economist concludes, *competition exists because of scarcity.* If there were enough resources to satisfy all our seemingly unlimited wants, people would not have to compete for the available but limited resources.

Second, the economist sees that competition takes the form of people trying to get more of the rationing device. If dollar price is the rationing device, people will compete to earn dollars. Look at your own case. You are a college student working for a degree. One reason (but perhaps not the only reason) you are attending college is to earn a higher income after graduation. But why do you want a higher income? You want it because it will allow you to satisfy more of your wants.

Suppose muscular strength (measured by lifting weights) were the rationing device instead of dollar price. People with more muscular strength would receive more resources and goods than people with less muscular strength would receive. In this situation, people would compete for muscular strength. (Would they spend more time at the gym lifting weights?) The lesson is simple: *Whatever the rationing device, people will compete for it.*

Finding ECONOMICS

At the Campus Book Store

To learn economics well, you must practice what you learn. One of the ways of "practicing economics" is to find economics in everyday scenes of life. With this in mind, consider the following scene: You are in the campus book store buying a book for your computer science course. You are currently handing over $65 to the cashier. Can you find the economics in this simple scene? Before you read on, think about it for a minute.

Let's work backward to find the economics. You are currently handing the cashier $65. We know that dollar price is a rationing device. But let's now ask ourselves why we would need a rationing device to get the book. The answer is scarcity. In other words, scarcity is casting its long shadow there in the book store when you buy a book. We have found one of the key economic concepts—scarcity—in the campus book store. (If you also said that a book is a good, then you have found even more economics in the book store. Can you find more than scarcity and a good?)

SELF-TEST

(Answers to Self-Test questions are in the Self-Test Appendix.)

1. Scarcity is the condition of finite resources. True or false? Explain your answer.
2. How does competition arise out of scarcity?
3. How does choice arise out of scarcity?

KEY CONCEPTS IN ECONOMICS

There are numerous key concepts in economics—concepts that define the field. We discuss a few of these concepts next.

Opportunity Cost

So far we have established the fact that people must make choices because scarcity exists. In other words, because our seemingly unlimited wants push up against limited resources, some wants must go unsatisfied. We must therefore *choose* which wants we will satisfy and which we will not. The most highly valued opportunity or alternative forfeited when a choice is made is known as **opportunity cost.** Every time you make a choice, you incur an opportunity cost. For example, you have chosen to read this chapter. In making this choice, you denied yourself the benefits of doing something else. You could have watched television, emailed a friend, taken a nap, eaten a few slices of pizza, read a novel, shopped for a new computer, and so on. Whatever you *would have chosen* to do had you decided not to read this chapter is the opportunity cost of your reading this chapter. For example,

Opportunity Cost
The most highly valued opportunity or alternative forfeited when a choice is made.

if you would have watched television had you chosen not to read this chapter—if this was your next best alternative—then the opportunity cost of reading this chapter is watching television.

Common Misconceptions

Think "No Free Lunch"

Economists are fond of saying that *there is no such thing as a free lunch.* This catchy phrase expresses the idea that opportunity costs are incurred when choices are made. Perhaps this is an obvious point, but consider how often people mistakenly assume there *is* a free lunch. For example, some parents think education is free because they do not pay tuition for their children to attend public elementary school. Sorry, but that is a misconception. Free implies no sacrifice and no opportunities forfeited, which is not true in regard to elementary school education. Resources that could be used for other things are used to provide elementary school education.

Consider the people who speak about free medical care, free housing, free bridges ("there is no charge to cross it"), and free parks. Sorry, again, but free medical care, free housing, free bridges, and free parks are misconceptions. The resources that provide medical care, housing, bridges, and parks could have been used in other ways.

Opportunity Cost and Behavior

Economists believe that a change in opportunity cost can change a person's behavior. For example, consider Ryan, who is a sophomore at Cornell University in Ithaca, New York. He attends classes Monday through Thursday of every week. Every time he chooses to go to class, he gives up the opportunity to do something else, such as the opportunity to earn $10 an hour working at a job. The opportunity cost of Ryan spending an hour in class is $10.

Now let's raise the opportunity cost of attending class. On Tuesday, we offer Ryan $70 to skip his economics class. He knows that if he attends his economics class, he will forfeit $70. What will Ryan do? An economist would predict that as the opportunity cost of attending class increases relative to the benefits of attending class, Ryan is less likely to attend class.

This is how economists think about behavior, whether it is Ryan's or your own. *The higher the opportunity cost of doing something, the less likely it will be done.* This is part of the economic way of thinking.

Before you continue, look at Exhibit 1, which summarizes some of the things about scarcity, choice, and opportunity cost up to this point.

exhibit 1

Scarcity and Related Concepts

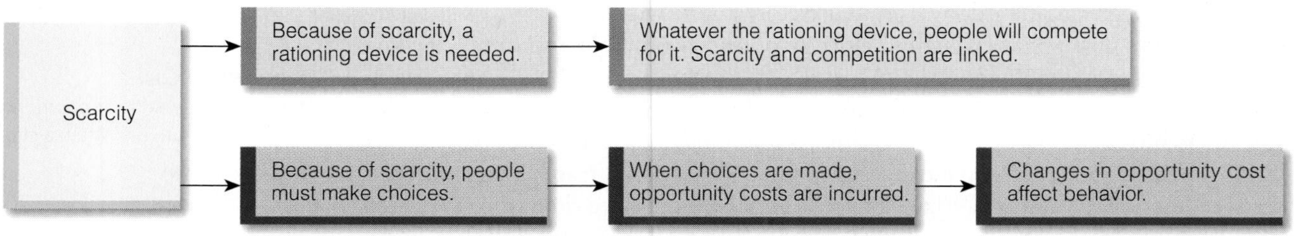
Scarcity
Because of scarcity, a rationing device is needed.
Whatever the rationing device, people will compete for it. Scarcity and competition are linked.
Because of scarcity, people must make choices.
When choices are made, opportunity costs are incurred.
Changes in opportunity cost affect behavior.

economics 24/7

WHY DIDN'T JESSICA ALBA GO TO COLLEGE?

Jessica Alba, the actress, was born on April 28, 1981. After graduating from high school, Jessica Alba chose not to go to college. But why didn't she go to college? It's not because she couldn't get into a college or couldn't afford college. Jessica Alba did not go to college because it was costlier for her to go to college than it is for most 18- to 25-year-olds to attend college.

© AP PHOTO/MATT SAYLES

To understand, think of what it costs you to attend college. If you pay $2,000 tuition a semester for eight semesters, the full tuition amounts to $16,000. However, $16,000 is not the full cost of your attending college because if you were not a student, you could be earning income working at a job. For example, you could be working at a full-time job earning $25,000 annually. Certainly, this $25,000, or at least part of it if you are currently working part time, is forfeited because you attend college. It is part of the cost of your attending college.

Thus, the *tuition* cost may be the same for everyone who attends your college, but the *opportunity cost* is not. Some people have higher opportunity costs for attending college than others do. Jessica Alba had high opportunity costs for attending college. She would have to give up the income she earned from commericals, TV shows, and movies.

This discussion illustrates two related points made in this chapter. First, *the higher the opportunity cost of doing something, the less likely it will be done.* The opportunity cost of attending college is higher for Jessica Alba than it (probably) is for you, and that is why you are in college and Jessica Alba did not go to college.

Second, according to economists, *individuals think and act in terms of costs and benefits and only undertake actions if they expect the benefits to outweigh the costs.* Jessica Alba was likely to see certain benefits to attending college—just as you see certain benefits to attending college. However, those benefits were insufficient for her to attend college because benefits are not all that matter. Costs matter too. For Jessica Alba, the costs of attending college were much higher than the benefits, and so she chose not to attend college. In your case, the benefits are higher than the costs, and so you have decided to attend college.

Benefits and Costs

If it were possible to eliminate air pollution completely, should all air pollution be eliminated? If your answer is yes, then you are probably focusing on the *benefits* of eliminating air pollution. For example, one benefit might be healthier individuals. Certainly, individuals who do not breathe polluted air have fewer lung disorders than people who do breathe polluted air.

But benefits rarely come without costs. The economist reminds us that although there are benefits to eliminating pollution, there are costs too. To illustrate, one way to eliminate all car pollution tomorrow is to pass a law stating that anyone caught driving a car will go to prison for 40 years. With such a law in place, and enforced, very few people would drive cars, and all car pollution would be a thing of the past. Presto! Cleaner air! However, many people would think that the cost of obtaining that cleaner air is too high. Someone might say, "I want cleaner air, but not if I have to completely give up driving my car. How will I get to work?"

What distinguishes the economist from the non-economist is that the economist thinks in terms of *both* costs *and* benefits. Often, the non-economist thinks in terms of one or the other. There are benefits from studying, but there are costs too. There are benefits from coming to class, but there are costs too. There are costs to getting up early each morning and exercising, but let's not forget that there are benefits too.

Decisions Made at the Margin

It is late at night and you have already studied three hours for your biology test tomorrow. You look at the clock and wonder if you should study another hour. How would you summarize your thinking process? What question or questions do you ask yourself to decide whether or not to study another hour?

Perhaps without knowing it, you think in terms of the costs and benefits of further study. You probably realize that there are certain benefits from studying an additional hour (you may be able to raise your grade a few points), but there are costs too (you will get less sleep or have less time to watch television or talk on the phone with a friend). Thinking in terms of costs and benefits, however, doesn't tell us *how* you think in terms of costs and benefits. For example, when deciding what to do, do you look at the total costs and total benefits of the proposed action, or do you look at something less than the total costs and benefits? According to economists, for most decisions, you think in terms of *additional,* or *marginal,* costs and benefits, not *total* costs and benefits. That's because most decisions deal with making a small, or additional, change.

To illustrate, suppose you just finished eating a hamburger and drinking a soda for lunch. You are still a little hungry and are considering whether or not to order another hamburger. An economist would say that in deciding whether or not to order another hamburger, you will compare the additional benefits of the additional hamburger to the additional costs of the additional hamburger. In economics, the word *marginal* is a synonym for *additional.* So we say that you will compare the **marginal benefits** of the (next) hamburger to the **marginal costs** of the (next) hamburger. If the marginal benefits are greater than the marginal costs, you obviously expect a net benefit to ordering the next hamburger, and therefore, you order the next hamburger. If, however, the marginal benefits are less than the marginal costs, you obviously expect a net cost to ordering the next hamburger, and therefore, you do not order the next hamburger.

Marginal Benefits
Additional benefits. The benefits connected to consuming an additional unit of a good or undertaking one more unit of an activity.

Marginal Costs
Additional costs. The costs connected to consuming an additional unit of a good or undertaking one more unit of an activity.

Condition	Action
MB of next hamburger > *MC* of next hamburger	Buy next hamburger
MB of next hamburger < *MC* of next hamburger	Do not buy next hamburger

What you don't consider when making this decision are the total benefits and total costs of hamburgers. That's because the benefits and costs connected with the first hamburger (the one you have already eaten) are no longer relevant to the current decision. You are not deciding between eating two hamburgers and eating no hamburgers; your decision is whether to eat a second hamburger after you have already eaten a first hamburger.

According to economists, when individuals make decisions by comparing marginal benefits to marginal costs, they are making **decisions at the margin**. The president of the United States makes a decision at the margin when deciding whether or not to talk another 10 minutes with the speaker of the House of Representatives, the employee makes a decision at the margin when deciding whether or not to work two hours overtime, and the economics professor makes a decision at the margin when deciding whether or not to put an additional question on the final exam.

Decisions at the Margin
Decision making characterized by weighing the additional (marginal) benefits of a change against the additional (marginal) costs of a change with respect to current conditions.

Efficiency

What is the right amount of time to study for a test? In economics, the "right amount" of anything is the "optimal" or "efficient" amount, and the efficient amount is the amount for which the marginal benefits equal the marginal costs. Stated differently, you have achieved **efficiency** when the marginal benefits equal the marginal costs.

Efficiency
Exists when marginal benefits equal marginal costs.

Suppose you are studying for an economics test, and for the first hour of studying, the marginal benefits (*MB*) are greater than the marginal costs (*MC*):

$$MB \text{ studying first hour} > MC \text{ studying first hour}$$

Given this condition, you will certainly study for the first hour. After all, it is worthwhile: The additional benefits are greater than the additional costs, so there is a net benefit to studying.

Suppose for the second hour of studying, the marginal benefits are still greater than the marginal costs:

$$MB \text{ studying second hour} > MC \text{ studying second hour}$$

You will study for the second hour because the additional benefits are still greater than the additional costs. In other words, it is worthwhile studying the second hour. In fact, you will continue to study as long as the marginal benefits are greater than the marginal costs. Exhibit 2 graphically illustrates this discussion.

The marginal benefit (*MB*) curve of studying is downward sloping because we have assumed that the benefits of studying for the first hour are greater than the benefits of studying for the second hour and so on. The marginal cost (*MC*) curve of studying is upward sloping because we assume that it costs a person more (in terms of goods forfeited) to study the second hour than the first, more to study the third than the second, and so on. (If we assume the additional costs of studying are constant over time, the *MC* curve is horizontal.)

In the exhibit, the marginal benefits of studying equal the marginal costs at three hours. So three hours is the efficient length of time to study in this situation. At fewer than three hours, the marginal benefits of studying are greater than the marginal costs; thus, at all these hours, there are net benefits from studying. At more than three hours, the marginal

exhibit 2

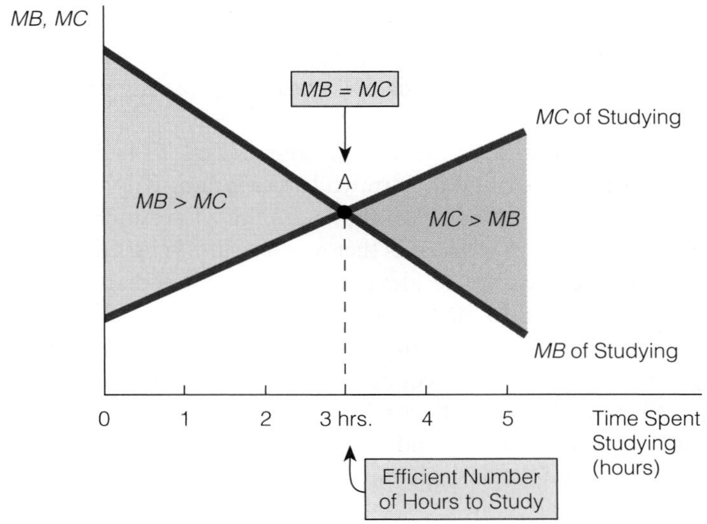

Efficiency

MB = marginal benefits and *MC* = marginal costs. In the exhibit, the *MB* curve of studying is downward sloping and the *MC* curve of studying is upward sloping. As long as *MB* > *MC*, the person will study. The person stops studying when *MB* = *MC*. This is where efficiency is achieved.

costs of studying are greater than the marginal benefits, and so it wouldn't be worthwhile to study beyond three hours.

MAXIMIZING NET BENEFITS Take another look at Exhibit 2. Suppose you had stopped studying after the first hour (or after the 60th minute). Would you have given up anything? Yes, you would have given up the net benefits of studying longer. To illustrate, notice that between the first and the second hour, the marginal benefits (*MB*) curve lies above the marginal costs (*MC*) curve. This means there are net benefits to studying the second hour. But if you hadn't studied that second hour—if you had stopped after the first hour—then you would have given up the opportunity to collect those net benefits. The same analysis holds for the third hour. We conclude that by studying three hours (but not one minute longer), you have maximized net benefits. In short, efficiency (which is consistent with $MB = MC$) is also consistent with maximizing net benefits.

Thinking like AN ECONOMIST

No $10 Bills on the Sidewalk

An economist says that people try to maximize their net benefits. You ask for proof. The economist says, "You don't find any $10 bills on the sidewalk." What is the economist getting at by making this statement? Well, keep in mind that the reason you don't find any $10 bills on the sidewalk is because if there were a $10 bill on the sidewalk, the first person to see it would pick it up, so that when you came along it wouldn't be there. But why would the first person to find the $10 bill pick it up? Because people don't pass by net benefits, and picking up the $10 bill comes with net benefits. The *benefits* of having an additional $10 are obvious; the *costs* of obtaining the additional $10 bill are simply what you give up during the time you are stooping down to pick it up. In short, the marginal benefits are likely to be greater than the marginal costs (giving us net benefits) and that is why the $10 bill is picked up. Saying there are no $10 bills on the sidewalk is the same as saying no one leaves net benefits on the sidewalk; instead, people try to maximize net benefits.

Unintended Effects

Economists think in terms of unintended effects. Consider an example. Andres, 16 years old, currently works after school at a grocery store. He earns $6.50 an hour. Suppose the state legislature passes a law specifying that the minimum dollar wage a person can be paid to do a job is $8.50 an hour. The legislators' intention in passing the law is to help people like Andres earn more income.

Will the $8.50 an hour legislation have the intended effect? Perhaps not. The manager of the grocery store may not find it worthwhile to continue employing Andres if she has to pay him $8.50 an hour. In other words, Andres may have a job at $6.50 an hour but not at $8.50 an hour. If the law specifies that no one will earn less than $8.50 an hour and the manager of the grocery store decides to fire Andres rather than pay this amount, then an unintended effect of the $8.50 an hour legislation is Andres' losing his job.

As another example, let's analyze mandatory seatbelt laws to see if they have any unintended effects. States have laws that require drivers to wear seatbelts. The intended effect is to reduce the number of car fatalities by making it more likely drivers will survive an accident.

Could these laws have an unintended effect? Some economists think so. They look at accident fatalities in terms of this equation:

$$\text{Total number of fatalities} = \text{Number of accidents} \times \text{Fatalities per accident}$$

For example, if there are 200,000 accidents and 0.10 fatalities per accident, the total number of fatalities is 20,000.

The objective of a mandatory seatbelt program is to reduce the total number of fatalities by reducing the fatalities per accident. Many studies have found that wearing seatbelts does just this. If you are in an accident, you have a better chance of not being killed if you are wearing a seatbelt.

Let's assume that with seatbelts, there are 0.08 instead of 0.10 fatalities per accident. If there are still 200,000 accidents, this means that the total number of fatalities falls from 20,000 to 16,000. Thus, there is a drop in the total number of fatalities if fatalities per accident are reduced and the number of accidents is constant.

Number of Accidents	Fatalities per Accident	Total Number of Fatalities
200,000	0.10	20,000
200,000	0.08	16,000

However, some economists wonder if the number of accidents stays constant. Specifically, they suggest that seatbelts may have an unintended effect: *The number of accidents may increase.* This happens because wearing seatbelts may make drivers feel safer. Feeling safer may cause them to take chances that they wouldn't ordinarily take—such as driving faster or more aggressively, or concentrating less on their driving and more on the music on the radio. For example, if the number of accidents rises to 250,000, then the total number of fatalities is 20,000.

Number of Accidents	Fatalities per Accident	Total Number of Fatalities
200,000	0.10	20,000
250,000	0.08	20,000

We conclude the following: If a mandatory seatbelt law reduces the number of fatalities per accident (intended effect) but increases the number of accidents (unintended effect), it may, contrary to popular belief, not reduce the total number of fatalities. In fact, some economic studies show just this.

What does all this mean for you? You may be safer if you know that this unintended effect exists and you adjust accordingly. To be specific, when you wear your seatbelt, your chances of getting hurt in a car accident are less than if you don't wear your seatbelt. But if this added sense of protection causes you to drive less carefully than you would otherwise, then you could unintentionally offset the measure of protection your seatbelt provides. To reduce the probability of hurting yourself and others in a car accident, *the best policy is to wear a seatbelt and to drive as carefully as you would if you weren't wearing a seatbelt.* Knowing about the unintended effect of wearing your seatbelt could save your life.

Exchange

Exchange or **trade** is the process of giving up one thing for something else. Economics is sometimes called the "science of exchange" because so much that is discussed in economics has to do with exchange.

Exchange (Trade)
The process of giving up one thing for another.

We start with a basic question: Why do people enter into exchanges? The answer is that they do so to make themselves better off. When a person voluntarily trades $100 for a jacket, she is saying, "I prefer to have the jacket instead of the $100." And of course, when the seller of the jacket voluntarily sells the jacket for $100, he is saying, "I prefer to have the $100 instead of the jacket." In short, through trade or exchange, each person gives up something he or she values less for something he or she values more.

ECONOMICS IN A COSMETIC SURGEON'S OFFICE?

According to the American Society for Aesthetic Plastic Surgery, cosmetic surgery is on the rise. In 1997, there were approximately 2.09 million surgical and non-surgical cosmetic procedures. In 2005, that number had risen to 11.42 million procedures. If we consider only surgical cosmetic procedures, the number was 972,996 in 1997, rising to 2.1 million in 2005. In 2006, the top five surgical cosmetic procedures (in order) were lipoplasty (liposuction), breast augmentation, eyelid surgery, rhinoplasty (nose reshaping), and abdominoplasty (tummy tuck). The top non-surgical procedure: Botox® injections.

But enough of the facts and figures of cosmetic surgery. In this chapter we have discussed a few key economic concepts. One way to test how many of these concepts we are learning is to try to find them in different settings. You are in a store buying a shirt. How many economic concepts can you find in the store? You are driving to work. How many economic concepts can you find on your drive? Or, as we have done here, someone has just brought up the subject of cosmetic surgery. How many economic concepts can you find that are relevant to cosmetic surgery?

One thing is that cosmetic surgery gives some people utility, so for those persons it is a good. (Could cosmetic surgery ever be a bad? Well, it might be if the surgery does not turn out the way a person intended.)

We know that goods do not fall from the sky, just waiting to be picked up. It takes resources to produce a good. What resources are needed to produce cosmetic surgery? Certainly there is the surgeon's labor and his or her use of some capital goods (such as scalpels).

Does cosmetic surgery have anything to do with rationing devices? People usually get cosmetic surgery to improve their appearance. But why would people want to improve their appearance? One reason might be to feel better about themselves. Another could be to use their improved looks to get more of what they may want in life. Whether it's true or not, if they believe that only the best looking people get into the entertainment industry, or only the best looking people get the job promotions, or only the best looking people get the choice of whom they will date, then cosmetic surgery might be the means for them to get what they want, in much the same way that money (a definite rationing device) might be necessary to buy a computer, a car, or a vacation to Barbados.

Is there an opportunity cost to cosmetic surgery? Whatever would have been done with the money paid for the surgery, and whatever would be done with the time spent during the surgery and recovery constitutes the opportunity cost of the cosmetic surgery.

How might benefits and costs be relevant to surgery? Probably no one undertakes cosmetic surgery unless he or she believes the benefits will be greater than the costs.

What about the economic concept of exchange or trade? The person getting the cosmetic surgery turns over dollars to the cosmetic surgeon and in return the cosmetic surgeon performs lipoplasty, rhinoplasty, or some other procedure on that person. The person getting the cosmetic surgery implicitly says through his actions that he values the cosmetic procedure more than the money he pays, and the cosmetic surgeon obviously values the money more than the time and labor he has to expend to perform the surgery.

Finally, consider the economic concept of efficiency. In this chapter we learned that efficiency has to do with the marginal benefits and the marginal costs of an activity. The efficient amount of an activity is that amount at which the marginal benefits of the activity equal the marginal costs. Obviously, the efficient amount of the activity will change as the marginal benefits and/or marginal costs change. For example, if you raise the marginal benefits of studying, and the marginal costs remain constant, the efficient amount of studying will rise.

Earlier in this feature we learned that the number of cosmetic procedures is on the rise. While the number of surgical and non-surgical cosmetic procedures was 2.09 million in 1997 that number had risen to 11.42 procedures in 2005. Either the marginal benefits of cosmetic procedures had risen during this time, or the marginal costs had fallen, or both had changed in the stated directions.

Some persons have suggested that the main variable that has changed is the marginal cost of cosmetic surgery. It has fallen during the time period specified earlier. Not in dollar terms, but in terms of how acceptable cosmetic surgery has become. Consumer surveys show that over time cosmetic surgery has become more acceptable, as evidenced by the number of surveyed persons who say they would "not be embarrassed" to have cosmetic surgery. In 2006, 82 percent of women and 79 percent of men said that they would have cosmetic surgery if they felt they needed it.

You can think of trade in terms of utility or satisfaction. Imagine a utility scale that goes from 1 to 10, with 10 being the highest utility you can achieve. Now suppose you currently have $40 in your wallet and you are at 7 on the utility scale. A few minutes later, you are in a store looking at some new CDs. The price of each is $10. You end up buying four CDs for $40.

Before you made the trade, you were at 7 on the utility scale. Are you still at 7 on the utility scale after you traded your $40 for the four CDs? The likely answer is no. If you expected to have the same utility after the trade as you did before, it is unlikely you would have traded your $40 for the four CDs. The only reason you entered into the trade is that you *expected* to be better off after the trade than you were before the trade. In other words, you thought trading your $40 for the four CDs would move you up the utility scale from 7 to, say, 8.

SELF-TEST

1. Give an example to illustrate how a change in opportunity cost can affect behavior.
2. There are both costs and benefits of studying. If you continue to study (say, for a test) as long as the marginal benefits of studying are greater than the marginal costs and stop studying when the two are equal, will your action be consistent with having maximized the net benefits of studying? Explain your answer.
3. You stay up an added hour to study for a test. The intended effect is to raise your test grade. What might be an unintended effect of staying up an added hour to study for the test?

ECONOMIC CATEGORIES

Economics is sometimes broken down into different categories according to the type of questions economists ask. Four common economic categories are positive economics, normative economics, microeconomics, and macroeconomics.

Positive and Normative Economics

Positive economics attempts to determine *what is.* **Normative economics** addresses *what should be.* Essentially, positive economics deals with cause-effect relationships that can be tested. Normative economics deals with value judgments and opinions that cannot be tested.

Positive Economics
The study of "what is" in economic matters.

Normative Economics
The study of "what should be" in economic matters.

Many topics in economics can be discussed within both a positive framework and a normative framework. Consider a proposed cut in federal income taxes. An economist practicing positive economics would want to know the *effect* of a cut in income taxes. For example, she may want to know how a tax cut will affect the unemployment rate, economic growth, inflation, and so on. An economist practicing normative economics would address issues that directly or indirectly relate to whether the federal income tax *should* be cut. For example, she may say that federal income taxes should be cut because the income tax burden on many taxpayers is currently high.

This book mainly deals with positive economics. For the most part, we discuss the economic world as it is, not the way someone might think it should be. Keep in mind, too, that no matter what your normative objectives are, positive economics can shed some light on how they might be accomplished. For example, suppose you believe that absolute poverty should be eliminated and the unemployment rate should be lowered. No doubt you have ideas as to how these goals can be accomplished. But will your ideas work? For example, will a greater redistribution of income eliminate absolute poverty? Will lowering taxes lower the unemployment rate? There is no guarantee that the means you think will bring about certain ends will do so. This is where sound positive economics can help. It helps us see what is. As someone once said, "It is not enough to want to do good; it is important also to know how to do good."

Microeconomics and Macroeconomics

Microeconomics
The branch of economics that deals with human behavior and choices as they relate to relatively small units—an individual, a firm, an industry, a single market.

Macroeconomics
The branch of economics that deals with human behavior and choices as they relate to highly aggregate markets (e.g., the goods and services market) or the entire economy.

It has been said that the tools of microeconomics are microscopes, and the tools of macroeconomics are telescopes. Macroeconomics stands back from the trees to see the forest. Microeconomics gets up close and examines the tree itself, its bark, its limbs, and its roots. **Microeconomics** is the branch of economics that deals with human behavior and choices as they relate to relatively small units—an individual, a firm, an industry, a single market. **Macroeconomics** is the branch of economics that deals with human behavior and choices as they relate to an entire economy. In microeconomics, economists discuss a single price; in macroeconomics, they discuss the price level. Microeconomics deals with the demand for a particular good or service; macroeconomics deals with aggregate, or total, demand for goods and services. Microeconomics examines how a tax change affects a single firm's output; macroeconomics looks at how a tax change affects an entire economy's output.

Microeconomists and macroeconomists ask different types of questions. A microeconomist might be interested in answering such questions as:

- How does a market work?
- What level of output does a firm produce?
- What price does a firm charge for the good it produces?
- How does a consumer determine how much of a good he or she will buy?
- Can government policy affect business behavior?
- Can government policy affect consumer behavior?

On the other hand, a macroeconomist might be interested in answering such questions as:

- How does the economy work?
- Why is the unemployment rate sometimes high and sometimes low?
- What causes inflation?
- Why do some national economies grow faster than other national economies?
- What might cause interest rates to be low one year and high the next?
- How do changes in the money supply affect the economy?
- How do changes in government spending and taxes affect the economy?

office hours

"I DON'T BELIEVE THAT EVERY TIME A PERSON DOES SOMETHING, HE COMPARES THE MARGINAL BENEFITS AND COSTS"

Student:

In class yesterday you said that individuals compare the marginal benefits (*MB*) of doing something (say, exercising) with the marginal costs (*MC*), and if the marginal benefits are greater than the marginal costs, they exercise; but if the marginal costs are greater than the marginal benefits, they don't. Here is what I am having a problem with: I don't believe that every time a person does something, he compares the marginal benefits and costs. I think people do some things without thinking of benefits and costs; they do some things instinctively or because they have always done them.

Instructor:

Can you give an example?

Student:

I don't think of the benefits and costs of eating breakfast in the morning, I just eat breakfast. I don't think of the benefits and costs of doing my homework, I just do the homework before it is due. For me, so many of my activities are automatic; I do them without thinking.

Instructor:

It doesn't necessarily follow that you are not considering benefits and costs when you do something automatically. All you have to do is "sense" whether doing something comes with net benefits (benefits greater than costs) or net costs (costs greater than benefits); all you have to do is "sense" whether something is likely to make you better off or worse off. You eat breakfast in the morning because you have "decided" that it makes you better off. But making you better off is no different than saying that you receive net benefits from eating breakfast, which is no different than saying that the benefits of eating breakfast are greater than the costs. In other words, better off = net benefits = benefits greater than costs.

Student:

I see what you're saying. But then how would you explain the fact that Smith smokes cigarettes and Jones does not. If both Smith and Jones consider the benefits and costs of smoking cigarettes, then it seems that both would have to either smoke, or both would have to not smoke. The fact that different people do different things tells me that not everyone is considering the costs and benefits of their actions, because if everyone did consider the costs and benefits of their actions, they would all do the same thing.

Instructor:

I disagree. Not everyone sees the costs and benefits of the same thing the same way. Jim and Bob may not see the benefits or costs of smoking the same way. For Jim, the benefits of smoking may be high, but for Bob they may be low. It is no different than saying different people estimate the benefits of playing chess, or eating a doughnut, or riding a bicycle differently. The same holds for costs. Not everyone will estimate the costs of playing chess, or eating a doughnut, or riding a bicycle the same way. The costs of a person with diabetes eating a doughnut are much higher than the costs of a person without diabetes eating a doughnut.

Student:

Let me see if I have this right. You are making two points. First, not everyone has the same benefits and costs of, say, running a mile. Second, everyone who does run a mile believes the benefits are greater than the costs and everyone who does not run a mile believes the costs are greater than the benefits.

Instructor:

Yes, that's it. It is really no different than saying that everybody is trying to make himself better off (reap net benefits), but not everybody will do X because not everybody will be made better off by doing X.

Points to Remember

1. If you undertake those actions for which you expect to receive net benefits, then you are "thinking" in terms of costs and benefits. Specifically, you expect the marginal benefits to be greater than the marginal costs.
2. The costs and benefits of doing any activity are not necessarily the same for everybody. Smith may expect higher benefits than Jones when it comes to doing X; Jones may expect higher costs than Smith when it comes to doing X.

a reader asks

What's in Store for an Economics Major?

This is my first course in economics. The material is interesting, and I have given some thought to majoring in economics. Please tell me something about the major and about job prospects for an economics graduate. What courses do economics majors take? What is the starting salary of economics graduates? Do the people who run large companies think highly of people who have majored in economics?

If you major in economics, you will certainly not be alone. Economics is one of the top majors at Yale, Harvard, Brown, the University of California at Berkeley, Princeton, Columbia, Cornell, Dartmouth, and Stanford. For the 2003–2004 academic year, the number of economics degrees granted by U.S. colleges and universities increased 40 percent from five years previously.

The popularity of economics is probably based on two major reasons. First, many people find economics an interesting course of study. Second, what you learn in an economics course is relevant and applicable to the real world.

Do executives who run successful companies think highly of economics majors? Well, a *BusinessWeek* survey found that economics was the second favorite undergraduate major of chief executive officers (CEOs) of major corporations. Engineering was their favorite undergraduate major.

An economics major usually takes a wide variety of economics courses, starting with introductory courses—principles of microeconomics and principles of macroeconomics—and then studying intermediate microeconomics and intermediate macroeconomics. Upper division electives usually include such courses as public finance, international economics, law and economics, managerial economics, labor economics, health economics, money and banking, environmental economics, public choice, and more.

According to the National Association of Colleges and Employers Salary Survey in Summer 2007, the average starting salary for a college graduate in economics was $48,483. For a college graduate in finance, the average starting salary was $47,239, and for a college graduate in accounting, the average starting salary was $46,718. The average starting salary for a college graduate in computer science was $53,396.

Finally, in the June 16, 2008, edition of *Forbes* magazine, an article reported on median salary by undergraduate major. The second highest median salary by major was economics (computer engineering was the first). Specifically, after 10–20 years of work experience, the median salary for persons who had majored in economics at college was higher than for persons who had completed a major in the following areas: electricial engineering, computer science, mechanical engineering, finance, mathematics, civil engineering, political science, marketing, accounting, history, business management, communications, english, biology, sociology, graphic design, psychology, and criminal justice.

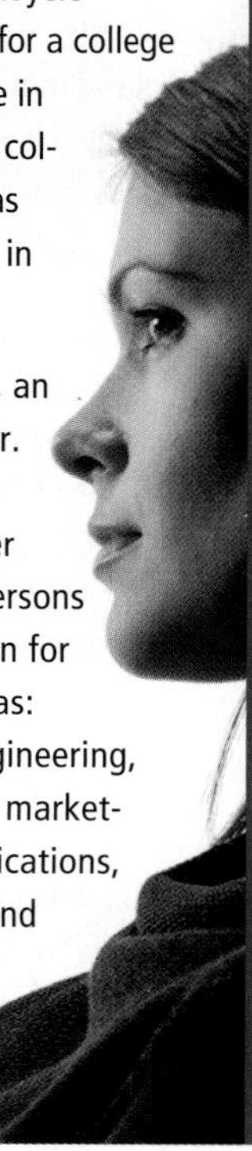

Chapter Summary

GOODS, BADS, AND RESOURCES

- A good is anything that gives a person utility or satisfaction.
- A bad is anything that gives a person disutility or dissatisfaction.
- Economists divide resources into four categories: land, labor, capital, and entrepreneurship.
- Land includes natural resources, such as minerals, forests, water, and unimproved land.
- Labor refers to the physical and mental talents that people contribute to the production process.
- Capital consists of produced goods that can be used as inputs for further production, such as machinery, tools, computers, trucks, buildings, and factories.
- Entrepreneurship refers to the particular talent that some people have for organizing the resources of land, labor, and capital to produce goods, seek new business opportunities, and develop new ways of doing things.

SCARCITY

- Scarcity is the condition in which our wants are greater than the limited resources available to satisfy them.

- Scarcity implies choice. In a world of limited resources, we must choose which wants will be satisfied and which will go unsatisfied.
- Because of scarcity, there is a need for a rationing device. A rationing device is a means of deciding who gets what quantities of the available resources and goods.
- Scarcity implies competition. If there were enough resources to satisfy all our seemingly unlimited wants, people would not have to compete for the available but limited resources.

OPPORTUNITY COST

- Every time a person makes a choice, he or she incurs an opportunity cost. Opportunity cost is the most highly valued opportunity or alternative forfeited when a choice is made. The higher the opportunity cost of doing something, the less likely it will be done.

COSTS AND BENEFITS

- What distinguishes the economist from the non-economist is that the economist thinks in terms of *both* costs and benefits. Asked what the benefits of taking a walk may be, an economist will also mention the costs of taking a walk. Asked what the costs of studying are, an economist will also point out the benefits of studying.

DECISIONS MADE AT THE MARGIN

- Marginal benefits and costs are not the same as total benefits and costs. When deciding whether to talk on the phone one more minute, an individual would not consider the total benefits and total costs of speaking on the phone. Instead, the individual would compare only the marginal benefits (additional benefits) of talking on the phone one more minute to the marginal costs (additional costs) of talking on the phone one more minute.

EFFICIENCY

- As long as the marginal benefits of an activity are greater than its marginal costs, a person gains by continuing to do the activity—whether the activity is studying, running, eating, or watching television. The net benefits of an activity are maximized when the marginal benefits of the activity equal its marginal costs. Efficiency exists at this point.

UNINTENDED EFFECTS

- Economists often think in terms of causes and effects. Effects may include both intended effects and unintended effects. Economists want to denote both types of effects when speaking of effects in general.

EXCHANGE

- Exchange or trade is the process of giving up one thing for something else. People enter into exchanges to make themselves better off.

ECONOMIC CATEGORIES

- Positive economics attempts to determine what is; normative economics addresses what should be.
- Microeconomics deals with human behavior and choices as they relate to relatively small units—an individual, a firm, an industry, a single market. Macroeconomics deals with human behavior and choices as they relate to an entire economy.

Key Terms and Concepts

Good
Utility
Bad
Disutility
Land
Labor
Capital
Entrepreneurship
Scarcity
Economics
Rationing Device
Opportunity Cost
Marginal Benefits
Marginal Costs
Decisions at the Margin
Efficiency
Exchange (Trade)
Positive Economics
Normative Economics
Microeconomics
Macroeconomics

Questions and Problems

1 The United States is considered a rich country because Americans can choose from an abundance of goods and services. How can there be scarcity in a land of abundance?

2 Give two examples for each of the following: (a) an intangible good, (b) a tangible good, (c) a bad.

3 Give an example of something that is a good for one person and a bad for someone else.

4 What is the difference between the resource labor and the resource entrepreneurship?

5 Can either scarcity or one of the effects of scarcity be found in a car dealership? Explain your answer.

6 Explain the link between scarcity and each of the following: (a) choice, (b) opportunity cost, (c) the need for a rationing device, (d) competition.

7 Is it possible for a person to incur an opportunity cost without spending any money? Explain.

8 Discuss the opportunity costs of attending college for four years. Is college more or less costly than you thought it was? Explain.

9 Explain the relationship between changes in opportunity cost and changes in behavior.

10 Smith says that we should eliminate all pollution in the world. Jones disagrees. Who is more likely to be an economist, Smith or Jones? Explain your answer.

11 A friend pays for your lunch. Is this an example of a "free lunch"? Why or why not?

12 A layperson says that a proposed government project simply costs too much and therefore shouldn't be undertaken. How might an economist's evaluation be different?

13 Economists say that individuals make decisions at the margin. What does this mean?

14 How would an economist define the efficient amount of time spent playing tennis?

15 Ivan stops studying before the point at which his marginal benefits of studying equal his marginal costs. Is Ivan forfeiting any net benefits? Explain your answer.

16 What does an economist mean if she says there are no $10 bills on the sidewalk?

17 A change in X will lead to a change in Y; the predicted change is desirable, so we should change X. Do you agree or disagree? Explain.

18 Why do people enter into exchanges?

19 When two individuals enter an exchange, you can be sure that one person benefits and the other person loses. Do you agree or disagree with this statement? Explain your answer.

20 What is the difference between positive economics and normative economics? between microeconomics and macroeconomics?

21 Would there be a need for a rationing device if scarcity did not exist? Explain your answer.

22 Jackie's alarm clock buzzes. She reaches over to the small table next to her bed and turns it off. As she pulls the covers back up, Jackie thinks about her 8:30 American history class. Should she go to the class today or sleep a little longer? She worked late last night and really hasn't had enough sleep. Besides, she's fairly sure her professor will be discussing a subject she already knows well. Maybe it would be okay to miss class today. Is Jackie more likely to miss some classes than she is to miss other classes? What determines which classes Jackie will attend and which classes she won't attend?

23 If you found $10 bills on the sidewalk regularly, we might then conclude that individuals don't try to maximize net benefits. Do you agree or disagree with this statement? Explain your answer.

24 The person who smokes cigarettes cannot possibly be thinking in terms of costs and benefits because it has been proven that cigarette smoking increases one's chances of getting lung cancer. Do you agree or disagree with the part of the statement that reads "the person who smokes cigarettes cannot possibly be thinking in terms of costs and benefits"? Explain your answer.

25 Janice decides to go out on a date with Kyle instead of Robert. Do you think Janice is using some kind of "rationing device" to decide who she dates? If so, what might that rationing device be?

WORKING WITH DIAGRAMS

A picture is worth a thousand words. With this familiar saying in mind, economists construct their diagrams or graphs. With a few lines and a few points, much can be conveyed.

TWO-VARIABLE DIAGRAMS

Most of the diagrams in this book represent the relationship between two variables. Economists compare two variables to see how a change in one variable affects the other variable.

Suppose our two variables of interest are *consumption* and *income.* We want to show how consumption changes as income changes. Suppose we collect the data in Table 1. By simply looking at the data in the first two columns, we can see that as income rises (column 1), consumption rises (column 2). Suppose we want to show the relationship between income and consumption on a graph. We could place *income* on the horizontal axis, as in Exhibit 1, and *consumption* on the vertical axis. Point A represents income of $0 and consumption of $60, point B represents income of $100 and consumption of $120, and so on. If we draw a straight line through the various points we have plotted, we have a picture of the relationship between income and consumption, based on the data we collected.

Notice that our line in Exhibit 1 slopes upward from left to right. Thus, as income rises, so does consumption. For example, as you move from point A to point B, income rises from $0 to $100 and consumption rises from $60 to $120. The line in Exhibit 1 also shows that as income falls, so does consumption. For example, as you move from point C to point B, income falls from $200 to $100 and consumption falls from $180 to $120. When two variables—such as consumption and income—change in the same way, they are said to be **directly related.**

Now let's take a look at the data in Table 2. Our two variables are *price of compact discs (CDs)* and *quantity demanded of CDs.* By simply looking at the data in the first two columns, we see that as price falls (column 1), quantity demanded rises (column 2).

exhibit 1

A Two-Variable Diagram Representing a Direct Relationship

In this exhibit, we have plotted the data in Table 1 and then connected the points with a straight line. The data represent a direct relationship: as one variable (say, income) rises, the other variable (consumption) rises too.

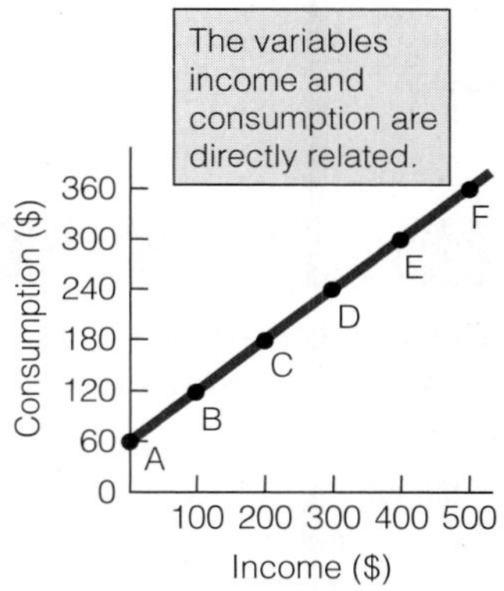

Directly Related
Two variables are directly related if they change in the same way.

table 1

(1) When Income Is:	(2) Consumption Is:	(3) Point
$ 0	$ 60	A
100	120	B
200	180	C
300	240	D
400	300	E
500	360	F

table 2

(1) When Price of CDs Is:	(2) Quantity Demanded of CDs Is:	(3) Point
$20	100	A
18	120	B
16	140	C
14	160	D
12	180	E

Inversely Related
Two variables are inversely related if they change in opposite ways.

Independent
Two variables are independent if as one changes, the other does not.

Slope
The ratio of the change in the variable on the vertical axis to the change in the variable on the horizontal axis.

Suppose we want to plot these data. We could place *price* (of CDs) on the vertical axis, as in Exhibit 2, and *quantity demanded* (of CDs) on the horizontal axis. Point A represents a price of $20 and a quantity demanded of 100, point B represents a price of $18 and a quantity demanded of 120, and so on. If we draw a straight line through the various points we have plotted, we have a picture of the relationship between price and quantity demanded, based on the data in Table 2.

Notice that as price falls, quantity demanded rises. For example, as price falls from $20 to $18, quantity demanded rises from 100 to 120. Also as price rises, quantity demanded falls. For example, when price rises from $12 to $14, quantity demanded falls from 180 to 160.

When two variables—such as price and quantity demanded—change in opposite ways, they are said to be **inversely related**.

As you have seen so far, variables may be directly related (when one increases, the other also increases), or they may be inversely related (when one increases, the other decreases). Variables can also be **independent** of each other. This condition exists if as one variable changes, the other does not.

In Exhibit 3(a), as the *X* variable rises, the *Y* variable remains the same (at 20). Obviously, the *X* and *Y* variables are independent of each other: as one changes, the other does not.

In Exhibit 3(b), as the *Y* variable rises, the *X* variable remains the same (at 30). Again, we conclude that the *X* and *Y* variables are independent of each other: as one changes, the other does not.

exhibit 2

A Two-Variable Diagram Representing an Inverse Relationship

In this exhibit, we have plotted the data in Table 2 and then connected the points with a straight line. The data represent an inverse relationship: as one variable (price) falls, the other variable (quantity demanded) rises.

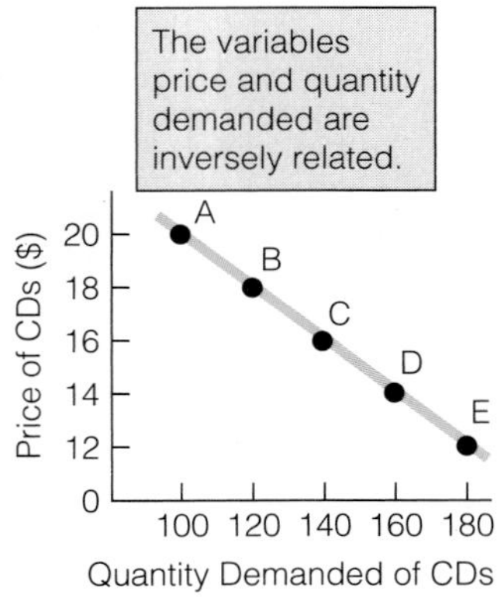

SLOPE OF A LINE

It is often important not only to know *how* two variables are related but also to know *how much* one variable changes as the other variable changes. To find out, we need only calculate the slope of the line. The **slope** is the ratio of the change in the variable on the vertical axis to the change in the variable on the horizontal axis. For example, if *Y* is on the vertical axis and *X* on the horizontal axis, the slope is equal to $\Delta Y/\Delta X$. (The symbol "Δ" means "change in.")

$$\text{Slope} = \frac{\Delta Y}{\Delta X}$$

Exhibit 4 shows four lines. In each case, we have calculated the slope. After studying (a)–(d), see if you can calculate the slope in each case.

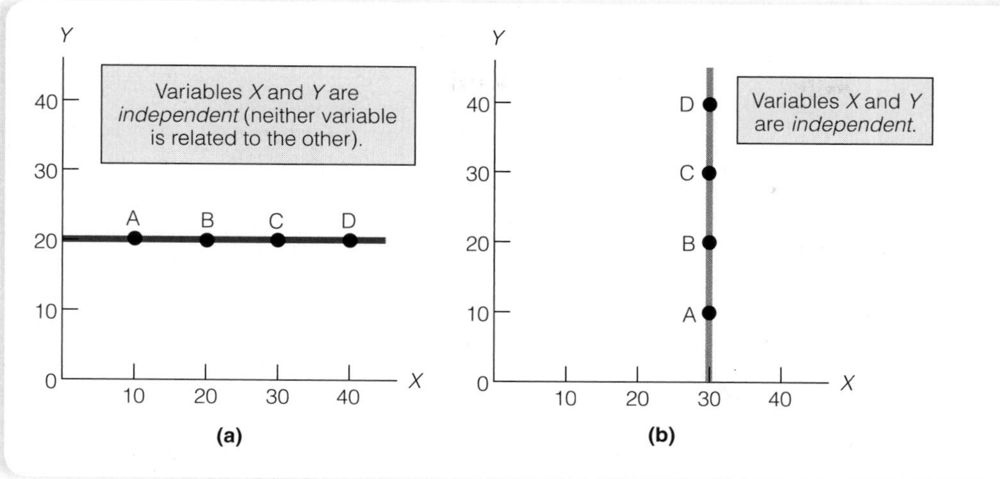

exhibit 3

Two Diagrams Representing Independence Between Two Variables

In (a) and (b), the variables *X* and *Y* are independent: as one changes, the other does not.

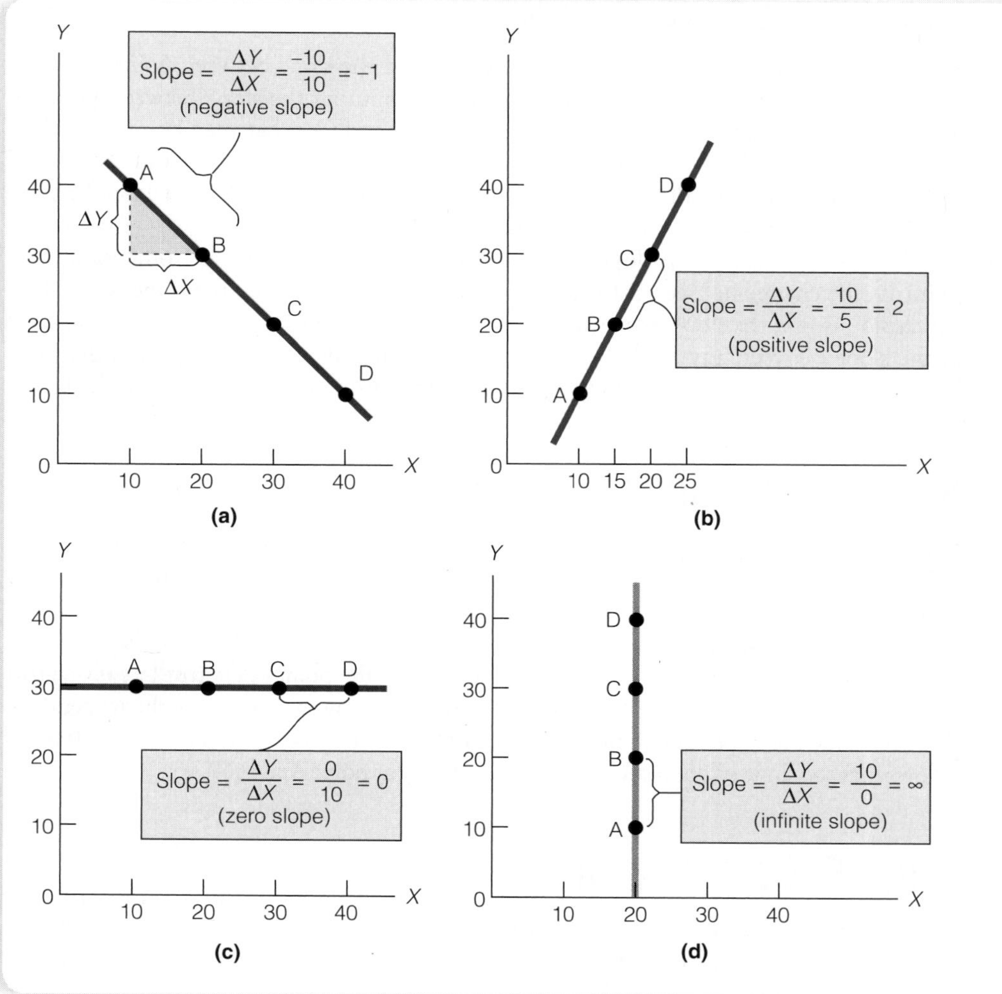

exhibit 4

Calculating Slopes

The slope of a line is the ratio of the change in the variable on the vertical axis to the change in the variable on the horizontal axis. In (a)–(d), we have calculated the slope.

exhibit 5

Calculating the Slope of a Curve at a Particular Point

The slope of the curve at point A is 0.67. This is calculated by drawing a line tangent to the curve at point A and then determining the slope of the line.

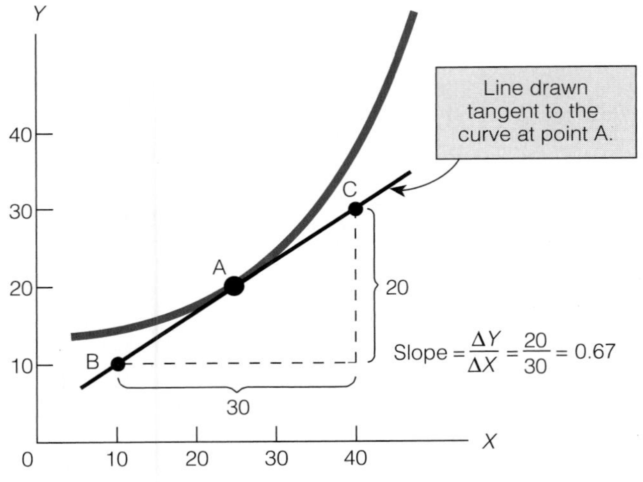

Slope of a Line Is Constant

Look again at the line in Exhibit 4(a). We computed the slope between points A and B and found it to be −1. Suppose that instead of computing the slope between points A and B, we had computed the slope between points B and C or between points C and D. Would the slope still be −1? Let's compute the slope between points B and C. Moving from point B to point C, the change in *Y* is −10 and the change in *X* is +10. So the slope is −1, which is what the slope was between points A and B.

Now let's compute the slope between points A and D. Moving from point A to point D, the change in *Y* is −30 and the change in *X* is +30. Again the slope is −1. Our conclusion is that the slope between any two points on a (straight) line is always the same as the slope between any other two points. To see this for yourself, compute the slope between points A and B and between points A and C using the line in Exhibit 4(b).

exhibit 6

The 45-Degree Line

Any point on the 45-degree line is equidistant from each axis. For example, point A is the same distance from the vertical axis as it is from the horizontal axis.

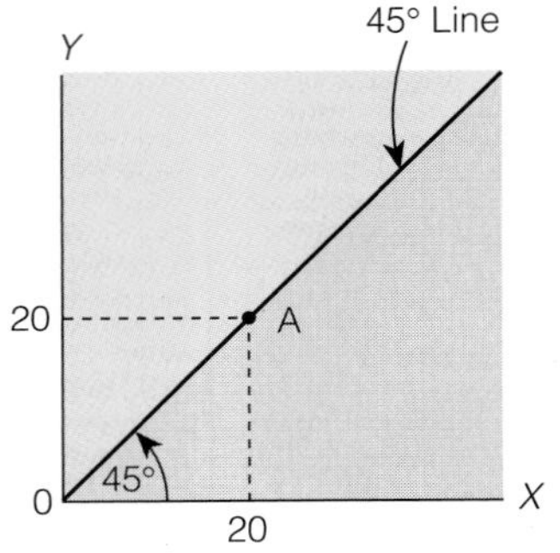

Slope of a Curve

Economic graphs use both straight lines and curves. The slope of a curve is not constant throughout as it is for a straight line. The slope of a curve varies from one point to another.

Calculating the slope of a curve at a given point requires two steps, as illustrated for point A in Exhibit 5. First, draw a line tangent to the curve at the point (a tangent line is one that just touches the curve but does not cross it). Second, pick any two points on the tangent line and determine the slope. In Exhibit 5 the slope of the line between points B and C is 0.67. It follows that the slope of the curve at point A (and only at point A) is 0.67.

The 45-Degree Line

Economists sometimes use a *45-degree line* to represent data. This is a straight line that bisects the right angle formed by the intersection of the vertical and horizontal axes (see Exhibit 6). As a result, the 45-degree line divides the space enclosed by the two axes into *two equal parts.* We have illustrated this by shading the two equal parts in different colors.

exhibit 7

A Pie Chart

The breakdown of activities for Charles Myers during a typical 24-hour weekday is represented in pie chart form.

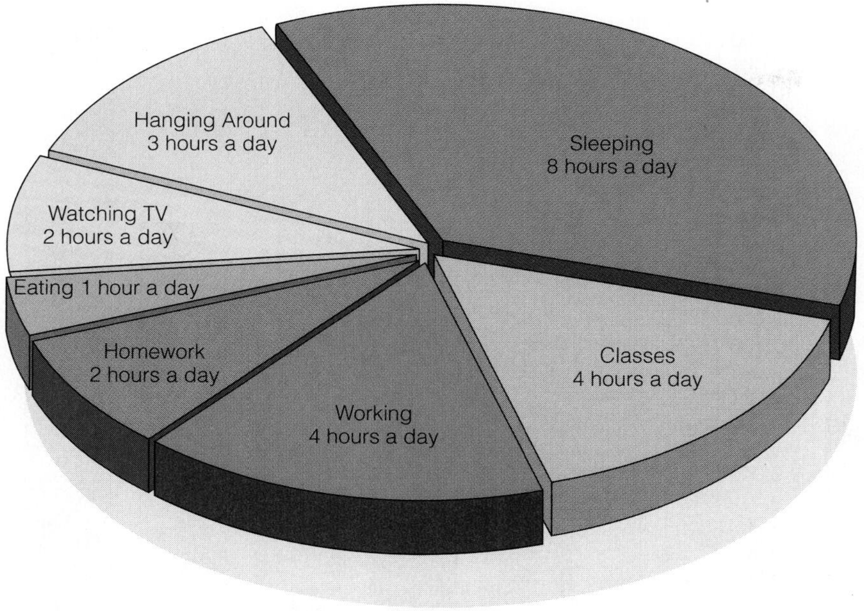

The major characteristic of the 45-degree line is that any point that lies on it is equidistant from both the horizontal and vertical axes. For example, point A is exactly as far from the horizontal axis as it is from the vertical axis. It follows that point A represents as much X as it does Y. Specifically, in the exhibit, point A represents 20 units of X and 20 units of Y.

Pie Charts

In numerous places in this text, you will come across a *pie chart.* A pie chart is a convenient way to represent the different parts of something that when added together equal the whole.

Let's consider a typical 24-hour weekday for Charles Myers. On a typical weekday, Charles spends 8 hours sleeping, 4 hours taking classes at the university, 4 hours working at his part-time job, 2 hours doing homework, 1 hour eating, 2 hours watching television, and 3 hours doing nothing in particular (we'll call it "hanging around"). Exhibit 7 shows the breakdown of a typical weekday for Charles in pie chart form.

Pie charts give a quick visual message as to rough percentage breakdowns and relative relationships. For example, it is easy to see in Exhibit 7 that Charles spends twice as much time working as doing homework.

Bar Graphs

The *bar graph* is another visual aid that economists use to convey relative relationships. Suppose we wanted to represent the gross domestic product for the United States in different years. The **gross domestic product (GDP)** is the value of the entire output produced annually within a country's borders. A bar graph can show the actual GDP for each year and can also provide a quick picture of the relative relationships between the GDP in

Gross Domestic Product (GDP)
The value of the entire output produced annually within a country's borders.

exhibit 8

A Bar Graph

U.S. gross domestic product for different years is illustrated in bar graph form.

Source: Bureau of Economic Analysis

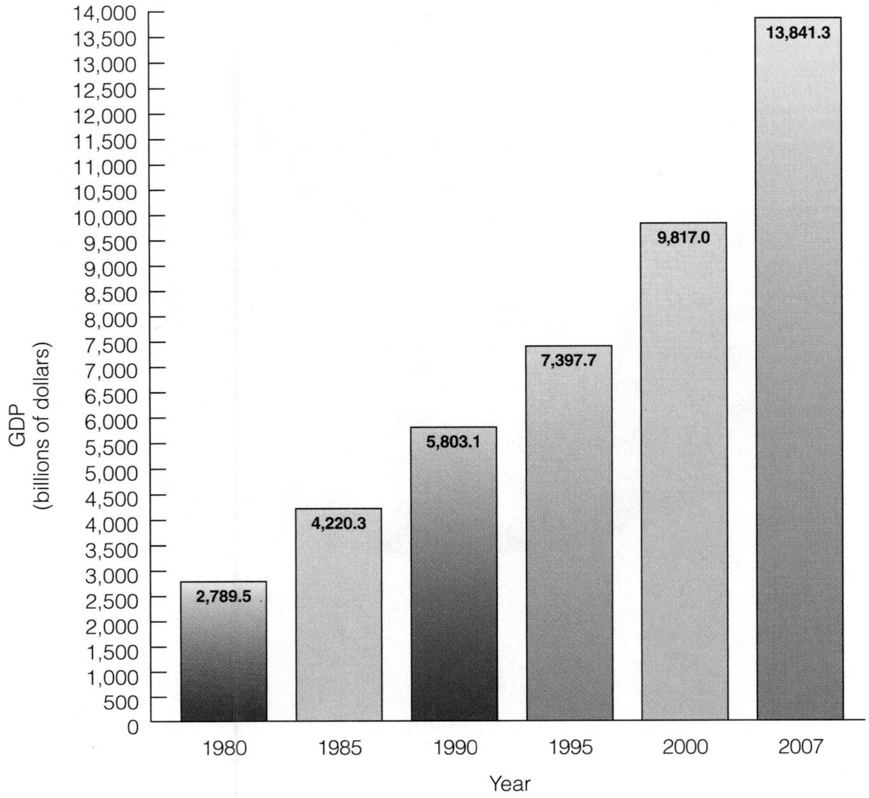

different years. For example, it is easy to see in Exhibit 8 that the GDP in 1990 was more than double what it was in 1980.

Line Graphs

Sometimes information is best and most easily displayed in a *line graph.* Line graphs are particularly useful for illustrating changes in a variable over some time period. Suppose we want to illustrate the variations in average points per game for a college basketball team in different years. As you can see from Exhibit 9(a), the basketball team has been on a roller coaster during the years 1996–2009. Perhaps the message transmitted here is that the team's performance has not been consistent from one year to the next.

Suppose we plot the data in Exhibit 9(a) again, except this time we use a different measurement scale on the vertical axis. As you can see in (b), the variation in the performance of the basketball team appears much less pronounced than in (a). In fact, we could choose some scale such that if we were to plot the data, we would end up with close to a straight line. Our point is simple: Data plotted in line graph form may convey different messages depending on the measurement scale used.

Sometimes economists show two line graphs on the same axes. Usually, they do this to draw attention to either (1) the *relationship* between the two variables or (2) the *difference* between the two variables. In Exhibit 10, the line graphs show the variation and trend in projected federal government expenditures and tax receipts for the years 2008–2013 and draw attention to what has been happening to the "gap" between the two.

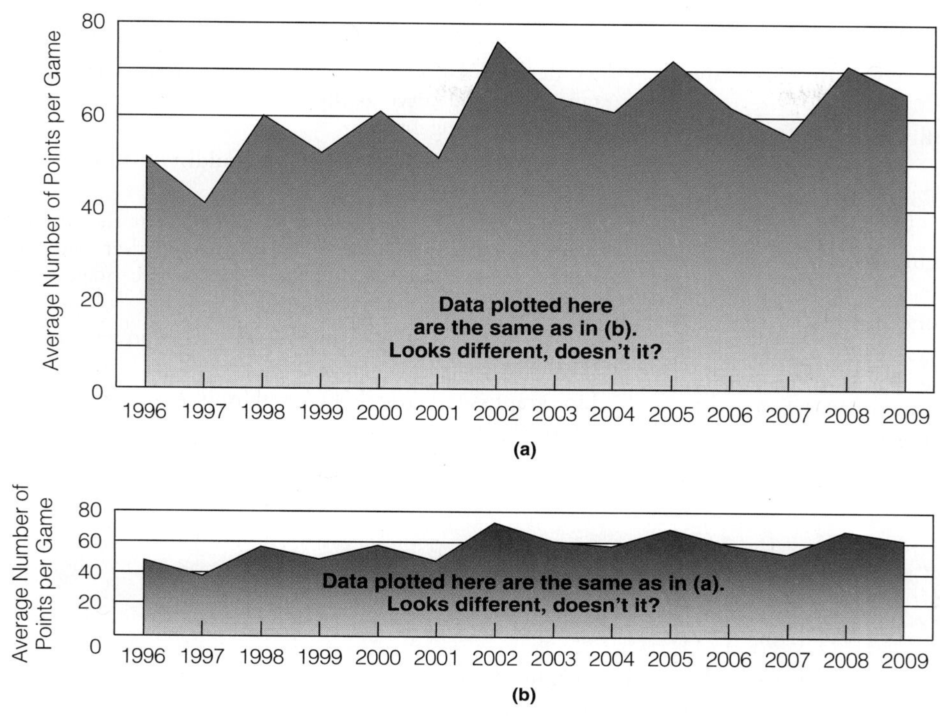

exhibit 9

The Two Line Graphs Plot the Same Data

In (a) we plotted the average number of points per game for a college basketball team in different years. The variation between the years is pronounced. In (b) we plotted the same data as in (a), but the variation in the performance of the team appears much less pronounced than in (a).

Year	Average Number of Points per Game
1996	50
1997	40
1998	59
1999	51
2000	60
2001	50
2002	75
2003	63
2004	60
2005	71
2006	61
2007	55
2008	70
2009	64

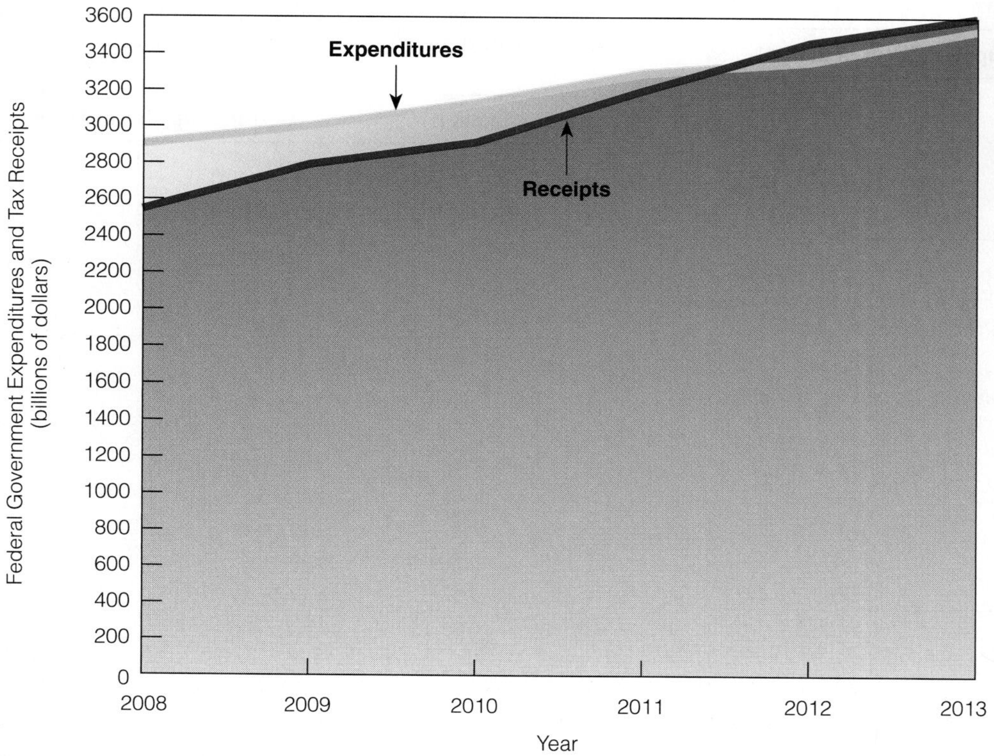

exhibit 10

Projected Federal Government Expenditures and Tax Receipts, 2008–2013

Projected federal government expenditures and tax receipts are shown in line graph form for the period 2008–2013.

Source: Congressional Budget Office

Appendix Summary

- Two variables are directly related if one variable rises as the other rises.
- An upward-sloping line (left to right) represents two variables that are directly related.
- Two variables are inversely related if one variable rises as the other falls.
- A downward-sloping line (left to right) represents two variables that are inversely related.
- Two variables are independent if one variable rises as the other remains constant.
- The slope of a line is the ratio of the change in the variable on the vertical axis to the change in the variable on the horizontal axis. The slope of a (straight) line is the same between every two points on the line.
- To determine the slope of a curve at a point, draw a line tangent to the curve at the point and then determine the slope of the tangent line.
- Any point on a 45-degree line is equidistant from the two axes.
- A pie chart is a convenient way to represent the different parts of something that when added together equal the whole. A pie chart visually shows rough percentage breakdowns and relative relationships.
- A bar graph is a convenient way to represent relative relationships.
- Line graphs are particularly useful for illustrating changes in a variable over some time period.

Questions and Problems

1 What type of relationship would you expect between the following: (a) sales of hot dogs and sales of hot dog buns, (b) the price of winter coats and sales of winter coats, (c) the price of personal computers and the production of personal computers, (d) sales of toothbrushes and sales of cat food, (e) the number of children in a family and the number of toys in a family.

2 Represent the following data in bar graph form.

Year	U.S. Money Supply (billions of dollars)
2003	1,273
2004	1,344
2005	1,371
2006	1,374
2007	1,369

3 Plot the following data and specify the type of relationship between the two variables. (Place "price" on the vertical axis and "quantity demanded" on the horizontal axis.)

Price of Apples ($)	Quantity Demanded of Apples
0.25	1,000
0.50	800
0.70	700
0.95	500
1.00	400
1.10	350

4 In Exhibit 4(a), determine the slope between points C and D.

5 In Exhibit 4(b), determine the slope between points A and D.

6 What is the special characteristic of a 45-degree line?

7 What is the slope of a 45-degree line?

8 When would it be preferable to illustrate data using a pie chart instead of a bar graph?

9 Plot the following data and specify the type of relationship between the two variables. (Place "price" on the vertical axis and "quantity supplied" on the horizontal axis.)

Price of Apples ($)	Quantity Supplied of Apples
0.25	350
0.50	400
0.70	500
0.95	700
1.00	800
1.10	1,000

SHOULD YOU MAJOR IN ECONOMICS?

You are probably reading this textbook as part of your first college course in economics. You may be taking this course because you need it to satisfy the requirements in your major. Economics courses are sometimes required for students who plan to major in business, history, liberal studies, social science, or computer science. Of course, you may also be taking this course because you plan to major in economics.

If you are like many college students, you may complain that not enough information is available to students about the various majors at your college or university. For example, students who major in business sometimes say they are not quite certain what a business major is all about, but then they go on to add that majoring in business is a safe bet. "After all," they comment, "you are pretty sure of getting a job if you have a business degree. That's not always the case with other degrees."

Many college students choose their majors based on their high school courses. History majors sometimes say that they decided to major in history because they "liked history in high school." Similarly, chemistry, biology, and math majors say they chose chemistry, biology, or math as a college major because they liked studying chemistry, biology, or math in high school. In addition, if a student had a hard time with chemistry in high school and found it boring, then he doesn't usually want to major in chemistry in college. If a student found both math and economics easy and interesting in high school, then she is likely to major in math or economics.

Students also often look to the dollars at the end of the college degree. A student may enjoy history and want to learn more history in college but tell herself that she will earn a higher starting salary after graduation if she majors in computer science or engineering. Thus, when choosing a major, students often consider (1) how much they enjoy studying a particular subject, (2) what they would like to see themselves doing in the future, and (3) income prospects.

Different people may weight these three factors differently. But no matter what weights you put on each of the factors, it is always better to have more information than less information, *ceteris paribus.* (We note *"ceteris paribus"* because it is not necessarily better having more information than less information if you have to pay more for the additional information than the additional information is worth. Who wants to pay $10 for a piece of information that only provides $1 in benefits?)

We believe this appendix is a fairly low-cost way of providing you with more information about an economics major than you currently have. We start by dispelling some of the misinformation you might possess about an economics major. Stated bluntly, some things that people think about an economics major and about a career in economics are just not true. For example, some people think that economics majors almost never study social relationships; instead, they only study such things as inflation, interest rates, and unemployment. Not true. Economics majors study some of the same things that sociologists, historians, psychologists, and political scientists study. We also provide you with some information about the major that you may not have.

Next, we tell you the specifics of the economics major—what courses you study if you are an economics major, how many courses you are likely to have to take, and more.

Finally, we tell you something about a career in economics. Okay, so you have opted to become an economics major. But the day will come when you have your degree in hand. What's next? What is your starting salary likely to be? What will you be doing? Are you going to be happy doing what economists do? (If you never thought economics was about happiness, you already have some misinformation about economics. Contrary to what most laypeople think, economics is not just about money. It is about happiness too.)

FIVE MYTHS ABOUT ECONOMICS AND AN ECONOMICS MAJOR

Myth 1: Economics Is All Mathematics and Statistics

Some students choose not to major in economics because they think economics is all mathematics and statistics. Math and statistics are used in economics, but at the undergraduate degree level, the math and statistics are certainly not overwhelming. Economics majors are usually required to take one statistics course and one math course (usually an introductory calculus course). Even students who say, "Math isn't my subject" are sometimes happy with the amount of math they need in economics. Fact is, at the undergraduate level at many colleges and universities, economics is not a very math-intensive course of study. There are many diagrams in economics, but there is not a large amount of math.

A proviso: The amount of math in the economics curriculum varies across colleges and universities. Some economics departments do not require their students to learn much math or statistics, but others do. Speaking for the majority of departments, we still hold to our original point that there isn't really that much math or statistics in economics at the undergraduate level. The graduate level is a different story.

Myth 2: Economics Is Only About Inflation, Interest Rates, Unemployment, and Other Such Things

If you study economics at college and then go on to become a practicing economist, no doubt people will ask you certain questions when they learn your chosen profession. Here are some of the questions they ask:

- Do you think the economy is going to pick up?
- Do you think the economy is going to slow down?
- What stocks would you recommend?
- Do you think interest rates are going to fall?
- Do you think interest rates are going to rise?
- What do you think about buying bonds right now? Is it a good idea?

People ask these kinds of questions because most people believe that economists only study stocks, bonds, interest rates, inflation, unemployment, and so on. Well, economists do study these things. But these topics are only a tiny part of what economists study. It is not hard to find many economists today, both inside and outside academia, who spend most of their time studying anything but inflation, unemployment, stocks, bonds, and so on.

As we hinted earlier, much of what economists study may surprise you. There are economists who use their economic tools and methods to study crime, marriage, divorce, sex, obesity, addiction, sports, voting behavior, bureaucracies, presidential elections, and much more. In short, today's economics is not your grandfather's economics. Many more topics are studied today in economics than were studied in your grandfather's time.

Myth 3: People Become Economists Only if They Want to "Make Money"

A while back we asked a few well-respected and well-known economists what got them interested in economics. Here is what some of them had to say:[1]

Gary Becker, the 1992 winner of the Nobel Prize in Economics, said: "I got interested in economics when I was an undergraduate in college. I came into college with a strong interest in mathematics, and at the same time with a strong commitment to do something to help society. I learned in the first economics course I took that economics could deal rigorously, à la mathematics, with social problems. That stimulated me because in economics I saw that I could combine both the mathematics and my desire to do something to help society."

Vernon Smith, the 2002 winner of the Nobel Prize in Economics, said: "My father's influence started me in science and engineering at Cal Tech, but my mother, who was active in socialist politics, probably accounts for the great interest I found in economics when I took my first introductory course."

Alice Rivlin, an economist and former member of the Federal Reserve Board, said: "My interest in economics grew out of concern for improving public policy, both domestic and international. I was a teenager in the tremendously idealistic period after World War II when it seemed terribly important to get nations working together to solve the world's problems peacefully."

Allan Meltzer said: "Economics is a social science. At its best it is concerned with ways (1) to improve well being by allowing individuals the freedom to achieve their personal aims or goals and (2) to harmonize their individual interests. I find working on such issues challenging, and progress is personally rewarding."

Robert Solow, the 1987 winner of the Nobel Prize in Economics, said: "I grew up in the 1930s and it was very hard not to be interested in economics. If you were a high school student in the 1930s, you were conscious of the fact that our economy was in deep trouble and no one knew what to do about it."

Charles Plosser said: "I was an engineer as an undergraduate with little knowledge of economics. I went to the University of Chicago Graduate School of Business to get an MBA and there became fascinated with economics. I was impressed with the seriousness with which economics was viewed as a way of organizing one's thoughts about the world to address interesting questions and problems."

Walter Williams said: "I was a major in sociology in 1963 and I concluded that it was not very rigorous. Over the summer I was reading a book by W.E.B. DuBois, *Black Reconstruction,* and somewhere in the book it said something along the lines that blacks could not melt into the mainstream of American society until they understood economics, and that was something that got me interested in economics."

Murray Weidenbaum said: "A specific professor got me interested in economics. He was very prescient: He correctly noted that while lawyers dominated the policy-making process up until then (the 1940s), in the future economics would be an important tool for developing public policy. And he was right."

Irma Adelman said: "I hesitate to say because it sounds arrogant. My reason [for getting into economics] was that I wanted to benefit humanity. And my perception at the time was that economic problems were the most important problems that humanity has to face. That is what got me into economics and into economic development."

Lester Thurow said: "[I got interested in economics because of] the belief, some would see it as naive belief, that economics was a profession where it would be possible to help make the world better."

1. See various interviews in Roger A. Arnold, *Economics,* 2d ed. (St. Paul, MN: West Publishing Company, 1992).

Myth 4: Economics Wasn't Very Interesting in High School, So It's Not Going to Be Very Interesting in College

A typical high school economics course emphasizes consumer economics and spends much time discussing this topic. Students learn about credit cards, mortgage loans, budgets, buying insurance, renting an apartment, and other such things. These are important topics because not knowing the "ins and outs" of such things can make your life much harder. Still, many students come away from a high school economics course thinking that economics is always and everywhere about consumer topics.

However, a high school economics course and a college economics course are usually as different as day and night. Simply leaf through this book and look at the variety of topics covered compared to the topics you might have covered in your high school economics course. Go on to look at texts used in other economics courses—courses that range from law and economics to history of economic thought to international economics to sports economics—and you will see what we mean.

Myth 5: Economics Is a Lot Like Business, But Business Is More Marketable

Although business and economics have some common topics, much that one learns in economics is not taught in business and much that one learns in business is not taught in economics. The area of intersection between business and economics is not large.

Still, many people think otherwise. And so thinking that business and economics are pretty much the same thing, they often choose to major in the subject they believe has greater marketability—which they believe is business.

Well, consider the following:

1. A few years ago *BusinessWeek* magazine asked the chief executive officers (CEOs) of major companies what they thought was the best undergraduate degree. Their first choice was engineering. Their second choice was economics. Economics scored higher than business administration.
2. The National Association of Colleges and Employers undertook a survey in 2007 in which they identified the average starting salary offers in different disciplines. The average starting salary in economics was $48,483. Here are average starting salaries for some other fields: computer science, $53,396; accounting, $46,718; finance, $47,239; civil engineering, $47,718; marketing, $41,323; electrical engineering, $54,599; and chemical engineering, $60,054.

WHAT AWAITS YOU AS AN ECONOMICS MAJOR?

If you become an economics major, what courses will you take? What are you going to study?

At the lower-division level, economics majors must take both the principles of macroeconomics course and the principles of microeconomics course. They usually also take a statistics course and a math course (usually calculus).

At the upper-division level, they must take intermediate microeconomics and intermediate macroeconomics, along with a certain number of electives. Some of the elective courses include: (1) money and banking, (2) law and economics, (3) history of economic thought, (4) public finance, (5) labor economics, (6) international economics, (7) antitrust and regulation, (8) health economics, (9) economics of development, (10) urban and regional economics, (11) econometrics, (12) mathematical economics, (13) environmental economics, (14) public choice, (15) global managerial economics, (16) economic approach to politics and sociology, (17) sports economics, and many more courses. Most economics majors take between 12 and 15 economics courses.

One of the attractive things about studying economics is that you will acquire many of the skills employers highly value. First, you will have the quantitative skills that are important in many business and government positions. Second, you will acquire the writing skills necessary in almost all lines of work. Third, and perhaps most importantly, you will develop the thinking skills that almost all employers agree are critical to success.

A study published in the 1998 edition of the *Journal of Economic Education* ranked economics majors as having the highest average scores on the Law School Admission Test (LSAT). Also, consider the words of the Royal Economic Society: "One of the things that makes economics graduates so employable is that the subject teaches you to think in a careful and precise way. The fundamental economic issue is how society decides to allocate its resources: how the costs and benefits of a course of action can be evaluated and compared, and how appropriate choices can be made. A degree in economics gives a training in decision making principles, providing a skill applicable in a very wide range of careers."

Keep in mind, too, that economics is one of the most popular majors at some of the most respected universities in the country. As of this writing, economics is the top major at Harvard, Princeton, Columbia, Stanford, the University of Pennsylvania, and the University of Chicago. It is the second most popular major at Brown, Yale, and the University of California at Berkeley. It is the third most popular major at Cornell and Dartmouth.

WHAT DO ECONOMISTS DO?

Employment for economists is projected to grow between 21 and 35 percent between 2000 and 2010. According to the *Occupational Outlook Handbook:*

> *Opportunities for economists should be best in private industry, especially in research, testing, and consulting firms, as more companies contract out for economic research services. The growing complexity of the global economy, competition, and increased reliance on quantitative methods for analyzing the current value of future funds, business trends, sales, and purchasing should spur demand for economists. The growing need for economic analyses in virtually every industry should result in additional jobs for economists.*

Today, economists work in many varied fields. Here are some of the fields and some of the positions economists hold in those fields:

Education
College professor
Researcher
High school teacher

Journalism
Researcher
Industry analyst
Economic analyst

Accounting
Analyst
Auditor
Researcher
Consultant

General Business
Chief executive officer
Business analyst
Marketing analyst
Business forecaster
Competitive analyst

Government
Researcher
Analyst
Speechwriter
Forecaster

Financial Services
Business journalist
International analyst
Newsletter editor
Broker
Investment banker

Banking
Credit analyst
Loan officer
Investment analyst
Financial manager

Other
Business consultant
Independent forecaster
Freelance analyst
Think tank analyst
Entrepreneur

Economists do a myriad of things. For example, in business, economists often analyze economic conditions, make forecasts, offer strategic planning initiatives, collect and analyze data, predict exchange rate movements, and review regulatory policies, among other things. In government, economists collect and analyze data, analyze international economic situations, research monetary conditions, advise on policy, and much more. As private consultants, economists work with accountants, business executives, government officials, educators, financial firms, labor unions, state and local governments, and others. Median annual wage and salary earnings of economists were $77,010 in May 2006. The middle 50 percent earned between $55,740 and $103,500. The lowest 10 percent earned less than $42,280, and the highest 10 percent earned more than $136,550.

Places to Find More Information

If you are interested in an economics major and perhaps a career in economics, here are some places where you can go and some people you can speak with to acquire more information:

- To learn about the economics curriculum, we urge you to speak with the economics professors at your college or university. Ask them what courses you would have to take as an economics major. Ask them what elective courses are available. In addition, ask them why they chose to study economics. What is it about economics that interested them?
- For more information about salaries and what economists do, you may want to visit the *Occupational Outlook Handbook* website at http://www.bls.gov/oco/.
- For starting salary information, you may want to visit the National Association of Colleges and Employers website at http://www.naceweb.org/.
- To see a list of famous people who have majored in economics, go to http://www.marietta.edu/~ema/econ/famous.html.

Concluding Remarks

Choosing a major is a big decision and therefore should not be made too quickly and without much thought. In this short appendix, we have provided you with some information about an economics major and a career in economics. Economics may not be for everyone (in fact, economists would say that if it were, many of the benefits of specialization would be lost), but it may be right for you. Economics is a major where many of today's most marketable skills are acquired—the skills of good writing, quantitative analysis, and thinking. It is a major in which professors and students daily ask and answer some very interesting and relevant questions. It is a major that is highly regarded by employers. It may just be the right major for you. Give it some thought.

© PHOTO ALTO/JUPITER IMAGES

CHAPTER 2

ECONOMIC ACTIVITIES: PRODUCING AND TRADING

Introduction In the last chapter you learned about various economic concepts—such as scarcity, choice, and opportunity cost. In this chapter we develop a graphical framework of analysis with which to understand these concepts and more. Specifically, we develop the production possibilities frontier. Next we go on to discuss one of the most important topics in economics—trade.

THE PRODUCTION POSSIBILITIES FRONTIER

This section discusses the production possibilities frontier (PPF) and numerous economic concepts that can be illustrated by it.

The Straight-Line PPF: Constant Opportunity Costs

Assume the following:

1. Only two goods can be produced in an economy: computers and television sets.
2. The opportunity cost of one television set is one computer.
3. As more of one good is produced, the opportunity cost between television sets and computers is constant.

In Exhibit 1(a), we have identified six combinations of computers and television sets that can be produced in our economy. For example, combination A is 50,000 computers and 0 television sets, combination B is 40,000 computers and 10,000 television sets, and so on. We plotted these six combinations of computers and television sets in Exhibit 1(b). Each combination represents a different point in Exhibit 1(b). For example, the combination of 50,000 computers and 0 television sets is represented by point A. The line that connects points A–F is the production possibilities frontier. A **production possibilities frontier (PPF)** represents the combination of two goods that can be produced in a certain period of time under the conditions of a given state of technology and fully employed resources.

Production Possibilities Frontier (PPF)
Represents the possible combinations of two goods that can be produced in a certain period of time under the conditions of a given state of technology and fully employed resources.

exhibit 1

Production Possibilities Frontier (Constant Opportunity Costs)

The economy can produce any of the six combinations of computers and television sets in part (a). We have plotted these combinations in part (b). The production possibilities frontier in part (b) is a straight line because the opportunity cost of producing either good is constant: for *every* 1 computer not produced, 1 television set is produced.

Combination	Computers	Television Sets	Point in Part (b)
A	50,000	0	A
B	40,000	10,000	B
C	30,000	20,000	C
D	20,000	30,000	D
E	10,000	40,000	E
F	0	50,000	F

(a)

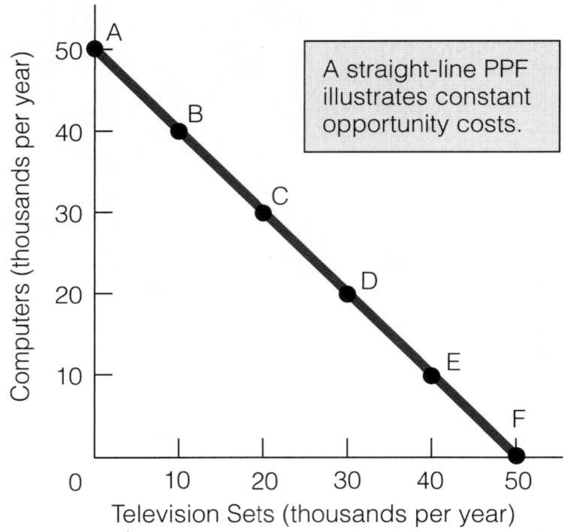

(b)

The production possibilities frontier is a straight line in this instance because the opportunity cost of producing computers and television sets is constant.

Straight-line PPF = Constant opportunity costs

For example, if the economy were to move from point A to point B, from B to C, and so on, the opportunity cost of each good would remain constant at 1 for 1. To illustrate, at point A, 50,000 computers and 0 television sets are produced. At point B, 40,000 computers and 10,000 television sets are produced.

We conclude that for every 10,000 computers not produced, 10,000 television sets are produced—a ratio of 1 to 1. The opportunity cost—1 computer for 1 television set—that exists between points A and B also exists between points B and C, C and D, D and E, and E and F. In other words, opportunity cost is constant at 1 computer for 1 television set.

The Bowed-Outward (Concave-Downward) PPF: Increasing Opportunity Costs

Assume two things:

1. Only two goods can be produced in an economy: computers and television sets.
2. As more of one good is produced, the opportunity cost between computers and television sets changes.

In Exhibit 2(a), we have identified four combinations of computers and television sets that can be produced in our economy. For example, combination A is 50,000 computers and 0 television sets, combination B is 40,000 computers and 20,000 television sets, and so on. We plotted these four combinations of computers and television sets in Exhibit 2(b).

exhibit 2

Production Possibilities Frontier (Increasing Opportunity Costs)

The economy can produce any of the four combinations of computers and televisions sets in part (a). We have plotted these combinations in part (b). The production possibilities frontier in part (b) is bowed outward because the opportunity cost of producing television sets increases as more television sets are produced.

Combination	Computers	Television Sets	Point in Part (b)
A	50,000	0	A
B	40,000	20,000	B
C	25,000	40,000	C
D	0	60,000	D

(a)

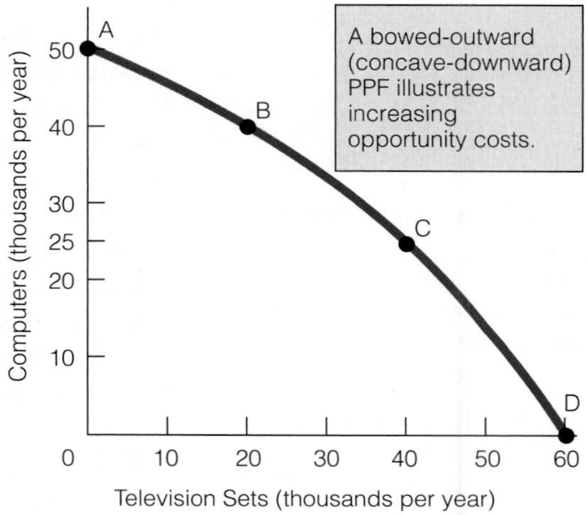

(b)

Each combination represents a different point. The curved line that connects points A–D is the production possibilities frontier.

In this case, the production possibilities frontier is bowed outward (concave downward) because the opportunity cost of television sets increases as more sets are produced.

Bowed-outward PPF = Increasing opportunity costs

To illustrate, let's start at point A, where the economy is producing 50,000 computers and 0 television sets, and move to point B, where the economy is producing 40,000 computers and 20,000 television sets.

What is the opportunity cost of a television set over this range? We see that 20,000 more television sets are produced by moving from point A to point B but *at the cost of 10,000 computers*. This means for every 1 television set produced, 1/2 computer is forfeited. Thus, the opportunity cost of 1 television set is 1/2 computer.

Now let's move from point B, where the economy is producing 40,000 computers and 20,000 television sets, to point C, where the economy is producing 25,000 computers and 40,000 television sets.

Point B: 40,000 computers, 20,000 television sets

Point C: 25,000 computers, 40,000 television sets

What is the opportunity cost of a television set over this range? In this case, 20,000 more television sets are produced by moving from point B to point C *but at the cost of 15,000 computers*. This means for every 1 television set produced, 3/4 computer is forfeited. Thus, the opportunity cost of 1 television set is 3/4 of a computer.

What statement can we make about the opportunity costs of producing television sets? Obviously, as the economy produces more television sets, the opportunity cost of producing television sets increases. This gives us the bowed-outward production possibilities frontier in Exhibit 2(b).

Law of Increasing Opportunity Costs

We know that the shape of the production possibilities frontier depends on whether opportunity costs (1) are constant or (2) increase as more of a good is produced. In Exhibit 1(b), the production possibilities frontier is a straight line; in Exhibit 2(b), it is bowed outward (curved). In the real world, most production possibilities frontiers are bowed outward. This means that for most goods, the opportunity costs *increase* as more of the good is produced. This is referred to as the **law of increasing opportunity costs.**

Law of Increasing Opportunity Costs
As more of a good is produced, the opportunity costs of producing that good increase.

But why (for most goods) do the opportunity costs increase as more of the good is produced? The answer is because people have varying abilities. For example, some people are better suited to building houses than other people are. When a construction company first starts building houses, it employs the people who are most skilled at house building. The most skilled persons can build houses at lower opportunity costs than others can. But as the construction company builds more houses, it finds that it has already employed the most skilled builders, so it must employ those who are less skilled at house building. These (less skilled) people build houses at higher opportunity costs. Where three skilled house builders could build a house in a month, as many as seven unskilled builders may be required to build it in the same length of time. Exhibit 3 summarizes the points in this section.

exhibit 3

A Summary Statement About Increasing Opportunity Costs and a Production Possibilities Frontier That Is Bowed Outward (Concave Downward)

Many of the points about increasing opportunity costs and a production possibilities frontier that is bowed outward are summarized here.

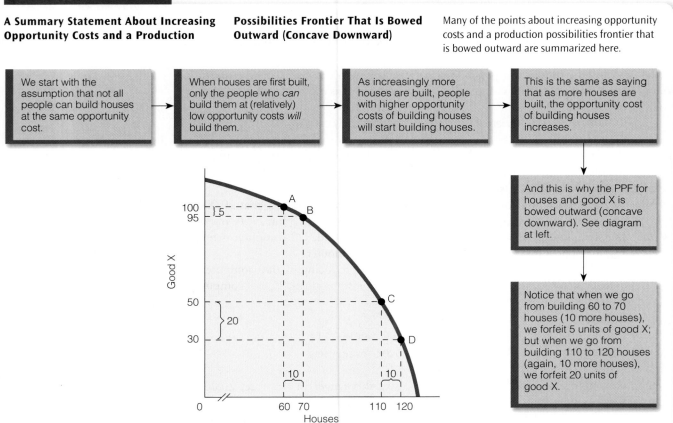

We start with the assumption that not all people can build houses at the same opportunity cost.

→ When houses are first built, only the people who *can* build them at (relatively) low opportunity costs *will* build them.

→ As increasingly more houses are built, people with higher opportunity costs of building houses will start building houses.

→ This is the same as saying that as more houses are built, the opportunity cost of building houses increases.

↓ And this is why the PPF for houses and good X is bowed outward (concave downward). See diagram at left.

↓ Notice that when we go from building 60 to 70 houses (10 more houses), we forfeit 5 units of good X; but when we go from building 110 to 120 houses (again, 10 more houses), we forfeit 20 units of good X.

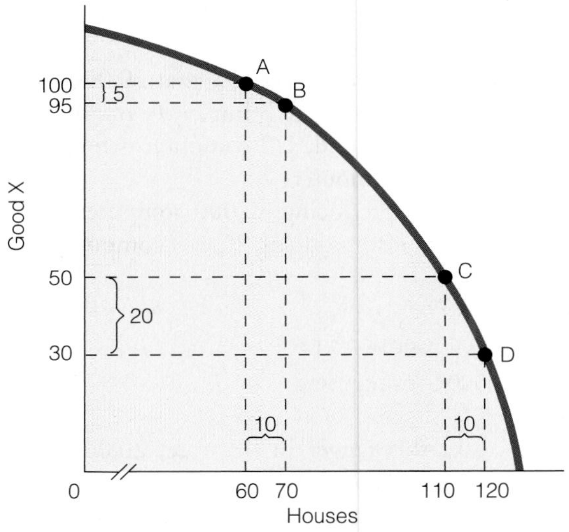

Economic Concepts Within a PPF Framework

The PPF framework is useful for illustrating and working with economic concepts. This section discusses seven economic concepts in terms of the PPF framework (see Exhibit 4).

exhibit 4

The PPF Economic Framework

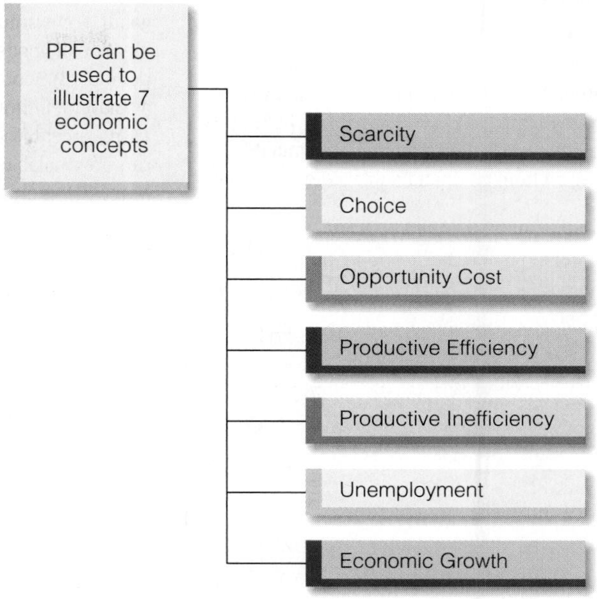
PPF can be used to illustrate 7 economic concepts
Scarcity
Choice
Opportunity Cost
Productive Efficiency
Productive Inefficiency
Unemployment
Economic Growth

SCARCITY Recall that scarcity is the condition where wants (for goods) are greater than the resources available to satisfy those wants. The finiteness of resources is graphically portrayed by the PPF in Exhibit 5. The frontier (itself) tells us: "At this point in time, that's as far as you can go. You cannot go any farther. You are limited to choosing any combination of the two goods on the frontier or below it."

The PPF separates the production possibilities of an economy into two regions: (1) an attainable region, which consists of the points on the PPF itself and all points below it (this region includes points A–F) and (2) an unattainable region, which consists of the points above and beyond the PPF (such as point G). Recall that scarcity implies that some things are attainable and others are unattainable. Point A on the PPF is attainable, as is point F; point G is not.

Choice and opportunity cost are also shown in Exhibit 5. Note that within the attainable region, individuals must choose the combination of the two goods they want to produce. Obviously, hundreds of different combinations exist, but let's consider only two, represented by points A and B. Which of the two will individuals choose? They can't be at both points; they must make a choice.

Opportunity cost is illustrated as we move from one point to another on the PPF in Exhibit 5. Suppose we are at point A and choose to move to point B. At A, we have 55,000 television sets and 5,000 cars, and at point B, we have 50,000 television sets and 15,000 cars. What is the opportunity cost of a car? Because 10,000 *more* cars come at a cost of 5,000 *fewer* television sets, the opportunity cost of 1 car is 1/2 television set.

PRODUCTIVE EFFICIENCY Economists often say that an economy is **productive efficient** if it is producing the maximum output with given resources and technology. In Exhibit 5, points A, B, C, D, and E are all productive efficient points. Notice that all these points lie on the production possibilities frontier. In other words, we are getting the most (in terms of output) from what we have (in terms of available resources and technology).

Productive Efficiency
The condition where the maximum output is produced with given resources and technology.

It follows that an economy is **productive inefficient** if it is producing less than the maximum output with given resources and technology. In Exhibit 5, point F is a productive inefficient point. It lies below the production possibilities frontier; it is below the outer limit of what is possible. In other words, we could produce more goods with the resources we have available to us. Or we can get more of one good without getting less of another good.

Productive Inefficiency
The condition where less than the maximum output is produced with given resources and technology. Productive inefficiency implies that more of one good can be produced without any less of another good being produced.

To illustrate, suppose we move from inefficient point F to efficient point C. We produce more television sets and no fewer cars. What if we move from F to D? We produce more television sets and more cars. Finally, if we move from F to E, we produce more cars and no fewer television sets. Thus, moving from F can give us more of at least one good and no less of another good. In short, productive inefficiency implies that gains are possible in one area without losses in another.

UNEMPLOYED RESOURCES When the economy exhibits productive inefficiency, it is not producing the maximum output with the available resources and technology.

exhibit 5

The PPF and Various Economic Concepts

The PPF can illustrate various economic concepts: (1) Scarcity is illustrated by the frontier itself. Implicit in the concept of scarcity is the idea that we can have some things but not all things. The PPF separates an attainable region from an unattainable region. (2) Choice is represented by our having to decide among the many attainable combinations of the two goods. For example, will we choose the combination of goods represented by point A or by point B? (3) Opportunity cost is most easily seen as movement from one point to another, such as movement from point A to point B. More cars are available at point B than at point A, but fewer television sets are available. In short, the opportunity cost of more cars is fewer television sets. (4) Productive efficiency is represented by the points on the PPF (such as A–E), while productive inefficiency is represented by any point below the PPF (such as F). (5) Unemployment (in terms of resources being unemployed) exists at any productive inefficient point (such as F), whereas resources are fully employed at any productive efficient point (such as A–E).

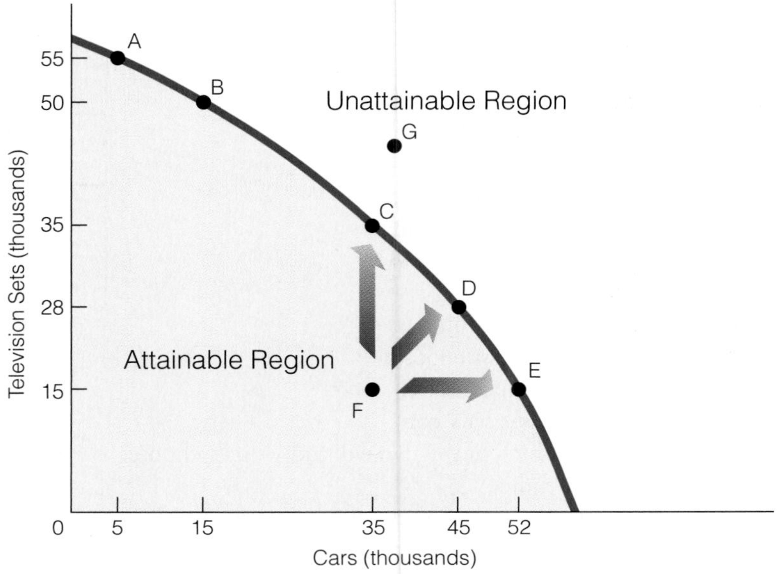

One reason may be that the economy is not using all its resources; that is, some of its resources are unemployed, as at point F in Exhibit 5.

When the economy exhibits productive efficiency, it is producing the maximum output with the available resources and technology. This means it is using all its resources to produce goods; its resources are fully employed, and none are unemployed. At the productive efficient points A–E in Exhibit 5, there are no unemployed resources.

ECONOMIC GROWTH Economic growth refers to the increased productive capabilities of an economy. It is illustrated by a shift outward in the production possibilities frontier. Two major factors that affect economic growth are (1) an increase in the quantity of resources and (2) an advance in technology.

With an increase in the quantity of resources (e.g., through a new discovery of resources), it is possible to produce a greater quantity of output. In Exhibit 6, an increase in the quantity of resources makes it possible to produce both more military goods and more civilian goods. Thus, the PPF shifts outward from PPF_1 to PPF_2.

Technology refers to the body of skills and knowledge concerning the use of resources in production. An advance in technology commonly refers to the ability to produce more output with a fixed quantity of resources or the ability to produce the same output with a smaller quantity of resources.

Technology
The body of skills and knowledge concerning the use of resources in production. An advance in technology commonly refers to the ability to produce more output with a fixed amount of resources or the ability to produce the same output with fewer resources.

Suppose an advance in technology allows more military goods and more civilian goods to be produced with the same quantity of resources. As a result, the PPF in Exhibit 6 shifts outward from PPF_1 to PPF_2. The outcome is the same as when the quantity of resources is increased.

Finding Economics

In an Attorney's Office

An attorney is sitting in his office working. Where is the economics?

Let's back up and first talk about farmers and a change in technology. During the twentieth century, many farmers left farming because farming experienced major technological advances. Where farmers once farmed with minimal capital equipment, today they use computers, tractors, pesticides, cellular phones, and much more. In 1910, the United States had 32.1 million farmers; today there are around 4.8 million farmers. Where did all the farmers go?

Because of technological advancements, fewer farmers were needed to produce food and so many farmers left the farmers for the cities, where they entered the manufacturing and service industries. In other words, people who were once farmers (or whose parents and grandparents were farmers) began to produce cars, airplanes, television sets, and computers. They became attorneys, accountants, and police officers.

What we learn here is that a technological advancement in one sector of the economy can have ripple effects throughout the economy. We also learn that a technological advancement can affect the composition of employment.

exhibit 6

Economic Growth Within a PPF Framework

An increase in resources or an advance in technology can increase the production capabilities of an economy, leading to economic growth and a shift outward in the production possibilities frontier.

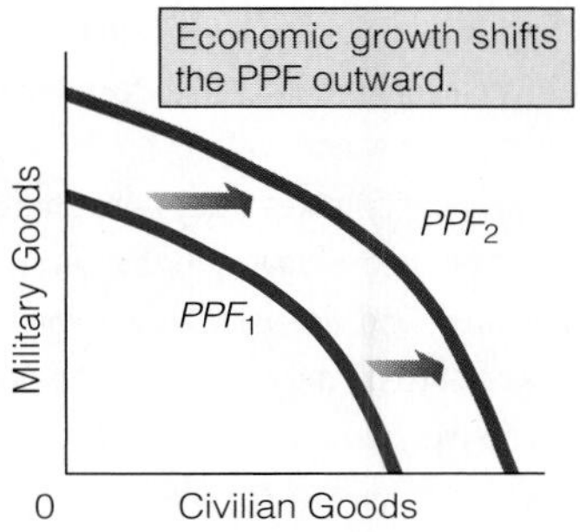

SELF-TEST

(Answers to Self-Test questions are in the Self-Test Appendix.)

1. What does a straight-line production possibilities frontier (PPF) represent? What does a bowed-outward PPF represent?
2. What does the law of increasing costs have to do with a bowed-outward PPF?
3. A politician says, "If you elect me, we can get more of everything we want." Under what condition(s) is the politician telling the truth?
4. In an economy, only one combination of goods is productive efficient. True or false? Explain your answer.

Exchange or Trade

Exchange (trade) is the process of giving up one thing for something else. Usually, money is traded for goods and services. Trade is all around us; we are involved with it every day. Few of us, however, have considered the full extent of trade.

Exchange (Trade)
The process of giving up one thing for something else.

Periods Relevant to Trade

There are three time periods relevant to the trading process. We discuss these relevant time periods next.

economics 24/7

THE PPF AND YOUR GRADES

You have your own PPF, you just may not know it. Suppose you are studying for two upcoming exams. You have only a total of eight hours before you have to take the first exam, after which you will immediately proceed to take the second exam. Time spent studying for the first exam (in economics) takes away from time that could be spent studying for the second exam (in math), and vice versa. Also, time studying is a resource in the production of a good grade; less time studying for the economics exam and more time spent studying for the math exam means a higher grade in math and a lower grade in economics. For you, the situation may look as it does in Exhibit 7(a). We have identified four points in the exhibit (1–4) corresponding to the four combinations of two grades (one grade in economics and one grade in English).

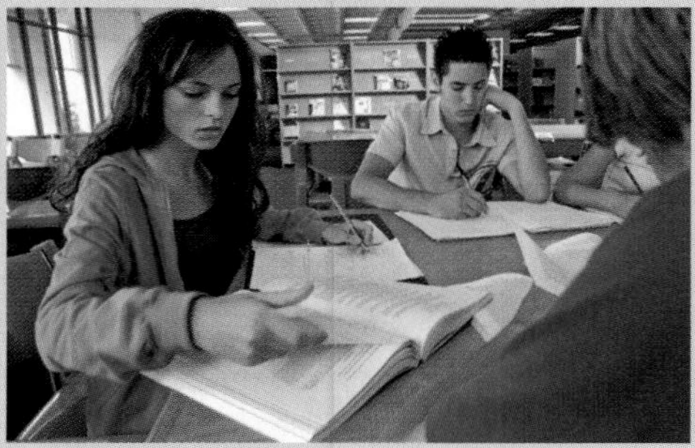

©PIXLAND/JUPITER IMAGES

You will notice also that each grade comes with a certain amount of time studying. This time is specified under the grade.

Given the resources you currently have (your labor and time) you can achieve any of the four combinations. For example, you can spend six hours studying for economics and get a B (point 1), but this means you study math for zero hours and get an F in that course. Or you can spend four hours studying for economics and get a C (point 2), leaving you two hours to study for math, in which you get a D.

What do you need to get a higher grade in one course without getting a lower grade in the other course? You need more resources, which in this case is more time. If you have eight hours to study, your PPF shifts rightward, as in Exhibit 7(b). Now point 5 is possible (whereas it was not possible before you got more time). At point 5, you can get a C in economics and in math, which was an impossible combination of grades when you had less time (a PPF closer to the origin).

exhibit 7

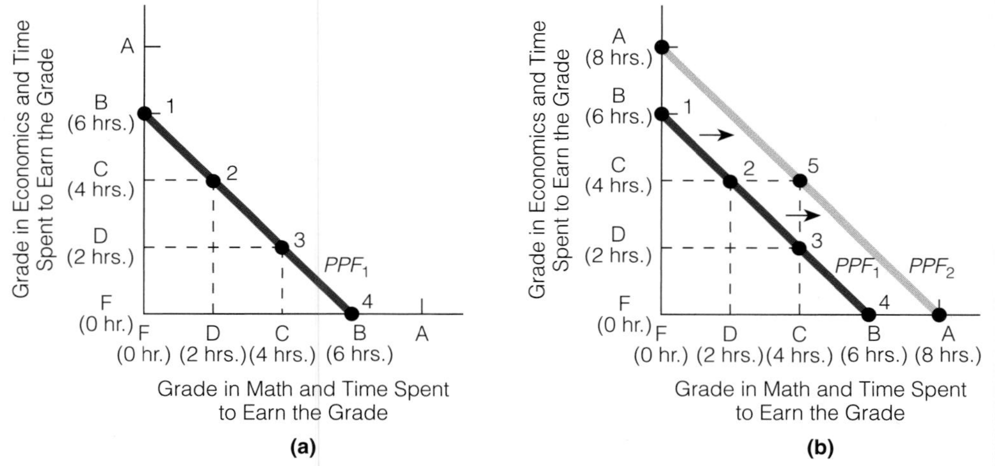

Ex Ante
Phrase that means "before," as in before a trade.

BEFORE THE TRADE Before a trade is made, a person is said to be in the **ex ante** position. For example, suppose Ramona has the opportunity to trade what she has, $2,000, for something she does not have, a plasma television set. In the ex ante position, she wonders if she will be better off with (1) the television set or with (2) $2,000 worth of other goods. If she concludes that she will be better off with the television set than with $2,000 worth of other goods, she will make the trade. Individuals will make a trade only if they believe ex ante (before) the trade that the trade will make them better off.

economics 24/7

TRADING PRISONERS

Earlier we said that no one enters into a trade unless he expects to be made better off by the trade. Let's now translate Rag this into *utility* (which we discussed in Chapter 1).

Suppose Bob has a radio and Jim has a book. The two men come together and trade: Bob gives Jim the radio in exchange for the book. Now ask yourself this question: For this trade to occur, what condition must hold? The answer for Bob is that the book must give him more utility than the radio.

For Bob: Utility of book (10 utils) $>$ Utility for radio (8 utils)

The answer for Jim is that the radio must give him more utility than the book.

For Jim: Utility of radio (10 utils) $>$ Utility for book (8 utils)

In other words, no one enters a trade unless he expects to be made better off (gain utility). In our example, each person is made better off by (or gains) 2 utils.

Economists assume that the one thing individuals want to do is maximize their utility. In other words, they want as much utility as possible. To help them in this endeavor, they trade. In fact, their desire for utility is so great that individuals will even end up trading with their enemies sometimes. To illustrate, in April 2007, the Israelis and Hezbollah were negotiating for prisoners, as were the Taliban and the government of Afghanistan. In both cases (Israeli-Hezbollah and Taliban-Afghani government) it wasn't the actual trade of prisoners that was being called into question, it was the *terms of trade*. In other words, all sides had agreed to a trade, it was simply how many prisoners would be traded on one side for prisoners on the other side.

AT THE POINT OF TRADE Suppose Ramona now gives $2,000 to the person in possession of the television set. Does Ramona still believe she will be better off with the television set than with the $2,000? Of course she does. Her action testifies to this fact.

AFTER THE TRADE After a trade is made, a person is said to be in the **ex post** position. Suppose two days have passed. Does Ramona still feel the same way about the trade as she did before the trade and at the point of trade? Maybe. Maybe not. She may look back on the trade and regret it. She may say that if she had it to do over again, she would not trade the $2,000 for a plasma television set. In general, though, people expect a trade to make them better off, and usually, the trade meets their expectations. But there are no guarantees that a trade will meet expectations because no one in the real world can see the future.

Ex Post
Phrase that means "after," as in after a trade.

Trade and the Terms of Trade

Trade refers to the process whereby "things" (money, goods, services, etc.) are given up to obtain something else. The **terms of trade** refer to *how much* of one thing is given up for *how much* of something else. For example, if $30 is traded for a bestselling book, the terms of trade are 1 bestseller for $30. If the price of a loaf of bread is $2.50, the terms of trade are 1 loaf of bread for $2.50. Buyers and sellers can always think of more advantageous terms of exchange. Buyers prefer lower prices, whereas sellers prefer higher prices.

Terms of Trade
How much of one thing is given up for how much of something else.

Thinking like AN ECONOMIST

It's Always Possible to Imagine Better Terms of Trade

A person buys a pair of shoes for $100. Later that day, the person says that he was "ripped off" by the shoe store owner; specifically, he says he paid too much for the shoes. Is this person arguing against trade or against the terms of trade? The economist knows that sometimes what sounds like a person arguing "against trade" is really his argument against the "terms of trade." Everyone can think of better terms of trade for himself. You buy a book for $40. Are there better terms of trade for you? Sure, you would have rather paid $30 for the book instead of $40. Sometimes, when it sounds as if we are arguing against trade, what we are really saying is this: "I wish I could have bought the good or service at better terms of trade than I did."

Costs of Trades

As always, economists consider both benefits and costs. They want to determine what costs are involved in a trade and whether the costs may prevent a trade from taking place.

UNEXPLOITED TRADES Suppose Smith wants to buy a red 1965 Ford Mustang in excellent condition. The maximum price she is willing and able to pay for the Mustang is $30,000. Also suppose that Jones owns a red 1965 Ford Mustang in excellent condition. The minimum price he is willing and able to sell the Mustang for is $23,000. Obviously, Smith's maximum buying price ($30,000) is greater than Jones's minimum selling price ($23,000), so a potential trade or exchange exists.

Transaction Costs
The costs associated with the time and effort needed to search out, negotiate, and consummate an exchange.

Will the potential trade between Smith and Jones become an actual exchange? The answer to this question may depend on the transaction costs. **Transaction costs** are the costs associated with the time and effort needed to search out, negotiate, and consummate a trade. To illustrate, neither Smith nor Jones may know that the other exists. Suppose Smith lives in Roanoke, Virginia, and Jones lives 40 miles away in Blacksburg, Virginia. Each needs to find the other, which may take time and money. Perhaps Smith can put an ad in the local Blacksburg newspaper stating that she is searching for a 1965 Ford Mustang in mint condition. Alternatively, Jones can put an ad in the local Roanoke newspaper stating that he has a 1965 Ford Mustang to sell. The ad may or may not be seen by the relevant party and then acted upon. Our point is a simple one: Transaction costs sometimes keep potential trades from turning into actual trades.

Consider another example. Suppose Kurt hates to shop for clothes because shopping takes too much time. He has to get in his car, drive to the mall, park the car, walk into the mall, look in different stores, try on different clothes, pay for the items, walk to and get back in his car, and drive home. Suppose Kurt spends an average of two hours when he shops, and he estimates that an hour of his time is worth $30. It follows, then, that Kurt incurs $60 worth of transaction costs when he buys clothes. Usually, he is not willing to incur the transaction costs necessary to buy a pair of trousers or a shirt.

Now, suppose we ask Kurt if he would be more willing to buy clothes if shopping was easier. Suppose, we say, the transaction costs associated with buying clothes could be lowered from $60 to less than $10. At lower transaction costs, Kurt says that he would be willing to shop more often.

How can transaction costs be lowered? Both people and computers can help lower the transaction costs of trades. For example, real estate brokers lower the transaction costs of selling and buying a house. Jim has a house to sell but doesn't know how to find a buyer. Karen wants to buy a house but doesn't know how to find a seller. Enter the real estate broker, who brings buyers and sellers together. In so doing, she lowers the transaction costs of buying and selling a house.

As another example, consider e-commerce on the Internet. Ursula can buy a book by getting in her car, driving to a bookstore, getting out of her car, walking into the bookstore, looking at the books on the shelves, taking a book to the cashier, paying for it, leaving the store, getting back in her car, and returning home. Or Ursula can buy a book over the Internet. She can click on one of the online booksellers, search for the book by title, read a short description of the book, and then click once to buy. Buying on the Internet has lower transaction costs than shopping at a store because online buying requires less time and effort. Before online book buying and selling, were there potential book purchases and sales that weren't being turned into actual book purchases and sales? There is some evidence that there were.

TURNING POTENTIAL TRADES INTO ACTUAL TRADES Some people are always looking for ways to earn a profit. It would seem that one way to earn a profit is to turn potential trades into actual trades by lowering transaction costs. Consider the following example. Buyer Smith is willing to pay a maximum price of $400 for good X; Seller Jones is willing to accept a minimum price of $200 for good X. Currently, the transaction costs of the exchange are $500, evenly split between Buyer Smith and Seller Jones.

Buyer Smith thinks, "Even if I pay the lowest possible price for good X, $200, I will still have to pay $250 in transaction costs, bringing my total to $450. The maximum price I am willing to pay for good X is $400, so I will not make this purchase."

Seller Jones thinks, "Even if I receive the highest possible price for good X, $400, I will still have to pay $250 in transaction costs, leaving me with only $150. The minimum price I am willing to accept for good X is $200, so I will not make this sale."

This potential trade will not become an actual trade unless someone can lower the transaction costs. One role of an entrepreneur is to try *to turn potential trades into actual trades by lowering transaction costs.* Suppose Entrepreneur Brown can lower the transaction costs for Buyer Smith and Seller Jones to $10 each, asking $60 from each person for services rendered. Also, Entrepreneur Brown negotiates the price of good X at $300. Will the potential exchange become an actual exchange?

Buyer Smith thinks, "I am willing to pay a maximum of $400 for good X. If I purchase good X through Entrepreneur Brown, I will pay $300 to Seller Jones, $10 in transaction costs, and $60 to Brown. This is a total of $370, leaving me better off by $30. It is worthwhile for me to purchase good X."

Seller Jones thinks, "I am willing to sell good X for a minimum of $200. If I sell good X through Entrepreneur Brown, I will receive $300 from Buyer Smith and will have to pay $10 in transaction costs and $60 to Brown. That will leave me with $230, or $30 better off. It is worthwhile for me to sell good X."

Thinking like AN ECONOMIST

Profit Motivates Action

In the example just given, Buyer Smith and Seller Jones were made better off by Entrepreneur Brown. Keep in mind that it was profit that motivated Entrepreneur Brown to turn a potential exchange into an actual exchange and, in the process, make both Smith and Jones better off. Simply put, the desire for profit (to help ourselves) can often prompt us to assist others. Thus, an entrepreneur can earn a profit by finding a way to lower transaction costs. As a result, a potential exchange turns into an actual exchange.

Trades and Third-Party Effects

Consider two trades. In the first, Harriet pays 80 cents to Taylor for a pack of chewing gum. In this trade, both Harriet and Taylor are made better off (they wouldn't have traded otherwise), and no one is made worse off.

In the second trade, Bob pays $5 to George for a pack of cigarettes. Bob takes a cigarette, lights it, and smokes it. It happens that he is near Caroline when he smokes the cigarette, and she begins to cough because she is sensitive to cigarette smoke. In this trade, both Bob, who buys the cigarettes, and George, who sells the cigarettes, are made better off. But Caroline, who had nothing to do with the trade, is made worse off. In this exchange, a third party, Caroline, is adversely affected by the exchange between George and Bob.

These examples show that some trades affect only the parties involved in the exchange, and some trades have *third-party effects* (someone other than the parties involved in the exchange is affected). In the cigarette example, the third-party effect was negative; there was an adverse effect on Caroline, the third party. Sometimes economists call adverse third-party effects *negative externalities*. A later chapter discusses this topic in detail.

SELF-TEST

1. What are transaction costs? Are the transaction costs of buying a house likely to be greater or less than those of buying a car? Explain your answer.
2. Smith is willing to pay a maximum of $300 for good X, and Jones is willing to sell good X for a minimum of $220. Will Smith buy good X from Jones?
3. Give an example of a trade without third-party effects. Next, give an example of a trade with third-party effects.

PRODUCTION, TRADE, AND SPECIALIZATION

The first section of this chapter discusses production; the second section discusses trade. From these two sections, you might conclude that production and trade are unrelated activities. However, they are not: Before you can trade, you need to produce something. This section ties production and trade together and also shows how the benefits one receives from trade can be affected by how one produces.

Producing and Trading

To show how a change in production can benefit traders, we eliminate anything and everything extraneous to the process. Thus, we eliminate money and consider a barter, or moneyless, economy.

In this economy, there are two individuals, Elizabeth and Brian. They live near each other, and each engages in two activities: baking bread and growing apples. Let's suppose that within a certain period of time, Elizabeth can produce 20 loaves of bread and no apples, or 10 loaves of bread and 10 apples, or no bread and 20 apples. See Exhibit 8. In other words, three points on Elizabeth's production possibilities frontier correspond to 20 loaves of bread and no apples, 10 loaves of bread and 10 apples, and no bread and 20 apples. As a consumer, Elizabeth likes to eat both bread and apples, so she decides to produce (and consume) 10 loaves of bread and 10 apples.

exhibit 8

Production by Elizabeth and Brian

This exhibit shows the combinations of goods each can produce individually in a given time period.

Elizabeth		Brian	
Bread	**Apples**	**Bread**	**Apples**
20	0	10	0
10	10	5	15
0	20	0	30

Within the same time period, Brian can produce 10 loaves of bread and no apples, or 5 loaves of bread and 15 apples, or no bread and 30 apples. In other words, these three combinations correspond to three points on Brian's production possibilities frontier. Brian, like Elizabeth, likes to eat both bread and apples, so he decides to produce and consume 5 loaves of bread and 15 apples. See Exhibit 8.

Elizabeth thinks that both she and Brian may be better off if each specializes in producing only one of the two goods and trading it for the other. In other words, Elizabeth should produce either bread or apples but not both. Brian thinks this may be a good idea but is not sure which good each person should specialize in producing.

An economist would advise each to produce the good that he or she can produce at a lower cost. In economics, a person who can produce a good at a lower cost than another person is said to have a **comparative advantage** in the production of that good.

Comparative Advantage
The situation where someone can produce a good at lower opportunity cost than someone else can.

Exhibit 8 shows that for every 10 units of bread Elizabeth does not produce, she can produce 10 apples. In other words, the opportunity cost of producing 1 loaf of bread (B) is 1 apple (A):

Opportunity costs for Elizabeth: 1B = 1A
1A = 1B

As for Brian, for every 5 loaves of bread he does not produce, he can produce 15 apples. So for every 1 loaf of bread he does not produce, he can produce 3 apples. It follows, then, that for every 1 apple he chooses to produce, he forfeits 1/3 loaf of bread.

Opportunity costs for Brian: 1B = 3A
1A = ⅓B

Comparing opportunity costs, we see that Elizabeth can produce bread at a lower opportunity cost than Brian can. (Elizabeth forfeits 1 apple when she produces 1 loaf of bread, whereas Brian forfeits 3 apples when he produces 1 loaf of bread.) On the other hand, Brian can produce apples at a lower opportunity cost than Elizabeth can. We conclude that Elizabeth has a comparative advantage in the production of bread, and Brian has a comparative advantage in the production of apples.

Suppose each person specializes in the production of the good in which he or she has a comparative advantage. This means Elizabeth produces only bread and produces 20 loaves. Brian produces only apples and produces 30 apples.

Now suppose that Elizabeth and Brian decide to trade 8 loaves of bread for 12 apples. In other words, Elizabeth produces 20 loaves of bread and then trades 8 of the loaves for 12 apples. After the trade, Elizabeth consumes 12 loaves of bread and 12 apples.

exhibit 9

Consumption for Elizabeth and Brian With and Without Specialization and Trade

A comparison of the consumption of bread and apples before and after specialization and trade shows that both Elizabeth and Brian benefit from producing the good in which each has a comparative advantage and trading for the other good.

		No Specialization and No Trade	Specialization and Trade	Gains from Specialization and Trade
Elizabeth	Consumption of Loaves of Bread	10	12	+2
	Consumption of Apples	10	12	+2
Brian	Consumption of Loaves of Bread	5	8	+3
	Consumption of Apples	15	18	+3

Compare this situation with what she consumed when she didn't specialize and didn't trade. In that situation, she consumed 10 loaves of bread and 10 apples. Clearly, Elizabeth is better off when she specializes and trades than when she does not. But what about Brian?

Brian produces 30 apples and trades 12 of them to Elizabeth for 8 loaves of bread. In other words, he consumes 8 loaves of bread and 18 apples. Compare this situation with what he consumed when he didn't specialize and didn't trade. In that situation, he consumed 5 loaves of bread and 15 apples. Thus, Brian is also better off when he specializes and trades than when he does not.

Exhibit 9 summarizes consumption for Elizabeth and Brian. It shows that both Elizabeth and Brian make themselves better off by specializing in the production of one good and trading for the other.

Finding ECONOMICS

At the Airport

You wake up in the morning and drive to the airport. Curbside at the airport you have your bags checked. You tip the person who checks your luggage. You then line up to go through security. Once on the plane you hear the pilot telling you the flying time for today's flight. Later in the flight, the flight attendant brings you a soft drink and a snack. What you see at the airport and on board the plane is different people performing different tasks. The pilot is flying the plane and the customer service person at the check-in counter is receiving your luggage, and so on. Can you find the economics? Think about it for a minute before you read on.

What you see at the airport and on board the plane is specialization. The pilot isn't flying the plane and checking your luggage too. He is only flying the plane. The flight attendant isn't serving you food and checking you through security too. He is only serving you food. Why do people specialize? Largely, it's because individuals have found that they are better off specializing than not specializing. And usually what people specialize in is that activity in which they have a comparative advantage.

JERRY SEINFELD, THE DOORMAN, AND ADAM SMITH

Oh, I get it. Why waste time making small talk with the doorman? I should just shut up and do my job, opening the door for you.

—The doorman, speaking to Jerry, in an episode of *Seinfeld*

© NBC TV/THE KOBAL COLLECTION

In a Seinfeld episode, Jerry comes across a doorman (played by actor Larry Miller) who seems to have a chip on his shoulder. While waiting for the elevator, Jerry sees the doorman reading a newspaper. Jerry looks over and says, "What about those Knicks?" (a reference to the New York Knicks professional basketball team). The doorman's response is, "What makes you think I wasn't reading the Wall Street page? Oh, I know, because I'm the uneducated doorman."

This exchange between the doorman and Jerry would be unlikely if Jerry had not lived in New York City or in some other large city. That's because doormen are usually found only in large cities. If you live in a city with a population less than 100,000, you may not find a single doorman in the entire city. There are few doormen even in cities with a population of one million.

This observation is not unique to us. It goes back to Adam Smith, who said that there is a direct relationship between the degree of specialization and the size of the market. Smith said: "There are some sorts of industry, even of the lowest kind, which can be carried on nowhere but in a great town. A porter, for example, can find employment and subsistence in no other place. A village is by much too narrow a sphere for him; even an ordinary market town is scarce large enough to afford him constant occupation."[1]

Smith's observation that "some sorts of industry . . . can be carried on nowhere but in a great town" seems true. Some occupations and some goods can only be found in big cities. Try to find a doorman in North Adams, Michigan (population 514), or restaurant chefs who only prepare Persian, Yugoslavian, or Caribbean entrées in Ipswich, South Dakota (population 943).

[1] Smith, Adam. *An Inquiry into the Nature and Causes of the Wealth of Nations.* Edwin Cannan, ed. New York: Modern Library, 1965.

Profit and a Lower Cost of Living

The last column of Exhibit 9 shows the gains from specialization and trade. One way to view these gains is in terms of Elizabeth and Brian being better off when they specialize and trade than when they do not specialize and do not trade. In short, specialization and trade make people better off.

Another way to view these gains is in terms of profit and a lower cost of living. To illustrate, let's look again at Elizabeth. Essentially, Elizabeth undertakes two actions by specializing and trading. The first action is to produce more of one good (loaves of bread) than she produces when she does not specialize. The second action is to trade, or "sell," some of the bread for a "price" higher than the cost of producing the bread. Specifically, she "sells" 8 of the loaves of bread (to Brian) for a "price" of 12 apples. In other words, she "sells" each loaf of bread for a "price" of 1 1/2 apples. But Elizabeth can produce a loaf of bread for a cost of 1 apple. So she "sells" the bread for a "price" (1 1/2 apples) that's higher than her cost of producing the bread (1 apple). The difference is her profit.

Common MISCONCEPTIONS

About Profits and Winners and Losers

Many people think that one person's profit is another person's loss. In other words, because Elizabeth earns a profit by specializing and trading, Brian must lose. But we have showed that this is not the case. The cost to Brian of producing a loaf of bread is 3 apples. But he "buys" bread from Elizabeth for a "price" of only 1 1/2 apples. In other words, while Elizabeth is earning a profit, Brian's cost of living (what he has to forfeit to get a loaf of bread) is declining.

A Benevolent and All-Knowing Dictator Versus the Invisible Hand

Suppose a benevolent dictator governs the country where Brian and Elizabeth live. We assume that this benevolent dictator knows everything about almost every economic activity in his country. In other words, he knows Elizabeth's and Brian's opportunity costs of producing bread and apples.

Because the dictator is benevolent and because he wants the best for the people who live in his country, he orders Elizabeth to produce only loaves of bread and Brian to produce only apples. Next, he tells Elizabeth and Brian to trade 8 loaves of bread for 12 apples.

Afterward, he shows Exhibit 9 to Elizabeth and Brian. They are both surprised that they are better off having done what the benevolent dictator told them to do.

Now in the original story about Elizabeth and Brian, there was no benevolent, all-knowing dictator. There were only two people who were guided by their self-interest to specialize and trade. In other words, self-interest did for Elizabeth and Brian what the benevolent dictator did for them.

Adam Smith, the eighteenth-century Scottish economist and founder of modern economics, spoke about the *invisible hand* that "guided" individuals' actions toward a positive outcome that they did not intend. That is what happened in the original story about Elizabeth and Brian. Neither intended to increase the overall output of society; each intended only to make himself or herself better off.

SELF-TEST

1. If George can produce either (a) 10X and 20Y or (b) 5X and 25Y, what is the opportunity cost to George of producing one more X?
2. Harriet can produce either (a) 30X and 70Y or (b) 40X and 55Y; Bill can produce either (c) 10X and 40Y or (d) 20X and 20Y. Who has a comparative advantage in the production of X? of Y? Explain your answers.

office hours

"WHAT PURPOSE DOES THE PPF SERVE?"

Student:

It seems that economists have many uses for the production possibilities frontier (PPF). For example, they can talk about scarcity, choice, opportunity costs, and many other topics in terms of the PPF. Beyond this, what purpose does the PPF serve?

Instructor:

One purpose is to ground us in reality. For example, the frontier (or boundary) of the PPF represents scarcity, which is a fact of life. In other words, the frontier of the PPF is essentially saying, "Here is scarcity. Work with it." One of the important effects of acknowledging this fact is that we come to understand *what is* and *what is not* possible. For example, if the economy is currently on the frontier of its PPF, producing 100 units of X and 200 units of Y, it follows that it's possible to get more of X, but it's impossible to get more of X without getting less of Y. In other words, the frontier of the PPF grounds us in reality: More of one thing means less of something else.

Student:

But isn't this something that we already knew?

Instructor:

We understand that more of X means less of Y once someone makes this point, but think of how often we might act as if we don't know it. John thinks he can work more hours at his job and get a good grade on his upcoming chemistry test. Well, he might be able to get a good grade (say, a 90), but this ignores how much higher the grade could have been (say, five points higher) if he hadn't worked more hours at his job. The frontier of the PPF reminds us that there are trade-offs in life. That is an important reality to be aware of. We ignore it at our own peril.

Student:

I've also heard that the PPF can show us what is necessary before the "average person" in a country can become richer. Is this true? And what kind of richer do we mean here?

Instructor:

We are talking about becoming richer in terms of having more goods and services. It's possible for the "average person" to become richer through economic growth. In other words, the average person in society becomes richer if the PPF shifts rightward by more than the population grows. To illustrate, suppose that a 100-person economy is currently producing 100 units of X and 200 units of Y. It follows that the average person can have 1 unit of X and 2 units of Y. Now suppose there is economic growth (shifting the PPF to the right) and the economy can now produce more of both goods, X and Y. It produces 200 units of X and 400 units of Y. If the population has not changed (if it is still 100 people), then the average person can now have 2 units of X and 4 units of Y. The average person is richer in terms of two goods, X and Y. If we change things, and let the population grow from 100 persons to, say, 125 persons, it is still possible for the average person to have more through economic growth. With a population of 125 people, the average person now has 1.6 units of X and 3.2 units of good Y. In other words, as long as the productive capability of the economy grows by a greater percentage than the population, it is possible for the average person to become richer (in terms of goods and services).

Student:

Just because the economy is producing more of both goods (X and Y), it doesn't necessarily follow that the average person is better off in terms of goods and services, does it? Can't all the extra output end up in the hands of only a few people instead of being evenly distributed across the entire population?

Instructor:

That's correct. What we are assuming when we say the "average person" can be made better off is that if we took the extra output and divided it evenly across the population, then the average person would be better off in terms of having more goods and services. By the way, this is what economists mean when they say that the output (goods and services) per capita in a population has risen.

Points to Remember

1. The production possibilities frontier (PPF) grounds us in reality. It tells us *what is* and *what is not* possible in terms of producing various combinations of goods and services.
2. The PPF tells us that when we have efficiency (we are at a point on the frontier itself), more of one thing means less of something else. In other words, the PPF tells us there are trade-offs in life.
3. If the PPF shifts rightward and the population does not change, then output per capita rises.

a reader asks

How Will Economics Help Me if I'm a History Major?

I'm a history major taking my first course in economics. But quite frankly, I don't see how economics will be of much use in my study of history. Any thoughts on the subject?

Economics often plays a major role in historical events. For example, many social scientists argue that economics played a large role in the collapse of communism. If communism had been able to produce the quantity and variety of goods and services that capitalism produces, perhaps the Soviet Union would still exist.

Fact is, understanding economics may help you understand many historical events or periods. If, as a historian, you study the Great Depression, you will need to know something about the stock market, tariffs, and more. If you study the California Gold Rush, you will need to know about supply, demand, and prices. If you study the history of prisoner-of-war camps, you will need to know about how and why people trade and about money. If you study the Boston Tea Party, you will need to know about government grants of monopoly and about taxes.

Economics can also be useful in another way. Suppose you learn in your economics course what can and cannot cause inflation. We'll say you learn that X can cause inflation and that Y cannot. Then, one day, you read an article in which a historian says that Y caused the high inflation in a certain country and that the high inflation led to a public outcry, which was then met with stiff government reprisals. Without an understanding of economics, you might be willing to accept what the historian has written. But with your understanding of economics, you know that events could not have happened as the historian reports because Y, which the historian claims caused the high inflation, could not have caused the high inflation.

In conclusion, a good understanding of economics will not only help you understand key historical events but will also help you discern inaccuracies in recorded history.

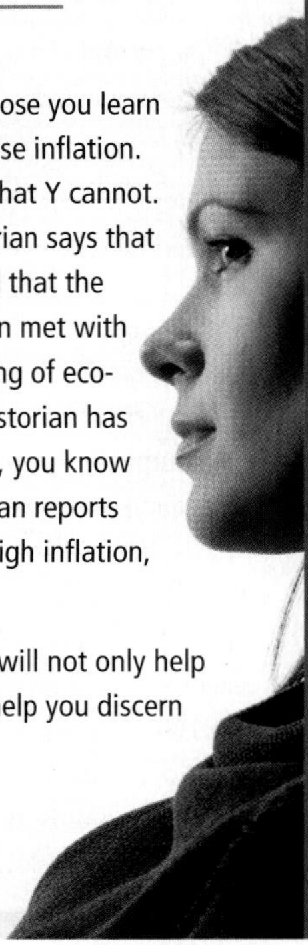

Chapter Summary

AN ECONOMY'S PRODUCTION POSSIBILITIES FRONTIER

- An economy's production possibilities frontier (PPF) represents the possible combinations of two goods that the economy can produce in a certain period of time under the conditions of a given state of technology and fully employed resources.

INCREASING AND CONSTANT OPPORTUNITY COSTS

- A straight-line PPF represents constant opportunity costs: Increased production of one good comes at constant opportunity costs.
- A bowed-outward (concave-downward) PPF represents the law of increasing opportunity costs: Increased production of one good comes at increased opportunity costs.

THE PRODUCTION POSSIBILITIES FRONTIER AND VARIOUS ECONOMIC CONCEPTS

- The PPF can be used to illustrate various economic concepts. Scarcity is illustrated by the frontier itself. Choice is illustrated by our knowing that we have to locate at some particular point either on the frontier or below it. In short, of the many attainable positions, one must be chosen. Opportunity cost is illustrated by a movement from one point on the PPF to another point on the PPF. Unemployed resources and productive inefficiency are illustrated by a point below the PPF. Productive efficiency and fully employed resources are illustrated by a point on the PPF. Economic growth is illustrated by a shift outward in the PPF.

EXCHANGE OR TRADE

- The three time periods relevant to the trading process are (1) the ex ante period, which is the time before the trade is made, (2) the point of trade, and (3) the ex post period, which is the time after the trade has been made.
- There is a difference between trade and the terms of trade. Trade refers to the act of giving up one thing for something else. For example, a person may trade money for a car. The terms of trade refer to *how much* of one thing is traded for *how much* of something else. For example, how much money ($25,000? $30,000?) is traded for one car.

TRANSACTION COSTS

- Transaction costs are the costs associated with the time and effort needed to search out, negotiate, and consummate a trade. Some potential exchanges are not realized because of high transaction costs. Lowering transaction costs can turn a potential exchange into an actual exchange.
- One role of an entrepreneur is to try to lower transaction costs.

COMPARATIVE ADVANTAGE AND SPECIALIZATION

- Individuals can make themselves better off by specializing in the production of the good in which they have a comparative advantage and then trading some of that good for other goods. A person has a comparative advantage in the production of a good if he or she can produce the good at a lower opportunity cost than another person can.
- Individuals gain by specializing and trading. Specifically, they earn a profit by specializing in the production of the goods in which they have a comparative advantage.

Key Terms and Concepts

Production Possibilities Frontier (PPF)
Law of Increasing Opportunity Costs
Productive Efficiency
Productive Inefficiency
Technology
Exchange (Trade)
Ex Ante
Ex Post
Terms of Trade
Transaction Costs
Comparative Advantage

Questions and Problems

1 Describe how each of the following would affect the U.S. production possibilities frontier: (a) an increase in the number of illegal immigrants entering the country, (b) a war that takes place on your country's soil, (c) the discovery of a new oil field, (d) a decrease in the unemployment rate, and (e) a law that requires individuals to enter lines of work for which they are not suited.

2 Explain how the following can be represented in a PPF framework: (a) the finiteness of resources implicit in the scarcity condition, (b) choice, (c) opportunity cost, (d) productive efficiency, and (e) unemployed resources.

3 What condition must hold for the production possibilities frontier to be bowed outward (concave downward)? to be a straight line?

4 Give an example to illustrate each of the following: (a) constant opportunity costs and (b) increasing opportunity costs.

5 Why are most production possibilities frontiers for goods bowed outward (concave downward)?

6 Within a PPF framework, explain each of the following: (a) a disagreement between a person who favors more domestic welfare spending and one who favors more national defense spending, (b) an increase in the population, and (c) a technological change that makes resources less specialized.

7 Explain how to derive a production possibilities frontier. For instance, how is the extreme point on the vertical axis identified? How is the extreme point on the horizontal axis identified?

8 If the slope of the production possibilities frontier is the same between any two points, what does this imply about costs? Explain your answer.

9 Suppose a nation's PPF shifts inward as its population grows. What happens, on average, to the material standard of living of the people? Explain your answer.

10 "A nation may be able to live beyond its means, but the world cannot." Do you agree or disagree? Explain your answer.

11 Can a technological advancement in sector X of the economy affect the number of people who work in sector Y of the economy? Explain your answer.

12 Use the PPF framework to explain something in your everyday life that was not mentioned in the chapter.

13 Describe the three time periods relevant to the trading process.

14 Are all exchanges or trades beneficial to both parties in the ex post position? Explain your answer.

15 A person who benefits from a trade can be disgruntled over the terms of trade. Do you agree or disagree? Explain your answer.

16 Give a numerical example that illustrates high transaction costs preventing an exchange or trade from taking place.

17 Give an example of a negative third-party effect (negative externality).

18 On any given day, 16 million items in 27,000 different categories are listed on sale on eBay.com. What does eBay do? It brings buyers and sellers together. But how does it do this?

19 Bob and Susan are married. Instead of splitting the various tasks in the home equally (you cook half the meals and I'll cook the other half of the meals), they end up specializing in certain tasks. For example, Susan does the cooking and Bob washes the dishes; Susan does the laundry and Bob mows the lawn. Why might Bob and Susan find it better to specialize in certain tasks instead of equally splitting each task?

20 Is it always possible to imagine better terms of trade? Give an example of why it is or why it is not.

21 "A profit for one person does not necessarily imply a loss for someone else." Do you agree or disagree? Explain your answer with an example.

22 What does it mean to say that someone has a comparative advantage in the production of good X?

23 The frontier or boundary of the PPF says "Here is scarcity." What does this mean?

24 Why might there be more people working as doormen in New York City than Topeka, Kansas?

Working with Numbers and Graphs

1 Tina can produce any of the following combinations of goods X and Y: (a) 100X and 0Y, (b) 50X and 25Y, and (c) 0X and 50Y. David can produce any of the following combinations of goods X and Y: (a) 50X and 0Y, (b) 25X and 40Y, and (c) 0X and 80Y. Who has a comparative advantage in the production of good X? of good Y? Explain your answer.

2 Using the data in problem 1, prove that both Tina and David can be made better off through specialization and trade.

3 Exhibit 6 represents an advance in technology that made it possible to produce more of both military and civilian goods. Represent an advance in technology that makes it possible to produce more of only civilian goods. Does this indirectly make it possible to produce more military goods? Explain your answer.

4 In the following figure, which graph depicts a technological breakthrough in the production of good X only?

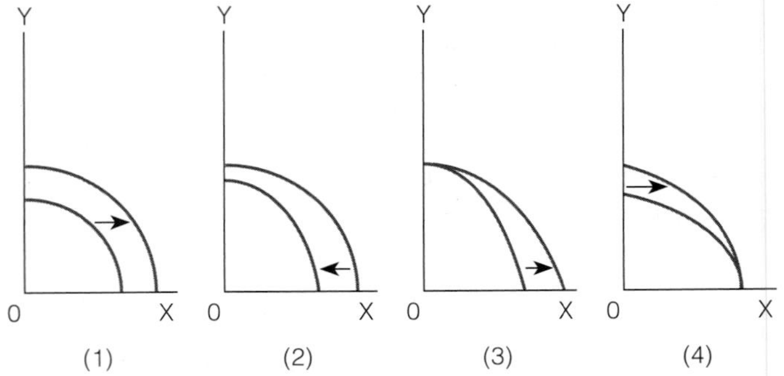

5 In the preceding figure, which graph depicts a change in the PPF that is a likely consequence of war?

6 If PPF_2 in the following graph is the relevant production possibilities frontier, then which points are unattainable? Explain your answer.

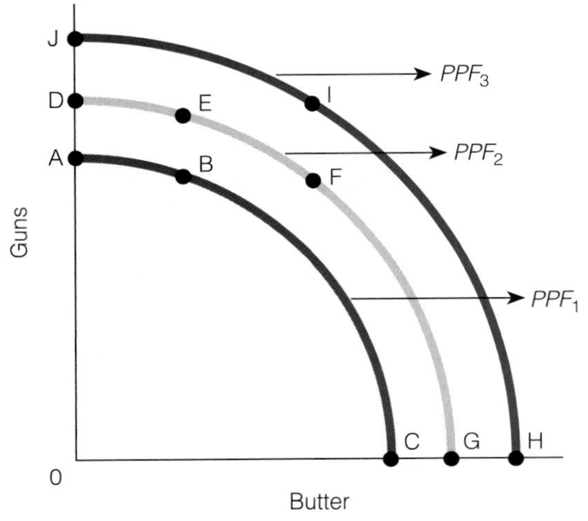

7 If PPF_1 in the preceding figure is the relevant production possibilities frontier, then which point(s) represent productive efficiency? Explain your answer.

CHAPTER 3

SUPPLY AND DEMAND: THEORY

Introduction Psychologists sometimes use a technique called word association to learn more about their patients. The psychologist says a word, then the patient says the first word that comes into his or her head: morning, night; boy, girl; sunrise, sunset. If a psychologist ever happened to say "supply" to an economist, the response would undoubtedly be "demand." To economists, supply and demand go together. (Thomas Carlyle, the historian and philosopher, said that "it is easy to train economists. Just teach a parrot to say Supply and Demand." Not funny, Carlyle.) Supply and demand have been called the "bread and butter" of economics. In this chapter, we discuss them, first separately and then together.

A NOTE ABOUT THEORIES

Economists often build theories. They build a **theory** to answer questions that do not have obvious answers. For example, they might build a theory to understand why interest rates rise at some times and fall at others, why the price of a car is $25,000 and not $27,000, or why some countries have higher economic growth rates than other countries. When building theories, economists omit certain variables or factors when trying to explain or understand something. To understand why, consider an analogy. Suppose you were to draw a map for a friend, showing him how to get from his house to your house. Would you draw a map that showed *every single thing* your friend would see on the trip from his house to yours, or would you simply draw the main roads and one or two landmarks? If you'd do the latter, you would be abstracting from reality; you would be omitting certain things.

Theory
An abstract representation of the real world designed with the intent to better understand the world.

You would "omit certain variables or factors" for two reasons. First, to get your friend from his house to yours, you don't need to include everything on your map. Simply noting main roads may be enough. Second, if you did note everything on your map, your friend might get confused. Giving too much detail could be as bad as giving too little.

(Back in Chapter 1, you learned there is an efficient amount of almost everything. There is also an efficient amount of detail. There can be too much, too little, or just the right amount. Just the right amount is the efficient amount.)

When economists build a theory, they do the same thing you do when you draw a map. They abstract from reality; they leave out certain things. They focus on the major factors or variables that they believe will explain the phenomenon they are trying to understand.

This chapter deals with the theory of supply and demand. The objective of the theory is to try to understand why prices are what they are—for instance, why bread's price is $2 a loaf and not $20 a loaf or why a computer's price is $1,000 and not $10,000.

WHAT IS DEMAND?

Market
Any place people come together to trade.

Demand
The willingness and ability of buyers to purchase different quantities of a good at different prices during a specific time period.

A **market** is any place people come together to trade. Economists often say that there are *two* sides to every market: a buying side and a selling side. The buying side of the market is usually referred to as the *demand* side; the selling side of the market is usually referred to as the *supply* side. Let's begin with a discussion of *demand.*

The word **demand** has a precise meaning in economics. It refers to:

1. the willingness and ability of buyers to purchase different quantities of a good
2. at different prices
3. during a specific time period (per day, week, etc.).[1]

For example, we can express part of John's demand for magazines by saying that he is willing and able to buy 10 magazines a month at $4 per magazine and that he is willing and able to buy 15 magazines a month at $3 per magazine.

Remember this important point about demand: Unless both willingness and ability to buy are present, there is no demand, and a person is not a buyer. For example, Josie may be willing to buy a computer but be unable to pay the price; Tanya may be able to buy a computer but be unwilling to do so. Neither Josie nor Tanya demands a computer, and neither is a buyer of a computer.

The Law of Demand

Law of Demand
As the price of a good rises, the quantity demanded of the good falls, and as the price of a good falls, the quantity demanded of the good rises, *ceteris paribus.*

Will people buy more units of a good at lower prices than at higher prices? For example, will people buy more shirts at $10 a shirt than at $70 a shirt? If your answer is yes, you instinctively understand the law of demand. The **law of demand** states that as the price of a good rises, the quantity demanded of the good falls, and as the price of a good falls, the quantity demanded of the good rises, *ceteris paribus.* Simply put, the law of demand states that the price of a good and the quantity demanded of the good are inversely related, *ceteris paribus:*

$$P\uparrow Q_d\downarrow$$
$$P\downarrow Q_d\uparrow \text{ ceteris paribus}$$

where P = price and Q_d = quantity demanded.

Quantity demanded is the number of units of a good that individuals are willing and able to buy at a particular price during some time period. For example, suppose individuals

1. Demand takes into account *services* as well as goods. A few examples of goods: shirts, books, and television sets. A few examples of services: dental care, medical care, an economics lecture. To simplify the discussion, we refer only to goods.

are willing and able to buy 100 TV dinners per week at a price of $4 per dinner. Therefore, 100 units is the quantity demanded of TV dinners at $4.

A warning: We know that the words "demand" and "quantity demanded" sound alike. But keep in mind that they do not speak to the same thing. Demand is different than quantity demanded. You need to keep that in mind as you continue to read this chapter. For now, remind yourself that demand speaks to the willingness and ability of buyers to buy different quantities of a good at different prices. Quantity demanded speaks to the willingness and ability of buyers to buy a specific quantity (say, 100 units of a good) at a specific price (say, $10 per unit).

What Does *Ceteris Paribus* Mean?

When we defined the law of demand, we used the term ***ceteris paribus***. This is a Latin term that means *all other things held constant* or *nothing else changes*. For example, an economist might say: "As the price of Pepsi-Cola rises, the quantity demanded of Pepsi-Cola falls, *ceteris paribus*." Translated: If we raise the price of Pepsi-Cola, and nothing else changes—in other words, people's preferences stay the same, the recipe for Pepsi-Cola stays the same, and so on—then in response to the higher price of Pepsi-Cola, people will buy less Pepsi-Cola.

Ceteris Paribus
A Latin term meaning "all other things constant" or "nothing else changes."

But some people ask, "Why would economists want to assume that when the price of Pepsi-Cola rises, nothing else changes? Don't other things change in the real world? Why assume things that we know are not true?"

Economists do not specify *ceteris paribus* because they want to say something false about the world. They specify it because they want to clearly define what they believe to be the real-world relationship between two variables. Look at it this way. If you drop a ball off the roof of a house, it will strike the ground *unless someone catches it.* This statement is true, and probably everyone would willingly accept it as true. But saying "unless someone catches it" is really no different than saying "assuming nothing else changes" or "*ceteris paribus.*"

Thinking like AN ECONOMIST

The Ceteris Paribus *Mindset*

Suppose John has eaten fat-free ice cream for the past two months but hasn't lost any weight. Does that mean that eating fat-free ice cream (instead of regular ice cream) won't help you lose weight? Not at all. We know that eating fat-free ice cream will help you lose weight "assuming nothing else changes" or "*ceteris paribus.*" In other words, if you were eating one bowl of regular ice cream twice a week, and you now replace it with one bowl of fat-free ice cream twice a week, and you change nothing else—you don't change how much you exercise, or how much you eat, or how much you sleep, and so on—then replacing regular ice cream with fat-free ice cream will cause you to lose weight. Of course, if you eat twice as much fat-free ice cream as regular ice cream, and stop exercising, and start eating more cookies (because you think you can take on more cookie calories because you are taking in fewer ice cream calories per serving), then you're not going to lose weight.

To the economist, all she is saying when she adds "*ceteris paribus*" to the end of a sentence (e.g., as the price of Pepsi-Cola rises, the quantity demanded of Pepsi-Cola falls, *ceteris paribus*) is the point we made in our ice cream example—namely, that if you change one thing (like eating fat-free ice cream and not regular ice cream), and nothing else changes, then you can expect a particular outcome (you will lose weight). The economist is not trying to get the results she wants by saying "*ceteris paribus*"; she is just trying to tell you what the relationship is between two variables.

Demand Schedule
The numerical tabulation of the quantity demanded of a good at different prices. A demand schedule is the numerical representation of the law of demand.

Demand Curve
The graphical representation of the law of demand.

Absolute (Money) Price
The price of a good in money terms.

Relative Price
The price of a good in terms of another good.

Four Ways to Represent the Law of Demand

Here are four ways to represent the law of demand.

- *In Words.* We can represent the law of demand in words; we have done so already. Earlier we said that as the price of a good rises, quantity demanded falls, and as price falls, quantity demanded rises, *ceteris paribus*. That was the statement (in words) of the law of demand.
- *In Symbols.* We can also represent the law of demand in symbols, which we have also done earlier. In symbols, the law of demand is:

$$P\uparrow Q_d\downarrow$$
$$P\downarrow Q_d\uparrow \text{ ceteris paribus}$$

- *In a Demand Schedule.* A **demand schedule** is the numerical representation of the law of demand. A demand schedule for good X is illustrated in Exhibit 1(a).
- *As a Demand Curve.* In Exhibit 1(b), the four price-quantity combinations in part (a) are plotted and the points connected, giving us a (downward-sloping) demand curve. A (downward-sloping) **demand curve** is the graphical representation of the inverse relationship between price and quantity demanded specified by the law of demand. In short, a demand curve is a picture of the law of demand.

exhibit 1

Demand Schedule and Demand Curve

Part (a) shows a demand schedule for good X. Part (b) shows a demand curve, obtained by plotting the different price-quantity combinations in part (a) and connecting the points. On a demand curve, the price (in dollars) represents price per unit of the good. The quantity demanded, on the horizontal axis, is always relevant for a specific time period (a week, a month, and so on).

Demand Schedule for Good X

Price (dollars)	Quantity Demanded	Point in Part (b)
4	10	A
3	20	B
2	30	C
1	40	D

(a)

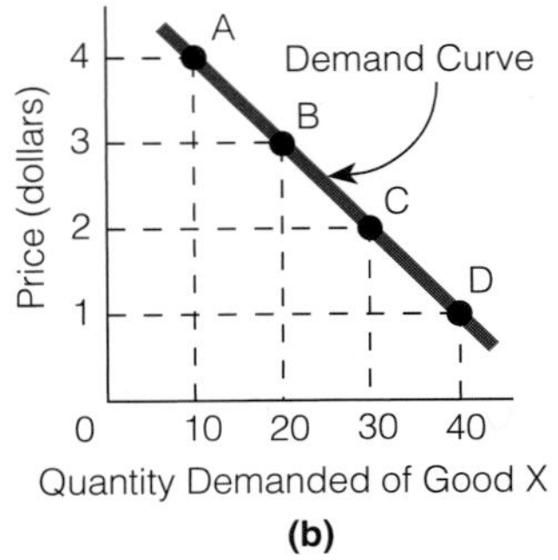

(b)

Finding ECONOMICS

In a Visit Home to See Mom

A friend tells you that she only flies home to see her mother once a year. You ask why. She says, "Because the price of the ticket to fly home is $1,100." She then adds, "If the price were, say, $600 instead of $1,100, I'd fly home twice a year instead of once." Can you find any economics in what she says? If you listen closely to what she says, she has identified two points on her demand curve for air travel home: one point corresponds to $1,100 and one ticket (home) and the other point corresponds to $600 and two tickets home.

Two Prices: Absolute and Relative

In economics, there are absolute (or money) prices and relative prices. The **absolute (money) price** is the price of the good in money terms. For example, the absolute price of a car might be $30,000. The **relative price** is the price of the good *in terms of another good.* For example, suppose the absolute price of a car is $30,000 and the absolute price of a computer is $2,000. The relative price of the car—that is, the price of the car *in terms of computers*—is 15 computers. A person gives up the opportunity to buy 15 computers when he or she buys a car.

$$\text{Relative price of a car (in terms of computers)} = \frac{\text{Absolute price of a car}}{\text{Absolute price of a computer}}$$
$$= \frac{\$30{,}000}{\$2{,}000}$$
$$= 15$$

Thus, the relative price of a car in this example is 15 computers.

Now let's compute the relative price of a computer—that is, the price of a computer in terms of a car:

$$\text{Relative price of a computer (in terms of cars)} = \frac{\text{Absolute price of a computer}}{\text{Absolute price of a car}} = \frac{\$2{,}000}{\$30{,}000} = \frac{1}{15}$$

Thus, the relative price of a computer in this example is 1/15 of a car. A person gives up the opportunity to buy 1/15 of a car when he or she buys a computer.

Now consider this question: What happens to the relative price of a good if its absolute price rises and nothing else changes? For example, if the absolute price of a car rises from $30,000 to $40,000, what happens to the relative price of a car? Obviously, it rises from 15 computers to 20 computers. In short, if the absolute price of a good rises and nothing else changes, then the relative price of the good rises too.

Thinking like An Economist

Higher Price Can Mean Cheaper

The economist knows that it is possible for a good to go up in price at the same time as it becomes cheaper. (How can this happen?) To illustrate, suppose the absolute price of a pen is \$1 and the absolute price of a pencil is 10 cents. The relative price of 1 pen, then, is 10 pencils. Now let the absolute price of a pen rise to \$1.20 at the same time that the absolute price of a pencil rises to 20 cents. As a result, the relative price of 1 pen falls to 6 pencils. In other words, the absolute price of pens rises (from \$1 to \$1.20) at the same time as pens become relatively cheaper (in terms of how many pencils you have to give up to get a pen). Who would have thought it?

Why Does Quantity Demanded Go Down as Price Goes Up?

The law of demand states that price and quantity demanded are inversely related. This much you know. But you do know *why* quantity demanded moves in the opposite direction of price? We identify two reasons. The first reason is that *people substitute lower priced goods for higher priced goods.*

Often, many goods serve the same purpose. Many different goods will satisfy hunger, and many different drinks will satisfy thirst. For example, both orange juice and grapefruit juice will satisfy thirst. On Monday, the price of orange juice equals the price of grapefruit juice, but on Tuesday, the price of orange juice rises. As a result, people will choose to buy less of the relatively higher priced orange juice and more of the relatively lower priced grapefruit juice. In other words, a rise in the price of orange juice will lead to a decrease in the quantity demanded of orange juice.

The second reason for the inverse relationship between price and quantity demanded has to do with the **law of diminishing marginal utility**, which states that for a given time period, the marginal (additional) utility or satisfaction gained by consuming equal successive units of a good will decline as the amount consumed increases. For example, you may receive more utility or satisfaction from eating your first hamburger at lunch than from eating your second and, if you continue, more utility from your second hamburger than from your third.

Law of Diminishing Marginal Utility
For a given time period, the marginal (additional) utility or satisfaction gained by consuming equal successive units of a good will decline as the amount consumed increases.

What does this have to do with the law of demand? Economists state that the more utility you receive from a unit of a good, the higher the price you are willing to pay for it;

economics 24/7

TICKET PRICES AT DISNEY WORLD

The Walt Disney Company operates two major theme parks in the United States: Disneyland in California and Disney World in Florida. Every year, millions of people visit each site. The ticket price for visiting Disneyland or Disney World differs depending on how many days a person visits the theme park. For example, Disney World sells one- to ten-day tickets. Here are the ticket prices:

Ticket	Price
1 day	$71
2 day	$139
3 day	$203
4 day	$212
5 day	$215
6 day	$217
7 day	$219
8 day	$221
9 day	$223
10 day	$225

Now if we take the price of a one-day ticket and multiply it by 2, we get $142, but oddly enough, the price of a two-day ticket is not $142 but $139. Of course, if we take the price of a one-day ticket and multiply it by 10, we get $710, but Disney World doesn't charge $710 for a ten-day ticket, it charges $225, which is $485 less than $710. Why does Disney World charge less than double the price of a one-day ticket for a two-day ticket, and why does Disney World charge less than 10 times the price of a one-day ticket for a ten-day ticket?

Disney World is effectively telling visitors that if they want to visit the theme park for one day, they have to pay $71. But if they want to visit the theme park for additional days they don't have to pay $71 for each additional day. They pay less for additional days. But why?

An economic concept, the law of diminishing marginal utility, is the reason. The law of diminishing marginal utility states that as a person consumes additional units of a good, eventually the utility from each additional unit of the good decreases. Assuming the law of diminishing marginal utility holds for Disney World, individuals will get more utility from the first day at Disney World than from, say, the second, third, or tenth day. The less utility or satisfaction a person gets from something, the lower the dollar amount he is willing to pay for it. Thus, a person would not be willing to pay as much for the second day at Disney World as the first, and he would not be willing to pay as much for the tenth day as the ninth and so on. Disney World knows this and therefore prices its tickets differently depending on how many days one wants to visit Disney World.

the less utility you receive from a unit of a good, the lower the price you are willing to pay for it. According to the law of diminishing marginal utility, individuals obtain less utility from additional units of a good. It follows that they will only buy larger quantities of a good at lower prices. And this is the law of demand.

Individual Demand Curve and Market Demand Curve

There is a difference between an individual demand curve and a market demand curve. An individual demand curve represents the price-quantity combinations of a particular good for a *single buyer.* For example, a demand curve could show Jones's demand for CDs. A market demand curve represents the price-quantity combinations of a particular good for *all buyers.* In this case, the demand curve would show all buyers' demand for CDs.

A market demand curve is derived by "adding up" individual demand curves, as we show in Exhibit 2. The demand schedules for Jones, Smith, and other buyers are shown in part (a). The market demand schedule is obtained by adding the quantities demanded at each price. For example, at $12, the quantities demanded are 4 units for Jones, 5 units for Smith, and 100 units for other buyers. Thus, a total of 109 units are demanded at $12.

exhibit 2

Deriving a Market Demand Schedule and a Market Demand Curve

Part (a) shows four demand schedules combined into one table. The market demand schedule is derived by adding the quantities demanded at each price. In (b), the data points from the demand schedule are plotted to show how a market demand curve is derived. Only two points on the market demand curve are noted.

Price	Quantity Demanded: Jones		Smith		Other Buyers		All Buyers
$15	1		2		20		23
14	2		3		45		50
13	3		4		70		77
12	4	+	5	+	100	=	109
11	5	+	6	+	130	=	141
10	6		7		160		173

(a)

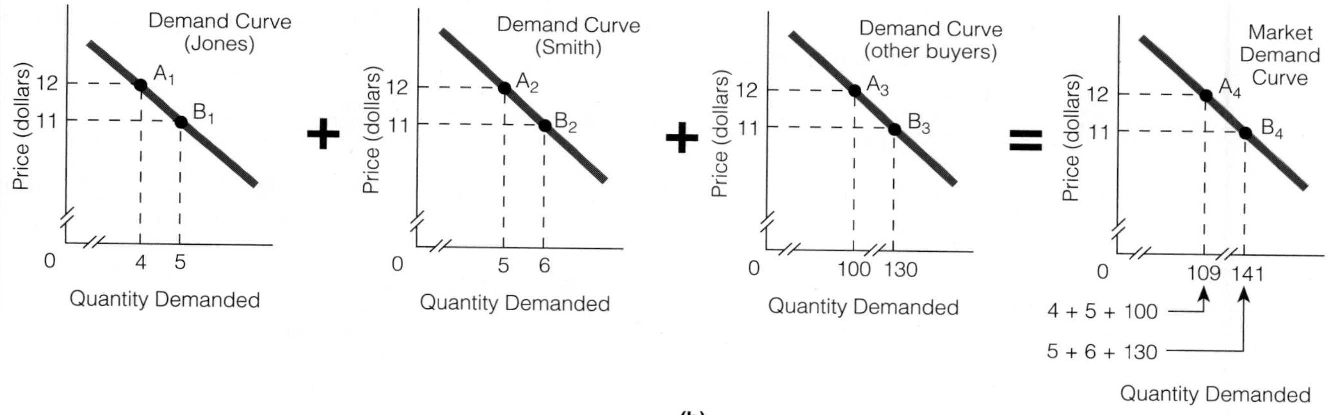

(b)

In part (b), the data points for the demand schedules are plotted and added to produce a market demand curve. The market demand curve could also be drawn directly from the market demand schedule.

A Change in Quantity Demanded Versus a Change in Demand

Economists often talk about (1) a change in quantity demanded and (2) a change in demand. As we stated earlier, although "quantity demanded" may sound like "demand," they are not the same. In short, a "change in quantity demanded" *is not* the same as a "change in demand." (Read the last sentence at least two more times.) We use Exhibit 1 to illustrate the difference between "a change in quantity demanded" and "a change in demand."

A CHANGE IN QUANTITY DEMANDED Look at the horizontal axis in Exhibit 1, which is labeled "quantity demanded." Notice that quantity demanded is a *number*—such as 10, 20, 30, 40, and so on. More specifically, it is the number of units of a good that individuals are willing and able to buy at a particular price during some time period. In

Exhibit 1, if the price is $4, then quantity demanded is 10 units of good X; if the price is $3, then quantity demanded is 20 units of good X.

Quantity demanded = The *number* of units of a good that individuals are willing and able to buy at a particular price

Now, again looking at Exhibit 1, what can change quantity demanded from 10 (which it is at point A) to 20 (which it is at point B)? Or what has to change before quantity demanded will change? The answer is on the vertical axis of Exhibit 1. The only thing that can change the quantity demanded of a good is the price of the good, which is called **own price**.

Own Price
The price of a good. For example, if the price of oranges is $1, this is its own price.

Change in quantity demanded = A *movement* from one point to another point on the same demand curve *caused* by a change in the price of the good

A CHANGE IN DEMAND Let's look again at Exhibit 1, this time focusing on the demand curve. Demand is represented by the *entire* curve. When an economist talks about a "change in demand," he or she is actually talking about a change—or shift—in the entire demand curve.

Change in demand = Shift in demand curve

Demand can change in two ways: Demand can increase, and demand can decrease. Let's look first at an *increase* in demand. Suppose we have the following demand schedule.

Demand Schedule *A*

Price	Quantity Demanded
$20	500
$15	600
$10	700
$ 5	800

The demand curve for this demand schedule will look like the demand curve labeled D_A in Exhibit 3(a).

What does an increase in demand mean? It means that individuals are willing and able to buy more units of the good at each and every price. In other words, demand schedule *A* will change as follows:

Demand Schedule *B* (increase in demand)

Price	Quantity Demanded
$20	~~500~~ 600
$15	~~600~~ 700
$10	~~700~~ 800
$ 5	~~800~~ 900

Whereas individuals were willing and able to buy 500 units of the good at $20, now they are willing and able to buy 600 units of the good at $20; whereas individuals were willing and able to buy 600 units of the good at $15, now they are willing and able to buy 700 units of the good at $15; and so on.

exhibit 3

Shifts in the Demand Curve

In part (a), the demand curve shifts rightward from D_A to D_B. This shift represents an increase in demand. At each price, the quantity demanded is greater than it was before. For example, the quantity demanded at $20 increases from 500 units to 600 units. In part (b), the demand curve shifts leftward from D_A to D_C. This shift represents a decrease in demand. At each price, the quantity demanded is less. For example, the quantity demand at $20 decreases from 500 units to 400 units.

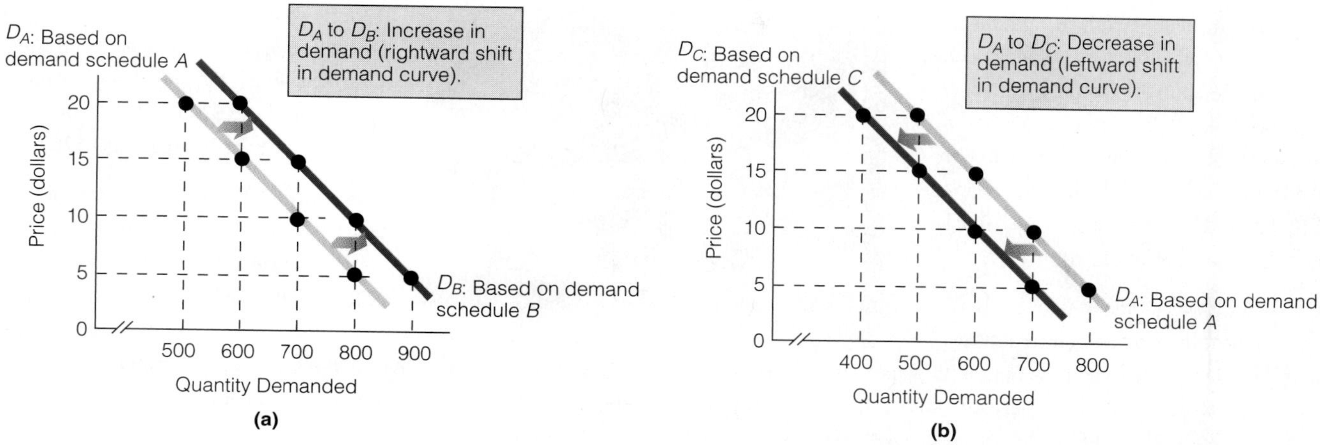

As shown in Exhibit 3(a), the demand curve that represents demand schedule *B* lies to the right of the demand curve that represents demand schedule *A*. We conclude that *an increase in demand is represented by a rightward shift in the demand curve and means that individuals are willing and able to buy more of a good at each and every price.*

Increase in demand = Rightward shift in the demand curve

Now let's look at a decrease in demand. What does a decrease in demand mean? It means that individuals are willing and able to buy less of a good at each and every price. In this case, demand schedule *A* will change as follows:

Demand Schedule *C* (decrease in demand)

Price	Quantity Demanded
$20	~~500~~ 400
$15	~~600~~ 500
$10	~~700~~ 600
$ 5	~~800~~ 700

As shown in Exhibit 3(b), the demand curve that represents demand schedule *C* obviously lies to the left of the demand curve that represents demand schedule *A*. We conclude that a *decrease in demand is represented by a leftward shift in the demand curve and means that individuals are willing and able to buy less of a good at each and every price.*

Decrease in demand = Leftward shift in the demand curve

economics 24/7

iPODS AND THE LAW OF DEMAND

The law of demand holds that the price of a good and the quantity demanded of the good are inversely related. But does the law of demand hold for an individual when it comes to a good like an iPod? Will the individual buy more iPods at $10 than at $200? Perhaps she will, if only to give some iPods to friends.

©AP PHOTO/PAUL SAKUMA

But suppose we assume that the person doesn't want to give away any iPods as gifts. She wants only an iPod for herself. How many more than one iPod does she need? Probably none since there is little use of buying two iPods if one iPod holds all the songs you want. In other words, instead of having a downward-sloping demand curve for iPods, an individual might have a demand curve that looks like the one in Exhibit 4(a). This curve says the individual will buy one iPod no matter what the price is between zero and $300. But if the price is above $300, she will not buy an iPod since the demand curve doesn't extend that high.

Suppose no person has a downward-sloping demand curve. Is it still possible for the *market demand curve* to be downward-sloping? The answer is yes. To understand why, let's suppose there is another person's demand curve for an iPod shown in Exhibit 4(b). This demand curve says she is willing and able to buy one iPod if the price is anywhere between zero and $200, but she won't buy an iPod if the price is higher than $200.

If we horizontally sum the two demand curves in panels (a) and (b) to get the market demand curve, we see that at a price of $300, one iPod will be purchased, and at $200, two iPods will be purchased. This is shown in Exhibit 4(c). Notice that this gives us a downward-sloping demand curve: More iPods are bought at a lower price than at a higher price.

exhibit 4

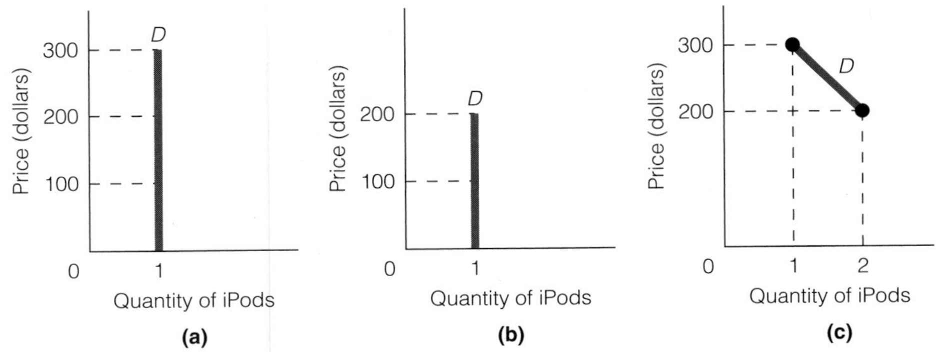

What Factors Cause the Demand Curve to Shift?

We know what an increase and decrease in demand mean: An increase in demand means consumers are willing and able to buy more of a good at every price. A decrease in demand means consumers are willing and able to buy less of a good at every price. We also know that an increase in demand is graphically portrayed as a rightward shift in a demand curve and a decrease in demand is graphically portrayed as a leftward shift in a demand curve.

But what factors or variables can increase or decrease demand? What factors or variables can shift demand curves? We identify and discuss these factors or variables in this section.

INCOME As a person's income changes (increases or decreases), his or her demand for a particular good may rise, fall, or remain constant.

economics 24/7

ADVERTISING AND THE DEMAND CURVE

A company produces a good that it hopes to sell. To help sell its product, the company hires an advertising firm to work up an advertising campaign. It takes out ads in magazines and newspapers and on the radio and television.

Now ask if the seller of a good would prefer the demand for its good to be high or low? Obviously, the answer is high. All other things being equal, the higher the demand for the good, the higher the equilibrium price of the good. But to change a low demand into a high demand, one or more of the factors that demand is dependent upon (income, preferences, price of related goods, and so on) will have to change.

Which of these demand factors does advertising try to change? An ad runs in a magazine stating that good X is just like good Y except it is priced lower. Obviously here the company placing the ad is comparing the price of a substitute (Y) with the good it sells (X). We know that if X and Y are substitutes, then the higher the price of Y, the higher the demand for X.

Some ads inform the public of a good it may not know about. When ads do this, which of the demand factors is the company placing the ad trying to change? Obviously it is trying to change the number of buyers: the more buyers, the higher the demand curve. By informing people of a good they may not be aware of, it is possible to change nonbuyers into buyers.

Some ads try to persuade—they try to change preferences in favor of a particular good. If they are successful, the demand for the good being advertised rises. It is perhaps this kind of advertising (the kind designed to persuade) that we reject as manipulative. People might argue: "Advertisers simply create a demand for certain goods that would not ordinarily exist. They get us to buy things we don't really want to buy. No one has a demand for a cell phone with 100 different ringtones."

Can advertising persuade? At times, probably. But is it wrong to persuade? Our guess is that you weren't born with a demand for higher education. No doubt your parents, high school teachers, and friends might have influenced your decision to attend college. Were they manipulating you when they were telling you about the advantages of college?

Here's a controversial issue to discuss or think about. Person X tries to raise your demand for higher education and attending the opera. Person Y tries to raise your demand for cocaine. In some sense, both persons are "advertising" the benefits of different goods. Is advertising all right if it is truthful and the good being advertised is "good for you" but not all right if the good is "bad for you"? Next controversial issue: Who decides what is good and bad for you?

For example, suppose Jack's income rises. As a consequence, his demand for CDs rises. For Jack, CDs are a normal good. For a **normal good**, as income rises, demand for the good rises, and as income falls, demand for the good falls.

Normal Good
A good the demand for which rises (falls) as income rises (falls).

X is a normal good: If income $\uparrow$ then $D_X \uparrow$
If income $\downarrow$ then $D_X \downarrow$

Now suppose Marie's income rises. As a consequence, her demand for canned baked beans falls. For Marie, canned baked beans are an inferior good. For an **inferior good**, as income rises, demand for the good falls, and as income falls, demand for the good rises.

Inferior Good
A good the demand for which falls (rises) as income rises (falls).

Y is an inferior good: If income $\uparrow$ then $D_y \downarrow$
If income $\downarrow$ then $D_y \uparrow$

Finally, suppose when George's income rises, his demand for toothpaste neither rises nor falls. For George, toothpaste is neither a normal good nor an inferior good. Instead,

exhibit 5

Substitutes and Complements

(a) Coca-Cola and Pepsi-Cola are substitutes: The price of one and the demand for the other are directly related. As the price of Coca-Cola rises, the demand for Pepsi-Cola increases. (b) Tennis rackets and tennis balls are complements: The price of one and the demand for the other are inversely related. As the price of tennis rackets rises, the demand for tennis balls decreases.

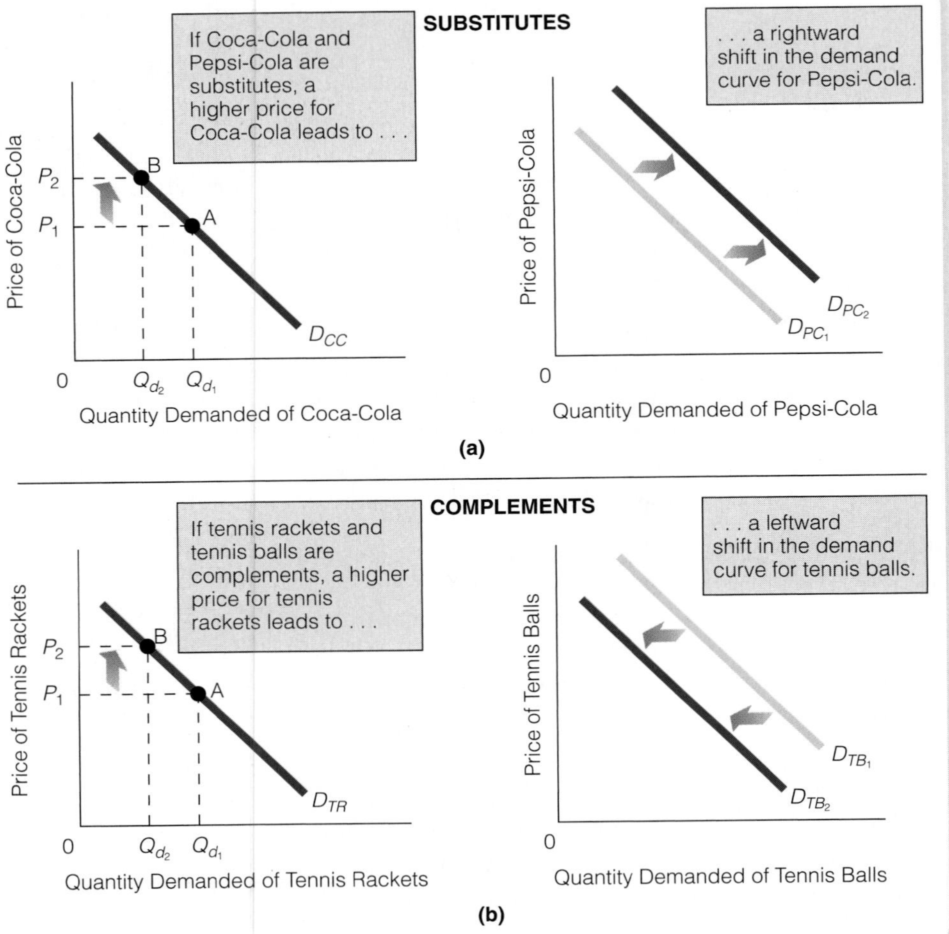

Neutral Good
A good the demand for which does not change as income rises or falls.

it is a neutral good. For a **neutral good**, as income rises or falls, the demand for the good does not change.

PREFERENCES People's preferences affect the amount of a good they are willing to buy at a particular price. A change in preferences in favor of a good shifts the demand curve rightward. A change in preferences away from the good shifts the demand curve leftward. For example, if people begin to favor Elmore Leonard novels to a greater degree than previously, the demand for Elmore Leonard novels increases, and the demand curve shifts rightward.

Substitutes
Two goods that satisfy similar needs or desires. If two goods are substitutes, the demand for one rises as the price of the other rises (or the demand for one falls as the price of the other falls).

PRICES OF RELATED GOODS There are two types of related goods: substitutes and complements. Two goods are **substitutes** if they satisfy similar needs or desires. For many people, Coca-Cola and Pepsi-Cola are substitutes. If two goods are substitutes, as the price of one rises (falls), the demand for the other rises (falls). For instance, higher Coca-Cola prices will increase the demand for Pepsi-Cola as people substitute Pepsi for the higher-priced Coke [Exhibit 5(a)]. Other examples of substitutes are coffee and tea, corn chips and potato chips, two brands of margarine, and foreign and domestic cars.

X and Y are substitutes: If $P_X \uparrow$ then $D_Y \uparrow$
If $P_X \downarrow$ then $D_Y \downarrow$

Two goods are **complements** if they are consumed jointly. For example, tennis rackets and tennis balls are used together to play tennis. If two goods are complements, as the price of one rises (falls), the demand for the other falls (rises). For example, higher tennis racket prices will decrease the demand for tennis balls, as Exhibit 5(b) shows. Other examples of complements are cars and tires, light bulbs and lamps, and golf clubs and golf balls.

Complements
Two goods that are used jointly in consumption. If two goods are complements, the demand for one rises as the price of the other falls (or the demand for one falls as the price of the other rises).

NUMBER OF BUYERS The demand for a good in a particular market area is related to the number of buyers in the area: more buyers, higher demand; fewer buyers, lower demand. The number of buyers may increase owing to a higher birthrate, increased immigration, the migration of people from one region of the country to another, and so on. The number of buyers may decrease owing to a higher death rate, war, the migration of people from one region of the country to another, and so on.

EXPECTATIONS OF FUTURE PRICE Buyers who expect the price of a good to be higher next month may buy the good now—thus increasing the current (or present) demand for the good. Buyers who expect the price of a good to be lower next month may wait until next month to buy the good—thus decreasing the current (or present) demand for the good. For example, suppose you are planning to buy a house. One day, you hear that house prices are expected to go down in a few months. Consequently, you decide to delay your purchase of a house for a few months. Alternatively, if you hear that prices are expected to rise in a few months, you might go ahead and purchase a house now.

Movement Factors and Shift Factors

Economists often distinguish between (1) factors that can move us along curves and (2) factors that can shift curves.

The factors that move us along curves are sometimes called *movement* factors. In many economic diagrams—such as the diagram of the demand curve in Exhibit 1—the movement factor (price) is on the vertical axis.

The factors that actually shift the curves are sometimes called *shift* factors. The shift factors for the demand curve are income, preferences, the price of related goods, and so on. Often, the shift factors do not appear in the economic diagrams. For example, in Exhibit 1, the movement factor—price—is on the vertical axis, but the shift factors do not appear anywhere in the diagram. We just know what they are and that they can shift the demand curve.

When you see a curve in this book, first ask what factor will move us along the curve. In other words, what is the movement factor? Second, ask what factors will shift the curve. In other words, what are the shift factors? Exhibit 6 summarizes the shift factors that can change demand and the movement factors that can change quantity demanded.

Finding ECONOMICS

Soft Drinks Go on Sale

Karen buys more soft drinks when soft drinks go on sale. Two people interpret this action differently. John says that if Karen buys more soft drinks when soft drinks go on sale, Karen's demand curve has shifted to the right. Laura says that if Karen buys more soft drinks when soft drinks go on sale, Karen is simply "moving down" her given demand curve. "In short," says Laura, "Karen's quantity demanded of soft drinks has increased." Who is right? Laura is. Saying that soft drinks went on sale is no more than saying that the price of soft drinks declined. As price declines, quantity demanded (not demand) increases.

exhibit 6

A Change in Demand Versus a Change in Quantity Demanded

(a) A change in demand refers to a shift in the demand curve. A change in demand can be brought about by a number of factors (see the exhibit and text). (b) A change in quantity demanded refers to a movement along a given demand curve. A change in quantity demanded is brought about only by a change in (a good's) own price.

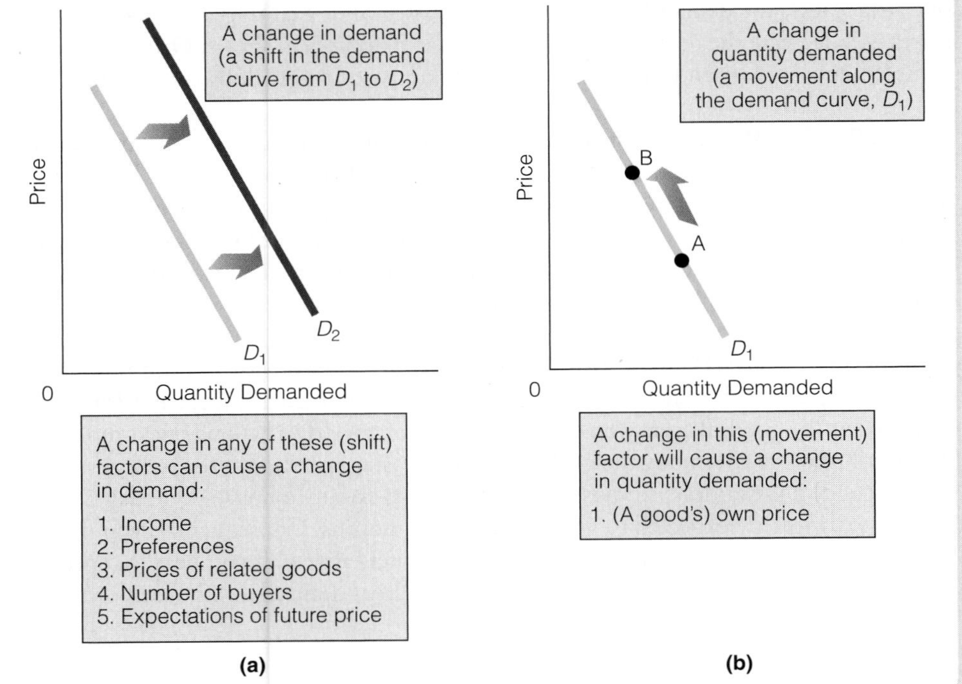
A change in demand (a shift in the demand curve from D_1 to D_2)
Price
D_1
D_2
0
Quantity Demanded
A change in any of these (shift) factors can cause a change in demand:
1. Income
2. Preferences
3. Prices of related goods
4. Number of buyers
5. Expectations of future price
(a)
A change in quantity demanded (a movement along the demand curve, D_1)
Price
B
A
D_1
0
Quantity Demanded
A change in this (movement) factor will cause a change in quantity demanded:
1. (A good's) own price
(b)

SELF-TEST

(Answers to Self-Test questions are in the Self-Test Appendix.)

1. As Sandi's income rises, her demand for popcorn rises. As Mark's income falls, his demand for prepaid telephone cards rises. What kinds of goods are popcorn and telephone cards for the people who demand each?
2. Why are demand curves downward sloping?
3. Give an example that illustrates how to derive a market demand curve.
4. What factors can change demand? What factors can change quantity demanded?

SUPPLY

Just as the word *demand* has a specific meaning in economics, so does the word *supply.* **Supply** refers to

1. the willingness and ability of sellers to produce and offer to sell different quantities of a good
2. at different prices
3. during a specific time period (per day, week, etc.).

Supply
The willingness and ability of sellers to produce and offer to sell different quantities of a good at different prices during a specific time period.

Law of Supply
As the price of a good rises, the quantity supplied of the good rises, and as the price of a good falls, the quantity supplied of the good falls, *ceteris paribus.*

The Law of Supply

The **law of supply** states that as the price of a good rises, the quantity supplied of the good rises, and as the price of a good falls, the quantity supplied of the good falls, *ceteris paribus.* Simply put, the price of a good and the quantity supplied of the good are directly related, *ceteris paribus.* (Quantity supplied is the number of units sellers are willing and able to produce and offer to sell at a particular price.) The (upward-sloping) **supply curve** is the graphical representation of the law of supply (see Exhibit 7). The law of supply can be summarized as follows:

$$P\uparrow\ Q_S\uparrow$$
$$P\downarrow\ Q_S\downarrow \textit{ ceteris paribus}$$

where P = price and Q_S = quantity supplied.

The law of supply holds for the production of most goods. It does not hold when there is no time to produce more units of a good. For example, suppose a theater in Atlanta is sold out for tonight's play. Even if ticket prices increased from $30 to $40, there would be no additional seats in the theater. There is no time to produce more seats. The supply curve for theater seats is illustrated in Exhibit 8(a). It is fixed at the number of seats in the theater, 500.[2]

The law of supply also does not hold for goods that cannot be produced over any period of time. For example, the violin maker Antonio Stradivari died in 1737. A rise in the price of Stradivarius violins does not affect the number of Stradivarius violins supplied, as Exhibit 8(b) illustrates.

Why Most Supply Curves Are Upward Sloping

Think back to the discussion of the *law of increasing opportunity costs* in Chapter 2. That discussion shows that if the production possibilities frontier (PPF) is bowed outward, increasing costs exist. In other words, increased production of a good comes at increased opportunity costs. An upward-sloping supply curve simply reflects the fact that costs rise when more units of a good are produced.

THE MARKET SUPPLY CURVE An individual supply curve represents the price-quantity combinations for a single seller. The market supply curve represents the price-quantity combinations for all sellers of a particular good. Exhibit 9 shows how a market supply curve can be derived by "adding" individual supply curves. In part (a), a **supply schedule,** the numerical tabulation of the quantity supplied of a good at different prices, is given for Brown, Alberts, and other suppliers. The market supply schedule is obtained by adding the quantities supplied at each price, *ceteris paribus.* For example, at $11, the

Supply Curve
The graphical representation of the law of supply.

exhibit 7

A Supply Curve

The upward-sloping supply curve is the graphical representation of the law of supply, which states that price and quantity supplied are directly related, *ceteris paribus.* On a supply curve, the price (in dollars) represents price per unit of the good. The quantity supplied, on the horizontal axis, is always relevant for a specific time period (a week, a month, and so on).

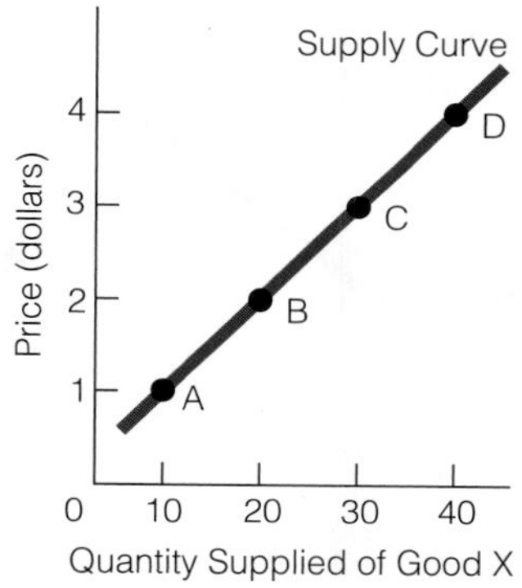

Supply Schedule
The numerical tabulation of the quantity supplied of a good at different prices. A supply schedule is the numerical representation of the law of supply.

exhibit 8

Supply Curves when There Is No Time to Produce More or No More Can Be Produced

The supply curve is not upward-sloping when there is no time to produce additional units or when additional units cannot be produced. In those cases, the supply curve is vertical.

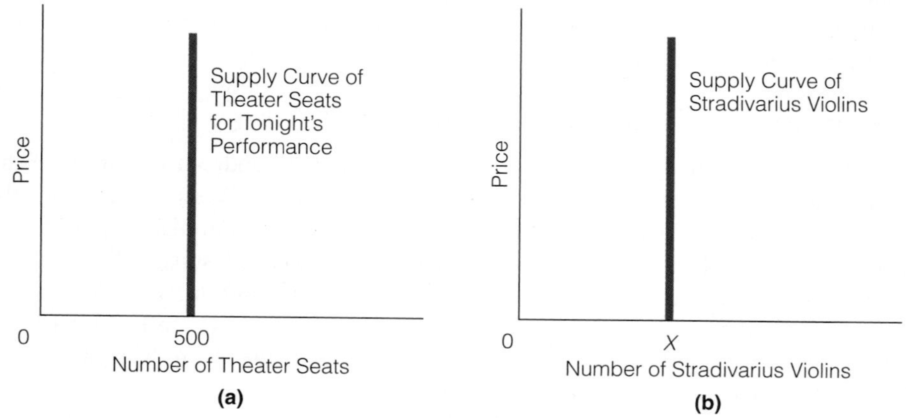

2. The vertical supply curve is said to be *perfectly inelastic.*

exhibit 9

Deriving a Market Supply Schedule and a Market Supply Curve

Part (a) shows four supply schedules combined into one table. The market supply schedule is derived by adding the quantities supplied at each price. In (b), the data points from the supply schedules are plotted to show how a market supply curve is derived. Only two points on the market supply curve are noted.

Price	Quantity Supplied: Brown		Alberts		Other Suppliers		All Suppliers
$10	1		2		96		99
11	2	+	3	+	98	=	103
12	3	+	4	+	102	=	109
13	4		5		106		115
14	5		6		108		119
15	6		7		110		123

(a)

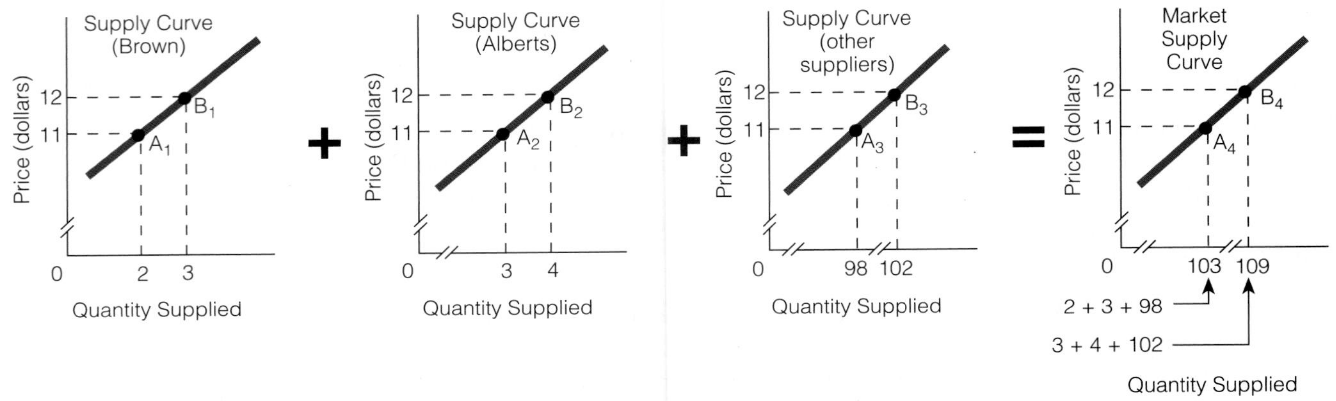

(b)

quantities supplied are 2 units for Brown, 3 units for Alberts, and 98 units for other suppliers. Thus, a total of 103 units are supplied at $11. In part (b), the data points for the supply schedules are plotted and added to produce a market supply curve. The market supply curve could also be drawn directly from the market supply schedule.

Changes in Supply Mean Shifts in Supply Curves

Just as demand can change, so can supply. The supply of a good can rise or fall. What does it mean if the supply of a good increases? It means that suppliers are willing and able to produce and offer to sell more of the good at all prices. For example, suppose that in January sellers are willing and able to produce and offer for sale 600 shirts at $25 each and that in February they are willing and able to produce and sell 900 shirts at $25 each. An increase in supply shifts the entire supply curve to the right, as shown in Exhibit 10(a).

The supply of a good decreases if sellers are willing and able to produce and offer to sell less of the good at all prices. For example, suppose that in January sellers are willing and able to produce and offer for sale 600 shirts at $25 each and that in February they are willing and able to produce and sell only 300 shirts at $25 each. A decrease in supply shifts the entire supply curve to the left, as shown in Exhibit 10(b).

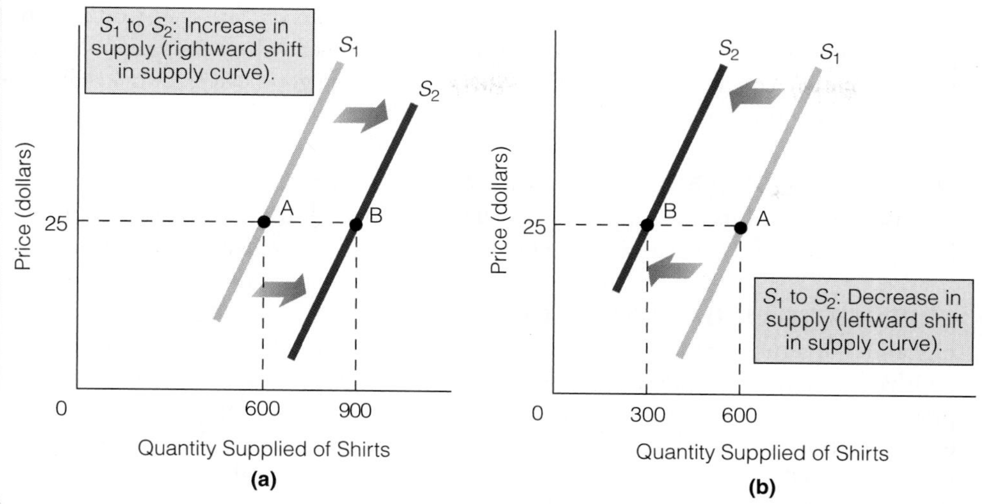

exhibit 10

Shifts in the Supply Curve

(a) The supply curve shifts rightward from S_1 to S_2. This represents an increase in the supply of shirts: At each price the quantity supplied of shirts is greater. For example, the quantity supplied at \$25 increases from 600 shirts to 900 shirts. (b) The supply curve shifts leftward from S_1 to S_2. This represents a decrease in the supply of shirts: At each price the quantity supplied of shirts is less. For example, the quantity supplied at \$25 decreases from 600 shirts to 300 shirts.

What Factors Cause the Supply Curve to Shift?

We know the supply of any good can change. But what causes supply to change? What causes supply curves to shift? The factors that can change supply include (1) prices of relevant resources, (2) technology, (3) prices of other goods, (4) number of sellers, (5) expectations of future price, (6) taxes and subsidies, and (7) government restrictions.

PRICES OF RELEVANT RESOURCES Resources are needed to produce goods. For example, wood is needed to produce doors. If the price of wood falls, it becomes less costly to produce doors. How will door producers respond? Will they produce more doors, the same number of doors, or fewer doors? With lower costs and prices unchanged, the profit from producing and selling doors has increased; as a result, there is an increased (monetary) incentive to produce doors. Door producers will produce and offer to sell more doors at each and every price. Thus, the supply of doors will increase, and the supply curve of doors will shift rightward. If the price of wood rises, it becomes more costly to produce doors. Consequently, the supply of doors will decrease, and the supply curve of doors will shift leftward.

TECHNOLOGY In Chapter 2, technology is defined as the body of skills and knowledge concerning the use of resources in production. Also, an advance in technology refers to the ability to produce more output with a fixed amount of resources, thus reducing per-unit production costs. To illustrate, suppose it currently takes \$100 to produce 40 units of a good. The per-unit cost is therefore \$2.50. If an advance in technology makes it possible to produce 50 units at a cost of \$100, then the per-unit cost falls to \$2.00.

If per-unit production costs of a good decline, we expect the quantity supplied of the good at each price to increase. Why? The reason is that lower per-unit costs increase profitability and therefore provide producers with an incentive to produce more. For example, if corn growers develop a way to grow more corn using the same amount of water and other resources, it follows that per-unit production costs will fall, profitability will increase, and growers will want to grow and sell more corn at each price. The supply curve of corn will shift rightward.

PRICES OF OTHER GOODS Think of a farmer who is producing wheat. Suddenly, the price of something he is not producing (say, corn) rises relative to wheat. It is possible that the farmer may shift his farming away from wheat to corn. In other words, as the price of corn rises relative to wheat, the farmer switches from wheat production to corn production. We conclude that a change in the price of one good can lead to a change in the supply of another good.

NUMBER OF SELLERS If more sellers begin producing a particular good, perhaps because of high profits, the supply curve will shift rightward. If some sellers stop producing a particular good, perhaps because of losses, the supply curve will shift leftward.

EXPECTATIONS OF FUTURE PRICES If the price of a good is expected to be higher in the future, producers may hold back some of the product today (if possible, but perishables cannot be held back). Then they will have more to sell at the higher future price. Therefore, the current supply curve will shift leftward. For example, if oil producers expect the price of oil to be higher next year, some may hold oil off the market this year to be able to sell it next year. Similarly, if they expect the price of oil to be lower next year, they might pump more oil this year than previously planned.

TAXES AND SUBSIDIES Some taxes increase per-unit costs. Suppose a shoe manufacturer must pay a $2 tax per pair of shoes produced. This tax leads to a leftward shift in the supply curve, indicating that the manufacturer wants to produce and offer to sell fewer pairs of shoes at each price. If the tax is eliminated, the supply curve shifts rightward.

Subsidy
A monetary payment by government to a producer of a good or service.

Subsidies have the opposite effect. Suppose the government subsidizes the production of corn by paying corn farmers $2 for every bushel of corn they produce. Because of the subsidy, the quantity supplied of corn is greater at each price, and the supply curve of corn shifts rightward. Removal of the subsidy shifts the supply curve of corn leftward. A rough rule of thumb is that we get more of what we subsidize and less of what we tax.

GOVERNMENT RESTRICTIONS Sometimes, government acts to reduce supply. Consider a U.S. import quota on Japanese television sets. An import quota, or quantitative restriction on foreign goods, reduces the supply of Japanese television sets in the United States. It shifts the supply curve leftward. The elimination of the import quota allows the supply of Japanese television sets in the United States to shift rightward.

Licensure has a similar effect. With licensure, individuals must meet certain requirements before they can legally carry out a task. For example, owner-operators of day-care centers must meet certain requirements before they are allowed to sell their services. No doubt, this reduces the number of day-care centers and shifts the supply curve of day-care centers leftward.

A Change in Supply Versus a Change in Quantity Supplied

It is important to remember that a change in *supply* is not the same as a change in *quantity supplied*. A change in supply refers to a shift in the supply curve, as illustrated in Exhibit 11(a). For example, saying that the supply of oranges has increased is the same as saying that the supply curve for oranges has shifted rightward. The factors that can change supply (shift the supply curve) include prices of relevant resources, technology, prices of other goods, number of sellers, expectations of future price, taxes and subsidies, and government restrictions.

A change in quantity supplied refers to a movement along a supply curve, as in Exhibit 11(b). The only factor that can directly cause a change in the quantity supplied of a good is a change in the price of the good, or own price.

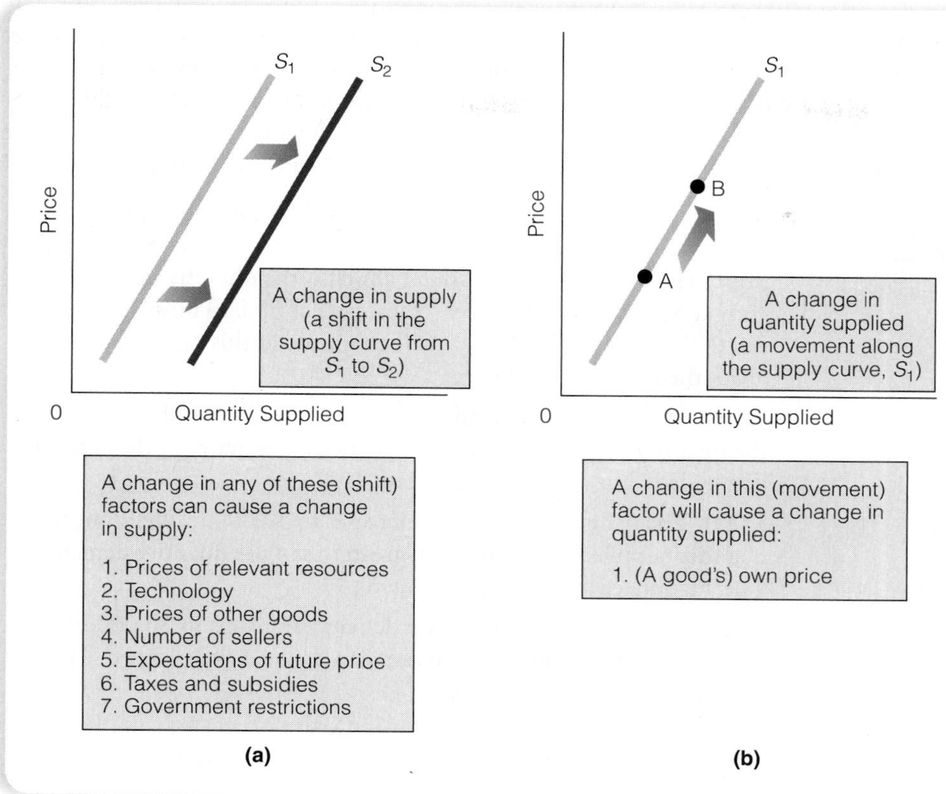

S_1
S_2
Price
A change in supply (a shift in the supply curve from S_1 to S_2)
0
Quantity Supplied
A change in any of these (shift) factors can cause a change in supply:
1. Prices of relevant resources
2. Technology
3. Prices of other goods
4. Number of sellers
5. Expectations of future price
6. Taxes and subsidies
7. Government restrictions
(a)
S_1
B
A
Price
A change in quantity supplied (a movement along the supply curve, S_1)
0
Quantity Supplied
A change in this (movement) factor will cause a change in quantity supplied:
1. (A good's) own price
(b)

exhibit 11

A Change in Supply Versus a Change in Quantity Supplied

(a) A change in supply refers to a shift in the supply curve. A change in supply can be brought about by a number of factors (see the exhibit and text). (b) A change in quantity supplied refers to a movement along a given supply curve. A change in quantity supplied is brought about only by a change in (a good's) own price.

SELF-TEST

1. What would the supply curve for houses (in a given city) look like for a time period of (a) the next ten hours and (b) the next three months?
2. What happens to the supply curve if each of the following occurs?
   a. There is a decrease in the number of sellers.
   b. A per-unit tax is placed on the production of a good.
   c. The price of a relevant resource falls.
3. "If the price of apples rises, the supply of apples will rise." True or false? Explain your answer.

THE MARKET: PUTTING SUPPLY AND DEMAND TOGETHER

In this section, we put supply and demand together and discuss the market. The purpose of the discussion is to gain some understanding about how prices are determined.

Supply and Demand at Work at an Auction

Imagine you are at an auction where bushels of corn are bought and sold. At this auction, the auctioneer will adjust the corn price to sell all the corn offered for sale. The supply curve of corn is vertical, as in Exhibit 12. It intersects the horizontal axis at

exhibit 12

Supply and Demand at Work at an Auction

Q_d = quantity demanded; Q_s = quantity supplied. The auctioneer calls out different prices, and buyers record how much they are willing and able to buy. At prices of $9.00, $8.00, and $7.00, quantity supplied is greater than quantity demanded. At prices of $4.25 and $5.25, quantity demanded is greater than quantity supplied. At a price of $6.10, quantity demanded equals quantity supplied.

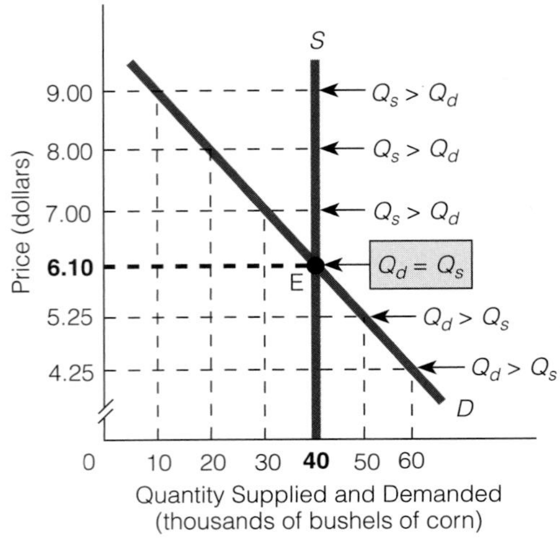

40,000 bushels; that is, quantity supplied is 40,000 bushels. The demand curve for corn is downward sloping. Furthermore, suppose each potential buyer of corn is sitting in front of a computer that immediately registers the number of bushels he or she wants to buy. For example, if Nancy Bernstein wants to buy 5,000 bushels of corn, she simply keys "5,000" into her computer. The auction begins. (Follow along in Exhibit 12 as we relay what is happening at the auction.) The auctioneer calls out the price:

- $9.00. The potential buyers think for a second, and then each registers the number of bushels he or she is willing and able to buy at that price. The total is 10,000 bushels, which is the quantity demanded of corn at $9.00. The auctioneer, realizing that 30,000 bushels of corn (40,000 − 10,000 = 30,000) will go unsold at this price, decides to lower the price per bushel to:
- $8.00. The quantity demanded increases to 20,000 bushels, but still the quantity supplied of corn at this price is greater than the quantity demanded. The auctioneer calls out:
- $7.00. The quantity demanded increases to 30,000 bushels, but the quantity supplied at $7.00 is still greater than the quantity demanded. The auctioneer drops the price down to:
- $4.25. At this price, the quantity demanded jumps to 60,000 bushels, but that is 20,000 bushels more than the quantity supplied. The auctioneer calls out a higher price:
- $5.25. The quantity demanded drops to 50,000 bushels, but buyers still want to buy more corn at this price than there is corn to be sold. The auctioneer calls out:
- $6.10. At this price, the quantity demanded of corn is 40,000 bushels and the quantity supplied of corn is 40,000 bushels. The auction stops. The 40,000 bushels of corn are bought and sold at $6.10 per bushel.

Surplus (Excess Supply)
A condition in which quantity supplied is greater than quantity demanded. Surpluses occur only at prices above equilibrium price.

Shortage (Excess Demand)
A condition in which quantity demanded is greater than quantity supplied. Shortages occur only at prices below equilibrium price.

Equilibrium Price (Market-Clearing Price)
The price at which quantity demanded of the good equals quantity supplied.

Equilibrium Quantity
The quantity that corresponds to equilibrium price. The quantity at which the amount of the good that buyers are willing and able to buy equals the amount that sellers are willing and able to sell, and both equal the amount actually bought and sold.

The Language of Supply and Demand: A Few Important Terms

If quantity supplied is greater than quantity demanded, a **surplus** or **excess supply** exists. If quantity demanded is greater than quantity supplied, a **shortage** or **excess demand** exists. In Exhibit 12, a surplus exists at $9.00, $8.00, and $7.00. A shortage exists at $4.25 and $5.25. The price at which quantity demanded equals quantity supplied is the **equilibrium price (market-clearing price)**. In our example, $6.10 is the equilibrium price. The quantity that corresponds to the equilibrium price is the **equilibrium quantity.** In our example, it is 40,000 bushels of corn. Any price at which quantity demanded is not equal to quantity supplied is a **disequilibrium price.**

A market that exhibits either a surplus ($Q_s > Q_d$) or a shortage ($Q_d > Q_s$) is said to be in **disequilibrium**. A market in which quantity demanded equals quantity supplied ($Q_d = Q_s$) is said to be in **equilibrium** (identified by the letter *E* in Exhibit 12).

Moving to Equilibrium: What Happens to Price when There Is a Surplus or a Shortage?

What did the auctioneer do when the price was $9.00 and there was a surplus of corn? He lowered the price. What did the auctioneer do when the price was $5.25 and there was a shortage of corn? He raised the price. The behavior of the auctioneer can be summarized this way: If a surplus exists, lower the price; if a shortage exists, raise the price. This is how the auctioneer moved the corn market into equilibrium.

Not all markets have auctioneers. (When was the last time you saw an auctioneer in the grocery store?) But many markets act *as if* an auctioneer were calling out higher and lower prices until equilibrium price is reached. In many real-world auctioneer-less markets, prices fall when there is a surplus and rise when there is a shortage. Why?

Disequilibrium Price
A price other than equilibrium price. A price at which quantity demanded does not equal quantity supplied.

Disequilibrium
A state of either surplus or shortage in a market.

Equilibrium
Equilibrium means "at rest." Equilibrium in a market is the price quantity combination from which there is no tendency for buyers or sellers to move away. Graphically, equilibrium is the intersection point of the supply and demand curves.

WHY DOES PRICE FALL WHEN THERE IS A SURPLUS? In Exhibit 13, there is a surplus at a price of $15: Quantity supplied (150 units) is greater than quantity demanded (50 units). Suppliers will not be able to sell all they had hoped to sell at $15. As a result, their inventories will grow beyond the level they hold in preparation for demand changes. Sellers will want to reduce their inventories. Some will lower prices to do so, some will cut back on production, others will do a little of both. As shown in the exhibit, there is a tendency for price and output to fall until equilibrium is achieved.

WHY DOES PRICE RISE WHEN THERE IS A SHORTAGE? In Exhibit 13, there is a shortage at a price of $5: Quantity demanded (150 units) is greater than quantity supplied (50 units). Buyers will not be able to buy all they had hoped to buy at $5. Some buyers will bid up the price to get sellers to sell to them instead of to other buyers. Some sellers, seeing buyers clamor for the goods, will realize that they can raise the price

exhibit 13

Moving to Equilibrium

If there is a surplus, sellers' inventories rise above the level they hold in preparation for demand changes. Sellers will want to reduce their inventories. As a result, price and output fall until equilibrium is achieved. If there is a shortage, some buyers will bid up price to get sellers to sell to them instead of to other buyers. Some sellers will realize they can raise the price of the goods they have for sale. Higher prices will call forth added output. Price and output rise until equilibrium is achieved.

(Note: Recall that price, on the vertical axis, is price per unit of the good, and quantity, on the horizontal axis, is for a specific time period. In this text, we do not specify this on the axes themselves, but consider it to be understood.)

Price	Q_s	Q_d	Condition
$15	150	50	Surplus
10	100	100	Equilibrium
5	50	150	Shortage

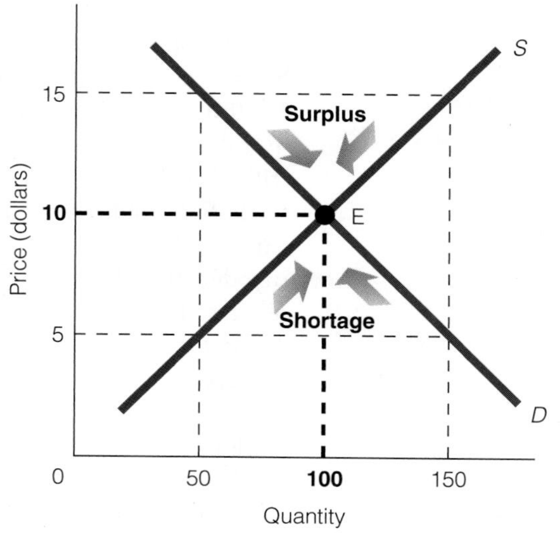

exhibit 14

A Summary Exhibit of a Market (Supply and Demand)

This exhibit ties together the topics discussed so far in this chapter. A market is composed of both supply and demand, as shown. Also shown are the factors that affect supply and demand and therefore indirectly affect the equilibrium price and quantity of a good.

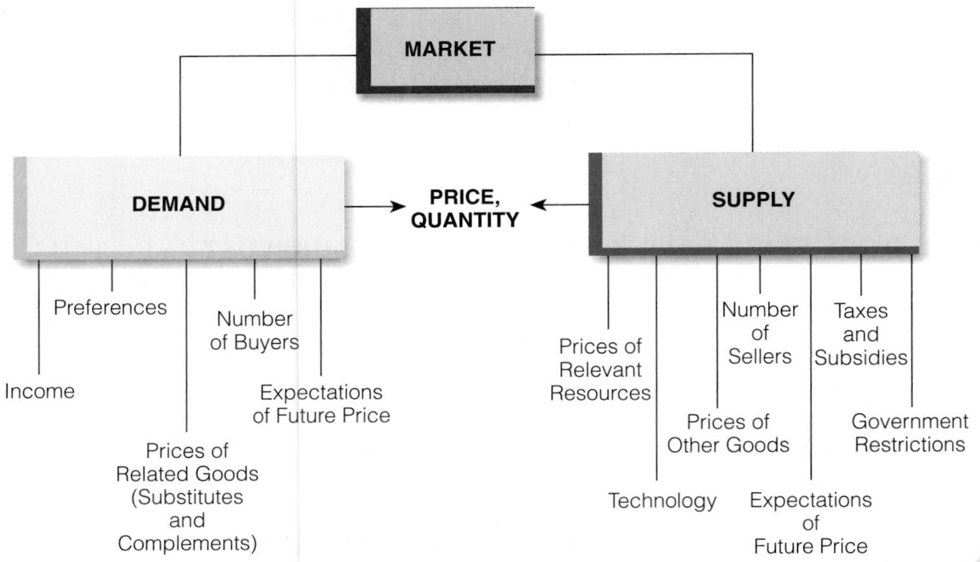

of the goods they have for sale. Higher prices will also call forth added output. Thus, there is a tendency for price and output to rise until equilibrium is achieved.

Take a look at Exhibit 14. It brings together much of what we have discussed about supply and demand.

Speed of Moving to Equilibrium

On July 16, 2008, at 12:00 p.m. (Eastern time), the price of a share of IBM stock was approximately $123. A few minutes later, the price had risen to $124. Obviously, the stock market is a market that equilibrates quickly. If demand rises, then initially there is a shortage of the stock at the current equilibrium price. The price is bid up, and there is no longer a shortage. All this happens in seconds.

Now consider a house offered for sale in any city in the United States. It is not uncommon for the sale price of a house to remain the same even though the house does not sell for months. For example, a person offers to sell her house for $400,000. One month passes, no sale; two months pass, no sale; three months pass, no sale; and so on. Ten months later, the house has still not sold, and the price is still $400,000.

Is $400,000 the equilibrium price of the house? Obviously not. At the equilibrium price, there would be a buyer for the house and a seller of the house (quantity demanded would equal quantity supplied). At a price of $400,000, there is a seller of the house but no buyer. The price of $400,000 is above equilibrium price. At $400,000, there is a surplus in the housing market; equilibrium has not been achieved.

Some people may be tempted to argue that supply and demand are at work in the stock market but not in the housing market. A better explanation, though, is that *not all markets equilibrate at the same speed.* While it may take only seconds for the stock market to go from surplus or shortage to equilibrium, it may take months for the housing market to do so.

economics 24/7

THE DOWRY AND MARRIAGE MARKET DISEQUILIBRIUM

It is generally accepted by men and women that monogamy is the ideal marriage practice. In other words, polygyny (the practice of one man being able to have more than one wife) is not the ideal marriage practice, and therefore should be deemed illegal. Some anthropologists and evolutionary biologists challenge orthodoxy by arguing that polygyny gives women greater choice. Here is how they structure their argument. Suppose there are 1,000 men and 1,000 women. Suppose each of the men and each of the women is given a ranking of between 1 and 1,000. The number 1 man is ranked higher than the number 2 man (and so on) in terms of a variety of characteristics. The same holds for women.

Currently the number 1 man is matched up with the number 1 woman, the number 2 man with the number 2 woman, and so on. The woman marries the man with whom she shares the same ranking. Now suppose the 404th-ranked woman (who is scheduled to marry the 404th-ranked man) prefers to be the second wife of the 40th-ranked man rather than the only wife of the 404th man. If polygyny were allowed, the 404th-ranked woman can marry the 40th-ranked man and share him with another wife. If polygyny is outlawed, she can't.

Now let's put things into economic terms. We know that a shortage exists if the quantity demanded of a good is greater than the quantity supplied. Think of the situation we have just discussed, where two women might want to marry the same man. Quantity supplied of the man is one, but the quantity demanded (of him) is two. This sounds like a shortage of the man, unless polygyny is permitted, because in that case it is possible for the two women to be married to the same man.

But suppose polygyny is not permitted, even though the two women still want to be married to the same man. Now we have the problem of a shortage (of this particular man) that cannot be eliminated through the adoption of polygyny. But what other way remains to eliminate the shortage? Normally we think of money as eliminating a shortage, and this is exactly what might be the purpose of the dowry. A dowry is a transfer of assets from the bride's family to the groom's family (usually) before the marriage takes place. If two women want to be married to the same man, but only one can be legally married to him, then the dowry may effectively take the place of polygyny (in eliminating the shortage of the man). All other things being equal, the prospective bride's family that offers the better dowry to the groom's family ends up with the groom as their son-in-law. This is consistent with the findings of anthropologists Gaulin and Boster, who have shown that the dowry is almost exclusively found in societies where monogamy has been imposed (and polygyny outlawed).

Moving to Equilibrium: Maximum and Minimum Prices

The discussion of surpluses illustrates how a market moves to equilibrium, but there is another way to demonstrate this. Exhibit 15 shows the market for good X. Look at the first unit of good X. What is the *maximum price buyers would be willing to pay* for it? The answer is $70. This can be seen by following the dotted line up from the first unit of the good to the demand curve. What is the *minimum price sellers need to receive before they would be willing to sell* this unit of good X? It is $10. This can be seen by following the dotted line up from the first unit to the supply curve. Because the maximum buying price is greater than the minimum selling price, the first unit of good X will be exchanged.

What about the second unit? For the second unit, buyers are willing to pay a maximum price of $60, and sellers need to receive a minimum price of $20. The second unit of good X will be exchanged. In fact, exchange will occur as long as the maximum buying price is greater than the minimum selling price. The exhibit shows that a total of four units of good X will be exchanged. The fifth unit will not be exchanged because the maximum buying price ($30) is less than the minimum selling price ($50).

exhibit 15

Moving to Equilibrium in Terms of Maximum and Minimum Prices

As long as the maximum buying price is greater than the minimum selling price, an exchange will occur. This condition is met for units 1–4. The market converges on equilibrium through a process of mutually beneficial exchanges.

Units of Good X	Maximum Buying Price	Minimum Selling Price	Result
1st	$70	$10	Exchange
2d	60	20	Exchange
3d	50	30	Exchange
4th	40	40	Exchange
5th	30	50	No Exchange

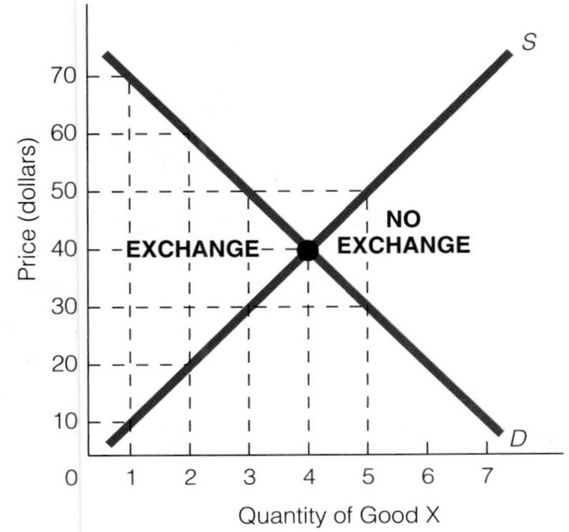

In the process just described, buyers and sellers trade money for goods as long as both benefit from the trade. The market converges on a quantity of 4 units of good X and a price of $40 per unit. This is equilibrium. In other words, mutually beneficial trade drives the market to equilibrium.

Equilibrium in Terms of Consumers' and Producers' Surplus

Equilibrium can be viewed in terms of two important economic concepts: consumers' surplus and producers' (or sellers') surplus. **Consumers' surplus** is the difference between the maximum buying price and the price paid by the buyer.

Consumers' Surplus (*CS*)
The difference between the maximum price a buyer is willing and able to pay for a good or service and the price actually paid. *CS* = Maximum buying price − Price paid.

Consumers' surplus = Maximum buying price − Price paid

For example, if the highest price you would pay to see a movie is $10 and you pay $7 to see the movie, then you have received $3 consumers' surplus. Obviously, the more consumers' surplus consumers receive, the better off they are. Wouldn't you have preferred to pay, say, $4 to see the movie instead of $7? If you had paid only $4, your consumers' surplus would have been $6 instead of $3.

Producers' (sellers') surplus is the difference between the price received by the producer or seller and the minimum selling price.

Producers' (Sellers') Surplus (*PS*)
The difference between the price sellers receive for a good and the minimum or lowest price for which they would have sold the good. *PS* = Price received − Minimum selling price.

Producers' (sellers') surplus = Price received − Minimum selling price

Suppose the minimum price the owner of the movie theater would have accepted for admission is $5. But she doesn't sell admission for $5; she sells it for $7. Her producers' or sellers' surplus is $2. A seller prefers a large producers' surplus to a small one. The theater owner would have preferred to sell admission to the movie for $8 instead of $7 because then she would have received $3 producers' surplus.

Total surplus is the sum of the consumers' surplus and producers' surplus.

Total Surplus (*TS*)
The sum of consumers' surplus and producers' surplus. $TS = CS + PS$.

Total surplus = Consumers' surplus + Producers' surplus

In Exhibit 16(a), consumers' surplus is represented by the shaded triangle. This triangle includes the area under the demand curve and above the equilibrium price. According to the definition, consumers' surplus is the highest price buyers are willing to pay (maximum buying price) minus the price they pay. For example, the window in (a) shows that buyers are willing to pay as high as $7 for the 50th unit but only pay $5. Thus, the consumers' surplus on the 50th unit of the good is $2. If we add the consumers' surplus on each unit of the good between and including the first and the 100th units (the equilibrium quantity), we obtain the shaded consumers' surplus triangle.

In Exhibit 16(b), producers' surplus is represented by the shaded triangle. This triangle includes the area above the supply curve and under the equilibrium price. Keep in mind the definition of producers' surplus—the price received by the seller minus the lowest price the seller would accept for the good. For example, the window in (b) shows that sellers would have sold the 50th unit for as low as $3 but actually sold it for $5. Thus, the producers' surplus on the 50th unit of the good is $2. If we add the producers' surplus on each unit of the good between and including the first and the 100th unit, we obtain the shaded producers' surplus triangle.

exhibit 16

Consumers' and Producers' Surplus

(a) Consumers' surplus. As the shaded area indicates, the difference between the maximum or highest amount buyers would be willing to pay and the price they actually pay is consumers' surplus. (b) Producers' surplus. As the shaded area indicates, the difference between the price sellers receive for the good and the minimum or lowest price they would be willing to sell the good for is producers' surplus.

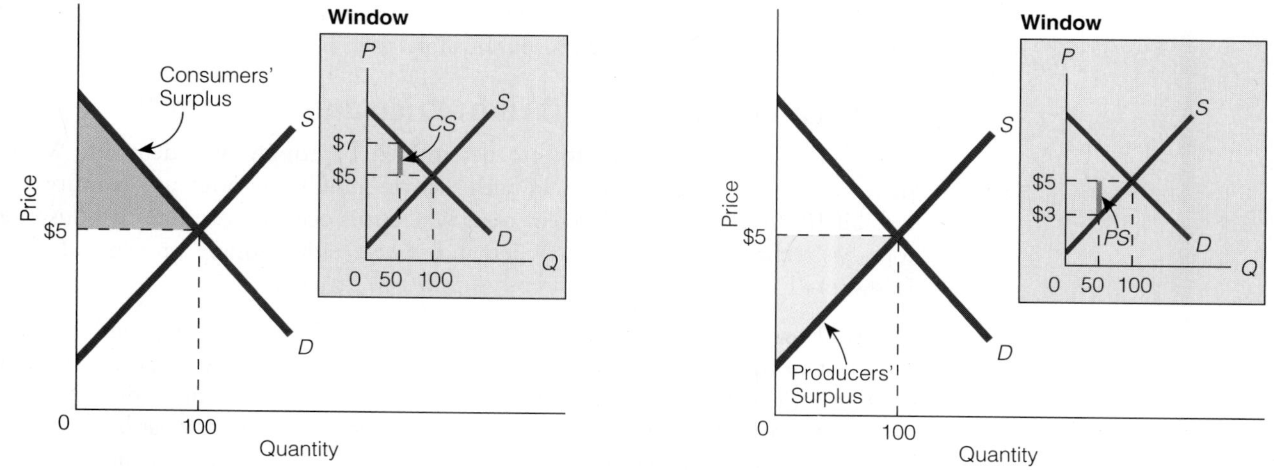

(a)
Consumers' Surplus (*CS*)

(b)
Producers' Surplus (*PS*)

exhibit 17

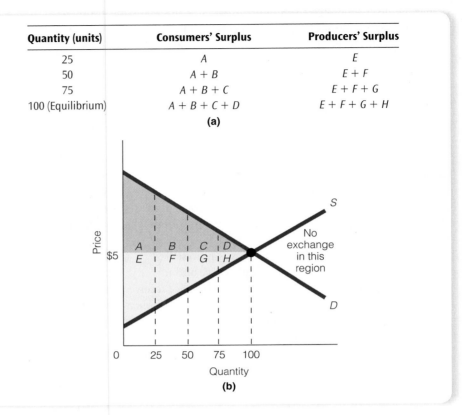

Equilibrium, Consumers' Surplus, and Producers' Surplus

Consumers' surplus is greater at equilibrium quantity (100 units) than at any other exchangeable quantity. Producers' surplus is greater at equilibrium quantity than at any other exchangeable quantity. For example, consumers' surplus is areas $A + B + C$ at 75 units, but areas $A + B + C + D$ at 100 units. Producers' surplus is areas $E + F + G$ at 75 units, but areas $E + F + G + H$ at 100 units.

Quantity (units)	Consumers' Surplus	Producers' Surplus
25	A	E
50	$A + B$	$E + F$
75	$A + B + C$	$E + F + G$
100 (Equilibrium)	$A + B + C + D$	$E + F + G + H$

(a)

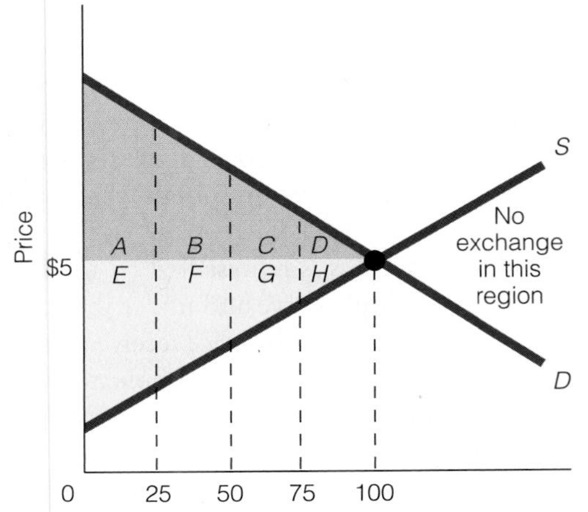

(b)

Now consider consumers' surplus and producers' surplus at the equilibrium quantity. Exhibit 17 shows that consumers' surplus at equilibrium is equal to areas $A + B + C + D$, and producers' surplus at equilibrium is equal to areas $E + F + G + H$. At any other exchangeable quantity, such as at 25, 50, or 75 units, both consumers' surplus and producers' surplus are less. For example, at 25 units, consumers' surplus is equal to area A, and producers' surplus is equal to area E. At 50 units, consumers' surplus is equal to areas $A + B$, and producers' surplus is equal to areas $E + F$.

Is there a special property to equilibrium? At equilibrium, both consumers' surplus and producers' surplus are maximized. In short, total surplus is maximized.

What Can Change Equilibrium Price and Quantity?

Equilibrium price and quantity are determined by supply and demand. Whenever demand changes, supply changes, or both change, equilibrium price and quantity change. Exhibit 18 illustrates eight different cases where this occurs. Cases (a)–(d) illustrate the four basic changes in supply and demand, where either supply or demand changes. Cases (e)–(h) illustrate changes in both supply and demand.

- (a) Demand rises (the demand curve shifts rightward from D_1 to D_2), and supply is constant (the supply curve does not move). As a result of demand rising and supply remaining constant, equilibrium price rises from P_1 to P_2 and equilibrium quantity rises from 10 units to 12 units. Now let's see if you can identify what has happened to quantity supplied (not supply) as price has risen from P_1 to P_2. (Remember, quantity supplied changes if *price* changes.) As price rises from P_1 to P_2, quantity supplied rises from 10 to 12 units. We see this as a movement up the supply curve from point 1 to point 2, which corresponds (on the horizontal axis) to a change from 10 to 12 units.

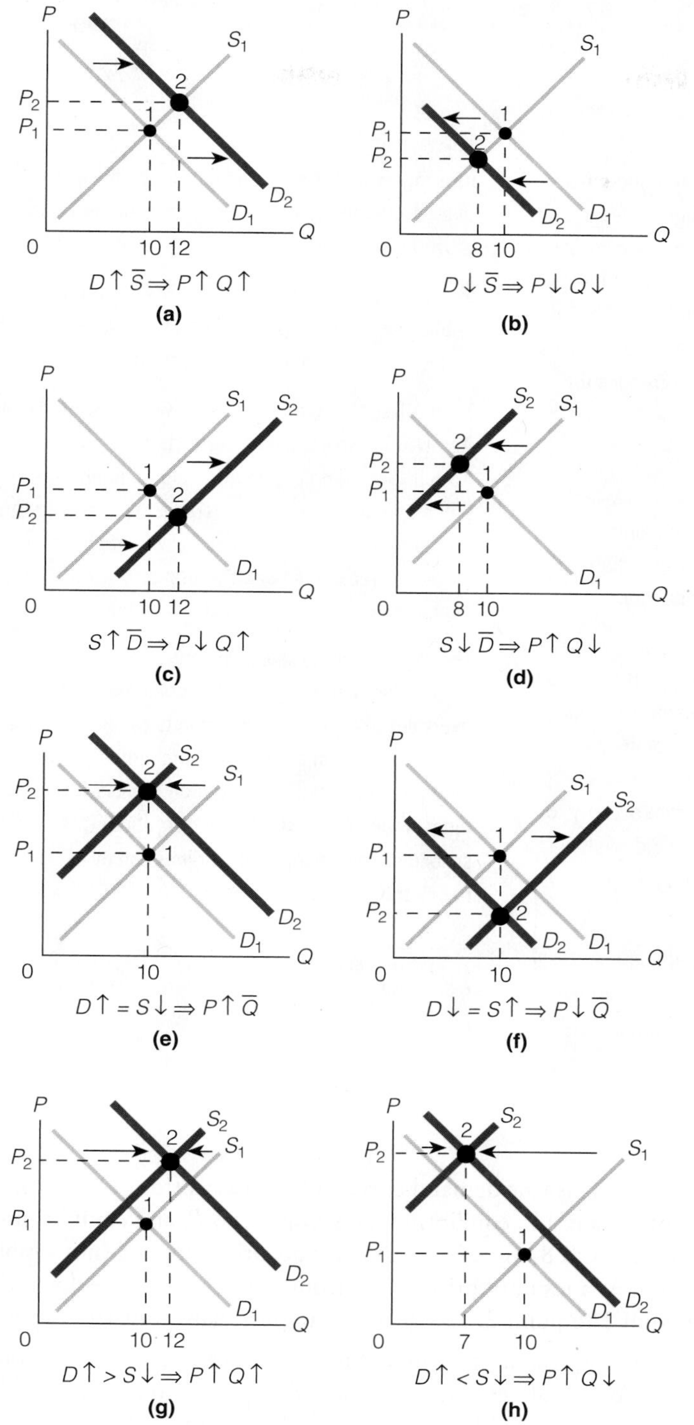

exhibit 18

Equilibrium Price and Quantity Effects of Supply Curve Shifts and Demand Curve Shifts

The exhibit illustrates the effects on equilibrium price and quantity of a change in demand, a change in supply, or change in both. Below each diagram the condition leading to the effects is noted, using the following symbols: (1) a bar over a letter means *constant* (thus, $\bar{S}$ means that supply is constant); (2) a downward-pointing arrow (↓) indicates a fall; (3) an upward-pointing arrow (↑) indicates a rise. A rise (fall) in demand is the same as a rightward (leftward) shift in the demand curve. A rise (fall) in supply is the same as a rightward (leftward) shift in the supply curve.

economics 24/7

OVERBOOKING AND THE AIRLINES

Airlines often overbook flights; that is, they accept more reservations than there are seats available on a flight. They do this because they know that a certain (usually small) percentage of individuals with reservations will not show up. An empty seat means that the airline's cost per actual passenger on board is higher than it would be if the seat were occupied by a paying passenger. So airlines try to make sure there are few empty seats. One way to reduce the number of empty seats is to overbook.

A while back, when an airline was confronted with more people with reservations showing up for a flight than there were seats available, it would simply "bump" passengers. In other words, the airline would tell some passengers that they could not fly on a particular flight. Obviously, the bumped passengers were disappointed and angry.

One day while shaving, economist Julian Simon (1932–1998) came up with a better way to deal with overbooking. He argued that the airline should enter into a market transaction with those persons who had reserved seats for an overbooked flight. Instead of bumping people randomly, an airline should ask passengers to sell their seats back to the airline. Passengers who absolutely had to get from one city to another would not sell their seats, but passengers who did not have to get from one city to another right away might be willing to sell their ticket for a given flight.

Simon wrote the executives of various airlines and outlined the details of his plan. He even told them that the first airline that enacted the plan would likely reap larger sales. It could, after all, guarantee its passengers that they would not get bumped. Most airline executives wrote back and told him it was a reasonably good idea but unworkable.

Simon contacted various economists asking them to support his idea publicly. Some did; some didn't. For years, Simon pushed his idea with airline executives and government officials.

Then Alfred Kahn, an economist, was appointed chairman of the Civil Aeronautics Board. Simon contacted Kahn with his plan, and Kahn liked it. According to Simon, "Kahn announced something like the scheme in his first press conference. He also had the great persuasive skill to repackage it as a 'voluntary' bumping plan, and at the same time to increase the penalties that airlines must pay to involuntary bumpees, a nice carrot-and-stick combination."[1]

The rest, as people say, is history. Simon's plan has been in operation since 1978. Simon wrote, "The volunteer system for handling airline oversales exemplifies how markets can improve life for all concerned parties. In case of an oversale, the airline agent proceeds from lowest bidder upwards until the required number of bumpees is achieved. Low bidders take the next flight, happy about it. All other passengers fly as scheduled, also happy. The airlines can overbook more, making them happy too."[2]

1. See Julian Simon, "Origins of the Airline Oversales Auction System," at http://www.cato.org/pubs/regulation/regv17n2/reg17n2-simon.html.

2. Ibid.

- (b) Demand falls (the demand curve shifts leftward from D_1 to D_2), and supply is constant. As a result, equilibrium falls from P_1 to P_2 and equilibrium quantity falls from 10 units to 8 units. Now ask: Has quantity supplied (not supply) changed? Yes it has. As a result of price falling from P_1 to P_2, we move down the supply curve from point 1 to point 2, and quantity supplied falls from 10 units to 8 units.
- (c) Supply rises (the supply curve shifts rightward from S_1 to S_2), and demand is constant. As a result, equilibrium price falls from P_1 to P_2 and equilibrium quantity rises from 10 units to 12 units. Now ask: Has quantity demanded (not demand) changed? Yes it has. As a result of price falling from P_1 to P_2, we move down the demand curve from point 1 to point 2, and quantity demanded rises from 10 to 12 units.
- (d) Supply falls (the supply curve shifts leftward from S_1 to S_2), and demand is constant. As a result, equilibrium price rises from P_1 to P_2 and equilibrium quantity falls

from 10 to 8 units. One last time: Has quantity demanded (not demand) changed? Yes it has. As a result of price rising from P_1 to P_2, we move up the demand curve from point 1 to point 2, and quantity demanded falls from 10 to 8 units.

- (e) Demand rises (the demand curve shifts from D_1 to D_2) and supply falls (the supply curve shifts leftward from S_1 to S_2) by an equal amount. As a result, equilibrium price rises from P_1 to P_2 and equilibrium quantity remains constant at 10 units.
- (f) Demand falls (the demand curve shifts leftward from D_1 to D_2) and supply rises (the supply curve shifts rightward from S_1 to S_2) by an equal amount. As a result, equilibrium price falls from P_1 to P_2 and equilibrium quantity is constant at 10 units.
- (g) Demand rises (the demand curve shifts rightward from D_1 to D_2) by a greater amount than supply falls (the supply curve shifts leftward from S_1 to S_2). As a result, equilibrium price rises from P_1 to P_2 and equilibrium quantity rises from 10 to 12 units.
- (h) Demand rises (the demand curve shifts rightward from D_1 to D_2) by a smaller amount than supply falls (the supply curve shifts leftward from S_1 to S_2). Equilibrium price rises from P_1 to P_2 and equilibrium quantity falls from 10 to 7 units.

DEMAND AND SUPPLY AS EQUATIONS

You are used to seeing demand and supply as curves. Let's now look at demand and supply as equations. Here is a demand equation:

$$Q_d = 1{,}500 - 32P$$

To see what this equation says, we let price (P) in the equation equal \$10 and then solve for quantity demanded (Q_d). We get 1,180.

$$Q_d = 1{,}500 - 32(10) = 1{,}180$$

So this equation says that if price is \$10, it follows that quantity demanded is 1,180 units. We could find other quantities demanded by plugging in different dollar amounts for price (P).

Now here is a supply equation:

$$Q_s = 1{,}200 + 43P$$

To find what quantity supplied (Q_S) equals at a particular price, we let \$5 equal price (P) and solve for quantity supplied. We get 1,415.

$$Q_s = 1{,}200 + 43(5) = 1{,}415$$

Now suppose we want to find equilibrium price and quantity given our demand and supply equations. How would we do it?

First, we know that in equilibrium the quantity demanded (Q_d) of a good is equal to the quantity supplied (Q_s), so let's set the two equations equal to each other this way:

$$1{,}500 - 32P = 1{,}200 + 43P$$

Now we can solve for P. We add $32P$ to both sides of the equal sign and subtract 1,200 from both sides. We are left with:

$$75P = 300$$

It follows then that $P = 300/75$ or \$4.00.

Once we know equilibrium price is \$4.00, we can place this value in either the demand or supply equation to find the equilibrium quantity. Let's place it in the demand equation:

$$Q_d = 1{,}500 - 32(4.00) = 1{,}372$$

Just to make sure that 1,372 is also the quantity supplied, we put the equilibrium price of \$4.00 into the supply equation:

$$Q_S = 1{,}200 + 43(4.00) = 1{,}372$$

In summary, given our demand and supply equations, equilibrium price is \$4.00 and equilibrium quantity is 1,372.

SELF-TEST

1. When a person goes to the grocery store to buy food, there is no auctioneer calling out prices for bread, milk, and other items. Therefore, supply and demand cannot be operative. Do you agree or disagree? Explain your answer.
2. The price of a given-quality personal computer is lower today than it was five years ago. Is this necessarily the result of a lower demand for computers? Explain your answer.
3. What is the effect on equilibrium price and quantity of the following?
   a. A decrease in demand that is greater than the increase in supply
   b. An increase in supply
   c. A decrease in supply that is greater than the increase in demand
   d. A decrease in demand
4. At equilibrium quantity, what is the relationship between the maximum buying price and the minimum selling price?
5. If the price paid is \$40 and the consumers' surplus is \$4, then what is the maximum buying price? If the minimum selling price is \$30 and producers' surplus is \$4, then what is the price received by the seller?

PRICE CONTROLS

Because scarcity exists, there is a need for a rationing device—such as dollar price. But price is not always permitted to be a rationing device. Sometimes, price is controlled. There are two types of price controls: price ceilings and price floors. In the discussion of price controls, the word *price* is used in the generic sense. It refers to the price of an apple, for example, the price of labor (wage), the price of credit (interest rate), and so on.

Price Ceiling: Definition and Effects

Price Ceiling
A government-mandated maximum price above which legal trades cannot be made.

A **price ceiling** is a government-mandated maximum price above which legal trades cannot be made. For example, suppose the government mandates that the maximum price at which good X can be bought and sold is \$8. It follows that \$8 is a price ceiling. If \$8 is below the equilibrium price of good X, as in Exhibit 19, any or all of the following effects may arise.[3]

SHORTAGES At the $12 equilibrium price in Exhibit 19, the quantity demanded of good X (150) is equal to the quantity supplied (150). At the $8 price ceiling, a shortage exists. The quantity demanded (190) is greater than the quantity supplied (100). When a shortage exists, there is a tendency for price and output to rise to equilibrium. But when a price ceiling exists, this tendency cannot be realized because it is unlawful to trade at the equilibrium price.

FEWER EXCHANGES At the equilibrium price of $12 in Exhibit 19, 150 units of good X are bought and sold. At the price ceiling of $8, 100 units of good X are bought and sold. (Buyers would prefer to buy 190 units, but only 100 are supplied.) We conclude that price ceilings cause fewer exchanges to be made.

exhibit 19

A Price Ceiling

The price ceiling is $8 and the equilibrium price is $12. At $12, quantity demanded = quantity supplied. At $8 quantity demanded > quantity supplied. (Recall that price, on the vertical axis, always represents price per unit. Quantity, on the horizontal axis, always holds for a specific time period.)

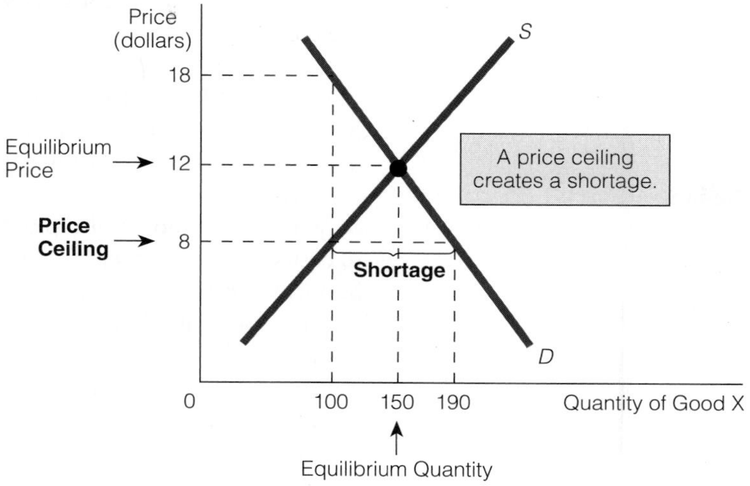

Notice in Exhibit 19 that the demand curve is above the supply curve for all quantities less than 150 units. (At 150 units, the demand curve and the supply curve intersect and thus share the same point in the two-dimensional space.) This means the maximum buying price is greater than the minimum selling price for all units less than 150. In particular, the maximum buying price is greater than the minimum selling price for units 101 to 149. For example, buyers might be willing to pay $17 for the 110th unit, and sellers might be willing to sell the 110th unit for $10. But no unit after the 100th unit (not the 110th unit, not the 114th unit, not the 130th unit) will be produced and sold because of the price ceiling. In short, the price ceiling prevents mutually advantageous trades from being realized.

NONPRICE RATIONING DEVICES If the equilibrium price of $12 fully rationed good X before the price ceiling was imposed, it follows that a (lower) price of $8 can only partly ration this good. In short, price ceilings prevent price from rising to the level sufficient to ration goods fully. But if price is responsible for only part of the rationing, what accounts for the rest? The answer is some other (nonprice) rationing device, such as first come, first served (FCFS).

In Exhibit 19, 100 units of good X will be sold at $8, although buyers are willing to buy 190 units at this price. What happens? Possibly, good X will be sold on an FCFS basis for $8 per unit. In other words, to buy good X, a person must not only pay $8 per unit but also be one of the first people in line.

BUYING AND SELLING AT A PROHIBITED PRICE Buyers and sellers may regularly circumvent a price ceiling by making their exchanges "under the table." For example, some buyers may offer some sellers more than $8 per unit for good X. No

3. If the price ceiling is above the equilibrium price (say, $8 is the price ceiling and $4 is the equilibrium price), it has no effects. Usually, however, a price ceiling is below the equilibrium price.

doubt, some sellers will accept the offers. But why would some buyers offer more than $8 per unit when they can buy good X for $8? The answer is because not all buyers can buy the amount of good X they want at $8. As Exhibit 19 shows, there is a shortage. Buyers are willing to buy 190 units at $8, but sellers are willing to sell only 100 units. In short, 90 fewer units will be sold than buyers would like to buy. Some buyers will go unsatisfied. How, then, does any one buyer make it more likely that sellers will sell to him or her instead of to someone else? The answer is by offering to pay a higher price. Because it is illegal to pay a higher price, the transaction must be made "under the table."

Tie-in Sale
A sale whereby one good can be purchased only if another good is also purchased.

TIE-IN SALES In Exhibit 19, the maximum price buyers would be willing and able to pay per unit for 100 units of good X is $18. (This is the price on the demand curve at a quantity of 100 units.) The maximum legal price, however, is $8. This difference between these two prices often prompts a **tie-in sale**, a sale whereby one good can be purchased only if another good is also purchased. For example, if Ralph's Gas Station sells gasoline to customers only if they buy a car wash, the two goods are linked together in a tie-in sale. Suppose that the sellers of good X in Exhibit 18 also sell good Y. They might offer to sell buyers good X at $8 only if the buyers agree to buy good Y at, say, $10. We choose $10 as the price for good Y because $10 is the difference between the maximum per-unit price buyers are willing and able to pay for 100 units of good X ($18) and the maximum legal price ($8).

In New York City and other communities with rent-control laws, tie-in sales sometimes result from rent ceilings on apartments. Occasionally, to rent an apartment, an individual must agree to buy the furniture in the apartment.

Common MISCONCEPTIONS

About the Prices That Buyers Prefer

Do buyers prefer lower prices to higher prices? "Of course," someone might say, "buyers prefer lower prices to higher prices. What buyer would want to pay a higher price for anything?" But wait a minute. Price ceilings are often lower than equilibrium prices. Does it follow that buyers prefer price ceilings to equilibrium prices? Not necessarily. Price ceilings have effects that equilibrium prices do not: shortages; use of first come, first served as a rationing device; tie-in sales; and so on. A buyer could prefer to pay a higher price (an equilibrium price) than to pay a lower price and have to deal with the effects of a price ceiling. All we can say for certain is that buyers prefer lower prices to higher prices, *ceteris paribus.* As in many cases, the *ceteris paribus* condition makes all the difference.

Thinking like AN ECONOMIST

Look for the Unintended Effects

Economists think in terms of unintended effects. For example, a price ceiling policy intended to lower prices for the poor may cause shortages, the use of nonprice rationing devices, illegal market transactions, and tie-in sales. When we consider both the price ceiling and its effects, it is not clear that the poor have been helped. The economist knows that wanting to do good (for others) is not sufficient. It is important to know how to do good too.

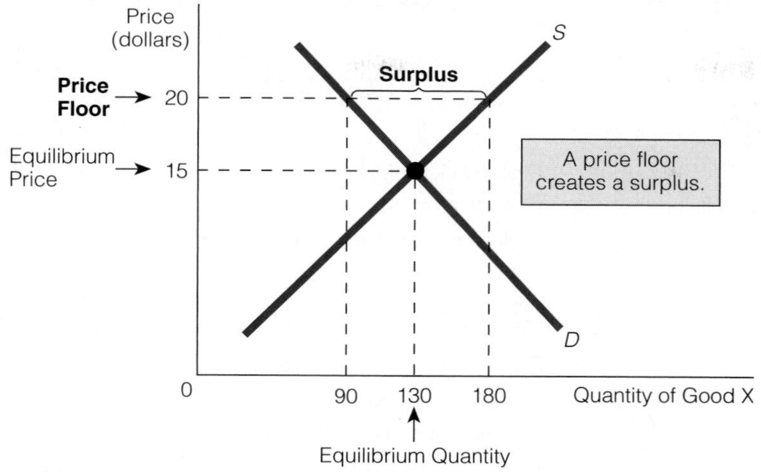

exhibit 20

A Price Floor

The price floor is \$20 and the equilibrium price is \$15. At \$15, quantity demanded = quantity supplied. At \$20, quantity supplied > quantity demanded.

Price Floor: Definition and Effects

A **price floor** is a government-mandated minimum price below which legal trades cannot be made. For example, suppose the government mandates that the minimum price at which good X can be sold is \$20. It follows that \$20 is a price floor (see Exhibit 20). If the price floor is above the equilibrium price, the following two effects arise.[4]

Price Floor
A government-mandated minimum price below which legal trades cannot be made.

SURPLUSES At the \$15 equilibrium price in Exhibit 20, the quantity demanded of good X (130) is equal to the quantity supplied (130). At the \$20 price floor, a surplus exists.

The quantity supplied (180) is greater than the quantity demanded (90). A surplus is usually a temporary state of affairs. When a surplus exists, there is a tendency for price and output to fall to equilibrium. But when a price floor exists, this tendency cannot be realized because it is unlawful to trade at the equilibrium price.

FEWER EXCHANGES At the equilibrium price in Exhibit 20, 130 units of good X are bought and sold. At the price floor, 90 units are bought and sold. (Sellers want to sell 180 units, but buyers buy only 90.) We conclude that price floors cause fewer exchanges to be made.

SELF-TEST

1. Do buyers prefer lower prices to higher prices?
2. When there are long-lasting shortages, there are long lines of people waiting to buy goods. It follows that the shortages cause the long lines. Do you agree or disagree? Explain your answer.
3. Who might argue for a price ceiling? a price floor?

4. If the price floor is below the equilibrium price (say, \$20 is the price floor and \$25 is equilibrium price), it has no effects. Usually, however, a price floor is above the equilibrium price.

office hours

"I THOUGHT PRICES EQUALED COSTS PLUS 10 PERCENT"

Student:

My uncle produces and sells lamps. I asked him once how he determines the price he sells his lamps for. He said he takes his costs and adds on 10 percent. In other words, if it cost him $200 to make a lamp, he sells it for a price of $220. If all sellers do the same thing, then prices aren't being determined by supply and demand, are they?

Instructor:

Supply and demand could still be at work even given what your uncle said. For example, it could be that $220 is the (supply-and-demand determined) equilibrium price for the type of lamps your uncle is producing and selling. Look at it this way: If your uncle could sell the lamps for, say, $250 each, then he would have told you that he takes his cost (of $200) and adds on 25 percent ($50) to get "his price" of $250.

Student:

Is the point that what looks like *cost plus 10 percent* to me could really be supply and demand?

Instructor:

Yes, that's the point. But there is something else we can add to make the point stronger. Think of the housing market for a minute. Are the prices of houses determined by *cost plus 10 percent* or by supply and demand? Let's see if we can think through an example together. Suppose you buy a house for $400,000 in one year and then decide to sell that house ten years later. What price do you charge for the house? Do you charge the (market) equilibrium price for that house, or do you charge what you paid for the house ($400,000) plus 10 percent (plus $40,000) for a total of $440,000?

Student:

Oh, I think I see what you mean. You mean that if the equilibrium price for the house happened to be $650,000, there would be no way I would charge only $440,000.

Instructor:

Exactly. In other words, the supply-and-demand-determined price would take precedence over the cost plus 10 percent price. Now going back to your uncle, he might have just thought that he was charging a price of cost plus 10 percent because the equilibrium price for the goods he produced and sold happened to be 10 percent higher than his cost. But as stated before, if that equilibrium price had been 25 percent higher, your uncle would have told you his price was determined by his taking his costs and adding on 25 percent. It was the equilibrium price that was determining what percentage your uncle said he added to costs, and not simply his picking a percentage out of thin air.

Points to Remember

1. What looks like cost plus 10 percent (cost plus some markup) could instead be supply and demand at work.
2. Supply and demand are obviously determining prices at, say, an auction. There is one good for sale (say, a painting) and numerous buyers. The bidding stops when there is only one buyer left. At the price the last bidder bid, the quantity demanded (of the painting) equals the quantity supplied and both equal one. Just because you might not see supply and demand at work in non-auction settings, it doesn't necessarily follow that supply and demand are not at work determining prices.

a reader asks — How Does Knowing About Supply and Demand Help Me?

Some things are interesting but not useful. Other things are useful but not interesting. For example, supply and demand are interesting but not useful. Learning how to fix a car is useful but not particularly interesting. Am I wrong? Have I missed something? Is knowledge of supply and demand useful? If it is, what can you do with it?

A knowledge of supply and demand can be used both to explain and to predict. Let's look at the issue of prediction first. Suppose you learn that the federal government is going to impose a quota on imported television sets. What will happen when the quota is imposed? With your knowledge of supply and demand, you can predict that the price of television sets will rise. In other words, you can use your knowledge of supply and demand to predict what *will happen.* Stated differently, you can use your knowledge of supply and demand to see into the *future.* Isn't the ability to see into the future useful?

Supply and demand also allows you to develop richer and fuller explanations of events. To illustrate, suppose there is a shortage of apples in country X. The cause of the shortage, someone says, is that apple growers in the country are simply growing too few apples. Well, of course, it's true that apple growers are growing "too few" apples compared to the number of apples consumers want to buy. But does this explanation completely account for the shortage of apples? Your knowledge of supply and demand will prompt you to ask *why* apple growers are growing too few apples. When you understand that quantity supplied is related to price, you understand that apple growers will grow more apples if the price of apples is higher. What is keeping the price of apples down? Could it be a price ceiling? Without a price ceiling, the price of apples would rise, and apple growers would grow (and offer to sell) more apples. The shortage of apples will vanish.

In other words, without a knowledge of supply and demand, you may have been content to explain the shortage of apples by saying that apple growers are growing too few apples. With your knowledge of supply and demand, you delve deeper into *why* apple growers are growing too few apples.

Chapter Summary

DEMAND

- The law of demand states that as the price of a good rises, the quantity demanded of the good falls, and as the price of a good falls, the quantity demanded of the good rises, *ceteris paribus.* The law of demand holds that price and quantity demanded are inversely related.
- Quantity demanded is the total number of units of a good that buyers are willing and able to buy at a particular price.
- A (downward-sloping) demand curve is the graphical representation of the law of demand.
- Factors that can change demand and cause the demand curve to shift include income, preferences, prices of related goods (substitutes and complements), number of buyers, and expectations of future price.
- The only factor that can directly cause a change in the quantity demanded of a good is a change in the good's own price.

ABSOLUTE PRICE AND RELATIVE PRICE

- The absolute price of a good is the price of the good in money terms.
- The relative price of a good is the price of the good in terms of another good.

SUPPLY

- The law of supply states that as the price of a good rises, the quantity supplied of the good rises, and as the price of a good falls, the quantity supplied of the good falls, *ceteris paribus.* The law of supply asserts that price and quantity supplied are directly related.
- The law of supply does not hold when there is no time to produce more units of a good or when goods cannot be produced at all (over any period of time).
- The upward-sloping supply curve is the graphical representation of the law of supply. More generally, a supply curve (no matter how it slopes) represents the relationship between price and quantity supplied.
- Factors that can change supply and cause the supply curve to shift include prices of relevant resources, technology, prices of other goods, number of sellers, expectations of future price, taxes and subsidies, and government restrictions.

- The only factor that can directly cause a change in the quantity supplied of a good is a change in the good's own price.

THE MARKET

- Demand and supply together establish equilibrium price and equilibrium quantity.
- A surplus exists in a market if, at some price, quantity supplied is greater than quantity demanded. A shortage exists if, at some price, quantity demanded is greater than quantity supplied.
- Mutually beneficial trade between buyers and sellers drives the market to equilibrium.

CONSUMERS' SURPLUS, PRODUCERS' SURPLUS, AND TOTAL SURPLUS

- Consumers' surplus is the difference between the maximum buying price and price paid by the buyer.

Consumers' surplus = Maximum buying price − Price paid

- Producers' (or sellers') surplus is the difference between the price the seller receives and minimum selling price.

Producers' surplus = Price received − Minimum selling price

- The more consumers' surplus that buyers receive, the better off they are. The more producers' surplus that sellers receive, the better off they are. Total surplus is the sum of consumers' surplus and producers' surplus.
- Total surplus (the sum of consumers' surplus and producers' surplus) is maximized at equilibrium.

PRICE CEILINGS

- A price ceiling is a government-mandated maximum price. If a price ceiling is below the equilibrium price, some or all of the following effects arise: shortages, fewer exchanges, nonprice rationing devices, buying and selling at prohibited prices, and tie-in sales.
- Consumers do not necessarily prefer (lower) price ceilings to (higher) equilibrium prices. They may prefer higher prices and none of the effects of price ceilings to lower prices and some of the effects of price ceilings. All we can say for sure is that consumers prefer lower prices to higher prices, *ceteris paribus.*

PRICE FLOORS

- A price floor is a government-mandated minimum price. If a price floor is above the equilibrium price, the following effects arise: surpluses and fewer exchanges.

Key Terms and Concepts

Theory
Market
Demand
Law of Demand
Ceteris Paribus
Demand Schedule
Demand Curve
Absolute (Money) Price
Relative Price
Law of Diminishing Marginal Utility
Own Price
Normal Good
Inferior Good
Neutral Good
Substitutes
Complements
Supply
Law of Supply
Supply Curve
Supply Schedule
Subsidy
Surplus (Excess Supply)
Shortage (Excess Demand)
Equilibrium Price (Market-Clearing Price)
Equilibrium Quantity
Disequilibrium Price
Disequilibrium
Equilibrium
Consumers' Surplus
Producers' (Sellers') Surplus
Total Surplus
Price Ceiling
Tie-in Sale
Price Floor

Questions and Problems

1 When economists build theories they abstract from reality. What does this mean?

2 What is wrong with this statement: Demand refers to the willingness of buyers to purchase different quantities of a good at different prices during a specific time period.

3 What is the difference between *demand* and *quantity demanded*?

4 True or false? As the price of oranges rises, the demand for oranges falls, *ceteris paribus.* Explain your answer.

5 What does *ceteris paribus* mean, and how is it used in terms of the law of demand?

6 "The price of a bushel of wheat, which was $3.00 last month, is $3.70 today. The demand curve for wheat must have shifted rightward between last month and today." Discuss.

7 "Some goods are bought largely because they have 'snob appeal.'" For example, the residents of Beverly Hills gain prestige by buying expensive items. In fact, they won't buy some items unless they are expensive. The law of demand, which holds that people buy more at lower prices than higher prices, obviously doesn't hold for the residents of Beverly Hills. The following rules apply in Beverly Hills: "high prices, buy; low prices, don't buy." Discuss.

8 "The price of T-shirts keeps rising and rising, and people keep buying more and more. T-shirts must have an upward-sloping demand curve." Identify the error.

9 With respect to each of the following changes, identify whether the demand curve will shift rightward or leftward:

a. an increase in income (the good under consideration is a normal good)
b. a rise in the price of a substitute good
c. a fall in the price of a complementary good
d. a fall in the number of buyers

10 What does a sale on shirts have to do with the law of demand (as applied to shirts)?

11 What is wrong with this statement: "As the price of a good falls, the supply of that good falls, *ceteris paribus*"?

12 In the previous chapter, you learned about the law of increasing opportunity costs. What does this law have to do with an upward-sloping supply curve?

13 How might the price of corn affect the supply of wheat?

14 What is the difference between supply and quantity supplied?

15 Predict what would happen to the equilibrium price of marijuana if it were legalized.

16 Compare the ratings for television shows with prices for goods. How are ratings like prices? How are ratings different from prices? (Hint: How does rising demand for a particular television show manifest itself?)

17 At equilibrium in a market, the maximum price buyers would be willing to pay for the good is equal to the minimum price sellers need to receive before they are willing to sell the good. Do you agree or disagree with this statement? Explain your answer.

18 Must consumers' surplus equal producers' surplus at equilibrium price? Explain your answer.

19 Many movie theaters charge a lower admission price for the first show on weekday afternoons than they do for a weeknight or weekend show. Explain why.

20 A Dell computer is a substitute for a Hewlett-Packard computer. What happens to the demand for Hewlett-Packard computers and the quantity demanded of Dell computers as the price of a Dell falls?

21 Describe how each of the following will affect the demand for personal computers: (a) a rise in incomes (assuming computers are a normal good), (b) a lower expected price for computers, (c) cheaper software, and (d) computers become simpler to operate.

22 Describe how each of the following will affect the supply of personal computers: (a) a rise in wage rates, (b) an increase in the number of sellers of computers, (c) a tax placed on the production of computers, and (d) a subsidy placed on the production of computers.

23 The law of demand specifies an inverse relationship between price and quantity demanded, *ceteris paribus*. Is the "price" in the law of demand absolute price or relative price? Explain your answer.

24 Use the law of diminishing marginal utility to explain why demand curves slope downward.

25 Explain how the market moves to equilibrium in terms of shortages and surpluses and in terms of maximum buying prices and minimum selling prices.

26 Identify what happens to equilibrium price and quantity in each of the following cases:

a. Demand rises and supply is constant
b. Demand falls and supply is constant
c. Supply rises and demand is constant
d. Supply falls and demand is constant
e. Demand rises by the same amount that supply falls
f. Demand falls by the same amount that supply rises
g. Demand falls by less than supply rises
h. Demand rises by more than supply rises
i. Demand rises by less than supply rises
j. Demand falls by more than supply falls
k. Demand falls by less than supply falls

27 Many of the proponents of price ceilings argue that government-mandated maximum prices simply reduce producers' profits and do not affect the quantity supplied of a good on the market. What must the supply curve look like before a price ceiling does not affect quantity supplied?

28 When speeding tickets were $100, there were usually 500 speeders on the roads each month in a given city; when ticket prices were raised to $250, there were usually 215 speeders on the roads in the city each month. Can you find any economics in this observation?

29 James lives in a rent-controlled apartment and has for the past few weeks been trying to get the supervisor to fix his shower. What does waiting to get one's shower fixed have to do with a rent-controlled apartment?

30 On most days there are more people who want to see the taping of the *Tonight Show with Jay Leno* (in Burbank, California) than there are seats in the studio where Jay Leno tapes the show. What might explain this shortage?

31 Explain why there are fewer exchanges made when a disequilibrium price (below equilibrium price) exists than when equilibrium price exists.

32 Buyers always prefer lower prices to higher prices. Do you agree or disagree with this statement? Explain your answer.

33 What is the difference between a price ceiling and a price floor? What effect is the same for both a price ceiling and a price floor?

Working with Numbers and Graphs

1 If the absolute price of good X is $10 and the absolute price of good Y is $14, then what is (a) the relative price of good X in terms of good Y and (b) the relative price of good Y in terms of good X?

2 Price is $10, quantity supplied is 50 units, and quantity demanded is 100 units. For every $1 rise in price, quantity supplied rises by 5 units and quantity demanded falls by 5 units. What is the equilibrium price and quantity?

3 Using numbers explain how a market demand curve is derived from two individual demand curves.

4 Draw a diagram that shows a larger increase in demand than the decrease in supply.

5 Draw a diagram that shows a smaller increase in supply than the increase in demand.

6 At equilibrium in the following figure, what area(s) does consumers' surplus equal? producers' surplus?

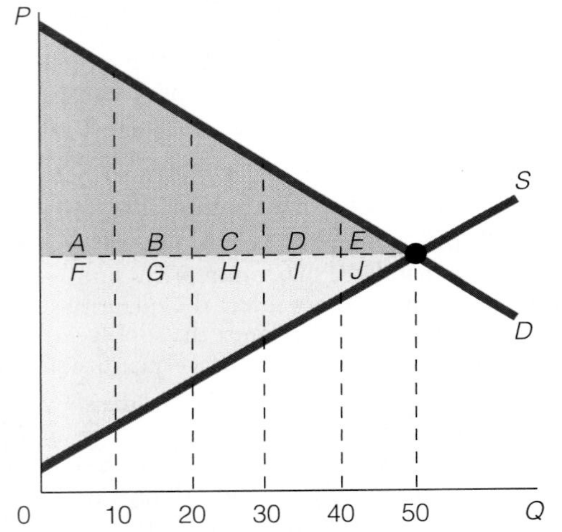

7 At what quantity in the preceding figure is the maximum buying price equal to the minimum selling price?

8 In the following figure, can the movement from point 1 to point 2 be explained by a combination of an increase in the price of a substitute and a decrease in the price of nonlabor resources? Explain your answer.

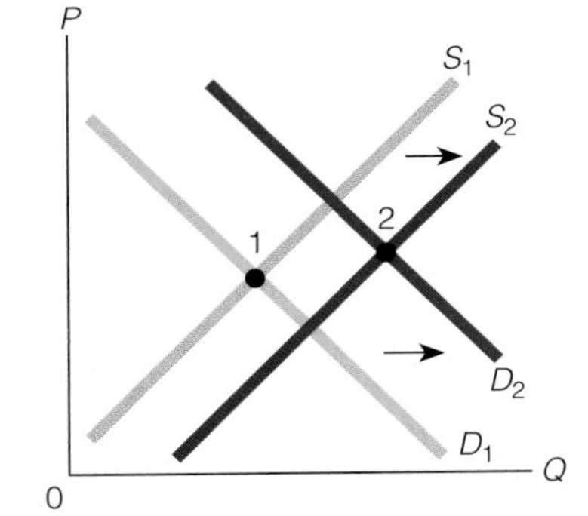

9 The demand curve is downward sloping, the supply curve is upward sloping, and the equilibrium quantity is 50 units. Show on a graph that the difference between the maximum buying price and minimum selling price is greater at 25 units than at 33 units.

10 Determine equilibrium price and quantity for the following supply and demand equations:

a. $Q_d = 1{,}800 - 60P$; $Q_s = 400 + 10P$

b. $Q_d = 950 - 23P$; $Q_s = 900 + 27P$

c. $Q_d = 2{,}250 - 12P$; $Q_s = 1{,}200 + 13P$

11 Using each of the supply and demand equations in problem 10, identify quantity demanded and quantity supplied if price equals $15.

12 Diagrammatically show and explain why a price ceiling that is above the equilibrium price will not prompt a tie-in sale.

CHAPTER 4

SUPPLY AND DEMAND: APPLICATIONS

Introduction In the last chapter we discussed the theory of supply and demand. In this chapter it is time to work with supply and demand. This is a chapter of applications. Each application has something to do with one of the topics we discussed in the last chapter. Many applications deal with supply and demand, some deal with price, and others deal with price ceilings and price floors.

The theory of supply and demand is not very useful to you unless you can use it to explain some of the things you see around you in everyday life. In this chapter we discuss medical care, changing house prices, college classes at 10 a.m., driving on a freeway, standardized tests (such as the SAT), college athletes, and more—all within the general framework of supply and demand.

APPLICATION 1: WHY IS MEDICAL CARE SO EXPENSIVE?

Think of the way you buy groceries. You go to the grocery store, place certain products in your basket, and then pay for them (usually with cash) at the cash register.

Now think of the way you buy medical care. You go to the doctor or hospital, give the doctor's office or hospital your health insurance card, perhaps pay a copayment of $10 or $20, and then receive medical care. Your doctor or the hospital ends up billing your insurance company for the bulk of your expenses.

Now what is the difference between the way you buy groceries and the way you buy medical care? Well, in the grocery store example there are only two parties: you (the buyer) and the grocery store (the seller). In the medical care example, there are three parties: you, the doctor or hospital, and the insurance company. The insurance company is often referred to as the "third party." So, we can put things this way: There is no third party in the grocery store example but there is a third party in the medical care example.

What the existence of a third party does is separate the buying of something from the paying for something. In the grocery store example, the person who bought the groceries and the person who paid for the groceries were the same person (you). In the medical care example, the person who bought and received the medical care (you) was different from the person or entity that paid for the medical care (the insurance company).

But wait a minute, you say. You indirectly pay for your medical care by paying monthly insurance premiums to the medical insurance company. Yes, that is partly true, but it is similar to what happens at a buffet. You pay a set dollar price for the buffet and then you can eat all you want. Our guess is that you will end up eating more food at the buffet than you would if you had to pay for each item at the buffet.

The same often happens with medical care. You pay a set premium to the insurance company (let's say $250 a month) and then you enter the health care buffet line. Might you end up buying more health care than you would if each item of the health care buffet were priced separately?

Before we continue on, there are perhaps two points that we need to get out of the way. You might say: But I don't buy medical care in the medical care buffet line as I buy food in the food buffet line. I like shrimp, steak, salads, and desserts, but who likes getting x-rays taken, being prodded and poked by doctors, and taking medicine? It is ridiculous to think that a person will buy shrimp cocktails the same way he or she buys MRIs.

That is true, of course. But that is not the point we are making. The point is that once you get sick, and go to the doctor or hospital, the existence of a third party (who pays for the medical care you receive) may give you, your doctor, and the hospital options for more medical examinations/procedures/care than you need. A conversation in your doctor's office may go like this:

Doctor: I think you have condition X but just to be sure let's order some blood tests and get an MRI too.

You: Whatever you think is best.

Now ask yourself what you might say if you had to pay—out of your pocket—for the blood test and MRI. You might ask, "How much is this going to cost me, doctor? And is all this really necessary?"

Our point is a simple one: Once you have paid your insurance premium, the price you pay for medical care amounts only to your copayment (which is usually minimal). For all practical purposes, the dollar amount you have to pay, out of pocket, to get medical care is zero. That is a fairly low price for health care. We can expect that the quantity demanded of medical care would be greater at zero than at some positive dollar amount.

Now let us link the *quantity demanded* of medical care (which will be high if the price of medical care is zero) with the *demand for specific items* that make up medical care. (In our buffet food example, it would be similar to linking the *quantity demanded* of food with the *demand* for specific food items—shrimp, chocolate ice cream, or a Caesar's salad.)

If the quantity demanded of medical care is higher at a zero price than at some positive price, then we would expect the demand for those *specific items* that make up health care to be higher than it would be if the quantity demanded of health care were lower. We show this diagrammatically in Exhibit 1. In Exhibit 1(a), we show the demand for medical care as downward sloping. Notice that if the price is zero for health care, then the quantity demanded of medical care is 100 units. But if the price is some positive dollar amount (such as P_1), then the quantity demanded of medical care is 50 units.

exhibit 1

The Price of Medical Care and the Demand for X-rays

(a) If the price of medical care is low (say, zero), the quantity demanded of medical care is 100 units. If the price of medical care for you is P_1, the quantity demanded of medical care is 50 units. (b) The lower the price of medical care and the higher the quantity demanded of medical care in panel (a), then the higher the demand curve for x-rays in (b). (c) The higher the demand for x-rays, the higher the price of x-rays.

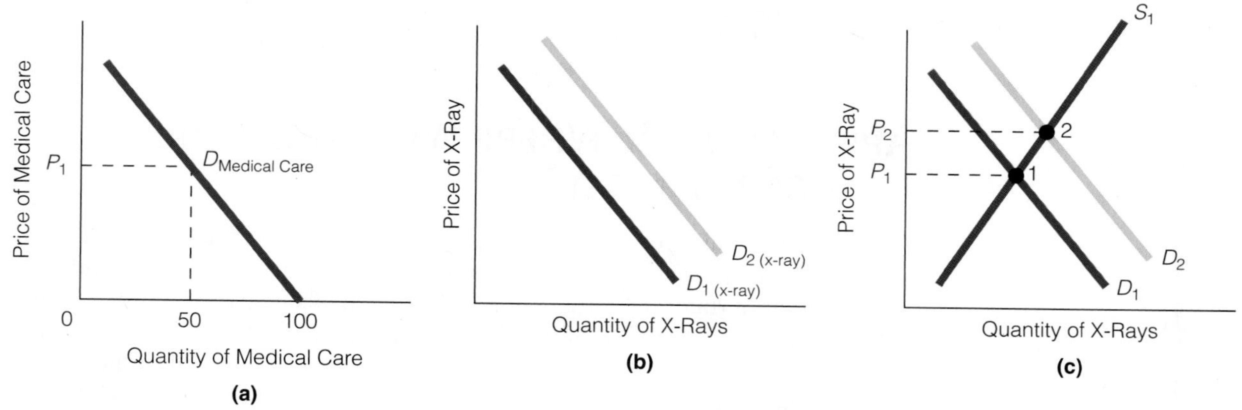

In Exhibit 1(b), we do not show the demand for medical care in general, but instead show the demand for a specific item of medical care—the demand for x-rays. There are two demand curves in panel (b). The first demand curve (D_1) is the demand that exists for x-rays if the *quantity demanded of medical care* is 50 units in panel (a). Stated differently, it is the demand for x-rays if the price for medical care (shown in panel a) is P_1. The second demand curve (D_2) is the demand curve that exists for x-rays if the *quantity demanded of medical care* is 100 units in panel (a). Stated differently, it is the demand for x-rays if the price for medical care (shown in panel a) is zero.

In a nutshell, what we are saying is this: The lower the price of medical care, the higher the quantity demanded of medical care, and the higher the demand for x-rays. The higher the price of medical care, the lower the quantity demanded of medical care, and the lower the demand for x-rays.

Price of medical care is low → Quantity demanded of medical care is high → Demand for x-rays is high

Price of medical care is high → Quantity demanded of medical care is low → Demand for x-rays is low

We have come to the point in the analysis where we must ask what does a high demand for x-rays end up doing to the price of an x-ray? Obviously, it pushes up the price of an x-ray. See Exhibit 1(c).

As a result, the health insurance company finds itself paying more for the x-rays (you receive). Can you see what will happen next? That's right, the health insurance company will make the argument that with rising medical costs, the premiums for your health insurance coverage will need to rise too.

Why is health insurance as expensive as it is, you ask. You now have a large part of the answer. Think buffet.

SELF-TEST

(Answers to Self-Test questions are in the Self-Test Appendix.)

1. Suppose food insurance exists. You pay the food insurance company a certain dollar amount each month and then you purchase all the food you want to purchase from your local grocery store. The grocery store sends the bill to your food insurance company. What will happen to the price of food and to the premium you pay for food insurance?
2. In Exhibit 1(a), suppose that the price a person has to pay for medical care is between P_1 and zero. Where would the demand for x-rays in panel (b) be in relationship to D_1 and D_2?

Application 2: Where Will House Prices Change the Most?

At one point in time you notice that house prices are rising. You also notice that house prices rise more in some areas of the country than in other areas. You wonder why. At another point in time you notice that house prices are falling. You also notice that house prices fall more in some areas of the country than in other areas. You wonder why.

Your knowledge of why prices change might lead you to say this: Obviously supply and demand changes are different in different areas of the country and that is why price changes are different too. To illustrate, in one area of the country the demand for houses rises by more than in another area and this explains why house prices rise by more in one area than in another area.

But suppose the demand for houses rises by the same in all areas of the country. What then? Well, the answer may have to do with the supply curve. To illustrate, look at the two supply curves in Exhibit 2. You will notice that we have drawn S_1 as steeper than S_2. Suppose S_1 represents the supply of houses in area 1 of the country and S_2 represents the supply of houses in area 2. Obviously, if the demand for houses rises in both areas by the same amount—identified by a shift in the demand curve from D_1 and D_2—we notice

exhibit 2

Where Will Prices Change the Most?

We start with two supply curves (S_1 and S_2) and one demand curve (D_1). If we increase demand from D_1 to D_2, you will notice that price rises no matter which supply curve is operational. However, price rises more the steeper the supply curve is. Since S_1 is steeper than S_2, price rises more using S_1 than it does using S_2. The same holds for a decrease in demand. If we decrease demand from D_2 to D_1, we see that price falls more along S_1 than S_2.

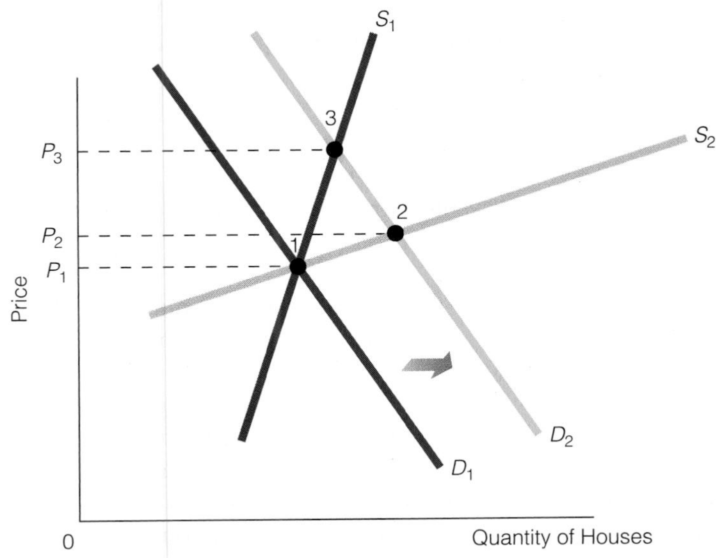

that house prices rise by more in area 1 (moving from P_1 to P_3) than in area 2 (moving from P_1 to P_2). We conclude that the shape of the supply curve affects how high price will rise for a given increase in demand. (In a later chapter, we will discuss the topic of price elasticity of supply, which is not the same as the steepness of the supply curve, but indirectly relates to it.)

The shape of the supply curve will also affect how low price will fall for a given decrease in demand. Using the same exhibit, suppose demand falls from D_2 to D_1. We notice that price falls more (from P_3 to P_1) if S_1 is the operational supply curve than if S_2 is the operational supply curve (from P_2 to P_1).

SELF-TEST

1. In city 1 the supply curve of housing is steeper than in city 2. Given an equal decrease in demand for housing in both cities, in which city will the price of housing fall by less?
2. In city 1 the supply curve of housing is steeper than in city 2. Given an equal increase in demand for housing in both cities, in which city will the (equilibrium) quantity of houses increase less?

APPLICATION 3: WHY DO COLLEGES USE GPAS, ACTS, AND SATS FOR PURPOSES OF ADMISSION?

At many colleges and universities, a student pays part of the price of his or her education (by way of tuition payments), and taxpayers and private donors pay part (by way of tax payments and charitable donations, respectively). Thus, the tuition that students pay to attend colleges and universities is usually less than the equilibrium tuition. To illustrate, suppose a student pays tuition T_1 at a given college or university. As shown in Exhibit 3, T_1 is below the equilibrium tuition, T_E. At T_1, the number of students who want to attend the university (N_1) is greater than the number of openings at the university (N_2); that is, quantity demanded is greater than quantity supplied. The university receives more applications for admission than there are places available. Something has to be done. But what?

The college or university is likely to ration its available space by a combination of money price and some other nonprice rationing devices. The student must pay the tuition, T_1, *and* meet the standards of the nonprice rationing devices. Colleges and universities usually use such things as GPAs (grade point averages), ACT scores, and SAT scores as rationing devices.

exhibit 3

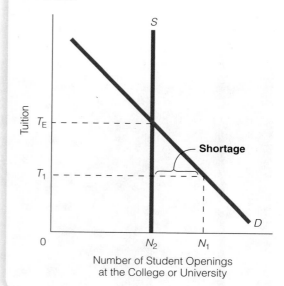

College and University Admissions

If the college or university charges T_1 in tuition (when T_E is the equilibrium tuition), a shortage will be generated. The college or university will then use some nonprice rationing device, such as GPAs, ACTs, and SATs, as admission criteria.

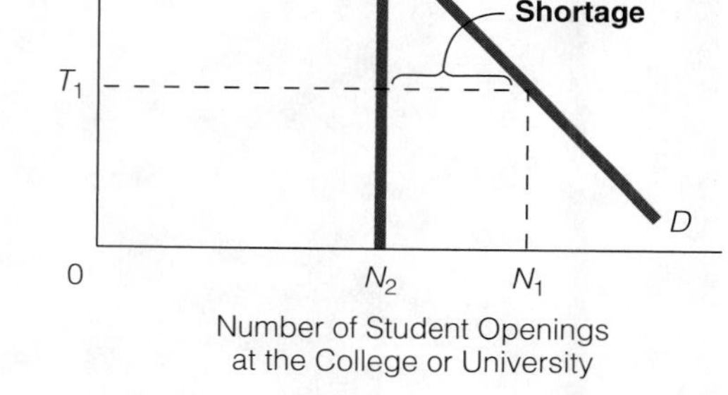

Thinking like AN ECONOMIST

Identifying Rationing Devices

The layperson sees a university that requires a GPA of 3.8 and an SAT score of 1,900 or better for admission. An economist sees a rationing device. The economist then goes on to ask why this particular nonprice rationing device is used. He reasons that there would be no need for a nonprice rationing device if (dollar) price were fully rationing the good or service.

SELF-TEST

1. Suppose the demand rises for admission to a university but both the tuition and the number of openings in the entering class remain the same. Will this affect the admission standards of the university? Explain your answer.
2. Administrators and faculty at state colleges and universities often say that their standards of admission are independent of whether there is a shortage or surplus of openings at the university. Do you think this is true? Do you think that faculty and administrators ignore surpluses and shortages of openings when setting admission standards? Explain your answer.

APPLICATION 4: SUPPLY AND DEMAND ON A FREEWAY

What does a traffic jam on a busy freeway in any large city have to do with supply and demand? Actually, it has quite a bit to do with supply and demand. Look at it this way: There is a demand for driving on the freeway and a supply of freeway space. The supply of freeway space is fixed (freeways do not expand and contract over a day, week, or month). The demand, however, fluctuates. It is higher at some times than at other times. For example, we would expect the demand for driving on the freeway to be higher at 8 a.m. (rush hour) than at 11 p.m. But even though the demand may vary, the money price for driving on the freeway is always the same—zero. A zero money price means that motorists do not pay tolls to drive on the freeway.

Exhibit 4 shows two demand curves for driving on the freeway: $D_{8\text{ a.m.}}$ and $D_{11\text{ p.m.}}$ We have assumed the demand at 8 a.m. is greater than at 11 p.m. We have also assumed that at $D_{11\text{ p.m.}}$ and zero money price the freeway market clears: Quantity demanded of freeway space equals quantity supplied of freeway space. At the higher demand, $D_{8\text{ a.m.}}$, however, this is not the case. At zero money price, a shortage of freeway space exists: Quantity demanded of freeway space is greater than quantity supplied of freeway space. The shortage appears in the form of freeway congestion and bumper-to-bumper traffic. One way to eliminate the shortage is through an increase in the money price of driving on the freeway at 8 a.m. For example, as Exhibit 4 shows, a toll of 70 cents would clear the freeway market at 8 a.m.

If charging different prices (tolls) at different times of the day on freeways sounds like an unusual idea, consider how Miami Beach hotels price their rooms. They charge different prices for their rooms at different times of the year. During the winter months when the demand for vacationing in Miami Beach is high, the hotels charge higher prices than when the demand is (relatively) low. If different prices were charged for freeway space at different times of the day, freeway space would be rationed the same way Miami Beach hotel rooms are rationed.

© DAVID PAUL MORRIS/GETTY IMAGES

Before we leave this topic, let's consider the three alternatives usually proposed for freeway congestion. Some people propose tolls, some propose building more freeways, and others propose encouraging carpooling. Tolls deal with the congestion problem by adjusting price to its equilibrium level, as shown in Exhibit 4. Building more freeways deals with the problem by increasing supply. In Exhibit 4, it would be necessary to shift the supply curve of freeway space to the right so there is no longer any shortage of space at 8 a.m. More carpooling deals with the problem by decreasing demand. Two people in one car take up less space on a freeway than two people in two cars. In Exhibit 4, if through carpooling the demand at 8 a.m. begins to look like the demand at 11 p.m., then there is no longer a shortage of freeway space at 8 a.m.

A final note: A fee to drive in the Central London area was introduced in 2003. Anyone going into or out of the Central London area between 7:00 a.m. and 6:30 p.m., Monday through Friday, must pay a fee of approximately $15. (Not everyone has to pay the fee. For example, taxi drivers, ambulance drivers, police vehicles, motorcycle drivers, and bicyclists do not have to pay the fee. The residents who live in the area receive a 90 percent discount.) Many people have claimed the fee a success because it has cut down on traffic and travel times and reduced pollution in the area.

Some people have urged New York City to institute a similar fee program to drive on certain streets in the city. On any given day in New York City, there are approximately 800,000 cars on the streets south of 60th Street in Manhattan. According to many, the city is "choking in traffic." We will have to wait to see if New York City goes the way of London.

exhibit 4

Freeway Congestion and Supply and Demand

The demand for driving on the freeway is higher at 8 a.m. than at 11 p.m. At zero money price and $D_{11\ p.m.}$, the freeway market clears. At zero money price and $D_{8\ a.m.}$, there is a shortage of freeway space, which shows up as freeway congestion. At a price (toll) of 70 cents, the shortage is eliminated and freeway congestion disappears.

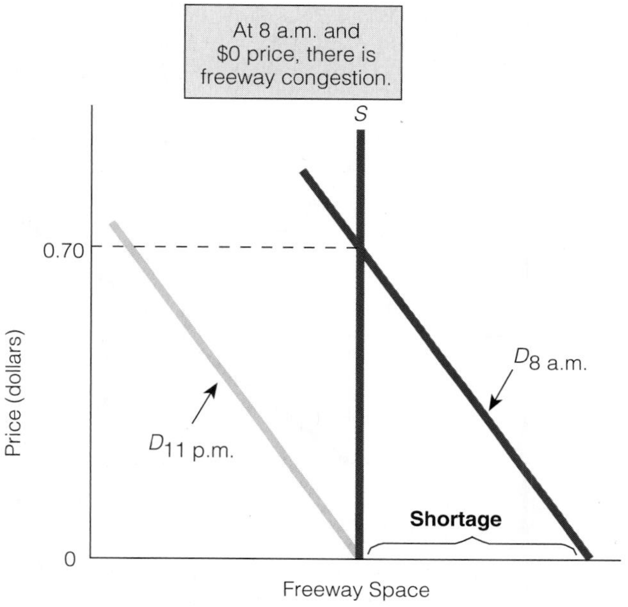

Thinking like AN ECONOMIST

It's One of Three

The economist knows that when there are buyers and sellers of anything (bread, cars, or freeway space), only three conditions are possible—equilibrium, shortage, or surplus. When the economist sees traffic congestion, the first thing that comes to mind is that there is a shortage of road space. But why is there a shortage? The economist knows that shortages occur at prices below equilibrium price. In other words, price is too low.

SELF-TEST

1. In Exhibit 4, at what price is there a surplus of freeway space at 8 a.m.?
2. If the driving population increases in an area and the supply of freeway space remains constant, what will happen to freeway congestion? Explain your answer.

APPLICATION 5: PRICE CEILINGS IN THE KIDNEY MARKET

Just as there are people who want to buy houses, computers, and books, there are people who want to buy kidneys. These people have kidney failure and either will die without a new kidney or will have to endure years of costly and painful dialysis. This demand for kidneys is shown as D_K in Exhibit 5.

The supply of kidneys is shown as S_K in Exhibit 5. Notice that at $0 price, the quantity supplied of kidneys is 350. These kidneys are from people who donate their kidneys

exhibit 5

The Market for Kidneys

We have identified the demand for kidneys as D_K and the supply of kidneys as S_K. Given the demand for and supply of kidneys, the equilibrium price of a kidney is P_1. It does not follow, though, that simply because there is an equilibrium price, people will be allowed to trade at this price. Today, it is unlawful to buy and sell kidneys at any positive price. In short, there is a price ceiling in the kidney market and the ceiling is \$0. At the price ceiling, there is a shortage of kidneys, a nonprice rationing device for kidneys (first-come-first-served), fewer kidney transplants (than there would be at P_1), and illegal purchases and sales of kidneys.

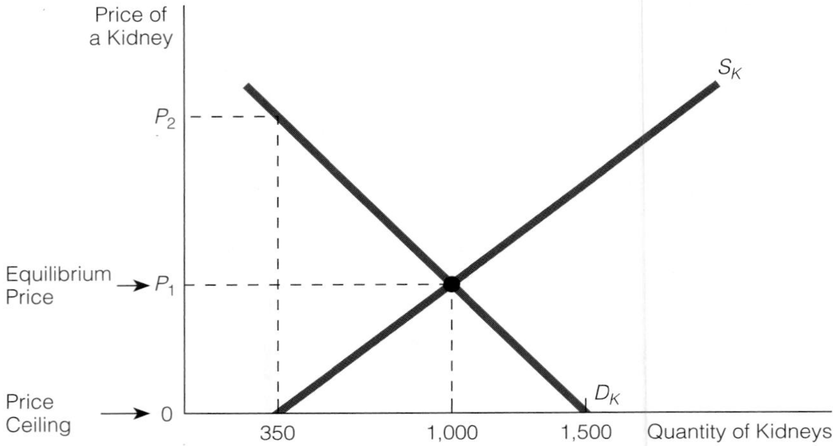

to others, asking nothing in return. They may donate their kidneys upon their death or may donate one of their two kidneys while living. We have drawn the supply curve as upward sloping because we assume that some people who today are unwilling to donate a kidney for \$0 might be willing to do so for some positive dollar amount. Specifically, we assume that as the price of a kidney rises, the quantity supplied of kidneys will rise.

If there were a free market in kidneys, the price of a kidney would be P_1 in Exhibit 5. At this price, 1,000 kidneys would be purchased and sold—1,000 kidney transplants would occur.

Today, there is no free market in kidneys. Buying or selling kidneys is illegal at any dollar amount. In essence, then, there is a price ceiling in the kidney market, and the ceiling is set at \$0. What is the effect of this price ceiling?

If the demand curve for kidneys and the supply curve of kidneys intersected at \$0, there would be neither a surplus nor a shortage of kidneys. But there is evidence that the demand and supply curves do not intersect at \$0; they look more like those shown in Exhibit 5. In other words, there is a shortage of kidneys at \$0: The quantity supplied of kidneys is 350 and the quantity demanded is 1,500. (Although these are not the actual numbers of kidneys demanded and supplied at \$0, they are representative of the current situation in the kidney market.)

The last chapter described the possible effects of a price ceiling set below equilibrium price: shortages, nonprice rationing devices, fewer exchanges, tie-in sales, and buying and selling at prohibited prices (in other words, illegal trades). Are any of these effects occurring in the kidney market?

First, there is evidence of a shortage. In almost every country in the world, there are more people on national lists who want a kidney than there are kidneys available. Some of these people die waiting for a kidney.

Second, as just indicated, the nonprice rationing device used in the kidney market is (largely) first come, first served. A person who wants a kidney registers on a national waiting list. How long one waits is a function of how far down the list one's name appears.

Third, there are fewer exchanges; not everyone who needs a kidney gets a kidney. With a price ceiling of \$0, only 350 kidneys are supplied. All these kidneys are from people who freely donate their kidneys. If P_1 were permitted, some people who are unwilling to supply a kidney (at \$0) would be willing to do so. In short, monetary payment would provide the incentive for some people to supply a kidney. At P_1, 1,000 kidneys are demanded and supplied, so more people would get kidney transplants when the price of a kidney is P_1 (1,000 in total) than when the price of a kidney is \$0 (350 in total). More transplants, of course, means fewer people die waiting for a kidney.

Fourth, kidneys are bought and sold at prohibited prices. People buy and sell kidneys today; they just do so illegally. There are stories of people paying between \$25,000 and \$200,000 for a kidney.

Some people argue that a free market in kidneys would be wrong. Such a system would place the poor at a disadvantage. Think of it: A rich person who needed a kidney could buy the kidney, but a poor person could not. The rich person would get a second chance at life, whereas the poor person would not. No one particularly enjoys contemplating this stark reality.

But consider another stark reality. If it is unlawful to pay someone for a kidney, fewer kidneys will be forthcoming. In other words, the quantity supplied of kidneys is less at $0 than at, say, $20,000. Fewer kidneys supplied mean fewer kidney transplants. And fewer kidney transplants mean more people will die from kidney failure.

Finding ECONOMICS

Not Getting a Kidney Transplant

A person dies because she does not receive a much-needed kidney transplant in time. Where is the economics here? To most people, this is simply a very sad fact of life. How unfeeling it might seem, then, when the economist points out that the person might have died because of a long string of events that started with a disequilibrium price. The economist's story goes like this: (1) The current price in the kidney market is a disequilibrium price (below equilibrium price). (2) As a result, the quantity supplied of kidneys is less than it would be if the equilibrium price existed in the kidney market. (3) It follows that there will be fewer kidneys supplied for transplants, and some people who might have gotten a kidney but don't now will end up dying.

SELF-TEST

1. A shortage of kidneys for transplants is a consequence of the price of a kidney being below equilibrium price. Do you agree or disagree? Explain your answer.
2. Assume the price ceiling in the kidney market is $0. Will there be a shortage of kidneys? Explain your answer.

APPLICATION 6: THE MINIMUM WAGE LAW

Recall that a price floor is a legislated minimum price below which trades cannot legally be made. The *minimum wage* is a price floor—a government-mandated minimum price for labor. It affects the market for unskilled labor. In Exhibit 6, we assume the minimum wage is W_M and the equilibrium wage is W_E. At the equilibrium wage, N_1 workers are employed. At the higher minimum wage, N_3 workers want to work but only N_2 actually do work. There is a surplus of workers equal to $N_3 - N_2$ in this unskilled labor market. In addition, fewer workers are working at the minimum wage (N_2) than at the equilibrium wage (N_1). Overall, the effects of the minimum wage are (1) a surplus of unskilled workers and (2) fewer workers employed.

Suppose two economists decide to test the theory that as the minimum wage rises, some unskilled workers will lose their jobs. They look at the number of unskilled workers before and after the minimum wage is raised, and surprisingly, they find that the number of unskilled workers is the same. Is this sufficient evidence to conclude that an increase in the minimum wage does not cause some workers to lose their jobs? We'll leave that question hanging while we consider whether or not the economists have adequately tested their theory. Instead of focusing on the number of people who lose their jobs, suppose they look at the people who keep their jobs but have their hours reduced as a result of the higher minimum wage. Let's look at an example. Suppose a local hardware store

exhibit 6

Effects of the Minimum Wage

At a minimum wage of W_M an hour, there is a surplus of workers and fewer workers are employed than would be at the equilibrium wage W_E.

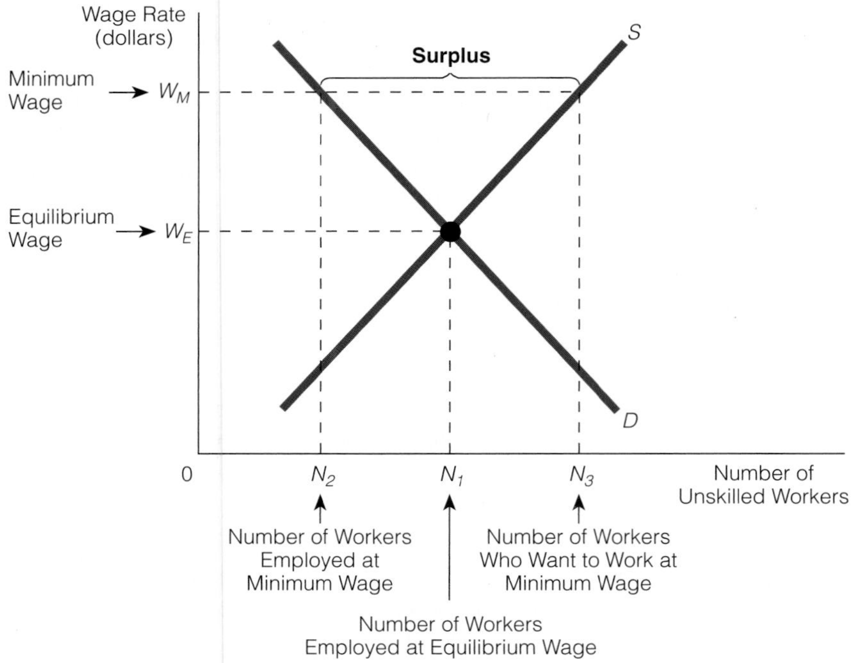

currently employs David and Francesca to work after school cleaning up and stocking shelves. The owner of the store pays each of them the minimum wage of, say, $6.55 an hour. Then, the minimum wage is raised to $8.25 an hour. Will either David or Francesca lose their jobs as a result? Not necessarily. Instead, the owner of the store could reduce the number of hours he employs the two workers. For example, instead of having each of them work 20 hours a week, he might ask each to work only 14 hours a week.

Now, let's reconsider our original question: Has the higher minimum wage eliminated jobs? In a way, no. It has, however, reduced the number of hours a person works in a job. (Of course, if we define a job as including both a particular task and a certain number of hours completing that task, then the minimum wage increase has eliminated "part" of the job.) This discussion argues for changing the label on the horizontal axis in Exhibit 6 from "Number of Unskilled Workers" to "Number of Unskilled Labor Hours."

Thinking like AN ECONOMIST

Direction Versus Magnitude

In economics, some questions relate to "direction" and some to "magnitude." For example, suppose someone asks, "If the demand for labor is downward sloping and the labor market is competitive, how will a minimum wage (above the equilibrium wage) affect employment?" This person is asking a question that relates to the direction of the change in employment. Usually, these types of questions can be answered by applying a theory. Applying the theory of demand, an economist might say, "At higher wages, the quantity demanded of labor, or the employment level, will be lower than at lower wages." The word *lower* speaks to the *directional change* in employment.

(continued)

Thinking Like An Economist (continued)

Now suppose someone asks, "How much will employment decline?" This person is asking a question that relates to *magnitude*. Usually, questions that deal with magnitude can be answered only through some kind of empirical (data-collecting and analyzing) work. In other words, we would have to collect employment figures at the equilibrium wage and at the minimum wage and then find the difference.

SELF-TEST

1. When the labor supply curve is upward sloping, a minimum wage law that sets the wage rate above its equilibrium level creates a surplus of labor. If the labor supply curve is vertical, does a surplus of labor still occur? Explain your answer.
2. Someone says that an increase in the minimum wage will not cause firms to hire fewer workers. What is this person assuming?

APPLICATION 7: PRICE FLOORS AND WINNERS AND LOSERS

Exhibit 7 shows the demand for and supply of an agricultural foodstuff (corn, wheat, soybeans, etc.). If the market is allowed to move to equilibrium, the equilibrium price will be P_1, and the equilibrium quantity will be Q_1. Consumers' surplus will equal the area under the demand curve and above the equilibrium price: areas 1 + 2 + 3. Producers' surplus will equal the area under the equilibrium price and above the supply curve: areas 4 + 5. Total surplus, of course, is the sum of consumers' surplus and producers' surplus: areas 1 + 2 + 3 + 4 + 5.

Now suppose that the suppliers of the foodstuff argue for (and receive) a price floor, P_F. At this higher price, consumers do not buy as much as they once did. They now buy Q_2, whereas they used to buy Q_1. In addition, consumers' surplus is now only area 1, and producers' surplus is areas 2 + 4.

Obviously, consumers have been hurt by the new higher (government-mandated) price of P_F; specifically, they have lost consumers' surplus equal to areas 2 + 3.

How have suppliers fared? Whereas their producers' surplus was equal to areas 4 + 5 at P_1, it is now equal to areas 2 + 4. (Area 2, which used to be part of consumers' surplus, has been transferred to producers and is now part of producers' surplus.) Whether or not producers are better off depends on whether or not area 2 (what they gain from P_F) is larger than area 5 (what they lose from P_F). Visually, we can tell that area 2 is larger than area 5, so producers are better off.

exhibit 7

Agricultural Price Floors

The demand for and supply of an agricultural foodstuff are shown in this exhibit. The equilibrium price is P_1; consumers' surplus (*CS*) is areas 1 + 2 + 3; producers' surplus is areas 4 + 5. A price floor of P_F effectively transfers some of the consumers' surplus to producers in the form of a gain in producers' surplus. Specifically, at P_F, consumers' surplus is area 1 and producers' surplus is areas 2 + 4. Consumers are net losers because consumers' surplus has decreased by areas 2 + 3. Producers are net gainers because producers' surplus has increased from areas 4 + 5 to areas 2 + 4 and area 2 is larger than area 5. Overall, the economic pie of *CS* + *PS* has decreased from areas 1 + 2 + 3 + 4 + 5 to areas 1 + 2 + 4.

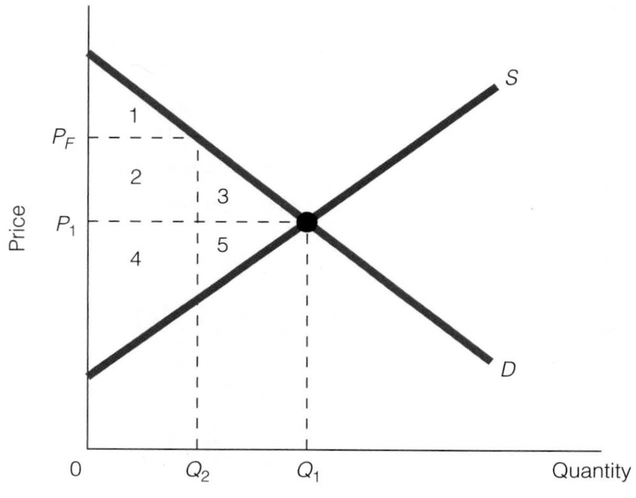

What is the overall effect of the price floor? Have producers gained more than consumers have lost, or have consumers lost more than producers have gained? To answer this question, we note that consumers lose areas 2 + 3 in consumers' surplus; producers gain area 2 in producers' surplus and lose area 5 in producers' surplus. So the gains and losses are:

Losses to consumers: areas 2 + 3
Gains to producers: area 2
Losses to producers: area 5

Part of the loss to consumers is offset by the gain to producers (area 2), so net losses amount to areas 3 + 5. In other words, total surplus—the sum of consumers' surplus and producers' surplus—is lower than it was. Whereas it used to be areas 1 + 2 + 3 + 4 + 5, it now is areas 1 + 2 + 4. The total surplus lost is areas 3 + 5.

In short, (1) consumers lose, (2) producers gain, and (3) society (which is the sum of consumers and producers) loses.

You can think of this example in terms of a pie. Initially, the pie was made up of areas 1 + 2 + 3 + 4 + 5. This rather large pie registered all the gains of consumers and producers. After the price floor of P_F was imposed, the pie shrank to areas 1 + 2 + 4; in other words, the pie was smaller by areas 3 + 5.

Deadweight Loss
The loss to society of not producing the competitive, or supply-and-demand-determined, level of output.

A loss in total surplus—in our example, areas 3 + 5—is sometimes called a **deadweight loss.** It is the loss to society of not producing the competitive, or supply-and-demand-determined, level of output. In terms of Exhibit 7, it is the loss to society of producing Q_2 instead of producing Q_1.

Common MISCONCEPTIONS

About Gains and Losses

Some persons argue that a price floor creates a situation in which (a) someone wins and someone loses and (b) the gains for the winner are equal to the losses for the loser (e.g., $5 is lost by one person and $5 is won by another person). A quick look at Exhibit 7 tells us that (b) is not true. The losses (for consumers) are not offset by the gains (for producers). A price ceilings ends with a *net loss* or *deadweight loss* of areas 3 + 5. Now think of how hard it would have been to identify this deadweight loss without the tools of supply, demand, consumers' surplus, and producers' surplus. Economic tools often have the ability to make what is invisible visible.

SELF-TEST

1. Look at the area equal to areas 3 + 5 in Exhibit 7. If there is a price floor, this area ends up being a deadweight loss. It is the loss to society of not producing Q_1. Are there mutually beneficial trades that exist between Q_2 and Q_1, and if so, how do you know this?
2. Why might producers argue for a price floor if it ends up making society worse off?

APPLICATION 8: ARE RENTERS BETTER OFF?

We begin with an analysis of two laws related to eviction of a renter. Under law 1, a renter has 30 days to vacate an apartment after being served with an eviction notice. Under law 2, the renter has 90 days to vacate.

Landlords will find it less expensive to rent apartments under law 1 than under law 2. Under law 1, the most money a landlord can lose after serving an eviction notice is 30 days' rent. Under law 2, a landlord can lose 90 days' rent. Obviously, losing 90 days' rent is more costly than losing 30 days' rent.

A different supply curve of apartments exists under each law. The supply curve under law 1 (S_1 in Exhibit 8) lies to the right of the supply curve under law 2 (S_2 in the exhibit). Again, that's because it is less expensive to supply apartments under law 1 than under law 2.

If the supply curve is different under the two laws, the equilibrium rent will be different too. As shown in Exhibit 8, the equilibrium rent will be lower under law 1 (R_1) than under law 2 (R_2).

In conclusion, under law 1, a renter pays lower rent (good) and has fewer days to vacate the apartment (bad). Under law 2, a renter pays a higher rent (bad) and has more days to vacate the apartment (good). Who pays for the additional days to vacate the apartment under law 2? The renter pays for these additional days by paying higher rent.

exhibit 8

Apartment Rent and the Law

Under law 1, a renter has 30 days to leave an apartment after receiving an eviction notice from his or her landlord. Under law 2, a renter has 90 days to leave an apartment after receiving an eviction notice from his or her landlord. The cost to the landlord of renting an apartment is higher under law 2 than law 1, and so the supply curve of apartments under law 1 lies to the right of the supply curve of apartments under law 2. Different supply curves mean different rents. Apartment rent is higher under law 2 (R_2) than under law 1 (R_1).

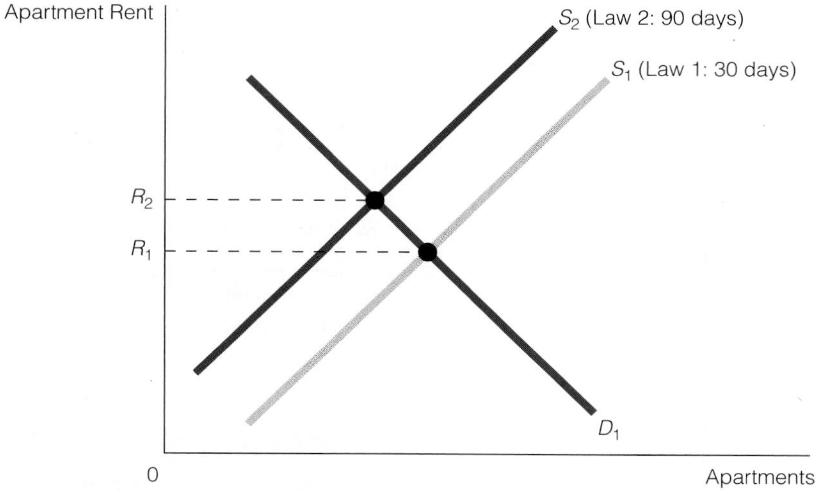

Finding ECONOMICS

In an HMO

You may frequently hear people complain about their health maintenance organizations (HMOs). The complaints are diverse and wide-ranging. One common complaint is that patients cannot sue their HMOs in state courts for denial of benefits and poor-quality care. Some people argue that patients should have the right to sue their HMOs.

Let's consider two settings: one in which patients cannot sue their HMOs and one in which patients can sue. If patients cannot sue, an HMO's liability cost is lower than if patients can sue. A difference in liability costs will be reflected in different supply curves.

To illustrate, recall that any single point on a supply curve is the minimum price sellers need to receive for them to be willing and able to sell that particular unit of a good. Suppose when patients cannot sue, an HMO is willing and able to provide health care to John for $300 a month. If patients can sue, is the HMO still willing and able to provide health care to John for $300 a month? Not likely. Because of the higher liability cost due to the patient's ability to sue, the HMO is no longer willing and able to provide health care to John for $300 month. It will, however, be willing and able to provide health care to John for, say, $350 a month.

Saying a seller's minimum price for providing a good or service rises is the same as saying the seller's supply curve has shifted upward and to the left. In other words, the supply curve of HMO-provided health care will shift upward and to the left if patients have the right to sue. This is the same way the supply curve of apartments moved in Exhibit 4.

(continued)

Finding Economics (continued)

Will a difference in supply curves affect the price patients pay for their HMO-provided health care coverage? Yes. One effect of moving from a setting where patients do not have the right to sue to one where patients do have the right to sue is that patients will have to pay more for their HMO-provided health care coverage.

Economists don't determine whether a patient having the right to sue is good or bad or right or wrong. Economists use their tools (in this instance, supply and demand) to point out that things people want, such as the right to sue their HMOs, often come with price tags. Individuals must decide whether the price they pay is worth what they receive in return.

SELF-TEST

1. Economists often say, "There is no such thing as a free lunch." How is this saying related to patients moving from a system where they cannot sue their HMOs to one where they can?
2. A professor tells her students that they can have an extra week to complete their research papers. Under what condition are the students better off with the extra week? Can you think of a case where the students would actually be worse off with the extra week?

APPLICATION 9: DO YOU PAY FOR GOOD WEATHER?

Some places in the country are considered to have better weather than other places. For example, most people would say the weather in San Diego, California, is better than the weather in Fargo, North Dakota. Often, a person in San Diego will say, "You can't beat the weather today. And the good thing about it is that you don't have to pay a thing for it. It's free."

In one sense, the San Diegan is correct: There is no weather market. Specifically, no one comes around and asks San Diegans to pay a certain dollar amount for the weather on a given day.

But in another sense, the San Diegan is incorrect. The fact is that San Diegans indirectly pay for their good weather. How do they pay? To enjoy the weather in San Diego on a regular basis, you have to live in San Diego—you need to have housing. There is a demand for housing in San Diego just as there is a demand for housing in other places. Is the demand for housing in San Diego higher than it would be if the weather were not so good? Without the good weather, living in San Diego would not be as pleasurable, and therefore, the demand to live there would be lower. See Exhibit 9. In short, the demand for housing in San Diego is higher because San Diego enjoys good weather. It follows that the price of housing is higher too (P_2 as opposed to P_1 in Exhibit 9). Thus, San Diegans indirectly pay for their good weather because they pay higher housing prices than they would if San Diego had bad weather.

Was our representative San Diegan right when he said the good weather was free?

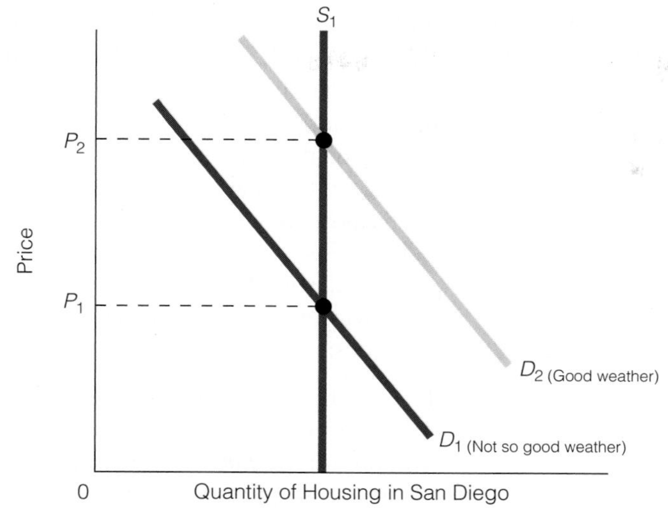

exhibit 9

The Price of Weather and Housing Prices

We show two demand curves, D_1 and D_2. D_1 represents the demand for housing in San Diego if the weather were not so good. The higher demand curve D_2 shows the demand for housing in San Diego if the weather is good. Notice that the price of housing in San Diego is higher if the weather is good than not so good. Lesson learned: You pay for good weather (in San Diego) in terms of higher house prices.

Finding ECONOMICS

Good Schools and House Prices

There are two neighborhoods, A and B. The kids who live in neighborhood A go to school A and the kids who live in neighborhood B go to school B. Currently, school A has a much better academic reputation than school B. Can you find the economics?

This is really no more than a disguised version of our good weather example. If school A is better than school B, then the equilibrium price of houses in neighborhood A is likely to be higher than the equilibrium price of (similar) houses in neighborhood B. Just as we pay for good weather in terms of house prices, we pay for good schools in terms of house prices too.

SELF-TEST

1. Give an example to illustrate that someone may "pay" for clean air in much the same way that she "pays" for good weather.
2. If people pay for good weather, who ultimately receives the "good-weather payment"?

APPLICATION 10: COLLEGE SUPERATHLETES

Let's consider a young man, 17 years old, who is one of the best high school football players in the country. As a superathlete, the young man will be recruited by many college and university football coaches. Every one of those colleges and universities will likely want its coach to be successful at getting the young athlete; after all, at many universities, athletics is a moneymaker.

Our superathlete decides to attend college A, where he receives a "full ride"—a full scholarship. How should this full scholarship be viewed? One way is to say the superathlete is charged zero tuition to attend the college. (In other words, whereas some students pay a price of $10,000 a year to attend the college, the superathlete pays nothing.)

exhibit 10

The College Athlete

The exhibit shows the demand for and supply of a college athlete. If the market wage for the college athlete is $15,000, then the buyer of the athlete—in this case, the college—receives consumers' surplus equal to area *A*. If the wage can be held down to the tuition cost of attending the college—$10,000 in this example—then the college receives consumers' surplus of areas *A* + *B*.

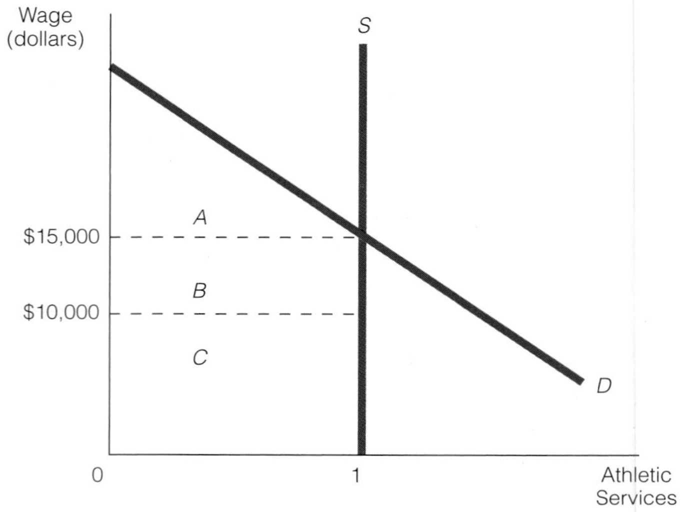

Another way to view the full scholarship involves a two-step process. First, the college pays the superathlete a dollar amount equal to the full tuition. Second, it then charges the superathlete the full tuition. (In other words, the college gives the athlete $10,000 with one hand and then collects the $10,000 with the other hand.)

Although it ends up being the same for the athlete regardless of which way we view the full scholarship, for purposes of our analysis, let's view the full scholarship the second way: as a payment to the athlete combined with full price being charged. This way of viewing the scholarship leads to two important questions:

1. Can the college pay the athlete more than the full tuition of the college? In other words, if the full tuition is $10,000 a year, can the college pay the athlete, say, $15,000 a year?
2. Is the superathlete being paid what he is worth?

Because of NCAA rules, the answer to the first question is essentially no. The NCAA states that a college or university cannot pay a student to attend, and for all practical purposes, the NCAA views payment as anything more than a full scholarship. The NCAA takes the position that college athletes are amateurs, and amateurs cannot be paid to play their sport.

How does the NCAA rule affect our second question? What if the athlete's worth to the college or university is greater than the dollar amount of the full tuition? For example, suppose the athlete will increase the revenues of the college by $50,000 a year, and the full tuition is only $10,000 a year. In this case, the NCAA rule sets a price ceiling for the college. It sets a ceiling on what the college can pay an athlete. What is the effect of this price ceiling?

Let's consider the demand (on the part of various colleges) for a single superathlete and the supply of this single superathlete (see Exhibit 10). We assume that the supply curve is vertical at 1 "athletic services."

Now suppose the representative college charges tuition of $10,000. Because of the NCAA rule, this dollar amount is the effective price ceiling (or wage ceiling). Furthermore, let's suppose that the single college athlete's market equilibrium wage is $15,000. So, if the NCAA rule did not exist, the athlete's wage would rise to $15,000. This dollar amount is equal to areas *B* + *C* in Exhibit 10. What is the consumers' surplus for the college that buys the athlete's services for $15,000? Obviously, it is equal to area *A*.

However, the NCAA rule stipulates that the college cannot pay the athlete more than $10,000 (full tuition). So, the athlete's payment falls from $15,000 to $10,000, or from areas *B* + *C* to simply area *C*. The college's consumers' surplus increases to areas *A* + *B*. Essentially, the NCAA rule transfers part of the athlete's income—area *B*—to the college in the form of greater consumers' surplus.

Just as the price floor in Application 7 leads to a transfer (from consumers to producers), a price ceiling leads to a transfer. The price ceiling set by the NCAA rule results in a transfer from the athlete to the college. In short, the athlete loses and the college gains. Moreover, in this case, the college gain in consumers' surplus equals the income loss for the athlete.

SELF-TEST

1. University X is a large university with a major football team. A new field house and track were just added to the university. How is this related to the discussion in this application?
2. Sometimes it is argued that if colleges paid student athletes, the demand for college sports would decline. In other words, the demand for college sports is as high as it is because student athletes are not paid (the way athletes in professional sports are paid). How would the analysis in this application change if we assume this argument is true?

APPLICATION 11: 10 A.M. CLASSES IN COLLEGE

Suppose an economics class is offered in the same classroom at 10 a.m. in the morning and at 8 p.m. at night. Most students would prefer the 10 a.m. class to the 8 p.m. class. Notice in Exhibit 11 that the supply of seats in the class is the same at each time, but the demand to occupy those seats is not. Because the demand is greater for the 10 a.m. class than for the 8 p.m. class, the equilibrium price for the 10 a.m. class is higher than the equilibrium price for the 8 p.m. class.

But the university or college charges the same tuition no matter what time students choose to take the class. The university doesn't charge students a higher tuition if they enroll in 10 a.m. classes than if they enroll in 8 p.m. classes.

Suppose tuition of T_1 is charged for all classes, and T_1 is the equilibrium tuition for 8 p.m. classes (see Exhibit 11). It follows that T_1 is below the equilibrium tuition for 10 a.m. classes. At T_1, the quantity demanded of seats for 10 a.m. classes will be greater than the quantity supplied; more students will want the 10 a.m. class than there is space available.

How will the university allocate the available seats? It may do it the same way that airlines ration aisle seats—that is, on a first come, first served basis. Students who are first to register get the 10 a.m. class; the latecomers have to take the 8 p.m. class. Or the university could ration these "high-demand classes" by giving their upper-class students (seniors) first priority.

Thinking like AN ECONOMIST

Remembering Price

The layperson sees students clamoring to get 10 a.m. classes and concludes that the demand is high for classes at this time. He then wonders why the university doesn't schedule more 10 a.m. classes. The economist knows that what the layperson sees is as much an effect of price as of demand. The demand for 10 a.m. classes may be high, but the quantity demanded may not be if the price is high enough. In fact, even though the demand for various classes at various times may be different, there is some set of prices that will make the quantity demanded of each class the same.

exhibit 11

The Supply and Demand for College Classes at Different Times

A given class is offered at two times, 10 a.m. and 8 p.m. The supply of seats in the classroom is the same at both times; however, the student demand for the 10 a.m. class is higher than the demand for the 8 p.m. class. The university charges the same tuition, T_1, regardless of which class a student takes. At this tuition, there is a shortage of seats for the 10 a.m. class. Seats are likely to be rationed on a first-come-first-served (first to register) basis or on seniority (seniors take precedence over juniors, etc.).

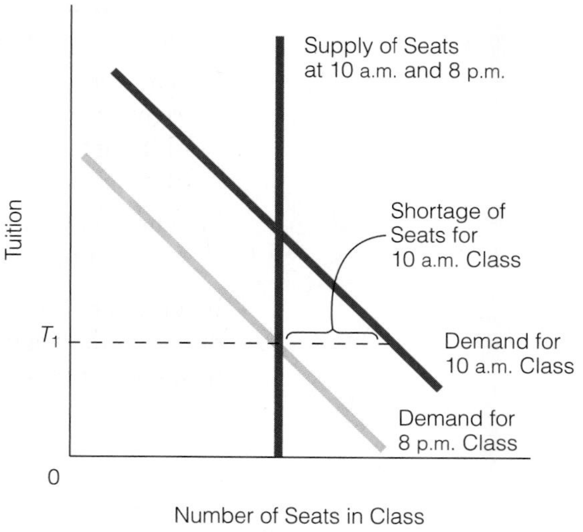

SELF-TEST

1. Suppose college students are given two options. With option A, the price a student pays for a class is always the equilibrium price. For example, if the equilibrium price to take Economics 101 is $600 at 10 a.m. and is $400 at 4 p.m., then students pay more for the 10 a.m. class than they do for the 4 p.m. class. With option B, the price a student pays for a class is the same regardless of the time the class is taken. When given the choice between options A and B, many students would say they prefer option B to option A. Is this the case for you? If so, why would this be your choice?
2. How is the analysis of the 10 a.m. class similar to the analysis of a price ceiling in the kidney market?

APPLICATION 12: WHAT WILL HAPPEN TO THE PRICE OF MARIJUANA IF THE PURCHASE AND SALE OF MARIJUANA ARE LEGALIZED?

In the United States, the purchase or sale of marijuana is unlawful. However, there is still a demand for and supply of marijuana. There is also an equilibrium price of marijuana. Let's say that price is P_1.

Suppose that beginning tomorrow, the purchase and sale of marijuana become legal. Will P_1 rise, fall, or remain the same?

The answer, of course, depends on what we think will happen to the demand for and supply of marijuana. If the purchase and sale of marijuana are legal, then some people currently producing corn and wheat will likely choose instead to produce and sell marijuana. So the supply of marijuana will rise. If nothing else changes, the price of marijuana will fall.

But something else is likely to change. If marijuana consumption is no longer illegal, then the number of people who want to buy and consume marijuana will likely rise. In other words, there will be more buyers of marijuana. This will increase the demand for marijuana.

Thus, decriminalizing the purchase and sale of marijuana is likely to shift both the marijuana demand and supply curves to the right. What happens to the price of marijuana depends on how much the curves shift. Three possibilities exist:

1. The demand curve shifts to the right by the same amount as the supply curve shifts to the right. In this case, the price of marijuana will not change. (Try to visualize the demand and supply curves shifting.)
2. The demand curve shifts to the right by more than the supply curve shifts to the right. In this case, the price of marijuana will rise. (Try to visualize the demand curve shifting to the right by more than the supply curve shifts to the right. Can you see the higher price on the vertical axis?)
3. The supply curve shifts to the right by more than the demand curve shifts to the right. In this case, the price of marijuana will fall.

If you can't visualize the shifts of the demand and supply curves for the three possibilities, draw the original demand and supply curves, then draw the shift in each curve, and finally, identify the new equilibrium price.

office hours

"DOESN'T HIGH DEMAND MEAN HIGH QUANTITY DEMANDED?"

Student:

The other day in class you said, "The demand for 10 a.m. classes may be high, but the quantity demanded may not be if the price is high enough." In other words, you were saying that high demand doesn't necessarily mean high quantity demanded. But I thought it did. Could you explain?

Instructor:

Let me explain what is going on by first showing you the demand schedule for two goods, A and B.

Good A Demand Schedule

Price	Quantity Demanded
$6	100
7	80
8	60
9	40

Good B Demand Schedule

Price	Quantity Demanded
$6	200
7	150
8	125
9	90

As you can see from the two demand schedules, the demand for good B is greater than the demand for good A. In other words, if we were to derive a demand curve for each good (based on its demand schedule) the demand curve for good B would lie farther to the right than the demand curve for good A.

Now suppose we look at quantity demanded for each good at the price of $6. The quantity demanded of good A (the low demand good) is 100 units and the quantity demanded of good B (the high demand good) is 200 units. What can we conclude? Namely, a*t the same price for each good* ($6), quantity demanded is higher when demand is higher.

But now let's consider quantity demanded for each good when the price of good A is $6 and the price of good B is $9. The quantity demanded of good A (the low demand good) is 100 units and the quantity demanded of good B (the high demand good) is 90 units. In other words, if the price is high enough for good B (the high demand good), the quantity demanded of good B may end up being lower than the quantity demanded of good A (the low demand good).

Now let's go back and repeat the statement I made in class: "The demand for 10 a.m. classes may be high, but the quantity demanded may not be if the price is high enough." Now do you understand what I was saying?

Student:

Yes, I think I do. You were saying that high demand doesn't necessarily mean high quantity demanded if we are dealing with different prices.

Instructor:

Yes, that's it.

Points to Remember

1. High demand means high quantity demanded, but only "necessarily so" if the price for the high demand good and the low demand good are the same. From our example: At a price of $6, quantity demanded for the high demand good B is greater than quantity demanded for the low demand good A.
2. Quantity demanded for the low demand good can be higher than quantity demanded for the high demand good if the prices for the two goods are not the same and the price for the high demand good is high enough. From our example: At a price of $9 for good B (the high demand good), quantity demanded is lower than quantity demand is for good A (the low demand good) at a price of $6.

a reader asks

How Do I Find My Own Supply-and-Demand Applications?

I can understand an economist's applications of supply and demand, but I don't know how to apply supply and demand myself. How do I find my own supply-and-demand applications?

You can proceed in several ways, two of which we discuss here. First, you can heed the words of Robert Solow: "I am a supply-and-demand economist. When I come across something, I ask myself what is being transferred here and where does the supply come from and where does the demand come from."[1]

We can reformulate what Solow has said into a single question: Is trade involved? This is the relevant supply-and-demand question because supply and demand are about trade. In other words, when you observe something, simply ask: Is this about trade? If you are driving on a freeway, ask: Is driving on a freeway about trade? Specifically, is something being "bought" and "sold"? If so, what? If you are applying to college, ask: Is this about trade? What is being bought and sold?

A second way to proceed is to look for surpluses and shortages around you. Surpluses and shortages are manifestations of market disequilibrium. If you find them, you can be fairly sure that supply and demand are relevant. If you are sitting in a classroom with empty seats, ask: Is there a surplus or shortage here? In this case, of course, there is a surplus, which should lead you to think about price. Surpluses exist when prices are too high. Why is the price too high? If you observe more people applying to a particular college than the college will admit, ask: Is there a surplus or shortage here? In this case, there is a shortage, which again should lead you to think about price. Shortages exist when prices are too low. Why is price too low?

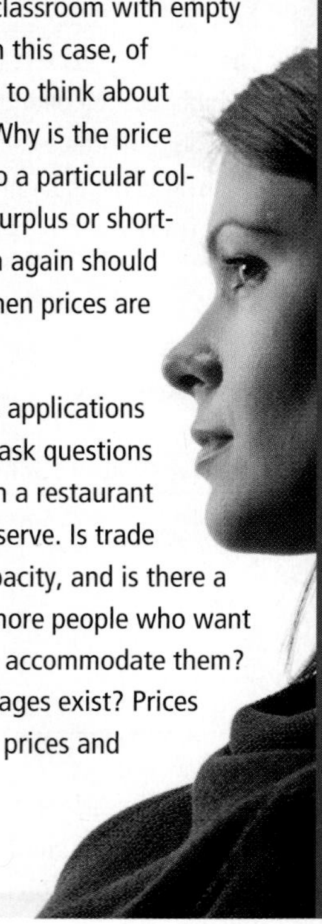

The key to finding your own supply-and-demand applications is to (1) observe things around you and then (2) ask questions about the things you observe. If you are sitting in a restaurant eating a meal, ask questions about what you observe. Is trade involved here? Yes. Is the restaurant filled to capacity, and is there a line of people waiting to get in? Yes. Are there more people who want to eat at this restaurant than there are spaces to accommodate them? Yes. Is there a shortage here? Yes. Why do shortages exist? Prices are too low. Why doesn't the restaurant raise its prices and eliminate the shortage?

The process isn't that hard, is it?

1. Interview with Robert Solow. The entire interview is in *Economics* by Roger A. Arnold (St. Paul, MN: West Publishing Company, 1992).

Chapter Summary

WHY IS MEDICAL CARE SO EXPENSIVE?

- When it comes to medical care, often there is the person who sells medical care, the person who buys medical care, and the person who (directly) pays for the medical care (the third party).
- Once a person has paid her (medical) insurance premium, the price she pays for medical care may amount to no more than her copayment (which is usually minimal). For all practical purposes, then, the dollar amount she has to pay out of pocket to get medical care is zero. We expect the quantity demanded of medical care to be greater than at some positive dollar amount.

WHERE WILL HOUSE PRICES CHANGE THE MOST?

- The supply curve for housing is steeper in city 1 than city 2. For an equal increase in demand for housing in each city, house prices will rise more in city 1. For an equal decrease in demand for housing in each city, house prices will fall more in city 2.

WHY DO COLLEGES USE GPAs, ACTs, AND SATs FOR PURPOSES OF ADMISSION?

- Colleges and universities charging students less than the equilibrium tuition for admission create a shortage of spaces at the colleges or universities. Consequently, colleges and universities have to impose some nonprice rationing device, such as GPAs or ACT or SAT scores.

SUPPLY AND DEMAND ON A FREEWAY

- The effect of a disequilibrium price for driving on a freeway is a traffic jam. If the price to drive on a freeway is \$0 and at this price the quantity demanded of freeway space is greater than the quantity supplied, then there will be a shortage of freeway space that will manifest itself as freeway congestion.

PRICE CEILING IN THE KIDNEY MARKET

- Currently, there is a price ceiling in the kidney market, and the price is set at \$0. Many of the effects of a price ceiling (shortages, fewer exchanges, etc.) are seen in the kidney market.

THE MINIMUM WAGE LAW

- A minimum wage (above equilibrium wage) reduces the number of unskilled workers working or reduces the number of unskilled labor hours purchased by employers.

PRICE FLOORS AND WINNERS AND LOSERS

- A price floor placed on an agricultural foodstuff ends up lowering consumers' surplus, raising producers' surplus, and creating a deadweight loss. In short, a price floor can transfer "surplus" from consumers to producers and leave society (as a whole) worse off too.

ARE RENTERS BETTER OFF?

- The supply curve of apartments will shift upward and to the left if renters have 90 days as opposed to 30 days to vacate an apartment. As a result, renters will pay higher rent when they have 90 days to vacate and apartment.

DO YOU PAY FOR GOOD WEATHER?

- If good weather gives people utility, then the demand for and the price of housing will be higher in a city with good weather than in a city with bad weather. Conclusion: People who buy houses in good-weather locations indirectly pay for the good weather.

COLLEGE SUPERATHLETES

- If a college superathlete receives a full scholarship to play a sport at a university and if the full scholarship is less than the equilibrium wage for the superathlete (because of a prohibition mandating that the athlete cannot be paid the difference between his higher equilibrium wage and the dollar amount of his full scholarship), then the university gains at the expense of the athlete.

10 A.M. CLASSES IN COLLEGE

- Colleges usually charge the same tuition for a class no matter when the class is taken. The supply of seats in the class may be the same at each time, but the demand for the class may be different at different times. At least for some classes, the quantity demanded of seats (in the class) will be greater than the quantity supplied. Thus, some nonprice rationing device will have to be used to achieve equilibrium.

LEGALIZATION OF MARIJUANA

- If the purchase and sale of marijuana are legalized, the price of marijuana may rise, fall, or remain the same. The price will depend on whether the rise in the demand for marijuana is more than, less than, or equal to the rise in the supply of marijuana.

Key Terms and Concepts

Deadweight Loss

Questions and Problems

1 If there were no third parties in medical care, medical care prices would be lower. Do you agree or disagree? Explain your answer.

2 What does the shape of the supply curve have to do with how much price will rise given an increase in demand?

3 Harvard, Yale, and Princeton all charge relatively high tuition. Still, each uses ACT and SAT scores as admission criteria. Are charging a relatively high tuition and using standardized test scores (as admission criteria) inconsistent? Explain your answer.

4 Suppose the purchase and sale of marijuana are legalized and the price of marijuana falls. What explains the lower price of marijuana?

5 The minimum wage in year 1 is $1 higher than the equilibrium wage. In year 2, the minimum wage is increased so that it is $2 above the equilibrium wage. We observe that the same number of people are working at the minimum wage in year 2 as in year 1. Does it follow that an increase in the minimum wage does not cause some workers to lose their jobs? Explain your answer.

6 In our discussion of the kidney market, we represent the demand curve for kidneys as downward sloping and the supply curve of kidneys as upward sloping. At the end of the discussion, we state, "If it is unlawful to pay someone for a kidney, fewer kidneys will be forthcoming. In other words, the quantity supplied of kidneys is less at $0 than at, say, $20,000. Fewer kidneys supplied mean fewer kidney

transplants." Would there be fewer kidney transplants if the supply curve of kidneys is vertical? Explain your answer.

7 What do the applications about freeway congestion and 10 a.m. classes have in common?

8 Economics has been called the "dismal science" because it sometimes "tells us" that things are true when we would prefer they were false. For example, although there are no free lunches, might we prefer that there were? Was there anything in this chapter that you learned was true that you would have preferred to be false? If so, identify it. Then explain why you would have preferred it to be false.

9 In the discussion of health care and the right to sue your HMO, we state, "Saying a seller's minimum price for providing a good or service rises is the same as saying the seller's supply curve has shifted upward and to the left." Does it follow that if a seller's minimum price falls, the supply curve shifts downward and to the right? Explain your answer.

10 Application 9 explains that even though no one directly and explicitly pays for good weather ("Here is $100 for the good weather"), it is still possible to pay for good weather indirectly, such as through housing prices. Identify three other things (besides good weather) that you believe people pay for indirectly.

11 Suppose there exists a costless way to charge drivers on the freeway. Under this costless system, tolls on the freeway would be adjusted according to traffic conditions. For example, when traffic is usually heavy, such as from 6:30 a.m. to 9:00 a.m. on a weekday, the toll to drive on the freeway would be higher than the toll would be when traffic is light. In other words, freeway tolls would be used to equate the demand for freeway space and the supply of freeway space. Would you be in favor of such a system to replace our current (largely, zero-price) system? Explain your answer.

12 Wilson walks into his economics class ten minutes late because he couldn't find a place to park. Because of his tardiness, he doesn't hear the professor tell the class there will be a quiz at the next class session. At the next class session, Wilson is unprepared for the quiz and ends up failing it. Might Wilson's failing the quiz have anything to do with the price of parking?

13 University A charges more for a class for which there is high demand than for a class for which there is low demand. University B charges the same for all classes. All other things being equal between the two universities, which university would you prefer to attend? Explain your answer.

14 Explain and diagrammatically represent how a price floor can bring about a transfer from consumers to producers.

15 Suppose the equilibrium wage for a college athlete is $40,000, but because of NCAA rules, the university can offer him only $22,000 (full tuition). How might the university administrators, coaches, or university alumni lure the college athlete to choose their school over others?

16 Consider the theater in which a Broadway play is performed. If tickets for all seats are the same price (say, $70), what economic effect might arise?

17 What is the relationship between the probability of a person being admitted to the college of his choice and the tuition the college charges?

18 Samantha is flying from San Diego, California, to Arlington, Texas, on a commercial airliner. She asks for an aisle seat but only middle-of-the-row seats are left. Why aren't any aisle seats left? (Hint: The airlines charges the same price for an aisle seat as a middle-of-the-row seat.)

Working with Numbers and Graphs

1 The price to drive on a freeway is $0 at all times of the day. This price establishes equilibrium at 3 a.m. but is too low to establish equilibrium at 5 p.m. There is a shortage of freeway space at 5 p.m.

a. Graphically show and explain how carpooling may eliminate the shortage.

b. Graphically show and explain how building more freeways may eliminate the shortage.

2 Diagrammatically show and explain why there is a shortage of classroom space for some college classes and a surplus for others.

3 Smith has been trying to sell his house for six months, but so far, there are no buyers. Draw the market for Smith's house.

©DAVID McNEW/GETTY IMAGES

CHAPTER 5

MACROECONOMIC MEASUREMENTS, PART I: PRICES AND UNEMPLOYMENT

Introduction Government economists often collect and analyze the latest economic data. Their analysis includes computing important economic measurements such as the inflation rate and the unemployment rate. Our elected representatives and certain government officials then use these in formulating economic policy. The structure, content, and timing of that economic policy will often affect you in the roles as buyer, seller, taxpayer, and employee.

HOW TO APPROACH THE STUDY OF MACROECONOMICS

Before we begin our discussion of macroeconomic measurements, we need to take some time to discuss what macroeconomics is about and how best to approach the study of macroeconomics.

Macroeconomics is the branch of economics that deals with the entire economy. Most discussions in macroeconomics focus on one or more of the following:

1. Macroeconomic problems
2. Macroeconomic theories
3. Macroeconomic policies
4. Different views of how the economy works

We briefly discuss each next (see Exhibit 1).

Macroeconomic Problems

Here are a few macroeconomic problems:

1. High inflation rate
2. High unemployment rate

exhibit 1

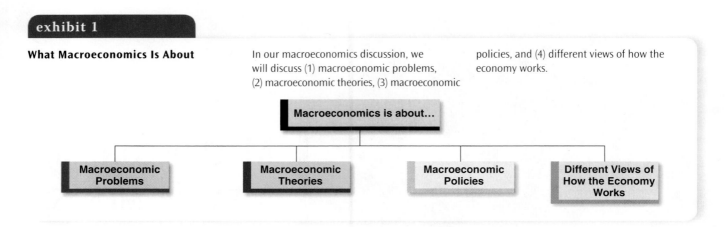

What Macroeconomics Is About

In our macroeconomics discussion, we will discuss (1) macroeconomic problems, (2) macroeconomic theories, (3) macroeconomic policies, and (4) different views of how the economy works.

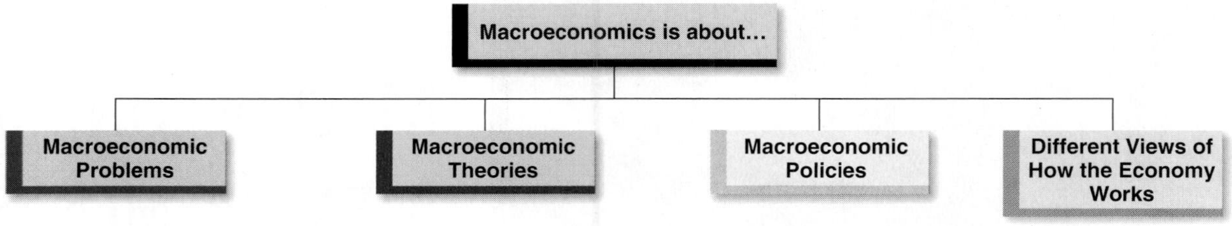
Macroeconomics is about...
Macroeconomic Problems
Macroeconomic Theories
Macroeconomic Policies
Different Views of How the Economy Works

3. High interest rates
4. Low economic growth

When it comes to these macroeconomics problems and others, macroeconomists want to know two things: (1) What is the cause of the problem? and (2) What needs to be done to end the problem?

It is really no different than your going to see a physician about some health problem—say a regular stomachache. You might want to know the cause of the stomachache and then how to end the stomachache.

In this text, we will discuss a number of macroeconomic problems, including inflation, high unemployment, stagflation, low economic growth, and more.

Macroeconomic Theories

When macroeconomists encounter macroeconomic problems, certain questions naturally come to mind. For example, if interest rates are unusually high, a macroeconomist might wonder why interest rates are high sometimes but low at other times. If the inflation rate has recently gone up, a macroeconomist might wonder why the inflation rate went up now. Many of the questions macroeconomists ask do not have obvious answers.

To answer these questions, then, macroeconomists often build theories. For example, a macroeconomist might build a theory to try to understand why interest rates are high in one year but not high in some other year; he or she might build a theory to try to understand why the inflation rate is low in one year but high in another year.

We will encounter a number of macroeconomic theories in our discussion of macroeconomics. We will encounter theories that attempt to explain such things as changes in the price level, changes in unemployment, changes in interest rates, and so on. Some of these theories will have names, such as the Keynesian theory, monetarist theory, or new classical theory. Often, the term that comes before the word *theory*, such as *Keynesian or monetarist theory of* . . . , refers to the macroeconomic school of thought that put forth the theory.

As you read through the macroeconomic chapters of this book, keep in mind that not all macroeconomists agree on the causes of certain macroeconomic problems. In other words, one macroeconomist might think that X is the cause of high unemployment, whereas another macroeconomist might think that the Y is the cause of high unemployment.

Macroeconomic Policies

To solve certain macroeconomic problems, macroeconomists often propose certain types of policies. Specifically, a macroeconomist might propose cutting tax rates to revive economic growth or cutting back the growth rate in the money supply to lower prices. The two types of macroeconomic policy that we will discuss include *fiscal policy and monetary policy*. Fiscal policy deals with changes in government expenditures and/or taxes. For example, a proposal to cut taxes is a fiscal policy measure. Monetary policy deals with changes in the money supply. For example, a proposal to decrease the rate of growth of the money supply is a monetary policy measure.

Different Views of How the Economy Works

We are not at the stage in the history of macroeconomics where we can say that all macroeconomists agree as to how the economy works. For example, some economists believe that the economy is inherently stable and self-regulating. A rough analogy comes from the field of medicine. For some illnesses, physicians believe that the human body has a way of curing itself. For example, in time, the human body usually heals itself of certain viruses (e.g., a cold or flu virus). In other words, the body is self-regulating; it can cure itself of certain ailments.

Some economists do not believe the economy is self-regulating. They see it as inherently unstable. In other words, the economy has certain forces within it that can (and sometimes do) cause it to get "ill" on its own.

Three Macroeconomic Organizational Categories

As we stated earlier, macroeconomics is the branch of economics that deals with the entire economy. The subject matter in macroeconomics includes (1) macroeconomic problems, (2) macroeconomic theories, (3) macroeconomic policies, and (4) different views of how the economy works. To help you categorize what you learn in macroeconomics and to give you a better idea of what macroeconomics is about, we outline three macroeconomic organizational categories. We call these categories the

- P-Q category
- Self-Regulating–Economic Instability category
- Effective-Ineffective category

THE P-Q CATEGORY Many of the topics discussed in macroeconomics relate directly or indirectly to the *price level* and *Real GDP*. The price level is the weighted average of the prices of all goods and services. **Real GDP** is the value of the entire output produced annually within a country's borders, adjusted for price changes. We discuss both the price level and Real GDP in depth later, but for now, you may simply want to view the price level as an average price and Real GDP as the quantity of output produced.

Real GDP
The value of the entire output produced annually within a country's borders, adjusted for price changes.

The symbol we use for the price level is *P*; the symbol we use for Real GDP is *Q*. Thus, we can talk about the P-Q category.

In macroeconomics, we have occasion to discuss numerous topics, such as inflation, deflation, unemployment, and so on. Many of these topics relate directly or indirectly to either *P* or *Q*. Here is a list of macroeconomic topics and how each relates to either *P* or *Q*.

- *Gross Domestic Product (GDP). P* times *Q*.
- *Unemployment.* Changes in unemployment are related to changes in *Q*.

- *Inflation.* A rising *P*.
- *Deflation.* A falling *P*.
- *Economic growth.* Related to increasing *Q*.
- *Stagflation.* A rising *P* combined with rising unemployment.
- *Business cycle.* Recurrent swings up and down in *Q*.
- *Inflationary gap.* The condition of the economy when *Q* is above its natural level.
- *Recessionary gap.* The condition of the economy when *Q* is below its natural level.
- *Fiscal policy.* Concerned with stabilizing *P* and increasing *Q*.
- *Monetary policy.* Concerned with stabilizing *P* and increasing *Q*.

THE SELF-REGULATING–ECONOMIC INSTABILITY CATEGORY Consider the Great Depression of 1929–1933. During this period in U.S. history, unemployment skyrocketed, the production of goods and services plummeted (*Q* fell), prices fell (*P* fell), banks closed, savings were lost, and companies went bankrupt. What does this period indicate about the inherent properties of a market economy? Some observers argue that the Great Depression is proof of the inherent instability of a market (or capitalist) economy and demonstrates that natural economic forces, if left to themselves, may bring on human suffering.

Other observers see things differently. They argue that left to itself, the economy would never have nosedived into the Great Depression. They argue that the economy is inherently stable or self-regulating. The Great Depression, they believe, was largely caused and made worse by government tampering with the self-regulating and wealth-producing properties of a market economy.

Which came first? Did the market economy turn down under the weight of its own forces, producing massive unemployment, with government later stepping in to restrain the destructive market forces? Or was the market economy pushed into depression, and held there, by government economic tampering? The answer largely depends on how the inherent properties of a market economy are viewed. As economist Axel Leijonhufvud notes:

> *The central issue in macroeconomic theory is—once again—the extent to which the economy, or at least its market sectors, may properly be regarded as a self-regulating system. . . . How well or badly do its "automatic" mechanisms perform?*[1]

Fiscal Policy
Changes in government expenditures and/or changes in taxes to achieve particular macroeconomic goals.

Monetary Policy
Changes in the money supply, or the rate of growth of the money supply, to achieve particular macroeconomic goals.

THE EFFECTIVE-INEFFECTIVE CATEGORY Here the words *effective* and *ineffective* describe *fiscal policy* and *monetary policy*. **Fiscal policy** refers to changes in government expenditures and/or changes in taxes to achieve particular macroeconomic goals (e.g., low unemployment, stable prices). **Monetary policy** refers to changes in the money supply, or the rate of growth of the money supply, to achieve particular macroeconomic goals.

Macroeconomists can take one of several positions with the effective-ineffective category. They can believe that fiscal and monetary policy are always effective (at meeting their goals), that both fiscal and monetary policy are ineffective, or that fiscal policy is effective and monetary policy is ineffective, and so on.

Often, a macroeconomist's position on the effectiveness-ineffectiveness of a policy is implicit in his or her view of how the economy works.

1. Axel Leijonhufvud, "Effective Demand Failures," *Swedish Journal of Economics* 75 (1973): 28.

MACROECONOMIC MEASURES

Earlier, we presented three distinct macroeconomic categories—boxes, if you will, in which much of our macroeconomic discussion can be placed. In this section, we discuss the *P* of the P-Q category; in other words, we discuss the price level. In this section, we discuss how economists measure the price level.

Measuring Prices Using the CPI

As stated earlier, the **price level** is a weighted average of the prices of all goods and services. Economists measure the price level by constructing a **price index**. One major price index is the **consumer price index (CPI)**.

Price Level
A weighted average of the prices of all good and services.

Price Index
A measure of the price level.

Consumer Price Index (CPI)
A widely cited index number for the price level; the weighted average of prices of a specific set of goods and services purchased by a typical household.

COMPUTING THE CPI The CPI is calculated by the Bureau of Labor Statistics (BLS) through its sampling of thousands of households and businesses. When a news report says that the "cost of living" increased by, say, 7 percent, it is usually referring to the CPI.[2]

The CPI is based on a representative group of goods and services purchased by a typical household. This representative group of goods is called the *market basket*. The market basket includes eight major categories of goods and services: food and beverages, housing, apparel, transportation, medical care, recreation, education and communication, and other goods and services. Some examples of these goods and services are breakfast cereal, milk, coffee, bedroom furniture, men's shirts, women's dresses, jewelry, new vehicles, airline fares, gasoline, prescription drugs, cable television, sports equipment, college tuition, postage, and haircuts.

To simplify our discussion, we assume the market basket includes only three goods instead of the many goods it actually contains. Our market basket consists of 10 pens, 5 shirts, and 3 pairs of shoes.

To calculate the CPI, we must first calculate the total dollar expenditure on the market basket in two years: the current year and the base year. The **base year** is a benchmark year that serves as a basis of comparison for prices in other years.

Base Year
The year chosen as a point of reference or basis of comparison for prices in other years; a benchmark year.

In Exhibit 2, we multiply the quantity of each good in the market basket (column 1) by its current-year price (column 2) to compute the current-year expenditure on each good (column 3). By adding the dollar amounts in column 3, we obtain the total dollar expenditure on the market basket in the current year. This amount is $167.

To find the total expenditure on the market basket in the base year, we multiply the quantity of each good in the market basket (column 1A) by its base-year price (column 2A) and then add these products (column 3A). This gives us $67.

To find the CPI, we use the formula:

$$\text{CPI} = \frac{\text{Total dollar expenditure on market basket in current year}}{\text{Total dollar expenditure on market basket in base year}} \times 100$$

As shown in Exhibit 2, the CPI for our tiny economy is 249.

The consumer price index for the United States for the years 1959 to 2007 is shown in Exhibit 3.

MORE ABOUT THE BASE YEAR Recall that the base year is a benchmark year that serves as a basis of comparison for prices in other years. The CPI in the base

2. Although changes in the CPI are often used to compute the change in the "cost of living," one's cost of living usually involves more than is measured by the CPI. For example, the CPI does not include income taxes, yet income taxes are a part of the cost of living for most people.

exhibit 2

Computing the Consumer Price Index

The exhibit uses hypothetical data to show how the CPI is computed. To find the "total dollar expenditure on market basket in current year," we multiply the quantities of goods in the market basket times their current-year prices and add these products. This gives us $167. To find the "total dollar expenditure on market basket in base year," we multiply the quantities of goods in the market basket times their base-year prices and add these products. This gives us $67. We then divide $167 by $67 and multiply the quotient by 100.

(1) Market Basket		(2) Current-Year Prices (per item)		(3) Current-Year Expenditures
10 pens	×	$ .70	=	$ 7.00
5 shirts	×	14.00	=	70.00
3 pairs of shoes	×	30.00	=	90.00
				$167.00
				Total dollar expenditure on market basket in current year

(1A) Market Basket		(2A) Base-Year Prices (per item)		(3A) Base-Year Expenditures
10 pens	×	$ .20	=	$ 2.00
5 shirts	×	7.00	=	35.00
3 pairs of shoes	×	10.00	=	30.00
				$67.00
				Total dollar expenditure on market basket in base year

$$\text{CPI} = \left(\frac{\text{Total dollar expenditure on market basket in current year}}{\text{Total dollar expenditure on market basket in base year}}\right) \times 100$$

$$= \left(\frac{\$167}{\$67}\right) \times 100$$

$$= 249$$

year is 100. How do we know this? Well, look again at the formula for calculating the CPI. The numerator is the "total dollar expenditure on market basket in current year" and the denominator is the "total dollar expenditure on market basket in base year." In the base year, the current year *is* the base year, so the numerator and denominator are the same. The ratio is 1, and 1 × 100 = 100.

But if you look at Exhibit 3, you will notice that there is no year where the CPI is 100. Does this mean that there is no base year? Not at all. The base year has been defined by the government to be the period 1982–1984. Look at the CPI in each of the years 1982, 1983, and 1984. If we add the CPIs for the three years and divide by 3, we get 100: (96.5 + 99.6 + 103.9)/3 = 100.

WHEN WE KNOW THE CPI FOR VARIOUS YEARS, WE CAN COMPUTE THE PERCENTAGE CHANGE IN PRICES To find the percentage change in prices between any two years, we use the following formula:

$$\text{Percentage change in prices} = \left(\frac{\text{CPI}_{\text{later year}} - \text{CPI}_{\text{earlier year}}}{\text{CPI}_{\text{earlier year}}}\right) \times 100$$

For example, Exhibit 3 shows that the CPI in 1990 was 130.7, and the CPI in 2005 was 195.3. What was the percentage change in prices over this period of time? It was 49.43 percent: [(195.3 − 130.7) ÷ 130.7] × 100 = 49.43. This means that from 1990 to 2005, prices increased 49.43 percent. You can think of the percentage change in prices this way: What cost $1 in 1990 cost approximately $1.49 in 2005.

Common MISCONCEPTIONS

About the CPI

A person might read in the newspaper or hear on radio news that the CPI has risen by 4.5 percent over the last year. The person might then think, *I guess my cost of living has risen by 4.5 percent.* Truth is, the person's "cost of living" may have gone up by more or less than 4.5 percent. What has increased in cost is the market basket that is used to compute the CPI. The person's market basket—the combination of goods and services he or she buys—might not be the same as "the" market basket. In short, although "the" market basket might consist of goods X, Y, and Z, his or her market basket might consist of goods X, Y, and B.

One other thing. Just because one might have to spend more to buy a given market basket in year 2007 than in, say, 2006, it doesn't follow that the price of every good and service in the market basket went up. For example, looking at the price of goods and services in the 2007 market basket, we know that the prices of some goods and services went down and some went up. For example, here is a partial list of some of the goods and services that went up in price over the year: rent (3.6 percent), electricity (3.7 percent), fast food (4.4 percent), cable (3.6 percent), used cars and trucks (2.1 percent), and college tuition and fees (6.1 percent). Here is a partial list of some of the goods and services that went down in price over the year: dishes (−0.6 percent), cell phone services (−0.8 percent), computers (−12 percent), toys (−5.2 percent), phones (−5.2 percent), and sports equipment (−1 percent).

exhibit 3

CPI, 1959–2007

Source: The data were reported at the Web site for the U.S. Department of Labor, Bureau of Labor Statistics. Site address: http://www.bls.gov/home.htm. Beginning in 2007, the Bureau of Labor Statistics began reporting the CPI to three decimal points.

Year	CPI	Year	CPI
1959	29.1	1984	103.9
1960	29.6	1985	107.6
1961	29.9	1986	109.6
1962	30.2	1987	113.6
1963	30.6	1988	118.3
1964	31.0	1989	124.0
1965	31.5	1990	130.7
1966	32.4	1991	136.2
1967	33.4	1992	140.3
1968	34.8	1993	144.5
1969	36.7	1994	148.2
1970	38.8	1995	152.4
1971	40.5	1996	156.9
1972	41.8	1997	160.5
1973	44.4	1998	163.0
1974	49.3	1999	166.6
1975	53.8	2000	172.2
1976	56.9	2001	177.1
1977	60.6	2002	179.9
1978	65.2	2003	184.0
1979	72.6	2004	188.9
1980	82.4	2005	195.3
1981	90.9	2006	201.6
1982	96.5	2007	207.342
1983	99.6		

Inflation and the CPI

Inflation is an increase in the price level and is usually measured on an annual basis. The *inflation rate* is the positive percentage change in the price level on an annual basis. For example, the inflation rate for 2000 is the percentage change in prices from the end of December 1999 through the end of December 2000. Although we do not show these data in a table, the CPI in December 1999 was 168.9, and the CPI in December 2000 was 174.6. This means the inflation rate in 2000 was approximately 3.4 percent.

When you know the inflation rate, you can find out whether your income is (1) keeping up with, (2) not keeping up with, or (3) more than keeping up with inflation. How you are doing depends on whether your income is rising by (1) the same percentage as, (2) a smaller percentage than, or (3) a greater percentage than the inflation rate, respectively. Another way to look at this is to compute and compare your real income for different years. **Real income** is a person's **nominal income** (or money income) adjusted for any change in prices. Real income is computed as follows:

$$\text{Real income} = \left(\frac{\text{Nominal income}}{\text{CPI}}\right) \times 100$$

Inflation
An increase in the price level.

Real Income
Nominal income adjusted for price changes.

Nominal Income
The current-dollar amount of a person's income.

CASE 1. KEEPING UP WITH INFLATION: REAL INCOME STAYS CONSTANT
Jim earns $50,000 in year 1 and $55,000 in year 2. The CPI is 100 in year 1 and 110 in year 2. Jim's income has risen by 10 percent [(($55,000 − $50,000)/$50,000) × 100 = 10], and the inflation rate is 10 percent [((110 − 100)/100) × 100 = 10]. Jim's income has risen by the same percentage as the inflation rate, so he has kept up with inflation. This is evident when we see that Jim's real income is the same in the two years. In year 1, it is $50,000, and in year 2, it is $50,000 too.

Real income year 1 = ($50,000/100) × 100 = $50,000

Real income year 2 = ($55,000/110) × 100 = $50,000

CASE 2. NOT KEEPING UP WITH INFLATION: REAL INCOME FALLS Karen earns $50,000 in year 1 and $52,000 in year 2. The CPI is 100 in year 1 and 110 in year 2. Karen's income has risen by 4 percent, and the inflation rate is 10 percent. Her income has risen by a smaller percentage than the inflation rate, so she has not kept up with inflation. Karen's real income has fallen from $50,000 in year 1 to $47,273 in year 2.

Real income year 1 = ($50,000/100) × 100 = $50,000

Real income year 2 = ($52,000/110) × 100 = $47,273

CASE 3. MORE THAN KEEPING UP WITH INFLATION: REAL INCOME RISES Carl earns $50,000 in year 1 and $60,000 in year 2. The CPI is 100 in year 1 and 110 in year 2. Carl's income has risen by 20 percent, and the inflation rate is 10 percent. His income has risen by a greater percentage than the inflation rate, so he has more than kept up with inflation. Carl's real income has risen from $50,000 in year 1 to $54,545 in year 2.

Real income year 1 = ($50,000/100) × 100 = $50,000

Real income year 2 = ($60,000/110) × 100 = $54,545

Finding ECONOMICS

In Your Paycheck

Sharon comments to a friend that she recently received a $5 an hour raise at work. Her friend congratulates her and then goes on to talk about how prices have been rising lately. Where is the economics? Obviously if Sharon's nominal (or money) income has risen, and prices have risen too, it follows that Sharon's real income has changed. Has her real income risen, fallen, or stayed the same? The answer depends upon how much her nominal income has risen relative to how much prices have risen. Let's say her nominal income has risen by 5 percent and prices have risen by 2 percent. As a result, Sharon's real income has gone up.

Thinking like AN ECONOMIST

Comparing One Thing with Another

Comparing one thing with something else can be extremely useful. For example, in each of the three cases we have just discussed, we compared the percentage change in a person's nominal income with the inflation rate. Through this comparison, we learned something that we could not have learned by looking at either factor alone: how a person fared under inflation. Making comparisons is part of the economic way of thinking.

economics 24/7

ECONOMICS AT THE MOVIES

Some movies do better at the box office than other movies. For example, *Spider-Man 3,* released in 2007, earned higher gross receipts than *The Bourne Ultimatum,* another movie released in 2007.

As of August 2008, the following list ranks the all-time top 10 movies in the United States in terms of domestic gross receipts:

1. *Titanic* (1997)
2. *The Dark Knight* (2008)
3. *Star Wars* (1977)
4. *Shrek 2* (2004)
5. *E.T.: The Extra-Terrestrial* (1982)
6. *Star Wars: Episode I—The Phantom Menace* (1999)
7. *Pirates of the Caribbean: Dead Man's Chest* (2006)
8. *Spider-Man* (2002)
9. *Star Wars: Episode III—Revenge of the Sith* (2005)
10. *The Lord of the Rings: The Return of the King* (2003)

Titanic, first on the list, earned gross receipts in the United States of $600 million, and *Star Wars,* in third place, earned $461 million. Comparing these two dollar amounts, it is easy to conclude that *Titanic* did better at the box office than *Star Wars* did.

But notice that *Titanic* was released in 1997 and *Star Wars* was released 20 years earlier in 1977. In other words, the receipts for *Titanic* are in 1997 dollars, and those for *Star Wars* are in 1977 dollars. To accurately compare the receipts of the two movies, we need to put them on an even footing. To do this, we need to change each movie's receipts into today's dollars. When we do this, *Star Wars* earned more than double what *Titanic* earned. Specifically, *Star Wars* earned $1.5 billion and *Titanic* earned $732 million.

What is the top grossing film of all time in today's dollars? It is *Gone with the Wind,* released in 1939. In today's dollars, it earned $2.7 billion.

The Substitution Bias in Fixed-Weighted Measures

Look at Exhibit 2, where the CPI was first calculated. Notice that the market basket in both the current year and the base year is the same: 10 pens, 5 shirts, and 3 pairs of shoes. In the base year, the person bought 10 pens, 5 shirts, and 3 pairs of shoes, and even though the prices of all three of these items increased, she continued to buy the *same quantity* of each. This is like saying that Michael purchased two pounds of beef a week in 2007, and even though the price of beef increased between, say, 2007 and 2008, he continued to buy two pounds of beef a week. In reality, what Michael is likely to have done is *substitute,* say, chicken for beef *if the price of beef increased relatively more than the price of chicken during the time period in question.* In other words, Michael's buying behavior is likely to have responded to changes in *relative prices.*

Any price index that uses fixed quantities of goods, and therefore does not reflect the fact that people might substitute one good for another as the price of one good rises relative to another, is called a *fixed-weighted price index.* All fixed-weighted price measures have a *substitution bias*—they do not regularly account for the substitutions that individuals are likely to make. As a result of the substitution bias, a fixed-weighted price index can "overstate the cost of living." We explain how a fixed-weighted price index overstates the cost of living, in the following paragraphs.

Suppose a fixed-weighted price index—such as the CPI—is 100 in year 1 and 110 in year 2. Some people would loosely say that there has been a rise in the cost of living. In this context, a rise in the cost of living means that it takes more money in year 2 to

exhibit 4

C-CPI, 2000–2007

Here we show the Chained CPI (C-CPI) for the years 2000–2007. Beginning in 2007, the Bureau of Labor Statistics began reporting the C-CPI to three decimal points.

Year	C-CPI
2000	102.0
2001	104.3
2002	105.6
2003	107.8
2004	110.5
2005	113.7
2006	117.0
2007	119.948

purchase the same bundle of goods that was purchased in year 1. But this implicitly assumes that one's standard of living is obtained in only one way: *by purchasing a constant, or fixed, bundle of goods.* In reality, this probably isn't true. Different bundles of goods may represent *equivalent* standards of living.

For example, assume bundle A consists of two pounds of beef, one loaf of bread, and three boxes of Frosted Flakes cereal, and bundle B consists of two pounds of chicken, one loaf of bread, and three boxes of Honey Nut Cheerios. Furthermore, assume (1) bundles A and B represent equivalent standards of living; (2) a buyer is currently purchasing bundle A, which costs $100 over some time period; (3) the cost of purchasing bundle A rises to $110, prompting the buyer to substitute bundle B for bundle A; and (4) bundle B costs $100.

Has the cost of living increased for this person? If we base our answer on purchasing a fixed bundle of goods—bundle A—the answer is yes because the price of purchasing bundle A has risen from $100 to $110. But if we allow for substitutions (of bundles) and bundles A and B represent equivalent standards of living, then the answer is no because the cost of buying an equivalent bundle remains constant at $100. Many economists believe that allowing for substitutions is the only justifiable way of measuring the cost of living. Any method that does not allow for substitutions can result in overstating the change in the cost of living.

For many years, economists criticized the use of the CPI (a fixed-weighted price index) largely because the expenditure weights of the various goods and services in the market basket did not change often enough. This meant that the market basket used to measure the CPI was the same even though substitutions were taking place. In July 2002, the BLS started releasing what is called a "chained CPI," which essentially is a price index (based on the CPI) that does incorporate substitutions made. Stated differently, the chained CPI is not a fixed-weighted measure. In Exhibit 4 we show the chained CPI—designated C-CPI—for the years 2000 to 2007.

GDP Implicit Price Deflator

Besides the CPI, there is another price index that is often cited: the *GDP deflator* or the *GDP implicit price deflator.* As you know, the CPI is based on a representative group of goods and services (the market basket) purchased by a typical household. Obviously, there are more goods and services produced in an economy than find their way into the market basket. The GDP implicit price deflator, unlike the CPI, is based on all goods and services produced in an economy.

Converting Dollars from One Year to Another

Suppose someone says, "Back in 1960, I had an annual salary of $10,000 a year. That sure isn't much these days." Of course, the person is right in one sense: An annual salary of $10,000 doesn't buy much these days. But was $10,000 a good salary back in 1960? It certainly could have been because prices in 1960 weren't as high as they are today. For example, the CPI was 29.6 in 1960, and it was 201.6 in 2006. In other words, one of the things that make a salary "good" or "not so good" is what the salary can buy.

Now suppose someone tells you that a $10,000 salary in 1960 is the same as a $70,047 salary today. Would you then better understand the 1960 $10,000 salary? Of course you would because you understand what it means to earn $70,047 today. Economists convert a past salary into a salary today by using this formula:

$$\text{Salary in today's (current) dollars} = \text{Salary}_{\text{earlier year}} \times \left(\frac{\text{CPI}_{\text{current year}}}{\text{CPI}_{\text{earlier year}}}\right)$$

economics 24/7

WOODSTOCK, 1969

Actin' funny, but I don't know why
'scuse me, while I kiss the sky
—***Purple Haze,* Jimi Hendrix**

It was officially called the Woodstock Music and Art Fair. It took place at Max Yasgur's 600-acre dairy farm in Bethel, New York, for a period of three days—August 15, 16, and 17 of 1969. Bethel is about 43 miles from Woodstock, New York. It was advertised as three days of peace and music. To many, it came to represent the counterculture and hippie era of the 1960s. It is simply known as Woodstock.

©BETTMANN/CORBIS

As to the performers, there were many. Here is a partial list:

Richie Havens
John Sebastian
Sweetwater
Ravi Shankar
Arlo Guthrie
Joan Baez
Santana
Canned Heat
Janis Joplin
Sly & the Family Stone
Grateful Dead
Creedence Clearwater Revival
The Who
Jefferson Airplane
Joe Cocker
The Band
Blood, Sweat & Tears
Crosby, Stills, Nash & Young
Jimi Hendrix

The price of a one-day ticket to Woodstock was $8 in 1969. That sounds like a cheap ticket nowadays. But what is $8 in 1969 comparable to in 2007? We use the following formula:

$$\text{Ticket in 2007 dollars} = \$8 \times (207.342/36.7)$$
$$= \$45.20$$

Buying a one-day ticket at Woodstock was the same as buying a $45.20 ticket in 2007. Not a bad price at all, especially for all the groups you could see on any given day. You may want to check eBay to see what a one-day or three-day Woodstock ticket is selling for as a memorabilia item today. On the day we checked, a three-day ticket sold for $250.

Assume the CPI today is the same as the most recent CPI in Exhibit 3 (which is the CPI for 2007). Using the formula, we get:

$$\text{Salary in 2007 dollars} = \$10{,}000 \times (207.342/29.6)$$
$$= \$70{,}047$$

Finding ECONOMICS

In What Grandfather Says

Ursula, who is 25, told her grandfather that she just got a job that pays $67,000 a year. Her grandfather said, "That's a lot of money. When I got my first real job I earned only $5,000 a year. You're earning a whole lot more than I did." Where is the economics? We have just finished discussing that income earned in one time period cannot always be adequately compared to income earned in another time period unless we convert the dollars earned in one period into dollars earned in another period. If Ursula's grandfather earned $5,000 in, say, 1932, that would be equal to earning $75,672 today (the CPI in 1932 was 13.7).

SELF-TEST

(Answers to Self-Test questions are in the Self-Test Appendix.)

1. Explain how the CPI is calculated.
2. What is a base year?
3. In year 1, your annual income is $45,000 and the CPI is 143.6; in year 2, your annual income is $51,232 and the CPI is 150.7. Has your real income risen, fallen, or remained constant? Explain your answer.

MEASURING UNEMPLOYMENT

Every month, the government surveys thousands of households to gather information about labor market activities. It uses the information from the survey to derive the number of Americans unemployed.

Who Are the Unemployed?

The total population of the United States can be divided into two broad groups (Exhibit 5). One group consists of persons who are (1) under 16 years of age, (2) in the armed forces, or (3) institutionalized—that is, they are in a prison, mental institution, or home for the aged. The second group, which consists of all others in the total population, is called the *civilian noninstitutional population.*

The civilian noninstitutional population, in turn, can be divided into two groups: persons *not in the labor force* and persons in the *civilian labor force.* (Economists often refer to the "labor force" instead of the "civilian labor force.")

Civilian noninstitutional population = Persons not in the labor force + Persons in the labor force

Persons not in the labor force are neither working nor looking for work. For example, people who are retired, who are engaged in own-home housework, or who choose not to work fall into this category.

Persons in the civilian labor force fall into one of two categories: *employed* or *unemployed.*

Civilian labor force = Employed persons + Unemployed persons

According to the BLS, employed persons consist of:

- All persons who did any work for pay or profit during the survey reference week.
- All persons who did at least 15 hours of unpaid work in a family-operated enterprise.

exhibit 5

Breakdown of the U.S. Population and the Labor Force

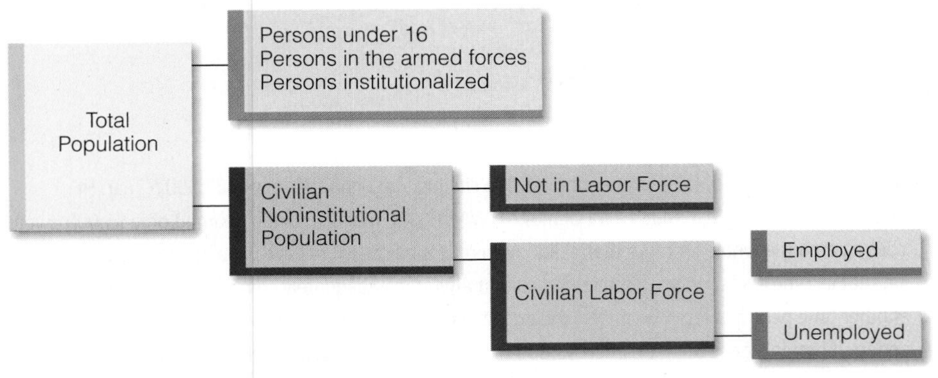

economics 24/7

WHAT WAS A PENNY WORTH?

You are walking and you look down and see a penny. Do you stop and pick it up? Many people will say no, stating that it isn't worth their stopping and picking up a penny. After all, a penny is not worth very much, they say.

You buy a magazine at your campus store. The total price (including tax) comes to $6.02. You hand the cashier a $10 bill. Instead of giving you $3.98 in change, she reaches into the cup next to the cash register and pulls out two pennies; she gives you back $4 in change. It is easier for her to get the two pennies from the cup than to count out $3.98 in change. You say "thank you" and go on your way.

Another day comes, and this time you buy something for $5.99. You hand the cashier $6. When the cashier gives you back one penny in change, you drop the penny in the cup next to the cash register. One day you take from the cup, another day you give to the cup.

Twenty years ago, there was no penny cup next to cash registers. Why no penny cups then, but penny cups now? It's because 20 years ago a penny had more purchasing power than it does today. If a penny today had greater purchasing power than it does have, then you'd be less likely to drop a penny change into the penny cup; instead, you'd drop it in your pocket.

The discussion of cups and pennies gets us thinking. What was a penny worth, say, in 1900? A different way of asking the question: What coin today is equal to the purchasing power a penny had in 1900? The answer is a quarter. In other words, having a penny in 1900 was equivalent of having a quarter (25 cents today). It follows then that having four pennies in 1900 was the equivalent of having $1 today.

We leave you with the question we started out with, but this time we change the date. It is 1900 and you are walking along and you look down and see a penny. Do you stop and pick it up?

- All persons who were temporarily absent from their regular jobs because of illness, vacation, bad weather, industrial dispute, or various personal reasons.

According to the BLS, unemployed persons consist of:

- All persons who did not have jobs, made specific active efforts to find a job during the prior four weeks, and were available for work.
- All persons who were not working and were waiting to be called back to a job from which they had been temporarily laid off.

The Unemployment and Employment Rates

The **unemployment rate** is the percentage of the civilian labor force that is unemployed. It is equal to the number of unemployed persons divided by the civilian labor force.

$$\text{Unemployment rate } (U) = \frac{\text{Number of unemployed persons}}{\text{Civilian labor force}}$$

The **employment rate** (sometimes referred to as the *employment/population ratio*) is the percentage of the civilian noninstitutional population that is employed. It is equal to the number of employed persons divided by the civilian noninstitutional population:

$$\text{Employment rate } (E) = \frac{\text{Number of employed persons}}{\text{Civilian noninstitutional population}}$$

Finally, the **labor force participation rate** (LFPR) is the percentage of the civilian noninstitutional population that is in the civilian labor force.

$$\text{Labor force participation rate (LFPR)} = \frac{\text{Civilian labor force}}{\text{Civilian noninstitutional population}}$$

Unemployment Rate
The percentage of the civilian force that is unemployed: Unemployment rate = Number of unemployed persons/Civilian labor force.

Employment Rate
The percentage of the civilian noninstitutional population that is employed: Employment rate = Number of employed persons/Civilian noninstitutional population.

Labor Force Participation Rate
The percentage of the civilian noninstitutional population that is in the civilian labor force. Labor force participation rate = Civilian labor force/Civilian noninstitutional population.

The LFPR may sound like the employment rate, but it is different. Although the denominator in both is the same, the numerator in the employment rate is the number of employed persons, and the numerator in the LFPR is the civilian labor force (which consists of both employed persons and unemployed persons). For this reason, some economists say that while the employment rate gives us the percentage of the population that is working, the LFPR gives us the percentage of the population that is *willing to work.*

Common MISCONCEPTIONS

About the Unemployment and Employment Rates

Many people mistakenly think that if the unemployment rate is, say, 7 percent, the employment rate must be 93 percent. They think this because they believe that the unemployment rate plus the employment rate must equal 100 percent. But the sum of the unemployment rate and the employment rate do not equal 100 percent. That's because the denominator of the unemployment rate is not the same as the denominator of the employment rate. The unemployment rate is a *percentage of the civilian labor force.* The employment rate is a *percentage of the civilian noninstitutional population,* which is a larger number than the civilian labor force.

Reasons for Unemployment

Usually, we think of an unemployed person as someone who has been fired or laid off from his or her job. Certainly, some unemployed persons fit this description, but not all of them do. According to the BLS, an unemployed person may fall into one of four categories.

1. *Job loser.* This is a person who was employed in the civilian labor force and was either fired or laid off. Most unemployed persons fall into this category.
2. *Job leaver.* This is a person employed in the civilian labor force who quits his or her job. For example, if Jim quit his job with company X and is looking for a better job, then he is a job leaver.
3. *Reentrant.* This is a person who was previously employed, hasn't worked for some time, and is currently reentering the labor force.
4. *New entrant.* This is a person who has never held a full-time job for two weeks or longer and is now in the civilian labor force looking for a job.

$$\text{Unemployed persons} = \text{Job losers} + \text{Job leavers} + \text{Reentrants} + \text{New entrants}$$

Discouraged Workers

Suppose Adam is fired from his job at company A in September. He looks for a job for about six months. During this time, he is considered an unemployed person and is counted in the unemployment rate. At the end of the sixth month, Adam is very discouraged; he doesn't think he will ever find a job, and so he stops looking. A month passes and he continues not to look for a job. Is Adam still considered an unemployed person? The answer is no. Remember, to be an unemployed person, you have to meet certain conditions, one of which is that you have to be actively looking for work. But Adam isn't actively looking for work, and he isn't waiting to be called back to a job or to report to a job. So Adam isn't unemployed. Because Adam is not unemployed, he does not get counted in the unemployment rate.

The BLS considers Adam a *discouraged worker.* You may think that for all practical purposes, a discouraged worker is the same as an unemployed person (because neither has a job). But they aren't the same for calculating the unemployment rate. The unemployed person gets counted, but the discouraged worker does not.

Some economists think that because discouraged workers are not considered unemployed, the unemployment rate is biased downward. Consequently, it doesn't really give us a good fix on the "real unemployment problem" in society.

Types of Unemployment

This section describes a few types of unemployment.

FRICTIONAL UNEMPLOYMENT Every day, demand conditions change in some markets, causing qualified individuals with transferable skills to leave some jobs and move to others. To illustrate, suppose there are two computer firms, A and B. For some reason, the demand falls for firm A's computers and the demand rises for firm B's computers. Consequently, firm A produces fewer computers. With fewer computers being produced, firm A doesn't need as many employees, so it fires some employees. On the other hand, firm B produces more computers. With more computers being produced, firm B hires additional employees. The employees fired from firm A have skills that they can transfer to firm B—after all, both firms produce computers. However, it takes time for people to transfer from one firm to another. During this time, they are said to be frictionally unemployed.

The unemployment owing to the natural "friction" of the economy, which is caused by changing market conditions and is represented by qualified individuals with transferable skills who change jobs, is called **frictional unemployment**. We use the symbol U_F to designate the frictional unemployment rate, which is the percentage of the labor force that is frictionally unemployed.

Frictional Unemployment
Unemployment due to the natural "friction" of the economy, which is caused by changing market conditions and is represented by qualified individuals with transferable skills who change jobs.

In a dynamic, changing economy like ours, there will always be frictional unemployment. Many economists believe that the basic cause of frictional unemployment is imperfect or incomplete information, which prevents individuals from leaving one job and finding another instantly.

Consider the situation where there are 1,000 job vacancies and 1,000 persons with the qualifications to fill the jobs. Will there be some unemployment? It is likely that there will be because not every one of the 1,000 job seekers will know where an available job is, nor will all employers give the job to the first applicant who knocks on the door (employers don't know if "better" applicants are around the corner). Matching qualified workers with jobs takes time.

STRUCTURAL UNEMPLOYMENT **Structural unemployment** is unemployment due to structural changes in the economy that eliminate some jobs and create other jobs for which the unemployed are unqualified. Most economists argue that structural unemployment is largely the consequence of automation (laborsaving devices) and long-lasting shifts in demand. The major difference between the frictionally unemployed and the structurally unemployed is that the latter do not have transferable skills. Their choice is between prolonged unemployment and retraining. For example, suppose there is a pool of unemployed automobile workers and a rising demand for computer analysts. If the automobile workers do not currently have the skills necessary to become computer analysts, they are structurally unemployed. We use the symbol U_S to designate the structural unemployment rate, which is the percentage of the labor force that is structurally unemployed.

Structural Unemployment
Unemployment due to structural changes in the economy that eliminate some jobs and create other jobs for which the unemployed are unqualified.

NATURAL UNEMPLOYMENT Adding the frictional unemployment rate and the structural unemployment rate gives the **natural unemployment** rate (or natural rate of unemployment). We use the symbol U_N to designate the natural unemployment rate. Currently, most economists estimate the natural unemployment rate at between 4 and 6.5 percent.

$$\text{Natural unemployment rate } (U_N) = \text{Frictional unemployment rate } (U_F) + \text{Structural unemployment rate } (U_S)$$

Natural Unemployment
Unemployment caused by frictional and structural factors in the economy. Natural unemployment rate = Frictional unemployment rate + Structural unemployment rate.

Cyclical Unemployment

Cyclical Unemployment Rate
The difference between the unemployment rate and the natural unemployment rate.

The unemployment rate that exists in the economy is not always the natural rate. The difference between the existing unemployment rate and the natural unemployment rate is the **cyclical unemployment rate** (U_C).

$$\text{Cyclical unemployment rate } (U_C) = \text{Unemployment rate } (U) - \text{Natural unemployment rate } (U_N)$$

When the unemployment rate (U) that exists in the economy is greater than the natural unemployment rate (U_N), the cyclical unemployment rate (U_C) is positive. For example, if $U = 8$ percent and $U_N = 5$ percent, then $U_C = 3$ percent. When the unemployment rate that exists in the economy is less than the natural unemployment rate, the cyclical unemployment rate is negative. For example, if $U = 4$ percent and $U_N = 5$ percent, then $U_C = -1$ percent.

Common MISCONCEPTIONS

About Full Employment

What do you think of when you hear the term *full employment*? Most people think *full employment* means that the actual or reported unemployment rate is zero. But a dynamic, changing economy can never have full employment of this type due to the frictional and structural changes that continually occur. In fact, it is natural for some unemployment to exist—some natural unemployment, that is. For this reason, economists *do not* equate full employment with a zero unemployment rate. Instead, for economists, **full employment** *exists when the economy is operating at its natural unemployment rate.* For example, if the natural unemployment rate is 5 percent, then full employment exists when the unemployment rate (in the economy) is 5 percent. In other words, the economy can be operating at full employment, and some people will be unemployed.

Full Employment
The condition that exists when the unemployment rate is equal to the natural unemployment rate.

SELF-TEST

1. What is the major difference between a person who is frictionally unemployed and one who is structurally unemployed?
2. If the cyclical unemployment rate is positive, what does this imply?

office hours

"IS THERE MORE THAN ONE REASON THE UNEMPLOYMENT RATE WILL FALL?"

Student:

If the unemployment rate drops, does it follow that some of the people who were once unemployed are now employed?

Instructor:

Not always. To see why, let's recall what the unemployment rate is equal to. It is equal to the number of unemployed persons divided by the civilian labor force.

$$\text{Unemployment Rate} = \frac{\text{Number of unemployed persons}}{\text{Civilian labor force}}$$

Now let's say there are 100 unemployed persons and the civilian labor force consists of 1,000 persons. The unemployment rate is 10 percent. Now suppose the number of unemployed persons rises to 105 (a 5 percent increase) at the same time that the civilian labor force rises to 1,120 (a 12 percent increase). The new unemployment rate is 9 percent, but you will notice that the number of unemployed persons has not decreased. In fact, it has increased from 100 to 105.

Student:

In other words, if the number of unemployed persons rises by a smaller percentage than the civilian labor force rises, the unemployment rate will decline—even though the number of unemployed persons has risen.

Instructor:

Yes, that's correct. Now consider something else. Suppose we return to 100 unemployed persons and a civilian labor force of 1,000 persons. These numbers give us an unemployment rate of 10 percent. Now suppose that 10 of the unemployed persons become discouraged workers and stop looking for work. The number of unemployed falls to 90 and the civilian labor force (which consists of employed plus unemployed persons) falls to 990. The unemployment rate now is 9.09 percent. The unemployment rate has dropped, but it hasn't dropped for the reason most people think the unemployment rate drops. It hasn't dropped because some of the unemployed persons found jobs. It has dropped because some of the unemployed became so discouraged that they stopped looking for jobs.

Student:

In other words, we might think that the unemployment rate has dropped because 10 of the 100 unemployed persons found work, whereas in reality these 10 persons did not find work. They just became so discouraged that they left the civilian labor force.

Instructor:

Yes, that's correct.

Student:

Does the government do anything to take into account these discouraged workers?

Instructor:

The Bureau of Labor Statistics does compute an alternative unemployment rate that adds in discouraged workers both to the ranks of the unemployed and to the civilian labor force. In short, it computes what it calls "total unemployed plus discouraged workers, as a percent of the civilian labor force plus discouraged workers."

$$\text{Alternative Unemployment Rate} = \frac{\text{Number of unemployed persons} + \text{Discouraged workers}}{\text{Civilian labor force} + \text{Discouraged workers}}$$

This alternative unemployment rate tells us what the unemployment rate would look like if we include discouraged workers in our calculation.

Points to Remember

1. The unemployment rate can decline even if the number of unemployed persons has not declined. For example, if the number of unemployed persons rises by a smaller percentage than the civilian labor force, the unemployment rate will decline (even though there are more, not fewer, unemployed persons).
2. There is an alternative unemployment rate defined as:

$$\text{Alternative Unemployment Rate} = \frac{\text{Number of unemployed persons} + \text{Discouraged workers}}{\text{Civilian labor force} + \text{Discouraged workers}}$$

a reader asks

Where Do I Go to Learn the Specifics of Jobs and Wages?

I'm a math major and I'll graduate from college in about a year. Is there a way for me to find out how much mathematicians earn and what types of jobs they perform?

No matter what your major is, you can learn about jobs and wages from the *Occupational Outlook Handbook.* The *Handbook* is on the Bureau of Labor Statistics website at http://stats.bls.gov/emp/.

According to the *Handbook,* mathematicians usually work as part of a team that includes economists, engineers, computer scientists, physicists, and others. In 2004, mathematicians held about 2,500 jobs. In addition, about 20,000 persons held faculty positions in mathematics at colleges and universities.

Many nonfaculty mathematicians work for the federal and state governments. The biggest employer of mathematicians in the federal government is the Department of Defense. In the private sector, major employers include research and testing services, educational services, security and commodity exchanges, and management and public relations services. In manufacturing, the pharmaceutical industry is the primary employer. Some mathematicians also work for banks, insurance companies, and public utilities.

Median annual earnings of mathematicians were $81,240 in 2004. The middle 50 percent earned between $60,050 and $101,360. The lowest 10 percent had earnings of less than $43,160, while the top 10 percent earned more than $120,900.

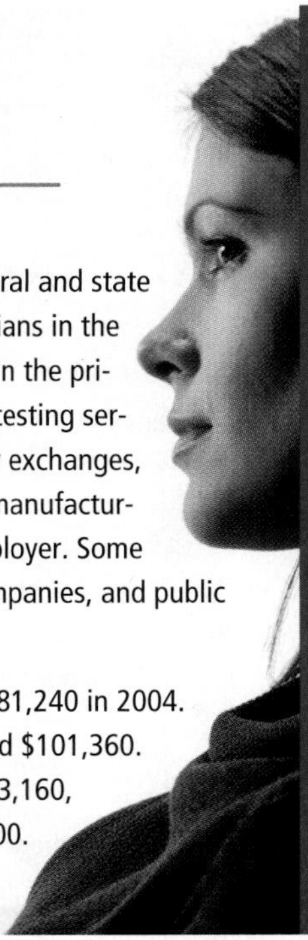

Chapter Summary

MEASURING PRICES

- One major price index is the consumer price index (CPI).
- Inflation is an increase in the price level or price index.
- Any price index that uses fixed quantities of goods, and therefore does not reflect the fact that people might substitute one good for another as the price of one good rises relative to another, is called a fixed-weighted price index. The substitution bias in a weighted price index can overstate the cost of living.
- A given dollar amount in an earlier year does not have the same purchasing power in a later year (or current year) if prices are different in the two years. To convert a dollar amount in an earlier year into today's (or current) dollars, we use the formula:

$$\text{Dollar amount in today's (current) dollars} = \text{Dollar amount}_{\text{earlier year}} \times \left(\frac{\text{CPI}_{\text{current year}}}{\text{CPI}_{\text{earlier year}}}\right)$$

UNEMPLOYMENT AND EMPLOYMENT

- An unemployed person may be a job loser, a job leaver, a reentrant, or a new entrant.
- The unemployment rate may be biased downward because discouraged workers are not considered unemployed.
- Frictional unemployment, due to the natural "friction" of the economy, is caused by changing market conditions and is represented by qualified individuals with transferable skills who change jobs.
- Structural unemployment is due to structural changes in the economy that eliminate some jobs and create others for which the unemployed are unqualified.
- Natural unemployment is caused by frictional and structural factors in the economy. The natural unemployment rate equals the sum of the frictional unemployment rate and the structural unemployment rate.
- Full employment is the condition that exists when the unemployment rate is equal to the natural unemployment rate.
- The cyclical unemployment rate is the difference between the existing unemployment rate and the natural unemployment rate.

Key Terms and Concepts

Real GDP	Consumer Price Index (CPI)	Unemployment Rate	Natural Unemployment
Fiscal Policy	Base Year	Employment Rate	Full Employment
Monetary Policy	Inflation	Labor Force Participation Rate	Cyclical Unemployment Rate
Price Level	Real Income	Frictional Unemployment	
Price Index	Nominal Income	Structural Unemployment	

Questions and Problems

1 What does the CPI in the base year equal? Explain your answer.

2 Show that if the percentage rise in prices is equal to the percentage rise in nominal income, then one's real income does not change.

3 What does it mean if the expenditure weights of the market basket used to compute the CPI are changed?

4 How does structural unemployment differ from frictional unemployment?

5 What does it mean to say that the country is operating at full employment?

6 What is "natural" about natural unemployment?

7 What is the difference between the employment rate and the labor force participation rate?

8 If the unemployment rate is 4 percent, it does not follow that the employment rate is 96 percent. Explain why.

9 What criteria must be met for a person to be characterized as unemployed?

10 What is the difference between a job leaver and a reentrant?

11 How is a discouraged worker different from an unemployed worker?

12 In the chapter we defined several economic topics in terms of the variables *P* (price level), *Q* (Real GDP), or both. Using the variables *P*, *Q*, or both, define the following: inflation, deflation, business cycles, fiscal policy, and deflation.

13 If the price of, say, oranges has risen, does it follow that the price level has risen too? Explain your answer.

14 What is the relationship between your nominal income and the inflation rate if you are more than keeping up with inflation?

15 The CPI is a fixed-weighted measure. What does this mean?

16 Explain how the CPI is computed.

Working with Numbers and Graphs

1 Suppose there are 60 million people employed, 10 million unemployed, and 30 million not in the labor force. What does the civilian noninstitutional population equal?

2 Suppose there are 100 million people in the civilian labor force and 90 million people employed. How many people are unemployed? What is the unemployment rate?

3 Change the current-year prices in Exhibit 2 to \$1 for pens, \$28 for shirts, and \$32 for a pair of shoes. What is the CPI for the current year based on these prices?

4 Jim earned an annual salary of \$15,000 in 1965. What is this equivalent to in 2005 dollars? (Use Exhibit 3 to find the CPI in the years mentioned.)

5 A house cost \$10,000 in 1976. What is this equivalent to in 2001 dollars? (Use Exhibit 3 to find the CPI in the years mentioned.)

6 Using the following data, compute (a) the unemployment rate, (b) the employment rate, and (c) the labor force participation rate.

Civilian noninstitutional population = 200 million

Number of employed persons = 126 million

Number of unemployed persons = 8 million

7 Based on the following data, compute (a) the unemployment rate, (b) the structural unemployment rate, and (c) the cyclical unemployment rate.

Frictional unemployment rate = 2 percent

Natural unemployment rate = 5 percent

Civilian labor force = 100 million

Number of employed persons = 82 million

8 Using Exhibit 3, compute the percentage change in prices between (a) 1966 and 1969, (b) 1976 and 1986, and (c) 1990 and 1999.

9 Assume the market basket contains 10X, 20Y, and 45Z. The current-year prices for goods X, Y, and Z are \$1, \$4, and \$6, respectively. The base-year prices are \$1, \$3, and \$5, respectively. What is the CPI in the current year?

10 If the CPI is 150 and nominal income is \$100,000, what does real income equal?

©WORKBOOK STOCK/JUPITER IMAGES

CHAPTER 6

MACROECONOMIC MEASUREMENTS, PART II: GDP AND REAL GDP

Introduction Each day in the United States many thousands of goods and services are produced. How do we measure all this economic activity? One of the principal ways is to compute GDP, or gross domestic product. GDP is one of the most important economic measurements used by economists. In this chapter we explain what GDP is and then discuss different ways of computing it. We also define and compute other economic measurements—such as national income, personal income, disposable income, and Real GDP.

GROSS DOMESTIC PRODUCT

In any given year, people in the United States produce goods and services. They produce television sets, books, pencil sharpeners, DVD players, attorney services, haircuts, and much more. Have you ever wondered what the total dollar value of all those goods and services is? In 2007, it was $13.84 trillion. In other words, in 2007, people living and working in the United States produced $13.84 trillion worth of goods and services. That dollar amount—$13.84 trillion—is what economists call the gross domestic product. Simply put, **gross domestic product (GDP)** is the *total market value of all final goods and services produced annually within a country's borders.*

Gross Domestic Product (GDP) The total market value of all final goods and services produced annually within a country's borders.

Three Ways to Compute GDP

Consider a simple economy in which one good is produced and sold.

1. Bob finds a seed and plants it. Sometime later, an orange tree appears.
2. Bob pays Harry $5 in wages to pick and box the oranges.
3. Next, Bob sells the oranges to Jim for $8.
4. Jim turns the oranges into orange juice and sells the orange juice to Caroline for $10. Caroline drinks the juice.

What is the GDP in this simple economy? Is it $5, $13, $10, $18, or some other dollar amount?

Economists use three approaches to compute GDP: the expenditure approach, the income approach, and the value-added approach. The following paragraphs describe each approach in terms of our simple economy.

EXPENDITURE APPROACH To compute GDP using the expenditure approach, add the amount of money spent by buyers on *final goods and services.* The words "final goods and services" are important in computing GDP because not all goods are final goods. Some goods are *intermediate goods.*

Final Good
A good in the hands of its final user.

A **final good** (or service) is a good in the hands of the final user, or ultimate consumer. Think of buyers standing in line one after another. The first buyer in our simple economy was Jim. He bought oranges from Bob. The second buyer was Caroline, who bought orange juice from Jim.

Caroline is the final buyer in this economy; she is the final user, the ultimate consumer. No buyer comes after her. The good that she buys is the final good. In other words, the orange juice is the final good.

Intermediate Good
A good that is an input in the production of a final good.

So, then, what are the oranges? Aren't they a final good too? No. The oranges are an *intermediate good.* An **intermediate good** is an input in the production of a final good. In other words, the oranges were used to produce orange juice (the final good).

So what does GDP equal if we use the expenditure approach to compute it? Again, it is the dollar amount spent by buyers for *final* goods and services. In our simple economy, there is only one buyer (Caroline), who spends $10 on one final good (orange juice). Thus, GDP in our tiny economy is $10.

Double Counting
Counting a good more than once when computing GDP.

You may be wondering why expenditures on only final goods are counted when computing GDP. The reason is because we would be *double counting* if we counted expenditures on both final goods and intermediate goods. **Double counting** refers to counting a good more than once when computing GDP. To illustrate, if we count both Caroline's purchase of the orange juice ($10) and Jim's purchase of the oranges ($8), we count the purchase of the oranges *twice*—once when the oranges are purchased by Jim and once when the oranges are in the orange juice.

INCOME APPROACH In our simple economy, income consists of wages and profits.[1] To compute GDP using the income approach, simply find the sum of all the wages and profits.

First, Harry earns $5 in wages.

Second, Bob's profit is $3: (1) Bob pays $5 to Harry, so the $5 is a cost to Bob; (2) Bob receives $8 for the oranges he sells to Jim; (3) $8 in revenue minus $5 in costs leaves Bob with $3 profit.

Third, Jim's profit is $2: (1) Jim pays $8 to Bob for the oranges, so the $8 is a cost to Jim; (2) Jim receives $10 for the orange juice he sells to Caroline; (3) $10 in revenue minus $8 in costs leaves Jim with $2 profit.

In our simple economy, the sum of Harry's wages, Bob's profit, and Jim's profit is $10. So GDP is equal to $10.

Value Added
The dollar value contributed to a final good at each stage of production.

VALUE-ADDED APPROACH In our tiny economy, orange juice is sold for, or has a market value of, $10. How much of the $10 market value is attributable to Jim? Stated differently, how much of the $10 market value is *value added* by Jim? If your intuition tells you $2, then your intuition is correct. **Value added** is the dollar value contributed to a final good at each stage of production. That is, it is the difference between the dollar value of the output the producer sells and the dollar value of the intermediate goods the producer buys.

1. Later in the chapter, you will learn that in a large economy, such as the U.S. economy, income consists of more than wages and profits. To simplify the explanation, we have defined a tiny economy where only wages and profits exist.

economics 24/7

GROSS FAMILY PRODUCT

One of the ways to understand GDP (gross domestic product) is to think of what GDP would be comparable to for a family. Instead of talking about what a country produces in a year, let's talk about what a family produces, and let's call the total market value of what the family produces gross family product (GFP).

Just as not every country has the same GDP, not every family has the same GFP. One family can have a higher or lower GFP than another family. Now ask yourself why one family's GFP might be higher than another family's GFP. It could be because there are more people producing in one family than in another family. For example, Family A is composed of five individuals and Family B is composed of eight individuals. With more family members (more resources), more output can be produced.

The same holds for countries. China might have a higher GDP than, say, France because China has a larger population than France. The Chinese family is larger than the French family.

Of course there are other reasons why one family might have a higher GFP than another family. For example, even with the same number of persons in two families, one family might have a higher GFP than the other. Perhaps this is because the members of, say, Family 1 work more hours than the members of Family 2. All other things equal, more work can result in more output.

The same holds for countries too. The GDP of one country might be higher than the GDP of another country because the workers in one country work more hours a week than the workers in another country.

Finally, consider that even though the size of two families is the same, and the number of hours worked each week by the two families is the same, still one family could have a higher GFP than another family. To understand why, keep in mind that GFP measures the total market value of the output the family produces. Emphasis here should be placed on "total market value." The total market value of the output one produces is computed by multiplying the price of each unit of output by the number of units produced. To illustrate, if a family is producing chairs, then its GFP will be equal to the price of each chair multiplied by the number of chairs produced. One hundred dollars ($100) per chair multiplied by, say, 100 chairs equals a GFP of $10,000. It follows that family's GFP might be higher than another family's GFP because the per-unit price of what it produces is higher.

To compute GDP using the value-added approach, find the sum of the values added at all the stages of production. Bob buys no intermediate goods (he simply found a seed, planted it, and then hired Harry to pick and box oranges), but he sells the oranges to Jim for $8. In other words, valued added at this stage of production is $8.

Jim takes the oranges (an intermediate good he buys from Bob for $8) and turns them into orange juice that he sells to Caroline for $10. Value added at this stage of production is $2.

The sum of the values added at all (two) stages of production is $10, so GDP is equal to $10.

Finding ECONOMICS

In a Factory, Restaurant, and Law Office

James works in a car factory in Detroit. Where is the economics? Obviously cars are being produced in the car factory in Detroit. The production of these cars will add to the GDP for the current year.

Marion works as a cook in a coffee house. Bill has just ordered an egg salad sandwich on rye (toasted) with cole slaw and a root beer. Where is the economics? Marion will make the sandwich and cole slaw. These two items plus the root beer are part of GDP for the current year.

Oliver is in his attorney's office talking about his upcoming court case. Where is the economics? The service the attorney is providing to Oliver is part of GDP for the current year.

exhibit 1

Size of the Underground Economy

Here we identify the size of the underground economy as a percentage of GDP for various countries in 2003.

Source: "Shadow Economies Around the World: What Do We Really Know?" Frederich Schneider, July 2004.

Country	Size of Underground Economy as Percentage of GDP
Australia	13.8%
Canada	15.4
France	14.8
Germany	16.8
Greece	28.3
Ireland	15.5
Italy	26.2
Japan	11.0
Norway	18.7
Spain	22.3
United States	8.6

What GDP Omits

Some exchanges that take place in an economy are not included in GDP. As the following paragraphs indicate, these trades range from sales of used cars to illegal drug deals.

CERTAIN NONMARKET GOODS AND SERVICES If a family hires a person through the classified section of the newspaper to cook and clean, the service is counted in GDP. If family members perform the same tasks, however, their services are not counted in GDP. The difference is that, in the first case, a service is actually bought and sold for a price in a market setting, and in the other case, it is not.

Some nonmarket goods are included in GDP. For example, the market value of food produced on a farm and consumed by the farm family is estimated, and this imputed value is part of GDP.

UNDERGROUND ACTIVITIES, BOTH LEGAL AND ILLEGAL The underground economy consists of unreported exchanges that take place outside the normal recorded market channels. Some underground activities involve illegal goods (e.g., cocaine), and others involve legal goods and tax evasion.

Illegal goods and services are not counted in GDP because no record exists of such transactions. There are no written records of illegal drug sales, illegal gambling, and illegal prostitution. Nor are there written records of some legal activities that individuals want to keep from government notice. For example, a gardener might agree to do some gardening work only on the condition that he is paid in cash. Obviously, it is not illegal for a person to buy or sell gardening services, but still, the transaction might not be recorded if one or both parties do not want it to be. Why might the gardener want to be paid in cash? Perhaps he doesn't want to pay taxes on the income received—an objective more easily accomplished if there is no written record of the income being generated.

In Exhibit 1, we show the size of the underground economy as a percentage of GDP for various countries in 2003.

SALES OF USED GOODS GDP measures *current production* (i.e., occurring during the current year). A used car sale, for example, does not enter into the current-year statistics because the car was counted when it was originally produced.

FINANCIAL TRANSACTIONS The trading of stocks and bonds is not counted in GDP because it does not represent the production of new assets. It is simply the trading of existing assets (the exchange of stocks or bonds for money).

Transfer Payment
A payment to a person that is not made in return for goods and services currently supplied.

GOVERNMENT TRANSFER PAYMENTS A **transfer payment** is a payment to a person that is not made in return for goods and services currently supplied. Government transfer payments—such as Social Security benefits and veterans' benefits—are not counted in GDP because they do not represent payments to individuals for *current production.*

LEISURE Leisure is a good in much the same way that cars, houses, and shoes are goods. New cars, houses, and shoes are counted in GDP, but leisure is not because it is too difficult to quantify. The length of the workweek has fallen in the United States over the past years, indicating that the leisure time individuals have to consume has increased. But GDP computations do not take leisure into account.

economics 24/7

HAPPINESS AND THE ECONOMIST

In one survey, students at Harvard University were asked whether they would prefer (a) $50,000 a year while others got $25,000 a year or (b) $100,000 a year while others got $200,000 a year.

©COMSTOCK RF/JUPITER IMAGES

A majority of the students chose (a). In other words, they chose a lower absolute income but a higher relative income. They chose to be poorer in absolute terms, as long as they could be richer in relative terms.

Sometimes, researchers conclude from such a survey that an increase in one's absolute standard of living (say, as measured by per capita GDP) does not matter as much to happiness as a rise in one's relative standard of living (say, as measured by moving up from being "poor" to being "middle income" or from being "middle income" to being "rich"). In short, what matters is not so much how we are doing but how we are doing relative to everyone else.

Now the real question is whether or not survey results—such as the Harvard University student survey—are meaningful. For example, let's ask ourselves what we would observe if people care more about their relative standing than their absolute standing. Some economists have suggested that we would see more affluent people moving into poorer neighborhoods so that they could experience higher relative incomes. They go on to say that since we don't see this very often, it follows that individuals do not care about their relative income as much as the survey results suggest. As to something we would not see if people cared about their relative incomes, we would not see poor immigrants coming to a rich country; after all, when poor immigrants come to a rich country, they know they will be near the bottom of the income scale. Yet they still come. Why? Perhaps it is because they enjoy a higher absolute income in the rich country than they would in the country they leave.

What can we learn about economists here? One key thing is economists don't always trust survey results—or what people say when answering certain questions. For economists, if we want to know something about people's preferences, we should observe how they act instead of noting what they say.

GDP Is Not Adjusted for Bads Generated in the Production of Goods

Economic growth often comes with certain *bads*. For example, producing cars, furniture, and steel often generates air and water pollution—considered bads by most people. (Remember from Chapter 1 that a bad is anything from which individuals receive disutility.) GDP counts the goods and services, but it does not net out the air and water pollution. Thus, some economists argue that GDP overstates our overall economic welfare.

Per Capita GDP

If we divide a country's GDP by the population in the country, we get *per capita GDP*. For example, if a country has a GDP of $5 trillion and its population is 200 million, GDP per capita is $25,000. Exhibit 2 shows the GDP (in billions of dollars) and per capita GDP (in dollars) for various countries in 2007.

Is Either GDP or Per Capita GDP a Measure of Happiness or Well-Being?

Are the people in a country with a higher GDP or higher per capita GDP better off or happier than the people in a country with a lower GDP or lower per capita GDP? We

exhibit 2

GDP and Per Capita GDP, Selected Countries, 2007

Source: CIA World Factbook, 2008.

Country	GDP (billions)	Per Capita GDP
Austria	$ 320	$39,000
China	7,043	5,300
Cuba	51	4,500
France	2,067	33,800
Germany	2,833	34,400
Mexico	1,353	12,500
Russia	2,076	14,600
United Kingdom	2,147	35,300
United States	13,840	46,000

cannot answer that question because well-being and happiness are subjective. A person with more goods may be happier than a person with fewer goods, but possibly not. The person with fewer goods but a lot of leisure, little air pollution, and a relaxed way of life may be much happier than the person with many goods, little leisure, and a polluted, stressful environment.

We make this point to warn against reading too much into GDP figures. GDP figures are useful for obtaining an estimate of the productive capabilities of an economy, but they do not necessarily measure happiness or well-being.

Common MISCONCEPTIONS

About GDP

Some people think that the higher a country's GDP, the richer the inhabitants of the country will be. Not true. GDP tells us what the total number of persons of a country produced in a given year. What it doesn't tell us is the share of GDP the "average person" receives. If GDP is large and the population of the country that produced the GDP is large, it is possible for the GDP per person (per capita GDP) to be small. For example, China has a much larger GDP than France, but the per capita GDP of France is over six times higher than the per capita GDP of China.

SELF-TEST

(Answers to Self-Test questions are in the Self-Test Appendix.)

1. Identify and explain the three approaches to computing GDP.
2. Suppose the GDP for a country is $0. Does this mean that there was no productive activity in the country? Explain your answer.

THE EXPENDITURE APPROACH TO COMPUTING GDP FOR A REAL-WORLD ECONOMY

The last section explains the expenditure, income, and value-added approaches to computing GDP for a simple economy. This simple economy consisted of one person producing oranges, one person producing orange juice, and one person buying orange juice. Obviously, the U.S. economy is much more complex than this tiny economy is.

This section explains how the expenditure approach is used to compute GDP in a real-world economy like the U.S. economy. The next section explains how the income approach is used.

Expenditures in a Real-World Economy

Economists often talk about four sectors of the economy: (1) household sector, (2) business sector, (3) government sector, and (4) foreign sector. Economic actors in these sectors buy goods and services; in other words, they spend. The expenditures of the sectors are called, respectively, (1) *consumption;* (2) gross private domestic investment, or simply *investment;* (3) government consumption expenditures and gross investment, or simply *government purchases;* and (4) *net exports.*

Consumption
The sum of spending on durable goods, nondurable goods, and services.

CONSUMPTION Consumption (C) includes (1) spending on durable goods, (2) spending on nondurable goods, and (3) spending on services. Durable goods are goods that are expected to last for more than three years, such as refrigerators, ovens, or cars.

economics 24/7

HOW ARE CALIFORNIA AND ITALY ALIKE?[1]

When it comes to countries, economists compute gross domestic product (GDP). When it comes to states, they compute gross domestic product by state (GDP by state).[2]

Once we have computed GDP and GDP by state, it is possible to compare states with countries. For example, in 2007 California's GDP was nearly equivalent to Italy's GDP. This means that in GDP terms, California and Italy are comparable. Or put it this way: In GDP terms, California *is* Italy.

What about Virginia? In 2007, its GDP was $383 billion. What country had a GDP comparable to this that year? The answer is Saudi Arabia. In GDP terms, Virginia is Saudi Arabia.

In the exhibit below, we show a map of the United States, where each state (in the map) has the name of a country. What are we saying here? That the state's GDP is comparable to the country's GDP. Looking at the map, we can see that California's GDP is comparable to Italy's; New York's is comparable to India's; and Florida's is comparable to the Netherland's GDP.

1. The source of the state data is the BEA; the source of the country data (GDP) is the *CIA World Fact Book*. All data are for 2007, and the GDP for countries is at the official exchange rate.

2. "GDP by state" used to be called gross state product (GSP).

exhibit 3

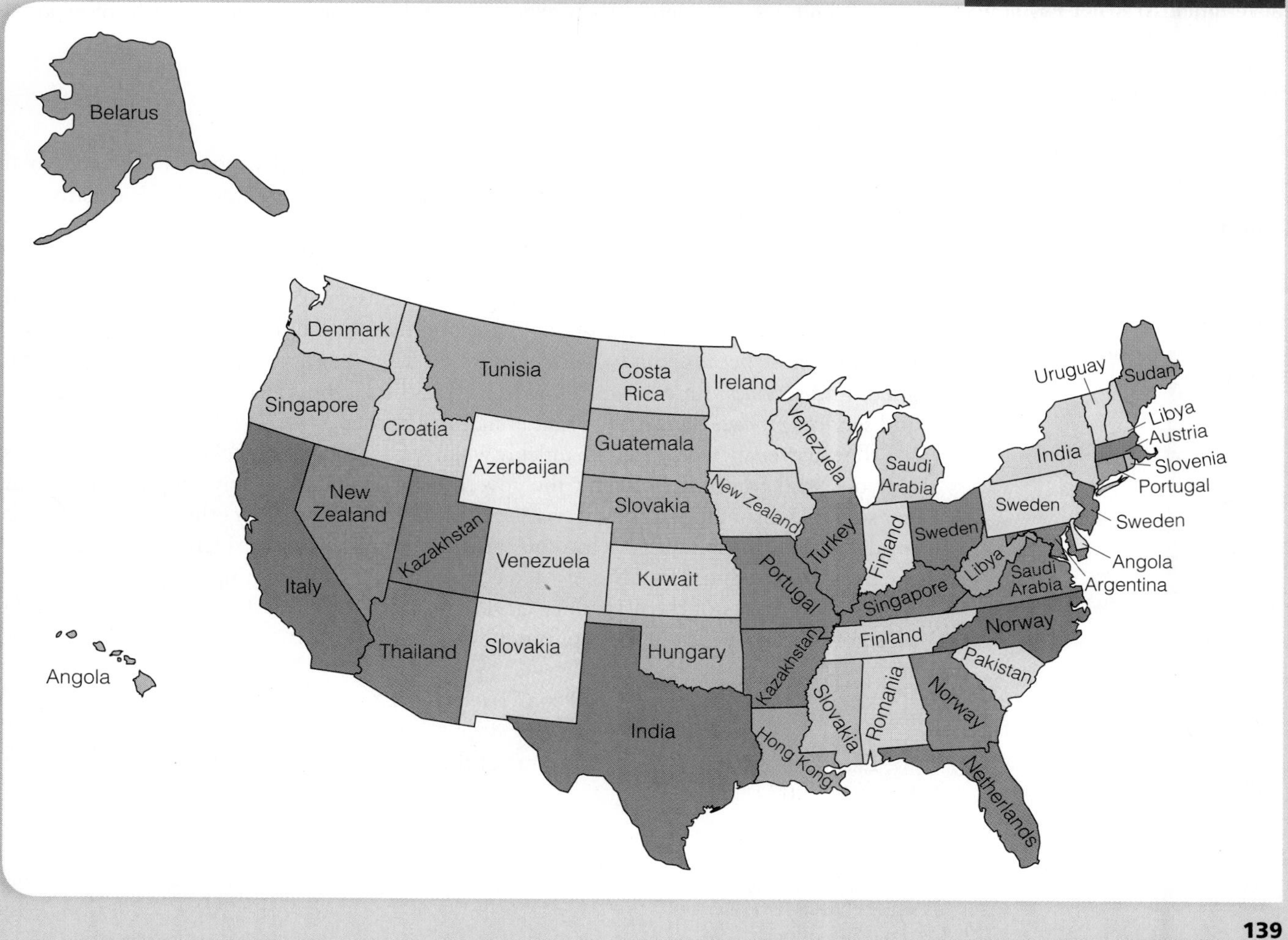

Nondurable goods are goods that are not expected to last for more than three years, such as food. Services are intangible items such as lawn care, car repair, and entertainment. Consumption expenditures in the United States usually account for 70 percent of GDP. In short, consumption is the largest spending component of GDP.

Investment
The sum of all purchases of newly produced capital goods, changes in business inventories, and purchases of new residential housing.

Inventory Investment
Changes in the stock of unsold goods.

Fixed Investment
Business purchases of capital goods, such as machinery and factories, and purchases of new residential housing.

Government Purchases
Federal, state, and local government purchases of goods and services and gross investment in highways, bridges, and so on.

Government Transfer Payments
Payments to persons that are not made in return for goods and services currently supplied.

Imports
Total domestic (U.S.) spending on foreign goods.

Exports
Total foreign spending on domestic (U.S.) goods.

Net Exports
Exports minus imports.

INVESTMENT **Investment** (I) is the sum of (1) the purchases of newly produced capital goods, (2) changes in business inventories, sometimes referred to as **inventory investment**, and (3) the purchases of new residential housing.[2] The sum of the purchases of newly produced capital goods and the purchases of new residential housing is often referred to as **fixed investment**. In other words, Investment = Fixed investment + Inventory investment. Fixed investment is the larger of the two components of investment.

GOVERNMENT PURCHASES **Government purchases** (G) include federal, state, and local government purchases of goods and services and gross investment in highways, bridges, and so on. **Government transfer payments**, which are payments to persons that are not made in return for goods and services currently supplied, are not included in government purchases. Social Security benefits and welfare payments are two examples of transfer payments; neither is a payment for current productive efforts.

NET EXPORTS People, firms, and governments in the United States sometimes purchase foreign-produced goods. These purchases are referred to as **imports** (IM). Foreign residents, firms, and governments sometimes purchase U.S.-produced goods. These purchases are referred to as **exports** (EX). If imports are subtracted from exports, we are left with **net exports** (NX).

$$NX = EX - IM$$

Obviously, net exports (NX) can be positive or negative. If exports are greater than imports, then NX is positive; if imports are greater than exports, then NX is negative.

Computing GDP Using the Expenditure Approach

The expenditure approach to computing GDP sums the purchases of final goods and services made by the four sectors of the economy (see Exhibit 4). This may give you reason to pause because our earlier definition of GDP did not mention *purchases* of final goods and services. Rather, we defined GDP as the total market value of all final goods and services *produced* annually within a nation's borders.

The discrepancy is cleared up quickly when we note that national income accountants (persons who compute GDP for the government) assume that anything produced but not sold to consumers is "bought" by the firm that produced it. In other words, if a car is produced but not sold, it goes into business inventory and is considered "purchased" by the firm that produced it. Thus, we can compute GDP by summing the purchases made by the four sectors of the economy. GDP equals consumption (C) plus investment (I) plus government purchases (G) plus net exports ($EX - IM$).

$$\text{GDP} = C + I + G + (EX - IM)$$

Exhibit 5 shows the dollar amounts of the four components of GDP for the United States in 2007.

2. For purposes of computing GDP, the purchases of new residential housing (although undertaken by members of the household sector) are considered investment.

exhibit 4

The Expenditure Approach to Computing GDP

The expenditure components of GDP are consumption, investment, government purchases, and net exports. The exhibit shows what is included in each of these components.

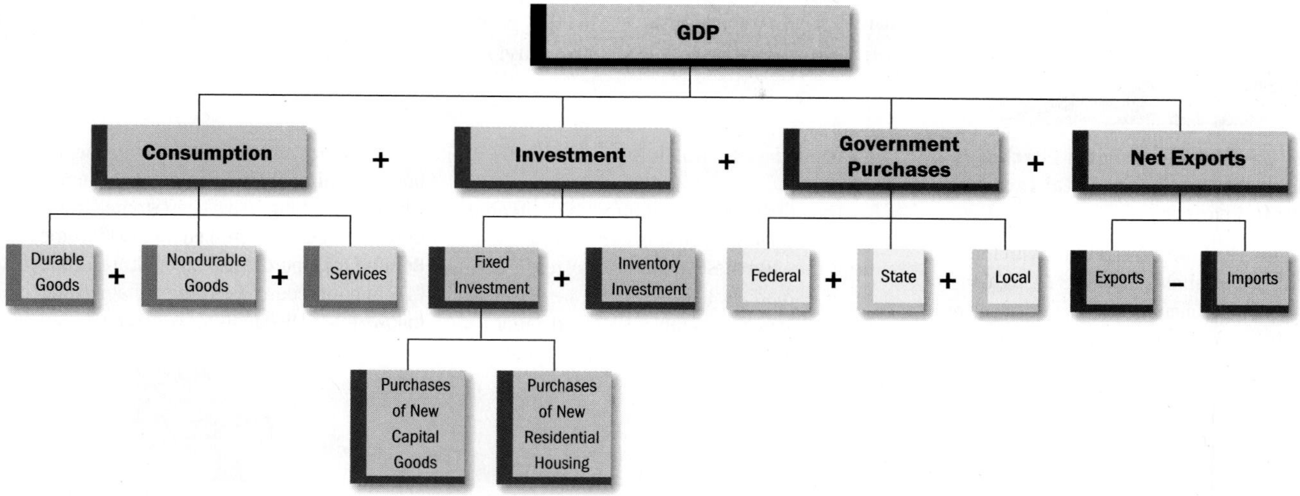

Common Misconceptions

About Increases in GDP

Are all increases in GDP alike? To answer this question, consider that if investment rises, and no other component of GDP declines, GDP will rise. Now recall that investment can rise for one of three reasons: (1) firms may purchase more newly produced capital goods (firms buy more factories and machinery), (2) individuals purchase new residential housing (someone buys a new house), or (3) firms' inventory investment rises. Now there are two ways firms' inventory investment can rise. The first is if firms deliberately produce more units of a good and add those units to inventory. The second is if consumers don't buy as many units of output as firms have produced and unsold units are added to inventory. The first is called planned inventory investment (because firms deliberately plan to add to their inventory). The second is called unplanned inventory investment (because firms have not planned to add to their inventory).

Now compare two settings. In setting 1, firms purchase more newly produced capital goods (more factories and machinery). As a result, investment rises and so GDP rises, all other things remaining constant. In setting 2, buyers don't buy as many units of output as firms have produced. The unsold units find their way into (unplanned) inventory investment. As a result, investment rises and so GDP rises, too, all other things remaining constant. Is the higher GDP in settings 1 and 2 equivalent? We think not. As far as the health and strength of the economy is concerned, the increase in GDP in setting 1 is superior to the increase in GDP in the second setting.

exhibit 5

Components of GDP (Expenditure Approach)

The expenditure approach to computing GDP sums the purchases made by final users of goods and services. The expenditure components include consumption, investment, government purchases, and net exports. The data are for 2007.

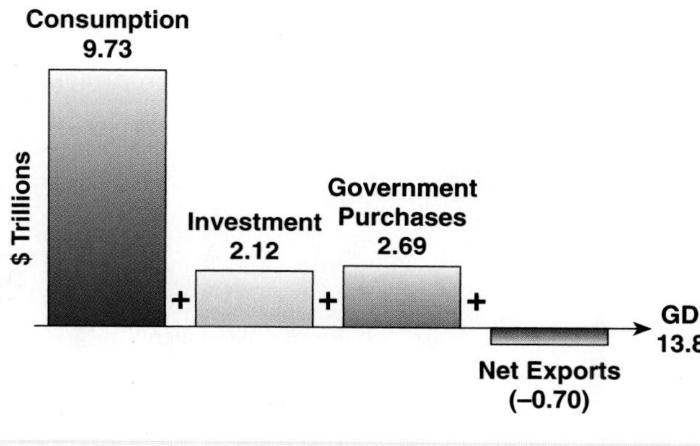

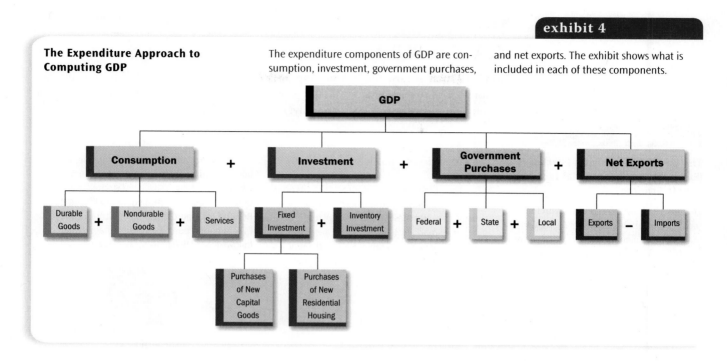

The Income Approach to Computing GDP for a Real-World Economy

Now let's look at how the income approach is used to compute GDP for a real-world economy. The two approaches should give us the same dollar figure for GDP. (Remember our simple orange juice economy?) Exhibit 6—a circular flow diagram of the

exhibit 6

The Circular Flow: Total Purchases (Expenditures) Equal Total Income in a Simple Economy

The exhibit shows an economy with four sectors: Households, Business Firms, Government, and Foreign Economies. Each sector purchases goods and services. The sum of these purchases is GDP [GDP = $C + I + G + (EX - IM)$].

The purchases (expenditures) made in product markets flow to business firms. Business firms then use these monies to buy resources in resource markets. In other words, these monies flow to the owners (suppliers) of land, labor, capital, and entrepreneurship. The sum of these resource payments is total income, which flows to households. In this simple economy, where some things have been ignored, total purchases (expenditures) equal total income. Because total purchases (expenditures) equal GDP and total purchases equal total income, it follows that GDP equals total income.

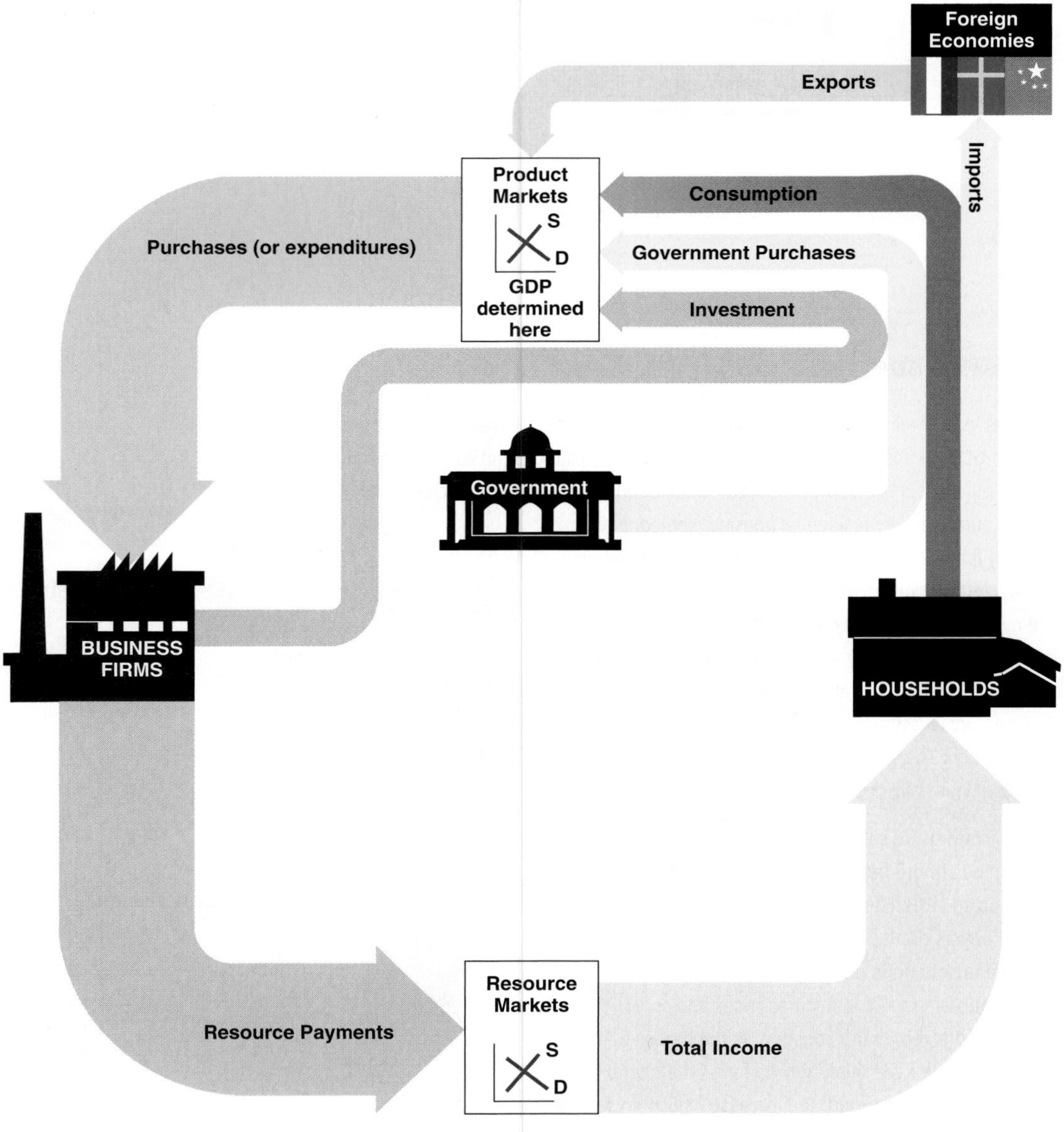

economics 24/7

1820

Most people are interested in knowing what the per capita GDP is today in different countries. Something else that is interesting, too, is the per capita GDP in different countries over the years. For example, wonder what country had the highest per capita GDP in, say, 1820?

©SUSAN VAN ETTEN

The answer is the Netherlands. What about 1900? That would be New Zealand. In the three tables in the exhibit, we identify the top 10 countries in various years in terms of per capita GDP.

Source: Angus Maddison at http://www.ggdc.net/maddison/.

exhibit 7

1820			1900			1950		
Rank	**Country**	**Per Capita GDP**	**Rank**	**Country**	**Per Capita GDP**	**Rank**	**Country**	**Per Capita GDP**
1	Netherlands	$1,561	1	New Zealand	$4,320	1	United States	$9,573
2	Australia	$1,528	2	Australia	$4,299	2	Switzerland	$8,939
3	Austria	$1,295	3	United States	$4,096	3	New Zealand	$8,495
4	Belgium	$1,291	4	Belgium	$3,652	4	Venezuela	$7,424
5	United States	$1,287	5	Netherlands	$3,533	5	Australia	$7,218
6	Denmark	$1,225	6	Switzerland	$3,531	6	Canada	$7,047
7	France	$1,218	7	Germany	$3,134	7	Sweden	$6,738
8	Sweden	$1,198	8	Denmark	$2,902	8	Denmark	$6,683
9	Germany	$1,112	9	Austria	$2,901	9	Netherlands	$5,850
10	Italy	$1,092	10	France	$2,849	10	Belgium	$5,346

economy—shows that in a simple economy, GDP computed by summing the purchases of the four sectors of the economy is equal to GDP computed by summing the income earned by the different resources. In other words, dollar purchases (or dollar expenditures) equal dollar income. Think of it in terms of a tiny economy where one person buys 10 oranges for $1 each. His expenditures equal $10. But the $10 also represents income for the person who sold the buyer the oranges. An expenditure for one person is income for another.

There are two steps involved in computing GDP using the income approach. First, we must compute national income. Second, we must adjust national income for certain things. The end result is GDP.

Computing National Income

National income is the sum of five components: (1) compensation of employees, (2) proprietors' income, (3) corporate profits, (4) rental income of persons, and (5) net interest. We discuss the details of each in the following paragraphs.

National Income
Total income earned by U.S. citizens and businesses, no matter where they reside or are located. National income is the sum of the payments to resources (land, labor, capital, and entrepreneurship). National income = Compensation of employees + Proprietors' income + Corporate profits + Rental income of persons + Net interest.

COMPENSATION OF EMPLOYEES Compensation of employees consists of wages and salaries paid to employees plus employers' contributions to Social Security and employee benefit plans plus the monetary value of fringe benefits, tips, and paid vacations. Compensation of employees is the largest component of national income. In 2007, compensation of employees in the United States was $7.85 trillion.

PROPRIETORS' INCOME Proprietors' income includes all forms of income earned by self-employed individuals and the owners of unincorporated businesses, including unincorporated farmers. Included in farm income is an estimate of the value of the food grown and consumed on farms.

CORPORATE PROFITS Corporate profits include all the income earned by the stockholders of corporations. Some of the profits are paid to stockholders in the form of dividends, some are kept within the firm to finance investments (these are called *undistributed profits* or *retained earnings*), and some are used to pay corporate profits taxes. (The portion of corporate profits used to pay corporate profits taxes is counted as income "earned" by households even though households do not receive the income.)

RENTAL INCOME (OF PERSONS) Rental income is the income received by individuals for the use of their nonmonetary assets (land, houses, offices). It also includes returns to individuals who hold copyrights and patents. Finally, it includes an imputed value to owner-occupied houses. For example, someone may own the house she lives in, and therefore not pay any rent, but for purposes of national income accounting, a rental value is imputed. In short, home ownership is viewed as a business that produces a service that is sold to the owner of the business.

NET INTEREST Net interest is the interest income received by U.S. households and government minus the interest they paid out.

NATIONAL INCOME We can summarize national income and its components as follows:

National income = Compensation of employees
+ Proprietors' income
+ Corporate profits
+ Rental income
+ Net interest

In 2007, national income in the United States was $12.2 trillion.

From National Income to GDP: Making Some Adjustments

After computing national income, you might think that there is nothing else to do—that national income should equal GDP. That's because we naturally think that every dollar spent is someone's income.

But when we check the actual figures for national income and GDP, we find that they are not equal. In other words, not every dollar spent is someone else's income. For example, if Jones spends $10 to buy a book, $9.50 of the $10 might end up in the seller's pocket as income, but 50 cents of the $10 might go for taxes.

With this in mind, the income approach to computing GDP requires us to add certain things to national income and to subtract certain things from national income. The following equation and Exhibit 8 shows what must be added to and subtracted

economics 24/7

GDP: PROCEED WITH CAUTION

Some people seem drawn to making incorrect comparisons between countries based on GDP figures. For example, a person might notice that Austria's GDP ($320 billion) is smaller than Germany's GDP ($2,833 billion) and conclude that Austrians are not as well off as Germans.

First, we would expect a country with a smaller population to have a smaller GDP than a country with a larger population. With fewer people, there is usually less output produced. Austria has a population of 8.2 million, whereas Germany has a population of 82.4 million. In other words, Germany has over 10 times the population of Austria, so we would expect it to have a higher GDP.

What we have said for GDP also holds for GDP by state or gross state product (GSP). For example, just as a country has a GDP, each state in the United States has a gross state product. The state with the largest GSP in 2004 was California with a GSP of $1.55 trillion. This is larger than the GDP of many countries, but then, California has a population greater than many countries.

Also, as we noted earlier in the chapter, it is not GDP (or GSP) that matters as much as it is per capita GDP (or per capita GSP). If you notice from Exhibit 2, Austria has a higher per capita GDP ($39,000) than does Germany ($34,400).

But even per capita GDP can be deceiving. When an economist states that the per capita GDP of, say, Austria, is $39,000, this is the dollar amount each person in Austria would have *if* the GDP of the country were divided up equally by the entire population—in other words, if everyone in the country had an equal slice of GDP.

But in actuality, not everyone in the country has an equal slice of GDP. Some people have a much smaller slice than other people. While one person may have a slice equal to $400,000, another person might have a slice equal to $7,000.

Finally, keep in mind the two ways we can witness an increase in GDP. GDP will rise if the inhabitants of a country actually produce more goods and services, and it will rise if output remains constant but only prices rise. A rise in GDP that is the result of only prices rising does not mean the same thing as a rise in GDP that is the result of prices remaining constant and output rising. Obviously, it means more to the overall standard of living of the people in the country if GDP rises because output is higher than because prices are higher.

The bottom line is that GDP is a useful economic variable, and it is readily measured and reported on. But we need to be careful that we don't use it incorrectly when making comparisons, discussing well-being, and so on.

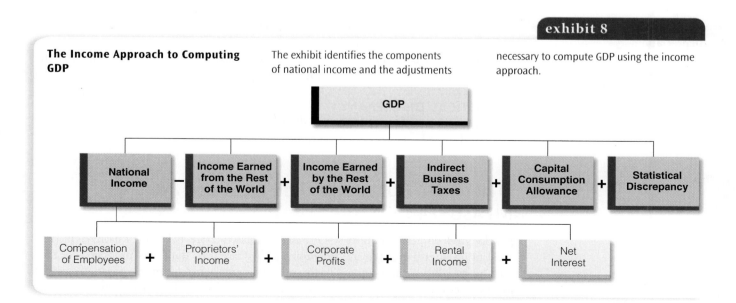

exhibit 8

The Income Approach to Computing GDP

The exhibit identifies the components of national income and the adjustments necessary to compute GDP using the income approach.

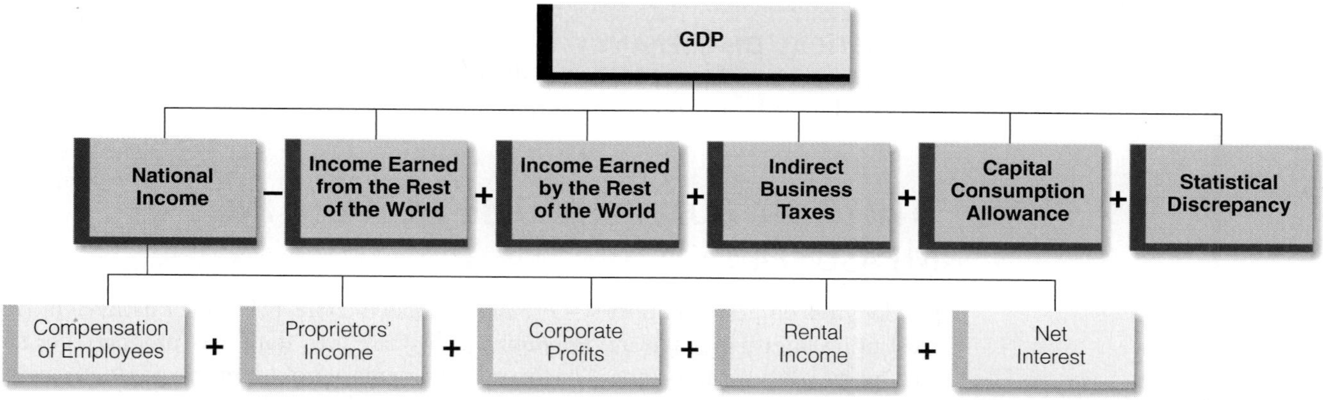

from national income to compute GDP. Keep the equation and exhibit in mind as you continue to read.

GDP = National income
− Income earned from the rest of the world
+ Income earned by the rest of the world
+ Indirect business taxes
+ Capital consumption allowance
+ Statistical discrepancy

INCOME EARNED FROM THE REST OF THE WORLD, INCOME EARNED BY THE REST OF THE WORLD Consider that when we compute national income, we include the income earned by U.S. citizens who work and live in other countries, but we do not include the income earned by foreigners who work and live in the United States. If we want to compute GDP, we have to adjust for both these incomes. We do so by (1) subtracting from national income the income earned from the rest of the world (this is income U.S. citizens living abroad earned by producing and selling goods) and (2) adding to national income the income earned by the rest of the world (this is income non-U.S. citizens earned by producing and selling goods in the United States).

INDIRECT BUSINESS TAXES The main items that comprise indirect business taxes are excise taxes, sales taxes, and property taxes. These taxes are not part of national income because they are not considered a payment to any resource (land, labor, etc.). You should think of them as "monies collected by government" and not as payment to land, labor, capital, or entrepreneurship.

These indirect taxes are included in purchases of goods and services (you pay a sales tax when you buy most goods) and so are included when the expenditure approach is used to compute GDP. Therefore, we must add indirect business taxes to national income.

CAPITAL CONSUMPTION ALLOWANCE Some capital goods are used up in the production process through natural wear, obsolescence, or accidental destruction (e.g., the machinery that breaks down and cannot be repaired). The cost to replace these capital goods is called the **capital consumption allowance**, or **depreciation**. We add the capital consumption allowance, or depreciation, to national income because we want a measure of all the income earned in the economy. National income, by itself, doesn't include the income payments implicit in the capital consumption allowance.

Capital Consumption Allowance (Depreciation)
The estimated amount of capital goods used up in production through natural wear, obsolescence, and accidental destruction.

STATISTICAL DISCREPANCY GDP and national income are computed using different sets of data. Hence, statistical discrepancies or pure computational errors often occur and must be accounted for in the national income accounts.

OTHER NATIONAL INCOME ACCOUNTING MEASUREMENTS

Besides gross domestic product (GDP) and national income, three other national income accounting measurements are important. They are net domestic product, personal income, and disposable income. The five measurements—gross domestic product, national income, net domestic product, personal income, and disposable income—are often used interchangeably to measure the output produced and income earned in an economy.

Net Domestic Product

If we use the expenditure approach to compute GDP, we add consumption, investment, government purchases, and net exports. Investment (or more specifically, gross private domestic investment) includes fixed investment and inventory investment. Some of the fixed investment, however, is used to replace worn-out or obsolete capital goods. It is not used for the production of new goods. In short, gross private domestic investment contains within it the capital consumption allowance. If we subtract the capital consumption allowance from GDP, we are left with **net domestic product (NDP)**. NDP measures the total value of new goods available in the economy in a given year after worn-out capital goods have been replaced.

Net Domestic Product (NDP)
GDP minus the capital consumption allowance.

Net domestic product (NDP) = GDP − Capital consumption allowance

Personal Income

Not all income earned is received, and not all income received is earned. An example of "income earned but not received" is undistributed profits. Undistributed profits are earned by stockholders but not received by them. Instead, the undistributed profits are usually reinvested by the corporation. An example of "income received but not earned" is Social Security benefits.

Personal income is the amount of income that individuals actually receive. It is equal to national income minus such major earned-but-not-received items as undistributed corporate profits, social insurance taxes (Social Security contributions), and corporate profits taxes, plus transfer payments (which are received but not earned).

Personal Income
The amount of income that individuals actually receive. It is equal to national income minus undistributed corporate profits, social insurance taxes, and corporate profits taxes, plus transfer payments.

Personal income = National income
− Undistributed corporate profits
− Social insurance taxes
− Corporate profits taxes
+ Transfer payments

In 2007, personal income in the United States was approximately $11.66 trillion.

Disposable Income

The portion of personal income that can be used for consumption or saving is referred to as disposable personal income or simply **disposable income**. It is equal to personal income minus personal taxes (especially income taxes). Sometimes, disposable income is referred to as spendable income, take-home pay, or after-tax income.

Disposable Income
The portion of personal income that can be used for consumption or saving. It is equal to personal income minus personal taxes (especially income taxes).

Disposable income = Personal income − Personal taxes

In 2007, disposable income in the United States was approximately $10.17 trillion.

SELF-TEST

1. Describe the expenditure approach to computing GDP in a real-world economy.
2. Will GDP be smaller than the sum of consumption, investment, and government purchases if net exports are negative? Explain your answer.
3. If GDP is $400 billion and the country's population is 100 million, does it follow that each individual in the country has $40,000 worth of goods and services?

REAL GDP

This section defines Real GDP, shows how to compute it, and then explains how it is used to measure economic growth.

Why We Need Real GDP

In 2006, U.S. GDP was about $13.19 trillion. One year later, in 2007, GDP was about $13.84 trillion. Although you know GDP was higher in 2007 than in 2006, do you know *the reason* GDP was higher in 2007 than in 2006?

As you think about your answer, let's look at GDP in a one-good economy. Suppose 10 units of this good are produced and each unit is sold for $10, so GDP in the economy is $100.

GDP = $10 × 10 units = $100

Now suppose GDP rises from $100 to $250. What caused it to rise? It could rise because price increased from $10 to $25:

GDP = $25 × 10 units = $250

Or it could rise because quantity of output produced increased from 10 units to 25 units:

GDP = $10 × 25 units = $250

Or it could rise because price increased to $12.50 and quantity increased to 20 units:

GDP = $12.50 × 20 units = $250

To gauge the health of the economy, economists want to know the reason for an increase in GDP. If GDP increased simply because price increased, then the economy is not growing. For an economy to grow, more output must be produced.

Because an increase in GDP can be due in part simply to an increase in price, a more meaningful measure is Real GDP. **Real GDP** is GDP adjusted for price changes.

Real GDP
The value of the entire output produced annually within a country's borders, adjusted for price changes.

Computing Real GDP

One way to compute Real GDP is to find the value of the output for the different years in terms of the same prices, the prices that existed in the base year. Let's look again at our one-good economy. Consider the following data.

Year	Price of Good X	Quantity Produced of Good X (units)	GDP
1	$10	100	$10 × 100 = **$1,000**
2	$12	120	$12 × 120 = **$1,440**
3	$14	140	$14 × 140 = **$1,960**

The data show why GDP is higher in subsequent years: GDP is higher because both price and quantity have increased. In other words, GDP rises because both price and quantity rise. Suppose we want to separate the part of GDP that is higher because quantity is higher from the part of GDP that is higher because price is higher. What we want then is Real GDP because Real GDP is the part of GDP that is higher because quantity (of output) is higher.

To compute Real GDP for any year, we simply multiply the quantity of the good produced in a given year by the price in the base year. Suppose we choose year 1 as the base year. So, to compute Real GDP in year 2, we simply multiply the quantity of the good produced in year 2 by the price of the good in year 1. To find Real GDP in year 3, we simply multiply the quantity of the good produced in year 3 by the price of the good in year 1.

Year	Price of Good X	Quantity Produced of Good X (units)	GDP	Real GDP
1 (Base Year)	$10	100	$10 × 100 = **$1,000**	$10 × 100 = **$1,000**
2	$12	120	$12 × 120 = **$1,440**	$10 × 120 = **$1,200**
3	$14	140	$14 × 140 = **$1,960**	$10 × 140 = **$1,400**

The General Equation for Real GDP

In the real world, there is more than one good and more than one price. The general equation used to compute Real GDP is:

$$\text{Real GDP} = \Sigma\ (\text{Base-year prices} \times \text{Current-year quantities})$$

Σ is the Greek capital letter sigma. Here it stands for summation. Thus, Real GDP is "the sum of all the current-year quantities times their base-year prices." In 2007, Real GDP in the United States was $11.56 trillion.

What Does It Mean if Real GDP Is Higher in One Year Than in Another Year?

If GDP is, say, $9 trillion in year 1 and $9.5 trillion in year 2, we cannot be sure why it has increased. Obviously, GDP can rise from one year to the next if (1) prices rise and output remains constant, (2) output rises and prices remain constant, or (3) prices and output rise.

However, if Real GDP is, say, $8 trillion in year 1 and $8.3 trillion in year 2, we know why it has increased. Real GDP rises only if output rises. In other words, Real GDP rises only if more goods and services are produced.

Real GDP, Economic Growth, and Business Cycles

Suppose there are two countries, A and B. In country A, Real GDP grows by 3 percent each year. In country B, Real GDP is the same each year: If Real GDP was $500 billion last year, it is $500 billion in the current year, and it will be $500 billion next year. In which of the two countries would you prefer to live, *ceteris paribus?*

Now consider another situation. Again suppose there are two countries, C and D. In country C, Real GDP takes a roller coaster ride: It alternates between rising and falling. It rises for some months, then falls, then rises again, then falls, and so on. In country D, Real GDP simply rises year after year. In which of the two countries would you prefer to live, *ceteris paribus?*

If you chose one country over the other in each of these two cases, then you are implicitly saying that Real GDP matters to you. One of the reasons economists study Real GDP is simply because Real GDP matters to you and others. In other words, because Real GDP is important to you, it is important to economists too.

Economists study two major macroeconomic topics that have to do with Real GDP. One topic is *economic growth;* the other is *business cycles.*

Economic Growth
Increases in Real GDP.

ECONOMIC GROWTH Annual **economic growth** has occurred if Real GDP in one year is higher than Real GDP in the previous year. For example, if Real GDP is $8.1 trillion in one year and $8.3 trillion in the next, the economy has witnessed economic growth. The growth rate is equal to the (positive) percentage change in Real GDP. The growth rate is computed using the following formula:

$$\text{Percentage change in Real GDP} = \left(\frac{\text{Real GDP}_{\text{later year}} - \text{Real GDP}_{\text{earlier year}}}{\text{Real GDP}_{\text{earlier year}}}\right) \times 100$$

Business cycle
Recurrent swings (up and down) in Real GDP.

THE "UPS AND DOWNS" IN THE ECONOMY, OR THE BUSINESS CYCLE If Real GDP is on a roller coaster—rising and falling and rising and falling—the economy is said to be incurring a **business cycle**. Economists usually talk about four or five phases of the business cycle. We identify five phases in the following list and in Exhibit 9.

1. *Peak.* At the *peak* of the business cycle, Real GDP is at a temporary high. In Exhibit 9, Real GDP is at a temporary high at Q_1.
2. *Contraction.* The *contraction* phase represents a decline in Real GDP. According to the standard definition of *recession,* two consecutive quarter declines in Real GDP constitute a recession.
3. *Trough.* The low point in Real GDP, just before it begins to turn up, is called the *trough* of the business cycle.
4. *Recovery.* The *recovery* is the period when Real GDP is rising. It begins at the trough and ends at the initial peak. The recovery in Exhibit 9 extends from the trough until Real GDP is again at Q_1.
5. *Expansion.* The *expansion* phase refers to increases in Real GDP beyond the recovery. In Exhibit 9, it refers to increases in Real GDP above Q_1.

exhibit 9

The Phases of the Business Cycle

The phases of a business cycle include the peak, contraction, trough, recovery, and expansion. A business cycle is measured from peak to peak.

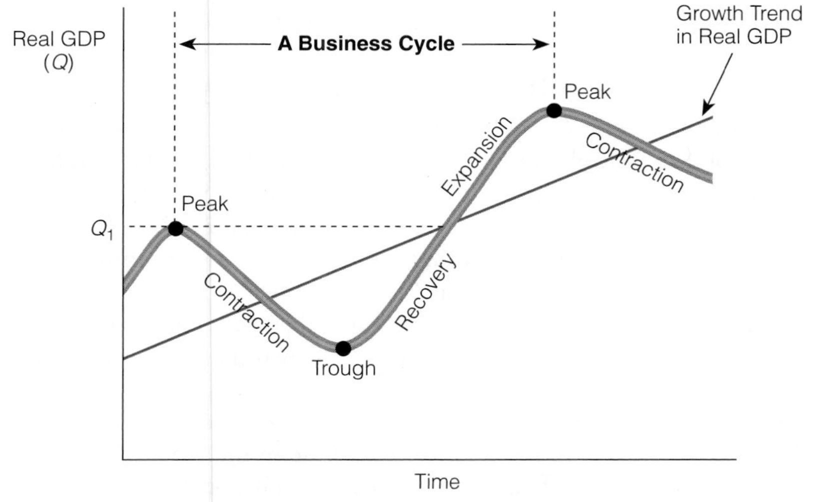

An entire business cycle is measured from peak to peak. The typical business cycle is approximately four to five years, although a few have been shorter and some have been longer.

Finding ECONOMICS

After Graduating from College

Yoram has just graduated from college. He has been searching for a job in his chosen field of accounting, but so far he hasn't been offered the job he would like. Where is the economics? The state (or health) of the economy is closely tied to whether business firms are hiring or firing. When the economy is growing, firms are usually hiring employees; when the economy is in a slump (a recession), firms are often firing employees. As far as one's job prospects go, it is better to be graduating when the economy is strong and growing than when it is weak and declining.

NBER AND RECESSIONS In the contraction stage of the business cycle, we state that the "standard" definition of a recession is two consecutive quarter declines in Real GDP. This is not, however, the only definition of a recession.

On November 26, 2001, the National Bureau of Economic Research, which dates the business cycle, issued a press release. The first paragraph read:

> *The NBER's Business Cycle Dating Committee has determined that a peak in business activity occurred in the U.S. economy in March 2001. A peak marks the end of an expansion and the beginning of a recession. The determination of a peak date in March is thus a determination that the expansion that began in March 1991 ended in March 2001 and a recession began. The expansion lasted exactly 10 years, the longest in the NBER's chronology.*

According to this statement, the U.S. economy entered a recession in March 2001. That's because according to the NBER "a peak marks the end of an expansion and the beginning of a recession," and March 2001 was dated by the NBER as the peak of the business cycle. In other words, the U.S. economy was in a recession even though Real GDP had not declined for two consecutive quarters.

The NBER definition is different from the standard definition of a recession. According to the NBER, "a recession is a significant decline in activity spread across the economy, lasting more than a few months, visible in industrial production, employment, real income, and wholesale-retail trade."

macro*theme* ➔ In the last chapter, we identified three macroeconomic categories, one of which was the P-Q category. The *P*, you may remember, stands for the price level, and the *Q* stands for Real GDP. In the last chapter, we discussed how to measure the price level, *P*. In this chapter, we have discussed how to measure GDP and Real GDP, and we have discussed economic growth and the business cycle. Everything we have discussed in this chapter can be translated into P-Q language and placed in the P-Q category. For example, GDP is really *P* times *Q*. Real GDP is *Q*. Economic growth is increasing *Q*, and the business cycle is recurrent swings up and down in *Q*.

SELF-TEST

1. Suppose GDP is $6 trillion in year 1 and $6.2 trillion in year 2. What has caused the rise in GDP?
2. Suppose Real GDP is $5.2 trillion in year 1 and $5.3 trillion in year 2. What has caused the rise in Real GDP?
3. Can an economy be faced with endless business cycles and still have its Real GDP grow over time? Explain your answer.

office hours

"WHY DO WE USE THE *EXPENDITURE* APPROACH TO MEASURE *PRODUCTION*?"

Student:

When GDP was first defined, emphasis was placed on goods and services being *produced*. The definition of GDP was "the total market value of all final goods and services *produced* annually within a country's borders."

Instructor:

Yes, that is correct.

Student:

But when we computed GDP, we simply summed the *expenditures* made by each of the four sectors of the economy. In other words, we added up consumption, investment, government purchases, and net exports.

Now here is my problem. When we define GDP we speak about production— final goods and services *produced*. But when we compute GDP, production doesn't seem to come up. Instead we sum *expenditures* made by the four sectors of the economy.

My point is a simple point: A good can be produced that is not purchased. So if we add up only expenditures (or purchases) aren't we underestimating production?

Instructor:

I see your point. What you are saying is that 100 chairs, say, are produced in the year, but if only 75 of the chairs are purchased, counting only purchases (or expenditures) underestimates production. And production is what we really want to get at because GDP is defined as the total market value of all final goods and services produced. . . .

Student:

Yes, that's right. That is what I am getting at.

Instructor:

Well, remember one important category of expenditures—investment. Investment consists of the expenditures of the business sector. Now we know that investment is the sum of fixed investment and inventory investment. Let's focus on inventory investment for a minute. Think of how goods might get into inventory. One way is for the firm to deliberately produce goods and put some into inventory. In other words, a company produces 1,000 chairs, sends 900 chairs to different retailers, and then puts 100 chairs in inventory. It places those 100 chairs in inventory in case there is an unexpected increase in demand for chairs. We'll call these 100 chairs that the firm deliberately puts into inventory "planned inventory."

Now think of another way that chairs can be added to inventory. Suppose when the firm sends those 900 chairs to different retailers, not all of the chairs sell. Suppose only 700 of the chairs sell. What will retailers do with the remaining 200 chairs? One thing they might do is return those chairs to the company they bought the chairs from. So 200 chairs are returned to the chair-producing firm. And what does the firm do with those 200 chairs. For now, they put those chairs into inventory. We'll call these 200 chairs that are returned to the firm "unplanned inventory."

Here is the important point: The 300 chairs in inventory (100 chairs that made up planned inventory and 200 chairs that made up unplanned inventory) are part of overall investment. In other words, if investment for the year equals $2.1 trillion (for the economy), the market value of the 300 chairs in inventory is part of that $2.1 trillion.

In other words, when computing GDP, we count those 300 chairs the same way we count the 700 chairs that were produced and were purchased. In short, everything produced in the economy is purchased by someone. The 300 chairs in our example were "purchased" by the firm that produced the chairs.

Student:

But isn't that cheating somehow? After all, the 300 chairs weren't actually sold to anyone. They certainly weren't sold in the way we usually think of something being sold.

Instructor:

That's true. But remember what we are trying to get at with GDP. We are trying to get at the total market value of all final goods and services produced, and those 300 chairs were certainly produced. Looking at the 300 chairs as being purchased by the firm that produced them is simply a way of counting those 300 chairs. And counting those 300 chairs is what we want to do when we are trying to measure GDP.

Student:

Yes, I see that now.

Points to Remember

1. GDP is the total market value of all final goods and services *produced* annually within a country's borders.
2. We can use the expenditure approach to measure production as long as all goods and services produced but not sold to final consumers are considered to be "purchased" by the firm that produced them.

a reader asks

Where Can I Find the Most Recent Economic Data?

I've been learning about the CPI, GDP, the components of GDP, national income, and so on. Where can I find the recent data on these economic variables and others?

Your best bet for finding recent economic data is the Internet. The Economic Report of the President website at http://www.gpoaccess.gov/eop/index.html is a good place to start. Once at the site, click "Downloadable Reports/Tables" and then on the most recent year under "Statistical Tables."

Another good website you may want to visit is Economagic.com at http://www.economagic.com/. If you click the "Most Requested Series" link at this site, you will find data on prices, GDP, Real GDP, and so on.

If you are interested in business cycle data, go to the National Bureau of Economic Research website at http://www.nber.org/, click "Data," and then "Business Cycle Dates."

Finally, here is a short list of other websites where you can find economic data:

- Economics Statistics Briefing Room at http://www.whitehouse.gov/fsbr/esbr.html
- Bureau of Economic Analysis at http://www.bea.gov/
- Bureau of Labor Statistics at http://stats.bls.gov/
- Congressional Budget Office at http://www.cbo.gov/
- U.S. Census Bureau at http://www.census.gov/

Chapter Summary

GROSS DOMESTIC PRODUCT

- Gross domestic product (GDP) is the total market value of all final goods and services produced annually within a country's borders.
- Any one of the following can be used to compute GDP: (1) expenditure approach, (2) income approach, or (3) value-added approach.
- To avoid the problem of double counting, only final goods and services are counted in GDP.
- GDP omits certain nonmarket goods and services, both legal and illegal underground activities, the sale of used goods, financial transactions, transfer payments, and leisure (even though leisure is a good). Finally, GDP is not adjusted for the bads (e.g., pollution) that sometimes accompany production.

EXPENDITURES

- The expenditures on U.S. goods and services include consumption; gross private domestic investment, or investment; government consumption expenditures and gross investment, or government purchases; and net exports (exports–imports).
- Consumption includes spending on durable goods, nondurable goods, and services.
- Investment includes purchases of newly produced capital goods (fixed investment), changes in business inventories (inventory investment), and the purchases of new residential housing (also fixed investment).
- Government purchases include federal, state, and local government purchases of goods and services and gross investment in highways, bridges, and so on. Government purchases do not include transfer payments.
- Net exports equal the total foreign spending on domestic goods (exports) minus the total domestic spending on foreign goods (imports).

COMPUTING GDP

- Using the expenditure approach, GDP $= C + I + G + (EX - IM)$. In other words, GDP equals consumption plus investment plus government purchases plus net exports.
- Using the income approach, GDP = National income − Income earned from the rest of the world + Income earned by the rest of the world + Indirect business taxes + Capital consumption allowance + Statistical discrepancy.

MEASUREMENTS OTHER THAN GDP

- Net domestic product (NDP) equals gross domestic product (GDP) minus the capital consumption allowance.

NDP = GDP − Capital consumption allowance

- National income equals the sum of resource, or factor, payments.

National income = Compensation of employees
+ Proprietors' income
+ Corporate profits
+ Rental income
+ Net interest

- Personal income equals national income minus undistributed corporate profits, social insurance taxes, and corporate profits taxes, plus transfer payments.

Personal Income = National income
− Undistributed corporate profits
− Social insurance taxes
− Corporate profits taxes
+ Transfer payments

- Disposable Income = Personal income − Personal taxes

REAL GDP

- Real GDP is GDP adjusted for price changes. It is GDP in base-year dollars.

ECONOMIC GROWTH AND BUSINESS CYCLES

- Annual economic growth has occurred if Real GDP in one year is higher than Real GDP in the previous year.
- There are five phases to the business cycle: peak, contraction, trough, recovery, and expansion. A complete business cycle is measured from peak to peak.

Key Terms and Concepts

Gross Domestic Product (GDP)
Final Good
Intermediate Good
Double Counting
Value Added
Transfer Payment
Consumption
Investment
Inventory Investment
Fixed Investment
Government Purchases
Government Transfer Payments
Imports
Exports
Net Exports
National Income
Capital Consumption Allowance (Depreciation)
Net Domestic Product (NDP)
Personal Income
Disposable Income
Real GDP
Economic Growth
Business Cycle

Questions and Problems

1 "I just heard on the news that GDP is higher this year than it was last year. This means that we're better off this year than last year." Comment.

2 Which of the following are included in the calculation of this year's GDP?

a. Twelve-year-old Johnny mows his family's lawn.
b. Dave Malone buys a used car.
c. Barbara Wilson buys a bond issued by General Motors.
d. Ed Ferguson receives a Social Security payment.
e. An illegal drug transaction takes place at the corner of Elm and Fifth.

3 Discuss the problems you see in comparing the GDPs of two countries, say, the United States and the People's Republic of China.

4 The manuscript for this book was keyed by the author. Had he hired someone to do the keying, GDP would have been higher than it was. What other activities would increase GDP if they were done differently? What activities would decrease GDP if they were done differently?

5 Why does GDP omit the sales of used goods? of financial transactions? of government transfer payments?

6 A business firm produces a good this year that it doesn't sell. As a result, the good is added to the firm's inventory. How does this inventory good find its way into GDP?

7 Economists prefer to compare Real GDP figures for different years instead of comparing GDP figures. Why?

8 What is the difference between a recovery and an expansion?

9 Define each of the following terms:

a. Contraction.
b. Business cycle.
c. Trough.
d. Disposable income.
e. Net domestic product.

10 Explain why GDP can be computed either by measuring spending or by measuring income.

11 Does the expenditure approach to computing GDP measure U.S. spending on all goods, U.S. spending on only U.S. goods, or U.S. and foreign spending on only U.S. goods? Explain your answer.

12 In the first quarter of the year, Real GDP was \$400 billion; in the second quarter, it was \$398 billion; in the third quarter, it was \$399 billion; and in the fourth quarter, it was \$395 billion. Has there been a recession? Explain your answer.

Working with Numbers and Graphs

1 Net exports are –$114 billion and exports are $857 billion. What are imports?

2 Consumption spending is $3.708 trillion, spending on nondurable goods is $1.215 trillion, and spending on services is $2.041 trillion. What does spending on durable goods equal?

3 Inventory investment is $62 billion and (total) investment is $1.122 trillion. What does fixed investment equal?

4 In year 1, the prices of goods X, Y, and Z are $2, $4, and $6 per unit, respectively. In year 2, the prices of goods X, Y, and Z are $3, $4, and $7, respectively. In year 2, twice as many units of each good are produced as in year 1. In year 1, 20 units of X, 40 units of Y, and 60 units of Z are produced. If year 1 is the base year, what does Real GDP equal in year 2?

5 Nondurable goods spending = $400 million, durable goods spending = $300 million, new residential housing spending = $200 million, and spending on services = $500 million. What does consumption equal?

6 According to the circular flow diagram in Exhibit 6, consumption spending flows into U.S. product markets but import spending does not. But U.S. households buy imported goods in U.S. markets, don't they? Explain.

7 How would you redraw the circular flow diagram in Exhibit 6 if you wanted to show (a) taxes that firms and households pay to government and (b) transfer payments that government makes to households?

8 National income = $500 billion, income earned from the rest of the world = $10 billion, income earned by the rest of the world = $12 billion, indirect business taxes = $2 billion, capital consumption allowance = $1 billion, and GDP = $525 billion. What does the statistical discrepancy equal?

9 GDP = $100 billion, NDP = $95 billion, and investment = $33 billion. What does the capital consumption allowance equal?

10 If Real GDP in year 1 is $487 billion and it is $498 billion in year 2, what is the economic growth rate equal to?

11 The following figure shows a business cycle. Identify each of the following as a phase of the business cycle:

a. Point A.

b. Between point A and point B.

c. Point B.

d. Between point B and point C.

e. Point D.

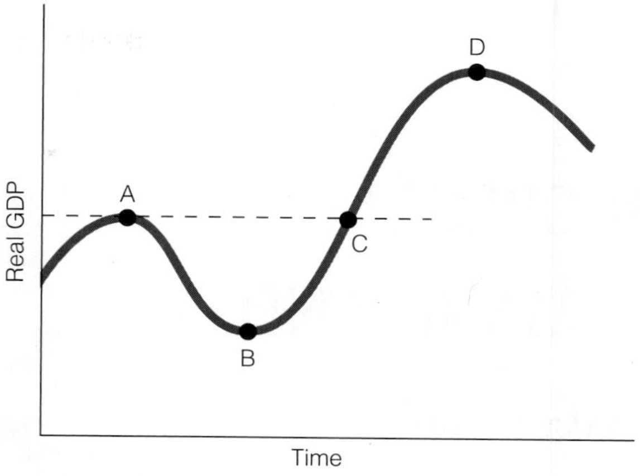

12 Using the following data, calculate (a) gross domestic product (GDP), (b) net domestic product (NDP), (c) national income (NI), (d) personal income (PI). All numbers are in billions of dollars.

Consumption	$1,149.5
Investment	400.3
Government purchases	425.3
Net exports	89.1
Capital consumption allowance	303.8
Indirect business taxes	213.3
Statistical discrepancy	4.4
Social Security insurance taxes	216.5
Transfer payments	405.6
Undistributed profits	91.0
Corporate profits taxes	77.7
Personal taxes	340.0
Dividends	0.0
Compensation of employees	800.0
Income earned from the rest of the world	50.0
Income earned by the rest of the world	56.0
Proprietors' income	400.0
Rental income	145.0
Net interest	23.0

© COMSTOCK/JUPITER IMAGES

CHAPTER 7

AGGREGATE DEMAND AND AGGREGATE SUPPLY

Introduction Businesses make decisions based on what is happening in the economy today and on what they expect will happen in the economy in the future. For example, their profitability is based in part on the wages they must pay their employees, the prices of their nonlabor inputs, the productivity of their workers, and business taxes. If they want to expand in the future, they must consider all these things and also try to predict their future sales. If they trade overseas, they must worry about exchange rates and foreign real national income. We examine all such things and more in this chapter.

THE TWO SIDES TO AN ECONOMY

Just as there are two sides to a market, a buying side (demand) and a selling side (supply), there are two sides to an economy. There is a demand side and a supply side. The demand in an economy is referred to as *aggregate demand* (*AD*); the supply is referred to as *aggregate supply* (*AS*).

The *AD-AS* framework has three parts: (1) aggregate demand (*AD*), (2) short-run aggregate supply (*SRAS*), and (3) long-run aggregate supply (*LRAS*). We begin with a discussion of aggregate demand.

AGGREGATE DEMAND

Aggregate Demand
The quantity demanded of all goods and services (Real GDP) at different price levels, *ceteris paribus.*

Recall from the last chapter that people, firms, and governments buy U.S. goods and services. **Aggregate demand** refers to the quantity demanded of these (U.S.) goods and services, or the quantity demanded of (U.S.) Real GDP, at various price levels, *ceteris paribus.* For example, the following whole set of data represents aggregate demand:

Aggregate Demand

Price Index	Quantity Demanded of Goods and Services (Quantity Demanded of Real GDP)
100	$1,200 billion worth of goods and services
110	$1,000 billion worth of goods and services
120	$800 billion worth of goods and services

An **aggregate demand (*AD*) curve** is the graphical representation of aggregate demand. An *AD* curve is shown in Exhibit 1. Notice that it is downward sloping, indicating an inverse relationship between the price level (*P*) and the quantity demanded of Real GDP (*Q*): As the price level rises, the quantity demanded of Real GDP falls, and as the price level falls, the quantity demanded of Real GDP rises, *ceteris paribus.*

Aggregate Demand (*AD*) Curve
A curve that shows the quantity demanded of all goods and services (Real GDP) at different price levels, *ceteris paribus.*

Real Balance Effect
The change in the purchasing power of dollar-denominated assets that results from a change in the price level.

Monetary Wealth
The value of a person's monetary assets. Wealth, as distinguished from monetary wealth, refers to the value of all assets owned, both monetary and nonmonetary. In short, a person's wealth equals his or her monetary wealth (e.g., $1,000 cash) plus nonmonetary wealth (e.g., a car or a house).

Purchasing Power
The quantity of goods and services that can be purchased with a unit of money. Purchasing power and the price level are inversely related: As the price level goes up (down), purchasing power goes down (up).

Why Does the Aggregate Demand Curve Slope Downward?

Asking why the *AD* curve slopes downward is the same as asking why there is an inverse relationship between the price level and the quantity demanded of Real GDP. This inverse relationship, and the resulting downward slope of the *AD* curve, is explained by the real balance effect, the interest rate effect, and the international trade effect.

REAL BALANCE EFFECT (DUE TO A CHANGE IN THE PRICE LEVEL) The **real balance effect** states that the inverse relationship between the price level and the quantity demanded of Real GDP is established through changes in the value of **monetary wealth**, or money holdings.

To illustrate, consider a person who has $50,000 in cash. Suppose the price level falls. As this happens, the **purchasing power** of the person's $50,000 rises. That is, the $50,000, which once could buy 100 television sets at $500 each, can now buy 125 sets at $400 each. An increase in the purchasing power of the person's $50,000 is identical to saying that his monetary wealth has increased. (After all, isn't the $50,000 more valuable when it can buy more than when it can buy less?) And as he becomes wealthier, he buys more goods.

In summary, a fall in the price level causes purchasing power to rise, which increases a person's monetary wealth. As people become wealthier, the quantity demanded of Real GDP rises.

Suppose the price level rises. As this happens, the purchasing power of the $50,000 falls. That is, the $50,000, which once could buy 100 television sets at $500 each, can now buy 80 sets at $625 each. A decrease in the purchasing power of the person's $50,000 is identical to saying that his monetary wealth has decreased. And as he becomes less wealthy, he buys fewer goods.

In summary, a rise in the price level causes purchasing power to fall, which decreases a person's monetary wealth. As people become less wealthy, the quantity demanded of Real GDP falls.

exhibit 1

The Aggregate Demand Curve

The aggregate demand curve is downward sloping, specifying an inverse relationship between the price level and the quantity demanded of Real GDP.

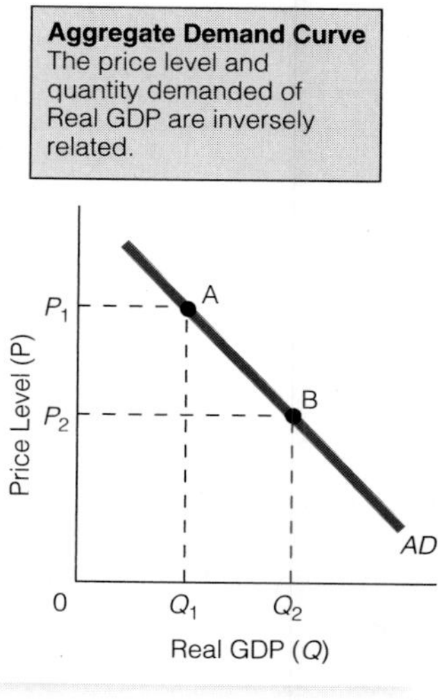

INTEREST RATE EFFECT (DUE TO A CHANGE IN THE PRICE LEVEL) The **interest rate effect** states that the inverse relationship between the price level and the quantity demanded of Real GDP is established through changes in household and business spending that is sensitive to changes in interest rates.

Let's consider a person who buys a fixed bundle of goods (food, clothing, and shelter) each week. Suppose the price level falls, increasing the purchasing power of the person's money. With more purchasing power (per dollar), she can purchase her fixed bundle of goods with less money. What does she do with (part of) this increase in her monetary wealth? She saves it. In terms of simple supply-and-demand analysis, the supply of credit increases. Subsequently, the price of credit, which is the interest rate, drops. As the

Interest Rate Effect
The changes in household and business buying as the interest rate changes (which, in turn, is a reflection of a change in the demand for or supply of credit brought on by price level changes).

interest rate drops, households and businesses borrow more, so they end up buying more goods. Thus, the quantity demanded of Real GDP rises.

Now suppose the price level rises, decreasing the purchasing power of the person's money. With less purchasing power (per dollar), she cannot purchase her fixed bundle of goods with the same amount of money. If she wants to continue to buy the fixed bundle of goods, she will need to acquire more money. In an effort to acquire more money, she goes to a bank and requests a loan. In terms of simple supply-and-demand analysis, the demand for credit increases. Subsequently, the interest rate rises. As the interest rate rises, households borrow less to finance, say, automobile purchases, and firms borrow less to finance new capital goods spending. Thus, the quantity demanded of Real GDP falls.

International Trade Effect
The change in foreign sector spending as the price level changes.

INTERNATIONAL TRADE EFFECT (DUE TO A CHANGE IN THE PRICE LEVEL) The **international trade effect** states that the inverse relationship between the price level and the quantity demanded of Real GDP is established through foreign sector spending, which includes U.S. spending on foreign goods (imports) and foreign spending on U.S. goods (exports).

Suppose the price level in the United States falls. As this happens, U.S. goods become relatively cheaper than foreign goods. As a result, both Americans and foreigners buy more U.S. goods. The quantity demanded of (U.S.) Real GDP rises.

Suppose the price level in the United States rises. As this happens, U.S. goods become relatively more expensive than foreign goods. As a result, both Americans and foreigners buy fewer U.S. goods. The quantity demanded of (U.S.) Real GDP falls.

For a review of the three effects—real balance, interest rate, and international trade—see Exhibit 2.

Finding ECONOMICS

While Buying a Swiss Watch

Jim is in a store buying a watch made in Switzerland. What does this have to do with a downward-sloping aggregate demand curve? Well, when we ask Jim why he's buying a Swiss watch, he tells us that it's because the Swiss watch is cheaper than the American watch. But why is this? It could very well be because the U.S. price level has recently risen relative to the Swiss price level. In other words, when Jim buys the Swiss watch instead of the American watch, what we could be watching is the international trade effect in action.

ONE IMPORTANT WORD ON THE THREE EFFECTS We explained that the aggregate demand curve is downward sloping because of the real balance, interest rate, and international trade effects. Keep in mind what caused these three effects: a change in the price level. In other words, when we were discussing, say, the interest rate effect, we were discussing the interest rate effect *of a change in the price level.*

Price level changes → Interest rate effect

Why is this an important point? Because the interest rate can change due to things *other than* the price level changing, and not everything that changes the interest rate leads to a movement from one point to another point on the *AD* curve. Some things that change the interest rate can lead to a shift in the *AD* curve instead. We will have more to say about this later. For now, though, we ask that you simply keep in mind the cause of each of the three effects we discussed. That cause was a change in the price level—the variable on the vertical axis in Exhibit 1.

exhibit 2

Why the Aggregate Demand Curve Is Downward Sloping

This exhibit outlines the three effects that explain why the *AD* curve is downward sloping. Each effect relates to a change in the price level (*P*) leading to a change in the quantity demanded of Real GDP (*Q*).

Type of Effect	How It Works	Graphical Representation of What Happens
Real Balance in Effect (due to a change in the price level)	***Price level falls*** → purchasing power rises → monetary wealth rises → **buy more goods.**	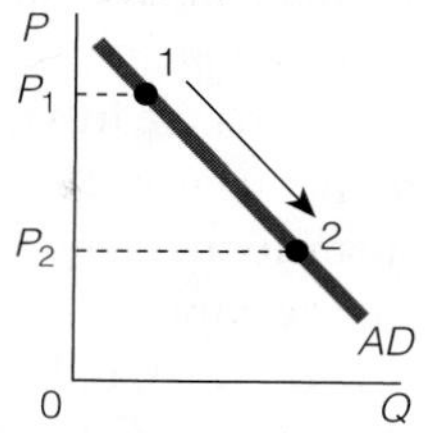
	Price level rises → purchasing power falls → monetary wealth falls → **buy fewer goods.**	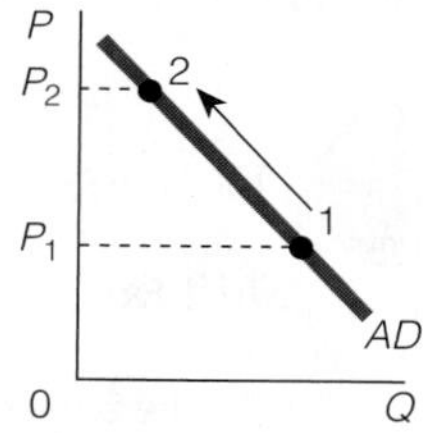
Interest Rate Effect (due to a change in the price level)	***Price level falls*** → purchasing power rises → less money needed to buy fixed bundle of goods → save more → supply of credit rises → interest rate falls → businesses and households borrow more at lower interest rate → **buy more goods.**	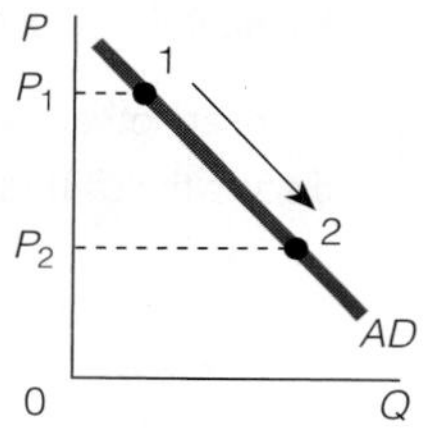
	Price level rises → purchasing power falls → borrow money in order to continue to buy fixed bundle of goods → demand for credit rises → interest rate rises → businesses and households borrow less at higher interest rate → **buy fewer goods.**	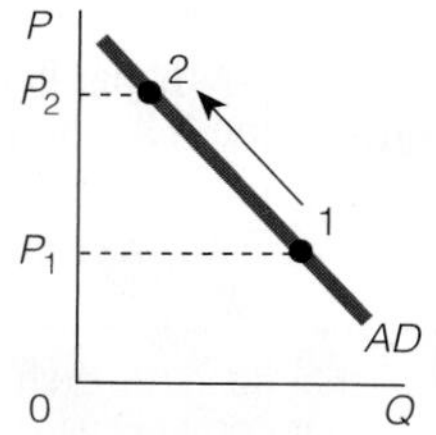
International Trade Effect (due to a change in the price level)	***Price level in U.S. falls*** relative to foreign price levels → U.S. goods relatively less expensive than foreign goods → both Americans and foreigners **buy more U.S. goods.**	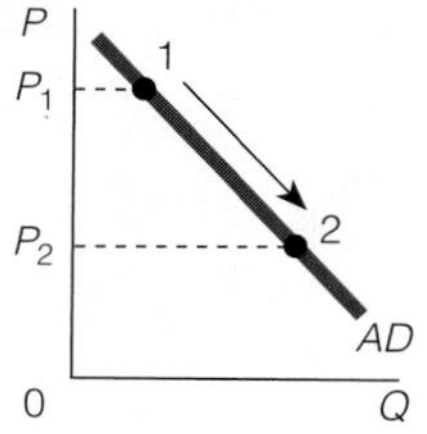
	Price level in U.S. rises relative to foreign price levels → U.S. goods relatively more expensive than foreign goods → both Americans and foreigners **buy fewer U.S. goods.**	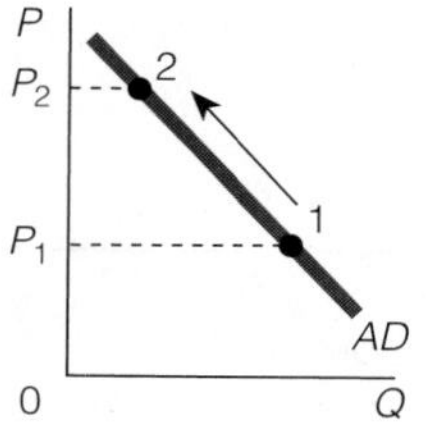

A Change in the Quantity Demanded of Real GDP Versus a Change in Aggregate Demand

A change in the quantity demanded of Real GDP is brought about by a change in the price level. As the price level falls, the quantity demanded of Real GDP rises, *ceteris paribus.* In Exhibit 3(a), a change in the quantity demanded of Real GDP is represented as a *movement* from one point (A) on AD_1 to another point (B) on AD_1.

A change in aggregate demand is represented in Exhibit 3(b) as a *shift* in the aggregate demand curve from AD_1 to AD_2. Notice that when the aggregate demand curve shifts, the quantity demanded of Real GDP changes even though the price level remains constant. For example, at a price level (index number) of 180, the quantity demanded of Real GDP on AD_1 in Exhibit 3(b) is \$6.0 trillion. But at the same price level (180), the quantity demanded of Real GDP on AD_2 is \$6.5 trillion.

Thinking like AN ECONOMIST

Shift Factors Versus Movement Factors, Once Again

To the economist, not all factors are alike. Some factors move us from one point on a curve to another point on the same curve. These are movement factors. The price level is a movement factor. Raise it, and we move up the *AD* curve; lower it, and we move down the *AD* curve.

There are other factors which, if they change, shift curves. These are shift factors. We turn now to discuss the shift factors with respect to the *AD* curve.

exhibit 3

A Change in the Quantity Demanded of Real GDP Versus a Change in Aggregate Demand

(a) A change in the quantity demanded of Real GDP is graphically represented as a *movement* from one point, A, on AD_1 to another point, B, on AD_1. A change in the quantity demanded of Real GDP is the result of a change in the price level. (b) A change in aggregate demand is graphically represented as a *shift* in the aggregate demand curve from AD_1 to AD_2.

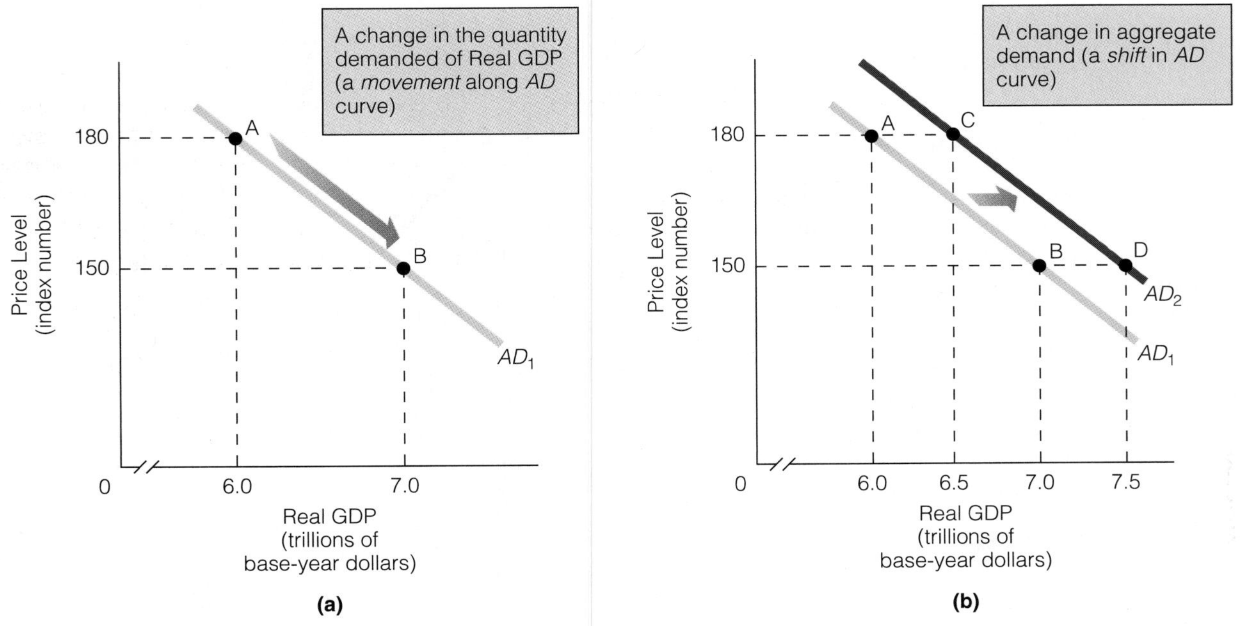

Changes in Aggregate Demand: Shifts in the *AD* Curve

What can change aggregate demand? In other words, what can cause aggregate demand to rise and what can cause it to fall?

The simple answer is that aggregate demand changes when the spending on U.S. goods and services changes. If spending increases at a given price level, aggregate demand rises; if spending decreases at a given price level, aggregate demand falls. For example, suppose the price level in the economy is represented by the consumer price index and the index is currently 150 (CPI = 150). At this price level, U.S. residents, firms, and governments, along with foreigners, foreign firms, and foreign governments, want to buy, say, $7.0 trillion worth of U.S. goods and services. Then something changes, and all of a sudden, they want to buy $7.5 trillion worth of U.S. goods and services. Now, before you conclude that they want to buy more goods and services because the prices of goods and services have fallen, keep in mind that we haven't lowered the price level. The price level is still represented by the CPI, and it is still 150. In other words, all these people, firms, and governments want to buy more U.S. goods even though the prices of the goods and services have not changed.

When individuals, firms, and governments want to buy more U.S. goods and services even though the prices of these goods have not changed, then we say that aggregate demand has increased. As a result, the *AD* curve shifts to the right. Of course, when individuals, firms, and governments want to buy fewer U.S. goods and services at a given price level, then we say that aggregate demand has decreased. As a result, the *AD* curve shifts to the left.

Let's look again at Exhibit 3(b), which shows a change in aggregate demand (a shift in the *AD* curve). At point B, the price level is 150, and total expenditures on U.S. goods and services are $7.0 trillion. At point D, the price level is still 150, but total expenditures on U.S. goods and services have increased to $7.5 trillion. Why has aggregate demand moved from point B to point D; that is, what has caused the increase in total expenditures? To find out, we have to look at the components of total expenditures.

How Spending Components Affect Aggregate Demand

The last chapter identified four major spending components: consumption, investment, government purchases, and net exports. Let's keep the numbers simple and let $C = \$100$, $I = \$100$, $G = \$100$, $EX = \$50$, and $IM = \$15$. If $EX = \$50$ and $IM = \$15$, it follows that net exports (NX) equal the difference, or $35.

Using these dollar figures, we calculate that $335 is spent on U.S. goods and services. We get this dollar amount by finding the sum of consumption, investment, government purchases, and net exports.

$$\text{Total expenditures on U.S. goods and services} = C + I + G + NX$$

Obviously, this dollar amount will go up if (1) C rises, (2) I rises, (3) G rises, or (4) NX rises. In other words, a rise in consumption, investment, government purchases, or net exports will raise spending on U.S. goods and services:

$$C\uparrow, I\uparrow, G\uparrow, NX\uparrow \rightarrow \text{Total expenditures on U.S. goods and services}\uparrow$$

Now, what will cause spending on U.S. goods to go down? Obviously, it will decline if (1) C falls, (2) I falls, (3) G falls, or (4) NX falls.

$$C\downarrow, I\downarrow, G\downarrow, NX\downarrow \rightarrow \text{Total expenditures on U.S. goods and services}\downarrow$$

exhibit 4

Changes in Aggregate Demand

The flow charts show how aggregate demand changes given changes in various spending components. C = Consumption, I = Investment, G = Government purchases, NX = Net exports, EX = Exports, IM = Imports. Keep in mind that $NX = EX - IM$.

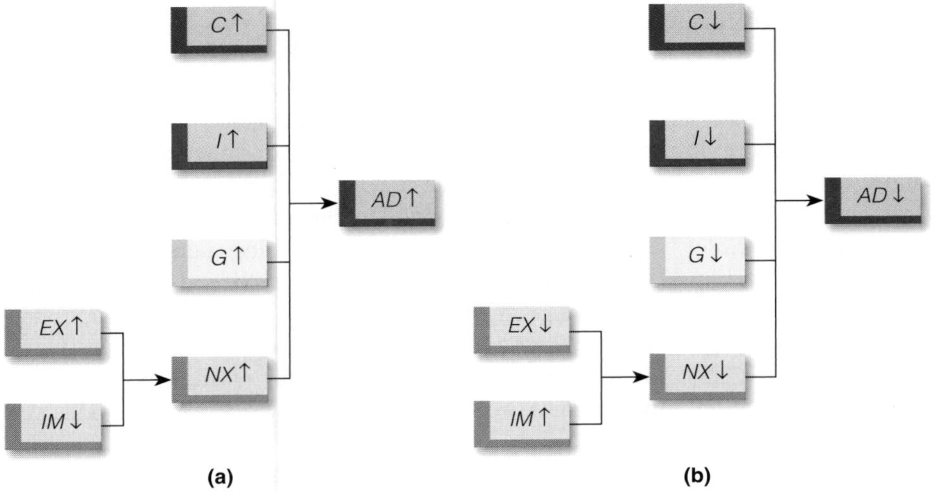

Because we now know what causes total expenditures on U.S. goods and services to change, we can relate the components of spending to (U.S.) aggregate demand. If, *at a given price level,* consumption, investment, government purchases, or net exports rise, aggregate demand will rise and the *AD* curve will shift to the right. If, *at a given price level,* consumption, investment, government purchases, or net exports fall, aggregate demand will fall and the *AD* curve will shift to the left. We can write these relationships as:

If, at a given price level, $C\uparrow$, $I\uparrow$, $G\uparrow$, $NX\uparrow$ then $AD\uparrow$

If, at a given price level, $C\downarrow$, $I\downarrow$, $G\downarrow$, $NX\downarrow$ then $AD\downarrow$

The flow charts in Exhibit 4 show how changes in spending components affect aggregate demand.

Factors That Can Change *C, I, G,* and *NX* (*EX* – *IM*) and Therefore Can Change *AD*

What can change aggregate demand (*AD*) in the economy? You know that the answer is a change in consumption, investment, government purchases, or net exports (exports minus imports). So, for example, if someone asks you why *AD* increased, you may say because consumption (*C*) increased.

But suppose the person then asks, "But what caused consumption to increase?" In other words, your answer to one question simply leads to another question. If a change in consumption changes aggregate demand, what changes consumption? The same question can be asked about changes in investment, government purchases, and net exports (which means exports and imports). For example, if aggregate demand increased because investment increased, then what caused investment to increase?

This section looks at some of the (many) factors that can change consumption, investment, and net exports. A later chapter considers the factors that can change government purchases.

CONSUMPTION Four factors that can affect consumption are wealth, expectations about future prices and income, the interest rate, and income taxes.

1. *Wealth.* Individuals consume not only on the basis of their present income but also on the basis of their **wealth.** Consider two individuals, each receiving an income of $80,000 a year. One has $75,000 in the bank, and the other has no assets at all. Which would you expect to spend more of her income on consumption goods this year? We would expect the person with the $75,000 in the bank to consume more. Greater wealth makes individuals feel financially more secure and thus more willing to spend.

   Increases in wealth lead to increases in consumption. If consumption increases, then aggregate demand rises and the *AD* curve shifts to the right. What will happen if wealth decreases? Decreases in wealth lead to a fall in consumption, which leads to a fall in aggregate demand. Consequently, the *AD* curve shifts to the left.

   Wealth ↑ → *C*↑ → *AD*↑
   Wealth ↓ → *C*↓ → *AD*↓

Wealth
The value of all assets owned, both monetary and nonmonetary.

2. *Expectations about future prices and income.* If individuals expect higher prices in the future, they increase current consumption expenditures to buy goods at the lower current prices. This increase in consumption leads to an increase in aggregate demand. If individuals expect lower prices in the future, they decrease current consumption expenditures. This reduction in consumption leads to a decrease in aggregate demand.

   Similarly, expectation of a higher future income increases consumption, which leads to an increase in aggregate demand. Expectation of a lower future income decreases consumption, which leads to a decrease in aggregate demand.

   Expect higher future prices → *C*↑ → *AD*↑
   Expect lower future prices → *C*↓ → *AD*↓
   Expect higher future income → *C*↑ → *AD*↑
   Expect lower future income → *C*↓ → *AD*↓

3. *Interest rate.* Current empirical work shows that spending on consumer durables is sensitive to the interest rate. Many of these items are financed by borrowing, so an increase in the interest rate increases the monthly payment amounts linked to their purchase and thereby reduces their consumption. This reduction in consumption leads to a decline in aggregate demand. Alternatively, a decrease in the interest rate reduces monthly payment amounts linked to the purchase of durable goods and thereby increases their consumption. This increase in consumption leads to an increase in aggregate demand.

   Interest rate ↑ → *C*↓ → *AD*↓
   Interest rate ↓ → *C*↑ → *AD*↑

4. *Income taxes.* Let's consider personal income taxes, the tax a person pays on the income he or she earns. As income taxes rise, disposable income decreases. When people have less take-home pay to spend, consumption falls. Consequently, aggregate demand decreases. A decrease in income taxes has the opposite effect; it raises disposable income. When people have more take-home pay to spend, consumption rises and aggregate demand increases.

   Income taxes ↑ → *C*↓ → *AD*↓
   Income taxes ↓ → *C*↑ → *AD*↑

Finding ECONOMICS

In a Housing Downturn

Suppose you read the following words in a newspaper: "Housing prices have fallen over the past six months and economists are concerned that this might lead to less overall demand in the economy." Can you find the economics here? Do housing prices have anything to do with aggregate demand? Well, let's work backward. We know that a decline in aggregate demand can be caused by a decline in consumption. Second, we know that a decline in consumption can be caused by a change in any of the four factors we have just discussed: wealth, expectations about future prices and income, the interest rate, and income taxes. Let's focus on wealth. We know that if housing prices fall, people who own houses will find themselves with less overall wealth. (Think of a person whose house is worth $500,000 one month and $450,000 six months later. She has suffered a decline in wealth.) As a result, these people will end up reducing their consumption and aggregate demand will fall.

INVESTMENT Three factors that can change investment are the interest rate, expectations about future sales, and business taxes.

1. *Interest rate.* Changes in interest rates affect business decisions. As the interest rate rises, the cost of a given investment project rises and businesses invest less. As investment decreases, aggregate demand decreases. On the other hand, as the interest rate falls, the cost of a given investment project falls and businesses invest more. Consequently, aggregate demand increases.

   Interest rate $\uparrow \rightarrow I\downarrow \rightarrow AD\downarrow$

   Interest rate $\downarrow \rightarrow I\uparrow \rightarrow AD\uparrow$

2. *Expectations about future sales.* Businesses invest because they expect to sell the goods they produce. If businesses become optimistic about future sales, investment spending grows and aggregate demand increases. If businesses become pessimistic about future sales, investment spending contracts and aggregate demand decreases.

   Businesses become optimistic about future sales $\rightarrow I\uparrow \rightarrow AD\uparrow$

   Businesses become pessimistic about future sales $\rightarrow I\downarrow \rightarrow AD\downarrow$

3. *Business taxes.* Businesses naturally consider expected after-tax profits when making their investment decisions. An increase in business taxes lowers expected profitability. With less profit expected, businesses invest less. As investment spending declines, aggregate demand declines. A decrease in business taxes, on the other hand, raises expected profitability and investment spending. This increases aggregate demand.

   Business taxes $\uparrow \rightarrow I\downarrow \rightarrow AD\downarrow$

   Business taxes $\downarrow \rightarrow I\uparrow \rightarrow AD\uparrow$

NET EXPORTS Two factors that can change net exports are foreign real national income and the exchange rate.

1. *Foreign real national income.* Just as Americans earn a national income, so do people in other countries. There is a foreign national income. By adjusting this foreign national income for price changes, we obtain foreign real national income. As foreign real national income rises, foreigners buy more U.S. goods and services. Thus, U.S. exports (EX) rise. As exports rise, net exports rise, *ceteris paribus.* As net exports rise, aggregate demand increases.

This process works in reverse too. As foreign real national income falls, foreigners buy fewer U.S. goods and exports fall. This lowers net exports, which reduces aggregate demand.

Foreign real national income ↑ → U.S. exports ↑ → U.S. net exports ↑ → *AD* ↑
Foreign real national income ↓ → U.S. exports ↓ → U.S. net exports ↓ → *AD* ↓

2. *Exchange rate.* The **exchange rate** is the price of one currency in terms of another currency; for example, $1.25 = 1 euro. A currency has **appreciated** in value if more of a foreign currency is needed to buy it. A currency has **depreciated** in value if more of it is needed to buy a foreign currency. For example, a change in the exchange rate from $1.25 = 1 euro to $1.50 = 1 euro means that more dollars are needed to buy 1 euro, and the euro has appreciated. And because more dollars are needed to buy 1 euro, the dollar has depreciated.

   Depreciation in a nation's currency makes foreign goods more expensive. Consider an Irish coat that is priced at 200 euros when the exchange rate is $1.25 = 1 euro. To buy the Irish coat for 200 euros, an American has to pay $250 ($1.25 for each of 200 euros for a total of $250). Now suppose the dollar depreciates to $1.50 = 1 euro. The American now has to pay $300 for the coat.

   This process is symmetrical, so an appreciation in a nation's currency makes foreign goods cheaper. For example, if the exchange rate goes from $1.25 = 1 euro to $1 = 1 euro, the Irish coat will cost the American $200.

   The depreciation and appreciation of the U.S. dollar affect net exports. As the dollar depreciates, foreign goods become more expensive, Americans cut back on imported goods, and foreigners (whose currency has appreciated) increase their purchases of U.S. exported goods. If exports rise and imports fall, net exports increase and aggregate demand increases.

   As the dollar appreciates, foreign goods become cheaper, Americans increase their purchases of imported goods, and foreigners (whose currency has depreciated) cut back on their purchases of U.S. exported goods. If exports fall and imports rise, net exports decrease, thus lowering aggregate demand.

   Dollar depreciates → U.S. exports ↑ and U.S. imports ↓ → U.S. net exports ↑ → *AD* ↑
   Dollar appreciates → U.S. exports ↓ and U.S. imports ↑ → U.S. net exports ↓ → *AD* ↓

   See Exhibit 5 for a summary of the factors that change aggregate demand.

Exchange Rate
The price of one currency in terms of another currency.

Appreciation
An increase in the value of one currency relative to other currencies.

Depreciation
A decrease in the value of one currency relative to other currencies.

Thinking like AN ECONOMIST

The W-X-Y-Z Explanation

Let's back up for a minute and look at the recent discussion. For example, we have said that if the dollar depreciates, U.S. exports will rise and U.S. imports will fall, which means in turn that U.S. net exports rise, which then causes aggregate demand to rise.

If we were to summarize this type of argument, we'd say that a change in W leads to a change in X, which leads to a change in Y, which leads to change in Z. Let's call this kind of explanation the W-X-Y-Z explanation.

Economists often think in terms of one thing changing something else, which in turn changes still something else, and so on. Some people find this kind of thinking difficult. They ask: Why not simply say that W leads to Z instead of saying that W leads to X, which leads to Y, which leads to Z?

Well, that might make things easier (there would be less to remember), but what it gains in ease, it loses in completeness. It is best to explain just how one thing eventually leads to something else happening.

economics 24/7

GISELE AND THE DOLLAR

In July 2007, Forbes.com reported that she was the highest-earning supermodel in the world, earning over $33 million during the period of January 2007 through June 2007. Her name: Gisele Bundchen.

In August 2007, Gisele signed a contract to represent Pantene hair products (owned by Cincinnati-based Procter & Gamble Co.). There was one thing unusual about this contract. Gisele asked that she be paid in euros instead of dollars.

© AP PHOTO/SILVIA IZQUIERDO

Why did she want to be paid in euros instead of dollars? Largely it is because the dollar had been depreciating in value, and Gisele (and her sister manager) thought the dollar's declining value would continue.

By asking for euros instead of dollars, Gisele had become a speculator (of sorts) in currencies. She was betting on the dollar's future decline in value (continued depreciation) vis-à-vis the euro. One often thinks of a currency speculator as a person who simply takes one currency and uses it to buy another currency (takes dollars and buys euros with the dollars). But one can speculate in a currency the way Gisele did; that is, by asking to be paid in the currency you believe will rise in value (relative to some other currencies). Of course, if your boss won't pay you in some other currency, then you can accomplish the same thing by either buying the currency you want (with dollars) or buying a stock or bond that pays off in a non-dollar currency.

exhibit 5

Factors That Change Aggregate Demand

Aggregate demand (*AD*) changes whenever consumption (*C*), investment (*I*), government purchases (*G*), or net exports (*EX* − *IM*) change. The factors that can affect *C*, *I*, and *EX* − *IM*, thereby indirectly affecting aggregate demand, are listed.

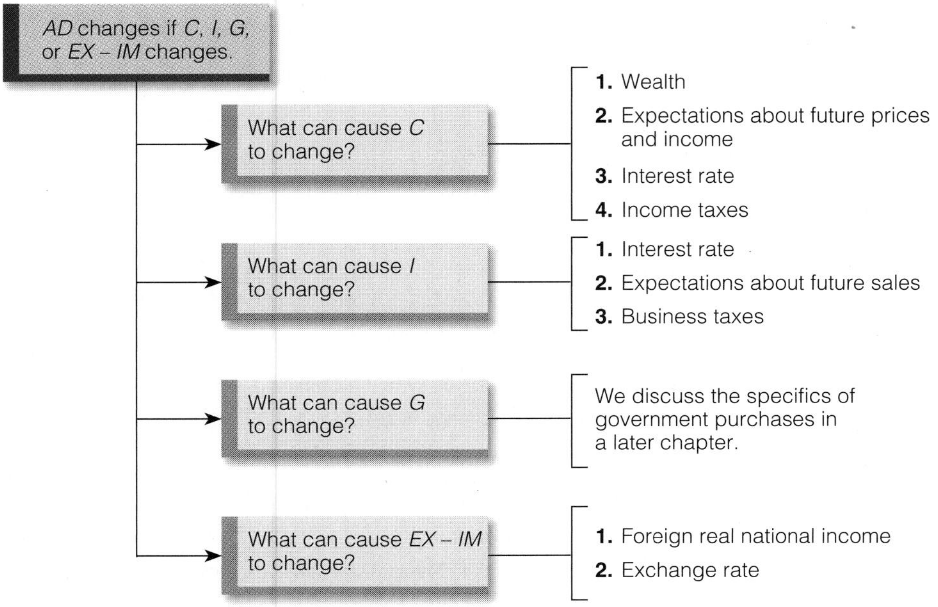

AD changes if C, I, G, or EX – IM changes.
What can cause C to change?
1. Wealth
2. Expectations about future prices and income
3. Interest rate
4. Income taxes
What can cause I to change?
1. Interest rate
2. Expectations about future sales
3. Business taxes
What can cause G to change?
We discuss the specifics of government purchases in a later chapter.
What can cause EX – IM to change?
1. Foreign real national income
2. Exchange rate

Can a Change in the Money Supply Change Aggregate Demand?

Changes in such factors as interest rates, business taxes, exchange rates, and so on can change aggregate demand (indirectly) by directly changing consumption, investment, and net exports. What about the money supply? Can a change in the money supply lead to a change in aggregate demand?

Suppose the money supply rises from, say, \$1,350 billion to \$1,400 billion. Will this result in an increase in aggregate demand? Most economists would say that it does, but they differ as to how the change in the money supply affects aggregate demand. One way to explain the effect (within the context of our discussion) is as follows: (1) a change in the money supply affects interest rates, (2) a change in interest rates changes consumption and investment, and (3) a change in consumption and investment affects aggregate demand. Therefore, a change in the money supply is a catalyst in a process that ends with a change in aggregate demand. (We will have much more to say about the money supply and interest rates in later chapters.)

exhibit 6

The Short-Run Aggregate Supply Curve

The short-run aggregate supply curve is upward sloping, specifying a direct relationship between the price level and the quantity supplied of Real GDP.

Short-Run Aggregate Supply Curve
The price level and quantity supplied of Real GDP are directly related.

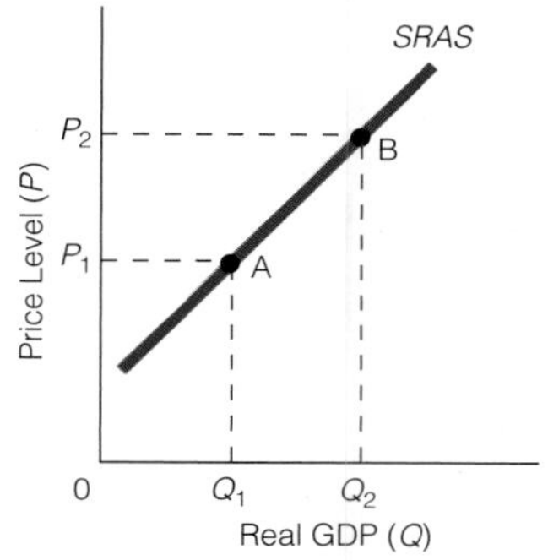

SELF-TEST

(Answers to Self-Test questions are in the Self-Test Appendix.)

1. Explain the real balance effect.
2. Explain what happens to the *AD* curve if the dollar appreciates relative to other currencies.
3. Explain what happens to the *AD* curve if personal income taxes decline.

SHORT-RUN AGGREGATE SUPPLY

Aggregate demand is one side of the economy; aggregate supply is the other side. **Aggregate supply** refers to the quantity supplied of all goods and services (Real GDP) at various price levels, *ceteris paribus.* Aggregate supply includes both short-run aggregate supply (*SRAS*) and long-run aggregate supply (*LRAS*). Short-run aggregate supply is discussed in this section.

Aggregate Supply
The quantity supplied of all goods and services (Real GDP) at different price levels, *ceteris paribus.*

Short-Run Aggregate Supply Curve: What It Is and Why It Is Upward Sloping

A **short-run aggregate supply (*SRAS*) curve** is illustrated in Exhibit 6. It shows the quantity supplied of all goods and services (Real GDP or output) at different price levels, *ceteris paribus.* Notice that the *SRAS* curve is upward sloping: As the price level rises, firms increase the quantity supplied of goods and services; as the price level drops, firms decrease the quantity supplied of goods and services. Why is the *SRAS* curve upward sloping? Economists have put forth a few explanations; we discuss two.

Short-Run Aggregate Supply (*SRAS*) Curve
A curve that shows the quantity supplied of all goods and services (Real GDP) at different price levels, *ceteris paribus.*

STICKY WAGES Some economists believe that wages are sticky, or inflexible. This may be because wages are "locked in" for a few years due to labor contracts entered into by workers and management. For example, management and labor may agree to lock in wages for the next one to three years. Both labor and management may see this as in their best interest. Management has some idea of what its labor costs will be during the time of the contract, and workers may have a sense of security knowing that their wages can't be lowered. Alternatively, wages may be sticky because of certain social conventions or perceived notions of fairness. Whatever the specific reason for sticky wages, let's see how they provide an explanation of an upward-sloping *SRAS* curve.

Firms pay *nominal wages* (e.g., \$30 an hour), but they often decide how many workers to hire based on real wages. *Real wages* are nominal wages divided by the price level.

Real wage = Nominal wage/Price level

For example, suppose the nominal wage is \$30 an hour, and the price level as measured by a price index is 1.50.[1] The real wage is therefore \$20.

The quantity supplied of labor is *directly related* to the real wage: As the real wage rises, the quantity supplied of labor rises; as the real wage falls, the quantity supplied of labor falls. In short, more individuals are willing to work, and current workers are willing to work more, at higher real wages than at lower real wages.

Real wage ↑ → *Quantity supplied* of labor ↑
Real wage ↓ → *Quantity supplied* of labor ↓

The quantity demanded of labor is *inversely related* to the real wage: As the real wage rises, the quantity demanded of labor falls; as the real wage falls, the quantity demanded of labor rises. Firms will employ more workers the cheaper it is to hire them.

Real wage ↑ → *Quantity demanded* of labor ↓
Real wage ↓ → *Quantity demanded* of labor ↑

With this as background, suppose a firm has agreed to pay its workers \$30 an hour for the next three years and it has hired 1,000 workers. When it agreed to this nominal wage, it thought the price index would remain at 1.50 and the real wage would stay at \$20.

Now suppose the price index *falls* to 1.25. When the price level falls to an index of 1.25, the real wage rises to \$24 (\$30/1.25). This is a higher real wage than the firm expected when it agreed to lock in nominal wages at \$30 an hour. If the firm had known that the real wage would turn out to be \$24 (and not remain at \$20), it would never have hired 1,000 workers. It would have hired, say, 800 workers instead.

So what does the firm do? As we stated, there is an inverse relationship between the real wage and the quantity demanded of labor (the number of workers that firms want to hire). Now that the real wage has risen (from \$20 to \$24), the firm cuts back on its labor (say, from 1,000 to 800 workers). With fewer workers working, less output is produced.

In conclusion, if wages are sticky, a decrease in the price level (which pushes real wages up) will result in a decrease in output. This is what an upward-sloping *SRAS* curve represents: As the price level falls, the quantity supplied of goods and services declines.

WORKER MISPERCEPTIONS Another explanation for the upward-sloping *SRAS* curve holds that workers may misperceive real wage changes. To illustrate, suppose the nominal wage is \$30 an hour and the price level as measured by a price index is 1.50. It follows that the real wage is \$20. Now suppose the nominal wage falls to \$25 and the price level falls to 1.25. The real wage is still \$20 (\$25/1.25 = \$20), *but workers may not know this.* They will know their nominal wage has fallen (they know they are earning \$25 an hour instead of \$30 an hour). They also may know the price level is lower. But they may not know initially *how much* lower the price level is. For example, suppose they mistakenly believe the price level has fallen from 1.50 to 1.39. They will then think that their real wage has actually fallen from \$20 (\$30/1.50) to \$17.98 (\$25/1.39). In response to (the misperceived) falling real wage, workers may reduce the quantity of labor they are willing to supply. With fewer workers (resources), firms will end up producing less.

In conclusion, if workers misperceive real wage changes, then a fall in the price level will bring about a decline in output, which is illustrative of an upward-sloping *SRAS* curve.

1. Alternatively, you can view the price index as 1.50 times 100, or 150. In this case, the formula for the real wage would change to Real wage = (Nominal wage/Price level) × 100.

What Puts the "Short Run" in *SRAS*?

According to most macroeconomists, the *SRAS* curve slopes upward because of sticky wages or worker misperceptions. No matter which explanation of the upward-sloping *SRAS* curve we accept, though, things are likely to change over time. Wages will not be sticky forever (labor contracts will expire), and workers will figure out that they misperceived real wage changes. It is only for a period of time—identified as the short run—that these issues are likely to be relevant.

Changes in Short-Run Aggregate Supply: Shifts in the *SRAS* Curve

A change in the quantity supplied of Real GDP is brought about by a change in the price level. A change in quantity supplied is shown as a *movement* along the *SRAS* curve. But what can change short-run aggregate supply? What can *shift* the *SRAS* curve? The factors that can shift the *SRAS* curve include wage rates, prices of nonlabor inputs, productivity, and supply shocks.

WAGE RATES Changes in wage rates have a major impact on the position of the *SRAS* curve because wage costs are usually a firm's major cost item. The impact of a rise or fall in equilibrium wage rates can be understood in terms of the following equation:

$$\text{Profit per unit} = \text{Price per unit} - \text{Cost per unit}$$

Higher wage rates mean higher costs and, at constant prices, translate into lower profits and a reduction in the number of units (of a given good) managers of firms will want to produce. Lower wage rates mean lower costs and, at constant prices, translate into higher profits and an increase in the number of units (of a given good) managers will decide to produce.

The impact of higher and lower equilibrium wages is shown in Exhibit 7. At the given price level, P_1 on $SRAS_1$, the quantity supplied of Real GDP is Q_1. When higher wage rates are introduced, a firm's profits at a given price level decrease. Consequently, the firm reduces production. In the diagram, this corresponds to moving from Q_1 to Q_2, which at the given price level is point B. Point B represents a point on a new aggregate supply curve ($SRAS_2$). Thus, a rise in equilibrium wage rates leads to a leftward shift in the aggregate supply curve. The steps are simply reversed for a fall in equilibrium wage rates.

PRICES OF NONLABOR INPUTS There are other inputs to the production process besides labor. Changes in their prices affect the *SRAS* curve in the same way as changes in wage rates do. An increase in the price of a nonlabor input (e.g., oil) shifts the *SRAS* curve leftward; a decrease in the price of a nonlabor input shifts the *SRAS* curve rightward.

PRODUCTIVITY *Productivity* describes the output produced per unit of input employed over some period of time. Although various inputs can become more productive, let's consider the input labor. An increase in labor productivity means businesses will produce more output with the same amount of labor. This causes the *SRAS* curve to shift rightward. A decrease in labor productivity means businesses will produce less output with the same amount of labor. This causes the *SRAS* curve to shift leftward. A host of factors lead to increased labor productivity, including a more educated labor force, a larger stock of capital goods, and technological advancements.

exhibit 7

Wage Rates and a Shift in the Short-Run Aggregate Supply Curve

A rise in wage rates shifts the short-run aggregate supply curve leftward. A fall in wage rates shifts the short-run aggregate supply curve rightward.

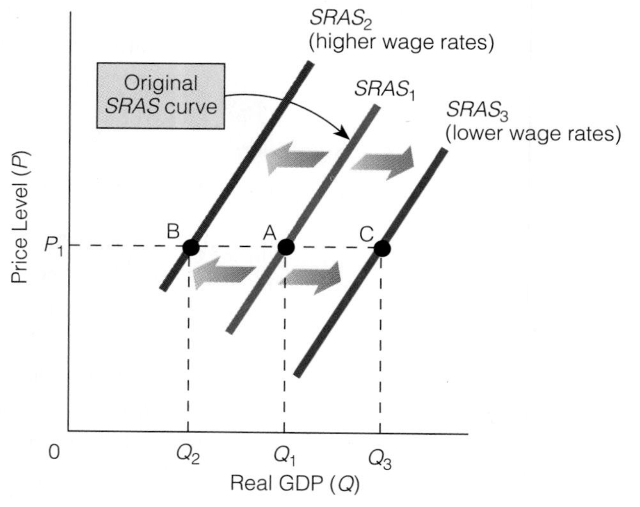

exhibit 8

Changes in Short-Run Aggregate Supply

The flow charts show how short-run aggregate supply changes given changes in several factors.

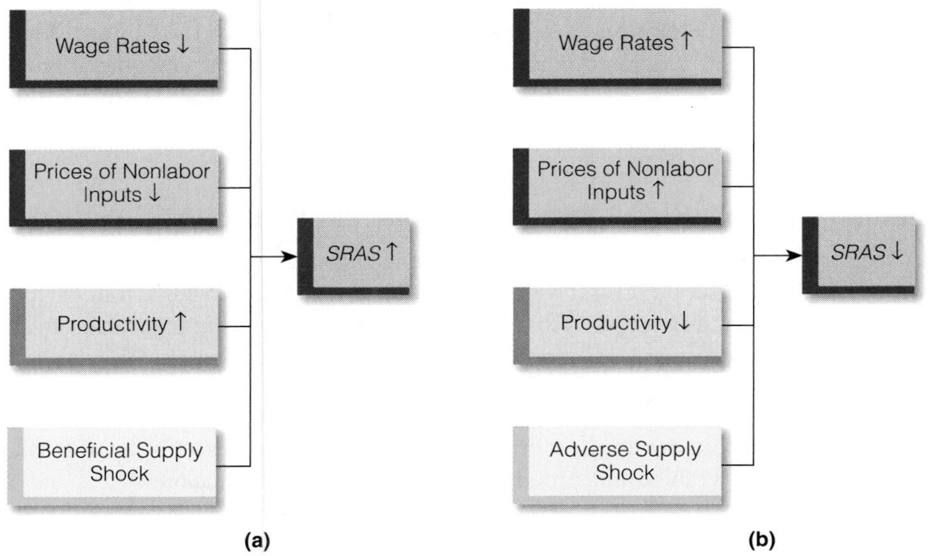

SUPPLY SHOCKS Major natural or institutional changes on the supply side of the economy that affect aggregate supply are referred to as *supply shocks*. Bad weather that wipes out a large part of the midwestern wheat crop would be considered a supply shock. So would a major cutback in the supply of oil coming to the United States from the Middle East.

Supply shocks are of two varieties. *Adverse supply shocks* (such as the examples just given) shift the *SRAS* curve leftward, and *beneficial supply shocks* shift it rightward. Examples of the latter include a major oil discovery and unusually good weather leading to increased production of a food staple. These supply shocks are reflected in resource or input prices.

Exhibit 8 summarizes the factors that affect short-run aggregate supply.

Something More to Come: People's Expectations

So far in this chapter we have said that several factors are capable of shifting the *SRAS* curve. Again, they are: wage rates, prices of nonlabor inputs, productivity, and supply shocks. In a later chapter (Chapter 15), we will begin to discuss how people's expectations (of certain key economic variables) can affect the price level and Real GDP. When we discuss expectations, we will add another factor that can shift the *SRAS* curve—the *expected price level.*

Common MISCONCEPTIONS

About the Price of Oil

As we just stated, a change in the price of a nonlabor input will shift the *SRAS* leftward. For example, an increase in the price of oil will shift the *SRAS* to the left. Now when it comes to oil, many people seem to believe that the price of oil almost always rises. But this is not true. For example, if we look at the period 1965–2004, not only did the nominal (or current dollar) price of oil (per barrel) sometimes fall, but so did the price of oil in 2004 dollars sometimes fall. To illustrate, in 1978, the nominal price of a barrel of oil was $13.60. If we convert this price into 2004 dollars, it equals $32.17. In 1986, the nominal price of oil had risen to $14.38, but the price in 2004 dollars had fallen to $21.84. The case in more recent years has been somewhat different. For example, in late 2007 and early 2008, not only was the nominal price of oil rising, but so was the price in 2004 dollars.

economics 24/7

THE SUBPRIME MORTGAGE MARKET

In recent years there has been talk about subprime lending (especially in the mortgage market). What is a subprime loan, and what is controversial about it? First, a subprime loan is simply a loan that involves elevated credit risk. In contrast, prime loans are made to persons who have a strong credit history and have a record of paying back loans. Subprime loans are usually made to persons who usually do not have a good credit history and may have been delinquent on paying back loans in the past.

A lender can research a person's credit risk by checking his or her FICO (Fair Issac Corporation) credit score. These scores usually run between 300 and 850. A score below 620 usually denotes a person as high risk and usually places that person in the subprime pool of borrowers.

One difference between a prime loan and a subprime loan is that the latter has a higher loan-to-value ratio. This means the loan is a greater percentage of the value of, say, the property the borrower is incurring the loan to buy. To illustrate, suppose the value of the property is $200,000 and the loan is $200,000. In this case the loan-to-value ratio is 1. If the loan is $100,000 and the value of the property is $200,000, then the loan-to-value ratio is 0.50. The higher loan-to-value ratio for subprime borrowers partly reflects the greater difficulty they have in making down payments.

In mortgage lending, subprime loans grew substantially during the period 1995–2003. For example, in 1994, subprime mortgage loans comprised only 4.5 percent of all mortgage loans. In 1995, this percentage had risen to 10.2 percent. It was higher in 1996 at 12.3 percent, and even higher in 1997 at 14.5 percent. As a consequence of the increase in subprime mortgage lending, home ownership increased. Nearly 9 million more people owned their homes in 2003 than in 1994.

In more recent years, subprime lending has come under discussion and review. This is largely due to many subprime borrowers being unable to pay off their loans. Why were they unable to pay off their loans? To a large degree, it was because the subprime loans were made at low interest rates that could change if interest rates in general were to rise. To illustrate, suppose you are a subprime borrower paying an initial rate of 5 percent on a $200,000 loan. Your monthly payment is $1,073. Now suppose your subprime loan agreement states that your interest rate will rise by the same percentage as some specified interest rate in the economy (such as the Treasury bill rate, or some other interest rate). And suppose that this interest rate rose by 300 basis points (or 3 percent). This means the new interest rate that you pay is 8 percent instead of 5 percent, and your monthly payment is now $1,467. This amounts to $394 more than you were previously paying. You would have been all right if interest rates hadn't risen (and you continued paying $1,073 a month), but they did rise, and now you end up having a hard time making your monthly mortgage payment. In such a situation, some subprime borrowers end up defaulting on their loans.

Things might not be so bad if the house you borrowed the money to buy has been rising in value. For example, suppose you took out a $200,000 loan to buy the house priced at $200,000 (no down payment) and now the house is worth $250,000. You could, of course, sell the house for $250,000, pay off the $200,000 loan, and pocket the $50,000. (This ignores such things as real estate commissions, taxes, etc.)

But this wasn't the situation many subprime mortgage borrowers found themselves in in 2007. In many cases, the value of the house had fallen. Now instead of the house being worth $200,000, it was worth, say, $185,000. In this case, many subprime borrowers ended up being either delinquent or defaulting on their loans.

SELF-TEST

1. If wage rates decline, explain what happens to the short-run aggregate supply (*SRAS*) curve.
2. Give an example of an increase in labor productivity.
3. Discuss the details of the worker misperceptions explanation for the upward-sloping *SRAS* curve.

PUTTING *AD* AND *SRAS* TOGETHER: SHORT-RUN EQUILIBRIUM

In this section, we put aggregate demand and short-run aggregate supply together to achieve short-run equilibrium in the economy. Aggregate demand and short-run aggregate supply determine the price level, Real GDP, and the unemployment rate in the short run.

How Short-Run Equilibrium in the Economy Is Achieved

Exhibit 9 hows an aggregate demand (*AD*) curve and a short-run aggregate supply (*SRAS*) curve. We consider the quantity demanded of Real GDP and the quantity supplied of Real GDP at three different price levels: P_1, P_2, and P_E.

At P_1, the quantity supplied of Real GDP (Q_2) is greater than the quantity demanded (Q_1). There is a surplus of goods. As a result, the price level drops, firms decrease output, and consumers increase consumption. Why do consumers increase consumption as the price level drops? (Hint: Think of the real balance, the interest rate, and the international trade effects.)

At P_2, the quantity supplied of Real GDP (Q_1) is less than the quantity demanded (Q_2). There is a shortage of goods. As a result, the price level rises, firms increase output, and consumers decrease consumption.

Short-Run Equilibrium
The condition that exists in the economy when the quantity demanded of Real GDP equals the (short-run) quantity supplied of Real GDP. This condition is met where the aggregate demand curve intersects the short-run aggregate supply curve.

In instances of both surplus and shortage, economic forces are moving the economy toward E, where the quantity demanded of Real GDP equals the (short-run) quantity supplied of Real GDP. This is the point of **short-run equilibrium**. P_E is the short-run equilibrium price level; Q_E is the short-run equilibrium Real GDP.

A change in aggregate demand, short-run aggregate supply, or both will obviously affect the price level and/or Real GDP. For example, an increase in aggregate demand

exhibit 9

Short-Run Equilibrium

At P_1, the quantity supplied of Real GDP is greater than the quantity demanded. As a result, the price level falls and firms decrease output. At P_2, the quantity demanded of Real GDP is greater than the quantity supplied. As a result, the price level rises and firms increase output. Short-run equilibrium occurs at point E, where the quantity demanded of Real GDP equals the (short-run) quantity supplied. This is at the intersection of the aggregate demand (*AD*) curve and the short-run aggregate supply (*SRAS*) curve. (Note: Although real-world *AD* and *SRAS* curves can, and likely do, have some curvature to them, we have drawn both as straight lines, This does not affect the analysis. Whenever the analysis is not disturbed, we follow suit throughout this text.)

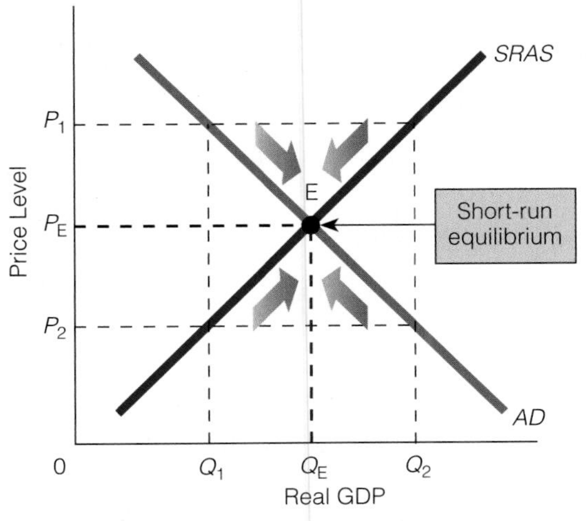

exhibit 10

Changes in Short-Run Equilibrium in the Economy

(a) An increase in aggregate demand increases the price level and Real GDP. (b) An increase in short-run aggregate supply decreases the price level and increases Real GDP. (c) A decrease in short-run aggregate supply increases the price level and decreases Real GDP.

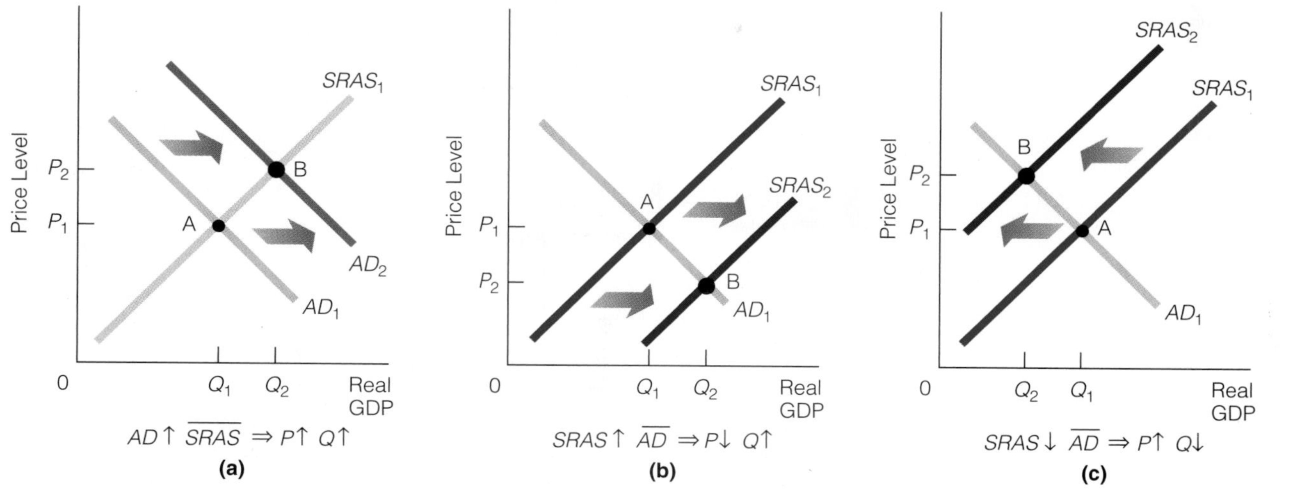

raises the equilibrium price level and, in the short run, Real GDP [Exhibit 10(a)]. An increase in short-run aggregate supply lowers the equilibrium price level and raises Real GDP [Exhibit 10(b)]. A decrease in short-run aggregate supply raises the equilibrium price level and lowers Real GDP [Exhibit 10(c)].

Thinking in Terms of Short-Run Equilibrium Changes in the Economy

Earlier, you learned that certain factors can lead to a change in aggregate demand. You also learned that certain factors can lead to a change in short-run aggregate supply. Then you learned that if either aggregate demand or short-run aggregate supply changes, the price level and Real GDP will all change in the short run.

Exhibit 11 shows us how changes in *AD* or *SRAS* can impact the economy and change *P* and *Q*. (Take a look at Exhibit 11 as we continue our discussion.) For example, when a factor changes, the first thing we ask ourselves is whether the factor affects the *AD* curve or the *SRAS* curve. If the answer is neither, then there will be no change in either curve.

If the answer is the *AD* curve, then we identify whether the *AD* curve shifts to the right or to the left. If the answer is the *SRAS* curve, we identify whether the *SRAS* curve shifts to the right or to the left.

After the shift in one or more curves, we identify the new equilibrium and identify what has happened to both the price level and Real GDP in the short run.

To illustrate, suppose there is an adverse supply shock in the economy. We know this will shift the *SRAS* curve leftward.

Nothing has changed on the demand side of the economy, so the *AD* curve remains stable.

A leftward shift in the *SRAS* curve in the face of an unchanged *AD* curve ends up increasing the price level and decreasing Real GDP.

exhibit 11

How a Factor Affects the Price Level and Real GDP in the Short Run

In the exhibit, P = price level and Q = Real GDP.

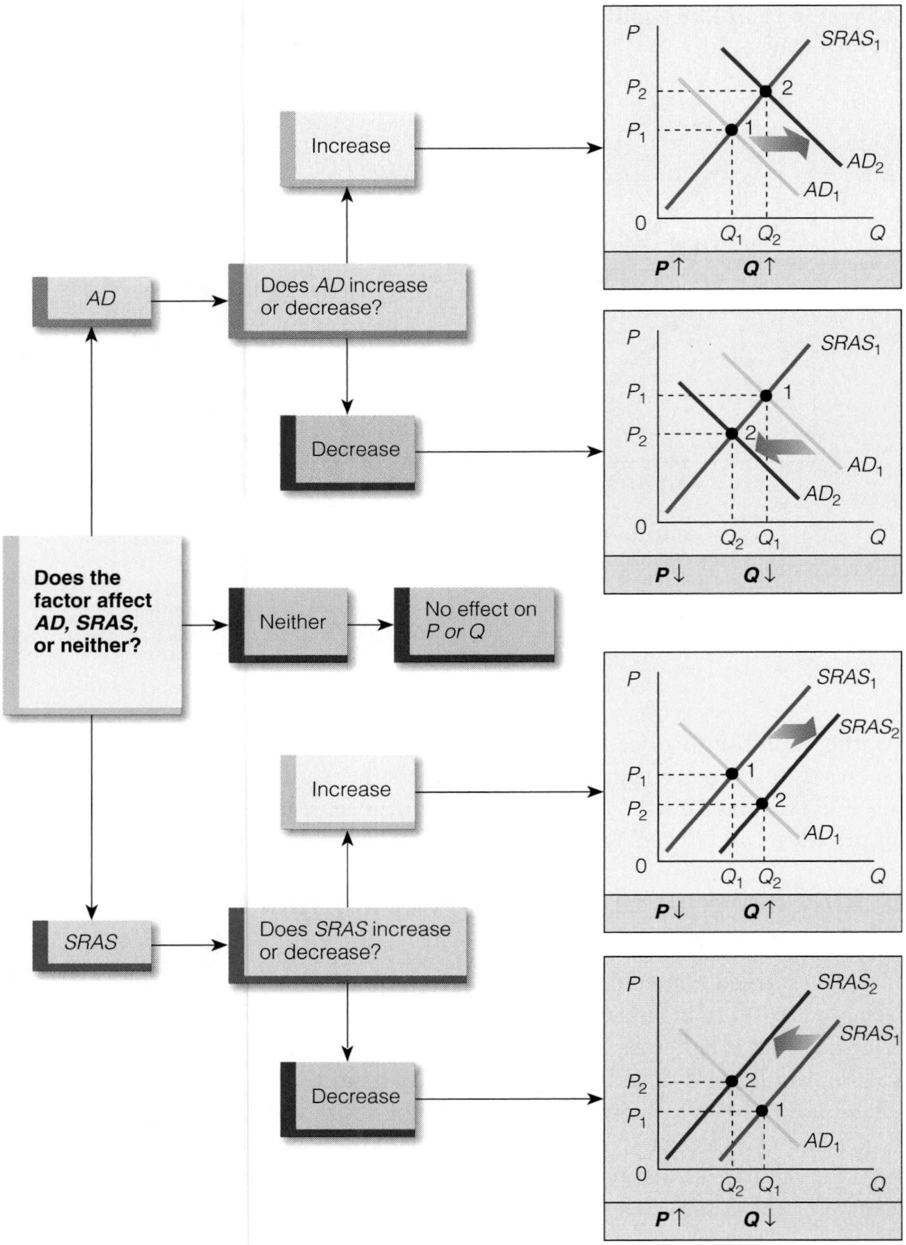

Finding ECONOMICS

In Dollars and in Oil

In November 2007 the (barrel) price of oil was rising. On November 1, 2007, it had risen to $96 a barrel. Also in November 2007 the value of the dollar was falling in foreign exchange markets. In fact, the value of the dollar had been falling for some time. Although the value of one dollar was 0.83 euros in January 2006, it had fallen to 0.69 euros by November 1, 2007. In other words, the

(continued)

THE VIETNAM WAR AND *AD-SRAS*

The tools of aggregate demand and aggregate supply are used in economics for explanatory and predictive purposes. Let's put ourselves in the position of an economist working with aggregate demand and aggregate supply. In the mid-1960s, the problem we are faced with is predicting the effect on Real GDP and the price level that will result from the economic actions associated with U.S. involvement in Vietnam. There are two main facts: (1) Beginning around 1965–1966, U.S. involvement in Vietnam escalated, with resulting increases in military spending. (2) During this period, the Federal Reserve increased the money supply. How would these actions affect Real GDP and the price level?

© AP PHOTO

First, if we assume that taxes were not being raised to finance increased military spending, it follows that an increase in government military spending shifts the *AD* curve rightward. The increase in the money supply also shifts the *AD* curve rightward. According to our *AD-SRAS* diagrammatics, a shift rightward in the *AD* curve will raise Real GDP and the price level. Did this actually happen? It did. During the period 1965–1969, Real GDP steadily increased, as did the inflation rate. It is interesting to look at the year-to-year changes in each factor. Here are the data:

Year	Real GDP (trillions of dollars)	Inflation Rate
1965	$3.2	1.7%
1966	$3.4	2.7%
1967	$3.5	2.8%
1968	$3.6	4.2%
1969	$3.8	4.9%

Finding Economics (continued)

dollar had depreciated over the time period specified. Now what does all this have to do with the predicted change in the price level and Real GDP?

We know that the falling value of the dollar would lead to greater U.S. exports, and this is exactly what was happening at the time. As a result, U.S. net exports were rising, pushing the *AD* curve in the economy to the right. But because oil prices were rising, the *SRAS* curve in the economy was shifting to the left. How will these two changes affect Real GDP? The answer depends on the relative shifts of the *AD* and *SRAS* curves. If the *AD* curve shifts rightward by more than the *SRAS* curve shifts leftward (can you see this happening in your mind's eye?), then Real GDP will rise. If the *AD* curve shifts rightward by less than the *SRAS* curve shifts leftward, then Real GDP will fall. But if the *AD* curve shifts rightward by the same amount as the *SRAS* curve shifts leftward, then Real GDP will remain unchanged. In all three cases, though, there would be an increase in the price level. Rising aggregate demand combined with falling short-run aggregate supply always results in a rising price level.

An Important Exhibit

Exhibit 12 brings together much of the material we have discussed in this chapter. To illustrate, much of our discussion up to this point has been about the economy in the short run; specifically, it has been about changes in the price level (P) and Real GDP (Q) in the short run.

exhibit 12

A Summary Exhibit of *AD* and *SRAS*

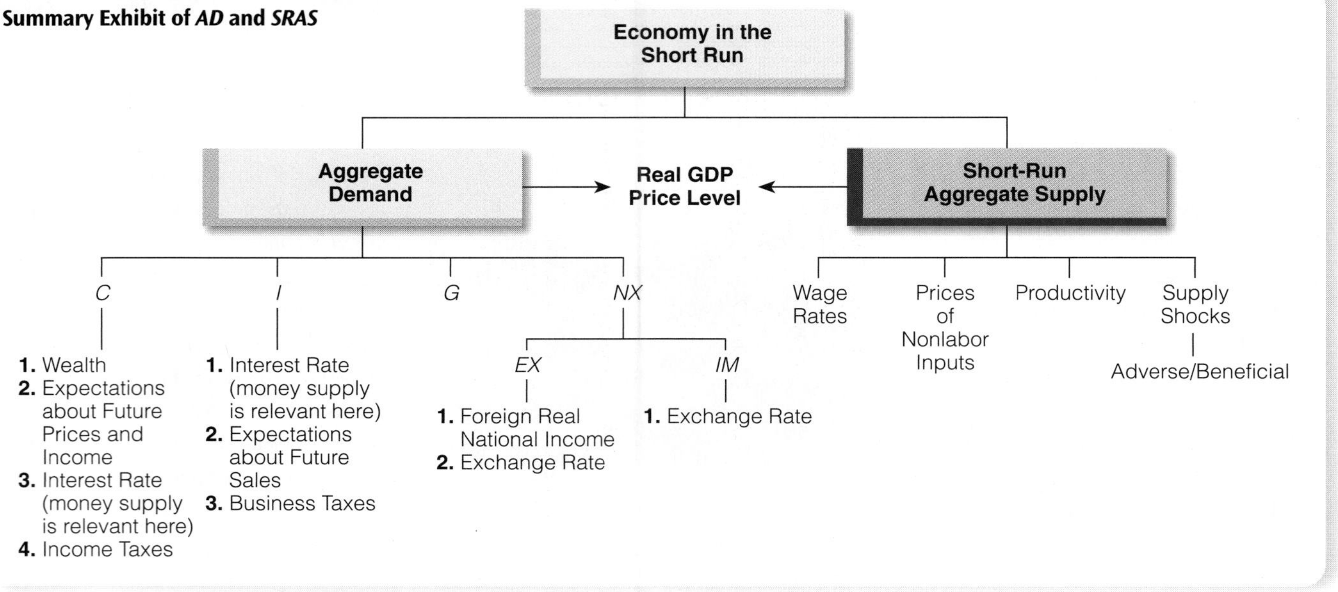

Exhibit 12 tells us that changes in *AD* and *SRAS* will change the price level and Real GDP in the short run. Then we see what factors will actually change *AD* and what factors will change *SRAS*.

While following the process in Exhibit 12, consider what a fall in the interest rate will do to *P* and *Q* in the short run. We know that if the interest rate falls, both consumption (*C*) and investment (*I*) will rise. If both *C* and *I* rise, the *AD* will rise or the *AD* curve will shift rightward. If the *AD* curve shifts rightward, the price level (*P*) will rise and so will Real GDP (*Q*).

Long-Run Aggregate Supply

In this section, we discuss long-run aggregate supply and draw a long-run aggregate supply (*LRAS*) curve. We also discuss long-run equilibrium and explain how it differs from short-run equilibrium.

Going from the Short Run to the Long Run

Graphically, short-run equilibrium is at the intersection of the *AD* curve and the (upward-sloping) *SRAS* curve. As an earlier section explains, economists give different reasons for an upward-sloping *SRAS* curve. Recall that those reasons have to do with:

1. Sticky wages
2. Worker misperceptions

It follows, then, that short-run equilibrium identifies the Real GDP the economy produces when either of these two conditions hold.

In time, though, wages will become unstuck and misperceptions will turn into accurate perceptions. When this happens, the economy is said to be in the *long run*. In other words, in the long run, these two conditions do not hold.

An important macroeconomic question is: *Will the level of Real GDP the economy produces in the long run be the same as in the short run?* Most economists say that it will not be. They argue that in the long run, the economy produces the full-employment Real GDP or the **Natural Real GDP** (Q_N). The aggregate supply curve that identifies the output

Natural Real GDP
The Real GDP that is produced at the natural unemployment rate. The Real GDP that is produced when the economy is in long-run equilibrium.

economics 24/7

REALITY CAN BE MESSY, AND CORRECT PREDICTIONS CAN BE DIFFICULT TO MAKE

In a textbook like this one, we can change one factor and then trace its effects through the economy, ultimately to the price level and Real GDP. To illustrate, suppose business taxes decline. We know this will lead to a rise in investment, which in turn will lead to a rise in *AD*. Now, assuming that *SRAS* has not changed, a rise in *AD* will lead to a rise in the price level and a rise in Real GDP. Here are the links again:

$$\text{Business taxes} \downarrow \rightarrow I\uparrow \rightarrow AD\uparrow \rightarrow P\uparrow\ Q\uparrow$$

where I = investment, AD = aggregate demand, P = price level, and Q = Real GDP.

In reality, though, more than one thing could change at a time. Or at a minimum, two or more things could change within a few days or weeks of each other. To illustrate, let's suppose there is a factor on the demand side of the economy that changes at about the same time as a factor on the supply side. Specifically, wealth rises at the same time as the price of nonlabor inputs rises. What will ultimately happen to the price level and Real GDP? Well, let's break the problem down into small parts and proceed to find out.

1. We know that a rise in wealth will raise *AD*. The *AD* curve shifts rightward.
2. We know that a rise in nonlabor input prices will lower *SRAS*. The *SRAS* curve will shift leftward.
3. Because we have both the *AD* and *SRAS* curves changing at the same time, or about the same time, the overall change in the price level and Real GDP will depend on the relative shifts of the *AD* and *SRAS* curves.
4. Let's suppose the *AD* curve shifts rightward by more than the *SRAS* curve shifts leftward. (You may want to draw this.) As a result, the price level and Real GDP will rise.
5. If, however, the *AD* curve shifts rightward by less than the *SRAS* curve shifts leftward, then the price level will rise and Real GDP will fall.
6. Finally, if the *AD* curve shifts rightward to the same degree that the *SRAS* curve shifts leftward, Real GDP will not change and the price level will rise.

Sometimes, all this has something to say about economists' predictions. It is quite easy to put forth correct predictions in economics when only one thing changes and everything else remains constant. What is hard to do is put forth correct predictions when more than one thing changes at a time and when the things that change pull the economy in opposite directions. We have seen this through our example. Specifically, although the increase in *AD* tends to raise Real GDP, the decrease in *SRAS* tends to lower Real GDP. What will be the final effect on Real GDP? As we have seen, it depends on the relative shifts in *AD* and *SRAS*.

the economy produces in the long run is the **long-run aggregate supply (*LRAS*) curve**. It is portrayed as the vertical line in Exhibit 13.

It follows that **long-run equilibrium** identifies the level of Real GDP the economy produces when wages and prices have adjusted to their (final) equilibrium levels and there are no misperceptions on the part of workers. Graphically, this occurs at the intersection of the *AD* and *LRAS* curves. Furthermore, the level of Real GDP that the economy produces in long-run equilibrium is Natural Real GDP (Q_N).

Long-Run Aggregate Supply (*LRAS*) Curve
The *LRAS* curve is a vertical line at the level of Natural Real GDP. It represents the output the economy produces when wages and prices have adjusted to their (final) equilibrium levels and neither producers nor workers have any relevant misperceptions.

Long-Run Equilibrium
The condition that exists in the economy when wages and prices have adjusted to their (final) equilibrium levels and workers do not have any relevant misperceptions. Graphically, long-run equilibrium occurs at the intersection of the *AD* and *LRAS* curves.

Short-Run Equilibrium, Long-Run Equilibrium, and Disequilibrium

There are two equilibrium states in an economy: short-run equilibrium and long-run equilibrium. These two equilibrium states are graphically shown in Exhibit 14.

In Exhibit 14(a), the economy is at point 1, producing Q_1 amount of Real GDP. Notice that at point 1, the quantity supplied of Real GDP (in the short run) is equal to the quantity demanded of Real GDP, and both are Q_1. The economy is in short-run equilibrium.

In Exhibit 14(b), the economy is at point 1, producing Q_N. In other words, it is producing Natural Real GDP. The economy is in long-run equilibrium when it produces Q_N.

Notice that in both short-run and long-run equilibrium, the quantity supplied of Real GDP equals the quantity demanded. So what is the difference between short-run equilibrium and long-run equilibrium? In long-run equilibrium, quantity supplied and demanded of Real GDP equal Natural Real GDP [see Exhibit 14(b)]. But in short-run equilibrium, quantity supplied and demanded of Real GDP are either more than or less than Natural Real GDP.

Let's illustrate with numbers. Suppose Q_N = \$9.0 trillion. In long-run equilibrium, quantity supplied of Real GDP = quantity demanded of Real GDP = \$9.0 trillion. In short-run equilibrium, quantity supplied of Real GDP equals quantity demanded, but neither equals \$9.0 trillion. For example, it could be that quantity supplied of Real GDP = quantity demanded of Real GDP = \$8.5 trillion.

When the economy is in neither short-run equilibrium nor long-run equilibrium, it is said to be in *disequilibrium.* Essentially, disequilibrium is the state of the economy as it moves from one short-run equilibrium to another or from short-run equilibrium to long-run equilibrium. In disequilibrium, quantity supplied of Real GDP and quantity demanded of Real GDP are not equal.

exhibit 13

Long-Run Aggregate Supply (*LRAS*) Curve

The *LRAS* curve is a vertical line at the level of Natural Real GDP. It represents the output the economy produces when all economywide adjustments have taken place and workers do not have any relevant misperceptions.

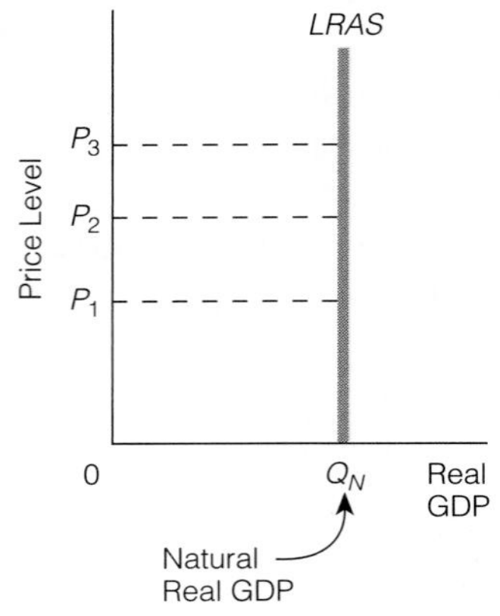

Something More to Come: Shifts in the *LRAS* Curve

In this chapter we have discussed both the *AD* curve and the *SRAS* curve. With respect to each curve, we have identified those factors that cause the curve to shift. Notice that while we have identified the *LRAS* curve (which is vertical), we have not identified those factors that will cause it to shift. We will in a later chapter. Shifts in the *LRAS* curve are important when we discuss long-run economic growth, the major topic of discussion in Chapter 16.

SELF-TEST

1. What is the difference between short-run equilibrium and long-run equilibrium?
2. Diagrammatically represent an economy that is in neither short-run equilibrium nor long-run equilibrium.

exhibit 14

Equilibrium States of the Economy

There are two equilibrium states in the economy: short-run equilibrium, shown in part (a), and long-run equilibrium, shown in part (b). During the time an economy moves from one equilibrium to another, it is said to be in disequilibrium.

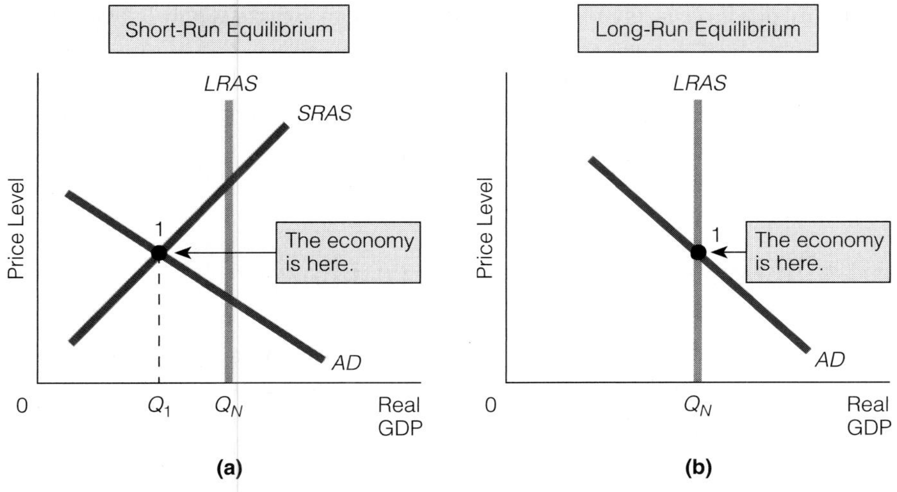

office hours

"WHAT PURPOSE DOES THE *AD-AS* FRAMEWORK SERVE?"

Student:
What purpose does the *AD-AS* framework serve?

Instructor:
One purpose is to link some variables to other variables.

Student:
How so?

Instructor:
Well, consider a rise in income taxes. We learned in this chapter that a rise in income taxes will lead to a decline in consumption. And we know that a decline in consumption will lead to a decline in aggregate demand. Finally, we know that a decline in aggregate demand will lead to a decline in both the price level and Real GDP. In other words, the *AD-AS* framework helps us to link a rise in *income taxes* to a decline in both the *price level* and *Real GDP*.

Student:
Oh, I see. It's sort of like the *AD-AS* framework is a road. We start at one point on the road (where income taxes are being raised) and then we follow the road until we come to the end (where the price level and Real GDP have declined).

Instructor:
That is a good way of putting it. Let's now start at another point along the road. Let's start with a decline in wage rates.

Student:
If there is a decline in wage rates, short-run aggregate supply increases (or the *SRAS* curve shifts to the right). As a result, the price level declines and Real GDP rises.

Instructor:
That's correct. Now let's go back to your original question: What purpose does the *AD-AS* framework serve? What would your answer be now?

Student:
I think I would say what you said—"that it links some variables to other variables"— but also add that it provides an explanation for changes in the price level and Real GDP, too.

Instructor:
Explain what you mean here.

Student:
Well, suppose someone were to ask me what might cause Real GDP to decline. Using the *AD-AS* framework, I would say that either a decline in *AD* or *SRAS* would lead to a decline in Real GDP. Then, if the person wanted more specificity, I could say that such things as an adverse supply shock, a decline in productivity, appreciation in the U.S. dollar, and so on could lead to a decline in Real GDP.

Instructor:
You make a good point.

Points to Remember

1. The *AD-AS* framework serves to link some variables to other variables. For example, a change in income taxes can ultimately be linked to a change in the price level and Real GDP.
2. The *AD-AS* framework helps us to understand changes in both the price level and Real GDP.

a reader asks | Do My Job Prospects Depend on *AD* and *SRAS*?

Aggregate demand (*AD*) and short-run aggregate supply (*SRAS*) appear to determine Real GDP in the short run. Will *AD* and *SRAS* also influence my job prospects after I graduate from college?

Your job prospects will depend in part on your major, your grades, and your performance in job interviews. But your prospects will also depend on where the *AD* curve and the *SRAS* curve "intersect." That is, your job prospects will depend on whether *AD* and *SRAS* have been increasing, decreasing, or remaining constant.

To illustrate, suppose that some months before you graduate, interest rates rise and the dollar appreciates. An increase in interest rates tends to reduce durable goods spending and investment spending—so both consumption and investment decline. If the dollar appreciates, U.S. goods become more expensive for foreigners, so they buy less. Also, foreign goods become cheaper for Americans, so they buy more. The result is that exports fall and imports rise, or net exports decline.

If consumption, investment, and net exports fall, aggregate demand in the U.S. economy declines. In other words, the *AD* curve shifts to the left.

As a result of declining aggregate demand in the economy, there is a new short-run equilibrium. The new short-run equilibrium is at a lower Real GDP level. In other words, firms have cut back on the quantity of goods and services they produce. Many of the firms that cut back may be the ones at which you hope to find a job after college. Your job prospects look slightly less rosy than they did before the changes in the economy.

A statement in the magazine *The Economist* provides further evidence of the connection between the state of the economy and your job prospects. In its November 1, 2001, edition, the magazine stated, "the downturn [in the economy] is plainly bad news for the [MBA] students, especially since banking and consulting—two of the industries which, in less interesting times, reliably hire hundreds of MBAs—have curtailed their recruiting."

Chapter Summary

AGGREGATE DEMAND

- Aggregate demand refers to the quantity demanded of all goods and services (Real GDP) at different price levels, *ceteris paribus.*
- The aggregate demand (*AD*) curve slopes downward, indicating an inverse relationship between the price level and the quantity demanded of Real GDP.
- The aggregate demand curve slopes downward because of the real balance, interest rate, and international trade effects.
- The real balance effect states that the inverse relationship between the price level and the quantity demanded of Real GDP is established through changes in the value of a person's monetary wealth or money holdings. Specifically, a fall in the price level causes purchasing power to rise, which increases a person's monetary wealth. As people become wealthier, they buy more goods. A rise in the price level causes purchasing power to fall, which reduces a person's monetary wealth. As people become less wealthy, they buy fewer goods.
- The interest rate effect states that the inverse relationship between the price level and the quantity demanded of Real GDP is established through changes in household and business spending that is sensitive to changes in interest rates. If the price level rises, a person needs more money to buy a fixed bundle of goods. In an effort to acquire more money, the demand for credit rises, as does the interest rate. As the interest rate rises, businesses and households borrow less and buy fewer goods. Thus, the quantity demanded of Real GDP falls. If the price level falls, a person needs less money to buy a fixed bundle of goods. Part of the increase in a person's monetary wealth is saved, so the supply of credit rises, and the interest rate falls. As the interest rate falls, businesses and households borrow more and buy more goods. Thus, the quantity demanded of Real GDP rises.

- The international trade effect states that the inverse relationship between the price level and the quantity demanded of Real GDP is established through foreign sector spending. Specifically, as the price level in the United States rises, U.S. goods become relatively more expensive than foreign goods, and both Americans and foreigners buy fewer U.S. goods. The quantity demanded of (U.S.) Real GDP falls. As the price level in the United States falls, U.S. goods become relatively less expensive than foreign goods, and both Americans and foreigners buy more U.S. goods. The quantity demanded of (U.S.) Real GDP rises.
- At a given price level, a rise in consumption, investment, government purchases, or net exports will increase aggregate demand and shift the *AD* curve to the right. At a given price level, a fall in consumption, investment, government purchases, or net exports will decrease aggregate demand and shift the *AD* curve to the left.

FACTORS THAT CAN CHANGE *C*, *I*, AND *NX* (*EX–IM*) AND THEREFORE CAN CHANGE *AD*

- The following factors can change consumption: wealth, expectations about future prices and income, the interest rate, and income taxes. The following factors can change investment: the interest rate, expectations about future sales, and business taxes. The following factors can change net exports (exports − imports): foreign real national income and the exchange rate. A change in the money supply can affect one or more spending components (e.g., consumption) and therefore affect aggregate demand.

SHORT-RUN AGGREGATE SUPPLY

- Aggregate supply refers to the quantity supplied of all goods and services (Real GDP) at different price levels, *ceteris paribus.*
- The short-run aggregate supply (*SRAS*) curve is upward sloping, indicating a direct relationship between the price level and the quantity supplied of Real GDP.
- A decrease in wage rates, a decrease in the price of nonlabor inputs, an increase in productivity, and beneficial supply shocks all shift the *SRAS* curve to the right. An increase in wage rates, an increase in the price of nonlabor inputs, a decrease in productivity, and adverse supply shocks all shift the *SRAS* curve to the left.

SHORT-RUN EQUILIBRIUM

- Graphically, short-run equilibrium exists at the intersection of the *AD* and *SRAS* curves. A shift in either or both of these curves can change the price level and Real GDP. For example, an increase in aggregate demand increases the price level and Real GDP, *ceteris paribus.*

LONG-RUN AGGREGATE SUPPLY AND LONG-RUN EQUILIBRIUM

- The long-run aggregate supply (*LRAS*) curve is vertical at the Natural Real GDP level.
- Graphically, long-run equilibrium exists at the intersection of the *AD* and *LRAS* curves. It is the condition that exists in the economy when all economy-wide adjustments have taken place and workers do not hold any (relevant) misperceptions. In long-run equilibrium, quantity demanded of Real GDP = quantity supplied of Real GDP = Natural Real GDP.

THREE STATES OF AN ECONOMY

- An economy can be in short-run equilibrium, long-run equilibrium, or disequilibrium.

Key Terms and Concepts

Aggregate Demand
Aggregate Demand (*AD*) Curve
Real Balance Effect
Monetary Wealth
Purchasing Power
Interest Rate Effect
International Trade Effect
Wealth
Exchange Rate
Appreciation
Depreciation
Aggregate Supply
Short-Run Aggregate Supply (*SRAS*) Curve
Short-Run Equilibrium
Natural Real GDP
Long-Run Aggregate Supply (*LRAS*) Curve
Long-Run Equilibrium

Questions and Problems

1 Is aggregate demand a specific dollar amount? For example, would it be correct to say that aggregate demand is $9 trillion this year?

2 Explain each of the following: (a) real balance effect, (b) interest rate effect, and (c) international trade effect.

3 Graphically portray each of the following: (a) a change in the quantity demanded of Real GDP and (b) a change in aggregate demand.

4 There is a difference between a change in the interest rate that is brought about by a change in the price level and

a change in the interest rate that is brought about by a change in some factor other than the price level. The first will change the quantity demanded of Real GDP, and the second will change the *AD* curve. Do you agree or disagree with this statement? Explain your answer.

5 The amount of Real GDP (real output) that households are willing and able to buy may change if there is a change in either (a) the price level or (b) some nonprice factor, such as wealth, interest rates, and so on. Do you agree or disagree? Explain your answer.

6 Explain what happens to aggregate demand in each of the following cases:
   a. The interest rate rises.
   b. Wealth falls.
   c. The dollar depreciates relative to foreign currencies.
   d. Households expect lower prices in the future.
   e. Business taxes rise.

7 Explain what is likely to happen to U.S. export and import spending as a result of the dollar depreciating in value.

8 Explain how expectations about future prices and income will affect consumption.

9 Explain how expectations about future sales will affect investment.

10 How will an increase in the money supply affect aggregate demand?

11 Will a direct increase in the price of U.S. goods relative to foreign goods lead to a change in the quantity demanded of Real GDP or to a change in aggregate demand? Will a change in the exchange rate that subsequently increases the price of U.S. goods relative to foreign goods lead to a change in the quantity demanded of Real GDP or to a change in aggregate demand? Explain your answers.

12 Explain how each of the following will affect short-run aggregate supply:
   a. An increase in wage rates.
   b. A beneficial supply shock.
   c. An increase in the productivity of labor.
   d. A decrease in the price of a nonlabor resource (e.g., oil).

13 What is the difference between a change in the quantity supplied of Real GDP and a change in short-run aggregate supply?

14 A change in the price level affects which of the following:
   a. The quantity demanded of Real GDP.
   b. Aggregate demand.
   c. Short-run aggregate supply.
   d. The quantity supplied of Real GDP.

15 In the short run, what is the impact on the price level and Real GDP of each of the following:
   a. An increase in consumption brought about by a decrease in interest rates.
   b. A decrease in exports brought about by an appreciation of the dollar.
   c. A rise in wage rates.
   d. A beneficial supply shock.
   e. An adverse supply shock.
   f. A decline in productivity.

16 Identify the details of each of the following explanations for an upward-sloping *SRAS* curve:
   a. Sticky-wage explanation.
   b. Worker-misperception explanation.

17 What is the difference between short-run equilibrium and long-run equilibrium?

18 An economist is sitting in the Oval Office of the White House, across the desk from the president of the United States. The president asks, "How does the unemployment rate look for the next quarter?" The economist answers, "It's not good. I don't think Real GDP is gong to be as high as we initially thought. The problem seems to be foreign income—it's just not growing at the rate we thought it was going to grow." How can foreign income affect U.S. unemployment?

Working with Numbers and Graphs

1 Suppose that at a price index of 154, the quantity demanded of (U.S.) Real GDP is $10.0 trillion worth of goods. Do these data represent aggregate demand or a point on an aggregate demand curve? Explain your answer.

2 Diagrammatically represent the effect on the price level and Real GDP in the short run of each of the following:
   a. An increase in wealth.
   b. An increase in wage rates.
   c. An increase in labor productivity.

3 Diagrammatically represent the following, and identify the effect on Real GDP and the price level in the short run:
   a. An increase in *SRAS* that is greater than the increase in *AD*.
   b. A decrease in *AD* that is greater than the increase in *SRAS*.
   c. An increase in *SRAS* that is less than the increase in *AD*.

4 In the following figure, which part is representative of each of the following:

a. A decrease in wage rates.
b. An increase in the price level.
c. A beneficial supply shock.
d. An increase in the price of nonlabor inputs.

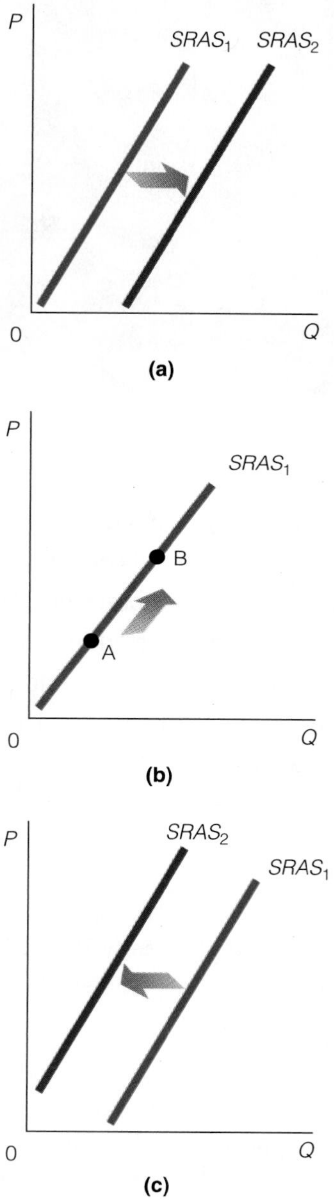

5 In the following figure, which of the points is representative of each of the following:

a. The lowest Real GDP.
b. The highest Real GDP.
c. A decrease in *SRAS* that is greater than an increase in *AD*.

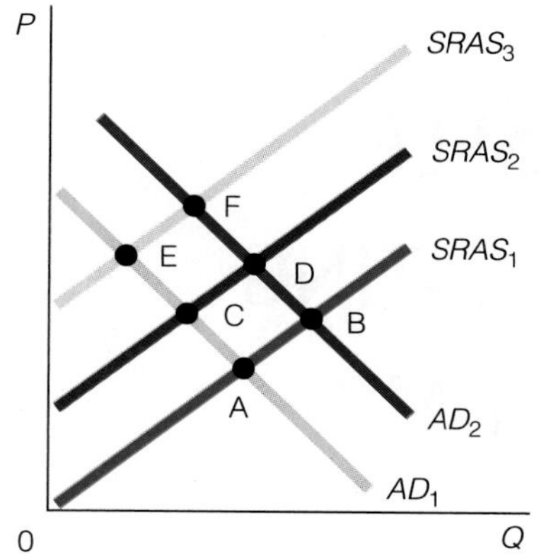

CHAPTER 8

IMAGE: NASA; © 2008 EUROPA TECHNOLOGIES; © 2008 TELE ATLAS; IMAGE: © 2008 TERRAMETRICS

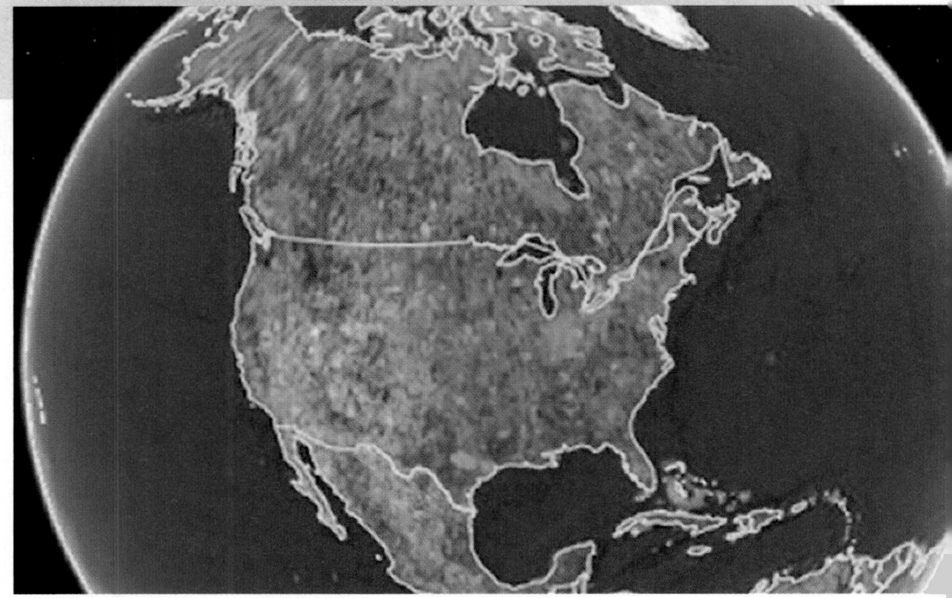

THE SELF-REGULATING ECONOMY

Introduction For hundreds of years, scientists have tried to understand themselves and their surroundings. Biologists have observed and conducted experiments to understand human and animal behavior. Ecologists have developed models to try to understand the relationships between plants and animals in forests and oceans. Astronomers have constructed increasingly powerful telescopes to try to understand phenomena in space. And economists have built and tested theories to try to understand the economy. This chapter presents one view about how the economy works.

THE CLASSICAL VIEW

The term *classical economics* is often used to refer to an era in the history of economic thought that stretched from about 1750 to the late 1800s or early 1900s. Although classical economists lived and wrote many years ago, their ideas are often employed by some modern-day economists.

Classical Economists and Say's Law

You know from your study of supply and demand that markets can experience temporary shortages and surpluses, such as a surplus in the apple market. But can the economy have a general surplus (a general glut of goods and services)? The classical economists thought not, largely because they believed in Say's law (named after J. B. Say). In its simplest version, **Say's law** states that supply creates its own demand.

Say's Law
Supply creates its own demand. Production creates demand sufficient to purchase all the goods and services produced.

This law is most easily understood in terms of a barter economy. Consider a person baking bread in a barter economy; the baker is a supplier of bread. According to Say, the baker works at his trade because he plans to demand other goods. As he is baking bread, the baker is thinking of the goods and services he will obtain in exchange for it. Thus, his act of supplying bread is linked to his demand for other goods. Supply creates its own demand.

If the supplying of some goods leads to a simultaneous demand for other goods, then Say's law implies that there cannot be either (1) a general overproduction of goods (where supply in the economy is greater than demand) or (2) a general underproduction of goods (where demand in the economy is greater than supply).

Now suppose the baker is baking bread in a money economy. Does Say's law hold? Over a period of time, the baker earns an income as a result of supplying bread, but what does he do with the income? One use of the money is to buy goods and services. However, his demand for goods and services does not necessarily match the income that he generates by supplying bread. The baker may spend less than his full income because he engages in saving. Noting this, we might think that Say's law does not hold in a money economy because the act of supplying goods and services—thus earning income—need not create an equal amount of demand.

But the classical economists disagreed. They argued that even in a money economy, where individuals sometimes spend less than their full incomes, Say's law still holds. Their argument was partly based on the assumption of interest rate flexibility.

Classical Economists and Interest Rate Flexibility

For Say's law to hold in a money economy, funds saved must give rise to an equal amount of funds invested; that is, what leaves the spending stream through one door must enter it through another door. If not, then some of the income earned from supplying goods may not be used to demand goods (good-bye Say's law). As a result, goods will be overproduced.

The classical economists argued that saving is matched by an equal amount of investment because of interest rate flexibility in the credit market. We explain their argument using Exhibit 1, where I represents investment and S represents saving. Notice that I_1 is downward sloping, indicating an inverse relationship between the amount of funds firms invest and the interest rate (i). The reason for this is straightforward. The interest rate is the cost of borrowing funds. The higher the interest rate is, the fewer funds firms borrow and invest; the lower the interest rate is, the more funds firms borrow and invest.

Notice also that S_1 is upward sloping, indicating a direct relationship between the amount of funds that households save and the interest rate. The reason is that the higher the interest rate is, the higher the reward is for saving (or the higher the opportunity cost of consuming), and therefore fewer funds are consumed and more funds are saved. Market-equilibrating forces move the credit market to interest rate i_1 and equilibrium point E_1. At E_1, the number of dollars households save ($100,000) equals the number of dollars firms invest ($100,000).

Suppose now that saving increases at each interest rate level. In Exhibit 1, we represent this by a rightward shift in the saving curve from S_1 to S_2. The classical economists believed that an increase in saving puts downward

exhibit 1

The Classical View of the Credit Market

In classical theory, the interest rate is flexible and adjusts so that saving equals investment. Thus, if saving increases and the saving curve shifts rightward from S_1 to S_2 (arrow 1), the increase in saving eventually puts pressure on the interest rate and moves it downward from i_1 to i_2 (arrow 2). A new equilibrium is established at E_2 (arrow 3), where once again the amount households save equals the amount firms invest.

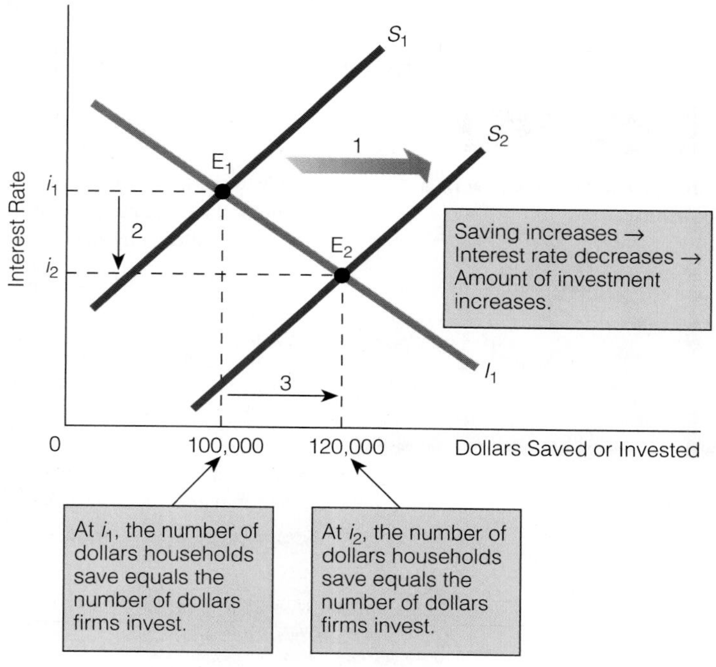

S1
S2
1
E1
E2
I1
2
3
Interest Rate
i1
i2
0
100,000
120,000
Dollars Saved or Invested
Saving increases →
Interest rate decreases →
Amount of investment increases.
At i1, the number of dollars households save equals the number of dollars firms invest.
At i2, the number of dollars households save equals the number of dollars firms invest.

pressure on the interest rate, moving it to i_2, thereby increasing the number of dollars firms invest. Ultimately, the number of dollars households save ($120,000) once again equals the number of dollars firms invest ($120,000). Interest rate flexibility ensures that saving equals investment. (What goes out one door comes in the other door.) In short, changes in the interest rate uphold Say's law in a money economy where there is saving.

Let's use a few numbers to illustrate what classical economists were saying. Suppose that at a given price level, total expenditures (TE) in a very tiny economy are $5,000. We know that total expenditures (total spending on domestic goods and services) equal the sum of consumption (C), investment (I), government purchases (G), and net exports ($EX - IM$). If $C = \$3{,}000$, $I = \$600$, $G = \$1{,}200$, and $EX - IM = \$200$, then

$$TE = C + I + G + (EX - IM)$$
$$\$5{,}000 = \$3{,}000 + \$600 + \$1{,}200 + \$200$$

Furthermore, let's assume the $5,000 worth of goods and services that the four sectors of the economy want to purchase also happens to be the exact dollar amount of goods and services that suppliers want to sell.

Next, let's increase saving in the economy. Saving (S) is equal to the amount of a person's disposable income (Y_d) minus consumption (C).

$$\text{Saving } (S) = \text{Disposable income } (Y_d) - \text{Consumption } (C)$$

For saving to increase, consumption must decrease (assuming disposable income remains constant). Let's say saving increases by $100; then, consumption must fall from $3,000 to $2,900. At first glance, this seems to imply that total expenditures will fall to $4,900. But classical economists disagreed. They said that investment will increase by $100, going from $600 to $700. Total expenditures will remain constant at $5,000 and will be equal to the dollar amount of the goods and services that suppliers want to sell.

$$TE = C + I + G + (EX - IM)$$
$$\$5{,}000 = \$2{,}900 + \$700 + \$1{,}200 + \$200$$

Exhibit 2 summarizes this discussion.

exhibit 2

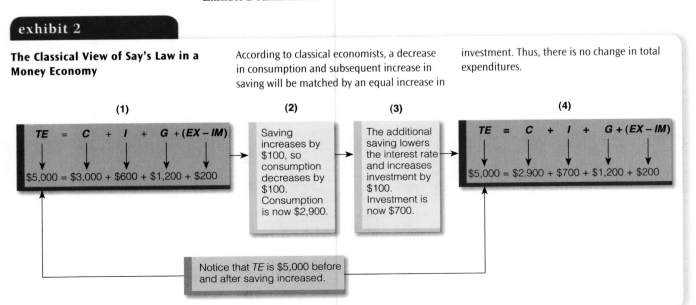

The Classical View of Say's Law in a Money Economy

According to classical economists, a decrease in consumption and subsequent increase in saving will be matched by an equal increase in investment. Thus, there is no change in total expenditures.

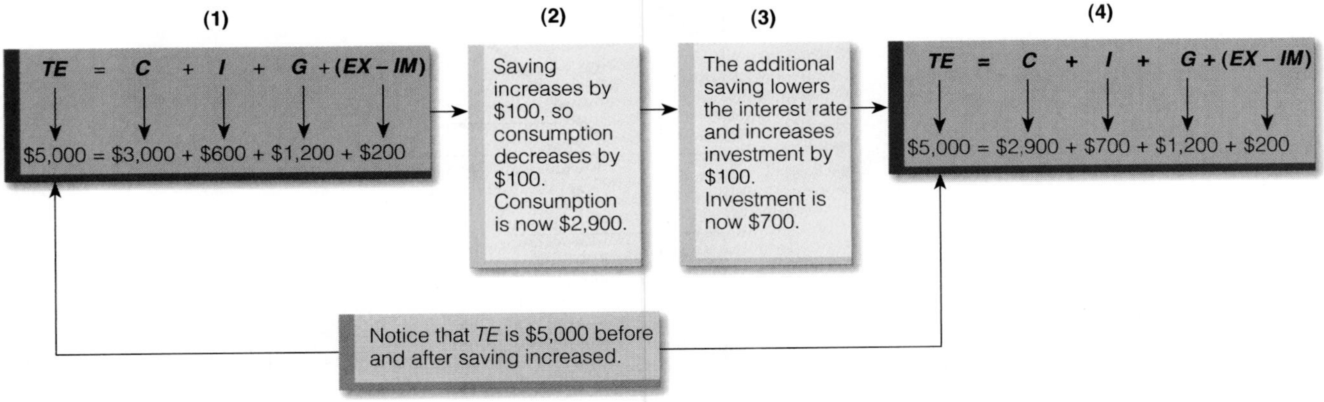
(1)
TE = C + I + G + (EX – IM)
$5,000 = $3,000 + $600 + $1,200 + $200
(2)
Saving increases by $100, so consumption decreases by $100. Consumption is now $2,900.
(3)
The additional saving lowers the interest rate and increases investment by $100. Investment is now $700.
(4)
TE = C + I + G + (EX – IM)
$5,000 = $2,900 + $700 + $1,200 + $200
Notice that TE is $5,000 before and after saving increased.

According to the classical view of the economy, then, Say's law holds both in a barter economy and in a money economy. In a money economy, according to classical economists, interest rates will adjust to equate saving and investment. Therefore, any fall in consumption (and consequent rise in saving) will be matched by an equal rise in investment. In essence, at a given price level, total expenditures will not decrease as a result of an increase in saving.

What does an increase in saving imply for aggregate demand (*AD*)? An earlier chapter explains that aggregate demand changes only if total spending in the economy changes at a given price level. Therefore, because there is no change in total spending as a result of an increase in saving, aggregate demand does not change.

macro*theme* ➔ Economists do not always agree on how the economy works. What you have just read is the classical position on interest rate flexibility and on an increase in saving matched by an equal increase in investment. What leaves the spending stream by one door enters through another. In the next chapter, you will learn about a group of economists who take issue with this classical position. The debates in macroeconomics are numerous, as you soon will find out.

Classical Economists on Prices and Wages

Classical economists believed that most, if not all, markets are competitive; that is, supply and demand operate in all markets. If, for example, the labor market has a surplus, it will be temporary. Soon, the wage rate will decline, and the quantity supplied of labor will equal the quantity demanded of labor. Similarly, given a shortage in the labor market, the wage rate will rise, and the quantity supplied will equal the quantity demanded.

What holds for wages in the labor market holds for prices in the goods and services market. Prices will adjust quickly to any surpluses or shortages, and equilibrium will be quickly reestablished.

SELF-TEST

(Answers to Self-Test questions are in the Self-Test Appendix.)

1. Explain Say's law in terms of a barter economy.
2. According to classical economists, if saving rises and consumption spending falls, will total spending in the economy decrease? Explain your answer.
3. What is the classical position on prices and wages?

THREE STATES OF THE ECONOMY

You will need the background information in this section to understand the views of economists who believe that the economy is self-regulating. Specifically, in this section, we discuss three states of the economy, the correspondence between the labor market and the three states of the economy, and more.

Real GDP and Natural Real GDP: Three Possibilities

In the last chapter, Natural Real GDP was defined as the Real GDP that is produced at the natural unemployment rate. The Real GDP is produced when the economy is in long-run equilibrium.

exhibit 3

Real GDP and Natural Real GDP: Three Possibilities

In (a), the economy is currently in short-run equilibrium at a Real GDP level of Q_1. Q_N is Natural Real GDP or the potential output of the economy. Notice that $Q_1 < Q_N$. When this condition ($Q_1 < Q_N$) exists, the economy is said to be in a recessionary gap.

In (b), the economy is currently in short-run equilibrium at a Real GDP level of Q_1. Q_N is Natural Real GDP or the potential output of the economy. Notice that $Q_1 > Q_N$. When this condition ($Q_1 > Q_N$) exists, the economy is said to be in an inflationary gap.

In (c), the economy is currently operating at a Real GDP level of Q_1, which is equal to Q_N. In other words, the economy is producing its Natural Real GDP or potential output. When this condition ($Q_1 = Q_N$) exists, the economy is said to be in long-run equilibrium.

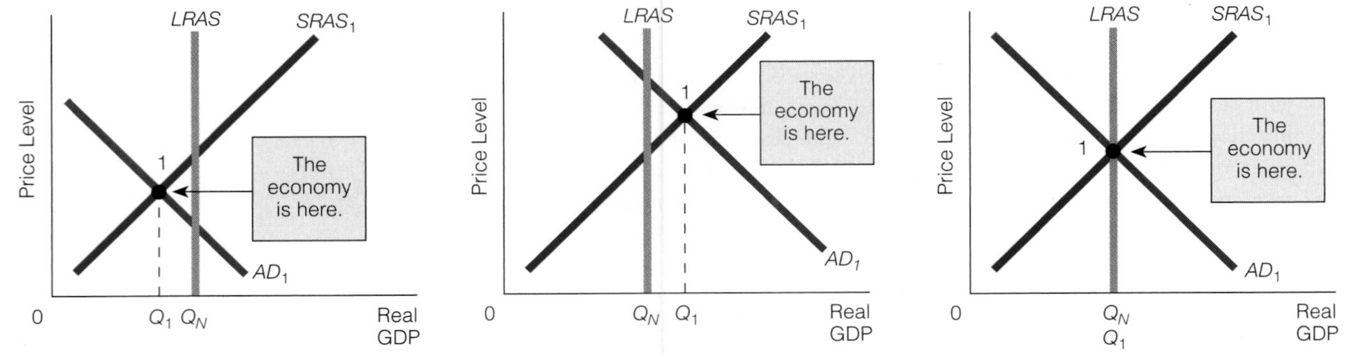

(a) (b) (c)

Economists often refer to the three possible states of an economy when they consider the relationship between Real GDP and Natural Real GDP. Three possible states of an economy are:

- Real GDP is less than Natural Real GDP.
- Real GDP is greater than Natural Real GDP.
- Real GDP is equal to Natural Real GDP.

Let's now name and graphically portray each of these three possible states of the economy.

REAL GDP IS LESS THAN NATURAL REAL GDP (RECESSIONARY GAP)

Exhibit 3(a) shows an *AD* curve, an *SRAS* curve, and the *LRAS* curve. It also shows that Natural Real GDP (Q_N) is produced in the long run.

Short-run equilibrium is at the intersection of the *AD* and *SRAS* curves; so, in Exhibit 3(a), short-run equilibrium is at point 1. The Real GDP level that the economy is producing at point 1 is designated by Q_1.

Now compare Q_1 with Q_N. Obviously, Q_1 is less than Q_N. In other words, the economy is currently producing a level of Real GDP in the short run that is less than its Natural Real GDP level.

When the Real GDP that the economy is producing is less than its Natural Real GDP, the economy is said to be in a **recessionary gap**.

Recessionary Gap
The condition in which the Real GDP that the economy is producing is less than the Natural Real GDP and the unemployment rate is greater than the natural unemployment rate.

REAL GDP IS GREATER THAN NATURAL REAL GDP (INFLATIONARY GAP) In Exhibit 3(b), the *AD* and *SRAS* curves intersect at point 1, so short-run equilibrium is at point 1. The Real GDP level that the economy is producing at point 1 is designated by Q_1. Compare Q_1 with Q_N. Obviously, Q_1 is greater than Q_N. In other words, the economy is currently producing a level of Real GDP in the short run that is greater than its Natural Real GDP level or potential output.

When the Real GDP that the economy is producing is greater than its Natural Real GDP, the economy is said to be in an **inflationary gap**.

Inflationary Gap
The condition in which the Real GDP that the economy is producing is greater than the Natural Real GDP and the unemployment rate is less than the natural unemployment rate.

REAL GDP IS EQUAL TO NATURAL REAL GDP (LONG-RUN EQUILIBRIUM) In Exhibit 3(c), the *AD* and *SRAS* curves indicate that short-run equilibrium is at point 1. The Real GDP level that the economy is producing at point 1 is designated by Q_1.

Again compare Q_1 and Q_N. This time, Q_1 is equal to Q_N. In other words, the economy is currently producing a level of Real GDP that is equal to its Natural Real GDP or potential output.

When the Real GDP that the economy is producing is equal to its Natural Real GDP, the economy is in *long-run equilibrium.*

Thinking like AN ECONOMIST

Thinking in Threes

The economist often thinks in threes. For the economist, a market has either (1) a shortage, (2) a surplus, or (3) equilibrium. Similarly, for the economist, an economy is either (1) in a recessionary gap producing a level of Real GDP lower than Natural Real GDP, (2) in an inflationary gap producing a level of Real GDP higher than Natural Real GDP, or (3) in long-run equilibrium producing a level of Real GDP equal to Natural Real GDP.

The Labor Market and the Three States of the Economy

If the economy can be in three possible states, so can the labor market. We identify the three possible states of the labor market and then tie each to a possible state of the economy.

We know that the labor market consists of the demand for and the supply of labor. Like a goods market, the labor market can manifest (1) equilibrium, (2) a shortage, or (3) a surplus. So three possible states of the labor market are:

- Equilibrium
- Shortage
- Surplus

When equilibrium exists in the labor market, the same number of jobs are available as the number of people who want to work. That is, the quantity demanded of labor is equal to the quantity supplied.

When the labor market has a shortage, more jobs are available than are people who want to work. That is, the quantity demanded of labor is greater than the quantity supplied.

When the labor market has a surplus, more people want to work than there are jobs available; the quantity supplied of labor is greater than the quantity demanded.

RECESSIONARY GAP AND THE LABOR MARKET If the economy is in a recessionary gap, is the labor market in equilibrium, shortage, or surplus? To simplify, suppose the economy is in a recessionary gap producing a Real GDP level of $9 trillion (worth of goods and services) when Natural Real GDP, or potential output, is $10 trillion.

The unemployment rate that exists when the economy produces Natural Real GDP is, of course, the natural unemployment rate. When the economy is in a recessionary gap, is the existing unemployment rate producing $9 trillion worth of goods and services greater or less than the natural unemployment rate that exists when the economy is producing \$10 trillion worth of goods and services? The answer is that the unemployment rate is greater than the natural unemployment rate because fewer workers are needed to produce a Real GDP of \$9 trillion than are needed to produce a Real GDP of \$10 trillion. *Ceteris paribus,* the unemployment rate will be higher at a Real GDP level of \$9 trillion than it is at a level of \$10 trillion.

We conclude that when the economy is in a recessionary gap, the unemployment rate is *higher* than the natural unemployment rate. This conclusion implies there is a surplus in the labor market: The quantity supplied of labor is greater than the quantity demanded, or more people want to work than there are jobs available.

If the economy is in a recessionary gap, the unemployment rate is higher than the natural unemployment rate, and a surplus exists in the labor market.

INFLATIONARY GAP AND THE LABOR MARKET Now suppose the economy is in an inflationary gap producing a Real GDP level of \$11 trillion (worth of goods and services) when Natural Real GDP, or potential output, is \$10 trillion.

Again, the unemployment rate that exists when the economy produces Natural Real GDP is the natural unemployment rate. Is the unemployment rate that exists when the economy is producing \$11 trillion worth of goods and services greater or less than the natural unemployment rate that exists when the economy is producing \$10 trillion worth of goods and services? The answer is that the unemployment rate is less than the natural unemployment rate because more workers are needed to produce a Real GDP of \$11 trillion than are needed to produce a Real GDP of \$10 trillion. *Ceteris paribus,* the unemployment rate will be lower at a Real GDP level of \$11 trillion than it is at a level of \$10 trillion.

We conclude that when the economy is in an inflationary gap, the unemployment rate is *lower* than the natural unemployment rate. This conclusion implies that there is a shortage in the labor market: The quantity demanded of labor is greater than the quantity supplied, or more jobs are available than there are people who want to work.

If the economy is in an inflationary gap, the unemployment rate is less than the natural unemployment rate, and a shortage exists in the labor market.

LONG-RUN EQUILIBRIUM AND THE LABOR MARKET Finally, suppose the economy is in long-run equilibrium. In other words, it is producing a Real GDP level equal to Natural Real GDP. In this state, the unemployment rate in the economy is the same as the natural unemployment rate. This conclusion implies that there is neither a shortage nor a surplus in the labor market; instead, equilibrium exists in the labor market.

If the economy is in long-run equilibrium, the unemployment rate equals the natural unemployment rate, and equilibrium exists in the labor market.

The following table summarizes three possible states of the economy and the related states of the labor market.

State of the Economy	What Do We Call It?	Relationship Between Unemployment Rate and Natural Unemployment Rate	State of the Labor Market
Real GDP < Natural Real GDP	Recessionary gap	Unemployment rate > Natural Unemployment rate	Surplus exists
Real GDP > Natural Real GDP	Inflationary gap	Unemployment rate < Natural Unemployment rate	Shortage exists
Real GDP = Natural Real GDP	Long-run equilibrium	Unemployment rate = Natural Unemployment rate	Equilibrium exists

Common Misconceptions

About the Unemployment Rate and the Natural Unemployment Rate

Some people mistakenly think that the economy's unemployment rate cannot be lower than the natural unemployment rate (as it is in an inflationary gap). In other words, if the natural unemployment rate is 5 percent, then the unemployment rate can never be 4 percent. But that opinion is a myth. To explain why, we need to use two production possibilities frontiers.

In Exhibit 4, the two production possibilities frontiers are the physical PPF (purple curve) and the institutional PPF (blue curve). The physical PPF illustrates different combinations of goods that the economy can produce, given the physical constraints of (1) finite resources and (2) the current state of technology.

The institutional PPF illustrates different combinations of goods that the economy can produce, given the physical constraints of (1) finite resources, (2) the current state of technology, and (3) any institutional constraints. Broadly defined, an institutional constraint is anything that prevents economic agents from producing the maximum Real GDP physically possible.

For example, the minimum wage law, which is an institutional constraint, specifies that workers must be paid a wage rate at least equal to the legislated minimum wage. One effect of this law is that unskilled persons whose value to employers falls below the legislated minimum wage will not be hired. Having fewer workers means less output, *ceteris paribus.* (This is why the institutional PPF lies closer to the origin than the physical PPF.)

Within the confines of society's physical and institutional constraints, there is a natural unemployment rate. This situation is represented by any point on the institutional PPF. In the exhibit, points A, B, and C are all such points.

exhibit 4

The Physical and Institutional PPFs

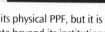

A society has both a physical PPF and an institutional PPF. The physical PPF illustrates different combinations of goods the economy can produce given the physical constraints of (1) finite resources and (2) the current state of technology. The institutional PPF illustrates different combinations of goods the economy can produce given the physical constraints of (1) finite resources, (2) the current state of technology, and (3) any institutional constraints. The economy is at the natural unemployment rate if it is located on its institutional PPF, such as at points A, B, or C. An economy can never operate beyond its physical PPF, but it is possible for it to operate beyond its institutional PPF because institutional constraints are not always equally effective. If the economy does operate beyond its institutional PPF, such as at point D, then the unemployment rate in the economy is lower than the natural unemployment rate.

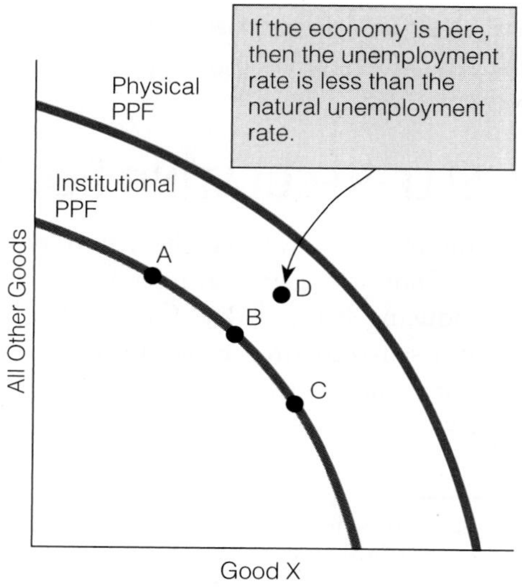

An economy can never operate beyond its physical PPF, but it can operate beyond its institutional PPF. For example, suppose inflation reduces the purchasing power of the minimum wage, thus reducing or eliminating the constraining properties of the minimum wage law on the unskilled labor market.[1] This would make one of society's institutional constraints ineffective, allowing the economy to temporarily move beyond the institutional constraint.

Logic dictates that if the economy is operating at the natural unemployment rate when it is located on its institutional PPF, then it must be operating at an unemployment rate lower than the natural rate when it is located beyond its institutional PPF (but below its physical PPF). Because society's institutional constraints are not always equally effective, an economy could be operating at an unemployment rate below the natural rate.

Finding ECONOMICS

In a Country's Institutional PPF

Assume that in year 1 Country A's unemployment rate was equal to its natural unemployment rate at 4.7 percent. In year 2 its unemployment rate was still equal to its natural unemployment rate at 5.4 percent. What was going on in the country between the two years? Where is the economics?

We learned earlier that if a country's unemployment rate is equal to its natural unemployment rate, then the country is operating on its institutional PPF. (It is also operating at long-run equilibrium.) Because country A's unemployment rate is equal to its natural unemployment rate in years 1 and 2, it follows that the country is operating on its institutional PPF in both years. But why are both the unemployment and natural unemployment rates higher (each at 5.4 percent) in year 2 than in year 1? What does this fact mean? Obviously, the country's institutional PPF has shifted inward between the two years. (We are assuming no change in the country's physical PPF.) In other words, some institutional changes came about between year 1 and year 2 that made it more difficult to produce goods and services. For example, perhaps changes in the regulatory climate in the country made it more difficult to produce output.

SELF-TEST

1. What is a recessionary gap? An inflationary gap?
2. What is the state of the labor market when the economy is in a recessionary gap? In an inflationary gap?
3. If the economy is in an inflationary gap, locate its position in terms of the two PPFs discussed in this section.

THE SELF-REGULATING ECONOMY

Some economists believe that the economy is self-regulating. In other words, if the economy is not at the natural unemployment rate (or full employment)—that is, it is not producing Natural Real GDP—then it can move itself to this position. The notion of a self-regulating economy is a very classical notion, but it is also a view held by some modern-day economists. This section describes how a self-regulating economy works.

1. Inflation reduces the real (inflation-adjusted) minimum wage. If the minimum wage rate is \$6 and the price level is 1.00, the real minimum wage is \$6 (\$6 divided by the price level, 1.00). If the price level rises to 2.00, then the real minimum wage rate falls to \$3. The lower the real minimum wage, the greater the number is of unskilled workers whom employers will hire, because the demand curve for unskilled workers is downward sloping.

What Happens if the Economy Is in a Recessionary Gap?

If the economy is in a recessionary gap,

1. it is producing a Real GDP level that is less than Natural Real GDP,
2. the unemployment rate is greater than the natural unemployment rate, and
3. a surplus exists in the labor market.

Exhibit 5(a) illustrates this case for a Real GDP of $9 trillion and a Natural Real GDP of $10 trillion. What, if anything, happens in the economy? According to economists who believe the economy is self-regulating, the surplus in the labor market begins to exert downward pressure on wages.[2] In other words, as old wage contracts expire, business firms will negotiate contracts that pay workers lower wage rates.

Recall from the last chapter that as wage rates fall, the *SRAS* curve begins to shift to the right, ultimately moving from $SRAS_1$ to $SRAS_2$ in Exhibit 5(b). As a result of the increase in short-run aggregate supply, the price level falls. But as the price level falls, the quantity demanded of Real GDP rises due to the real balance, interest rate, and international trade effects (all of which were discussed in the last chapter). As the price level falls, the economy moves from one point on the *AD* curve to a point farther down on the same curve. In Exhibit 5(b), this is a move from point 1 to point 2.

As long as the economy's Real GDP is less than its Natural Real GDP, the price level will continue to fall. Ultimately, the economy moves to long-run equilibrium at point 2, corresponding to P_2 and a Natural Real GDP of $10 trillion.

Recessionary gap →
Unemployment rate > Natural unemployment rate →
Surplus in labor market → Wages fall → *SRAS* curve shifts to the right →
Economy moves into long-run equilibrium

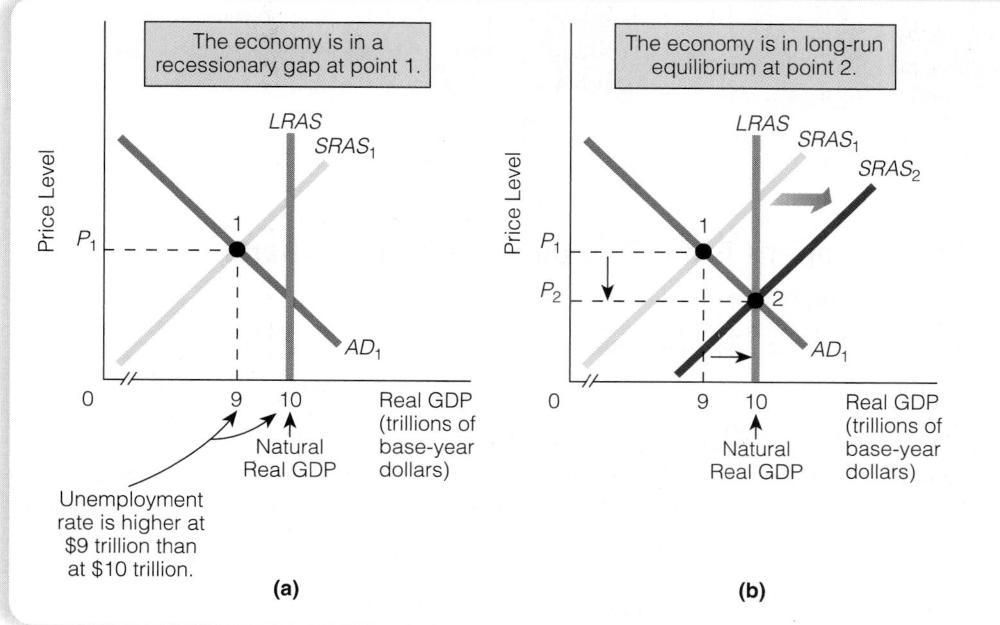

exhibit 5

The Self-Regulating Economy: Removing a Recessionary Gap

(a) The economy is at P_1 and Real GDP of $9 trillion. Because Real GDP is less than Natural Real GDP ($10 trillion), the economy is in a recessionary gap and the unemployment rate is higher than the natural unemployment rate. (b) Wage rates fall, and the short-run aggregate supply curve shifts from $SRAS_1$ to $SRAS_2$. As the price level falls, the real balance, interest rate, and international trade effects increase the quantity demanded of Real GDP. Ultimately, the economy moves into long-run equilibrium at point 2.

2. In this discussion of how the self-regulating economy eliminates a recessionary gap, we have emphasized wages (in the labor market) adjusting downward. Resource prices other than wages may fall as well.

economics 24/7

NATURAL DISASTERS AND THE ECONOMY

Do natural disasters (such as hurricanes, tornadoes, earthquakes, and some fires) affect the economy? Hurricane Katrina was a major hurricane that hit the central Gulf Coast on the morning of August 29, 2005. Katrina caused catastrophic damage along the coastlines of Louisiana, Mississippi, and Alabama. The levees that separated Lake Pontchartrain from the city of New Orleans were damaged by Katrina, ultimately leading to the flooding of about 80 percent of the city.

©AP PHOTO/RIC FIELD

How does something like Hurricane Katrina affect the economy? Is it possible to translate Katrina (or any natural disaster) into our aggregate demand–aggregate supply framework of analysis?

Katrina is an adverse supply shock to the economy, thus shifting the *SRAS* curve to the left. Katrina essentially destroyed lives (labor) and capital (production facilities, oil platforms) and thus adversely affected the economy's ability to produce goods and services.

Think of what a shift leftward in the *SRAS* curve means in terms of Real GDP. Either there will be an absolute decline in Real GDP, or Real GDP will not grow by as much as it would have had Katrina not occurred. (With respect to the latter possibility, think of Katrina as shifting the *SRAS* curve leftward at the same time that some forces in the economy are shifting the *SRAS* curve rightward. Even if the forces shifting the *SRAS* curve rightward are stronger than the leftward forces, like Katrina, still the left-shifting forces have an effect on the final position of the *SRAS* curve.)

Soon after Katrina, both private and government economic groups changed their predictions of growth in Real GDP. For example, both Merrill Lynch and Bank of America revised their growth figures for Real GDP downward. The Congressional Budget Office (CBO) reported that the growth rate in Real GDP would decline by 0.5 to 1 percent due to Hurricane Katrina. The CBO also predicted that employment would fall by 400,000 persons due to Katrina.

What about the self-regulating properties of the economy? Could a natural disaster destabilize the economy permanently, thus producing an economy that became so destabilized that it couldn't find its way back to Natural Real GDP without, say, government intervention? According to economists who believe the economy is self-regulating, the answer is no. Even if a natural disaster moved the economy into a recessionary gap, the self-regulating properties of the economy would soon exert themselves and remove the economy from the recessionary gap. In other words, if a natural disaster happened to move Real GDP below its natural level, in time wages would fall, the *SRAS* curve would shift rightward, and the economy would have self-regulated itself at its Natural Real GDP level.

What Happens if the Economy Is in an Inflationary Gap?

If the economy is in an inflationary gap,

1. it is producing a Real GDP level that is greater than Natural Real GDP,
2. the unemployment rate is less than the natural unemployment rate, and
3. a shortage exists in the labor market.

Exhibit 6(a) illustrates this case for a Real GDP of $11 trillion and a Natural Real GDP of $10 trillion. What happens in the economy in this situation? Again, according to economists who believe the economy is self-regulating, the shortage in the labor market begins to exert upward pressure on wages. In other words, as old wage contracts expire, business firms will negotiate contracts that pay workers higher wage rates.

As wage rates rise, the *SRAS* curve begins to shift to the left, ultimately moving from $SRAS_1$ to $SRAS_2$ in Exhibit 6(b). As a result of the decrease in short-run aggregate supply, the price level rises. But as the price level rises, the quantity demanded

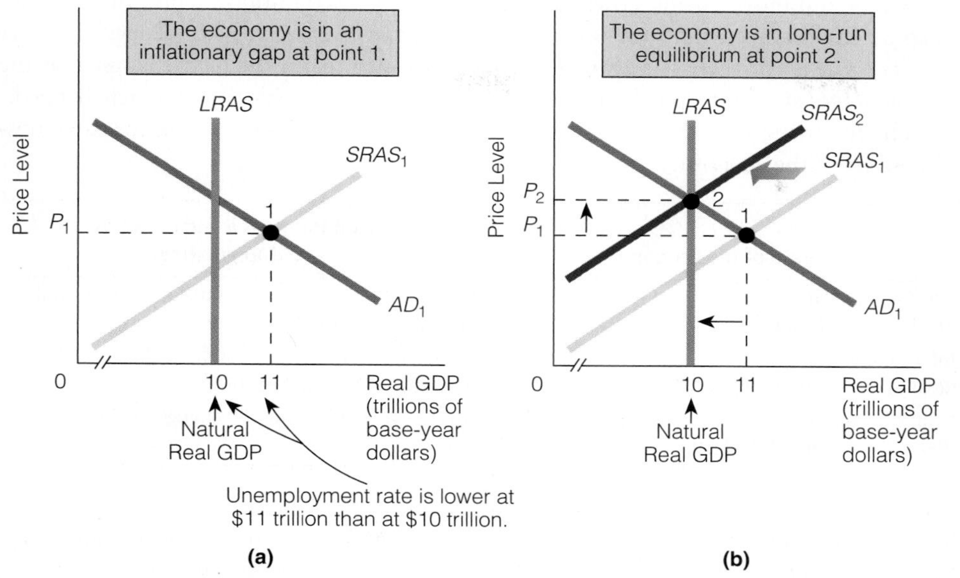

exhibit 6

The Self-Regulating Economy: Removing an Inflationary Gap

(a) The economy is at P_1 and Real GDP of \$11 trillion. Because Real GDP is greater than Natural Real GDP (\$10 trillion), the economy is in an inflationary gap and the unemployment rate is lower than the natural unemployment rate. (b) Wage rates rise, and the short-run aggregate supply curve shifts from $SRAS_1$ to $SRAS_2$. As the price level rises, the real balance, interest rate, and international trade effects decrease the quantity demanded of Real GDP. Ultimately, the economy moves into long-run equilibrium at point 2.

of Real GDP falls due to the real balance, interest rate, and international trade effects. As the price level rises, the economy moves from one point on the *AD* curve to a point farther up on the same curve. In Exhibit 6(b), this is a move from point 1 to point 2.

As long as the economy's Real GDP is greater than its Natural Real GDP, the price level will continue to rise. Ultimately, the economy moves to long-run equilibrium at point 2, corresponding to P_2, and a Natural Real GDP of \$10 trillion.

Inflationary gap →
Unemployment rate < Natural unemployment rate →
Shortage in labor market → Wages rise → *SRAS* curve shifts to the left →
Economy moves into long-run equilibrium

The Self-Regulating Economy: A Recap

We have shown that if the economy is in a recessionary gap, wage rates fall (along with other resource prices), and the *SRAS* curve shifts to the right. As this happens, the price level falls and the economy moves down the *AD* curve. The economy moves in the direction of long-run equilibrium, ultimately achieving the Natural Real GDP level.

If the economy is in an inflationary gap, wage rates rise (along with other resource prices), and the *SRAS* curve shifts to the left. As this happens, the price level rises and the economy moves up the *AD* curve. The economy moves in the direction of long-run equilibrium, ultimately achieving the Natural Real GDP level.

Flexible wage rates (and other resource prices) play a critical role in the self-regulating economy. For example, suppose wage rates are not flexible and do not fall in a recessionary gap. Then, the *SRAS* curve will not shift to the right. But if the *SRAS* curve does not shift to the right, the price level will not fall. And if the price level does not fall, the economy won't move down the *AD* curve toward long-run equilibrium. Similarly, if wage rates are not flexible and do not rise in an inflationary gap, then the economy won't move up the *AD* curve toward long-run equilibrium.

The economists who believe in a self-regulating economy—classical economists, monetarists, and new classical economists—believe that wage rates and other resource prices are *flexible* and move up and down in response to market conditions. Thus, these economists believe that *wage rates will fall* when there is a *surplus of labor*. They believe that *wage rates will rise* when there is a *shortage of labor*. You will see in the next chapter that the flexible wages and prices position taken by these economists has not gone unchallenged.

The following table summarizes how a self-regulating economy works for three possible states of the economy.

State of the Economy	What Happens if the Economy Is Self-Regulating?
Recessionary gap (Real GDP < Natural Real GDP)	Wages fall and *SRAS* curve shifts to the right until Real GDP = Natural Real GDP.
Inflationary gap (Real GDP > Natural Real GDP)	Wages rise and *SRAS* curve shifts to the left until Real GDP = Natural Real GDP.
Long-run equilibrium (Real GDP = Natural Real GDP)	No change in wages and no change in *SRAS*.

macro*theme* ➔ One of the macroeconomic categories we introduced in an earlier chapter was the *self-regulating–economic instability* category. We said then that some economists believe the economy is self-regulating and that other economists believe the economy is inherently unstable (or *not* self-regulating). This macro theme has been started in this chapter. You just heard from economists who believe the economy is self-regulating. In later chapters, you will hear from economists who believe the economy is inherently unstable.

Policy Implication of Believing the Economy Is Self-Regulating

Classical, new classical, and monetarist economists believe that the economy is self-regulating. For these economists, full employment is the norm: The economy always moves back to Natural Real GDP. Stated differently, if the economy becomes "ill"—in the form of a recessionary or an inflationary gap—it certainly is capable of healing itself through changes in wages and prices. This belief in how the economy works has led these economists to advocate a macroeconomic policy of **laissez-faire**, or noninterference. In these economists' view, government does not have an economic management role to play.

Laissez-faire
A public policy of not interfering with market activities in the economy.

Changes in a Self-Regulating Economy: Short Run and Long Run

Let's consider how a change in aggregate demand affects the economy in the short run and the long run if the economy is self-regulating. In Exhibit 7(a), the economy is initially in long-run equilibrium at point 1. Suppose an increase in aggregate demand is brought about by, say, an increase in government purchases (a possibility discussed in the last chapter). The *AD* curve shifts right from AD_1 to AD_2, and in the short run, the economy moves to point 2 with both Real GDP and the price level each higher than at point 1. Now at point 2, the economy is in an inflationary gap. If the economy is self-regulating, wages will soon rise, and the *SRAS* curve will shift to the left—ultimately from $SRAS_1$ to $SRAS_2$. The economy will end up at point 3 in long-run equilibrium.

Now let's examine the changes in the short run and the long run. As a result of an increase in aggregate demand, Real GDP rises, and the price level rises in the short run. In addition, because Real GDP rises, the unemployment rate falls. In the long run, when the economy is at point 3, it is producing exactly the same level of Real GDP that it was producing originally (Q_N) but at a higher price level.

exhibit 7

Changes in a Self-Regulating Economy: Short Run and Long Run

In (a) the economy is initially at point 1 in long-run equilibrium. Aggregate demand rises and the *AD* curve shifts right from AD_1 to AD_2. The economy is at point 2 in the short run, with a higher Real GDP and a higher price level than at point 1. The economy is also in an inflationary gap at point 2. If the economy is self-regulating, wages will soon rise, the *SRAS* curve will shift left from $SRAS_1$ to $SRAS_2$, and the economy will be in long-run equilibrium at point 3. At point 3, the economy is producing the same Real GDP as it did at point 1. In other words, in the long run, an increase in aggregate demand only raises the price level. In (b) the economy is initially at point 1 in long-run equilibrium. Aggregate demand falls and the *AD* curve shifts left from AD_1 to AD_2. The economy is at point 2 in the short run, with a lower Real GDP and a lower price level than at point 1. The economy is also in a recessionary gap. If the economy is self-regulating, wages will soon fall, the *SRAS* curve will shift right from $SRAS_1$ to $SRAS_2$, and the economy will be in long-run equilibrium at point 3. At point 3, the economy is producing the same Real GDP as it did at point 1. In other words, in the long run, a decrease in aggregate demand only lowers the price level.

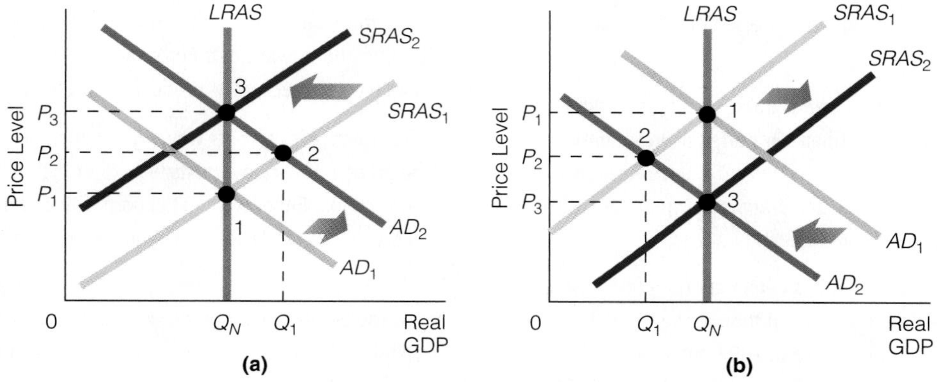

Conclusion: If the economy is self-regulating, an increase in aggregate demand can raise the price level and Real GDP in the short run, but in the long run the only effect of an increase in aggregate demand is a rise in the price level. In other words, in the long run, all that we have is only higher prices to show for an increase in aggregate demand.

Now let's consider what happens if aggregate demand falls. In Exhibit 7(b), the economy is initially in long-run equilibrium at point 1. Suppose aggregate demand decreases. The *AD* curve shifts left from AD_1 to AD_2, and in the short run the economy moves to point 2 with both Real GDP and the price level lower than each was at point 1.

Now at point 2, the economy is in a recessionary gap. If the economy is self-regulating, wages will soon fall and the *SRAS* curve will shift to the right—ultimately from $SRAS_1$ to $SRAS_2$. The economy will end up at point 3 in long-run equilibrium.

Again, let's examine the changes in the short run and the long run. As a result of a decrease in aggregate demand, Real GDP falls, and the price level falls in the short run. In addition, because Real GDP falls, the unemployment rate rises. In the long run, when the economy is at point 3, it is producing exactly the same level of Real GDP that it was producing originally (Q_N) but at a lower price level.

Conclusion: If the economy is self-regulating, a decrease in aggregate demand can lower the price level and Real GDP in the short run, but in the long run the only effect of a decrease in aggregate demand is a lower price level.

Change in *AD*	In the Short Run	In the Long Run
AD ↑	*P* ↑, *Q* ↑	*P* ↑, *Q* does not change
AD ↓	*P* ↓, *Q* ↓	*P* ↓, *Q* does not change

Let's return to Exhibit 7(a) to clarify a point about long-run equilibrium. In the exhibit, the economy starts at point 1 in long-run equilibrium and then moves to point 2.

economics 24/7

THE STORY BEHIND THE CURVES ON THE BLACKBOARD

The economics professor stands at the front of the classroom and draws some curves on the blackboard. The first curve is a downward-sloping *AD* curve; the second, an upward-sloping *SRAS* curve; the third, a vertical *LRAS* curve. "Starting in long-run equilibrium," the professor asks, "what happens if net exports rise? That's right, the *AD* curve shifts to the right and we see that the economy moves into an inflationary gap. . . ."

In the classroom, economics often comes down to curves shifting and new equilibrium points being identified. This often makes it easy to forget the real story behind the shifting curves. To illustrate, consider a story of two European companies, the European Commission (EC) of the European Union (EU), tariffs, and China.[3]

In recent years, the European Union has been importing fairly cheap, energy-saving light bulbs from China, even though the EU had imposed tariffs on these light bulbs. In Fall 2007, the EC considered removing the tariffs. Then things changed, and the Commission ended its discussions and postponed any removal of tariffs. What happened?

The European Commission was being pulled in opposite directions. Philips Electronics of the Netherlands was lobbying the Commission to remove the tariffs. Philips Electronics manufactures many of its light bulbs in China and stood to gain between $20 and $29 million a year if the tariffs were removed. But Osram, a German company that competes with Philips Electronics, manufactures few of its light bulbs in China. For Osram, removing the tariffs would compromise its competitive position in the light bulb market. Osram lobbied the EC to keep the tariffs. In trying to strengthen its position, Osram argued that Philips Electronics was not a European producer of light bulbs because it outsourced so much of its production to China.

If Philips Electronics gets its way, light bulb imports to EU countries will be greater; if Osram gets its way, light bulb imports will either stay the same or fall. Either way, net exports will be affected, and, according to the *AD-AS* model in this chapter, so will aggregate demand and Real GDP.

What is the point? On one level, we have a story of shifting curves on a blackboard. At another level, we have a story of real-world politicking, profits, and jobs.

3. This feature is based on "Europe Weighs the Trade-Offs: Even as Imports from China Have Benefited the European Economy, There Is a Growing Inclination Toward Protectionism in Its Trade Policy" by Stephen Castle, *International Herald Tribune*, November 7, 2007.

At point 2, both the price level and Real GDP are higher than they were at point 1. In other words, if *AD* rises, both the price level and Real GDP rise in the short run. If the economy is self-regulating, it will not remain at point 2 but rather move to point 3, where it is again in long-run equilibrium. At point 3, the price level is higher than it was at point 2, but Real GDP is lower. Why, then, don't we say that Real GDP is lower in the long run than it is in the short run, instead of saying that Real GDP does not change in the long run? The answer is that the long run is measured from one long-run equilibrium point to another long-run equilibrium point. In terms of Exhibit 7(a), we look at the long run by comparing point 1 and point 3. When we make this comparison, we notice two things: The price level is higher at point 3 than at point 1, and Real GDP is the same at both points.

SELF-TEST

1. If the economy is self-regulating, what happens if it is in a recessionary gap?
2. If the economy is self-regulating, what happens if it is in an inflationary gap?
3. If the economy is self-regulating, how do changes in aggregate demand affect the economy in the long run?

office hours

"DO ECONOMISTS REALLY KNOW WHAT THE NATURAL UNEMPLOYMENT RATE EQUALS?"

Student:

Do economists know what the natural unemployment rate equals at any given moment?

Instructor:

They estimate it but can't be absolutely sure that their estimate of the natural unemployment rate is the same as the natural unemployment rate. After all, not all economists get the same estimate for the natural unemployment rate. One economist might estimate the natural unemployment rate at 4.3 percent, whereas another estimates it at 4.6 percent.

Student:

Well, if that's true, then not every economist would agree the economy is in, say, a recessionary gap if the unemployment rate is, say, 4.5 percent. Am I correct?

Instructor:

You are correct. For example, the economist who thinks the natural unemployment rate is 4.3 percent will think the economy is in a recessionary gap if the actual unemployment rate is 4.5 percent, but the economist who thinks the natural unemployment rate is 4.6 percent will not. Here's an analogy: Smith thinks that Brown's normal body temperature is 98.9 degrees and Jones thinks it is only 98.6 degrees. If Brown's body temperature today is 98.9 degrees, Jones will think Brown is running a low-grade fever, but Smith will not.

Student:

Does getting a too-high or too-low estimate of the natural unemployment rate matter to the economy? In other words, do the incorrect estimates (that economists sometimes make) matter?

Instructor:

Actually, there is a yes and a no answer to that question. The answer is no if the economy is self-regulating and government doesn't plan to try to move the economy out of either a recessionary or inflationary gap by implementing economic policies. As in the example of misestimating Brown's normal body temperature, if no one plans to give Brown any medicine, then misestimating his body temperature probably doesn't matter.

But in later chapters you are going to read about the government implementing certain economic policies to try to remove the economy from either a recessionary or inflationary gap. Then misestimating the natural unemployment rate does matter.

To illustrate, suppose the natural unemployment rate has fallen from 5.0 percent to 4.7 percent, but economists and government economic policy makers have not figured this out yet. In other words, they still believe that the natural unemployment rate is 5.0 percent. Now if the actual unemployment rate is 4.7 percent, then the economy is in long-run equilibrium. Economists and government economic policy makers, however, mistakenly believe that the economy is in an inflationary gap (with the actual unemployment rate of 4.7 percent lower than their too-high estimate of 5.0 percent for the natural unemployment rate). Thinking the economy is in an inflationary gap, economists expect prices to rise in the future. To offset the higher prices in the future, they propose a reduction in the growth rate of the money supply in the hopes of reducing aggregate demand (shifting the *AD* curve to the left). The Federal Reserve (the monetary authority) follows suit and reduces the growth rate of the money supply, and the *AD* curve shifts leftward. But notice the effect of this in terms of our *AD-AS* model. A reduction in aggregate demand throws the economy into a recessionary gap. (Remember, the economy was actually in long-run equilibrium when the monetary policy action was carried out.)

Our conclusion is simple: A misestimate of the natural unemployment rate, if acted on, can move an economy from long-run equilibrium into a recessionary gap.

Back to the original question: Does getting a too-high or too-low estimate of the natural unemployment rate matter to the economy? The answer is yes, it certainly can matter to the economy.

Points to Remember

1. It is possible for economists to misestimate the natural unemployment rate.
2. Acting on a misestimated natural unemployment rate can affect the economy. For example, if a misestimated natural unemployment rate influences economic policy actions, then it can affect the economy (sometimes adversely).

a reader asks — Why Don't All Economists Agree?

According to the text, not all economists believe the economy is self-regulating. Why don't all economists agree on how the economy works?

One (but not the only) reason is that economists can't undertake controlled experiments. In a controlled experiment, they could change one variable, leave all other variables unchanged, and then see what happens. Then whatever happens must be the result of the one variable they changed.

To illustrate, suppose you want to know whether increasing your intake of vitamin C will reduce the number of colds you get in a year. In a controlled experiment, you would increase your intake of vitamin C and keep everything else in your life the same: the amount of sleep you get each night, the amount of exercise you get, the people you are around, and so on. Then you would observe whether you got fewer colds. If you did, you could be reasonably sure that it was because of your increased intake of vitamin C.

Now let's see what happens in economics because economists cannot run controlled experiments. Suppose Real GDP falls in February 2007. Economist A argues that the decline in Real GDP was due to high interest rates in July 2006, not to higher taxes in August 2006. Economist B argues just the opposite: The decline in Real GDP was due to high taxes in August 2006, not to high interest rates in July 2006.

Obviously, economist A's theory states that a change in interest rates affects Real GDP but a change in taxes does not. Economist B has a theory that a change in taxes affects Real GDP but a change in interest rates does not. It would be nice to test each theory in a controlled environment: Change taxes and nothing else, and see what happens; or change interest rates and nothing else, and see what happens. You can see that if we could do this, some of the disagreements between economists A and B are likely to disappear.

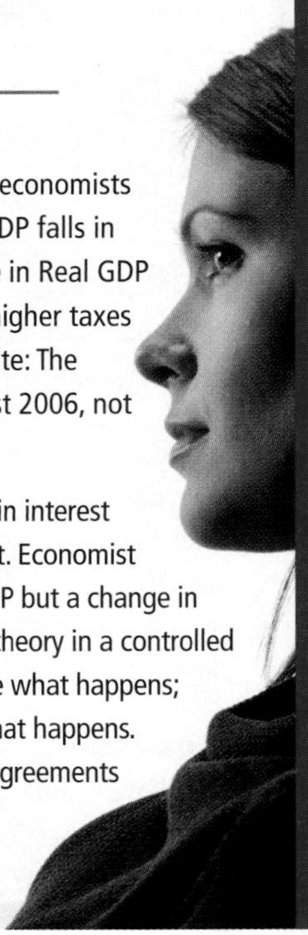

Chapter Summary

SAY'S LAW

- Say's law states that supply creates its own demand. All economists believe that Say's law holds in a barter economy, where there can be no general overproduction or underproduction of goods. Classical economists believed that Say's law also holds in a money economy. In their view, even if consumption drops and saving rises, economic forces are at work producing an equal increase in investment. According to classical economists, interest rates are flexible, and they move to a level that equates the amount of saving and the amount of investment in an economy.

CLASSICAL ECONOMISTS ON MARKETS, WAGES, AND PRICES

- Classical economists believed that most, if not all, markets are competitive and that wages and prices are flexible.

THREE STATES OF THE ECONOMY

- Natural Real GDP is the level of Real GDP that is produced when the economy is operating at the natural unemployment rate.
- The economy can be producing a Real GDP level that (1) is equal to Natural Real GDP, (2) is greater than Natural Real GDP, or (3) is less than Natural Real GDP. In other words, the economy can be in (1) long-run equilibrium, (2) an inflationary gap, or (3) a recessionary gap, respectively.
- In long-run equilibrium, the Real GDP that the economy is producing is equal to the Natural Real GDP. The unemployment rate in the economy is equal to the natural unemployment rate, and the labor market is in equilibrium.
- In a recessionary gap, the Real GDP that the economy is producing is less than the Natural Real GDP. The unemployment rate in the economy is greater than the natural unemployment rate, and a surplus exists in the labor market.
- In an inflationary gap, the Real GDP that the economy is producing is greater than the Natural Real GDP. The unemployment rate in the economy is less than the natural unemployment rate, and a shortage exists in the labor market.

THE INSTITUTIONAL AND PHYSICAL PRODUCTION POSSIBILITIES FRONTIERS

- The physical PPF illustrates different combinations of goods that the economy can produce, given the physical constraints of (1) finite resources and (2) the current state of technology. The institutional PPF illustrates different combinations of goods that the economy can produce, given the physical constraints of (1) finite resources, (2) the current state of technology, and (3) any institutional constraints.

- If an economy is operating on its institutional PPF, it is operating at the natural unemployment rate. If it is operating at a point beyond the institutional PPF but below the physical PPF, it is operating at an unemployment rate less than the natural unemployment rate.

THE SELF-REGULATING ECONOMY

- Some economists (classical, new classical, monetarists) contend that the economy can eliminate both recessionary and inflationary gaps smoothly and quickly by itself.
- If the economy is self-regulating and in a recessionary gap, then the unemployment rate in the economy is greater than the natural unemployment rate, and a surplus exists in the labor market. As wage contracts expire, wage rates fall. As a result, the *SRAS* curve shifts to the right, and the price level falls. As the price level falls, the quantity demanded of Real GDP rises. Ultimately, the economy will move into long-run equilibrium, where it will be producing Natural Real GDP.
- If the economy is self-regulating and in an inflationary gap, then the unemployment rate in the economy is less than the natural unemployment rate, and a shortage exists in the labor market. As wage contracts expire, wage rates rise. As a result, the *SRAS* curve shifts to the left and the price level rises. As the price level rises, the quantity demanded of Real GDP falls. Ultimately, the economy will move into long-run equilibrium, where it will be producing Natural Real GDP.

Key Terms and Concepts

Say's Law | Recessionary Gap | Inflationary Gap | Laissez-faire

Questions and Problems

1 What is the classical economics position on (a) wages, (b) prices, and (c) interest rates?

2 According to classical economists, does Say's law hold in a money economy? Explain your answer.

3 What is the explanation for why investment falls as the interest rate rises?

4 What is the explanation for why saving rises as the interest rate rises?

5 According to classical economists, does an increase in saving shift the *AD* curve to the left? Explain your answer.

6 What does it mean to say the economy is in a recessionary gap? In an inflationary gap? In long-run equilibrium?

7 What is the state of the labor market in each of the following states: (a) a recessionary gap, (b) an inflationary gap, (c) long-run equilibrium?

8 Describe the relationship of the (actual) unemployment rate to the natural unemployment rate in each of the following economic states: (a) a recessionary gap, (b) an inflationary gap, and (c) long-run equilibrium.

9 Diagrammatically represent an economy in (a) an inflationary gap, (b) a recessionary gap, and (c) long-run equilibrium.

10 Explain how an economy can operate beyond its institutional PPF but not beyond its physical PPF.

11 According to economists who believe in a self-regulating economy, what happens—step by step—when the economy is in a recessionary gap? What happens when the economy is in an inflationary gap?

12 If wage rates are not flexible, can the economy be self-regulating? Explain your answer.

13 Explain the importance of the real balance, interest rate, and international trade effects to long-run (equilibrium) adjustment in the economy.

14 Suppose that the economy is self-regulating, that the price level is 132, that the quantity demanded of Real GDP is \$4 trillion, that the quantity supplied of Real GDP in the short run is \$3.9 trillion, and that the quantity supplied of Real GDP in the long run is \$4.3 trillion. Is the economy in short-run equilibrium? Will the price level in long-run equilibrium be greater than, less than, or equal to 132? Explain your answers.

15 Suppose that the economy is self-regulating, that the price level is 110, that the quantity demanded of Real GDP is \$4 trillion, that the quantity supplied of Real GDP in the short run is \$4.9 trillion, and that the quantity supplied of Real GDP in the long run is \$4.1 trillion. Is the economy in short-run equilibrium? Will the price level in long-run equilibrium be greater than, less than, or equal to 110? Explain your answers.

16 Yvonne is telling her friend Wendy that wages are rising but that then so is the unemployment rate. She tells Wendy that she may be the next person to be fired at her company and that she may have to move back in with her parents. What does the economy have to do with Yvonne's possibly having to move back in with her parents?

17 Jim says, "I think it's a little like when you have a cold or the flu. You don't need to see a doctor. In time, your body heals itself. That's sort of the way the economy works too. We don't really need government coming to our rescue every time the economy gets a cold." According to Jim, how does the economy work?

18 Beginning in long-run equilibrium, explain what will happen to the price level and Real GDP in the short run and in the long run as a result of (a) a decline in *AD*, (b) a rise in *AD*, (c) a decline in *SRAS*, and (d) a rise in *SRAS*.

Working with Numbers and Graphs

1 In the following figure, which point is representative of
   a. The economy on its *LRAS* curve.
   b. The economy in a recessionary gap.
   c. The economy in an inflationary gap.

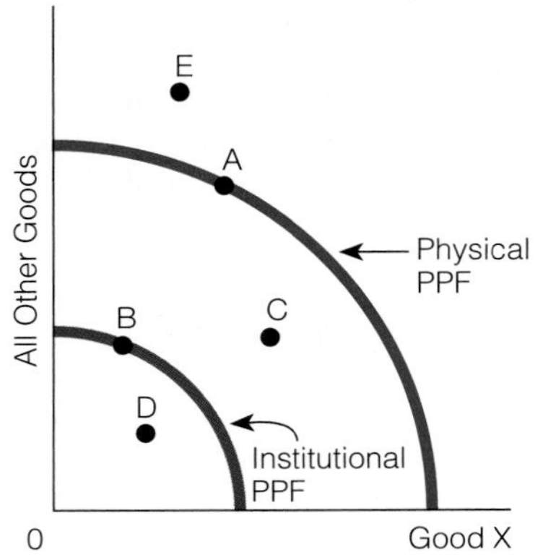

2 In the following figure, which of parts (a)–(c) is consistent with or representative of:
   a. The economy operating at the natural unemployment rate.
   b. A surplus in the labor market.
   c. A recessionary gap.
   d. A cyclical unemployment rate of zero.

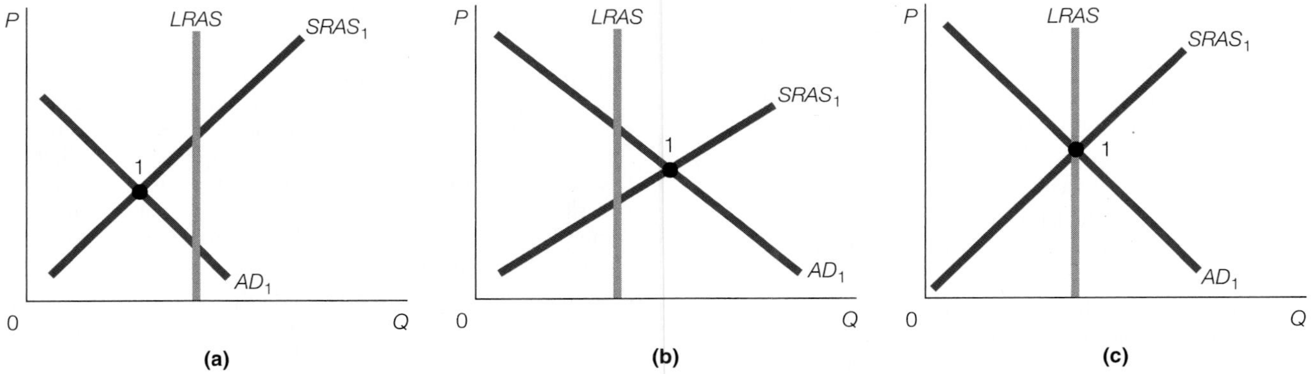

3 Diagrammatically represent the following:
   a. An economy in which *AD* increases as it is self-regulating out of a recessionary gap.
   b. An economy in which *AD* decreases as it is self-regulating out of an inflationary gap.

4 Economist Jones believes there is always sufficient (aggregate) demand in the economy to buy all the goods and services supplied at full employment. Diagrammatically represent what the economy looks like for Jones.

5 Diagrammatically show what happens when the institutional constraints in the economy become less effective.

©JACK SCRIVENER/SUTTERSTOCK

CHAPTER 9

ECONOMIC INSTABILITY: A CRITIQUE OF THE SELF-REGULATING ECONOMY

Introduction In the last chapter we discussed the economy as a self-regulating mechanism. For example, we learned that an economy can remove itself from a recessionary gap. In this chapter we challenge that assertion and discuss the views of economists who believe that the economy may not be able to self-regulate at Natural Real GDP. In other words, the economy may not be able to move itself out of a recessionary gap. The ideas in this chapter are mostly those of one man, John Maynard Keynes, who taught economics at Cambridge University in England.

QUESTIONING THE CLASSICAL POSITION

John Maynard Keynes, an English economist, changed how many economists viewed the economy. Keynes's major work, *The General Theory of Employment, Income and Money*, was published in 1936. Just prior to its publication, the Great Depression had plagued many countries of the world. Looking around at the world during that time, one had to wonder if the classical view of the economy wasn't wrong. After all, unemployment was sky high in many countries, and numerous economies had been contracting. Where was Say's law, with its promise that there would be no general gluts? Where was the self-regulating economy that was supposed to heal itself of its depression illness? Where was full employment? And, given the depressed state of the economy, could anyone any longer believe that laissez-faire was the right policy? With the Great Depression as recent history, Keynes and the Keynesians thought that, although their theory may not be right in every detail, they certainly had enough evidence to say that the classical view of the economy was wrong.

Keynes challenged all four of the following classical position beliefs: (1) Say's law holds, so that insufficient demand in the economy is unlikely. (2) Wages, prices, and interest rates are flexible. (3) The economy is self-regulating. (4) Laissez-faire is the right and sensible economic policy.

Keynes's Criticism of Say's Law in a Money Economy

According to classical economists and Say's law, if consumption spending falls because saving increases, then total spending will not fall, because the added saving will simply bring about more investment spending. This will happen through changes in the interest rate. The added saving will put downward pressure on the interest rate, and at a lower interest rate businesses will borrow and invest more. Through changes in the interest rate, the amount of saving will always equal the amount invested.

Keynes disagreed. He didn't think that added saving will necessarily stimulate an equal amount of added investment spending. Exhibit 1 illustrates Keynes's point of view. As in the last chapter, we let consumption equal \$3,000, investment equal \$600, government purchases equal \$1,200, and net exports equal \$200. Then saving increases by \$100, which lowers consumption to \$2,900. According to the classical economists, investment will rise by \$100 at the same time, going from \$600 to \$700. Keynes asked what guarantee is there that an increase in saving will be equally matched by an increase in investment? What if saving rises by \$100 (which means consumption goes down by \$100), but investment rises by, say, only \$40 (instead of \$100)? In this situation, the equation $TE = C + I + G + (EX - IM)$ changes from

$$TE = \$3{,}000 + \$600 + \$1{,}200 + \$200 = \$5{,}000$$

to

$$TE = \$2{,}900 + \$640 + \$1{,}200 + \$200 = \$4{,}940$$

exhibit 1

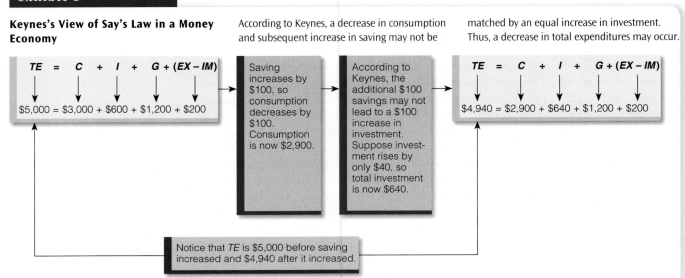

Keynes's View of Say's Law in a Money Economy

According to Keynes, a decrease in consumption and subsequent increase in saving may not be matched by an equal increase in investment. Thus, a decrease in total expenditures may occur.

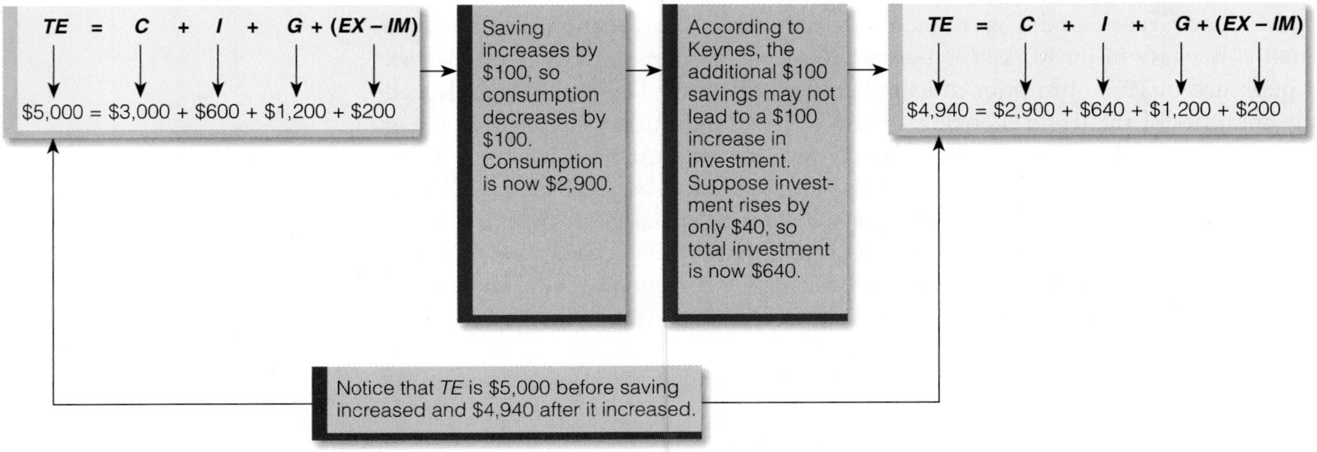
TE = C + I + G + (EX – IM)
\$5,000 = \$3,000 + \$600 + \$1,200 + \$200
Saving increases by \$100, so consumption decreases by \$100. Consumption is now \$2,900.
According to Keynes, the additional \$100 savings may not lead to a \$100 increase in investment. Suppose investment rises by only \$40, so total investment is now \$640.
TE = C + I + G + (EX – IM)
\$4,940 = \$2,900 + \$640 + \$1,200 + \$200
Notice that TE is \$5,000 before saving increased and \$4,940 after it increased.

Thus, total expenditures decrease from \$5,000 to \$4,940. And if, at a given price level, total spending falls, so will aggregate demand. In other words, according to Keynes, saving could increase and aggregate demand could fall.

Of course, a classical economist would retort that, as a result of a \$100 increase in saving, interest rates will fall enough to guarantee that investment will increase by \$100. But Keynes countered by saying that individuals save and invest for a host of reasons and that no single factor, such as the interest rate, links these activities.

Furthermore, Keynes believed that saving is more responsive to changes in income than to changes in the interest rate and that investment is more responsive to technological changes, business expectations, and innovations than to changes in the interest rate. In summary, whereas the classical economists believed that saving and investment depend on the interest rate, Keynes believed that both saving and investment depend on a number of factors that may be far more influential than the interest rate.

Consider the difference between Keynes and the classical economists on saving. As noted, the classical economists held that saving is directly related to the interest rate: As the interest rate goes up, saving rises; as the interest rate goes down, saving falls, *ceteris paribus*.

Keynes thought this assumption might not always be true. Suppose individuals are saving for a certain goal—say, a retirement fund of \$100,000. They might save less per period at an interest rate of 10 percent than at an interest rate of 5 percent because a higher interest rate means that they can save less per period and still meet their goal within a set time. For example, if the interest rate is 5 percent, \$50,000 in savings is needed to earn \$2,500 in interest income per year. If the interest rate is 10 percent, only \$25,000 in savings is needed to earn \$2,500 in interest.

As for investment, Keynes believed that the interest rate is important in determining the level of investment, but not as important as other variables, such as the expected rate of profit on investment. Keynes argued that if business expectations are pessimistic, then much investment is unlikely, regardless of how low the interest rate is.

Keynes on Wage Rates

As stated in the last chapter, if the unemployment rate in the economy is greater than the natural unemployment rate, a surplus exists in the labor market: The number of job seekers is high relative to the number of jobs available. Consequently, according to classical economists, wage rates will fall.

Keynes didn't believe the adjustment was so simple. Instead, he said, employees will naturally resist an employer's efforts to cut wages, and labor unions may resist wage cuts. In short, wage rates may be inflexible in a downward direction.

Suppose Keynes is correct and wage rates won't fall. Does this mean that the economy cannot get itself out of a recessionary gap? The unequivocal answer is yes. If employee and labor union resistance prevents wage rates from falling, then the *SRAS* curve will not shift to the right. If the *SRAS* curve doesn't shift to the right, the price level won't come down. If the price level doesn't come down, buyers will not purchase more goods and services and move the economy out of a recessionary gap. In terms of Exhibit 2, the economy is stuck at point 1. It cannot get to point 2.

In summary, Keynes believed that the economy is inherently unstable and that it may not automatically cure itself of a recessionary gap. It may not be self-regulating.

exhibit 2

The Economy Gets Stuck in a Recessionary Gap

If the economy is in a recessionary gap at point 1, Keynes held that wage rates may not fall. The economy may be stuck in the recessionary gap.

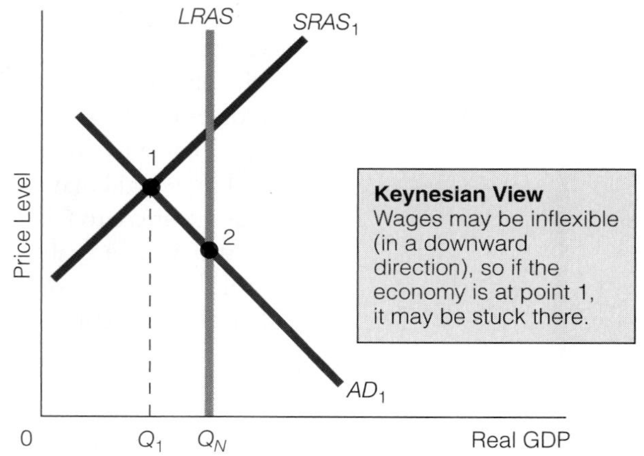
LRAS
SRAS1
1
2
Price Level
Keynesian View
Wages may be inflexible (in a downward direction), so if the economy is at point 1, it may be stuck there.
AD1
0
Q1
QN
Real GDP

New Keynesians and Wage Rates

Many economists criticized early versions of the Keynesian theory on the ground that it didn't offer a rigorous and complete explanation for inflexible wages. Some of the later versions—put forth by New Keynesian economists—made up for this deficiency by focusing on, among other things, long-term contracts and efficiency reasons for firms paying higher-than-market wages.

For example, New Keynesians argue that long-term labor contracts are often advantageous for both employers and workers. Firms may perceive such benefits in the form of (1) fewer labor negotiations (labor negotiations can be costly) and (2) a decreased likelihood of worker strikes (the firms avoid strikes during the time of the contract). Workers may perceive such benefits as (1) fewer strikes (which can be costly for them too) and (2) the sense of security that long-term contracts provide.

Long-term contracts have costs as well as benefits for both firms and workers, but some economists believe that in many instances the benefits outweigh the costs and that firms and workers enter into the long-term contracts for mutually advantageous reasons. When they do, wage rates are locked in for the period of the contract and therefore cannot adjust downward. As a result, the economy may get stuck at point 1 in Exhibit 2 for a long time and experience high levels of unemployment for many years.

Efficiency Wage Models
These models hold that it is sometimes in the best interest of business firms to pay their employees higher-than-equilibrium wage rates.

As another example, New Keynesian economists who work with **efficiency wage models** believe that there are solid microeconomic reasons for inflexible wages. They argue that firms sometimes find it in their best interest to pay wage rates above market-clearing levels. According to efficiency wage models, labor productivity depends on the wage rate that the firm pays its employees. Specifically, a cut in wages can cause labor productivity to decline, which, in turn, raises the firm's costs. (Basically, these models say that you are more productive when you are paid a higher wage than when you are paid a lower one.) By paying a higher-than-market wage, firms provide an incentive to workers to be productive and to do less shirking, among other things. If shirking declines, so do the monitoring (management) costs of the firm.

Economist Robert Solow has argued that "the most interesting and important line of work in current macroeconomic theory is the attempt to reconstruct plausible microeconomic underpinnings for a recognizably Keynesian macroeconomics."[1] Many Keynesian economists believe that efficiency wage models can perform this task. They believe that these models provide a solid microeconomic explanation for inflexible wages and thus are capable of explaining why continuing unemployment problems exist in some economies.

Keynes on Prices

Again, think back to the process that classical economists (among others) believe occurs when a recessionary gap exists. Wage rates fall, the *SRAS* curve shifts to the right, and the price level begins to decrease. . . . Stop right there! The phrase "and the price level begins to decrease" tells us that classical economists believe that prices in the economy are flexible: They move up and down in response to market forces.

Keynes said that the internal structure of an economy is not always competitive enough to allow prices to fall. Recall from Chapter 3 how the forces of supply and demand operate when price is above equilibrium. In this case, a surplus is generated, and price falls until the quantity supplied of the good equals the quantity demanded. Keynes suggested that anticompetitive or monopolistic elements in the economy sometimes prevent price from falling.

---

1. Robert Solow, "Another Possible Source of Wage Stickiness," in *Efficiency Wage Models of the Labor Market*, ed. by George Akerlof and Janet Yellen (New York: Cambridge University Press, 1986), p. 41

Before continuing, use the following chart to quickly review some of the differences in the views of the classical economists and Keynes.

	Classical Economists	Keynes
Say's Law	Holds in a money economy. In other words, all output produced will be demanded.	May not hold in a money economy. In other words, more output may be produced than will be demanded.
Savings	Amount saved and interest rate are directly related. Savers save more at higher interest rates and save less at lower interest rates.	Savers may not save more at higher interest rates or save less at lower interest rates. If savers have a savings goal in mind, then a higher interest rate means savers can save less and still reach their goal.
Investment	Amount invested is inversely related to interest rate. Businesses invest more at lower interest rates and invest less at higher interest rates.	If expectations are pessimistic, a lower interest rate may not stimulate additional investment.
Prices	Flexible	May be inflexible downward.
Wages	Flexible	May be inflexible downward.

Is It a Question of the Time It Takes for Wages and Prices to Adjust?

Classical economists believed that both wages and prices are flexible and adjust downward in a recessionary gap. Keynes, however, suggested that wages and prices are not flexible (in a downward direction) and may not adjust downward in a recessionary gap.

Many economists today take a position somewhere between Keynes's and that of the classical economists. For them, the question is not whether wages and prices are flexible downward, but *how long it takes for wages and prices to adjust downward.*

Consider Exhibit 3. Suppose the economy is currently in a recessionary gap at point 1. The relevant short-run aggregate supply curve is $SRAS_1$, where the wage rate is \$10 per hour and the price level is P_1. Now, classical economists said that the wage rate and price level will fall, whereas Keynes said this may not happen.

Did Keynes mean that if the economy is in a recessionary gap, *the wage rate will never fall and the price level will never adjust downward?* Most economists think not. The question is *how long* the wage rate and price level will take to fall. Will they fall in just a few weeks? Will they fall in a few months? Or will they take five years to fall? The question is relevant because the answer determines how long an economy will be in a recessionary gap and thus how long the economy takes to self-regulate.

Let's look at the question this way: If it takes only a few weeks or months for wage rates to fall (say, to \$8 an hour), for the short-run aggregate supply curve to shift from $SRAS_1$ to $SRAS_2$, and for the price level to fall from P_1 to P_2, then for all practical purposes, the

exhibit 3

A Question of How Long It Takes for Wage Rates and Prices to Fall

Suppose the economy is in a recessionary gap at point 1. Wage rates are \$10 per hour, and the price level is P_1. The issue may not be whether wage rates and the price level fall, but how long they take to reach long-run levels. If they take a short time, then classical economists are right: the economy is self-regulating. If they take a long time—perhaps years—then Keynes is right: the economy is not self-regulating over any reasonable period of time.

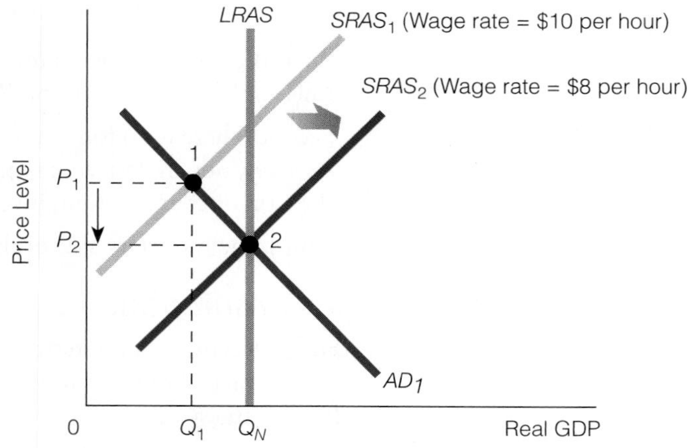

economy is almost instantaneously self-regulating. But if it takes years for all this to happen, the economy can hardly be considered self-regulating over any reasonable amount of time.

The classical position is that the time required for wages and prices to adjust downward is short enough to call the economy self-regulating. The Keynesian position is that the time is long enough to say that the economy is not self-regulating. Instead, the Keynesians believe that the economy is inherently unstable: It can exist in a recessionary gap for a long time.

Thinking like AN ECONOMIST

Different Assumptions, Different Conclusions

The economist knows that assumptions affect conclusions. For example, we know from the last chapter that classical economists assumed that wages are flexible, and now in this chapter we learn that Keynes assumed that wages (at times) might be inflexible. This difference in assumptions makes a difference to our policy conclusions. For example, classical economists, assuming wages are flexible, will reach different policy conclusions than will Keynes, who is assuming wages are inflexible.

SELF-TEST

(Answers to Self-Test questions are in the Self-Test Appendix.)

1. What do Keynesians mean when they say the economy is inherently unstable?
2. "What matters is not whether the economy is self-regulating or not, but whether prices and wages are flexible and adjust quickly." Comment.
3. According to Keynes, why might aggregate demand be too low?

THE SIMPLE KEYNESIAN MODEL

Economists build models and theories to better understand the economic world. Of the many you will find in economics, we have already discussed a few: the theory of supply and demand, the theory of comparative advantage, and the classical theory of interest rates. We turn now to a prominent macroeconomics model: the simple Keynesian model. In this section, we identify and discuss a few of its key components and themes.

Assumptions

In the simple Keynesian model, certain simplifying assumptions hold.

First, the price level is assumed to be constant until the economy reaches its full-employment or Natural Real GDP level.

Second, there is no foreign sector. In other words, the model represents a *closed economy*, not an *open economy*. It follows, then, that total spending in the economy is the sum of consumption, investment, and government purchases.

Third, the monetary side of the economy is excluded.

The Consumption Function

Although Keynes was interested in the level of total spending in general, he was particularly concerned about consumption. Consumption (*C*) was a major concern because it is by far the largest slice of the total spending pie.

Keynes made three basic points about consumption:

1. Consumption depends on disposable income (income minus taxes).
2. Consumption and disposable income move in the same direction.
3. When disposable income changes, consumption changes by less.

These three points make a specific statement about the relationship between consumption and disposable income. The statement specifying this relationship is called the **consumption function**, which we can write as:

$$C = C_0 + (MPC)(Y_d)$$

Consumption Function
The relationship between consumption and disposable income. In the consumption function used in this text, consumption is directly related to disposable income and is positive even at zero disposable income: $C = C_0 + (MPC)(Y_d)$.

To understand the consumption function, you need to know what the variables represent. You know that C is consumption, and we use Y_d to specify disposable income. Let's look at MPC and C_0.

MPC stands for **marginal propensity to consume (*MPC*)**, which is the ratio of the change in consumption to the change in disposable income:

Marginal Propensity to Consume (*MPC*)
The ratio of the change in consumption to the change in disposable income: $MPC = \Delta C/\Delta Y_d$.

$$\text{Marginal propensity to consume} = \frac{\text{Change in consumption}}{\text{Change in disposable income}}$$

$$MPC = \frac{\Delta C}{\Delta Y_d}$$

The symbol "Δ" stands for "change in." Thus, the *MPC* is equal to the change in consumption divided by the change in disposable income. To illustrate, suppose consumption rises from \$800 to \$900 as disposable income rises from \$1,000 to \$1,200. If we divide the change in consumption, which is \$100, by the change in disposable income, which is \$200, we see that the *MPC* equals 0.50. (Notice that the *MPC* is always a positive number between 0 and 1 because of Keynes's points 2 and 3.)

C_0 is **autonomous consumption**, which changes *not* as disposable income changes, but rather due to factors other than disposable income. Think of consumption (as specified by the consumption function) as made up of two parts. The C_0 part, which is independent of disposable income, is called *autonomous consumption*. The second part, the $MPC(Y_d)$ part, depends on disposable income and is called *induced consumption.*

Autonomous Consumption
The part of consumption that is independent of disposable income.

The difference between autonomous and induced consumption can be illustrated with an example. Suppose your taxes are lowered; consequently, your disposable income rises. With more disposable income, you buy more goods and services (e.g., entertainment, books, DVDs). The increase in disposable income has *induced* you to consume more; hence the name *induced consumption*. Next, suppose your disposable income has not changed, but for some reason you are consuming more. You might be consuming more medicine because you have recently become ill, or you might be consuming more car maintenance services because your car just broke down. In short, you are consuming more of various goods and services even though your disposable income has not changed at all. This type of consumption is autonomous (i.e., independent) of disposable income; hence the name *autonomous consumption*.

Now let's look again at the consumption function:

$$\text{Consumption} = \text{Autonomous consumption} + (\text{Marginal propensity to consume})(\text{Disposable income})$$

$$C = C_0 + (MPC)(Y_d)$$

exhibit 4

Consumption and Saving at Different Levels of Disposable Income (in billions)

Our consumption function is $C = C_0 + (MPC)(Y_d)$, where C_0 has been set at \$200 billion and $MPC = 0.80$. Saving is the difference between Y_d and C: $S = Y_d - [C_0 + (MPC)(Y_d)]$. All dollar amounts are in billions.

(1) Disposable Income Y_d	(2) Change in Disposable Income ΔY_d	(3) Consumption $C = C_0 + (MPC)(Y_d)$	(4) Change in Consumption	(5) Saving $S = Y_d - [C_0 + (MPC)(Y_d)]$	(6) Change in Saving
\$ 800	\$___	\$ 840	\$___	−\$40	\$___
1,000	200	1,000	160	0	40
1,200	200	1,160	160	40	40
1,400	200	1,320	160	80	40
1,600	200	1,480	160	120	40
1,800	200	1,640	160	160	40

Suppose C_0 is \$800, the *MPC* is 0.80, and Y_d is \$1,500. By substituting these numbers into the consumption function, we find that

$$C = \$800 + (0.80)(\$1{,}500) = \$800 + \$1{,}200 = \$2{,}000$$

What will cause an increase in consumption? Consumption, *C*, will increase if any of the variables (C_0, *MPC*, or Y_d) increases. Thus, *C* can be increased in three ways:

1. *Raise autonomous consumption.* Suppose in our example that autonomous consumption, C_0, goes from \$800 to \$1,000. This will raise consumption to \$2,200: $C = \$1{,}000 + (0.80)(\$1{,}500) = \$2{,}200$.
2. *Raise disposable income.* Suppose disposable income, Y_d, goes from \$1,500 to \$1,800. This will raise consumption to \$2,240: $C = \$800 + (0.80)(\$1{,}800) = \$2{,}240$. This increase in consumption from \$2,000 to \$2,240 is due to an increase of \$240 in induced consumption. Specifically, the increased consumption was induced by an increase in disposable income.
3. *Raise the MPC.* Suppose the *MPC* rises to 0.90. This will raise consumption to \$2,150: $C = \$800 + (0.90)(\$1{,}500) = \$2{,}150$.

In Exhibit 4, we set C_0 equal to \$200 billion and the *MPC* equal to 0.80; thus, C = \$200 billion + $(0.8)(Y_d)$. We then calculated different levels of consumption (column 3) for different levels of disposable income (column 1).

Finding ECONOMICS

In Bustling Sales Figures

Stores report that sales are bustling. Where is the economics? With so little to go on, we can only guess where the economics might be. Here is one guess: The bustling sales are simply the consumption function playing out. The consumption function $[C = C_0 + (MPC)(Y_d)]$ states that consumption rises as disposable income rises. So suppose income taxes are lowered. This decrease (in taxes) will increase disposable income; as disposable income rises, consumption does too. Maybe what the stores are reporting are bustling sales due to previously enacted tax cuts, embedded in the consumption function.

Consumption and Saving

In Exhibit 4, we also calculated the saving levels (column 5) at the different disposable income levels. How did we calculate these levels? We know that $C = C_0 + (MPC)(Y_d)$ and that households can only consume or save. So it follows that saving, S, is the difference between disposable income and consumption:

$$\begin{aligned}\text{Saving} &= \text{Disposable income} - \text{Consumption}\\ &= \text{Disposable income} - [\text{Autonomous consumption}\\ &\quad + (\text{Marginal propensity to consume})(\text{Disposable income})]\\ S &= Y_d - [C_0 - (MPC)(Y_d)]\end{aligned}$$

The **marginal propensity to save (*MPS*)** is the ratio of the change in saving to the change in disposable income:

Marginal Propensity to Save (*MPS*)
The ratio of the change in saving to the change in disposable income: $MPS = \Delta S/\Delta Y_d$.

$$\text{Marginal propensity to save} = \frac{\text{Change in saving}}{\text{Change in disposable income}}$$

$$MPS = \frac{\Delta S}{\Delta Y_d}$$

Disposable income can be used only for consumption or saving; that is, $C + S = Y_d$. So any change to disposable income can change only consumption or saving. Therefore, the marginal propensity to consume (*MPC*) plus the marginal propensity to save (*MPS*) must equal 1.

$$\text{Marginal propensity to consume} + \text{Marginal propensity to save} = 1$$

$$MPC + MPS = 1$$

In Exhibit 4, the *MPC* is 0.80; so the *MPS* is 0.20.

Common MISCONCEPTIONS

About a Low Savings Rate and Retirement

Savings is equal to disposable income minus consumption: $S = Y_d - [C_0 - (MPC)(Y_d)]$. To derive the savings rate, we simply divide S by Y_d: Savings rate $= S/Y_d$. Now during the period 1980–1994, the savings rate in the United States averaged about 8 percent. After 1994, the savings rate began to fall. For the period 2000–2004, it averaged around 2 percent; for the period 2005–2007, it averaged slightly less than 1 percent. Newspapers around the country ran headlines that decried the low savings rate in the United States. Some persons argued that the sharply declining savings rate meant that Americans weren't planning for their retirement. But that is not necessarily true. To illustrate, consider the person with a low savings rate whose house or stock portfolio has just appreciated in value. Let's say that the person's house value has increased by $100,000 over the last two years and her stock portfolio has appreciated by $17,000 in the last year. As far as our person is concerned, some percentage of the total dollar value of $117,000 may be available for her at retirement. (We say "some percentage" and not the total dollar amount because asset values can go down as well as up.) The problem is that the government's measure of savings excludes the change in the market value of such assets. Lesson learned: Even with a low savings rate, individuals could still be planning for their retirement.

economics 24/7

NEGATIVE SAVINGS AND HOUSE WEALTH

©THINKSTOCK IMAGES/JUPITER IMAGES (RF)

In 1932 and 1933, the savings rate in the United States was negative. These were years of the Great Depression, when the unemployment rate was high and businesses were collapsing.

The savings rate in the United States was also negative in 2005. But unemployment was not high in 2005, and businesses weren't collapsing. So what explains the negative savings rate? Why were many Americans spending their entire income and then borrowing more to spend?

Some have suggested that the explanation has to do with rising house prices. In many places in the United States during the late 1990s and early 2000s, real estate prices rose dramatically. In some parts of the country, the price of a home could double in a matter of a few years. As a result, a couple who had bought a house for, say, $150,000 now owned a house worth $300,000. Was there as much need to save when the booming real estate market had added $150,000 to the couple's net worth?

You can think of the explanation this way: A couple in their mid-forties is busy working, earning an income, and saving part of that income for retirement and old age. All of a sudden, the house they own increases in value at a rate many times greater than the inflation rate. As a result of the rise in real estate prices, the house owners become wealthier than they were before. Now there is not as great a need to save because they have just been handed a monetary bonus—special delivery, compliments of the real estate market. (Of course, whether they maintain their current house wealth depends on what happens to house prices in the future.)

In 2006, some people were wondering whether real estate prices weren't ripe for a fall. What happens when people, having spent their entire incomes and gone into debt too, find themselves living in houses that are declining in value? What happens if their so-called house wealth begins to dissipate? Do they dramatically reduce their consumption spending and shift the *AD* curve in the economy leftward? And does this reaction reduce Real GDP? Some economists thought so.

The Multiplier

We know from the consumption function that a rise in autonomous consumption (C_0) will raise consumption (C) and, in turn, raise total spending. But *how much* will total spending rise? If C_0 rises by $40 billion, will total spending rise by $40 billion? According to Keynes, total spending would not rise by only $40 billion in this case. The rise in C_0 will act as a catalyst to additional spending, and total spending will rise by *more than* $40 billion.

Let's illustrate with a simple example. Suppose there are ten people in the economy, represented by the letters *A–J*. Person A increases his autonomous consumption by buying $40 more additional goods from person B. Now person B has witnessed an increase in his income of $40. According to Keynes, person B will spend some fraction of this additional income. How much he spends depends on his marginal propensity to consume (*MPC*). If his *MPC* is 0.80, then he will spend 80 percent of $40, or $32. Let's say he spends this additional $32 on purchasing goods from person C. Thus, person C's income rises by $32, and now she will spend some percentage of her additional income. Again, how much she will spend depends on her *MPC*. If we again assume that the *MPC* is 0.80, then person C spends $25.60.

Person A increases his *autonomous consumption* by \$40 →
This generates \$40 *additional income* for person B →
Person B increases his *consumption* by \$32 →
This generates \$32 *additional income* for person C →
Person C increases her *consumption* by \$25.60 →
And so on and so on.

This process—whereby an initial rise in autonomous consumption leads to a rise in consumption for one person, generating additional income for another person, and leading to additional consumption spending by that person, and so on and so on—is called the *multiplier process.*

Suppose we sum the initial rise in autonomous spending (\$40) and all the additional spending it generates through the multiplier process. When the multiplier process ends, how much additional spending will have been generated? In other words, by how much will total expenditures rise?

The answer depends on the value of the multiplier. The **multiplier** (m) is equal to 1 divided by 1 − MPC.

Multiplier
The number that is multiplied by the change in autonomous spending to obtain the overall change in total spending. The multiplier (m) is equal to $1/(1-MPC)$. If the economy is operating below Natural Real GDP, then the multiplier turns out to be the number that is multiplied by the change in autonomous spending to obtain the change in Real GDP.

$$\text{Multiplier } (m) = \frac{1}{1 - MPC}$$

For example, if the $MPC = 0.80$ (in each round of spending), then the multiplier equals 5:

$$\begin{aligned}\text{Multiplier } (m) &= \frac{1}{1 - MPC} \\ &= \frac{1}{1 - 0.80} \\ &= \frac{1}{0.20} \\ &= 5\end{aligned}$$

Our original increase in autonomous consumption (\$40), multiplied by the multiplier (5), equals \$200. So in our example, a \$40 increase in autonomous consumption would increase total spending by \$200.

Just as consumption has an autonomous spending component, so do investment and government purchases. The multiplier process holds for these sectors too. The process also holds for a *decrease* in autonomous spending by one of the sectors of total spending. So, in general,

$$\text{Change in total spending} = \text{Multiplier} \times \text{Change in autonomous spending}$$

To illustrate, suppose many business owners become optimistic about the future of the economy. They believe that members of the household and government sectors will soon start buying more goods and services. In expectation of better times, businesses buy more factories and capital goods, and so investment spending rises. In this case, investment spending has risen, even without any change in income or Real GDP; hence, the rise is in autonomous investment spending. According to the multiplier analysis, this additional autonomous investment spending will change total spending by some multiple. For example, if the multiplier is 5, then a \$1 increase in autonomous investment will raise total spending by \$5.

The Multiplier and Reality

We have discussed the multiplier in simple terms: A change in autonomous spending leads to a *greater change* in total spending. Also, in the simple Keynesian model, the change in total spending is *equal to* the change in Real GDP (assuming that the economy is

economics 24/7

THE MULTIPLIER ON SPRING BREAK

During the weeklong spring break, many college students put away their books; pack their shorts, swimsuits, and tanning oil; jump into their cars; and head for the beaches. As they are driving to Fort Lauderdale, Galveston, Myrtle Beach, Daytona Beach, San Diego, and other coastal cities, the multiplier is getting ready to go to work.

©AP PHOTO/DAYTONA BEACH NEWS-JOURNAL

Look at it this way. When college students from around the country head for, say, Daytona Beach, they have dollars in their pockets. They will spend many of these dollars in Daytona Beach—on food and drink, motel rooms, dance clubs, and so on. As far as Daytona Beach is concerned, those dollars represent autonomous spending. More important, those dollars can raise the total income of Daytona Beach by some multiple of itself. College students buy pizzas, beer, and sodas. The people who sell these items find their incomes rising, and they, in turn, spend some fraction of their increase in income, which generates additional income for still others, who spend some fraction of their increase in income, and so on and so on.

Let's take a hypothetical example. Suppose college students spend \$7 million in Daytona Beach during spring break. If the *MPC* is, say, 0.60 in Daytona Beach and if all the added income generated is spent in Daytona Beach, then college students will increase (nominal) income in Daytona Beach by \$17.5 million (1/1 − *MPC* × \$7 million = 1/0.40 × \$7 million = 2.5 × \$7 million = \$17.5 million).

Do the people who live in Daytona Beach want college students to visit their city during spring break? Many of them do because it means extra dollars in their pockets. College students from out of town, together with the multiplier, often make for robust economic times.

operating below Natural Real GDP). The reason is that, in the model, prices are assumed to be constant until Natural GDP is reached; so any change in (nominal) total spending is equal to the change in *real* total spending.

We must note two points, however. First, the multiplier takes time to have an effect. In a textbook, it takes only seconds to go from an initial increase in autonomous spending to a multiple increase in either total spending or Real GDP. In the real world, this process takes many months.

Second, for the multiplier to increase Real GDP, *idle resources must exist at each spending round.* After all, if Real GDP is increasing (output is increasing) at each spending round, *idle resources must be available to be brought into production.* If this is not the case, then increased spending will simply result in higher prices without an increase in Real GDP. Simply put, there will be an increase in GDP but not in Real GDP.

SELF-TEST

1. How is autonomous consumption different from consumption?
2. If the *MPC* is 0.70, what does the multiplier equal?
3. What happens to the multiplier as the *MPC* falls?

THE SIMPLE KEYNESIAN MODEL IN THE *AD-AS* FRAMEWORK

The first section of this chapter presented a few of Keynes's criticisms of the self-regulating economy, or classical position. The second section identified and discussed some of the key components of the simple Keynesian model—in particular, the consumption function and the multiplier. In this section, we analyze the simple Keynesian model in terms of the aggregate demand and aggregate supply (*AD-AS*) framework. In the next section, we discuss the simple Keynesian model in terms of the total expenditures and total production (*TE-TP*) framework.[2]

Shifts in the Aggregate Demand Curve

Because there is no foreign sector in the simple Keynesian model, total spending consists of consumption (*C*), investment (*I*), and government purchases (*G*). Because the economy has no monetary side, it follows that changes in any of these variables (*C, I, G*) can shift the *AD* curve. For example, a rise in consumption will shift the *AD* curve to the right; a decrease in investment will shift the *AD* curve to the left.

Let's consider aggregate demand in terms of what we know about the consumption function and the multiplier. We know that a rise in autonomous consumption (C_0) will raise consumption (*C*) and therefore shift the *AD* curve to the right. How much the *AD* curve will shift due to the rise in autonomous consumption depends on the multiplier. In our earlier example, autonomous consumption C_0 increases by $40, and the multiplier (*m*) is 5.

$$\begin{aligned}\text{Change in total spending} &= \text{Multiplier} \times \text{Change in autonomous spending}\\ &= m \times \Delta C_0\\ &= 5 \times \$40\\ &= \$200\end{aligned}$$

Exhibit 5 illustrates how the *AD* curve shifts in this situation. We start with the original aggregate demand curve AD_1. Now autonomous consumption (C_0) rises by $40, shifting the aggregate demand curve to AD_2. But the *AD* curve does not stay here. Because of the multiplier, the initial autonomous consumption spending generates more spending, eventually pushing the *AD* curve to AD_3. In other words, at the end of the process, the *AD* curve has shifted from AD_1 to AD_3. Part of this shift ($40) is due to the initial rise in autonomous consumption, and part ($160) is due to the multiplier.

exhibit 5

The Multiplier and Aggregate Demand

An initial increase in autonomous consumption raises total spending and shifts the aggregate demand curve from AD_1 to AD_2. The *AD* curve does not end here, however. Because of the multiplier, the increase in autonomous spending generates additional incomes and additional spending, shifting the aggregate demand curve to AD_3.

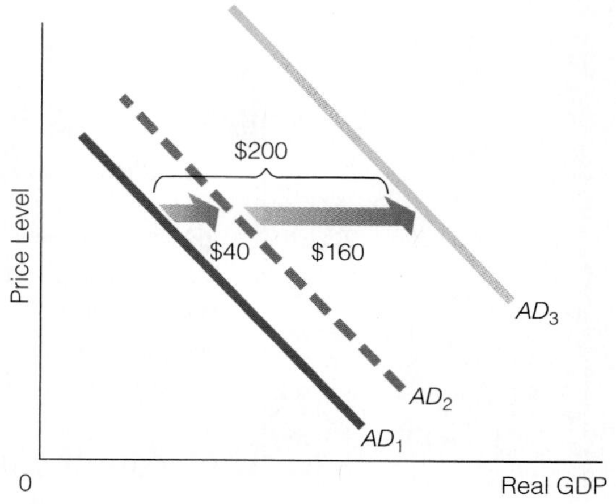

The Keynesian Aggregate Supply Curve

As noted earlier, in the simple Keynesian model, the price level is assumed to be constant until it reaches its full-employment or Natural Real GDP level. What does this assertion tell us about the Keynesian aggregate supply curve?

2. Some instructors may choose to assign only one of these two sections. It is clear at the end of the chapter which questions and problems go with which sections.

exhibit 6

The *AS* Curve in the Simple Keynesian Model

The *AS* curve in the simple Keynesian model is horizontal until Q_N (Natural Real GDP) and vertical at Q_N. It follows that any changes in aggregate demand in the horizontal section do not change the price level, but any changes in aggregate demand in the vertical section do change the price level.

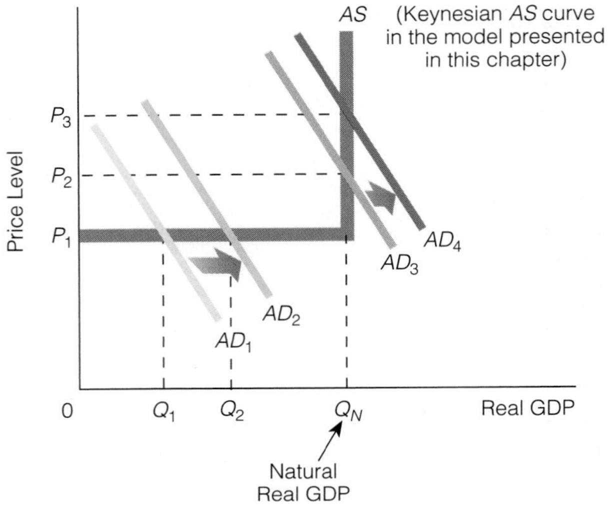

Think back to the discussions of aggregate demand and aggregate supply in the last two chapters and in the first section of this chapter. The *AD* curve is downward sloping, and the *SRAS* curve is upward sloping. Given that the *SRAS* curve is upward sloping, any shift in the *AD* curve (rightward or leftward) will automatically change (raise or lower) the price level. If the price level is assumed to be constant, then the Keynesian aggregate supple curve must have a horizontal section to it.

As shown in Exhibit 6, the Keynesian aggregate supply curve (outlined in this chapter and implicit in the simple Keynesian model) has both a horizontal section and a vertical section. The aggregate supply curve is horizontal until Q_N, or Natural Real GDP, because the simple Keynesian model assumes that the price level is constant until Q_N is reached. Given this *AS* curve, what happens in the economy when the *AD* curve shifts?

An increase in aggregate demand from AD_1 to AD_2 raises Real GDP from Q_1 to Q_2 but does not change the price level. (The price level remains at P_1.) On the other hand, once the economy has reached Q_N, any increases in aggregate demand change the price level. For example, an increase in aggregate demand from AD_3 to AD_4 raises the price level from P_2 to P_3.

According to Keynes, a change in autonomous spending (e.g., a change in autonomous consumption) will stimulate additional spending in the economy. In our example, a rise in autonomous consumption of $40 generated an additional $160 worth of spending so that total spending increased by $200. (The multiplier was 5 because we assumed the *MPC* was 0.80.)

Consider this question: Under what condition will a $200 *increase in total spending* lead to a $200 *increase in Real GDP?* That happens when the aggregate supply curve is horizontal, that is (in the simple Keynesian model), when the economy is currently producing less than Natural Real GDP. In other words, the *AD* curve in the economy must be shifting rightward (due to the increased spending) but must be within the *horizontal section* of the Keynesian *AS* curve.

Finding ECONOMICS

In Unchanging Prices

Suppose you read in the newspaper that the three sectors of a closed economy (household, business, and government) are all spending more but that, so far, there has been little to no change in the price level. Where is the economics? The picture that should come to mind is the Keynesian aggregate supply curve—in particular, the horizontal section of the curve. Increases in aggregate demand in the horizontal section of the aggregate supply curve do not raise the price level.

The Economy in a Recessionary Gap

According to classical and other economists (as discussed in the last chapter), the economy is self-regulating. A recessionary gap or an inflationary gap is only a temporary state of affairs. In time, the economy moves into long-run equilibrium and produces Natural Real GDP (Q_N).

Keynes did not believe that the economy always works this way. He believed that the economy could get stuck in a recessionary gap. As shown in Exhibit 7, this means the economy could be stuck at Q_1 (its equilibrium position) and be unable to get to Q_N on its own. In other words, the economy is at point A, and it is not able to get to point B. Keynes believed that the private sector—consisting of the household and business sectors—may not be able to move the economy from point A to point B. Stated differently, neither consumption nor investment will rise enough to shift the aggregate demand curve from its current position (AD_1).

But suppose the interest rate in the economy falls. Won't this be enough to get businesses to invest more, and thus won't the *AD* curve begin to shift rightward, headed for point B? Not necessarily, said Keynes, who didn't believe that investment spending was always responsive to changes in interest rates. For example, suppose businesses are pessimistic about future sales, and the interest rate drops. Are businesses going to invest more just because interest rates have dropped, or might their pessimistic expectations of future sales be so strong that they don't invest more at the lower interest rate? Keynes believed that the latter scenario could be the case.

exhibit 7

Can the Private Sector Remove the Economy from a Recessionary Gap?

The economy is at point A producing Q_1. Q_1 is less than Q_N, so the economy is in a recessionary gap. The questions is whether the private sector (consisting of consumption and investment spending) can remove the economy from the recessionary gap by increasing spending enough to shift the aggregate demand curve rightward to go through point B. Keynes believed that sometimes it could not. No matter how low interest rates fell, investment spending would not rise because of pessimistic business expectations with respect to future sales.

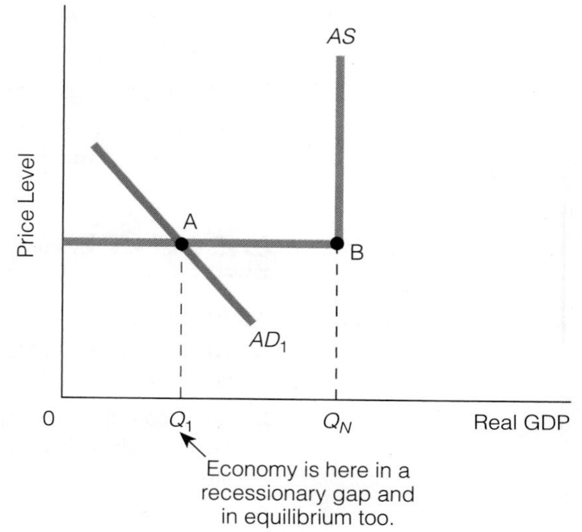

Government's Role in the Economy

In the self-regulating economy of the classical economists, government did not have a management role to play. The private sector (households and businesses) was capable of self-regulating the economy at its Natural Real GDP level. On the other hand, Keynes believed that the economy was not self-regulating and that economic instability was a possibility. In other words, the economy could get stuck in a recessionary gap.

Economic instability opens the door to government's playing a role in the economy. According to Keynes and to many Keynesians, if the private sector cannot self-regulate the economy at its Natural Real GDP level, then maybe the government must help. In terms of Exhibit 7, maybe the government has a role to play in shifting the *AD* curve rightward so that it goes through point B. We discuss the role government might play in the economy in the next chapter.

Thinking like AN ECONOMIST

From How the Economy Works to One's Policy Positions

An economist's view of the economy (how the economy works) and his policy suggestions are often linked. For example, classical economists and their modern-day counterparts, who view the economy as inherently stable, believe in a policy of laissez-faire: Government should keep its hands off the economy. Keynesians, however, who view the economy as inherently unstable, suggest that government has an economic role to play. In short, policy suggestions are sometimes a consequence of how one views the internal, or inherent, workings of an economy.

The Theme of the Simple Keynesian Model

As portrayed in terms of *AD* and *AS*, the essence of the simple Keynesian model can be summarized in five statements:

1. The price level is constant until Natural Real GDP is reached.
2. The *AD* curve shifts if there are changes in *C, I,* or *G*.
3. According to Keynes, the economy could be in equilibrium and in a recessionary gap, too. In other words, the economy can be at point A in Exhibit 7.
4. The private sector may not be able to get the economy out of a recessionary gap. In other words, the private sector (households and businesses) may not be able to increase *C* or *I* enough to get the *AD* curve in Exhibit 7 to intersect the *AS* curve at point B.
5. The government may have a management role to play in the economy. According to Keynes, government may have to raise aggregate demand enough to stimulate the economy to move it out of the recessionary gap and to its Natural Real GDP level.

SELF-TEST

1. What was Keynes's position on the self-regulating properties of an economy?
2. What will happen to Real GDP if autonomous spending rises and the economy is operating in the horizontal section of the Keynesian *AS* curve? Explain your answer.
3. An economist who believes the economy is self-regulating is more likely to advocate laissez-faire than one who believes the economy is inherently unstable. Do you agree or disagree? Explain your answer.

The Simple Keynesian Model in the *TE-TP* Framework

Just as a story can be translated into different languages, an economic model can be presented in various frameworks. The last section presented the simple Keynesian model in terms of the familiar (diagrammatic) *AD-AS* framework of analysis.

But the simple Keynesian model was not first presented in terms of *AD-AS*. It was first presented in terms of the framework discussed in this section. This framework has been known by different names, three of which are the Keynesian cross, income expenditure, and total expenditure-total production. In our discussion, we will refer to it as total expenditure–total production, or simply the *TE-TP* framework.

Deriving a Total Expenditures (*TE*) Curve

Just as we derived *AD* and *AS* curves in the *AD-AS* framework, we want to derive a total expenditures (*TE*) curve in the *TE-TP* framework. Total expenditures are the sum of its parts: consumption, investment, and government purchases. To derive a *TE* curve, we must first derive a diagrammatic representation of consumption, investment, and government purchases, as shown in Exhibit 8.

1. *Consumption.* As disposable income rises, so does consumption. This is shown arithmetically in columns (1) and (3) of Exhibit 4. Exhibit 4 also shows that because the *MPC* is less than 1, consumption rises by less than disposable income rises. Consumption also rises as Real GDP rises but again by a smaller percentage. For example, if Real GDP rises by $100, consumption may rise by $80. In Exhibit 8(a), we have

exhibit 8

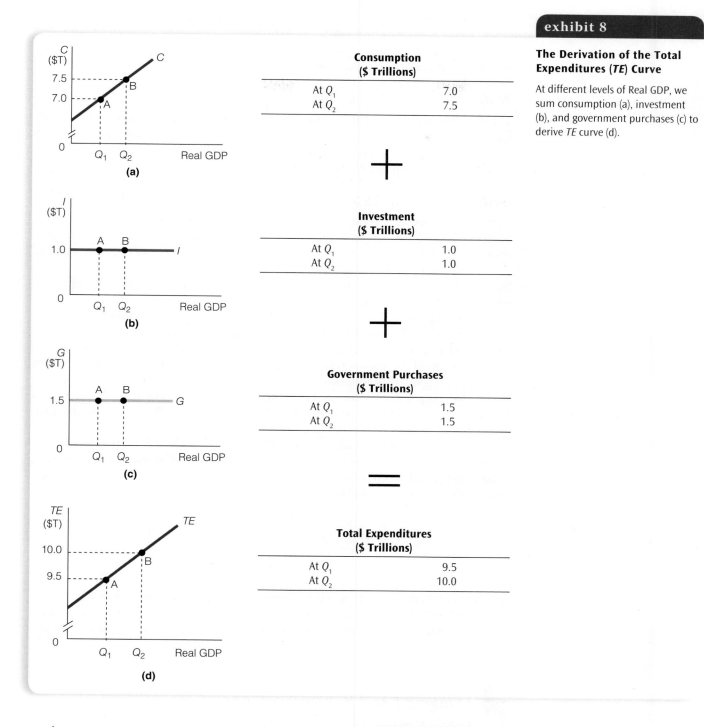

The Derivation of the Total Expenditures (*TE*) Curve

At different levels of Real GDP, we sum consumption (a), investment (b), and government purchases (c) to derive *TE* curve (d).

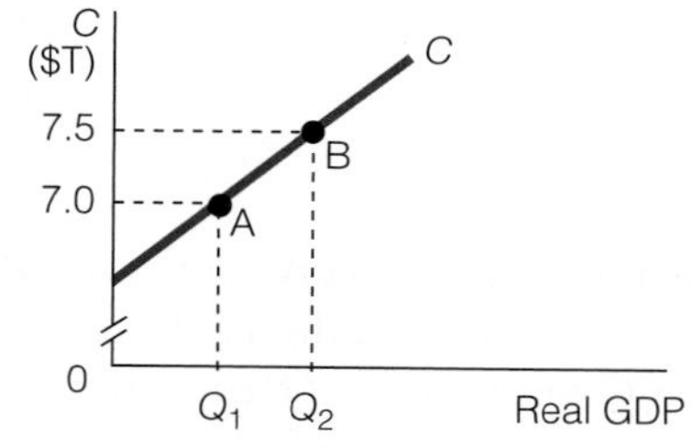

(a)

Consumption ($ Trillions)	
At Q_1	7.0
At Q_2	7.5

+

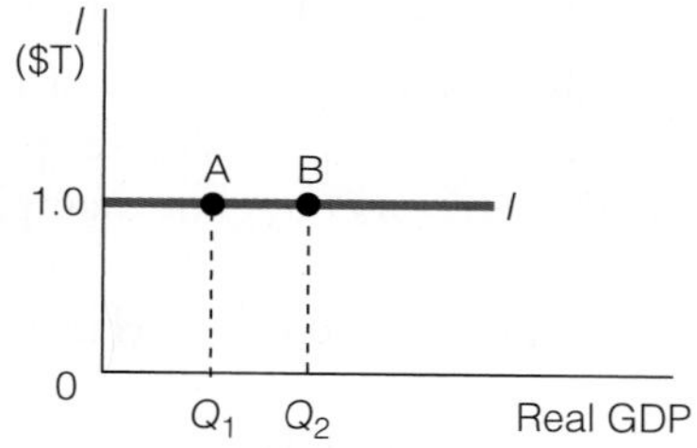

(b)

Investment ($ Trillions)	
At Q_1	1.0
At Q_2	1.0

+

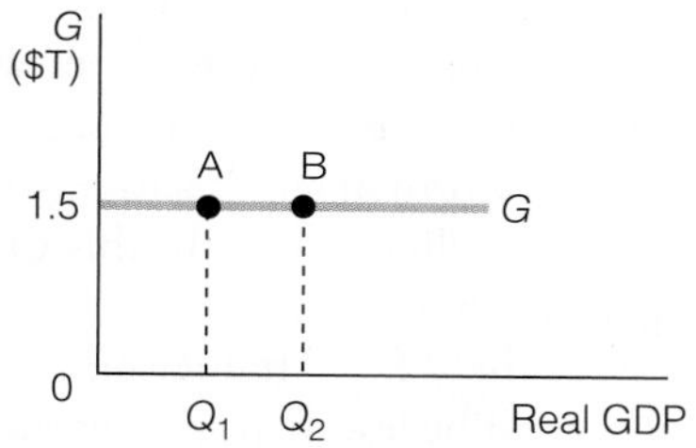

(c)

Government Purchases ($ Trillions)	
At Q_1	1.5
At Q_2	1.5

=

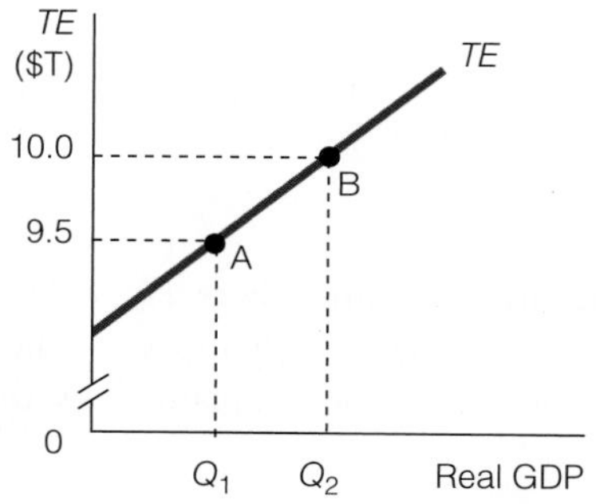

(d)

Total Expenditures ($ Trillions)	
At Q_1	9.5
At Q_2	10.0

drawn consumption as an upward-sloping curve. Notice that as Real GDP rises from Q_1 to Q_2, consumption rises from \$7 trillion to \$7.5 trillion.

2. *Investment.* To simplify things in deriving *TE*, in the investment curve in Exhibit 8(b), we assume investment is constant at \$1 trillion, whether Real GDP is Q_1 or Q_2.
3. *Government purchases.* We simplify the government spending curve too. In Exhibit 8(c), government purchases are constant at \$1.5 trillion, regardless of the amount of Real GDP.

In Exhibit 8(d), we derived a *TE* curve. We simply added the components of total expenditures at the two Real GDP levels (Q_1 and Q_2), plotted the relevant points, and then drew a line through the points. We see that at Q_1 total expenditures are $9.5 trillion, and at Q_2 they are $10.0 trillion. The *TE* curve is upward sloping.

What Will Shift the *TE* Curve?

The *TE* curve in the *TE-TP* framework plays the same role as the *AD* curve in the *AD-AS* framework. Just as the *AD* curve shifts if there is a change in *C, I,* or *G,* the *TE* curve shifts if there is a change in *C, I,* or *G.* For example, a rise in *C* will shift the *TE* curve upward; a decline in *I* will shift the *TE* curve downward.

Comparing Total Expenditures (*TE*) and Total Production (*TP*)

Businesses produce the goods and services that are bought in the three sectors of the economy (household, business, and government). Sometimes, though, businesses produce too much or too little in comparison to what the three sectors buy. For example, suppose businesses produce $10 trillion worth of goods and services, but the three sectors buy only $9.5 trillion worth. In this case, businesses have produced too much relative to what the three sectors of the economy buy.

Alternatively, businesses might produce $10 trillion worth of goods and services, but the three sectors of the economy buy $10.5 trillion worth. In this case, businesses have produced too little relative to what the three sectors of the economy buy. (If you are wondering how the three sectors of the economy can possibly buy more than businesses produce, the answer has to do with goods that businesses hold in inventory. We will soon explain the process.)

Finally, it is possible for businesses to produce $10 trillion worth of goods and services and for the three sectors of the economy to buy exactly $10 trillion worth. In this case, businesses have produced exactly the right amount of goods and services.

Thus, there are three possible states of the economy in the *TE-TP* framework. The total expenditures (*TE*) of the three sectors of the economy can be less than, greater than, or equal to the dollar value of total production (*TP*). In other words, each of the following states of the economy is possible:

$$TE < TP$$
$$TE > TP$$
$$TE = TP$$

According to many economists, if the economy is currently operating where $TE < TP$ or $TE > TP$ (both states are described as disequilibrium), it will eventually move to where $TE = TP$ (where the economy is in equilibrium). The next section explains how this happens.

Thinking like AN ECONOMIST

Thinking in Threes

The concept of threes came up when we discussed a single market (in Chapter 3), when we said that a market could be in equilibrium, shortage, or surplus. In other words, there were three possible states of a market. In Chapter 8, we said the economy could be producing a Real GDP level either greater than, less than, or equal to Natural Real GDP; that is, an economy may have three possible states. Now we are saying that total expenditures (*TE*) can be either less than, greater than, or equal to total production. Once again, we are dealing with three possible states of an economy.

Moving from Disequilibrium to Equilibrium

Business firms hold an inventory of their goods to guard against unexpected changes in the demand for their product. For example, General Motors may hold an inventory of a certain type of car in case the demand for it suddenly increases unexpectedly.

Although we know why business firms hold an inventory of their goods, we don't know *how much* inventory they will hold. For example, we don't know whether General Motors will hold an inventory of 1,000 cars, 2,000 cars, or 10,000 cars. (Inventories are usually held in terms of, say, a 45- or 60-day supply, but we have simplified things here.) However, we do know that, for General Motors and all other business firms, there is some *optimum inventory*. This is "just the right amount" of inventory—not too much and not too little. With this in mind, consider two cases that illustrate how business inventory levels play an important role in the economy's adjustment from disequilibrium to equilibrium in the *TE-TP* framework.

CASE 1: *TE* < *TP* Assume that business firms hold an optimum inventory level of $300 billion worth of goods, that the firms produce $11 trillion worth of goods and services, and that the three sectors of the economy buy $10.8 trillion worth of goods and services. In this case, producers produce more than individuals buy (*TE* < *TP*). The difference is added to inventories, and inventory levels rise unexpectedly to $500 billion, which is $200 billion more than the $300 billion firms see as optimal.

This unexpected rise in inventories signals to firms that they have *overproduced*. Consequently, they cut back on the quantity of goods they produce. The cutback in production causes Real GDP to fall, bringing Real GDP closer to the (lower) output level that the three sectors of the economy are willing and able to buy. Ultimately, *TP* will equal *TE*.

CASE 2: *TE* > *TP* Assume that business firms hold their optimum inventory level ($300 billion worth of goods), that the firms produce $10.4 trillion worth of goods, and that members of the three sectors buy $10.6 trillion worth of goods. How can individuals buy more than firms produce? Firms make up the difference out of inventory. In our example, inventory levels fall from $300 billion to $100 billion because individuals purchase $200 billion more of goods than firms produced (to be sold). This example illustrates why firms maintain inventories in the first place: to be able to meet an unexpected increase in sales.

The unexpected fall in inventories signals to firms that they have *underproduced*. Consequently, they increase the quantity of goods they produce. The rise in production causes Real GDP to rise, in the process bringing Real GDP closer to the (higher) real output that the three sectors are willing and able to buy. Ultimately, *TP* will equal *TE*.

The Graphical Representation of the Three States of the Economy in the *TE-TP* Framework

The three states of the economy are represented in Exhibit 9. The exhibit shows a *TE* curve, which we derived earlier, and a *TP* curve, which is simply a 45-degree line. (It is a 45-degree line because it bisects the 90-degree angle at the origin.) Notice that, at any point on the *TP* curve, total production is equal to Real GDP (*TP* = Real GDP).[3] This is because *TP* and Real GDP are different names for the same thing. Real GDP, remember, is simply the total market value of all final goods and services produced annually within a country's borders, adjusted for price changes.

---

3. Earlier, we said that the *TE* curve plays the role in the *TE-TP* framework that the *AD* curve plays in the *AD-AS* framework. In other words, roughly speaking, the *AD* curve is the *TE* curve. Similarly, the *TP* curve plays the role in the *TE-TP* framework that the *AS* curve plays in the *AD-AS* framework. In other words, roughly speaking, the *TP* curve is the *AS* curve. In the *AD-AS* framework, equilibrium is at the intersection of the *AD* and *AS* curves. As you will soon learn, in the *TE-TP* framework, equilibrium is at the intersection of the *TE* and *TP* curves.

exhibit 9

The Three States of the Economy in the *TE-TP* Framework

At Q_E, $TE = TP$ and the economy is in equilibrium. At Q_1, $TE < TP$. This results in an unexpected increase in inventories, which signals firms that they have overproduced, which leads firms to cut back production. The cutback in production reduces Real GDP. The economy tends to move from Q_1 to Q_E. At Q_2, $TE > TP$. This results in an unexpected decrease in inventories, which signals firms that they have underproduced, which leads firms to raise production. The increased production raises Real GDP. The economy tends to move from Q_2 to Q_E.

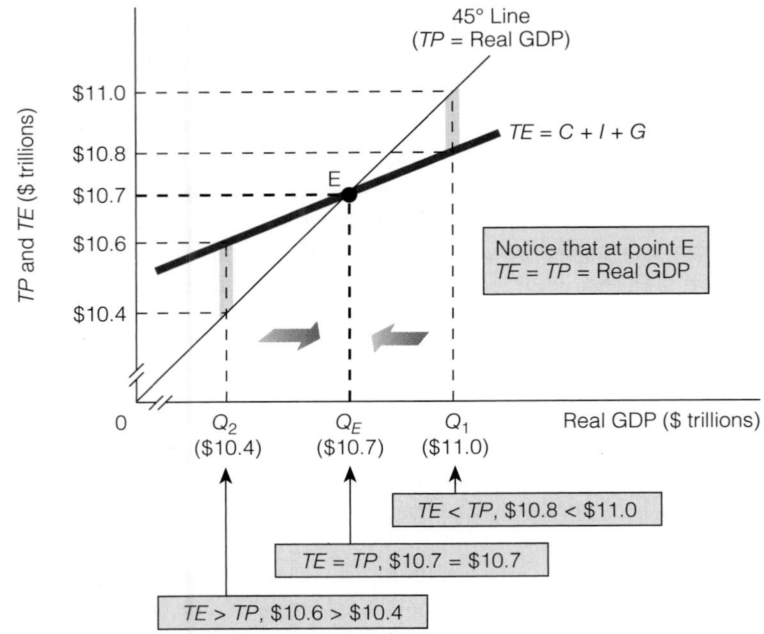

Now let's look at three different Real GDP levels in the exhibit. We start with Q_1, where Real GDP is $11 trillion. At this Real GDP level, what do *TE* and *TP* equal? We see that *TE* is $10.8 trillion and *TP* is $11 trillion. This illustrates Case 1, in which producers produce more than individuals buy ($TE < TP$), where the difference is added to inventories. This unexpected rise in inventories signals to firms that they have overproduced, and consequently they cut back on the quantity of goods they produce. The cutback in production causes Real GDP to fall, ultimately bringing Real GDP down to Q_E ($10.7 trillion in the exhibit).

Now we look at Q_2, where Real GDP is $10.4 trillion. At this Real GDP level, *TE* equals $10.6 trillion and *TP* equals $10.4 trillion. This illustrates Case 2, in which the three sectors of the economy buy more goods and services than business firms have produced ($TE > TP$). Business firms make up the difference between what they have produced and what the three sectors of the economy buy through inventories. Inventories then fall below optimum levels, and consequently businesses increase the quantity of goods they produce. The rise in production causes Real GDP to rise, ultimately moving Real GDP up to Q_E (again, $10.7 trillion).

When the economy is producing Q_E, or $10.7 trillion worth of goods and services, it is in equilibrium. At this Real GDP level, *TP* and *TE* are the same at $10.7 trillion. The following table summarizes some key points about the state of the economy in the *TE-TP* framework.

State of the Economy	What Happens to Inventories?	What Do Firms Do?
$TE < TP$ Individuals are buying less output than firms produce.	Inventories rise above optimum levels.	Firms cut back production to reduce inventories to their optimum levels.
$TE > TP$ Individuals are buying more output than firms produce.	Inventories fall below optimum levels.	Firms increase production to raise inventories to their optimum levels.
$TE = TP$	Inventories are at their optimum levels.	Firms neither increase nor decrease production.

The Economy in a Recessionary Gap and the Role of Government

According to Keynes, the economy can be in equilibrium and in a recessionary gap, too, as explained in the section on the simple Keynesian model in the *AD-AS* framework. (To review, look back at Exhibit 7.) The same situation can exist in the *TE-TP* framework. For example, in Exhibit 9, the economy equilibrates at point E and thus produces a Real GDP level of \$10.7 trillion worth of goods and services.

However, is there any guarantee that the Real GDP level of \$10.7 trillion is the Natural Real GDP level? None at all. The economy could be in a situation like that shown in Exhibit 10. The economy is in equilibrium at point A, producing Q_E, but the Natural Real GDP level is Q_N. Because the economy is producing at a Real GDP level that is less than Natural Real GDP, it is in a recessionary gap.

How does the economy get out of the recessionary gap? Will the private sector (households and businesses) be capable of pushing the *TE* curve in Exhibit 10 upward so that it goes through point B, and so that Q_N is produced? According to Keynes, the economy is not necessarily going to do so. Keynes believed that government may be necessary to get the economy out of a recessionary gap. For example, government may have to raise its purchases (raise *G*) so that the *TE* curve shifts upward and goes through point B.

exhibit 10

The Economy: In Equilibrium, and in a Recessionary Gap, Too

Using the *TE-TP* framework, the economy is currently in equilibrium at point A, producing Q_E. Natural Real GDP, however, is greater than Q_E, so the economy is in a recessionary gap as well as being in equilibrium.

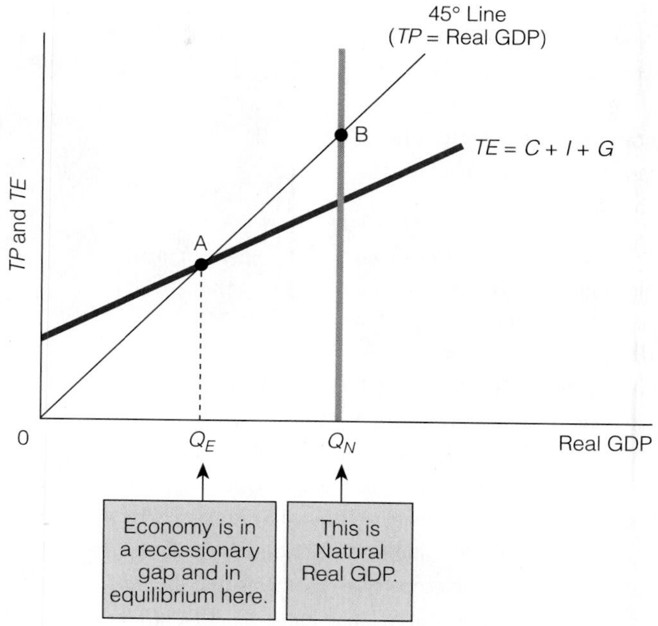

macro*theme* ➔ Of the many debates in macroeconomics, one concerns the issue of equilibrium in the economy: where the economy naturally ends up after all adjustments have been made. In the last chapter, we read about economists who believe that the economy is self-regulating and that an economy naturally ends up in the long run producing Natural Real GDP. In this chapter, we have read about economists who believe that the economy can be inherently unstable and that it can naturally end up producing a level of Real GDP less than Natural Real GDP. To the first group of economists, equilibrium is a desirable state of affairs; to the second group, equilibrium (where Real GDP is less than Natural Real GDP) is not.

The Theme of the Simple Keynesian Model

As portrayed in terms of *TE* and *TP*, the essence of the simple Keynesian model can be summed up in five statements:

1. The price level is constant until Natural Real GDP is reached.
2. The *TE* curve shifts if there are changes in *C, I,* or *G*.

economics 24/7

WHY ECONOMISTS MIGHT DISAGREE

As you have learned in this chapter, economists don't always agree. One economist might say the economy can remove itself from a recessionary gap, and another economist might say it cannot.

©GETTY IMAGES

Disagreements among economists of different schools of thought are not uncommon. But can economists of the same school of thought disagree, too? For example, suppose that two economists both believe that the simple Keynesian model is an accurate portrayal of how the economy works. Are they ever going to disagree? They just might. For example, suppose both believe that a change in autonomous spending will increase Real GDP by some multiple of the change in autonomous spending. What they might disagree on is the multiple by which autonomous spending will change Real GDP. One economist might think that the *MPC* is smaller than what the other thinks. If one thinks the *MPC* is 0.80, then she will think the multiplier is 5. If the other thinks the *MPC* is 0.60, then she will think the multiplier is 2.5. Will Real GDP change by 5 times or 2.5 times the change in autonomous spending? The answer is that the change depends on the value of the *MPC*.

Or suppose that two economists believe that the aggregate supply curve is as represented in Exhibit 7: It has a horizontal section followed by a vertical section. Are the two economists always going to agree as to what will happen if aggregate demand rises? One economist might think the increase in aggregate demand will move the economy out of the horizontal section of the aggregate supply curve and into the vertical section. This economist is going to predict a rise in both the price level and Real GDP as a result of a rise in aggregate demand. The other economist, however, might predict only a change in Real GDP because he believes the increase in aggregate demand falls within the horizontal section of the aggregate supply curve.

Finally, suppose two economists believe that savings will rise as the interest rate rises. What they might not agree on is how much savings will rise as the interest rate rises. One economist might think that savings will increase by 10 percent if the interest rate rises by from 6 percent to 7 percent; the other economist might think that savings will increase by only 1 percent.

As you can see, there is plenty of room for disagreement.

3. According to Keynes, the economy could be in equilibrium and in a recessionary gap, too. In other words, the economy can be at point A in Exhibit 10.
4. The private sector may not be able to get the economy out of a recessionary gap. In other words, the private sector (households and businesses) may not be able to increase *C* or *I* enough to get the *TE* curve in Exhibit 10 to rise and pass through point B.
5. The government may have a management role to play in the economy. According to Keynes, government may have to raise *TE* enough to stimulate the economy to move it out of the recessionary gap and to its Natural Real GDP level.

SELF-TEST

1. What happens in the economy if total production (*TP*) is greater than total expenditures (*TE*)?
2. What happens in the economy if total expenditures (*TE*) are greater than total production (*TP*)?

office hours

"DOES A LOT DEPEND ON WHETHER WAGES ARE FLEXIBLE OR INFLEXIBLE?"

Student:
Can what we learned in this chapter be seen as a criticism of what we learned in the last chapter?

Instructor:
Much of it can be viewed as a criticism. Specifically, in the last chapter you learned the views of economists who believe that the economy *is* self-regulating. In this chapter you learned the views of economists who believe that the economy *is not* always self-regulating.

Student:
What is at the heart of the disagreement between these two groups of economists?

Instructor:
That is a good question. One thing at the heart of the disagreement is whether wages are flexible or inflexible. To illustrate, look back at Exhibit 2. There you see an economy in a recessionary gap. Now if wages are flexible (as stated in the last chapter), then they will soon fall, and the *SRAS* curve in Exhibit 2 will shift to the right. In time, the economy will remove itself from a recessionary gap, to point 2 in the exhibit. However, if wages are inflexible downward (as stated in this chapter), then wages will not fall, the *SRAS* will not shift to the right, and the economy will remain stuck—at point 1 in the exhibit—in a recessionary gap.

Student:
Suppose the economists who say the economy can get stuck in a recessionary gap are right. What then? Does the economy just stay stuck forever?

Instructor:
What these economists usually propose is some government response. Specifically, they advocate fiscal or monetary policy to get the economy unstuck. We haven't discussed either fiscal or monetary policy yet, but we plan to in the next chapter.

Student:
It seems to me that a lot depends on whether wages are flexible or inflexible. If wages are flexible, the economy self-regulates, removes itself from a recessionary gap, and thus requires no government response. On the other hand, if wages are inflexible (downward), the economy can get stuck in a recessionary gap, and a government response may be needed.

Instructor:
That's right. And because much depends on whether wages are flexible or inflexible, economists research such things as wages in various industries. For example, trying to find out whether wages in industries X and Y are flexible or inflexible may seem abstruse and esoteric to many people (who cares?), but, as you have just pointed out, a lot can depend on the answers.

Points to Remember

1. Not all economists agree as to how the economy works. In the last chapter you learned the views of economists who believe that the economy is self-regulating. In this chapter you learned the views of economists who believe that the economy is not always self-regulating.
2. Often, much depends on what may appear to be a small issue. An economist tells you she is researching the degree of flexibility of wages in industry X. You may think, "What a small issue to research. Who cares about the degree of flexibility of wages? After all, they are what they are." However, as we have shown, sometimes these so-called small issues can make a big difference—such as whether government becomes involved in the economy.

a reader asks

Was Keynes a Revolutionary in Economics?

Even before I enrolled in an economics course, I had heard of the economist John Maynard Keynes. Could you tell me a little about his life? Also, I'd like to know whether economists consider him a revolutionary in economics. If so, what did he revolutionize?

John Maynard Keynes was born in Cambridge, England, on June 5, 1883, and died at Tilton (in Sussex) on April 21, 1946. His father was John Neville Keynes, an eminent economist and author of *The Scope and Method of Political Economy.* Keynes's mother was one of the first female students to attend Cambridge University and for a time presided as mayor of the city of Cambridge.

Keynes was educated at Eton and at King's College, Cambridge, where he received a degree in mathematics in 1905. At Cambridge, he studied under the well-known and widely respected economist Alfred Marshall. In 1925, Keynes married Russian ballerina Lydia Lopokova. He was prominent in British social and intellectual circles and enjoyed art, theater, opera, debate, and collecting rare books.

Many economists rank Keynes's *The General Theory of Employment, Interest and Money* alongside Adam Smith's *Wealth of Nations* and Karl Marx's *Das Kapital* as the most influential economic treatises ever written. The book was published on February 4, 1936.

Before the publication of *The General Theory,* Keynes presented the ideas contained in the work in a series of university lectures that he gave between October 10, 1932, and December 2, 1935. Ten days after his last lecture, he sent off the manuscript of what was to become *The General Theory.*

Keynes's lectures were said to be both shocking (he was pointing out the errors of the classical school) and exciting (he was proposing something new). One of the students at these lectures was Lorie Tarshis, who later wrote the first Keynesian introductory textbook, *The Elements of Economics.* In another venue, Tarshis wrote about the Keynes lectures and specifically about why Keynes's ideas were revolutionary.

> I attended that first lecture, naturally awed but bothered. As the weeks passed, only a stone would not have responded to the growing excitement these lectures generated. So I missed only two over the four years—two out of the thirty lectures. And like others, I would feel the urgency of the task. No wonder! These were the years when everything came loose; when sober dons and excitable students seriously discussed such issues as: Was capitalism not doomed? Should Britain not take the path of Russia or Germany to create jobs? Keynes obviously believed his analysis led to a third means to prosperity far less threatening to the values he prized, but until he had developed the theory and offered it in print, he knew that he could not sway government. So he saw his task as supremely urgent. I was also a bit surprised by his concern over too low a level of output. I had been assured by all I had read that the economy would bob to the surface, like a cork held under water—and output would rise, of its own accord, to an acceptable level. But Keynes proposed something far more shocking: that the economy could reach an equilibrium position with output far below capacity. That was an exciting challenge, sharply at variance with the views of Pigou and Marshall who represented "The Classical (Orthodox) School" in Cambridge, and elsewhere.[4]

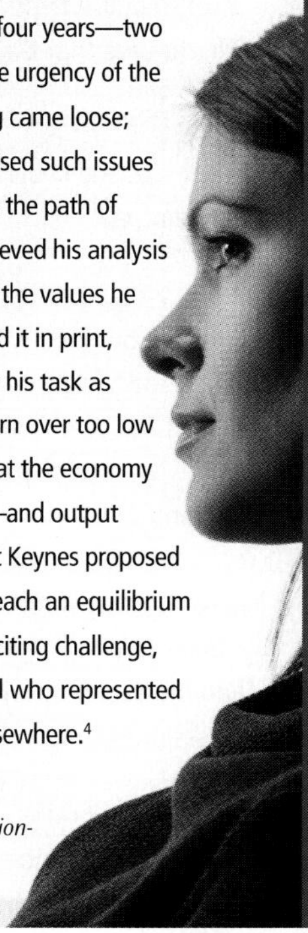

4. L. Tarshis, "Keynesian Revolution," in *The New Palgrave: A Dictionary of Economics*, vol. 3 (London: Macmillan Press, 1987), p. 48.

Chapter Summary

KEYNES ON WAGE RATES AND PRICES

- Keynes believed that wage rates and prices may be inflexible downward. He said that employees and labor unions will resist employer's wage cuts and that, because of anticompetitive or monopolistic elements in the economy, prices will not fall.

KEYNES ON SAY'S LAW

- Keynes did not agree that Say's law would necessarily hold in a money economy. He thought it was possible for consumption to fall (for saving to increase) by more than investment increased. Consequently, a decrease in consumption (or increase in saving) could lower total expenditures and aggregate demand in the economy.

CONSUMPTION FUNCTION

- Keynes made three points about consumption and disposable income: (1) Consumption depends on disposable income. (2) Consumption and disposable income move in the same direction. (3) As disposable income changes, consumption changes by less. These three ideas are incorporated into the consumption function, $C = C_0 + (MPC)(Y_d)$, where C_0 is autonomous consumption, *MPC* is the marginal propensity to consume, and Y_d is disposable income.

THE MULTIPLIER

- A change in autonomous spending will bring about a multiple change in total spending. The overall change in spending is equal to the multiplier $[1/(1-MPC)]$ times the change in autonomous spending.

THE SIMPLE KEYNESIAN MODEL IN THE *AD-AS* FRAMEWORK

- Changes in consumption, investment, and government purchases will change aggregate demand.
- A rise in *C*, *I*, or *G* will shift the *AD* curve to the right.
- A decrease in *C*, *I*, or *G* will shift the *AD* curve to the left.
- The aggregate supply curve in the simple Keynesian model has both a horizontal section and a vertical section. The kink between the two sections is at the Natural Real GDP level. If aggregate demand changes in the horizontal section of the curve (when the economy is operating below Natural Real GDP), there is a change in Real GDP but no change in the price level. If aggregate demand changes in the vertical section of the curve (when the economy is operating at Natural Real GDP), the price level changes but not Real GDP.

THE SIMPLE KEYNESIAN MODEL IN THE *TE-TP* FRAMEWORK

- Changes in consumption, investment, and government purchases will change total expenditures.
- A rise in *C*, *I*, or *G* will shift the *TE* curve upward.
- A decrease in *C*, *I*, or *G* will shift the *TE* curve downward.
- If total expenditures (*TE*) equal total production (*TP*), the economy is in equilibrium. If $TE < TP$, the economy is in disequilibrium and inventories will unexpectedly rise, signaling firms to cut back production. If $TE > TP$, the economy is in disequilibrium and inventories will unexpectedly fall, signaling firms to increase production.
- Equilibrium occurs where $TE = TP$. The equilibrium level of Real GDP may be less than the Natural Real GDP level, and the economy may be stuck at this lower level of Real GDP.

A KEYNESIAN THEME

- Keynes proposed that the economy could reach its equilibrium position with Real GDP below Natural Real GDP; that is, the economy could be in equilibrium and in a recessionary gap, too. Furthermore, he argued that the economy may not be able to get out of a recessionary gap by itself. Government may need to play a management role in the economy.

Key Terms and Concepts

Efficiency Wage Models
Consumption Function
Marginal Propensity to Consume (*MPC*)
Autonomous Consumption
Marginal Propensity to Save (*MPS*)
Multiplier

Questions and Problems

Questions 1–5 are based on the first section of the chapter, questions 6–12 are based on the second section, questions 13–20 are based on the third section, and questions 21–25 are based on the fourth section.

1 How is Keynes's position different from the classical position with respect to wages, prices, and Say's law?

2 Classical economists assumed that wage rates, prices, and interest rates are flexible and will adjust quickly. Consider an extreme case: Suppose classical economists believed that wage rates, prices, and interest rates will adjust instantaneously. What would the classical aggregate supply (*AS*) curve look like? Explain your answer.

3 Give two reasons explaining the possibility that wage rates may not fall.

4 How was Keynes's position different from the classical position with respect to saving and investment?

5 According to New Keynesian economists, why might business firms pay wage rates above market-clearing levels?

6 Given the Keynesian consumption function, how would a cut in income tax rates affect consumption? Explain your answer.

7 Look at the Keynesian consumption function: $C = C_0 + (MPC)(Y_d)$. What part of it relates to autonomous consumption? What part of it relates to induced consumption? Define autonomous consumption and induced consumption.

8 Using the Keynesian consumption function, prove numerically that as the *MPC* rises, saving declines.

9 Explain the multiplier process.

10 What is the relationship between the *MPC* and the multiplier?

11 Explain how a rise in autonomous spending can increase total spending by some multiple.

12 In which factors will a change lead to a change in consumption?

13 According to Keynes, can an increase in saving shift the *AD* curve to the left? Explain your answer.

14 What factors will shift the *AD* curve in the simple Keynesian model?

15 According to Keynes, an increase in saving and a decrease in consumption may lower total spending in the economy. But how could this happen if the increased saving lowers interest rates (as shown in the last chapter)? Wouldn't a decrease in interest rates increase investment spending, thus counteracting the decrease in consumption spending?

16 Can a person believe that wages are inflexible downward for, say, one year and also believe in a self-regulating economy? Explain your answer.

17 According to Keynes, can the private sector always remove the economy from a recessionary gap? Explain your answer.

18 What does the aggregate supply curve look like in the simple Keynesian model?

19 "In the simple Keynesian model, increases in *AD* that occur below Natural Real GDP will have no effect on the price level." Do you agree or disagree with this statement? Explain your answer.

20 Suppose consumption rises while investment and government purchases remain constant. How will the *AD* curve shift in the simple Keynesian model? Under what condition will the rise in Real GDP be equal to the rise in total spending?

21 Explain how to derive a total expenditures (*TE*) curve.

22 What role do inventories play in the equilibrating process in the simple Keynesian model (as described in the *TE-TP* framework)?

23 Identify the three states of the economy in terms of *TE* and *TP*.

24 If Real GDP is $10.4 trillion in Exhibit 9, what is the state of business inventories?

25 How will a rise in government purchases change the *TE* curve in Exhibit 9?

Working with Numbers and Graphs

Questions 1–2 are based on the second section of the chapter, questions 3–4 are based on the third section, and questions 5–8 are based on the fourth section.

1 Compute the multiplier in each of the following cases:
   a. *MPC* = 0.60.
   b. *MPC* = 0.80.
   c. *MPC* = 0.50.

2 Write an investment function (equation) that specifies two components:
   a. Autonomous investment spending.
   b. Induced investment spending.

3 Economist Smith believes that changes in aggregate demand affect only the price level, and economist Jones believes that changes in aggregate demand affect only Real GDP. What do the *AD* and *AS* curves look like for each economist?

4 Explain the following using the following figure.
   a. According to Keynes, aggregate demand may be insufficient to bring about the full-employment output level (or Natural Real GDP).
   b. A decrease in consumption (due to increased saving) is not matched by an increase in investment spending.

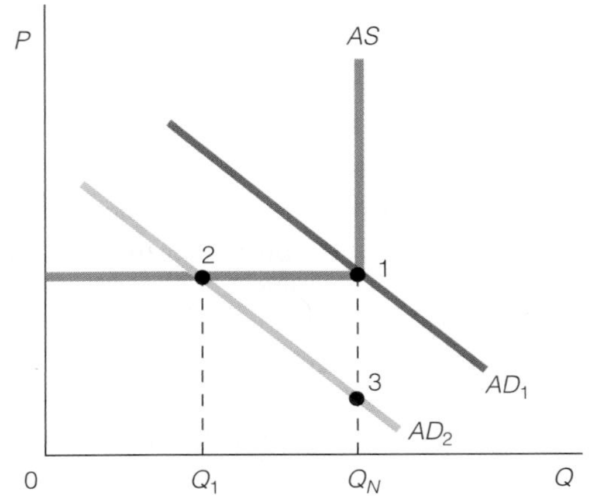

5 The *TE* curve in Exhibit 8(d) is upward sloping because the consumption function is upward sloping. Explain.

6 In Exhibit 8(d), what does the vertical distance between the origin and the point at which the *TE* curve cuts the vertical axis represent?

7 In the following figure, explain what happens if:
   a. The economy is at Q_1.
   b. The economy is at Q_2.

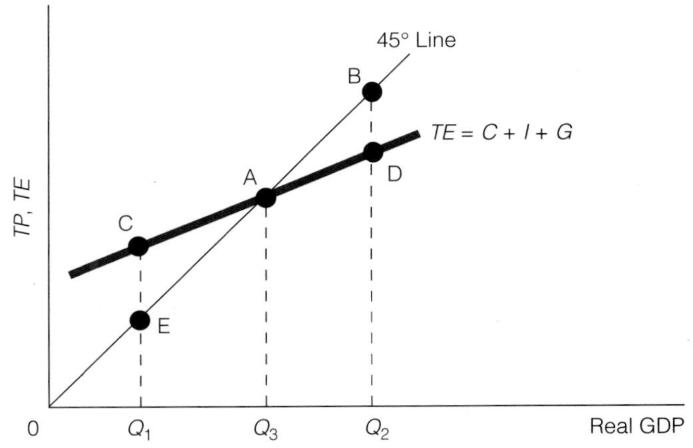

8 In the previous figure, if Natural Real GDP is Q_2, in what state is the economy at point A?

©JOE GOUGH/SHUTTERSTOCK

CHAPTER 10

FISCAL POLICY AND THE FEDERAL BUDGET

Introduction This chapter deals with fiscal policy and the federal budget. Fiscal policy deals with changes in government expenditures and/or taxes to achieve particular economic goals, such as low unemployment, stable prices, and economic growth. In the United States, the Congress and the president, together, fashion fiscal policy. We begin our discussion with some facts and figures about government expenditures and taxation, and we then go on to discuss the effect of fiscal policy on the economy.

THE FEDERAL BUDGET

The federal budget is composed of two, not necessarily equal, parts: government expenditures and tax revenues. You are familiar with the term *government purchases* from earlier chapters. Government expenditures—sometimes simply called government spending—are not the same as government purchases. Government expenditures include government purchases and (government) transfer payments.[1]

Government Expenditures

In 2007, the federal government spent $2.731 trillion—about 20 percent of GDP for that year. The following table shows government spending as a percentage of GDP in a few other years.

---

1. Remember from an earlier chapter that government purchases are the purchases of goods and services by government at all levels. Transfer payments are payments to persons that are not made in return for goods and services currently supplied, such as Social Security payments. In this chapter, the terms *government expenditures, government spending, government purchases,* and *transfer payments* all refer to the *federal* government.

Year	Government Spending as a Percentage of GDP
2000	18.4
2001	18.5
2002	19.4
2003	19.9
2004	19.9
2005	20.2
2006	20.3
2007	20.0
2008	20.4 (projected)
2009	20.3 (projected)

The bulk of the $2.731 trillion in government spending in 2007 was spent on four programs: national defense, Social Security, Medicare, and Medicaid. These four programs together accounted for 63.6 percent of all government spending in 2007. The following table shows the actual dollar amounts spent in various spending program categories.

Spending Program Category	Billions of Dollars
National Defense	$530
Social Security	577
Medicare	440
Medicaid	191
Other Programs and Activities	741
Net Interest on the Public Debt	252

Government Tax Revenues

The federal government imposes taxes and fees that generate revenue. In 2007, government revenues totaled $2.568 trillion. This was 18.8 percent of GDP for the year. The following table shows government tax revenues as a percentage of GDP in a few other years.

Year	Government Tax Revenues as a Percentage of GDP
2000	20.9
2001	19.8
2002	17.9
2003	16.5
2004	16.3
2005	17.5
2006	18.4
2007	18.8
2008	17.9 (projected)
2009	18.9 (projected)

The bulk of government tax revenues comes from three taxes: the individual income tax, the corporate income tax, and Social Security taxes. These three taxes accounted for 93.6 percent of total government tax revenues in 2007. The following table shows the actual dollar amount raised in tax revenue by each tax, and the tax revenue for each tax as a percentage of GDP.

Tax	Billions of Dollars	Percentage of 2007 GDP
Individual Income Tax	$1,163	8.5
Corporate Income Tax	370	2.7
Social Security Taxes	870	6.3
Other	163	1.2

You can see from these numbers that the individual income tax is a large portion of the government tax revenue pie. Let's look at this tax in more detail.

INCOME TAX STRUCTURES An income tax structure can be progressive, proportional, or regressive. Under a **progressive income tax**, the tax rate increases as a person's taxable income level rises. To illustrate, suppose Davidson pays taxes at the rate of 15 percent on a taxable income of $20,000. When his (taxable) income rises to, say, $30,000, he pays at a rate of 28 percent. And when his income rises to, say, $55,000, he pays at a rate of 31 percent. A progressive income tax is usually capped at some rate. Currently, the U.S. income tax structure is progressive, with six (marginal) tax rates, ranging from a low of 10 percent to a high (or cap) of 35 percent.

Progressive Income Tax
An income tax system in which one's tax rate rises as one's taxable income rises (up to some point).

Under a **proportional income tax**, the same tax rate is used for all income levels. A proportional income tax is sometimes referred to as a *flat tax.* For example, if Kuan's taxable income is $10,000, she pays taxes at a rate of 10 percent; if her taxable income rises to $100,000, she still pays at a rate of 10 percent.

Proportional Income Tax
An income tax system in which a person's tax rate is the same no matter what his or her taxable income is.

Under a **regressive income tax**, the tax rate decreases as a person's taxable income level rises. For example, Lowenstein's tax rate is 10 percent when her taxable income is $10,000 and 8 percent when her taxable income rises to $20,000.

Regressive Income Tax
An income tax system in which a person's tax rate declines as his or her taxable income rises.

See Exhibit 1 for a review of the three income tax structures.

Finding ECONOMICS

A Presidential Candidate Speaks

A presidential candidate is speaking before a large group in Des Moines, Iowa. He has just called the current income tax structure unfair. Someone from the crowd asks him what he means by "unfair." The candidate says that individuals shouldn't pay a higher tax rate just because they earn a higher income. We should all pay the same tax rate, he argues. Where is the economics? Obviously the candidate favors a proportional income tax (i.e., a flat tax). Under both a progressive and a regressive income tax structure, individuals pay different tax rates at different taxable income levels. Only with a proportional income tax do individuals pay the same tax rate no matter what their taxable income is.

exhibit 1

Three Income Tax Structures

The three income tax structures outlined are the progressive, proportional, and regressive.

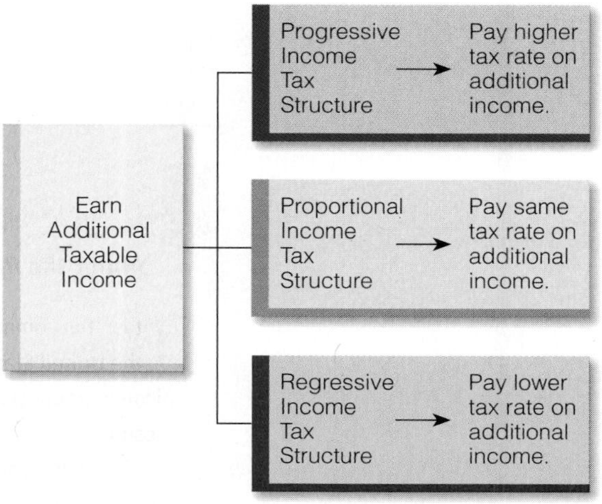

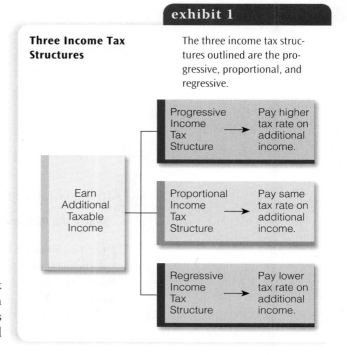

WHO PAYS THE INCOME TAX? Economists often look at the tax situations of different income groups. For example, in 2005, the top 1 percent of income earners in the United States earned 21.20 percent of the total income earned that year and

economics 24/7

TWO PLUMBERS, NEW YEAR'S EVE, AND PROGRESSIVE TAXATION

Many people believe that if two people do the same job, they should be paid the same dollar amount. This notion of equal pay for equal work often arises in discussions about the jobs performed by men and women. In other words, if a man and a woman do the same job, many people say that they should be paid the same dollar amount.

Sometimes the question of equal pay for equal work is extended to equal after-tax pay for equal work. That is, if two people do the same job, then they should earn the same after-tax income. However, a progressive income tax structure sometimes makes this impossible.

To illustrate, suppose under a progressive income tax structure, a person who earns between $50,000 and $60,000 pays income tax at a tax rate of 20 percent. For every dollar earned over $60,000 but under $70,000, a person pays at a tax rate of 30 percent.

Consider two plumbers, Smith and Jones. By December 30, Jones has earned $58,000 for the year, and Smith has earned $60,000. Each is asked to do the same kind of plumbing job on December 31, New Year's Eve. Each plumber charges $1,000 for the job. So Jones and Smith receive equal pay for equal work.

The after-tax income that each receives for the job makes for a different story. On the additional $1,000 that Jones earns, she pays at a tax rate of 20 percent. So she pays $200 in taxes and gets to keep $800 in after-tax income. Smith, on the other hand, now has an annual income of $61,000 and thus falls into a higher marginal tax bracket. He pays at a tax rate of 30 percent on the additional $1,000. So Smith pays $300 in taxes and has $700 in after-tax income. Smith does the same job as Jones but earns only $700 in after-tax pay, whereas Jones earns $800 in after-tax pay.

Our conclusion: The progressive income tax structure can turn equal pay for equal work into unequal after-tax pay for equal work. Stated differently, a person can be in favor of progressive income taxes or equal after-tax pay for equal work but not both. Sometimes, it is a matter of one or the other.

paid 39.38 percent of the total federal income taxes. The following data show the income and taxes for various income groups in 2005:

Income Group	Group's Share of Total Income	Group's Share of Federal Income Taxes
Top 1%	21.20	39.38
Top 5%	35.75	59.67
Top 10%	46.44	70.30
Top 25%	67.52	85.99
Top 50%	87.17	96.93
Bottom 50%	12.83	3.07

Common MISCONCEPTIONS

About the Rich and Taxes

It isn't uncommon to hear people say the rich do not pay a high percentage of income taxes in the United States. Often, many of these people do not know exactly what percentages different income groups pay in federal income taxes. If we define the rich as those in the top 1 percent of income earners, then we see that in 2005, they paid 39.38 percent of all federal income taxes. Or consider this: From looking at the income and tax data, we see that the bottom 95 percent of income earners paid 40.33 percent (100.00 – 59.67) of all federal income taxes in 2005. This percentage is

(continued)

Common Misconceptions (continued)

very close to 39.38 percent, which is the percentage of federal income taxes paid by the top 1 percent of income earners. In other words, in 2005 the top 1 percent of income earners paid approximately the same percentage of income taxes as the bottom 95 percent. By the way, you had to earn more than $364,657 to be in the top 1 percent of income earners in 2005.

Budget Deficit, Surplus, or Balance

If government expenditures are greater than tax revenues, the federal government runs a **budget deficit.** If tax revenues are greater than government expenditures, the federal government runs a **budget surplus.** If government expenditures equal tax revenues, the federal government runs a **balanced budget.**

Budget Deficit
Government expenditures greater than tax revenues.

Budget Surplus
Tax revenues greater than government expenditures.

Balanced Budget
Government expenditures equal to tax revenues.

In 2007, government expenditures were $2.731 trillion, and tax revenues were $2.568 trillion; so the federal government ran a budget deficit that year of $163 billion. Budget deficits are projected for upcoming years. For the period 2008 to 2011, the government is projected to run budget deficits. On July 29, 2008, the Congressional Budget Office estimated the federal budget deficit for 2008 at $422 billion.

If the government spends more than its tax revenue and thus runs a budget deficit, where does it get the money to finance the deficit? In other words, if the government spends $100 and only has $70 in taxes, where does it get the $30 difference? The answer is that the federal government—actually the U.S. Treasury—borrows the $30; that is, it finances the budget deficit with borrowed funds.

Structural and Cyclical Deficits

Suppose the budget is currently balanced, and then Real GDP in the economy drops. As Real GDP drops, the tax base of the economy falls, and, if tax rates are held constant, tax revenues will fall. Also as a result of the decline in Real GDP, transfer payments (e.g., unemployment compensation) will rise. Thus, government expenditures will rise, and tax revenues will fall. As a result, a balanced budget turns into a budget deficit. This budget deficit results from the downturn in economic activity, not from any current spending and taxing decisions by the government.

Economists use the term **cyclical deficit** to refer to the part of the budget deficit that is a result of a downturn in economic activity. The remainder of the deficit—or the part of the deficit that would exist if the economy were operating at full employment—is called the **structural deficit.** In other words,

Cyclical Deficit
The part of the budget deficit that is a result of a downturn in economic activity.

Structural Deficit
The part of the budget deficit that would exist even if the economy were operating at full employment.

$$\text{Total budget deficit} = \text{Structural deficit} + \text{Cyclical deficit}$$

To illustrate, suppose the economy is in a recessionary gap, government expenditures are currently $2.3 trillion, and tax revenues are $2.0 trillion. Thus, the (total) budget deficit is $300 billion. Economists estimate what government expenditures and tax revenues would be if the economy were operating at full employment. Assume they estimate that government expenditures would be only $2.2 trillion and that tax revenues would be $2.1 trillion. The structural deficit—the deficit that would exist at full employment—is therefore $100 billion. The cyclical deficit—the part of the budget deficit that is a result of economic downturn—is $200 billion.

The Public Debt

A budget deficit occurs when government expenditures are greater than tax revenues for a *single year.* The **public debt,** which is sometimes called the federal or national debt, is the *total* amount the federal government owes its creditors. Some of this debt is held by agencies

Public Debt
The total amount that the federal government owes its creditors.

Q&A: GOVERNMENT SPENDING AND TAXES

Economics is not all about concepts, theories, and policies. Sometimes it is about facts and figures. A complete knowledge of the economic scene requires us to know some of those facts and figures, which are presented here as the answer to questions that individuals often ask.

What are the two largest federal taxes that U.S. households pay?
The Social Security tax and the federal income tax. The average household paid $7,069 in Social Security taxes in 2004 and $7,062 in federal income taxes. If we add all federal taxes, the average household paid a total of $17,338 in federal taxes in 2004.

What are the three largest state and local taxes that U.S. households pay?
Property taxes, general sales taxes, and individual income taxes. In 2004, the average household paid $2,906 in property taxes, $2,240 in general sales taxes, and $1,984 in income taxes. If we add all state and local taxes, the average household paid a total of $9,400.

How much do U.S. households pay in taxes?
The total dollar amount in 2004 (including federal, state, and local taxes) was $3 trillion. This was an average of $26,778 per household.

Do different income groups in the United States pay the same dollar amount in taxes?
No. In 2004, the average household in the bottom 20 percent of income-earning households paid $4,325 in taxes; the average household in the top 20 percent of income-earning households paid $81,933 in taxes. Households in the so-called middle class (the middle 20 percent of income-earning households) paid $21,194 in taxes.

Do low-income and high-income households alike pay approximately the same percentage of their taxes to the federal government as they do to the state and local governments?
No. The lowest-earning households (bottom 20 percent) pay more in state and local taxes than in federal taxes. The highest-earning households (top 20 percent) pay more in federal taxes than in state and local taxes. Here are the percentages: The lowest-earning households pay 39 cents out of each tax dollar to the federal government and 61 cents out of each tax dollar to the state and local governments. The highest-earning households pay 70 cents out of each tax dollar to the federal government and 30 cents to the state and local governments.

We've talked about taxes, but not about government spending. Is there any information on how much different people receive in government spending benefits compared to how much they pay in taxes?
Yes. In 2004, the bottom 20 percent of income-earning households paid an average of $2,642 in state and local taxes and received an average of $10,650 in (state and local) government spending benefits. In fact, the bottom 60 percent of income-earning households received more in government spending benefits than they paid in taxes. The top 40 percent of income-earning households paid more (on average) in state and local taxes than they received in state and local government spending. For example, the top 20 percent paid an average of $24,421 in state and local taxes and received an average of $14,911 in spending benefits.

What about federal taxes and federal government spending benefits? Do some households pay more in taxes than they receive in spending benefits?
Yes. Some households pay more in federal taxes than they receive in federal government spending benefits, and some households pay less in federal taxes than they receive in spending benefits. To illustrate, the top 20 percent of income-earning households paid an average of $57,512 in federal taxes in 2004 and received an average of $18,573 in spending benefits. The bottom 20 percent of households paid an average of $1,684 in federal taxes and received an average of $24,860 in spending benefits. Overall, the bottom 60 percent of households receive a greater dollar worth of spending benefits than they pay in taxes, and the top 40 percent pay a greater dollar amount in taxes than they receive in spending benefits.

If I receive something from the government that costs the government $10, does it follow that I receive at least $10 worth of benefits from the good or service?
No. To illustrate, a middle school student might be receiving a lunch at school that is paid for by the government, and it might cost the government $3 to provide the lunch. However, the middle school student does not necessarily value the benefits of the lunch at $3. The value of the benefits (the student receives from the lunch) could be either much higher or much lower than $3. It would be no different than my giving you a watch that I paid $100 for. You might not value the watch at $100. In other words, you might tell me that you receive only $40 worth of benefits from the watch (and that you would have never paid $100 for the watch if it were up to you).

of the United States government—one entity in the government owes it to another. The remainder of the debt is held by the public and is referred to either as *public debt held by the public* or as *net public debt.* The public debt was $9.5 trillion on July 29, 2008. The public debt held by the public was $5.3 trillion. You can find the current public debt on the Bureau of the Public Debt website at http://www.publicdebt.treas.gov/opd/opd.htm. The public debt was at its lowest on January 1, 1835, totaling $33,733.05 on that day.

SELF-TEST

(Answers to Self-Test questions are in the Self-Test Appendix.)

1. Explain the differences among progressive, proportional, and regressive income tax structures.
2. What percentage of all income taxes was paid by the top 5 percent of income earners in 2005? What percentage of total income did this income group receive in 2005?
3. What three taxes account for the bulk of federal tax revenues?
4. What is the cyclical budget deficit?

FISCAL POLICY

As explained in the last chapter, some economists believe that the economy is inherently unstable. These economists argue that government should play a role in managing the economy because the economy can get stuck in a recessionary gap. They believe government should try to move the economy out of the recessionary gap and toward Natural Real GDP.

One of the major ways government can influence the economy is through its *fiscal policy.* **Fiscal policy** consists of changes in government expenditures and/or taxes to achieve particular economic goals, such as low unemployment, price stability, and economic growth. We discuss fiscal policy in the following sections.

Fiscal Policy
Changes in government expenditures and/or taxes to achieve economic goals, such as low unemployment, stable prices, and economic growth.

Some Relevant Fiscal Policy Terms

Expansionary fiscal policy consists of increases in government expenditures and/or decreases in taxes to achieve macroeconomic goals. **Contractionary fiscal policy** is implemented through decreases in government expenditures and/or increases in taxes to achieve these goals.

Expansionary Fiscal Policy
Increases in government expenditures and/or decreases in taxes to achieve particular economic goals.

Contractionary Fiscal Policy
Decreases in government expenditures and/or increases in taxes to achieve economic goals.

Expansionary fiscal policy: Government expenditures up and/or taxes down

Contractionary fiscal policy: Government expenditures down and/or taxes up

When deliberate government actions bring about changes in its expenditures and taxes, fiscal policy is said to be *discretionary.* For example, if Congress decides to increase government spending by, say, $10 billion in an attempt to lower the unemployment rate, this is an act of **discretionary fiscal policy**. In contrast, a change in either government expenditures or in taxes that occurs automatically in response to economic events is referred to as **automatic fiscal policy**. To illustrate, suppose Real GDP in the economy turns down, causing more people to become unemployed, and, as a result, automatically receive unemployment benefits. These added unemployment benefits automatically boost government spending.

Discretionary Fiscal Policy
Deliberate changes of government expenditures and/or taxes to achieve economic goals.

Automatic Fiscal Policy
Changes in government expenditures and/or taxes that occur automatically without (additional) congressional action.

Two Important Notes

In your study of this chapter, keep in mind the following two important points:

1. In this chapter, we deal only with *discretionary fiscal policy.* In other words, we consider deliberate actions on the part of policy makers to affect the economy through changes in government spending and/or taxes.

2. We assume that any change in government spending is due to a change in government purchases, not to a change in transfer payments. Stated differently, we assume that transfer payments are constant so that changes in government spending are a reflection only of changes in government purchases.

DEMAND-SIDE FISCAL POLICY

Fiscal policy can affect the demand side of the economy, that is, aggregate demand. This section focuses on how government spending and taxes can affect aggregate demand.

Shifting the Aggregate Demand Curve

How do changes in government purchases (*G*) and taxes (*T*) affect aggregate demand? Recall that a change in consumption, investment, government purchases, or net exports can change aggregate demand and therefore shift the *AD* curve. For example, an increase in government purchases (*G*) increases aggregate demand and shifts the *AD* curve to the right. A decrease in *G* decreases aggregate demand and shifts the *AD* curve to the left.[2]

A change in taxes (*T*) can affect consumption, investment, or both, and it therefore can affect aggregate demand. For example, a decrease in income taxes increases disposable (after-tax) income, which permits individuals to increase their consumption. As consumption rises, the *AD* curve shifts to the right. An increase in taxes decreases disposable income, lowers consumption, and shifts the *AD* curve to the left.

Fiscal Policy: Keynesian Perspective (Economy Is Not Self-Regulating)

The model of the economy in Exhibit 2(a) shows a downward-sloping *AD* curve and an upward-sloping *SRAS* curve. As you can see, the economy is initially in a recessionary gap at point 1. Aggregate demand is too low to move the economy to equilibrium at the Natural Real GDP level. The Keynesian *perspective* of the economy here is that the economy is not self-regulating. So the Keynesian *prescription* is to enact expansionary fiscal policy measures (an increase in government purchases or a decrease in taxes) to shift the aggregate demand curve rightward from AD_1 to AD_2 and to move the economy to the Natural Real GDP level at point 2.

At this point, the question might be, why not simply wait for the short-run aggregate supply curve to shift rightward and intersect the aggregate demand curve at point 2′? Again, the Keynesians usually respond that the economy is not self-regulating. They argue that either (1) the economy is stuck at point 1 and won't move naturally to point 2′—perhaps because wage rates won't fall—or (2) the short-run aggregate supply curve takes too long to shift rightward, and in the interim we must deal with the high cost of unemployment and a lower level of Real GDP. In Exhibit 2(b), the economy is initially in an inflationary gap at point 1. In this situation, Keynesians are likely to propose a contractionary fiscal measure (a decrease in government purchases or an increase in taxes) to shift the aggregate demand curve leftward from AD_1 to AD_2 and move the economy to point 2.

In Exhibit 2, fiscal policy has worked as intended. In (a), the economy was in a recessionary gap, and expansionary fiscal policy eliminated the recessionary gap. In (b), the economy was in an inflationary gap, and contractionary fiscal policy eliminated the inflationary gap. In (a) and (b), fiscal policy is at its best and working as intended.

---

2. Later in this chapter, when we discuss crowding out, we question the effect of an increase in government purchases on aggregate demand.

exhibit 2

Fiscal Policy in Keynesian Theory: Ridding the Economy of Recessionary and Inflationary Gaps

(a) In Keynesian theory, expansionary fiscal policy eliminates a recessionary gap. Increased government purchases, decreased taxes, or both lead to a rightward shift in the aggregate demand curve from AD_1 to AD_2, restoring the economy to the natural level of Real GDP, Q_N.

(b) Contractionary fiscal policy is used to eliminate an inflationary gap. Decreased government purchases, increased taxes, or both lead to a leftward shift in the aggregate demand curve from AD_1 to AD_2, restoring the economy to the natural level of Real GDP, Q_N.

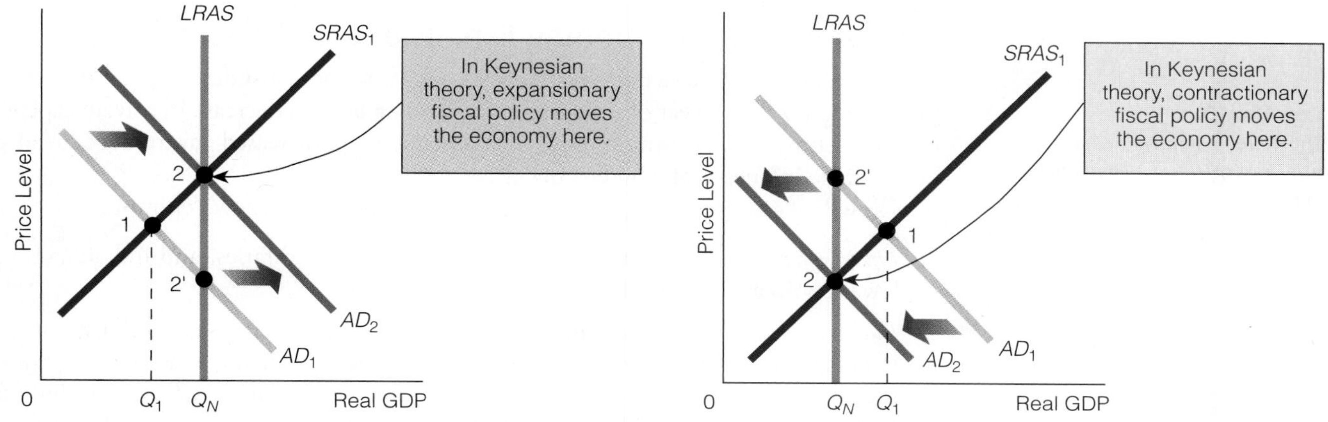

(a)
Expansionary Fiscal Policy for a Recessionary Gap

(b)
Contractionary Fiscal Policy for an Inflationary Gap

Common Misconceptions

About Fiscal Policy

In 1962, John F. Kennedy was president of the United States, and Walter Heller was one of Kennedy's economic advisors. Heller told the president that the economy needed a tax cut (a form of expansionary fiscal policy) to keep it from sputtering. In December, in a speech before the Economic Club of New York, President Kennedy said, "An economy hampered by restrictive tax rates will never produce enough revenue to balance our budget just as it will never produce enough jobs or enough profits."

Then in January 1963, he said, "It has become increasingly clear that the largest single barrier to full employment . . . and to a higher rate of economic growth is the unrealistically heavy drag of federal income taxes on private purchasing power, initiative and incentive." Kennedy proposed expansionary fiscal policy—in the form of a tax cut—to raise economic growth and lower the unemployment rate. He proposed lowering the top individual income tax rate, the bottom individual income tax rate, the corporate income tax, and the capital gains tax. He was assassinated in Dallas before Congress passed his tax program, but Congress did pass it. What was the result?

When the tax bill passed in 1964, the unemployment rate was 5.2 percent; in 1965, it was down to 4.5 percent; in 1966, it was down further to 3.8 percent. The tax cut is widely credited with bringing the unemployment rate down. As for economic growth, when the tax cut was passed in 1964, it was 5.8 percent; one year later, in 1965, the growth rate was up to 6.4 percent; and in 1966, the growth rate was even higher, at 6.6 percent. Again, the tax cut received much of the credit for stimulating economic growth.

macro*theme* ➔ In an earlier chapter, we said that economists don't always agree that economic policy is effective at, say, removing an economy from a recessionary or inflationary gap. Specifically, some economists say that fiscal policy is effective, whereas others say that it is ineffective. You have just heard from the economists who say fiscal policy is effective. Now we turn to those who say it is not.

Crowding Out: Questioning Expansionary Fiscal Policy

Crowding Out
The decrease in private expenditures that occurs as a consequence of increased government spending or the financing needs of a budget deficit.

Not all economists believe that fiscal policy works as we have just described. Some economists bring up the subject of *crowding out.* **Crowding out** is a decrease in private expenditures (consumption, investment, etc.) as a consequence of increased government spending or the financing needs of a budget deficit.

Crowding out can be direct or indirect, as described in these two examples:

1. *Direct effect.* The government spends more on public libraries, and individuals buy fewer books at bookstores.[3]
2. *Indirect effect.* The government spends more on social programs and defense without increasing taxes; as a result, the size of the budget deficit increases. Consequently, the government must borrow more funds to finance the larger deficit. This increase in borrowing causes the demand for credit (i.e., the demand for loanable funds) to rise, which in turn causes the interest rate to rise. As a result, investment drops. More government spending indirectly leads to less investment spending.

TYPES OF CROWDING OUT In our first example, the government spends more on public libraries. To be specific, let's say that the government spends $2 billion more on public libraries and that consumers choose to spend not $1 less on books at bookstores. Obviously, then, there is no crowding out, or *zero crowding out.*

Now suppose that, after the government has spent $2 billion more on public libraries, consumers choose to spend $2 billion less on books at bookstores. Obviously, crowding out exists, and the degree of crowding out is dollar for dollar. When $1 of government spending offsets $1 of private spending, **complete crowding out** is said to exist.

Complete Crowding Out
A decrease in one or more components of private spending that completely offsets the increase in government spending.

Incomplete Crowding Out
The decrease in one or more components of private spending that only partially offsets the increase in government spending.

Finally, suppose that, after the government has spent $2 billion more on public libraries, consumers spend $1.2 billion less on books at bookstores. Again, there is crowding out, but it is not dollar for dollar, not complete crowding out. In this case, incomplete crowding out exists. **Incomplete crowding out** occurs when the decrease in one or more components of private spending only partially offsets the increase in government spending.

The following table summarizes the different types of crowding out.

Type of Crowding Out	Example
Zero crowding out (sometimes called "no crowding out")	Government spends $2 billion more, and private sector spending stays constant.
Complete crowding out	Government spends $2 billion more, and private sector spends $2 billion less.
Incomplete crowding out	Government spends $2 billion more, and private sector spends $1.2 billion less.

3. We are not saying that, for example, if the government spends more on public libraries, individuals will necessarily buy fewer books at bookstores; rather, if they do, this would be an example of crowding out. The same holds for example 2.

exhibit 3

Zero (No), Incomplete, and Complete Crowding Out

The exhibit shows the effects of zero, incomplete, and complete crowding out in the *AD-AS* framework. Starting at point 1, expansionary fiscal policy shifts the aggregate demand curve to AD_2 and moves the economy to point 2 and Q_N. The Keynesian theory that predicts this outcome assumes zero, or no, crowding out; an increase in, say, government spending does not reduce private expenditures. With incomplete crowding out, an increase in government spending causes private expenditures to decrease by less than the increase in government spending. The net result is a shift in the aggregate demand curve to AD'_2. The economy moves to point 2′ and Q'_2. With complete crowding out, an increase in government spending is completely offset by a decrease in private expenditures, and the net result is that aggregate demand does not increase at all. The economy remains at point 1 and Q_1.

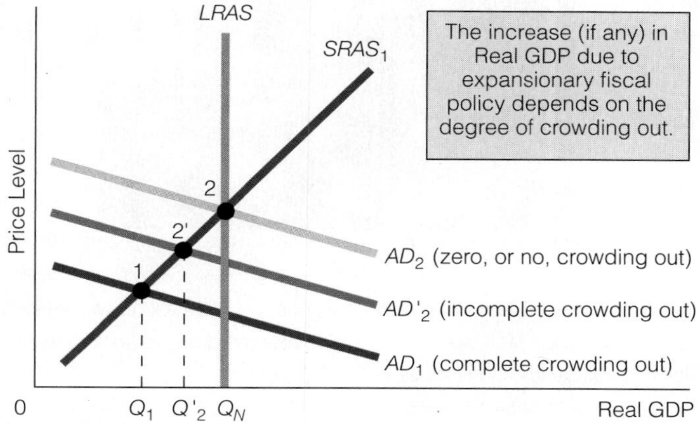

GRAPHICAL REPRESENTATION OF CROWDING OUT If *complete* or *incomplete crowding out* occurs, then expansionary fiscal policy will have less impact on aggregate demand and Real GDP than Keynesian theory predicts. Let's look at the graphical representation of crowding out.

Exhibit 3 illustrates the consequences of complete and incomplete crowding out. For comparison, the exhibit also includes the case of zero crowding out in Keynesian theory. As shown in Exhibit 3, keep in mind the three possibilities concerning crowding out:

- Zero crowding out (no crowding out)
- Incomplete crowding out
- Complete crowding out

In Exhibit 3, the economy is initially at point 1, with Real GDP at Q_1. In Keynesian theory, expansionary fiscal policy shifts the aggregate demand curve to AD_2 and moves the economy to point 2. Among other things, the implicit assumption is that there is zero crowding out (no crowding out). Notice that Real GDP has increased from Q_1 to Q_N. It follows that the unemployment rate will fall from its level at Q_1 to a lower level at Q_N. Summary: If there is no crowding out, expansionary fiscal policy increases Real GDP and lowers the unemployment rate.

With incomplete crowding out, the aggregate demand curve shifts (on net) only to AD'_2 because a fall in private expenditures *partially offsets* the initial stimulus in aggregate demand due to increased government spending. The economy moves to point 2′. Notice that Real GDP has increased from Q_1 to Q'_2. It follows that the unemployment rate will fall from what it was at Q_1 to what it is at Q'_2. Also notice that the changes in both Real GDP and the unemployment rate are smaller, with incomplete crowding out than they are with zero crowding out. Summary: Given incomplete crowding out, expansionary fiscal policy increases Real GDP and lowers the unemployment rate but not as much as if there is zero crowding out.

economics 24/7

MOVIE CROWDING OUT: THE CASE OF *THE DARK KNIGHT*

The blockbuster movie *The Dark Knight* made its U.S. premiere release on July 18, 2008. In its first three days at the theaters, it took in $158 million in gross receipts.

WARNER BROS/DC COMICS/THE KOBAL COLLECTION

As movie releases go, $158 million (in three days) is an extraordinarily large dollar amount. Some people said this dollar amount indicated that the public was spending more money on going to the movies.

But is this statement necessarily true? Certainly, it doesn't have to be. There may be such a thing as movie crowding out. To illustrate, we assume that the moviegoing public spends $70 million each weekend on ten movies. Let's say this dollar amount is evenly distributed across all ten movies so that each movie earns $7 million. A blockbuster movie may simply have a larger share of the $70 million pie. The blockbuster may earn, say, $20 million, and the nine remaining movies evenly divide the remaining $50 million. In other words, spending on the blockbuster comes at the expense of other movies on a dollar-for-dollar basis. Blockbuster spending crowds out nonblockbuster spending in much the same way as government spending can crowd out household spending.

Movie crowding out could also work another way. Perhaps because of the blockbuster, total spending on movies rises when the blockbuster is released; that is, the moviegoing public increases the amount spent on movies in the first few weekends after a blockbuster is released. Thus, spending may rise to, say, $100 million each weekend for three consecutive weekends after the release of a blockbuster. But then what we might call the blockbuster effect fades away, and spending on movies falls below the usual $70 million per weekend. It may fall to, say, $50 million per weekend for a few weekends. Blockbuster spending has still crowded out nonblockbuster spending, but not as quickly as in the first case.

There is also a related issue. Perhaps a blockbuster doesn't crowd out other movie spending but does crowd out nonmovie spending. To illustrate, suppose that, because of a blockbuster, spending on movies actually rises (over a year). The new average goes from $70 million each weekend to, say, $80 million. But because people are spending more on movies, they spend less on other things. In other words, movie spending crowds out nonmovie spending. People spend less on books, restaurant meals, clothes, and the like. One sector of the economy (the movie sector) expands as another contracts.

In the case of complete crowding out, a fall in private expenditures *completely offsets* the initial stimulus in aggregate demand due to increased government spending, and the aggregate demand curve does not move (on net) at all. Notice that Real GDP does not change, and neither does the unemployment rate. Summary: If there is complete crowding out, expansionary fiscal policy has no effect on the economy. The economy remains at point 1.

See Exhibit 4 for a summary flow chart of the different types of crowding out.

Thinking like AN ECONOMIST

Policy Is Not Necessarily Effective

An ill person goes to the doctor and asks for medicine. The doctor prescribes the medicine, and the person goes home. After a few days, the medicine has not made the person well. The same can be sometimes said of certain types of economic policy. Keep in mind what we are and are not saying. We are not saying that economic policy is never effective; we are simply saying it is not necessarily effective. In our discussion of fiscal policy so far, crowding out is simply one reason fiscal policy may not be effective at times. Lags, which we discuss next, are another.

exhibit 4

Expansionary Fiscal Policy (Government Spending Increases), Crowding Out, and Changes in Real GDP and the Unemployment Rate

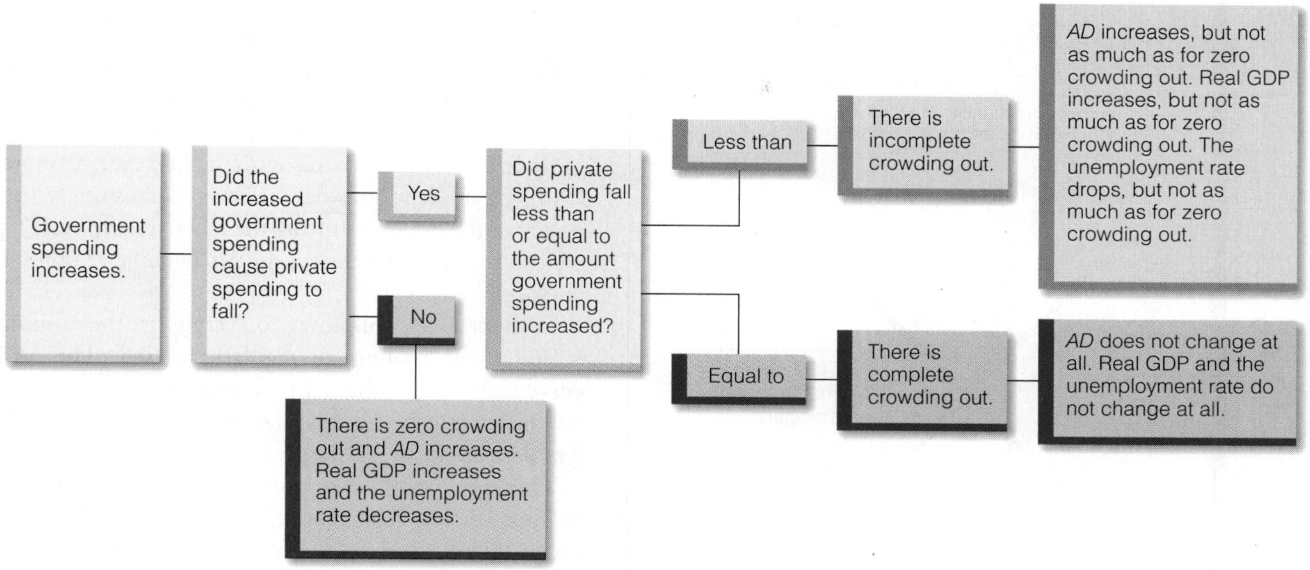

Lags and Fiscal Policy

Suppose we proved beyond a shadow of a doubt that no (zero) crowding out is taking place. Should fiscal policy then be used to solve the problems of inflationary and recessionary gaps? Many economists would answer not necessarily. The reason is that *lags* exist. There are five types of lags:

1. *The data lag.* Policy makers are not aware of changes in the economy as soon as they happen. For example, if the economy turns down in January, the decline may not be apparent for two to three months.
2. *The wait-and-see lag.* After policy makers are aware of a downturn in economic activity, they rarely enact counteractive measures immediately. Instead, they usually adopt a relatively cautious wait-and-see attitude. They want to be sure that the observed events are not just short-run phenomena.
3. *The legislative lag.* After policy makers decide that some type of fiscal policy measure is required, Congress or the president has to propose the measure, build political support for it, and get it passed. The legislative lag can take many months.
4. *The transmission lag.* After enacted, a fiscal policy measure takes time to go into effect. For example, a discretionary expansionary fiscal policy measure mandating increased spending for public works projects requires construction companies to submit bids for the work, prepare designs, negotiate contracts, and so on.
5. *The effectiveness lag.* After a policy measure is actually implemented, it takes time to affect the economy. If government spending is increased on Monday, the aggregate demand curve does not shift rightward on Tuesday.

exhibit 5

Fiscal Policy May Destabilize the Economy

In this scenario, the *SRAS* curve is shifting rightward (healing the economy of its recessionary gap), but this information is unknown to policy makers. Policy makers implement expansionary fiscal policy, and the *AD* curve ends up intersecting $SRAS_2$ at point 2 instead of intersecting $SRAS_1$ at point 1′. Policy makers thereby move the economy into an inflationary gap, thus destabilizing the economy.

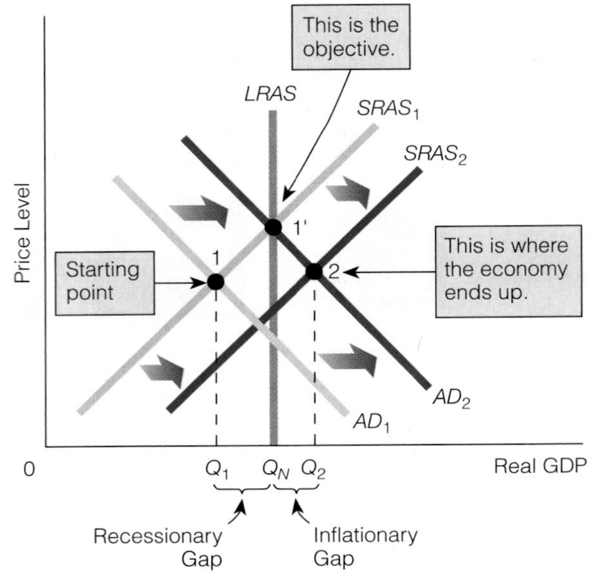

Taking these five lags together, some economists argue that discretionary fiscal policy is not likely to have the impact on the economy that policy makers hope for. By the time the full impact of the policy is felt, the economic problem it was designed to solve (1) may no longer exist, (2) may not exist to the degree it once did, or (3) may have changed altogether.

Exhibit 5 illustrates the effect of lags. Suppose the economy is currently in a recessionary gap at point 1. The recession is under way before government officials recognize it. After it is recognized, however, Congress and the president consider enacting expansionary fiscal policy in the hope of shifting the *AD* curve from AD_1 to AD_2 so that it will intersect the *SRAS* curve at point 1′, at Natural Real GDP.

In the interim, unknown to everybody, the economy is said to be healing, or regulating, itself: The *SRAS* curve is shifting to the right. Government officials don't see this change because it takes time to collect and analyze data about the economy.

Thinking that the economy is not healing itself or not healing itself quickly enough, the government enacts expansionary fiscal policy. In time, the *AD* curve shifts rightward. But by the time the increased demand is felt in the goods and services market, the *AD* curve intersects the *SRAS* curve at point 2. In short, the government has moved the economy from point 1 to point 2, not, as it had desired, from point 1 to point 1′. The government has moved the economy into an inflationary gap. Instead of stabilizing and moderating the ups and downs in economic activity (the business cycle), the government has intensified the fluctuations.

Crowding Out, Lags, and the Effectiveness of Fiscal Policy

Economists who believe that there is zero crowding out and that lags are insignificant conclude that fiscal policy is effective at moving the economy out of a recessionary gap. Economists who believe that crowding out is complete and/or that lags are significant conclude that fiscal policy is ineffective at moving the economy out of a recessionary gap.

SELF-TEST

1. How does crowding out create questions about the effectiveness of expansionary demand-side fiscal policy? Give an example.
2. How might lags reduce the effectiveness of fiscal policy?
3. Give an example of the indirect effect of crowding out.

SUPPLY-SIDE FISCAL POLICY

Fiscal policy effects may be felt on the supply side as well as on the demand side of the economy. For example, a reduction in tax rates may alter an individual's incentive to work and produce, thus altering aggregate supply.

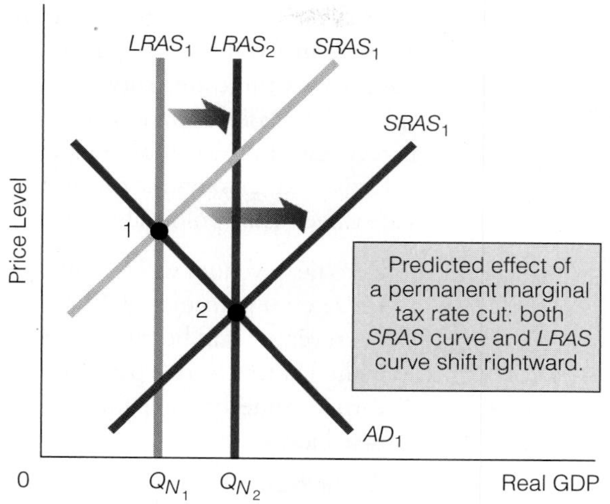
LRAS1
LRAS2
SRAS1
SRAS1
Price Level
1
2
Predicted effect of a permanent marginal tax rate cut: both SRAS curve and LRAS curve shift rightward.
AD1
0
QN1
QN2
Real GDP

exhibit 6

The Predicted Effect of a Permanent Marginal Tax Rate Cut on Aggregate Supply

A cut in marginal tax rates increases the attractiveness of productive activity relative to leisure and tax-avoidance activities and shifts resources from the latter to the former, thus shifting rightward both the short-run and the long-run aggregate supply curves.

Marginal Tax Rates and Aggregate Supply

When fiscal policy measures affect tax rates, they may affect both aggregate supply and aggregate demand. Consider a reduction in an individual's marginal tax rate. The **marginal (income) tax rate** is equal to the change in a person's tax payment divided by the change in the person's taxable income.

Marginal (Income) Tax Rate
The change in a person's tax payment divided by the change in his or her taxable income: ΔTax payment/ΔTaxable income.

$$\text{Marginal tax rate} = \frac{\Delta\text{Tax payment}}{\Delta\text{Taxable income}}$$

For example, if Serena's taxable income increases by $1 and her tax payment increases by $0.28, her marginal tax rate is 28 percent; if her taxable income increases by $1 and her tax payment increases by $0.35, then her marginal tax rate is 35 percent.

All other things held constant, lower marginal tax rates increase the incentive to engage in productive activities (work) relative to leisure and tax-avoidance activities.[4] As resources shift from leisure to work, short-run aggregate supply increases. If the lower marginal tax rates are permanent and not simply a one-shot affair, most economists predict that not only will the short-run aggregate supply curve shift rightward, but the long-run aggregate supply curve will shift rightward too. Exhibit 6 illustrates the predicted effect of a permanent marginal tax rate cut on aggregate supply.

The Laffer Curve: Tax Rates and Tax Revenues

> High tax rates are followed by attempts of ingenious men to beat them as surely as snow is followed by little boys on sleds.
>
> —Arthur Okun, economist (1928–1980)

If (marginal) income tax rates are reduced, will income tax revenues increase or decrease? Most people think the answer is obvious: Lower tax rates mean lower tax revenues.

4. When marginal tax rates are lowered, two things happen: (1) Individuals will have more disposable income, and (2) the amount of money that individuals can earn (and keep) by working increases. As a result of the first effect, individuals will choose to work less. As a result of the second effect, individuals will choose to work more. Whether an individual works less or more on net depends on whether effect 1 is stronger than or weaker than effect 2. We have assumed that effect 2 is stronger than effect 1; so, as marginal tax rates decline, the net effect is that individuals work more.

exhibit 7

The Laffer Curve

When the tax rate is either 0 or 100 percent, tax revenues are zero. Starting from a zero tax rate, increases in tax rates first increase (region A to B) and then decrease (region B to C) tax revenues. Starting from a 100 percent tax rate, decreases in tax rates first increase tax revenues (region C to B) and then decrease tax revenues (region B to A). This suggests there is some tax rate that maximizes tax revenues.

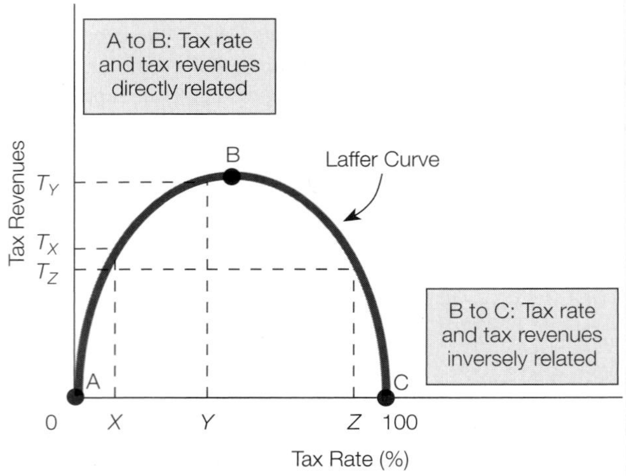

Economist Arthur Laffer explained why this may not be the case. As the story is told, Laffer, while dining with a journalist at a restaurant in Washington, D.C., drew the curve in Exhibit 7 on a napkin. The curve came to be known as the **Laffer curve**. Laffer's objective was to explain the possible relationships between tax rates and tax revenues. In the exhibit, tax revenues are on the vertical axis, and tax rates are on the horizontal axis. Laffer made three major points about the curve:

1. Zero tax revenues will be collected at two (marginal) tax rates: 0 percent and 100 percent. Obviously, no tax revenues will be raised if the tax rate is zero, and if the tax rate is 100 percent, no one will work and earn income because the entire amount would be taxed away.
2. An increase in tax rates could cause tax revenues to increase. For example, an increase in tax rates from *X* percent to *Y* percent will increase tax revenues from T_X to T_Y.
3. A decrease in tax rates could cause tax revenues to increase. For example, a decrease in tax rates from *Z* percent to *Y* percent will increase tax revenues from T_Z to T_Y. This was the point that brought public attention to the Laffer curve.

Laffer Curve
The curve, named after Arthur Laffer, that shows the relationship between tax rates and tax revenues. According to the Laffer curve, as tax rates rise from zero, tax revenues rise, reach a maximum at some point, and then fall with further increases in tax rates.

Tax Base
In terms of income taxes, the total amount of taxable income.
Tax revenue = Tax base × (average) Tax rate.

How can an *increase* in tax rates and a *decrease* in tax rates at different times both increase tax revenues? This can happen because of the interrelationship of tax rates, the **tax base**, and tax revenues.

Tax revenues equal the tax base times the (average) tax rate:[5]

$$\text{Tax revenues} = \text{Tax base} \times \text{(average) Tax rate}$$

For example, a tax rate of 20 percent multiplied by a tax base of $100 billion generates $20 billion of tax revenues.

Obviously, tax revenues are a function of two variables: (1) the tax rate and (2) the tax base. Whether tax revenues increase or decrease as the average tax rate is lowered depends on whether the tax base expands by a greater or lesser percentage than the percentage reduction in the tax rate. Exhibit 8 illustrates the point. We start with a tax rate of 20 percent, a tax base of $100 billion, and tax revenues of $20 billion. We assume that as the tax rate is reduced, the tax base expands: The rationale is that individuals work more, invest more, enter into more trades, and shelter less income from taxes at lower tax rates.

However, the real question is *how much* does the tax base expand following the tax rate reduction? Suppose the tax rate in Exhibit 8 is reduced to 15 percent. In Case 1, the reduction increases the tax base to $120 billion: A 25 percent decrease in the tax rate (from 20 to 15 percent) causes a 20 percent increase in the tax base (from $100 billion

5. First, the average tax rate is equal to an individual's tax payment divided by his or her taxable income (tax payment/taxable income). Second, a lower average tax rate requires a lower marginal tax rate. This follows from the average-marginal rule, which states that if the marginal magnitude is below the average magnitude, then the average is pulled down; if the marginal is above the average, the average is pulled up. Simply put, if an individual pays less tax on an additional taxable dollar (which is evidence of a marginal tax rate reduction), then his or her average tax naturally falls.

exhibit 8

	(1) Tax Rate	(2) Tax Base	(3) Tax Revenues (1) × (2)	Summary
Start with:	20%	$100	$20	—
Case 1:	15	120	18	↓ Tax rate ↓ Tax revenues
Case 2:	15	150	22.5	↓ Tax rate ↑ Tax revenues

Tax Rates, the Tax Base, and Tax Revenues

Tax revenues equal the tax base times the (average) tax rate. If the percentage reduction in the tax rate is greater than the percentage increase in the tax base, tax revenues decrease (Case 1). If the percentage reduction in the tax rate is less than the percentage increase in the tax base, tax revenues increase (Case 2). All dollar amounts are in billions of dollars.

to $120 billion). Tax revenues drop to $18 billion. In Case 2, the tax base expands by 50 percent to $150 billion. Because the tax base increases by a greater percentage than the percentage decrease in the tax rate, tax revenues increase (to $22.5 billion).

Of course, either case is possible. In the Laffer curve, tax revenues increase if a tax rate reduction is made in the downward-sloping portion of the curve (between points B and C in Exhibit 8); tax revenues decrease following a tax rate reduction in the upward-sloping portion of the curve (between points A and B).

Thinking like AN ECONOMIST

Incentives Matter

Contrast how economist Laffer thinks about a tax cut with the way the layperson thinks about it. The layperson probably believes that a reduction in tax rates will reduce tax revenues, focusing on the arithmetic of the situation. Laffer, however, focuses on the economic incentives. He asks what does a lower tax rate imply in terms of a person's incentive to engage in productive activity? How does a lower tax rate affect one's trade-off between work and leisure? The layperson likely sees only the arithmetic effect of a tax cut; the economist sees the incentive effect.

SELF-TEST

1. Give an arithmetic example to illustrate the difference between the marginal and average tax rates.
2. If income tax rates rise, will income tax revenues rise too?

office hours

"IS THERE A LOOMING FISCAL CRISIS?"

Student:

I've been reading what some economists have been saying about the future state of the federal budget. They say there is a looming fiscal crisis ahead. What do they mean by "a looming fiscal crisis"?

Instructor:

They are looking at the changing demographics in the United States, combined with rising health costs. As baby boomers retire and become eligible for Social Security and Medicare (and to a lesser extent, Medicaid), we can expect that Social Security, Medicare, and Medicaid spending will rise.

Student:

Will it rise by much? Is this a big spending problem headed our way?

Instructor:

Well, if our current federal tax burden (18.8 percent of GDP) were to remain constant over the years, it has been estimated that we will be able to pay for only three federal programs and nothing else by the year 2050: Social Security, Medicare, and Medicaid. In short, the so-called looming fiscal crisis is the expected growth in Social Security, Medicare, and Medicaid spending in the future. Or let's put it a slightly different way. If the nation's current federal spending and tax policies are continued (without change), the budget deficit is projected to be 20 percent of GDP in 2050. Compare this with the budget deficit as a share of GDP in 2006: 2 percent.

Student:

That will mean the public debt will grow, won't it?

Instructor:

Not only will it grow in absolute terms, but it will grow as a percentage of GDP. Today, the public debt held by the public is 38 percent of GDP. If current federal spending and tax policies continue, the public debt is projected to be 231 percent of GDP—more than twice the size of GDP.

Student:

Let me see if I have this correct. You're saying that (1) Social Security, Medicare, and Medicaid spending are likely to grow in the future and that these three programs will comprise a larger share of the federal budget than they do today; (2) if current spending and tax policies continue, both the budget deficit and the national debt will grow as a percentage of GDP. Budget deficits will rise to 20 percent of GDP, and the national debt will grow to more than twice the size of GDP. This is the looming fiscal crisis.

Instructor:

Yes, that's correct.

Student:

So what does this mean for our future? Are taxes going to have to be raised? Is spending going to have to be cut? Or are we just going to continue on course and end up having to deal with large budget deficits and debt (as a percentage of GDP)?

Instructor:

We are not sure what will happen. What we do know is that some stark fiscal realities are awaiting us. One way of identifying the problem (or the stark reality ahead) is to measure the *fiscal gap*. This is the amount of spending reductions or tax revenue increases needed (say, over the next four decades) if we want to keep our debt-to-GDP ratio at what it is today (38 percent). It has been estimated that the fiscal gap requires annual tax revenue increases or spending cuts totaling 3.2 percent of projected GDP for the next four decades. Here's what that means. The Congressional Budget Office forecasts 2009 GDP at $15.306 trillion. If we take 3.2 percent of this, we get $490 billion. The federal government would need to either (1) cut spending by this amount in 2009, or (2) raise tax revenues by this amount in 2009, or (3) raise tax revenues by, say, $200 billion and cut spending benefits by $290 billion (for a total of $490 billion), and so on.

Points to Remember

1. It is likely that in future years the combined spending on Social Security, Medicare, and Medicaid will grow as a percentage of the federal budget.
2. If the nation's current spending and tax policies continue, both the budget deficit and the public debt in the hands of the public will grow as a percentage of GDP. Today's deficit-to-GDP ratio is 2 percent; it is projected to be 20 percent in 2050. Today's debt-to-GDP ratio is 38 percent; it is projected to be 231 percent in 2050.

a reader asks | Are Americans Overtaxed?

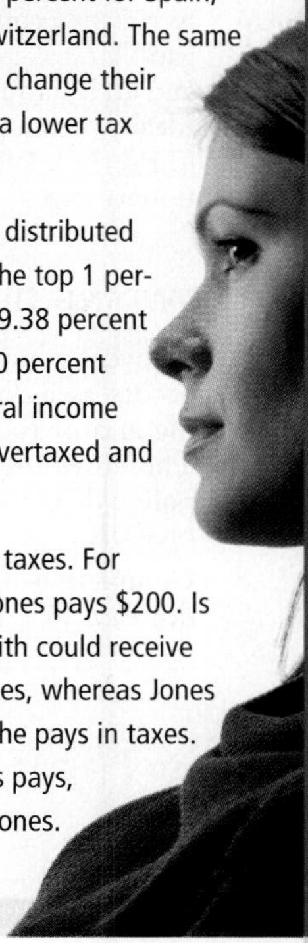

On a television news program the other day, a person said that Americans are overtaxed. He went on to back this up by saying that Americans work from January 1 to around the end of April just to pay their taxes. If this is true, then perhaps Americans are overtaxed. What do the economists say? Do they agree that Americans are overtaxed?

Most economists do not usually comment on whether Americans are overtaxed, undertaxed, or taxed just the right amount. Instead, they mainly report on which taxes people pay, how much taxes people pay, and so on.

For example, what you heard on the television news program about how many days Americans work each year to pay their taxes is essentially correct. In 2007, the average American taxpayer worked from January 1 to April 30 to pay all her taxes (federal, state, and local). That is a total of 120 days out of a 365-day year. Is that too much? Some people, speaking for themselves, would say yes. After all, they might say, working almost one-third of the year just to pay your taxes is too much.

But consider a different measure of the tax burden: the ratio of tax revenues to GDP. This tax ratio for the United States in 2006 was 28.2 percent, whereas the same ratio (and same year) was 50.1 percent for Sweden, 49 percent for Denmark, 36.7 percent for Spain, 35.7 percent for Germany, and 30.1 percent for Switzerland. The same people who said Americans were overtaxed might change their minds when they learn that the United States has a lower tax burden than many other countries have.

Another issue to consider is how the tax burden is distributed among American workers. For example, in 2007, the top 1 percent of income earners in the United States paid 39.38 percent of all federal income taxes, whereas the bottom 50 percent of all income earners paid 3.07 percent of all federal income taxes. Were the top 1 percent of income earners overtaxed and the bottom 50 percent undertaxed?

Finally, there is the issue of who benefits from the taxes. For example, suppose Smith pays $400 in taxes and Jones pays $200. Is Smith overtaxed relative to Jones? Maybe not. Smith could receive $500 worth of benefits for the $400 he pays in taxes, whereas Jones could receive $100 worth of benefits for the $200 he pays in taxes. Even though Smith pays twice the taxes that Jones pays, Smith may consider himself much better off than Jones. And Jones may agree.

Chapter Summary

GOVERNMENT SPENDING

- In 2007, the federal government spent $2.731 trillion. This was 20 percent of the country's GDP. About 63.6 percent of the money went for Social Security, Medicare, Medicaid, and national defense.
- With a proportional income tax, everyone pays taxes at the same rate, whatever his or her income level. With a progressive income tax, a person pays taxes at a higher rate (up to some top rate) as his or her income level rises. With a regressive income tax, a person pays taxes at a lower rate as his or her income level rises.
- The federal income tax is a progressive income tax.

TAXES

- In 2007, the federal government took in $2.568 trillion in tax revenues. Most of this came from three taxes: the individual income tax, the corporate income tax, and Social Security taxes.

DEFICITS, SURPLUSES, AND THE PUBLIC DEBT

- If government expenditures are greater than tax revenues, a budget deficit results; if government expenditures are less than tax revenues, a budget surplus results. If government expenditures equal tax revenues, the budget is balanced. Budget deficits are predicted for the near future.
- A cyclical deficit is the part of the budget deficit that is a result of a downturn in economic activity.
- A structural deficit is the part of the deficit that would exist if the economy were operating at full employment.
- Total budget deficit = Structural deficit + Cyclical deficit.
- The public debt is the total amount that the federal government owes its creditors.

FISCAL POLICY: GENERAL REMARKS

- Fiscal policy consists of changes in government expenditures and/or taxes to achieve economic goals. Expansionary fiscal policy is composed of increases in government expenditures and/or decreases in taxes. Contractionary fiscal policy entails decreases in government expenditures and/or increases in taxes.

DEMAND-SIDE FISCAL POLICY: A KEYNESIAN PERSPECTIVE

- In Keynesian theory, demand-side fiscal policy can be used to rid the economy of a recessionary gap or an inflationary gap. A recessionary gap calls for expansionary fiscal policy, and an inflationary gap calls for contractionary fiscal policy. Ideally, fiscal policy changes aggregate demand by enough to rid the economy of either a recessionary gap or an inflationary gap.

CROWDING OUT

- Crowding out is the decrease in private expenditures that occurs as a consequence of increased government spending and/or the greater financing needs of a budget deficit. The crowding-out effect suggests that expansionary fiscal policy does not work to the degree that Keynesian theory predicts.
- Complete (incomplete) crowding out occurs when the decrease in one or more components of private spending completely (partially) offsets the increase in government spending.

WHY DEMAND-SIDE FISCAL POLICY MAY BE INEFFECTIVE

- Demand-side fiscal policy may be ineffective at achieving certain macroeconomic goals because of (1) crowding out and (2) lags.

SUPPLY-SIDE FISCAL POLICY

- When fiscal policy measures affect tax rates, they may affect both aggregate supply and aggregate demand. It is generally accepted that a marginal tax rate reduction increases the attractiveness of work relative to leisure and tax-avoidance activities and thus leads to an increase in aggregate supply.
- Tax revenues equal the tax base multiplied by the (average) tax rate. Whether tax revenues decrease or increase as a result of a tax rate reduction depends on whether the percentage increase in the tax base is greater or less than the percentage reduction in the tax rate. If the percentage increase in the tax base is greater than the percentage reduction in the tax rate, then tax revenues will increase. If the percentage increase in the tax base is less than the percentage reduction in the tax rate, then tax revenues will decrease.

Key Terms and Concepts

Progressive Income Tax
Proportional Income Tax
Regressive Income Tax
Budget Deficit
Budget Surplus
Balanced Budget
Cyclical Deficit
Structural Deficit
Public Debt
Fiscal Policy
Expansionary Fiscal Policy
Contractionary Fiscal Policy
Discretionary Fiscal Policy
Automatic Fiscal Policy
Crowding Out
Complete Crowding Out
Incomplete Crowding Out
Marginal (Income) Tax Rate
Laffer Curve
Tax Base

Questions and Problems

1 What is the difference between government expenditures and government purchases?

2 How much were government expenditures in 2007? How much were government tax revenues in 2007?

3 The bulk of federal government expenditures go for four programs. What are they?

4 What percentage of total income did the top 5 percent of income earners earn in 2005? What percentage of federal income taxes did this group pay in 2005?

5 Is it true that under a proportional income tax structure, a person who earns a high income will pay more in taxes than a person who earns a low income? Explain your answer.

6 A progressive income tax always raises more revenue than a proportional income tax. Do you agree or disagree? Explain your answer.

7 Jim favors progressive taxation and equal after-tax pay for equal work. Comment.

8 What is the difference between a structural deficit and a cyclical deficit?

9 What is the difference between discretionary fiscal policy and automatic fiscal policy?

10 Explain two ways crowding out may occur.

11 Why is crowding out an important issue in the debate over the use of fiscal policy?

12 Some economists argue for the use of fiscal policy to solve economic problems; others argue against its use. What are some of the arguments on both sides?

13 Give a numerical example to illustrate the difference between complete crowding out and incomplete crowding out.

14 Give an example to illustrate the difference between indirect and direct crowding out.

15 The debate over using government spending and taxing powers to stabilize the economy involves more than technical economic issues. Do you agree or disagree? Explain your answer.

16 Is crowding out equally likely under all economic conditions? Explain your answer.

17 Tax cuts will likely affect aggregate demand and aggregate supply. Does it matter which is affected more? Explain in terms of the *AD-AS* framework.

18 Explain how expansionary fiscal policy can, under certain conditions, destabilize the economy.

19 Identify and explain the five lags associated with fiscal policy.

20 The economy is in a recessionary gap, and both Smith and Jones advocate expansionary fiscal policy. Does it follow that both Smith and Jones favor so-called big government?

21 Will tax cuts that are perceived to be temporary (by the public) affect the *SRAS* and *LRAS* curves differently than tax cuts that are perceived to be permanent? Explain your answer.

22 What is the difference between a marginal tax rate and an average tax rate?

23 Will tax revenue necessarily rise if tax rates are lowered? Explain your answer.

24 Georgia Dickens is sitting with a friend at a coffee shop. Georgia and her fiend are talking about the new tax bill. Georgia thinks it would be wrong to cut tax rates at this time: "Lower tax rates," she says, "will lead to a larger budget deficit, and the budget deficit is already plenty big." Do lower tax rates mean a larger deficit? Why or why not?

Working with Numbers and Graphs

Use the following table to answer questions 1–4.

Taxable	Income Taxes
$1,000–$5,000	10% of taxable income
$5,001–$10,000	$500 + 12% of everything over $5,000
$10,001–$15,000	$1,100 + 15% of everything over $10,000

1 If a person's income is $6,000, how much does he pay in taxes?

2 If a person's income is $14,000, how much does she pay in taxes?

3 What is the marginal tax rate on the 10,001st dollar? What is the marginal tax rate on the 10,000th dollar?

4 What is the average tax rate of someone with a taxable income of $13,766?

5 There are three income earners in a hypothetical society, and all three must pay income taxes. The taxable income of Smith is $40,000, the taxable income of Jones is $100,000, and the taxable income of Brown is $200,000.

a. How much tax revenue is raised under a proportional income tax where the tax rate is 10 percent? How much is raised if the tax rate is 15 percent?

b. Would a progressive tax with a rate of 5 percent on an income of $0–$40,000, a rate of 8 percent on everything over $40,000 and under $100,000, and a rate of 15 percent of everything over $100,000 raise more or less tax revenue than a proportional tax rate of 10 percent? Explain your answer.

6 Graphically show how fiscal policy works in the ideal case.

7 Graphically illustrate how government can use supply-side fiscal policy to get an economy out of a recessionary gap.

8 Graphically illustrate the following:

a. Fiscal policy destabilizes the economy.

b. Fiscal policy eliminates an inflationary gap.

c. Fiscal policy only partly eliminates a recessionary gap.

CHAPTER 11

MONEY AND BANKING

© SUSAN VAN ETTEN

Introduction Banks are more important for what you don't see than for what you do see. When you enter a bank, you may see a customer depositing a paycheck, a loan officer talking to a prospective borrower, or a teller handing $200 to a customer who needs cash for the weekend. All very ordinary. But what isn't so ordinary is what most of us don't see: banks creating money. No, there are no printing presses in the back room. Nevertheless, money is being created, as this chapter explains.

MONEY: WHAT IS IT AND HOW DID IT COME TO BE?

The story of money starts with a definition and a history lesson. This section discusses what money is and isn't (the definition) and how money came to be (the history lesson).

Money: A Definition

To the layperson, the words *income, credit,* and *wealth* are synonyms for *money*. In each of the next three sentences, the word *money* is used incorrectly; the word in parentheses is the word an economist would use.

1. How much money (income) did you earn last year?
2. Most of her money (wealth) is tied up in real estate.
3. It sure is difficult to get money (credit) in today's tight mortgage market.

In economics, the words *money, income, credit,* and *wealth* are not synonyms. The most general definition of **money** is any good that is widely accepted for purposes of exchange (payment for goods and services) and in the repayment of debts.

Money
Any good that is widely accepted for purposes of exchange and in the repayment of debt.

Three Functions of Money

Money has three major functions. It functions as a

1. medium of exchange,
2. unit of account, and
3. store of value.

MONEY AS A MEDIUM OF EXCHANGE If money did not exist, goods would have to be exchanged by **barter**. If you wanted a shirt, you would have to trade some good in your possession, say, a jackknife, for the shirt. But first you would have to locate a person who has a shirt and who wants to trade it for a knife. In a money economy, this step is not necessary. You can simply (1) exchange money for a shirt or (2) exchange the knife for money and then the money for the shirt. The buyer of the knife and the seller of the shirt do not have to be the same person. Money is the medium through which the exchange occurs; hence, it acts as a **medium of exchange**. As such, money reduces the *transaction costs* of exchanges. Exchange is easier and less time consuming in a money economy than in a barter economy.

Barter
Exchanging goods and services for other goods and services without the use of money.

Medium of Exchange
A function of money, anything that is generally acceptable in exchange for goods and services.

MONEY AS A UNIT OF ACCOUNT A **unit of account** is a common measure in which values are expressed. In a barter economy, the value of every good is expressed in terms of all other goods, and there is no common unit of measure. For example, 1 horse might equal 100 bushels of wheat, or 200 bushels of apples, or 20 pairs of shoes, or 10 suits, or 55 loaves of bread, and so on. In a money economy, a person doesn't have to know the price of an apple in terms of oranges, pizzas, chickens, or potato chips, as in a barter economy. He or she only needs to know the price in terms of money. And because all goods are denominated in money, determining relative prices is easy and quick. For example, if 1 apple is $1 and 1 orange is 50 cents, then 1 apple is worth 2 oranges.

Unit of Account
A function of money, a common measure in which relative values are expressed.

MONEY AS A STORE OF VALUE The **store of value** function is related to a good's ability to maintain its value over time. This is the least exclusive function of money because other goods—for example, paintings, houses, and stamps—can store value too. At times, money has not maintained its value well, such as during high-inflationary periods. For the most part, though, money has served as a satisfactory store of value. This function allows us to accept payment in money for our productive efforts and to keep that money until we decide how we want to spend it.

Store of Value
A function of money, the ability of an item to hold value over time.

From a Barter to a Money Economy: The Origins of Money

> The thing that differentiates man and animals is money.
>
> —Gertrude Stein

At one time, there was trade but no money. Instead, people bartered. They traded 1 apple for 2 eggs, a banana for a peach.

Today we live in a money economy. How did we move from a barter to a money economy? Did a king or queen issue the edict, "Let there be money"? Actually, money evolved in a much more natural, market-oriented manner.

Making exchanges takes longer (on average) in a barter economy than in a money economy because the *transaction costs* of making exchanges are higher in a barter economy. Stated differently, the time and effort incurred to consummate an exchange are greater in a barter economy than in a money economy.

To illustrate, suppose Smith, living in a barter economy, wants to trade apples for oranges. He locates Jones, who has oranges. Smith offers to trade apples for oranges, but Jones tells Smith that she does not like apples and would rather have peaches. Smith must

Double Coincidence of Wants
In a barter economy, a requirement that must be met before a trade can be made. It specifies that a trader must find another trader who is willing to trade what the first trader wants and at the same time wants what the first trader has.

either (1) find someone who has oranges and who wants to trade oranges for apples or (2) find someone who has peaches and who wants to trade peaches for apples, after which he must return to Jones and trade peaches for oranges. Suppose Smith continues to search and finds Brown, who has oranges and wants to trade oranges for (Smith's) apples. In economics terminology, Smith and Brown are said to have a **double coincidence of wants.** Two people have a double coincidence of wants if what the first person wants is what the second person has and what the second person wants is what the first person has. A double coincidence of wants is a necessary condition for a trade to take place.

In a barter economy, some goods are more readily accepted than others in exchange. This characteristic may originally be the result of chance, but when traders notice the difference in marketability, their behavior tends to reinforce the effect. Suppose there are 10 goods, A–J, and good G is the most marketable (most acceptable) of the 10. On average, good G is accepted 5 of every 10 times it is offered in an exchange, whereas the remaining goods are accepted, on average, only 2 of every 10 times. Given this difference, some individuals accept good G simply because of its relatively greater acceptability, even though they have no plans to consume it. They accept good G because they know it can easily be traded for most other goods at a later time (unlike the item originally in their possession). Thus the effect snowballs. The more people there are who accept good G for its relatively greater acceptability, the greater its relative acceptability becomes, in turn causing more people to agree to accept it.

This is how money evolved. When good G's acceptance evolves to the point where it is widely accepted for purposes of exchange, good G is money. Historically, goods that have evolved into money include gold, silver, copper, cattle, salt, cocoa beans, and shells.

Thinking like AN ECONOMIST

The Effects of Self-Interest

In our description of the emergence of money, we said that the people in a barter economy "accept good G because they know it can easily be traded for most other goods at a later time (unlike the item originally in their possession)." This tendency brings up the role of self-interest. People in a barter economy simply wanted to make life easier on themselves; they wanted to cut down on the time and energy required to obtain their preferred bundle of goods. In other words, it was out of self-interest that they began to accept the most marketable or acceptable of all goods—a process that eventually ended with money.

Finding ECONOMICS

In a POW Camp

You wouldn't think you could find money in a prisoner of war (POW) camp, but you can. During World War II, an American, R. A. Radford, was captured and imprisoned in a POW camp. While in the camp, he made some observations about economic developments, which he later described in the journal *Economica.* He noted that the Red Cross would periodically distribute packages to the prisoners that contained such goods as cigarettes, toiletries, chocolate, cheese, jam, margarine, and tinned beef. Not all the prisoners had the same preferences for the goods. For example, some liked chocolate more than others; some smoked cigarettes, and others did not. Because of their preferences, the prisoners began to trade, say, a chocolate bar for cheese, and a barter system emerged. After a short while, money appeared in the camp, but it was not U.S. dollars or any other government currency. The good that emerged as money—the good that was widely accepted for purposes of exchange—was cigarettes. As Radford noted, "The cigarette became the standard of value. In the permanent camp people started by wandering through the bungalows calling their offers—'cheese for seven [cigarettes]. . . .' "

economics 24/7

ENGLISH AND MONEY

In a world of barter, some goods are more widely accepted than others.

In a world of languages, some languages may be more widely used than others. Today, the most widely used language appears to be English.

© BRUCE AMOS/SHUTTERSTOCK

English is spoken not only by native English speakers but by many other people around the world. English is the language of computers and the Internet. You can see English on posters everywhere in the world. You can hear it in pop songs sung in Tokyo. English is the working language of the Asian trade group ASEAN (Association of Southeast Asian Nations). It is the language of 98 percent of German research physicists and of 83 percent of German research chemists. It is the official language of the European Central Bank, even though the bank is in Frankfurt, Germany. It is found in official documents in Phnom Penh, Cambodia. Singers all over the world sing in English. Alcatel, a French telecommunications company, uses English as its internal language. By 2050, half the world's population is expected to be proficient in English.

In a barter economy, if more people accept a good in exchange, then more people will want to accept it. Might the same be true of a language? That is, if more people speak English, then will more non-English-speaking people want to learn English? Just as money lowers the transaction costs of making exchanges, English might lower the transaction costs of communicating.

Is the world evolving toward one universal language, and is that language English?

Money, Leisure, and Output

Exchanges take less time in a money economy than in a barter economy because a double coincidence of wants is unnecessary: Everyone is willing to trade what he or she has for money. The movement from a barter to a money economy therefore frees up some of the transaction time, which people can use in other ways.

To illustrate, suppose making trades takes 10 hours a week in a barter economy, but only 1 hour in a money economy. In a money economy, then, each week has 9 hours that don't have to be spent making exchanges. How will people use these 9 hours? Some will use them to work, others will use them for leisure, and still others will divide the 9 hours between work and leisure. Thus, there is likely to be both more output (because of the increased production) and more leisure in a money economy than in a barter economy. In other words, a money economy is likely to be richer in both goods and leisure than a barter economy.

A person's standard of living is, to a degree, dependent on the number and quality of goods consumed and the amount of leisure consumed. We would expect the average person's standard of living to be higher in a money economy than in a barter economy.

Finding ECONOMICS

With William Shakespeare in London (1595)

It is 1595, and William Shakespeare is sitting at a desk writing the Prologue to *Romeo and Juliet.* Where is the economics? More specifically, can you see the connection between Shakespeare's writing a play and the emergence of money out of a barter economy? Look at it this way: In a money

(continued)

Finding Economics (continued)

economy, individuals usually specialize in the production of one good or service because they can do so. In a barter economy, specializing is extremely costly. For Shakespeare, it would mean writing plays all day and then going out and trying to trade what he had written that day for apples, oranges, chickens, and bread. Would the baker trade two loaves of bread for two pages of *Romeo and Juliet*? Had Shakespeare lived in a barter economy, he would have soon learned that he did not have a double coincidence of wants with many people and that therefore, if he was going to eat and be housed, he would need to spend time baking bread, raising chickens, and building a shelter instead of thinking about Romeo and Juliet.

In a barter economy, trade is difficult; so people produce for themselves. In a money economy, trade is easy, and so individuals produce one thing, sell it for money, and then buy what they want with the money. A William Shakespeare who lived in a barter economy no doubt spent his days very differently from the William Shakespeare who lived in England in the sixteenth century. Put bluntly: Without money, the world might never have enjoyed *Romeo and Juliet.*

Common Misconceptions

About What Gives Money Its Value

In the days when gold backed the dollar, people said that gold gave paper money its value. Very few ever asked, "What gives gold its value?"

It is a myth that paper money has to be backed by a commodity (e.g., gold) before it can have value. Today, our money is not backed by gold. Our money has value because of its *general acceptability.* You accept a dollar bill in payment for your goods and services because you know others will accept the dollar bill in payment.

This system may sound odd, but suppose our money was not generally accepted. Suppose one day that the supermarket clerk would not accept the paper dollars you offered as payment for groceries or that the plumber and the gas station attendant would not take your paper dollars for fixing your kitchen drain and for servicing your car. In such a case, would you be as likely to accept paper dollars in exchange for what you sell? We think not. You accept paper dollars because you know that other people will accept them when you spend them. Money has value to people because it is widely accepted in exchange for other valuable goods.

Defining the Money Supply

If money is any good that is widely accepted for purposes of exchange, is a $10 bill money? Is a dime money? Is a checking account or a savings account money? What constitutes money? In other words, what is included in the money supply? Two of the more frequently used definitions of the money supply are M1 and M2.

M1

M1
Currency held outside banks plus checkable deposits plus traveler's checks.

M1 is sometimes referred to as the *narrow definition of the money supply* or as *transactions money*. It is money that can be directly used for everyday transactions—to buy gas for the car, groceries to eat, and clothes to wear. **M1** consists of currency held outside banks (by

economics 24/7

IS MONEY THE BEST GIFT?

Consider what happens when one person gives another a gift. First, the gift giver has to decide how much money to spend. Is it an amount between $10 and $20 or between $50 and $80? After the dollar range is decided, the gift giver has to decide what to buy. Will it be a book, a shirt, a gift certificate to a restaurant, or what? Deciding what to buy requires the gift giver to guess the preferences of the recipient. This is no easy task, even if the giver knows the recipient fairly well. Often, guessing preferences is done poorly, which means that each year hundreds of thousands of people end up with gifts they would prefer not to have received. Every year, shirts go unworn, books go unread, and closets fill up with unwanted items.

At the end of a holiday season in 1993, Joel Waldfogel, then an economist at Yale University, asked a group of students two questions. First, he asked them to estimate the dollar value of all the holiday gifts they received. Second, he asked the students how much they would have paid to get the gifts they received. Waldfogel learned that, on average, gift recipients were willing to pay less for the gifts they received than gift givers paid for them. For example, a gift recipient might be willing to pay $25 for a book that a gift giver bought for $30. The most conservative estimate put the average gift recipient's valuation at 90 percent of the buying price. So, if the gift giver had given the cash value of the purchase instead of the gift itself, the recipient could then buy something that he or she really wanted and would be better off at no additional cost. In other words, some economists have concluded that when you don't know the preferences of the gift recipient very well, money might be the best gift.

members of the public for use in everyday transactions), checkable deposits, and traveler's checks.

M1 = Currency held outside banks
+ Checkable deposits
+ Traveler's checks

How are the components of M1 defined? **Currency** includes coins minted by the U.S. Treasury and paper money. About 99 percent of the paper money in circulation is in the form of **Federal Reserve notes** issued by the Federal Reserve District Banks. **Checkable deposits** are deposits on which checks can be written. There are different types of checkable deposits, including demand deposits, which are checking accounts that pay no interest, and NOW (negotiated order of withdrawal) and ATS (automatic transfer from savings) accounts, which do pay interest on their balances.

Currency
Coins and paper money.

Federal Reserve Notes
Paper money issued by the Fed.

Checkable Deposits
Deposits on which checks can be written.

On July 14, 2008, checkable deposits equaled $603 billion, currency held outside banks equaled $773 billion, and traveler's checks were $6 billion. M1, the sum of these figures, was $1,382 billion. The M1 money supply figures for the years 2003–2007 are shown in the following table.

Year	M1 Money Supply (billions of dollars)
2003	$1,273
2004	1,344
2005	1,372
2006	1,374
2007	1,369

Common MISCONCEPTIONS
About Money and Currency

When a layperson hears the word *money,* she usually thinks of currency—paper money (dollar bills) and coins. For example, if you're walking along a dark street at night and a thief stops you and says, "Your money or your life," you can be sure he wants your currency. People often equate money and currency. To an economist, though, money is more than simply currency. One definition of money (the M1 definition) is that it is currency, checkable deposits, and traveler's checks. (However, if robbed by a thief, an economist would be unlikely to hand over his currency and then write a check too.)

M2

M2 is most commonly referred to as the *broad definition of the money supply.* **M2** is made up of M1 plus savings deposits (including money market deposit accounts), small-denomination time deposits, and money market mutual funds (retail).

M2 = M1
+ Savings deposits (including money market deposit accounts)
+ Small-denomination time deposits
+ Money market mutual funds (retail)

Let's look at some of the components of M2. A **savings deposit**, sometimes called a *regular savings deposit,* is an interest-earning account at a commercial bank or thrift institution. (Thrift institutions include savings and loan associations, mutual savings banks, and credit unions.) Normally, checks cannot be written on savings deposits, and the funds in savings deposits can be withdrawn (at any time) without a penalty payment.

A **money market deposit account** (MMDA) is an interest-earning account at a bank or thrift institution, and usually a minimum balance is required. Most MMDAs offer limited check-writing privileges. For example, the owner of an MMDA might be able to write only a certain number of checks each month, and/or each check may have to be above a certain dollar amount (e.g., $500).

A **time deposit** is an interest-earning deposit with a *specified maturity date.* Time deposits are subject to penalties for early withdrawal. Small-denomination time deposits are deposits of less than $100,000.

A **money market mutual fund** (MMMF) is an interest-earning account at a *mutual fund company.* MMMFs held by large institutions are referred to as institutional MMMFs. MMMFs held by all others (e.g., by individuals) are referred to as retail MMMFs. *Only retail MMMFs are part of M2.* Usually, a minimum balance is required for an MMMF account, and most offer limited check-writing privileges.

On July 14, 2008, M2 was $7,698 billion. The M2 money supply figures for the years 2003–2007 are as follows:

Year	M2 Money Supply (billions of dollars)
2003	$5,984
2004	6,266
2005	6,545
2006	6,859
2007	7,264

M2
M1 plus savings deposits (including money market deposit accounts) plus small-denomination time deposits plus (retail) money market mutual funds.

Savings Deposit
An interest-earning account at a commercial bank or thrift institution. Normally, checks cannot be written on savings deposits, and the funds in a savings deposit can be withdrawn (at any time) without a penalty payment.

Money Market Deposit Account
An interest-earning account at a bank or thrift institution. Usually, a minimum balance is required for an MMDA, and most offer limited check-writing privileges.

Time Deposit
An interest-earning deposit with a specified maturity date. Time deposits are subject to penalties for early withdrawal. Small-denomination time deposits are deposits of less than $100,000.

Money Market Mutual Fund
An interest-earning account at a mutual fund company. Usually, a minimum balance is required for an MMMF account. Most MMMF accounts offer limited check-writing privileges. Only retail MMMFs are part of M2.

Where Do Credit Cards Fit in?

A credit card is commonly referred to as plastic money, but it is not money. A credit card is an instrument or document that makes it easier for the holder to obtain a loan. When Tina Ridges hands the department store clerk her MasterCard or Visa, she is, in effect, spending someone else's money (which already existed). The department store submits the claim to the bank, the bank pays the department store, and then the bank bills the holder of its credit card. By using her credit card, Tina spends someone else's money, and she ultimately must repay her credit card debt with money. These transactions shift around the existing quantity of money among individuals and firms, but they do not change the total.

SELF-TEST

(Answers to Self-Test questions are in the Self-Test Appendix.)

1. Why (not how) did money evolve out of a barter economy?
2. If individuals remove funds from their checkable deposits and transfer them to their money market accounts, will M1 fall and M2 rise? Explain your answer.
3. How does money reduce the transaction costs of making trades?

How Banking Developed

Just as money evolved, so did banking. This section discusses the origins of banking and sheds some light on and aids in understanding modern banking.

The Early Bankers

Our money today is easy to carry and transport, but it was not always so portable. For example, when money was principally gold coins, carrying it about was neither easy nor safe. First, gold is heavy. Second, gold was not only inconvenient for customers to carry, but it was also inconvenient for merchants to accept. Third, a person transporting thousands of gold coins can easily draw the attention of thieves. Yet storing gold at home can also be risky. Most individuals therefore turned to their local goldsmith for help because he was already equipped with safe storage facilities. Goldsmiths were the first bankers. They took in other people's gold and stored it for them. To acknowledge that they held deposited gold, goldsmiths issued receipts, called *warehouse receipts*, to their customers.

Once people's confidence in the receipts was established, they used the receipts to make payments instead of using the gold itself. In time, the paper warehouse receipts circulated as money. For instance, if Franklin wanted to buy something from Mason that was priced at ten gold pieces, he could simply give his warehouse receipt to Mason instead of going to the goldsmith, obtaining the gold, and then delivering it to Mason. For both Franklin and Mason, using the receipts was easier than dealing with the actual gold.

At this stage of banking, warehouse receipts were fully backed by gold; they simply represented gold in storage. Goldsmiths later began to recognize that, on an average day, few people came to redeem their receipts for gold. Many individuals were simply trading the receipts for goods and seldom requested the gold itself. In short, the receipts had become money, widely accepted for purposes of exchange.

Sensing opportunity, some goldsmiths began to lend some of the stored gold, realizing that they could earn interest on the loans without defaulting on their pledge to redeem the warehouse receipts when presented. In most cases, however, the borrowers of the gold also preferred warehouse receipts to the actual gold. Thus the amount of gold represented

economics 24/7

EBAY AND MATCH.COM

In our description of money emerging out of a barter economy, we learned that money lowered the transaction costs of making exchanges. In a barter economy, transaction costs are relatively high because no one can be sure that the person who has what you want wants what you have. With the emergence of money, the transaction costs of making exchanges drop because everyone is willing to trade for money.

Just as money has lowered the transaction costs of making exchanges, so has the Internet. Through the Internet, people can faster and more easily find other people they might want to exchange with.

Consider life before the Internet and before both eBay and Match.com. Suppose a person in London has an old Rolling Stones album for sale. The problem is that he is not sure how to find someone who might want to buy it. Today, the seller simply goes online to eBay and posts the Rolling Stones album for sale. In perhaps a matter of hours, people who want to buy the album are bidding on it. eBay and the Internet lower the transaction costs of bringing buyer and seller together.

Or consider Match.com, an online dating service. When people date each other, there is an exchange of sorts going on. Each person is effectively saying to the other, "I demand some of your time, which I hope you will supply to me."

One of the transaction costs of dating is actually finding a person to date. Match.com and the Internet, however, lower the transaction costs. The dating service is a little like eBay, in that you are offering to "sell" yourself. Instead of describing a Rolling Stones album, you describe yourself. Then, in a sense, people bid on you by getting in touch—and you bid on others.

What do money, eBay, and Match.com tell us about life? People want to trade with each other, and part of being able to trade with each other is lowering the transaction costs of trading. Money, eBay, and Match.com fill the bill.

by the warehouse receipts was greater than the actual amount of gold on deposit. Consequently, the money supply increased—now measured in terms of gold and the paper warehouse receipts issued by the goldsmith-bankers.

Fractional Reserve Banking
A banking arrangement that allows banks to hold reserves equal to only a fraction of their deposit liabilities.

This was the beginning of **fractional reserve banking**. In a fractional reserve system, banks create money by holding on reserve only a fraction of the money deposited with them and lending the remainder. Our modern-day banking system operates within a fractional reserve banking arrangement.

The Federal Reserve System

Federal Reserve System (the Fed)
The central bank of the United States.

The next chapter discusses the structure of the **Federal Reserve System (the Fed**, its popular name) and the tools it uses to change the money supply. For now, we need only note that the Federal Reserve System is the central bank, essentially a bank's bank. Its chief function is to control the nation's money supply.

THE MONEY CREATION PROCESS

This section describes the important money supply process, specifically, how the banking system, working under a fractional reserve requirement, creates money.

The Bank's Reserves and More

Many banks have an account with the Fed in much the same way that an individual has a checking account with a commercial bank. Economists refer to this account with the Fed as either a reserve account or bank deposits at the Fed. Banks also have currency or cash in their vaults—called vault cash—on the bank premises. The sum of (1) bank deposits at the Fed and (2) the bank's vault cash is (total bank) **reserves.**

Reserves
The sum of bank deposits at the Fed and vault cash.

Reserves = Bank deposits at the Fed + Vault cash

For example, if a bank currently has $4 million in deposits at the Fed and $1 million in vault cash, it has $5 million in reserves.

THE REQUIRED RESERVE RATIO AND REQUIRED RESERVES The Fed mandates that member commercial banks must hold a certain fraction of their checkable deposits in reserve form. The term *reserve form* means in the form of bank deposits at the Fed and/or vault cash because the sum of these two accounts equals reserves.

The fraction of checkable deposits that banks must hold in reserve form is called the **required reserve ratio (r).** The dollar amount of those deposits is called **required reserves.** In other words, to find the required reserves for a given bank, multiply the required reserve ratio by checkable deposits (in the bank):

Required Reserve Ratio (r)
A percentage of each dollar deposited that must be held on reserve (at the Fed or in the bank's vault).

Required Reserves
The minimum amount of reserves a bank must hold against its checkable deposits as mandated by the Fed.

Required reserves = r × Checkable deposits

For example, assume that customers have deposited $40 million in a neighborhood bank and that the Fed has set the required reserve ratio at 10 percent. Required reserves for the bank equal $4 million (0.10 × $40 million = $4 million).

EXCESS RESERVES The difference between a bank's (total) reserves and its required reserves is its **excess reserves:**

Excess Reserves
Any reserves held beyond the required amount. The difference between (total) reserves and required reserves.

Excess reserves = Reserves – Required reserves

For example, if the bank's (total) reserves are $5 million and its required reserves are $4 million, then it holds excess reserves of $1 million.

The important point about excess reserves is that banks use them to make loans. In fact, banks have a monetary incentive to use their excess reserves to make loans: If the bank uses the $1 million excess reserves to make loans, it earns interest income. If it does not make any loans, it does not earn interest income.

The Banking System and the Money Expansion Process

Banks in the banking system are prohibited from printing their own currency. Nevertheless, the banking system can create money by increasing checkable deposits. (Checkable deposits are a component of the money supply; e.g., M1 equals currency held outside banks plus checkable deposits plus traveler's checks.)

The process starts with the Fed. For hypothetical purposes, suppose the Fed prints $1,000 in new paper money and gives it to Bill. Bill takes the newly created $1,000 and deposits it in bank A. We can see this transaction in the following T-account. A **T-account** is a simplified balance sheet that records the *changes* in the bank's assets and liabilities.

T-Account
A simplified balance sheet that shows the changes in a bank's assets and liabilities.

Bank A

Assets		Liabilities	
Reserves	+$1,000	Checkable deposits (Bill)	+$1,000

Because the deposit initially is added to vault cash, *the bank's reserves have increased by $1,000.* The bank's liabilities also have increased by $1,000 because it owes Bill the $1,000 he deposited.

Next, the banker divides the $1,000 reserves into two categories: required reserves and excess reserves. The amount of required reserves depends on the required reserve ratio specified by the Fed; let's say it is 10 percent. This means the bank holds $100 in required reserves against the deposit and holds $900 in excess reserves. The previous T-account can be modified to show this:

Bank A			
Assets		**Liabilities**	
Required reserves	+$100	Checkable deposits (Bill)	+$1,000
Excess reserves	+$900		

On the left or right side of the T-account, the total is $1,000. By dividing total reserves into required reserves and excess reserves, we can see how many dollars the bank is holding above the Fed requirements. These excess reserves can be used to make new loans.

Suppose bank A makes a loan of $900 to Jenny. The left (assets) side of the bank's T-account looks like this:

Bank A		
Assets		**Liabilities**
Required reserves	+$100	See the next T-account.
Excess reserves	+$900	
Loans	+$900	

Now, when bank A gives Jenny a $900 loan, it doesn't give her $900 cash. Instead, it opens a checking account for Jenny at the bank, and the balance in the account is $900. This is how things are shown in the T-account:

Bank A		
Assets	**Liabilities**	
See the previous T-account.	Checkable deposits (Bill)	+$1,000
	Checkable deposits (Jenny)	+$ 900

Before we continue, *notice that the money supply has increased.* When Jenny borrowed $900 and the bank put that amount in her checking account, *no one else in the economy had any less money, and Jenny had more than before*. Consequently, the money supply has increased. (Again, think of M1 as equal to currency plus checkable deposits plus traveler's checks. Through the lending activity of the bank, checkable deposits have increased by $900, with no change in the amount of currency or traveler's checks. M1 has increased.) In other words, the money supply is $900 more than it was.

Now suppose Jenny spends the $900 on a new computer. She writes a $900 check to the computer retailer, who deposits the full amount of the check in bank B. First, what happens to bank A? It uses its excess reserves to honor Jenny's check when bank B presents it and simultaneously reduces her checking account balance from $900 to zero. Bank A's situation is:

Bank A			
Assets		**Liabilities**	
Required reserves	+$100	Checkable deposits (Bill)	+$1,000
Excess reserves	$0		
Loans	+$900	Checkable deposits (Jenny)	$0

The situation for bank B is different. Because of the computer retailer's deposit, bank B now has $900 that it didn't have previously. This increases bank B's reserves and liabilities by $900:

Bank B			
Assets		**Liabilities**	
Reserves	+$900	Checkable deposits (Computer Retailer)	+$900

Note that the computer purchase has not changed the overall money supply. Dollars have simply moved from Jenny's checking account to the computer retailer's checking account.

The process continues in much the same way for bank B as it did earlier for bank A. Only a fraction (10 percent) of the computer retailer's $900 needs to be kept on reserve (required reserves on $900 = $90). The remainder ($810) constitutes excess reserves that can be lent to still another borrower. That loan will create $810 in new checkable deposits and thus expand the money supply by that amount. The process continues with banks C, D, E, and so on until the dollar figures become so small that the process comes to a halt. Exhibit 1 summarizes what happens as the $1,000 originally created by the Fed works its way through the banking system.

Looking back over the entire process, this is what has happened:

- The Fed created $1,000 worth of new money and gave it to Bill, who then deposited it in bank A.
- The reserves of bank A increased. The reserves of no other bank decreased.
- The banking system, with the newly created $1,000 in hand, made loans and, in the process, created checkable deposits for the people who received the loans.
- Because checkable deposits are part of the money supply, by extending loans and, in the process, creating checkable deposits, the banking system increases the money supply.

exhibit 1

The Banking System Creates Checkable Deposits (Money)

In this exhibit, the required reserve ratio is 10 percent. We have assumed that there is no cash leakage and that excess reserves are fully lent out; that is, banks hold zero excess reserves.

(1) Bank	(2) New Deposits (new reserves)	(3) New Required Reserves	(4) Checkable Deposits Created by Extending New Loans (equal to new excess reserves)
A	$1,000.00	$100.00	$900.00
B	900.00	90.00	810.00
C	810.00	81.00	729.00
D	729.00	72.90	656.10
E	656.10	65.61	590.49
⋮	⋮	⋮	⋮
TOTALS (rounded)	$10,000	$1,000	$9,000

The $1,000 in new funds deposited in bank A is the basis of several thousand dollars' worth of new bank loans and new checkable deposits. In this instance, the $1,000 initially injected into the economy ultimately causes bankers to create $9,000 in new checkable deposits. When this amount is added to the newly created $1,000 that the Fed gave to Bill, the money supply has expanded by $10,000. A formula that shows this result is

$$\text{Maximum change in checkable deposits} = \frac{1}{r} \times \Delta R$$

where r = the required reserve ratio and ΔR = the change in reserves resulting from the original injection of funds.[1] In the equation, the reciprocal of the required reserve ratio ($1/r$) is known as the **simple deposit multiplier**. The arithmetic for this example is

Simple Deposit Multiplier
The reciprocal of the required reserve ratio, $1/r$.

$$\begin{aligned}\text{Maximum change in checkable deposits} &= \frac{1}{0.10} \times \$1{,}000 \\ &= 10 \times \$1{,}000 \\ &= \$10{,}000\end{aligned}$$

Finding ECONOMICS

In Filling Out a Loan Application

You go to a bank, fill out an application for a loan, and receive a $20,000 loan. Where is the economics? The economics has to do with the money creation process and the part you play in it. The loan is given to you in the form of a new checkable deposit, which is part of the money supply. (Recall that M1 is equal to currency held outside banks plus checkable deposits plus traveler's checks.) As a result of your receiving the loan (the new checkable deposit), the money supply rises.

Why Maximum? Answer: No Cash Leakages and Zero Excess Reserves

We made two important assumptions in our discussion of the money expansion process.

First, we assumed that all monies were deposited in bank checking accounts. For example, when Jenny wrote a check to the computer retailer, the retailer endorsed the check and deposited the full amount in bank B. In reality, the retailer might have deposited less than the full amount and kept a few dollars in cash, a practice that is called **cash leakage**. If there had been a cash leakage of $300, then bank B would have received only $600, not $900. The different deposit would change the second number in column 2 in Exhibit 1 to $600 and the second number in column 4 to $540. So the total in column 2 of Exhibit 1 would be much smaller. A cash leakage that reduces the flow of dollars into banks means that banks have fewer dollars to lend. Fewer loans mean banks put less into borrowers' accounts, and so less money is created than when cash leakages equal zero.

Cash Leakage
Occurs when funds are held as currency instead of deposited into a checking account.

Second, we assumed that every bank lent all its excess reserves, leaving every bank with zero excess reserves. After Bill's $1,000 deposit, for example, bank A had excess reserves of $900 and made a new loan for the full amount. Banks generally want to lend all of their excess reserves to earn additional interest income, but there is no law, natural or legislated, that says every bank has to lend every penny of excess reserves. If banks do not lend all

1. Because only checkable deposits and no other components of the money supply change in this example, we could write, "Maximum change in checkable deposits = $(1/r) \times \Delta R$" as "Maximum $\Delta M = (1/r) \times \Delta R$," where ΔM = the change in the money supply. In this chapter, the only component of the money supply that we allow to change is checkable deposits. For this reason, we can talk about changes in checkable deposits and the money supply as if they are the same—which they are, given our specification.

economics 24/7

ECONOMICS ON THE YELLOW BRICK ROAD

I'll get you, my pretty.
Wicked Witch of the West in The Wizard of Oz

©MGM/THE KOBAL COLLECTION

In 1893, the United States fell into economic depression. The stock market crashed, banks failed, workers were laid off, and many farmers lost their farms. Some people blamed the depression on the gold standard. They proposed that, instead of only gold backing U.S. currency, there should be a bimetallic monetary standard in which both gold and silver backed the currency. This, they said, would lead to an increase in the money supply. Many people thought that with more money in circulation, economic hard times would soon be a thing of the past.

One of the champions of silver was William Jennings Bryan, who was the Democratic candidate for the U.S. presidency in 1896. Bryan had established himself as a friend to the many Americans who had been hurt by the economic depression—especially farmers and industrial workers. Bryan's views were shared by L. Frank Baum, the author of *The Wonderful Wizard of Oz,* the book that was the basis for the 1939 movie *The Wizard of Oz.*

Baum blamed the gold standard for the hardships faced by farmers and workers during the depression. Baum saw the farmer and the industrial worker as the common man, and he saw William Jennings Bryan as the best possible hope for the common man in this country.

Numerous persons believe that Baum's most famous work, *The Wonderful Wizard of Oz,* is an allegory for the presidential election of 1896.[2] Some say that Dorothy, in the book and the movie, represents Bryan. Both Dorothy and Bryan were young (Bryan was a 36-year-old presidential candidate). Like the cyclone in the movie that transported Dorothy to the Land of Oz, the delegates at the 1896 Democratic convention lifted Bryan into a new political world, the world of presidential politics.

As Dorothy begins her travels to the Emerald City (Washington, D.C.) with Toto (who represents the Democratic party) to meet the Wizard of Oz, she travels down a yellow brick road (the gold standard). On her way, she meets the scarecrow (who represents the farmer), the tin man (who represents the industrial worker), and the cowardly lion, who some believe represents the Populist party of the time. (The Populist party was sometimes represented as a lion in cartoons of the time. It was a cowardly lion in that, as some say, it did not have the courage to fight an independent campaign for the presidency in 1896.) The message is clear: Bryan, with the help of the Democratic and Populist parties and the votes of the farmers and the industrial workers, will travel to Washington.

But then, when Dorothy and the others reach the Emerald City, they are denied their wishes, just as Bryan is denied the presidency. He loses the election to William McKinley.

But all is not over. There is still the battle with the Wicked Witch of the West, who wears a golden cap (the gold standard). When the Wicked Witch sees Dorothy's silver shoes—they were changed to ruby shoes in the movie—she desperately wants them for their magical quality. But that is not to happen. Dorothy kills the Wicked Witch of the West; she then clicks her silver shoes together, and they take her back home, where all is right with the world.

2. This interpretation is based on "William Jennings Bryan on the Yellow Brick Road" by John Geer and Thomas Rochon, *Journal of American Culture* (Winter 1993) and "The Wizard of Oz: Parable on Populism" by Henry Littlefield, *American Quarterly* (1964).

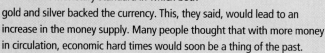

their excess reserves, then checkable deposits and the money supply will increase by less than when banks do lend all their excess reserves.

If we had not made our two assumptions, the change in checkable deposits would have been much smaller. Because we assumed no cash leakages and zero excess reserves, the change in checkable deposits is the *maximum* possible change.

Who Created What?

The money expansion process involves two major players: (1) the Fed, which created the new $1,000, and (2) the banking system. Together they expanded the money supply by $10,000. The Fed directly created $1,000 and thus made it possible for banks to create \$9,000 in new checkable deposits as a by-product of extending new loans.

An easy formula for finding the maximum change in checkable deposits brought about by the banking system (and *only* by the banking system) is

$$\text{Maximum change in checkable deposits (brought about by the banking system)} = \frac{1}{r} \times \Delta ER$$

where r = the required reserve ratio and ΔER = the change in excess reserves of the first bank to receive the new injection of funds. The arithmetic for our example is

$$\begin{aligned}\text{Maximum change in checkable deposits (brought about by the banking system)} &= \frac{1}{0.10} \times \$900 \\ &= 10 \times \$900 \\ &= \$9{,}000\end{aligned}$$

It Works in Reverse: The Money Destruction Process

In the preceding example, the Fed created \$1,000 of new money and gave it to Bill, who then deposited it in bank A, creating a multiple increase in checkable deposits and the money supply. The process also works in reverse. Suppose Bill withdraws the \$1,000 and gives it back to the Fed, which then destroys the \$1,000. As a result, bank reserves decline. The multiple deposit contraction process is symmetrical to the multiple deposit expansion process.

Again, we set the required reserve ratio at 10 percent. The situation for bank A looks like this:

Bank A			
Assets		**Liabilities**	
Reserves	−\$1,000	Checkable deposits (Bill)	−\$1,000

Losing \$1,000 in reserves places bank A in a *reserve deficiency position*. Specifically, it is \$900 short. Because bank A held \$100 reserves against the initial \$1,000 deposit, it loses \$900 in reserves that backed other deposits (\$1,000 – \$100 = \$900). If this is not immediately obvious, consider the following example.

Suppose the checkable deposits in a bank total \$10,000, and the required reserve ratio is 10 percent. The bank must hold \$1,000 in reserve form. Now let's suppose that the bank holds exactly \$1,000 in reserves (let's assume as vault cash). Is the bank reserve deficient at this point? No, it is holding exactly the right amount of reserves given its checkable deposits. Not one penny more, not one penny less.

Now a bank customer withdraws \$1,000. The bank teller goes to the vault, collects \$1,000, and hands it to the customer. Two things have happened: (1) The bank reserves have fallen by \$1,000, and (2) checkable deposits in the bank have fallen by the same amount. In other words, checkable deposits go from \$10,000 to \$9,000.

Does the bank currently have reserves? No. The bank's reserves of \$1,000 were given to the customer; so the bank has \$0 in reserves. If the required reserve ratio is 10 percent, how much does the bank need in reserves, given that checkable deposits are now \$9,000? The answer is \$900. Until it has that amount in reserve, the bank is \$900 reserve deficient.

When a bank is reserve deficient, it must take immediate corrective measures. One such measure is to reduce its outstanding loans. Funds from loan repayments can be applied to the reserve deficiency rather than used to extend new loans. As borrowers repay $900 worth of loans, they reduce their checking account balances by that amount, causing the money supply to decline by $900.

Let's assume that the $900 loan repayment to bank A is written on a check issued by bank B. After the check has cleared, reserves and customer deposits at bank B fall by $900. This situation is reflected in bank B's T-account:

Bank B			
Assets		**Liabilities**	
Reserves	−$900	Checkable deposits	−$900

Bank B now faces a situation similar to bank A's earlier one. Losing $900 in reserves places bank B in reserve deficiency; it is $810 short. Bank B had held $90 in reserve form against the $900 deposit; so it loses $810 that backed other deposits ($900 – $90 = $810). Bank B seeks to recoup $810 by reducing its outstanding loans by an equal amount. If a customer is asked to pay off an $810 loan and does so by writing a check on his or her account at bank C, that bank's reserves and deposits both decline by $810. As a result, bank C is now in reserve deficiency; it is $729 short. Remember, bank C held $81 in reserve form against the $810 deposit; so it is short the $729 that backed other deposits ($810 – $81 = $729).

As you can see, the figures are the same ones given in Exhibit 1, except that each change is negative rather than positive. When Bill withdrew $1,000 from his account and returned it to the Fed (which then destroyed the $1,000), the money supply declined by $10,000.

Exhibit 2 shows the money supply expansion and contraction processes in brief.

We Change Our Example

To change the example somewhat, suppose the Fed does not create new money. Instead, Jack, who currently has $1,000 in cash in a shoebox in his bedroom, decides that he doesn't want to keep this much cash around the house, and so he takes it to bank A and opens a checking account. So far, he does not change the money supply. Initially, the $1,000 in the shoebox was currency outside a bank and thus was part of

exhibit 2

The Money Supply Expansion and Contraction Processes

The money supply expands if reserves enter the banking system; the money supply contracts if reserves exit the banking system. In expansion, reserves rise; thus, excess reserves rise, more loans are made, and checkable deposits rise. Because checkable deposits are part of the money supply, the money supply rises. In contraction, reserves fall; thus, excess reserves fall, fewer loans are made, and checkable deposits fall. Because checkable deposits are part of the money supply, the money supply falls.

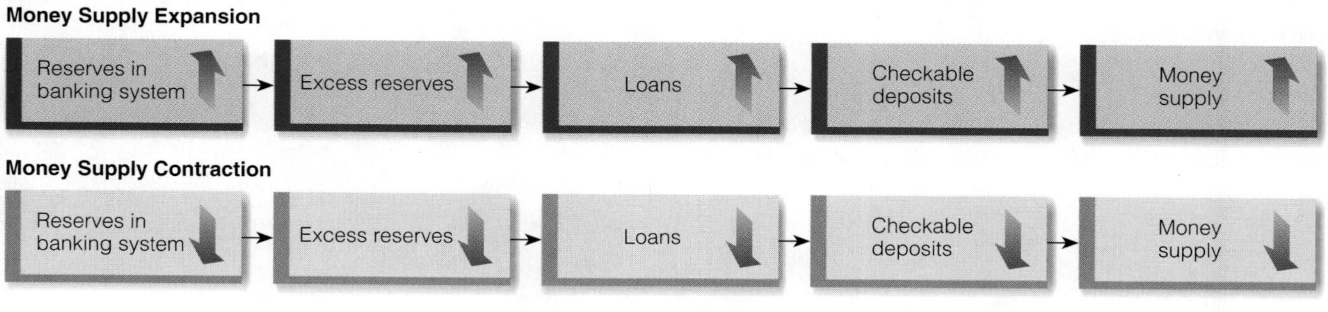

office hours

"CAN SOMETHING I DO END UP CHANGING THE MONEY SUPPLY?"

Student:
Let me see if I have this right: If I put $100 in my checking account at a bank, the bank then takes that $100 and adds it to vault cash, so that $100 becomes part of the bank's reserves, right?

Instructor:
Yes, that's right.

Student:
And then the bank holds a percentage of that $100 in reserve form and lends out the rest. So it might hold ten of the $100 dollars in its vault and lend out the remaining $90.

Instructor:
That's correct.

Student:
Now here's the part I am unsure of. When a bank gives out a loan of $90, does it actually lend out the $90 of currency (let's say nine $10 bills) or simply create a new checkable deposit of $90 for someone?

Instructor:
It creates a new checkable deposit of $90.

Student:
But then that means the full $100 currency is still in the bank's vault, right? When does $90 of the $100 leave the vault?

Instructor:
Suppose the person who received the $90 loan (or new checkable deposit) writes a check to Marie. Marie then deposits the $90 check in another bank. When the check clears, the $90 is transferred from the first bank (in which you deposited your money) to Marie's bank. And then Marie's takes a fraction of that $90 and creates a loan with it, and the process continues.

Student:
So, in the end, some portion of that $100 that I deposited into the bank ends up creating loans for a lot of people. Is that correct?

Instructor:
That is correct.

Student:
But this makes it sound like I can change the money supply by simply deciding to put $100 currency into a bank instead of keeping that $100 in my wallet. Is this true?

Instructor:
Let's put it this way: By putting $100 currency into a bank, you change the composition of the money supply. Specifically, there is $100 less in currency held outside banks and $100 more in checkable deposits. Then the banking system does the rest: It takes the $100 and creates a multiple of it in terms of new checkable deposits, which raises the money supply.

Points to Remember

1. An individual (any member of the public) can change the composition of the money supply.
2. A change in the composition of the money supply can lead to a dollar change in the money supply.

the money supply. When Jack took the $1,000 from his shoebox and placed it in a bank, there was $1,000 less currency outside a bank and $1,000 more checkable deposits. So far, his deposit has changed the *composition* of the money supply but not its *size*.

The $1,000 could not create a multiple of itself while it was in a shoebox. When the $1,000 is placed in a checking account, however, the banking system has $1,000 more reserves than before and thus has excess reserves that can be used to extend new loans and to create new checkable deposits. Thus the money supply can expand in much the same way as if the Fed had created $1,000 in money. At maximum, the banking system can create $9,000 worth of new loans and checkable deposits (assuming again that $r = 0.10$). The primary difference between the two examples is their *starting point*. The first example started with the Fed creating new money, the second with Jack removing $1,000 from a shoebox and depositing it in a bank. Despite this difference, in both examples, the banking system created the identical maximum amount of new checkable deposits.

SELF-TEST

1. If a bank's deposits equal $579 million and the required reserve ratio is 9.5 percent, what dollar amount must the bank hold in reserve form?
2. If the Fed creates $600 million in new reserves, what is the maximum change in checkable deposits that can occur if the required reserve ratio is 10 percent?
3. Bank A has $1.2 million in reserves and $10 million in deposits. The required reserve ratio is 10 percent. If bank A loses $200,000 in reserves, by what dollar amount is it reserve deficient?

a reader asks — Do People Want to Economize on Time?

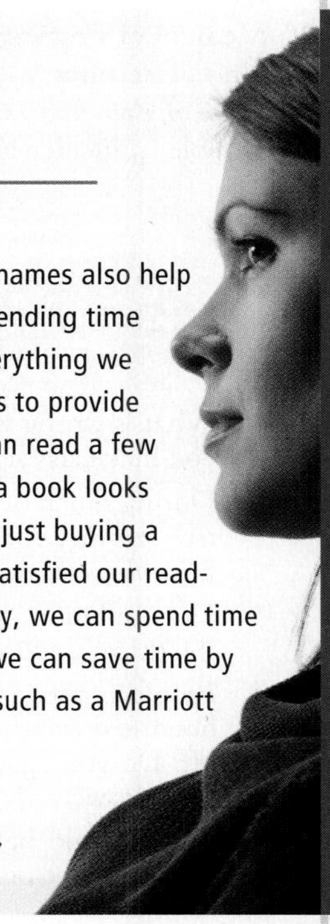

Making exchanges in a money economy takes less time than it does in a barter economy. In other words, by moving from a barter economy to a money economy, individuals economize on time. Are there other examples in economics of individuals economizing on time?

Some economists have argued that one of the hallmarks of a money economy is the gradual reduction of so-called dead time spent to consume a good or service. Examples abound. Today, the use of bar codes and scanners permits consumers to get through supermarket and department store lines very quickly. Touch-tone telephones allow people to refill prescriptions without going to the pharmacy. With the Internet, we can make price comparisons without traveling from store to store, and we can order a wide variety of goods and services.[3]

Some economists go on to argue that brand names also help individuals economize on time. Instead of spending time making price and quality comparisons on everything we purchase, we sometimes rely on brand names to provide an expected level of service or quality. We can read a few pages of every book in a bookstore to see if a book looks good enough to buy, or we can save time by just buying a book written by an author who has already satisfied our reading propensities. When traveling to a new city, we can spend time learning about the different local hotels, or we can save time by checking into a well-known hotel franchise, such as a Marriott or Holiday Inn.

[3] Many of the examples in this feature come from "Time: Economics' Neglected Stepchild," by Gene Epstein, *Barron's*, December 31, 2001.

Chapter Summary

WHAT MONEY IS

- Money is any good that is widely accepted for purposes of exchange and in the repayment of debts.
- Money serves as a medium of exchange, a unit of account, and a store of value.
- Money evolved out of a barter economy as traders attempted to make exchange easier. A few goods that have been used as money are gold, silver, copper, cattle, rocks, and shells.
- Our money today has value because of its general acceptability.

THE MONEY SUPPLY

- M1 includes currency held outside banks, checkable deposits, and traveler's checks.
- M2 includes M1, savings deposits (including money market deposit accounts), small-denomination time deposits, and money market mutual funds (retail).
- Credit cards are not money. When a credit card is used to make a purchase, a liability is incurred. This is not the case when money is used to make a purchase.

THE MONEY CREATION PROCESS

- Banks in the United States operate under a fractional reserve system, in which they must maintain only a fraction of their deposits in the form of reserves (i.e., in the form of deposits at the Fed and vault cash). Excess reserves are typically used to extend loans to customers. When banks make these loans, they credit borrowers' checking accounts and thereby increase the money supply. When banks reduce the volume of loans outstanding, they reduce checkable deposits and reduce the money supply.
- A change in the composition of the money supply can change the size of the money supply. For example, suppose M1 = $1,000 billion, where the breakdown is $300 billion currency outside banks and $700 billion in checkable deposits. Now suppose the $300 billion in currency is put into a checking account in a bank. Initially, this changes the composition of the money supply but not its size. M1 is still $1,000 billion but now includes $0 in currency and $1,000 billion in checkable deposits. Later, when the banks have had time to create new loans (checkable deposits) with the new reserves provided by the $300 billion deposit, the money supply expands.

Key Terms and Concepts

Money
Barter
Medium of Exchange
Unit of Account
Store of Value
Double Coincidence of Wants
M1
Currency
Federal Reserve Notes
Checkable Deposits
M2
Savings Deposit
Money Market Deposit Account
Time Deposit
Money Market Mutual Fund
Fractional Reserve Banking
Federal Reserve System (the Fed)
Reserves
Required Reserve Ratio (*r*)
Required Reserves
Excess Reserves
T-Account
Simple Deposit Multiplier
Cash Leakage

Questions and Problems

1 What is wrong with this statement: How much money did you make last year?

2 During much of 2007, the value of the dollar declined relative to other currencies (such as the euro, the pound, etc.). How does this affect the three functions of money?

3 Does inflation, which is an increase in the price level, affect the three functions of money? If so, how?

4 People in a barter economy came up with the idea of money because they wanted to do something to make society better off. Do you agree or disagree with this statement? Explain your answer.

5 There would be very few comedians in a barter economy. Do you agree or disagree with this statement? Explain your answer.

6 Some economists have proposed that the Fed move to a 100 percent required reserve ratio. This would make the simple deposit multiplier 1 ($1/r = 1/1.00 = 1$). Do you think banks would argue for or against the move? Explain your answer.

7 Money makes trade easier. Would having a money supply twice as large as it is currently make trade twice as easy? Would having a money supply half its current size make trade half as easy?

8 Explain why gold backing is not necessary to give paper money value.

9 Money is a means of lowering the transaction costs of making exchanges. Do you agree or disagree? Explain your answer.

10 If you were on an island with ten other people and there was no money, do you think money would emerge on the scene? Why or why not?

11 Can M1 fall as M2 rises? Can M1 rise without M2 rising too? Explain your answers.

12 Why isn't a credit card money?

13 Define the following:

a. Time deposit.

b. Money market mutual fund.

c. Money market deposit account.

d. Fractional reserve banking.

e. Reserves.

14 If Smith, who has a checking account at bank A, withdraws his money and deposits all of it into bank B, do reserves in the banking system change? Explain your answer.

15 If Jones, who has a checking account at bank A, withdraws her money, deposits half of it into bank B, and keeps the other half in currency, do reserves in the banking system change? Explain your answer.

16 Give an example that illustrates a change in the composition of the money supply.

17 The smaller the required reserve ratio is, the larger the simple deposit multiplier is. Do you agree or disagree with this statement. Explain your answer.

18 How does a bank's reserve deficiency affect the amount of loans it is likely to extend?

19 Describe the money supply expansion process.

20 Describe the money supply contraction process.

21 Does a cash leakage affect the change in checkable deposits and the money supply expansion process? Explain your answer.

Working with Numbers and Graphs

1 Suppose $10,000 in new dollar bills (never seen before) falls magically from the sky into the hands of Joanna Ferris. What minimum increase and what maximum increase in the money supply may result? Assume the required reserve ratio is 10 percent.

2 Suppose Joanna Ferris receives $10,000 from her friend Ethel and deposits the money in a checking account. Ethel gave Joanna the money by writing a check on her checking account. Would the maximum increase in the money supply still be what you found it to be in question 1, where Joanna received the money from the sky? Explain your answer.

3 Suppose that instead of Joanna getting $10,000 from the sky or through a check from a friend, she gets the money from her mother, who had buried it in a can in her backyard. In this case, would the maximum increase in the money supply be what you found it to be in question 1? Explain your answer.

4 Suppose r = 10 percent and the Fed creates $20,000 in new money that is deposited in someone's checking account in a bank. What is the maximum change in the money supply?

5 Suppose r = 10 percent and John walks into his bank, withdraws $2,000 in cash, and burns the money. What is the maximum change in the money supply as a result?

6 The Fed creates $100,000 in new money that is deposited in someone's checking account in a bank. What is the maximum change in the money supply if the required reserve ratio is

a. 5 percent?

b. 10 percent?

c. 20 percent?

CHAPTER 12

©LEE SNIDER/PHOTOIMAGES/CORBIS

THE FEDERAL RESERVE SYSTEM

Introduction Tourists in Washington, D.C., usually visit the White House, the Capitol building, and the Supreme Court building, buildings in which major decisions are made that affect people's lives. Major decisions that affect people's lives are also made in another building in Washington, D.C., but tourists rarely visit it. It is the Federal Reserve building. In this building, the Board of Governors of the Federal Reserve System and the members of the Federal Open Market Committee determine U.S. monetary policy. We provide you with many of the details of the Federal Reserve System in this chapter.

THE STRUCTURE AND FUNCTIONS OF THE FEDERAL RESERVE SYSTEM (THE FED)

The Federal Reserve System is the central bank of the United States. Other nations have central banks, such as the Bank of Sweden, the Bank of England, the Banque de France, the Bank of Japan, the Deutsche Bundesbank, and the like.

The Structure of the Fed

The Federal Reserve System came into existence with the Federal Reserve Act of 1913 and began operations in November 1914. The act divided the country into Federal Reserve Districts. As Exhibit 1 shows, there are 12 districts, each with a Federal Reserve Bank and its own president.

Board of Governors
The governing body of the Federal Reserve System.

Within the Fed, a seven-member **Board of Governors** coordinates and controls the activities of the Federal Reserve System. The board members serve 14-year terms and are appointed by the president with U.S. Senate approval. To limit political influence on Fed policy, the terms of the governors are staggered—with one new appointment every other year—so that a president cannot "pack" the board. The president also designates one member as chairman of the board for a four-year term.

exhibit 1

Federal Reserve Districts and Federal Reserve Bank Locations

The boundaries of the Federal Reserve Districts, the cities in which a Federal Reserve Bank is located, and the location of the Board of Governors (Washington, D.C.) are all noted on the map.

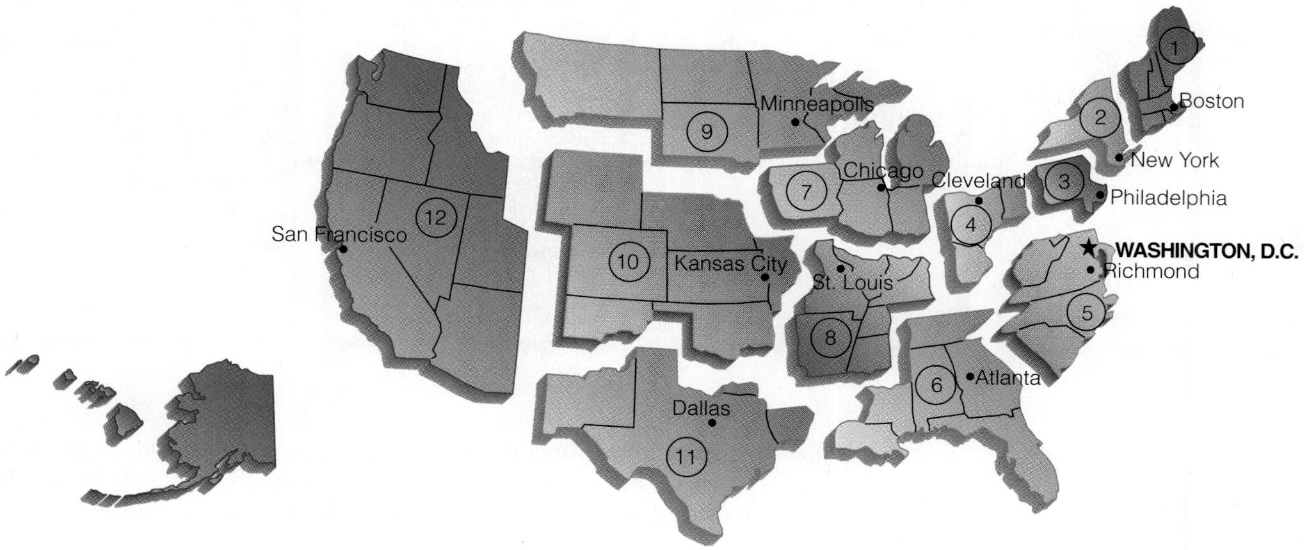

The major policy-making group within the Fed is the **Federal Open Market Committee (FOMC)**. Authority to conduct **open market operations**—the buying and selling of government securities—rests with the FOMC (more on open market operations later in the chapter). The FOMC has 12 members: the seven-member Board of Governors and five Federal Reserve District Bank presidents. The president of the Federal Reserve Bank of New York holds a permanent seat on the FOMC because a large amount of financial activity takes place in New York City and because the New York Fed is responsible for executing open market operations. The other four positions are rotated among the Federal Reserve District Bank presidents.

The most important responsibility of the Fed is to conduct monetary policy, or control the money supply. **Monetary policy** consists of changes in the money supply. More specifically, *expansionary monetary policy* aims to increase the money supply, and *contractionary monetary policy* aims to decrease the money supply. The Fed has tools at its disposal to both increase and decrease the money supply. In a later chapter, we will discuss monetary policy in detail and show how, under certain conditions, it can remove an economy from both recessionary and inflationary gaps.

Federal Open Market Committee (FOMC)
The 12-member policy-making group within the Fed. The committee has the authority to conduct open market operations.

Open Market Operations
The buying and selling of government securities by the Fed.

Monetary Policy
Changes in the money supply, or in the rate of change of the money supply, to achieve particular macroeconomic goals.

Functions of the Fed

The Fed has eight major responsibilities or functions:

1. *Controlling the money supply* (as noted in the previous section). A full explanation of how the Fed does this comes later in the chapter.
2. *Supplying the economy with paper money (Federal Reserve notes).* The Federal Reserve Banks have Federal Reserve notes on hand to meet the demands of the banks and the public. During the Christmas season, for example, more people withdraw larger-than-usual amounts of $1, $5, $20, $50, and $100 notes from banks. Needing to replenish their vault cash, banks turn to their Federal Reserve Banks. The Federal Reserve Banks meet

exhibit 2

The Check-Clearing Process

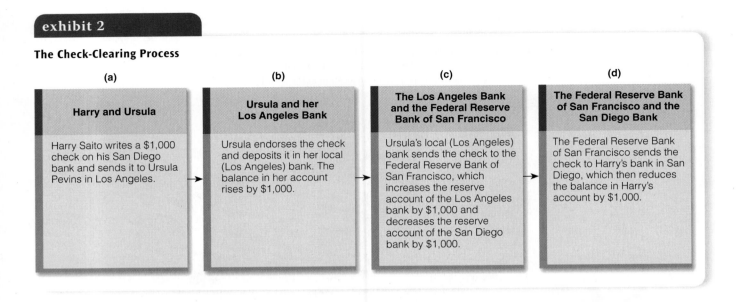

(a) Harry and Ursula

Harry Saito writes a $1,000 check on his San Diego bank and sends it to Ursula Pevins in Los Angeles.

→

(b) Ursula and her Los Angeles Bank

Ursula endorses the check and deposits it in her local (Los Angeles) bank. The balance in her account rises by $1,000.

→

(c) The Los Angeles Bank and the Federal Reserve Bank of San Francisco

Ursula's local (Los Angeles) bank sends the check to the Federal Reserve Bank of San Francisco, which increases the reserve account of the Los Angeles bank by $1,000 and decreases the reserve account of the San Diego bank by $1,000.

→

(d) The Federal Reserve Bank of San Francisco and the San Diego Bank

The Federal Reserve Bank of San Francisco sends the check to Harry's bank in San Diego, which then reduces the balance in Harry's account by $1,000.

cash needs by issuing more paper money (acting as passive suppliers of paper money). The money is actually printed at the Bureau of Engraving and Printing in Washington, D.C., but it is issued to commercial banks by the 12 Federal Reserve Banks.

3. *Providing check-clearing services.* When someone in San Diego writes a check to a person in Los Angeles, what happens to the check? The process by which funds change hands when checks are written is called the *check-clearing process.* The following process is summarized in Exhibit 2.
   a. Harry Saito writes a $1,000 check on his San Diego bank account and sends it to Ursula Pevins in Los Angeles.
   b. Ursula takes the check to her local bank, endorses it, and deposits it in her checking account. The balance in her account rises by $1,000.
   c. Ursula's Los Angeles bank sends the check to its Federal Reserve District Bank, which is located in San Francisco. The Federal Reserve Bank of San Francisco increases the reserve account of the Los Angeles bank by $1,000 and decreases the reserve account of the San Diego bank by $1,000.
   d. The Federal Reserve Bank of San Francisco sends the check to Harry's bank in San Diego, which then reduces the balance in Harry's checking account by $1,000. Harry's bank in San Diego either keeps the check on record or sends it to Harry with his monthly bank statement.
4. *Holding depository institutions' reserves.* As noted in the last chapter, banks are required to keep reserves against customer deposits either in their vaults or in reserve accounts at the Fed. These accounts are maintained by the 12 Federal Reserve Banks for member banks in their respective districts.
5. *Supervising member banks.* Without warning, the Fed can examine the books of member commercial banks to see the nature of the loans the banks have made, monitor compliance with bank regulations, check the accuracy of bank records, and so on. If the Fed finds that a bank has not been maintaining established banking standards, it can pressure it to do so.
6. *Serving as the government's banker.* The federal government collects and spends large sums of money. As a result, it needs a checking account for many of the same reasons an individual does. Its primary checking account is with the Fed, which is the government's banker.

economics 24/7

SOME HISTORY OF THE FED

Slightly before the passage of the Federal Reserve Act in 1913, there was disagreement about how many districts and banks there should be. Many people thought there should be as few banks as possible—6 to 8—because concentrating activities in only a few cities would enhance efficiency and ease of operation. The Secretary of State at the time, William Jennings Bryan, wanted 50 district banks. He called for a "branch at every major crossroad." It was to be neither 6 nor 50; instead, there was a compromise. Section 2 of the Federal Reserve Act states that "not less than eight nor more than twelve cities" would be designated as Federal Reserve cities.

After the number of cities was determined to be 8 to 12, a commission was set up to identify both the boundaries of the Federal Reserve Districts and the locations of the district banks. The commission was composed of the Comptroller of the Currency, the Secretary of the Treasury, and the Secretary of Agriculture. They had to choose from among the 37 cities that had applied to be locations of a district bank. The commission settled on a 12-bank, 12-city plan. It decided the boundaries of the districts on the basis of trade. In other words, the commission decided the boundaries should include cities or towns that traded the most with each other. If the residents of cities X and Y traded a lot with each other but the residents of city Z did not trade much with the residents of cities X and Y, then cities X and Y should be included in the same district but Z should not. Instead, city Z should be part of the district that included cities with which it traded.

Some commercial banks protested both the number of district banks and the boundaries decided on by the committee. These banks filed petitions for review of the plan with the Federal Reserve Board, thought to be the only group that could alter the plan.[1]

The petitions for review are said to have rekindled the debate about the actual number of district cities. Three members of the Federal Reserve Board wanted to reduce the number of district banks because they thought that one half of the banks were stronger than the other half were, and they wanted all banks to be of equal strength. Three other members of the Board wanted to stay with the original plan of 12 district banks. This left one member of the Board to break the tie. When it looked like that person's vote was going to be cast for a reduction in the number of district banks, one of the supporters of the original 12-bank plan went to the Attorney General of the United States. He asked the Attorney General for an opinion stating that the Board did not have the authority to alter the original plan. The Attorney General gave that opinion. The Board, afraid of attracting any negative publicity by disagreeing and challenging the opinion, accepted it.

1. Before there was a Board of Governors of the Federal Reserve System, there was the Federal Reserve Board. The Banking Act of 1935, approved on August 23, 1935, changed the name of the Federal Reserve Board to the Board of Governors of the Federal Reserve System.

7. *Serving as the lender of last resort.* A traditional function of a central bank is to serve as the lender of last resort for banks suffering cash management, or liquidity, problems.
8. *Handling the sale of U.S. Treasury securities (auctions).* **U.S. Treasury securities** (bills, notes, and bonds) are sold to raise funds to pay the government's bills. The Federal Reserve District Banks receive the bids for these securities and process them in time for weekly auctions.

U.S. Treasury Securities
Bonds and bond-like securities issued by the U.S. Treasury when it borrows.

Common MISCONCEPTIONS

About the U.S. Treasury and the Fed

Some persons confuse the U.S. Treasury with the Fed. They mistakenly believe that the U.S. Treasury does some of the things that the Fed does. However, there are major differences between the Treasury and the Fed.

- The U.S. Treasury is a budgetary agency; the Fed is a monetary agency.
- When the federal government spends funds, the Treasury collects the taxes and borrows the funds needed to pay suppliers and others. In short, the Treasury has an obligation to manage the

(continued)

Common Misconceptions (continued)

financial affairs of the federal government. Except for coins, the Treasury does not issue money. It cannot create money out of thin air as the Fed can. (We will soon explain exactly how this happens.)

- The Fed is principally concerned with the availability of money and credit for the entire economy. It does not issue Treasury securities. It does not have an obligation to meet the financial needs of the federal government. Its responsibility is to provide a stable monetary framework for the economy.

SELF-TEST

(Answers to Self-Test questions are in the Self-Test Appendix.)

1. The president of which Federal Reserve District Bank holds a permanent seat on the Federal Open Market Committee (FOMC)?
2. What is the most important responsibility of the Fed?
3. What does it mean to say the Fed acts as lender of last resort?

FED TOOLS FOR CONTROLLING THE MONEY SUPPLY

The money supply is, say, $1.35 trillion one month and $1.40 trillion a few months later. It changed because the Fed can change the money supply; it can cause the money supply to rise and to fall. The Fed has three major tools at its disposal to change (or control) the money supply:

1. open market operations,
2. the required reserve ratio, and
3. the discount rate.

This section explains how the Fed uses these tools to control the money supply.

Open Market Operations

Open Market Purchase
The buying of government securities by the Fed.

Open Market Sale
The selling of government securities by the Fed.

When the Fed buys or sells U.S. government securities in the financial markets, it is said to be engaged in *open market operations.*[2] Specifically, when it buys securities, it is engaged in an **open market purchase**; when it sells securities, it is engaged in an **open market sale**. Both open market purchases and open market sales affect the money supply.

OPEN MARKET PURCHASES When the Fed buys securities, someone has to sell securities. Suppose bank ABC in Denver is the seller; that is, suppose the Fed buys $5 million worth of government securities from bank ABC.[3] When this happens, the securities leave the possession of bank ABC and go to the Fed.

Bank ABC, of course, wants something in return for the securities: $5 million. The Fed pays for the government securities by increasing the balance in bank ABC's reserve account. In other words, if before bank ABC sold the securities to the Fed, it had $0 on deposit with the Fed, then after it sells the securities to the Fed, it has $5 million on deposit.

2. Actually, what the Fed buys and sells when it conducts open market operations are U.S. Treasury bills, notes, and bonds and government agency bonds. *Government securities* is a broad term that includes all of these financial instruments.

3. If the Fed purchases a government security from a bank, where did the bank get the security in the first place? Banks often purchase government securities from the U.S. Treasury, and so it is possible that the bank purchased the government security from the U.S. Treasury months ago.

Where did the Fed get the $5 million to put into bank ABC's reserve account? The answer, as odd as it seems, is *out of thin air.* The Fed has the legal authority to create money. What the Fed is effectively doing is deleting the $0 balance in bank ABC's account and, with a few keystrokes, replacing it with the number "5" and six zeroes: $5,000,000.

T-accounts are a good way to show how the transactions affect the accounts. After the open market purchase, the Fed's T-account looks like this:

The Fed	
Assets	**Liabilities**
Government securities + $5 million	Reserves on deposit in bank ABC's account + $5 million

After the open market purchase, bank ABC's T-account looks like this:

Bank ABC	
Assets	**Liabilities**
Government securities −$5 million	No change
Reserves on deposit at the Fed +$5 million	

Recall that as the reserves of one bank increase with no offsetting decline in reserves for other banks, the money supply expands through a process of increased loans and checkable deposits. In summary, an open market purchase by the Fed ultimately increases the money supply.

OPEN MARKET SALES Sometimes the Fed sells government securities to banks and others. Suppose the Fed sells $5 million worth of government securities to bank XYZ in Atlanta. The Fed surrenders the securities to bank XYZ and is paid with $5 million previously deposited in bank XYZ's reserve account at the Fed. In other words, the Fed simply reduces the balance in bank XYZ's reserve account by $5 million.

After the open market sale, the Fed's T-account looks like this:

The Fed	
Assets	**Liabilities**
Government securities −$5 million	Reserves on deposit in bank XYZ's account −$5 million

Bank XYZ's T-account looks like this:

Bank XYZ	
Assets	**Liabilities**
Government securities +$5 million	No change
Reserves on deposit at the Fed −$5 million	

Now that bank XYZ's reserves have declined by $5 million, it is reserve deficient. As bank XYZ and other banks adjust to the lower level of reserves, they reduce their total loans outstanding, which reduces the total volume of checkable deposits and money in the economy.

A nagging question remains: What happened to the $5 million the Fed got from bank XYZ's account? The answer is that it disappears from the face of the earth; it no longer exists. This is simply the other side of the Fed's ability to create money out of thin air. The Fed can destroy money too; it can cause money to disappear into thin air.

exhibit 3

Open Market Operations

An open market purchase increases reserves, which leads to an increase in the money supply. An open market sale decreases reserves, which leads to a decrease in money supply. (Note: We have assumed here that the Fed purchases government securities from and sells government securities to commercial banks.)

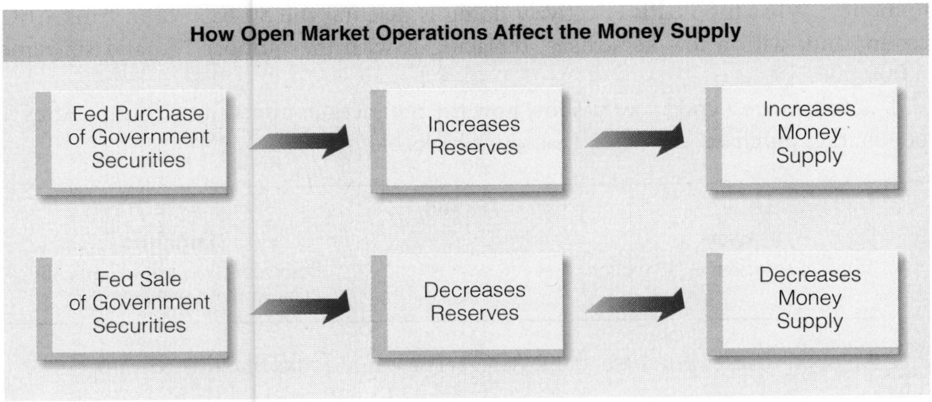

Exhibit 3 summarizes how open market operations affect the money supply.

Common MISCONCEPTIONS

About Money and Dollar Bills

Some people mistakenly equate money with coins and paper money (Federal Reserve notes). As we learned in the last chapter, money is more than coins and Federal Reserve notes, as just reinforced in our discussion of open market operations. To illustrate, in conducting an open market purchase, the Fed purchases government securities from and bank, and the bank's reserve account balance rises. As a result of having greater reserves, the bank extends more loans and creates more checkable deposits. The money supply rises without one new dollar bill being printed.

The Required Reserve Ratio

The Fed can influence the money supply by changing the required reserve ratio. Recall from the last chapter that we can find the maximum change in checkable deposits (for a given change in reserves) by using the following formula:

$$\text{Maximum change in checkable deposits} = \frac{1}{r} \times \Delta R$$

For example, if reserves (*R*) increase by $1,000 and the required reserve ratio (*r*) is 10 percent, then the maximum change in checkable deposits is $10,000:

$$\begin{aligned}\text{Maximum change in checkable deposits} &= \frac{1}{0.10} \times \$1{,}000 \\ &= 10 \times \$1{,}000 \\ &= \$10{,}000\end{aligned}$$

Now suppose Fed officials increase the required reserve ratio from 10 percent to 20 percent. How does this change the amount of checkable deposits? The amount of checkable deposits declines:

$$\begin{aligned}\text{Maximum change in checkable deposits} &= \frac{1}{0.20} \times \$1{,}000 \\ &= 5 \times \$1{,}000 \\ &= \$5{,}000\end{aligned}$$

economics 24/7

INSIDE AN FOMC MEETING

The major policy-making group in the Federal Reserve System is the Federal Open Market Committee (FOMC). The FOMC meets eight times a year, each time on a Tuesday. The meeting is held in the board room of the Federal Reserve Building. Decisions about monetary policy are, to a large degree, made by the FOMC. The following events occur at a typical FOMC meeting.

©JAY MARTIN/BLOOMBERG NEWS/LANDOV

8:00 a.m.
The board room is swept for electronic bugs.

8:45–9:00 a.m.
People begin to arrive for the meeting. In addition to the 12 members of the FOMC, about 37 other people will be present at the meeting.

8:59 a.m.
The chairman of the Board of Governors of the Federal Reserve System walks through the door that connects his office to the board room and takes his place at the table.

9:00 a.m.
The FOMC meeting commences. The first agenda item is a presentation by the manager of the System Open Market Account at the Federal Reserve Bank of New York. He discusses the financial and foreign exchange markets and provides certain details about open market operations.

A Little Later . . .
The director of research and statistics at the Federal Reserve Board presents the forecast of the U.S. economy. The forecast has previously been circulated to the FOMC members in the Greenbook (because the cover of the document is green). The latest economic data are reviewed and discussed.

A Little Later . . .
The 12 members of the FOMC present their views of local and national economic conditions.

A Little Later . . .
The director of monetary affairs presents policy options. These policy options have been previously circulated in the Bluebook (because the cover of the document is blue). The chairman of the Board of Governors gives his opinion of the economy and of the policy options.

A Little Later . . .
A general discussion among all the members of the FOMC takes place. At issue is the state of the U.S. economy and current policy options. After the discussion, the chairman summarizes his sense of the policy options. Then the members vote on the options. The chair votes first, the vice chair votes second, and the remaining FOMC members vote in alphabetical order.

A Little Later . . .
The FOMC discusses the wording of the announcement it will make regarding what it has decided.

Between 11:30 a.m. and 1:30 p.m.
The meeting usually adjourns.

2:15 p.m.
The decision of the FOMC is released to the public.

If, instead, the Fed lowers the required reserve ratio to 5 percent, the maximum change in checkable deposits increases:

$$\begin{aligned}\text{Maximum change in checkable deposits} &= \frac{1}{0.05} \times \$1{,}000 \\ &= 20 \times \$1{,}000 \\ &= \$20{,}000\end{aligned}$$

Thus, an increase in the required reserve ratio leads to a decrease in the money supply, and a decrease in the required reserve ratio leads to an increase in the money supply. In other words, there is an inverse relationship between the required reserve ratio and the money supply. As *r* goes up, the money supply goes down; as *r* goes down, the money supply goes up.

The Discount Rate

In addition to providing loans to customers, banks themselves borrow funds when they need them. Consider bank ABC, currently with zero excess reserves. Then either of the following two events occurs:

- *Case 1:* Brian applies for a loan to buy new equipment for his horse ranch. The bank loan officer believes that he is a good credit risk and that the bank could profit by granting him the loan. But the bank has no funds to lend.
- *Case 2:* Jennifer closes her checking account. As a result, the bank loses reserves and now is reserve deficient.

Reserve Requirement
The rule that specifies the amount of reserves a bank must hold to back up deposits.

Federal Funds Market
A market where banks lend reserves to one another, usually for short periods.

Federal Funds Rate
The interest rate in the federal funds market; the interest rate banks charge one another to borrow reserves.

Discount Rate
The interest rate the Fed charges depository institutions that borrow reserves from it.

In Case 1, the bank wants funds so that it can make a loan to Brian and increase its profits. In Case 2, the bank needs funds to meet its **reserve requirement**. In either case, the bank can turn to two major sources to acquire a loan: (1) the **federal funds market**, which means the bank goes to another bank for a loan, or (2) the Fed (the bank's Federal Reserve District Bank). At both places, the bank pays an interest rate. The rate it pays for a loan in the federal funds market is called the **federal funds rate**. The rate it pays for a (discount) loan from the Fed is called the **discount rate** (also known as the *primary credit rate*). Bank ABC tries to minimize its costs by borrowing where the interest rate is lower, *ceteris paribus.* Usually, the discount rate is set higher than the federal funds rate; so banks borrow in the federal funds market.

Let us suppose, though, that the discount rate is lowered so that it is below the federal funds rate. What would happen? Banks would go to the Fed for loans instead of going to each other. Let's suppose bank ABC gets a loan from the Fed. If the Fed grants the bank a loan, the Fed's T-account looks like this:

The FED	
Assets	**Liabilities**
Loan to bank ABC +$1 million	Reserves on deposit in bank ABC's account +$1 million

Bank ABC's T-account reflects the same transaction from its perspective.

Bank ABC	
Assets	**Liabilities**
Reserves on deposit at the Fed +$1 million	Loan from the Fed +$1 million

Notice that when bank ABC borrows from the Fed, its reserves increase, whereas the reserves of no other bank decrease. The result is increased reserves for the banking system as a whole; so the money supply increases. In summary, when a bank borrows at the Fed's discount window, the money supply increases.

On the other hand, when the discount rate is raised above the federal funds rate, banks do not borrow from the Fed. However, as the banks pay back their Fed loans that they previously had taken out, reserves fall, and ultimately the money supply declines. A summary of the effects of the Fed's different monetary tools is shown in Exhibit 4.

Term Auction Facility (TAF) Program
Under the Term Auction Facility (TAF) Program, the Federal Reserve auctions funds to depository institutions. Each TAF auction is for a fixed amount, with the TAF rate determined by the auction process (subject to a minimum bid rate).

Term Auction Facility (TAF) Program: One More Monetary Tool

In addition to the Fed's three traditional tools for changing the money supply (open market operations, the required reserve ratio, and the discount rate), the Fed made use of another tool in late 2007. It created the **term auction facility (TAF) program**. In this program, instead of banks asking for a specific dollar loan (as they would if they were to get a discount loan), the Fed states the total amount of credit it wants to extend. For example,

economics 24/7

FLYING IN WITH THE MONEY[4]

A banker at a commercial bank located about 200 miles from the Federal Reserve Bank of Minneapolis was frantic. There was a large crowd outside his bank, and the people wanted their money now. The banker got on the phone and called the Federal Reserve Bank in Minneapolis. He told the people at the Minneapolis Fed that there was a "mad run" on his bank. If the Fed did not come to his rescue soon, he would be out of currency and unable to give the customers of his bank their money.

Where was their money? Why didn't he have it to give to them? As the last chapter explained, banks need to have on hand only a fraction of their customers' deposits.

The Federal Reserve System responded to the call for currency. The Federal Reserve Bank of Minneapolis chartered a small plane, and two Fed officials took it, along with a half-million dollars in small-denomination bills, to the nearby town.

Upon approaching the town, the pilot flew the plane over Main Street to dramatize its arrival in the town: The Federal Reserve was flying in to the rescue. The plane landed at a nearby field. From the field, the Fed officials were escorted into town by the police, and the money was stacked in the bank's windows. The sight of all the money calmed the bank's customers, who were now assured they could get their money if they wanted. A banking panic was averted in a very dramatic way.

4. This feature is based on "Born of a Panic: Forming the Federal Reserve System," *The Region* (August 1998).

the Fed might state that it is willing to extend $20 billion worth of credit. Next, the Fed allows banks to bid on the funds. The bidding process determines the TAF rate (interest rate) for the loans.

exhibit 4

Fed Monetary Tools and Their Effects on the Money Supply

The following Fed actions increase the money supply: purchasing government securities on the open market, lowering the required reserve ratio, and lowering the discount rate relative to the federal funds rate. The following Fed actions decrease the money supply: selling government securities on the open market, raising the required reserve ratio, and raising the discount rate relative to the federal funds rate.

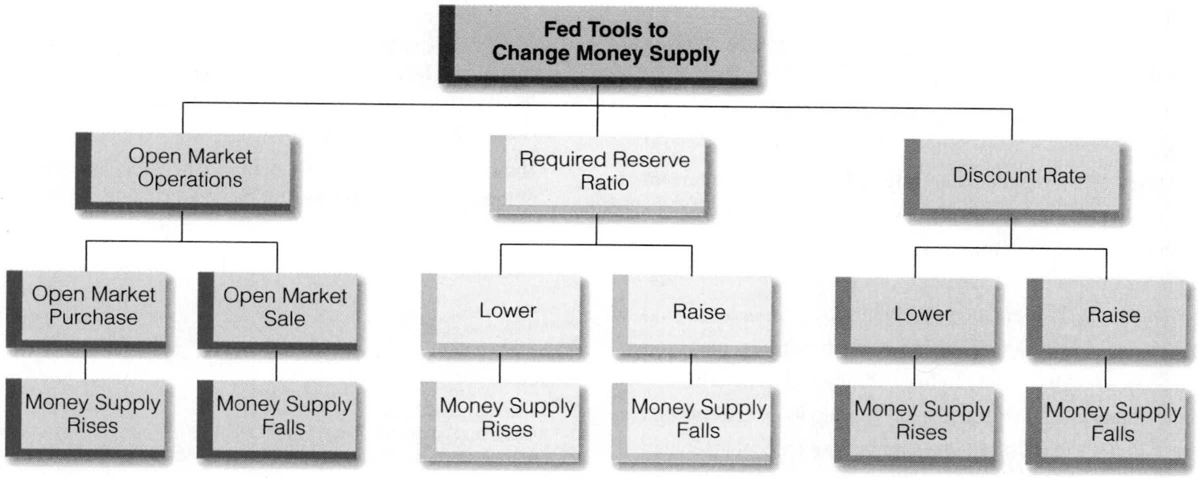

office hours

"IN THE PRESS TALK IS ABOUT INTEREST RATES, NOT THE MONEY SUPPLY"

Student:
When I listen to the news, I often hear about the Fed changing interest rates. For example, a news reporter might say, "Today the Fed decided to lower the federal funds rate by one-half of one percent." Rarely do I hear about the Fed changing the money supply. Why does this chapter go on about how the Fed changes the money supply?

Instructor:
Often what is missing from the news is this fact: The Fed doesn't change an interest rate (such as the federal funds rate) by issuing an order ("Lower the federal funds rate, now!"[5]) but by changing the amount of reserves in the banking system, which we know affects the money supply.

Student:
How so?

Instructor:
Consider the federal funds rate. We said in our lectures that the federal funds rate is determined in the federal funds market. That market consists of the demand for reserves and the supply of reserves, just as the apple market consists of the demand for and the supply of apples. Do you understand so far?

Student:
Yes, the federal funds rate is determined in the federal funds market.

Instructor:
Now some people mistakenly think the Fed can simply issue a directive to change the federal funds rate. But it can't. If the federal funds rate is, say, 4.75 percent today, the Fed *cannot* simply tell banks to start charging a federal funds rate of, say, 4.50 percent. That is not how things work. If the Fed wants the federal funds rate to decline, it can inject more reserves into the banking system. But ask yourself how it can do this. One way is to conduct an open market purchase.

Let's work through the process. Suppose that on day 1 the federal funds rate is 4.75 percent. In other words, this is the percentage rate at which the demand curve for reserves and the supply curve of reserves intersect. Now let's suppose that the Fed wants the federal funds rate to be lower, say, at 4.50 percent. To this end, the Fed could undertake an open market purchase, which increases the supply of reserves in the banking system. As a result of the increase in the supply of reserves, the federal funds rate declines.

Student:
Oh, I see things now. You're saying that what the press says is something like this: "Today the Fed decided to lower the federal funds rate." But what really is happening is that the Fed wants to lower the federal funds rate. It therefore conducts an open market purchase, which increases the supply of reserves in the banking system, leading to a decline in the federal funds rate.

Instructor:
That's correct. But now let's go back to your original observation, which was that the press talks about the Fed changing interest rates, but not about the Fed changing the money supply. Ask yourself this: Did the Fed change the money supply in its pursuit of lowering the federal funds rate?

Student:
I guess it did. After all, we just learned that it conducted an open market purchase to lower the federal funds rate, and earlier we learned that an open market purchase leads to an increase in the money supply.

Instructor:
Exactly. In other words, the press could say, "Today the Fed decided to lower the federal funds rate," which is essentially the same thing as saying, "Today the Fed decided to increase the money supply."

Points to Remember

1. The press often talks about the Fed changing interest rates (in particular, the federal funds rate). Sometimes this leaves members of the public with the mistaken impression (a) that the Fed can change the federal funds rate by issuing an order or directive and (b) that changing the federal funds rate has nothing to do with changing the money supply.
2. The Fed can change the discount rate by issuing an order to raise or lower the discount rate, but it cannot change the federal funds rate this way.

5. Although the Fed cannot change the federal funds rate by issuing an order, it can change the discount rate this way. If the Board of Governors of the Federal Reserve System wants to lower or raise the discount rate, it can simply do it.

SELF-TEST

1. How does the money supply change as a result of (a) an increase in the discount rate, (b) an open market purchase, (c) an increase in the required reserve ratio?
2. What is the difference between the federal funds rate and the discount rate?
3. If bank A borrows $10 million from bank B, what happens to the reserves in bank A? What happens in the banking system?
4. If bank A borrows $10 million from the Fed, what happens to the reserves in bank A? What happens in the banking system?

a reader asks | How Do I Get a Job at the Fed?

I'm a junior in college, majoring in economics. Are there any career opportunities at the Fed that I might apply for while I'm still a student?

The Fed operates both summer internships and a Cooperative Education Program for college students. The Fed's summer internship program is "designed to provide valuable work experience for undergraduate and graduate students considering careers in economics, finance, and computer science." Two major divisions at the Federal Reserve Board in Washington, D.C., regularly offer internships: Economic Research Divisions and Information Technology.

Summer internships are usually available to college sophomores, juniors, and seniors. The internships are usually unpaid and run from June 1 to September 1. As an economics major, you may be interested in applying for an internship in the Division of Research and Statistics. This division collects economic and financial information and develops economic analyses that are used by the Board of Governors, the Federal Open Market Committee, and other Fed officials in formulating monetary and regulatory policies. The Fed's Cooperative Education Program provides paid and unpaid professional work experience to undergraduate and graduate students in economics, finance and accounting, information systems, and law. Here are the assignments in three of these areas:

1. *Economics.* Students have the opportunity to apply their quantitative skills to projects in financial and nonfinancial areas, bank structure and competition, international trade, and foreign and exchange markets.
2. *Finance and accounting.* Students analyze the financial condition of domestic and foreign banking organizations and process applications filed by these financial institutions.
3. *Information systems.* Student assignments include creating public and intranet Web pages and assisting application developers in program maintenance, design, and coding.

Generally, employment in the Cooperative Education Program is for a summer or a year, although other assignment lengths are considered. Candidates are selected on the basis of scholastic achievement, recommendations, and completed coursework in relevant areas of study.

To obtain more information about the summer internships and the Cooperative Education Program, go to the Federal Reserve website at http://www.federalreserve.gov/, and click Career Opportunities. You can also call the Fed's 24-hour job vacancy line at 1-202-872-4984.

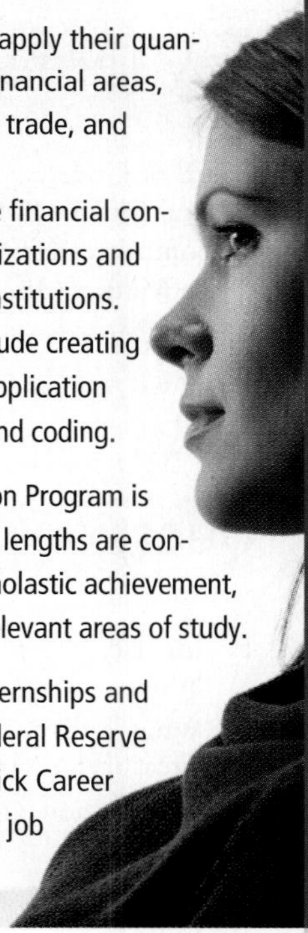

Chapter Summary

THE FEDERAL RESERVE SYSTEM

- There are 12 Federal Reserve Districts. The Board of Governors controls and coordinates the activities of the Federal Reserve System. The Board is made up of seven members, each appointed to a 14-year term. The major policy-making group within the Fed is the Federal Open Market Committee (FOMC). It is a 12-member group made up of the seven members of the Board of Governors and five Federal Reserve District Bank presidents.
- The major responsibilities of the Fed are to (1) control the money supply, (2) supply the economy with paper money (Federal Reserve notes), (3) provide check-clearing services, (4) hold depository institutions' reserves, (5) supervise member banks, (6) serve as the government's banker,

(7) serve as the lender of last resort, and (8) serve as a fiscal agent for the Treasury.

CONTROLLING THE MONEY SUPPLY

- The following Fed actions increase the money supply: lowering the required reserve ratio, purchasing government securities on the open market, and lowering the discount rate relative to the federal funds rate. The following Fed actions decrease the money supply: raising the required reserve ratio, selling government securities on the open market, and raising the discount rate relative to the federal funds rate.

OPEN MARKET OPERATIONS

- An open market purchase by the Fed increases the money supply. An open market sale by the Fed decreases the money supply.

THE REQUIRED RESERVE RATIO

- An increase in the required reserve ratio leads to a decrease in the money supply. A decrease in the required reserve ratio leads to an increase in the money supply.

THE DISCOUNT RATE

- An increase in the discount rate relative to the federal funds rate leads to a decrease in the money supply.
- A decrease in the discount rate relative to the federal funds rate leads to an increase in the money supply.

Key Terms and Concepts

Board of Governors
Federal Open Market Committee (FOMC)
Open Market Operations
Monetary Policy
U.S. Treasury Securities
Open Market Purchase
Open Market Sale
Reserve Requirement
Federal Funds Market
Federal Funds Rate
Discount Rate
Term Auction Facility (TAF) Program

Questions and Problems

1 Identify the major responsibilities of the Federal Reserve System.

2 What are the differences between the Fed and the U.S. Treasury?

3 Explain how an open market purchase increases the money supply.

4 Explain how an open market sale decreases the money supply.

5 Suppose the Fed raises the required reserve ratio, a move that is normally thought to reduce the money supply. However, banks find themselves with a reserve deficiency after the required reserve ratio is increased and are likely to react by requesting a loan from the Fed. Does this action prevent the money supply from contracting as predicted? Explain your answer.

6 Suppose bank A borrows reserves from bank B. Now that bank A has more reserves than previously, will the money supply increase? Explain your answer.

7 Explain how a decrease in the required reserve ratio increases the money supply.

8 Suppose you read in the newspaper that all last week the Fed conducted open market purchases and that on Tuesday of last week it lowered the discount rate. What would you say the Fed was trying to do?

9 Explain how a check is cleared through the Federal Reserve System.

10 The Fed can change the discount rate directly and the federal funds rate indirectly. Explain.

11 What does it mean to say the Fed serves as the lender of last resort?

12 The Fed has announced a new lower target for the federal funds rate. In other words, it wants to lower the federal funds rate from its present level. What does setting a lower target for the federal funds rate have to do with open market operations?

Working with Numbers and Graphs

1 If reserves increase by $2 million and the required reserve ratio is 8 percent, what is the maximum change in checkable deposits?

2 If reserves increase by $2 million and the required reserves ratio is 10 percent, what is the maximum change in checkable deposits?

3 If the federal funds rate is 6 percent and the discount rate is 5.1 percent, to whom will a bank be more likely to go for a loan—another bank or the Fed? Explain your answer.

4 Complete the following table:

Federal Reserve Action	Effect on the Money Supply (up or down?)
Lower the discount rate	A
Conduct open market purchase	B
Lower required reserve ratio	C
Raise the discount rate	D
Conduct open market sale	E
Raise the required reserve ratio	F

© RAFAEL RAMIREZ LEE/SHUTTERSTOCK

CHAPTER 13

MONEY AND THE ECONOMY

Introduction Does the money supply matter? Does a rise or fall in the money supply matter to the economy? In this chapter we talk about the money supply and its effects on the economy. We discuss changes in the money supply and in the price level, changes in the money supply and in real GDP, and changes in the money supply and interest rates.

MONEY AND THE PRICE LEVEL

Do changes in the money supply affect the price level in the economy? Classical economists believed so. Their position was based on the equation of exchange and on the simple quantity theory of money.

The Equation of Exchange

Equation of Exchange
An identity stating that the money supply times velocity must be equal to the price level times Real GDP.

The **equation of exchange** is an identity stating that the money supply (M) multiplied by velocity (V) must be equal to the price level (P) times Real GDP (Q).

$$MV \equiv PQ$$

where ≡ means "must be equal to." This is an identity, and an identity is valid for all values of the variables.

Velocity
The average number of times a dollar is spent to buy final goods and services in a year.

You are familiar with the money supply, the price level, and Real GDP but not with velocity. **Velocity** is the average number of times a dollar is spent to buy final goods and services in a year. For example, assume an economy has only five \$1 bills. In January, the first of the \$1 bills moves from Smith's hands to Jones's hands to buy good X. Then in June, it goes from Jones's hands to Brown's hands to buy good Y. And in December, it goes from Brown's hands to Peterson's hands to buy good Z. Over the course of the year, this dollar bill has changed hands three times.

The other dollar bills also change hands during the year. The second dollar bill changes hands five times; the third, six times; the fourth, two times; and the fifth, seven times.

Given this information, we can calculate the average number of times a dollar changes hands in purchases. In this case, the number is 4.6, which is velocity.

In a large economy such as ours, simply counting how many times each dollar changes hands is impossible; so calculating velocity as in our example is impossible. For a large economy, we use a different method. First, we calculate GDP, next we calculate the average money supply, and finally we divide GDP by the average money supply to obtain velocity. For example, if $4,800 billion worth of transactions occur in a year and the average money supply during the year is $800 billion, a dollar must have been used an average of six times during the year to purchase goods and services. Mathematically, we have

$$V \equiv \frac{GDP}{M}$$

GDP is equal to $P \times Q$; so this identity can be written

$$V \equiv \frac{P \times Q}{M}$$

Multiplying both sides by *M,* we get

$$MV \equiv PQ$$

which is the equation of exchange. Thus, the equation of exchange is derived from the definition of velocity.

The equation of exchange can be interpreted in different ways:

1. The money supply multiplied by velocity must equal the price level times Real GDP: $M \times V \equiv P \times Q$.
2. The money supply multiplied by velocity must equal GDP: $M \times V \equiv$ GDP (because $P \times Q =$ GDP).
3. Total spending or expenditures (measured by *MV*) must equal the total sales revenues of business firms (measured by *PQ*): $MV \equiv PQ$.

The third way of interpreting the equation of exchange is perhaps the most intuitively easy to understand: The total expenditures (of buyers) must equal the total sales (of sellers). Consider a simple economy where there is only one buyer and one seller. If the buyer buys a book for $20, then the seller receives $20. Stated differently, the money supply in the example, or $20, times velocity, 1, is equal to the price of the book, $20, times the quantity of the book.

From the Equation of Exchange to the Simple Quantity Theory of Money

The equation of exchange is an identity, not an economic theory. To turn it into a theory, we make some assumptions about the variables in the equation. Many eighteenth-century classical economists, as well as American economist Irving Fisher (1867–1947) and English economist Alfred Marshall (1842–1924), made the following assumptions:

1. Changes in velocity are so small that for all practical purposes velocity can be assumed to be constant (especially over short periods of time).
2. Real GDP, or *Q*, is fixed in the short run.

Hence, they turned the equation of exchange, which is simply true by definition, into a theory by assuming that both *V* and *Q* are fixed, or constant. With these two assumptions, we have the **simple quantity theory of money**: If *V* and *Q* are constant, we would predict that changes in *M* will bring about *strictly proportional* changes in *P*. In other

Simple Quantity Theory of Money
The theory assuming that velocity (*V*) and Real GDP (*Q*) are constant and predicting that changes in the money supply (*M*) lead to strictly proportional changes in the price level (*P*).

exhibit 1

Assumptions and Predictions of the Simple Quantity Theory of Money

The simple quantity theory of money assumes that both V and Q are constant. (A bar over each indicates this in the exhibit.) The prediction is that changes in M lead to strictly proportional changes in P. (Note: For purposes of this example, think of Q as "so many units of goods" and of P as the "average price paid per unit of these goods.")

Assumptions of Simple Quantity Theory							Predictions of Simple Quantity Theory	
M	×	$\bar{V}$	=	P	×	$\bar{Q}$	% Change in M	% Change in P
$ 500		4		$2		1,000		
1,000		4		4		1,000	+ 100%	+ 100%
1,500		4		6		1,000	+ 50	+ 50
1,200		4		4.80		1,000	− 20	− 20

words, the simple quantity theory of money predicts that changes in the money supply will bring about strictly proportional changes in the price level.

Exhibit 1 shows the assumptions and predictions of the simple quantity theory. On the left side of the exhibit, the key assumptions of the simple quantity theory are noted: V and Q are constant. Also, $M \times V = P \times Q$ is noted. We use the equals sign (=) instead of the identity sign (≡) because we are speaking about the simple quantity theory, not the equation of exchange. (The equals sign can be read as "is predicted to be equal"; i.e., given our assumptions, $M \times V$, or MV, is predicted to be equal to $P \times Q$, or PQ.)

Starting with the first row, the money supply is $500, velocity is 4, Real GDP (Q) is 1,000 units, and the price level, or price index, is $2.[1] Therefore, GDP equals $2,000. In the second row, the money supply increases by 100 percent, from $500 to $1,000, and both V and Q are constant, at 4 and 1,000, respectively. The price level moves from $2 to $4. On the right side of the exhibit, we see that a 100 percent increase in M predicts a 100 percent increase in P. Changes in P are predicted to be strictly proportional to changes in M.

In the third row, M increases by 50 percent, and P is predicted to increase by 50 percent. In the fourth row, M decreases by 20 percent, and P is predicted to decrease by 20 percent.

In summary, the simple quantity theory assumes that both V and Q are constant in the short run and therefore predicts that changes in M lead to strictly proportional changes in P.

How well does the simple quantity theory of money predict? That is, do changes in the money supply actually lead to *strictly proportional* changes in the price level? For example, if the money supply goes up by 7 percent, does the price level go up by 7 percent? If the money supply goes down by 4 percent, does the price level go down by 4 percent? The answer is that the strict proportionality between changes in the money supply and the price level does not show up in the data (at least not very often). Generally, though, evidence supports the spirit (or essence) of the simple quantity theory of money: the higher the growth rate in the money supply, the greater the growth rate in the price level. To illustrate, we would expect that a growth rate in the money supply of, say, 40 percent would generate a greater increase in the price level than, say, a growth rate in the money supply of 4 percent. Generally this is what we see. For example, countries with more rapid increases in their money supplies often witness more rapid increases in their price levels than do countries that witness less rapid increases in their money supplies.

---

1. You are used to seeing Real GDP expressed as a dollar figure and a price index as a number without a dollar sign in front of it. We have switched things for purposes of this example because it is easier to think of Q as "so many units of goods" and P as "the average price paid per unit of these goods."

economics 24/7

THE CALIFORNIA GOLD RUSH, OR REALLY EXPENSIVE APPLES

Soon there was too much money in California and too little of everything else.

—J. S. Holiday, *The World Rushed In*

The only peacetime rise [in prices] comparable in total magnitude [to the 40 to 50 percent in prices from 1897 to 1914] followed the California gold discoveries in the early 1850s. . . .

—Milton Friedman and Anna Schwartz, *A Monetary History of the United States, 1867–1960*

© BETTMANN/CORBIS

John Sutter was a Swiss immigrant who arrived in California in 1839. James Marshall, a carpenter, was building a sawmill for Sutter. On the chilly morning of January 24, 1848, Marshall was busy at work when something glistening caught his eye, and he reached down and picked it up. Marshall said to the workers he had hired, "Boys, by God I believe I have found a gold mine." Marshall later wrote, "I reached my hand down and picked it up; it made my heart thump, for I was certain it was gold. The piece was about half the size and shape of a pea. Then I saw another."

In time, Marshall and his workers came across more gold, and before long people from all across the United States and from many other countries headed to California. The California gold rush had begun.

The California gold rush, which resulted in an increase in the amount of money in circulation, provides an illustration of how a fairly dramatic increase in the money supply can affect prices. As more gold was mined and the supply of money increased, prices began to rise. Although prices rose generally across the country, the earliest and most dramatic increases in prices occurred in and near the areas where gold was discovered. Near the gold mines, the prices of food and clothing sharply increased. For example, whereas a loaf of bread sold for 4 cents in New York (equivalent to 84 cents today), near the mines the price was 75 cents (the equivalent of $15.67 today). Eggs sold for about $2 each ($41 today), apples for $4 ($83.59), a butcher's knife for $30 ($626), and boots went for $100 a pair ($2,089).

In San Francisco, land prices rose dramatically because of the city's relative closeness to the mines. In 18 months, real estate that cost $16 (the equivalent of $334 today) before gold was discovered jumped to $45,000 ($940,000 today).

The sharp rise in prices that followed the California gold discoveries followed other gold discoveries too. For example, the gold stock of the world is estimated to have doubled from 1890 to 1914, due both to discoveries (in South Africa, Alaska, and Colorado) and to improved methods of mining and refining gold. During this period, world prices increased too.

Common MISCONCEPTIONS

About the Money Supply and Various GDP Levels

Some people think that GDP cannot be greater than the money supply; that is, they believe that a money supply of say, $100, can support a GDP of only $100. Not true. What this belief fails to take into account is velocity. To illustrate, suppose the money supply is $100 and velocity is 2. It follows that GDP is $200. Let velocity rise to 3, and GDP rises to $300. In short, a given money supply of $100 is consistent with a GDP of $200 and with a GDP of $300.

macro*theme* → In Chapter 5, we noted that macroeconomists are very interested in what changes the variables P and Q. The simple quantity theory of money seeks to explain what leads to changes in P. The answer is fairly simple: Changes in the money supply lead to changes in the price level.

The Simple Quantity Theory of Money in an *AD-AS* Framework

In this section, we analyze the simple quantity theory of money in the *AD-AS* framework.

THE *AD* CURVE IN THE SIMPLE QUANTITY THEORY OF MONEY The simple quantity theory of money builds on the equation of exchange. Recall that one way of interpreting the equation of exchange is that the total expenditures of buyers (measured by *MV*) must equal the total sales of sellers (measured by *PQ*). Thus, *MV* is the total expenditures of buyers and *PQ* is the total sales of sellers. For now, we concentrate on *MV* as the total expenditures of buyers:

$$MV = \text{Total expenditures}$$

In an earlier chapter, total expenditures (*TE*) is defined as the sum of the expenditures made by the four sectors of the economy. In other words,

$$TE = C + I + G + (EX - IM)$$

Because $MV = TE$,

$$MV = C + I + G + (EX - IM)$$

Now recall that at a given price level, anything that changes *C*, *I*, *G*, *EX*, or *IM* changes aggregate demand and thus shifts the aggregate demand (*AD*) curve. But *MV* equals $C + I + G + (EX - IM)$; so it follows that *a change in the money supply (M) or a change in velocity (V) will change aggregate demand and therefore lead to a shift in the AD curve.* Another way to say this is that aggregate demand depends on *both* the money supply and velocity. Specifically:

- An increase in the money supply will increase aggregate demand and shift the *AD* curve to the right.
- A decrease in the money supply will decrease aggregate demand and shift the *AD* curve to the left.
- An increase in velocity will increase aggregate demand and shift the *AD* curve to the right.
- A decrease in velocity will decrease aggregate demand and shift the *AD* curve to the left.

But *in the simple quantity theory of money, velocity is assumed to be constant.* Thus, we are left with only changes in the money supply being able to shift the *AD* curve.

The *AD* curve for the simple quantity theory of money is shown in Exhibit 2(a). The $M, \overline{V}$ in parentheses next to the curve is a reminder of which factors can shift the *AD* curve. The bar over *V* (for velocity) indicates that velocity is assumed to be constant.

THE *AS* CURVE IN THE SIMPLE QUANTITY THEORY OF MONEY In the simple quantity theory of money, the level of Real GDP is assumed to be constant in the short run. Exhibit 2(b) shows Real GDP fixed at Q_1. The *AS* curve is vertical at this level of Real GDP.

***AD* AND *AS* IN THE SIMPLE QUANTITY THEORY OF MONEY** Exhibit 2(c) shows both the *AD* and *AS* curves in the simple quantity theory of money. Suppose AD_1 is initially operational. In the exhibit, AD_1 is based on a money supply of $800 billion and a velocity of 2. The price level is P_1.

exhibit 2

The Simple Quantity Theory of Money in the *AD-AS* Framework

(a) In the simple quantity theory of money, the *AD* curve is downward sloping. Velocity is assumed to be constant, so changes in the money supply will change aggregate demand. (b) In the simple quantity theory of money, Real GDP is fixed in the short run. Thus, the *AS* curve is vertical. (c) In the simple quantity theory of money, an increase in the money supply will shift the *AD* curve rightward and increase the price level. A decrease in the money supply will shift the *AD* curve leftward and decrease the price level.

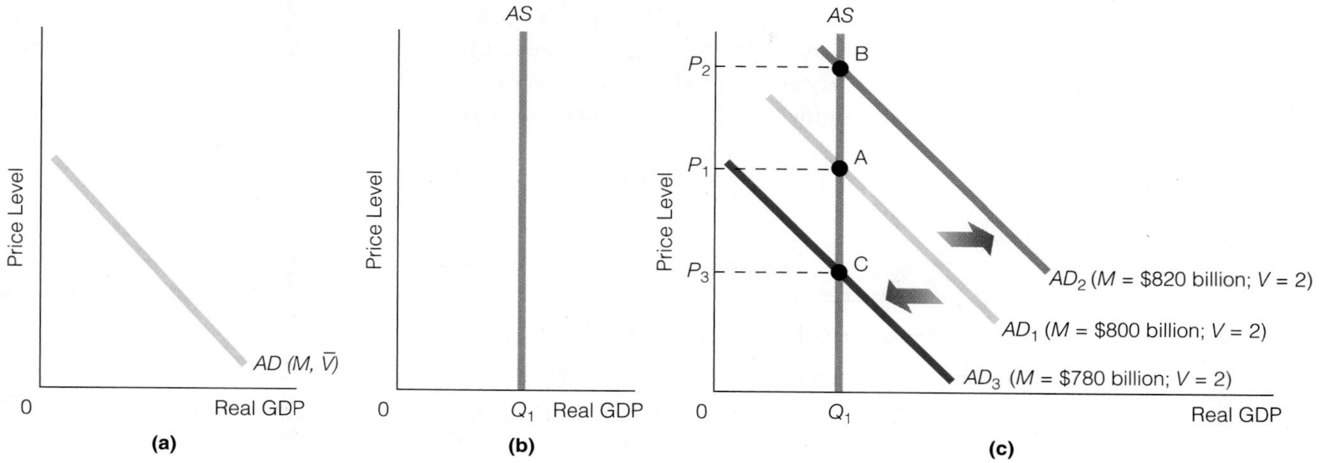

Now suppose we increase the money supply to \$820 billion, and velocity remains constant at 2. According to the simple quantity theory of money, the price level will increase, and it does. The increase in the money supply shifts the *AD* curve from AD_1 to AD_2 and pushes up the price level from P_1 to P_2.

Suppose that instead of increasing the money supply, we decrease it to \$780 billion, again with velocity remaining constant at 2. According to the simple quantity theory of money, the price level will decrease, and it does. The decrease in the money supply shifts the *AD* curve from AD_1 to AD_3 and pushes the price level down from P_1 to P_3.

Dropping the Assumptions That *V* and *Q* Are Constant

If we drop the assumptions that velocity (*V*) and Real GDP (*Q*) are constant, we have a more general theory of the factors that cause changes in the price level. Stated differently, changes in the price level depend on three variables:

1. money supply,
2. velocity, and
3. Real GDP.

Let's again start with the equation of exchange.

$$M \times V \equiv P \times Q \quad (1)$$

If the equation of exchange holds, it follows that:

$$P \equiv \frac{M \times V}{Q} \quad (2)$$

Looking at equation 2, we can see that the money supply, velocity, and Real GDP determine the price level. In other words, the price level depends on the money supply, velocity, and Real GDP.

What kinds of changes in M, V, and Q will bring about inflation (an increase in the price level)? Obviously, *ceteris paribus,* an increase in M or V or a decrease in Q will cause the price level to rise. For example, if velocity rises, *ceteris paribus,* the price level will rise. In other words, an increase in velocity is inflationary, *ceteris paribus.*

Inflationary Tendencies: $M\uparrow$, $V\uparrow$, $Q\downarrow$

What will bring about deflation (a decrease in the price level)? Obviously, *ceteris paribus,* a decrease in M or V or an increase in Q will cause the price level to fall. For example, if the money supply declines, *ceteris paribus,* the price level will drop. In other words, a decrease in the money supply is deflationary, *ceteris paribus.*

Deflationary Tendencies: $M\downarrow$, $V\downarrow$, $Q\uparrow$

SELF-TEST

(Answers to Self-Test questions are in the Self-Test Appendix.)

1. If M times V increases, why does P times Q have to rise?
2. What is the difference between the equation of exchange and the simple quantity theory of money?
3. Predict what will happen to the *AD* curve as a result of each of the following:
   a. The money supply rises.
   b. Velocity falls.
   c. The money supply rises by a greater percentage than velocity falls.
   d. The money supply falls.

MONETARISM

Economists who call themselves *monetarists* have not been content to rely on the simple quantity theory of money. They do *not* hold that velocity is constant, nor do they hold that output is constant. Monetarist views on the money supply, velocity, aggregate demand, and aggregate supply are discussed in this section.

Monetarist Views

We begin with a brief explanation of the four positions held by monetarists. Then we discuss how, based on these positions, monetarists view the economy.

VELOCITY CHANGES IN A PREDICTABLE WAY In the simple quantity theory of money, velocity is assumed to be constant; therefore, only changes in the money supply bring about changes in aggregate demand. Monetarists do not assume velocity is constant. Instead, they assume that velocity can and does change. However, monetarists believe that velocity changes in a predictable way; that is, velocity changes not randomly, but rather in a way that can be understood and predicted. Monetarists hold that velocity is a function of certain variables—the interest rate, the expected inflation rate, the frequency with which employees receive paychecks, and more—and that changes in it can be predicted.

AGGREGATE DEMAND DEPENDS ON THE MONEY SUPPLY AND ON VELOCITY Earlier, we showed that total expenditures in the economy (*TE*) equal *MV*. To better understand the economy, some economists—such as Keynesians—focus on the spending components of *TE*—*C*, *I*, *G*, *EX*, and *IM*. Other economists—such as monetarists—focus on the money supply (*M*) and velocity (*V*). For example, Keynesians often argue that changes in *C*, *I*, *G*, *EX*, or *IM* can change aggregate demand, whereas monetarists often argue that *M* and *V* can change aggregate demand.

THE *SRAS* CURVE IS UPWARD SLOPING In the simple quantity theory of money, the level of Real GDP (*Q*) is assumed to be constant in the short run. So the aggregate supply curve is vertical, as shown in Exhibit 2. According to monetarists, Real GDP may change in the short run, and therefore the *SRAS* curve is upward sloping.

THE ECONOMY IS SELF-REGULATING (PRICES AND WAGES ARE FLEXIBLE) Monetarists believe that prices and wages are flexible. It follows that monetarists believe the economy is self-regulating; it can move itself out of a recessionary or an inflationary gap and into long-run equilibrium, producing Natural Real GDP.

> **macro*theme*** ➜ Recall that some economists believe the economy is self-regulating, and other economists believe the economy is inherently unstable. For example, both classical economists and monetarists believe the economy is inherently stable (or self-regulating), whereas Keynesians believe the economy can be inherently unstable (not self-regulating).

Monetarism and *AD-AS*

If monetarists tend to stress velocity and the money supply when discussing how the economy works, what effect does this view have in the *AD-AS* framework? Exhibit 3 helps to explain some of the highlights of monetarism. Each of the four parts [(a)−(d)] is considered separately.

PART (a) The economy is initially in long-run equilibrium, producing Natural Real GDP (Q_N) at price level P_1. Monetarists believe that changes in the money supply will change aggregate demand. For example, suppose the money supply rises from $800 billion to $820 billion. If velocity is constant, the *AD* curve shifts to the right, from AD_1 to AD_2 in the exhibit. As a result, Real GDP rises to Q_1, and the price level rises to P_2. And, of course, if Real GDP rises, the unemployment rate falls, *ceteris paribus.*

According to monetarists, the economy is in an inflationary gap at Q_1. Monetarists, however, believe in a self-regulating economy. So, because the unemployment rate is less than the natural unemployment rate in an inflationary gap, soon wages will be bid up. This will cause the *SRAS* curve to shift leftward, from $SRAS_1$ to $SRAS_2$. The economy will return to long-run equilibrium, producing the same level of Real GDP as it did originally (Q_N), but at a higher price level.

We can separate what monetarists predict will happen to the economy in the short run due to an increase in the money supply from what they predict will happen in the long run. In the short run, Real GDP will rise and the unemployment rate will fall. In the long run, Real GDP will return to its natural level, as will the unemployment rate, and the price level will be higher.

PART (b) The economy is initially in long-run equilibrium, producing Natural Real GDP (Q_N) at price level P_1. A decrease in the money supply, holding velocity constant, will shift the *AD* curve to the left, from AD_1 to AD_2. This will reduce Real GDP to Q_1

exhibit 3

Monetarism in an *AD-AS* Framework

According to monetarists, changes in the money supply and velocity can change aggregate demand. In (a), an increase in the money supply shifts the *AD* curve to the right and raises Real GDP and the price level. Monetarists believe the economy is self-regulating; in time it moves back to its Natural Real GDP level at a higher price level. The same self-regulating properties are present in (b)–(d).

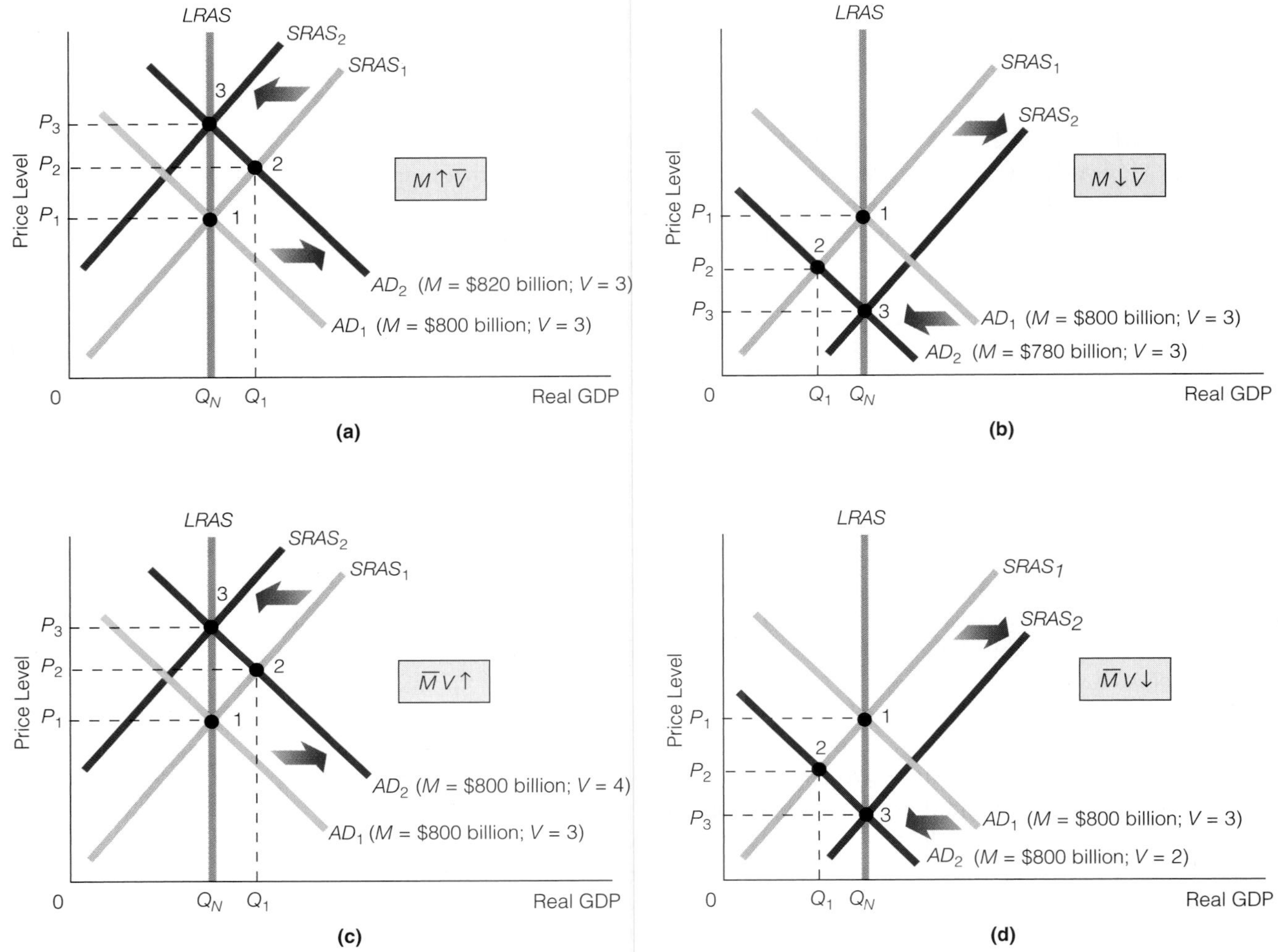

and reduce the price level to P_2. Because Real GDP has fallen, the unemployment rate will rise.

According to monetarists, the economy in part (b) is in a recessionary gap. Monetarists hold that the economy can get itself out of a recessionary gap because the economy is self-regulating. In time, wages will fall, the *SRAS* curve will shift to the right, and the economy will be back in long-run equilibrium producing Q_N, albeit at a lower price level.

Again, we separate the short-run and long-run effects of a decrease in the money supply according to monetarists. In the short run, Real GDP will fall and the unemployment rate will rise. In the long run, Real GDP will return to its natural level, as will the unemployment rate, and the price level will be lower.

PART (c) Again, we start with the economy in long-run equilibrium. Now, instead of changing the money supply, we change velocity. An increase in velocity causes the *AD* curve to shift to the right, from AD_1 to AD_2. As a result, Real GDP rises, as does the price level. The unemployment rate falls as Real GDP rises.

According to monetarists, the economy is in an inflationary gap, but in time it will move back to long-run equilibrium. So in the short run, an increase in velocity raises Real GDP and lowers the unemployment rate. In the long run, Real GDP returns to its natural level, as does the unemployment rate, and the price level is higher.

PART (d) We start with the economy in long-run equilibrium. A decrease in velocity causes the *AD* curve to shift to the left, from AD_1 to AD_2. As a result, Real GDP falls, as does the price level. The unemployment rate rises as Real GDP falls.

According to monetarists, the economy is in a recessionary gap, but in time it will move back to long-run equilibrium. So in the short run, a decrease in velocity lowers Real GDP and increases the unemployment rate. In the long run, Real GDP returns to its natural level, as does the unemployment rate, and the price level is lower.

The Monetarist View of the Economy

Based on our diagrammatic exposition of monetarism so far, we know the following about monetarists:

- Monetarists believe the economy is self-regulating.
- Monetarists believe changes in velocity and the money supply can change aggregate demand.
- Monetarists believe changes in velocity and the money supply will change the price level and Real GDP in the short run but only the price level in the long run.

We need to make one other important point with respect to monetarists, but first consider this question: Can a change in velocity offset a change in the money supply? To illustrate, suppose velocity falls and the money supply rises. By itself, a decrease in velocity will shift the *AD* curve to the left. And, by itself, an increase in the money supply will shift the *AD* curve to the right. Can the decline in velocity shift the *AD* curve to the left by the same amount as the increase in the money supply shifts the *AD* curve to the right? This is, of course, possible. If it happens, then a change in the money supply would have no effect on Real GDP, on the short-run price level, and on the long-run price level. In other words, we would have to conclude that changes in monetary policy may be ineffective at changing Real GDP and the price level.

Monetarists think that this condition—a change in velocity completely offsetting a change in the money supply—does not occur often. They believe (1) velocity does not change very much from one period to the next (i.e., it is relatively stable) and (2) changes in velocity are predictable (as mentioned earlier). In other words, monetarists believe velocity is relatively stable and predictable.

So in the monetarist view of the economy, changes in velocity are not likely to offset changes in the money supply. Therefore, *changes in the money supply will largely determine changes in aggregate demand and thus changes in Real GDP and the price level.* For all practical purposes, an increase in the money supply will raise aggregate demand, increase both Real GDP and the price level in the short run, and increase the price level in the long run. A decrease in the money supply will lower aggregate demand, decrease both Real GDP and the price level in the short run, and decrease the price level in the long run.

SELF-TEST

1. What do monetarists predict will happen in the short run and in the long run as a result of each of the following? (In each case, assume the economy is currently in long-run equilibrium.)
   a. Velocity rises.
   b. Velocity falls.
   c. The money supply rises.
   d. The money supply falls.
2. Can a change in velocity offset a change in the money supply (on aggregate demand)? Explain your answer.

INFLATION

In everyday usage, the word *inflation* refers to any increase in the price level. Economists, though, like to differentiate between two types of increases in the price level: a one-shot increase and a continued increase.

One-Shot Inflation

One-Shot Inflation
A one-time increase in the price level. An increase in the price level that does not continue.

One-shot inflation is exactly what it sounds like: a one-shot, or one-time, increase in the price level. Suppose the CPI for years 1 to 5 is as follows:

Year	CPI
1	100
2	110
3	110
4	110
5	110

Notice that the price level is higher in year 2 than in year 1, but after year 2 it does not change. In other words, it takes a one-shot jump in year 2 and then stabilizes. This is an example of one-shot inflation, which can originate on either the demand side or the supply side of the economy.

ONE-SHOT INFLATION: DEMAND-SIDE INDUCED In Exhibit 4(a), the economy is initially in long-run equilibrium at point 1. Suppose the aggregate demand curve shifts rightward from AD_1 to AD_2. As this happens, the economy moves to point 2, where the price level is P_2. At point 2 in Exhibit 4(b), the Real GDP the economy is producing (Q_2) is greater than Natural Real GDP; so the unemployment rate in the economy is lower than the natural unemployment rate. Consequently, as old wage contracts expire, workers are paid higher wage rates because unemployment is relatively low. As wage rates rise, the *SRAS* curve shifts leftward from $SRAS_1$ to $SRAS_2$. The long-run equilibrium position is at point 3. The price level and Real GDP at each of the three points are as follows:

Point	Price Level	Real GDP
1 (start)	P_1	$Q_1 = Q_N$
2	P_2	Q_2
3 (end)	P_3	$Q_1 = Q_N$

Notice that at point 3 the economy is at a higher price level than at point 1 but at the same Real GDP level.

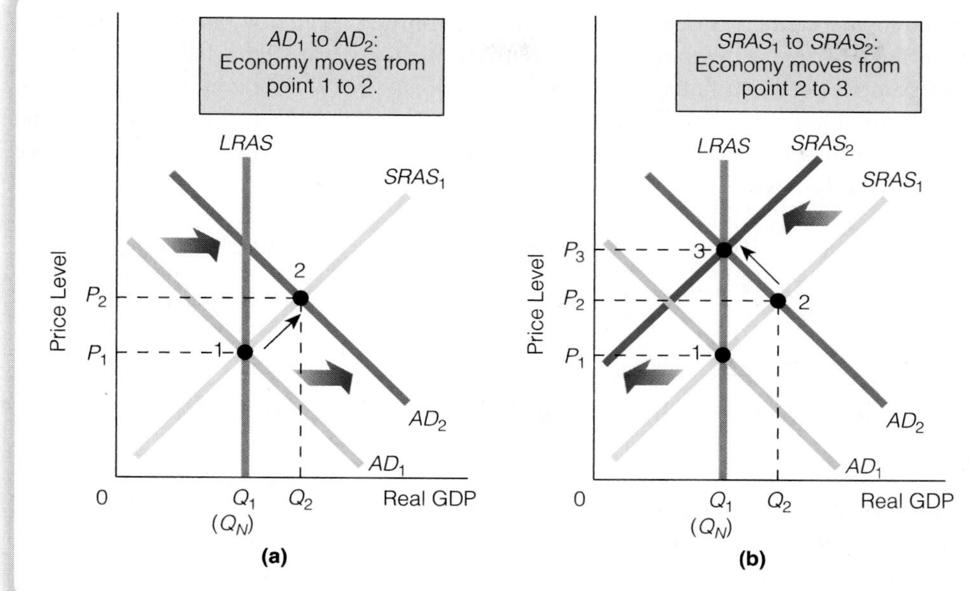

exhibit 4

One-Shot Inflation: Demand-Side Induced

(a) The aggregate demand curve shifts rightward from AD_1 to AD_2. As a result, the price level increases from P_1 to P_2; the economy moves from point 1 to point 2. (b) Because the Real GDP the economy produces (Q_2) is greater than Natural Real GDP, the unemployment rate that exists is less than the natural unemployment rate. Wage rates rise, and the short-run aggregate supply curve shifts leftward from $SRAS_1$ to $SRAS_2$. Long-run equilibrium is at point 3.

Because the price level goes from P_1 to P_2 to P_3, you may think we have more than a one-shot increase in the price level. But because the price level stabilizes (at P_3), we cannot characterize it as continually rising. So the change in the price level is representative of one-shot inflation.

ONE-SHOT INFLATION: SUPPLY-SIDE INDUCED In Exhibit 5(a), the economy is initially in long-run equilibrium at point 1. Suppose the short-run aggregate supply curve shifts leftward from $SRAS_1$ to $SRAS_2$, say, because oil prices increase. As this happens, the economy moves to point 2, where the price level is P_2.

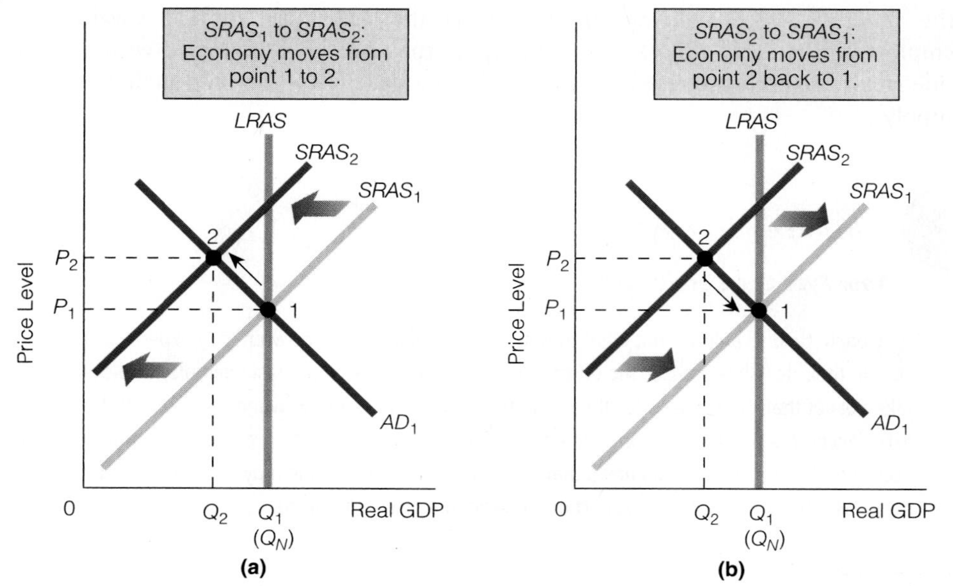

exhibit 5

One-Shot Inflation: Supply-Side Induced

(a) The short-run aggregate supply curve shifts leftward from $SRAS_1$ to $SRAS_2$. As a result, the price level increases from P_1 to P_2; the economy moves from point 1 to point 2.
(b) Because the Real GDP the economy produces (Q_2) is less than Natural Real GDP, the unemployment rate that exists is greater than the natural unemployment rate. Some economists argue that when this happens, wage rates will fall and the short-run aggregate supply curve will shift rightward from $SRAS_2$ (back to $SRAS_1$). Long-run equilibrium is at point 1.

At point 2 in Exhibit 5(b), the Real GDP the economy is producing (Q_2) is less than Natural Real GDP; so the unemployment rate in the economy is greater than the natural unemployment rate. Consequently, as old wage contracts expire, workers are paid lower wage rates because unemployment is relatively high. As wage rates fall, the short-run aggregate supply curve shifts rightward from $SRAS_2$ to $SRAS_1$. The long-run equilibrium position is at point 1 again. (If wage rates are somewhat inflexible, it may take a long time to move from point 2 back to point 1.) The price level and Real GDP at each of the three points are as follows:

Point	Price Level	Real GDP
1 (start)	P_1	$Q_1 = Q_N$
2	P_2	Q_2
1 (end)	P_1	$Q_1 = Q_N$

Because the price level initially increased from P_1 to P_2, this case is descriptive of one-shot inflation.

CONFUSING DEMAND-INDUCED AND SUPPLY-INDUCED ONE-SHOT INFLATION Demand-induced and supply-induced types of one-shot inflation are easy to confuse.[2] To illustrate, suppose the Federal Reserve System increases the money supply. With more money in the economy, there can be greater total spending at any given price level. Consequently, the *AD* curve shifts rightward.

Next, prices begin to rise. Soon after, wage rates begin to rise (because the economy is in an inflationary gap). Many employers, perhaps unaware that the money supply has increased, certainly are aware that they are paying their employees higher wages. Thus, the employers may think the higher price level is due to higher wage rates, not to the increased money supply that preceded the higher wage rates. But they would be wrong. What may look like a supply-induced rise in the price level is really a demand-induced rise in the price level.

We can tell this same story in terms of the diagrams in Exhibit 4. In (a), the *AD* curve shifts rightward because, as we said, the money supply increases. Employers, however, are unaware of what has happened in part (a). What they see is part (b). They end up paying higher wage rates to their employees, and the *SRAS* curve shifts leftward. Unaware that the *AD* curve shifted rightward in (a) and that the *SRAS* curve shifted leftward in (b), employers mistakenly conclude that the rise in the price level originated with a supply-side factor (higher wage rates), not with a demand-side factor (an increase in the money supply).

Thinking like AN ECONOMIST

Your Eyes Can Deceive You

People tend to believe that what they see with their own eyes or what they experience directly in their daily lives causes the effects they notice. Witness, in our last example, employers' mistaken belief that the stimulus for the rise in the price level is a rise in wage rates (which they had experienced firsthand), not an increase in the money supply (which they probably did not know had occurred). But the economist knows that the cause of a phenomenon may be far removed from our personal orbit. This awareness is part of the economic way of thinking.

2. Sometimes the terms *demand-side inflation* and *supply-side inflation* are used.

economics 24/7

GRADE INFLATION: IT'S ALL RELATIVE

Inflation can sometimes be deceptive. To illustrate, suppose Jones produces and sells motorcycles. The average price for one of his motorcycles is $10,000. Unknown to Jones, the Fed increases the money supply. Months pass, and then one day Jones notices that the demand for his motorcycles has increased. Jones raises the prices of his motorcycles and earns a higher dollar income.

©NAJLAH FEANNY/CORBIS

Jones is excited about earning more income, but soon he realizes that the prices of many of the things he buys have increased too. Food, clothing, and housing prices have all gone up. Jones is earning a higher dollar income, but he is also paying higher prices. In relative terms, Jones's financial position may be the same as it was before the price of motorcycles increased.

Now let's consider grade inflation. Beginning in the 1960s, the average GPA at most colleges and universities across the country began to rise. Whereas professors once gave out the full range of grades—A, B, C, D, and F—today many professors give only As and Bs and a few Cs. It's been said that the so-called Gentleman's C, once a mainstay on many college campuses, has been replaced by the Gentleperson's B.

Grade inflation can deceive you, just as general price inflation deceived Jones. To illustrate, suppose you get higher grades (without studying more or working harder). Your average grade goes from, say, C+ to B, and you believe you have an advantage over other college and university students. You reason that, with higher grades, you will have a better chance of getting a good job or of getting into graduate school.

But this is true only if your grades go up *and no one else's do.* In other words, your relative position must improve. But grade inflation at thousands of colleges and universities across the country prevents this from happening. You get higher grades, but so does everyone else. Your GPA increases from, say, 2.90 to 3.60, but other students' GPAs also increase similarly.

So, as long as other students are getting higher grades too, better grades for you do not necessarily make it easier for you to compete with others for a job or for admission to graduate school. In essence, grade inflation, like general price inflation, is deceptive. With price inflation, you may initially think your financial position has improved because you are earning more for what you sell, but then you realize that you have to pay more for the things you buy. With grade inflation, you may initially think you have an advantage over other students because you are receiving higher grades, but then you learn that everyone else is getting higher grades too. Your relative position may be the same as it was before grade inflation boosted your grades.

Finding ECONOMICS

In a Remodeling Job

Jan is getting her house remodeled. Today her contractor told her that the price he pays for many of his supplies has increased and that the remodeling is going to end up costing "a little more." That night, Jan says to her husaband, Mike, "I guess that is the way life is sometimes. Costs go up, so prices go up." Where is the economics? Could Jan be the reason her contractor's costs went up?

What Jan may not see is that she and others who want their houses remodeled are increasing the demand for remodeling. As a result, the demand for things such as tile, wood, nails, cement, and other such things rises. The higher prices for tile, nails, and wood are the higher costs the remodeler is talking about; so when he tells Jan his costs have risen, he is telling the truth. Jan then blames the higher costs for her having to pay more for her remodeling job. Actually, the higher demand stemming from her and others starts the process that ends in higher costs for the remodeler and higher prices for her.

exhibit 6

Changing One-Shot Inflation into Continued Inflation

(a) The aggregate demand curve shifts rightward from AD_1 to AD_2. The economy initially moves from point 1 to point 2 and finally to point 3. Continued increases in the price level are brought about through continued increases in aggregate demand. (b) The short-run aggregate supply curve shifts leftward from $SRAS_1$ to $SRAS_2$. The economy initially moves from point 1 to point 2. The economy will return to point 1 unless there is an increase in aggregate demand. We see here, as in (a), that continued increases in the price level are brought about through continued increases in aggregate demand.

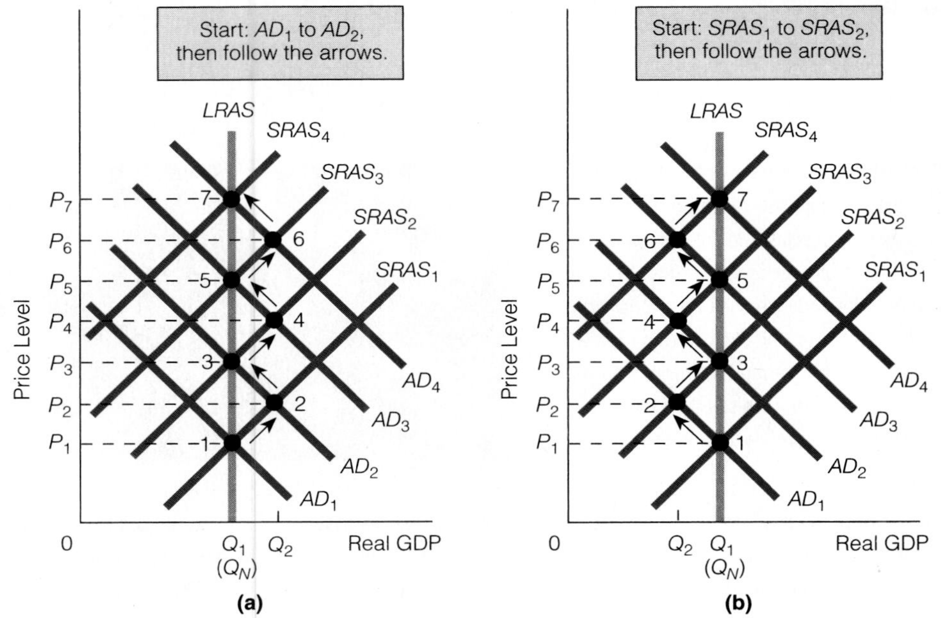

Continued Inflation

Suppose the CPI for years 1 to 5 is as follows:

Year	CPI
1	100
2	110
3	120
4	130
5	140

Notice that the CPI goes from 100 to 110, then from 110 to 120, and so on. Each year the CPI is higher than the year before. There is a continued increase in the price level. This is an example of **continued inflation.**

Continued Inflation
A continued increase in the price level.

FROM ONE-SHOT INFLATION TO CONTINUED INFLATION Continued increases in aggregate demand can turn one-shot inflation into continued inflation. (Later we describe what leads to continued increases in aggregate demand.) The process is illustrated in Exhibit 6. (The diagram looks scary, but it isn't when you take it one step at a time.)

Beginning at point 1 in Exhibit 6(a), the aggregate demand curve shifts rightward from AD_1 to AD_2. The economy moves from point 1 to point 2. At point 2, the unemployment rate in the economy is less than the natural unemployment rate. As a result, wage rates rise and cause the short-run aggregate supply curve to shift leftward from $SRAS_1$ to $SRAS_2$. The economy moves from point 2 to point 3. At point 3, the economy is in long-run equilibrium.

Suppose that at point 3 the economy experiences *another* rightward shift in the aggregate demand curve (to AD_3). The process repeats itself, and the economy moves from point 3 to point 4 to point 5. Still *another* rightward shift in the aggregate demand curve moves the economy from point 5 to point 6 to point 7. We have stopped at point 7, but we could have continued. Notice that the result of this process is a *continually rising price level*—from P_1 to P_7 and beyond. Continued increases in aggregate demand cause continued inflation.

Now let's look at continued inflation from the supply side of the economy. Beginning at point 1 in Exhibit 6(b), the short-run aggregate supply curve shifts leftward from $SRAS_1$ to $SRAS_2$. The economy moves from point 1 to point 2. At point 2, the unemployment rate in the economy is greater than the natural unemployment rate. According to some economists, there is a natural tendency for wage rates to fall and for the *SRAS* curve to shift rightward, moving the economy back to point 1.

This natural tendency of the economy to return to point 1 will be offset, however, if the aggregate demand curve shifts rightward. Then, instead of moving from point 2 back to point 1, the economy moves from point 2 to point 3. At point 3, the economy is in long-run equilibrium, and a higher price level exists than existed at point 2.

Suppose the economy experiences another leftward shift in the aggregate supply curve (to $SRAS_3$). The economy moves from point 3 to point 4 and would naturally return to point 3 unless the aggregate demand curve shifts rightward. If the latter occurs, the economy moves to point 5. The same process moves the economy from point 5 to point 6 to point 7, where we have decided to stop. Notice that this process results in a continually rising price level—from P_1 to P_7 and beyond. Again, *continued increases in aggregate demand cause continued inflation.*

CAN CONTINUED DECLINES IN *SRAS* CAUSE CONTINUED INFLATION?
A natural question might be, can continued declines in *SRAS* cause continued inflation? For example, suppose a labor union continually asks for and receives higher wages. As wages continually increase, the *SRAS* curve will continually shift leftward, leading to a continually rising price level. This could happen, but it isn't likely. Every time workers ask for and receive higher wages—shifting the *SRAS* curve leftward—Real GDP declines. And not as many workers are needed to produce a lower Real GDP as are needed to produce a higher Real GDP; so some of the workers will lose their jobs. It is doubtful labor unions would adopt a policy that put increasingly more of their members out of work.

Let's consider another argument against continued declines in *SRAS* causing continued inflation. If you check the CPI and the Real GDP level for, say, 1960, you will find that both CPI and Real GDP today are higher than they were in 1960. The higher price level means that, since 1960, we have experienced continued inflation in the United States but that this continued inflation has accompanied (generally) a rising Real GDP. If the continued inflation of the past few decades had been caused by continued declines in *SRAS*, we wouldn't have had a rising Real GDP. We would have had a falling Real GDP (as *SRAS* declines, the price level rises and Real GDP falls). In short, the continued inflation in the United States had to be caused by continued increases in *AD*, not by continued decreases in *SRAS*.

THE BIG QUESTION: WHAT CAUSES CONTINUED INCREASES IN AGGREGATE DEMAND? If continued increases in aggregate demand cause continued inflation, what causes continued increases in aggregate demand? At a given price level, anything that increases total expenditures increases aggregate demand and shifts the *AD* curve to the right. With this in mind, consider an increase in the money supply. With more money in the economy, there can be greater total expenditures at a given price level. Consequently, aggregate demand increases, and the *AD* curve shifts rightward.

Economists are widely agreed that the only factor that can change continually in such a way as to bring about continued increases in aggregate demand is the money supply.

economics 24/7

GLOBALIZATION AND INFLATION

The specialization brought about by economic integration may raise an economy's growth rate if it prompts specialization in dynamic sectors.

—Mark A. Wynne and Erasmus K. Kersting[3]

In recent years economists have been studying the effects of globalization on the domestic price level. Before we discuss the relationship between globalization and inflation, let's define what we mean by globalization. Globalization is the increased interdependence of national economies, as evidenced by greater flows of goods and services and capital across borders. Put simply, in a fully globalized world, goods and services and capital move as easily between countries as they currently do within them.

Given that defintion, how does globalization affect the domestic price level? We can reach one answer by combining what we know about the exchange equation with what we know about the benefits of specialization.

1. In Chapter 2, we explained how specialization could increase output. In short, if individuals specialize in the production of a good or service in which they have a comparative advantage (that is, if they produce their good or service at lower opportunity cost than that at which others can produce it), overall output will increase. So specialization leads to increased output.
2. With respect to globalization and specialization, there is some empirical evidence that globalization (increased economic integration) leads to more specialization. Some economists, dating back to Adam Smith, argue that this comes from the increased size of the market that comes with globalization. In other words, specialization is greater when the market is potentially one billion customers than when it is 100 million potential customers.

Combining these two points, we can say that globalization leads to greater specialization, which leads to greater output.

Globalization →

Increased specialization →

Greater output

With respect to the price level, according to the equation of exchange ($MV \equiv PQ$), the greater the rise is in the quantity of output (Q), the less the price level will rise for any given rise in the money supply (M). To illustrate, suppose that velocity (V) is constant, the money supply increases by 5 percent, and quantity of output (Q) rises by 2 percent. According to the equation of exchange, the price level will rise by 3 percent. But now consider how much the price level would rise if the quantity of output (Q) rises by 4 percent instead of 2 percent. The price level would rise by only 1 percent. In other words, the greater the rise in output is, the smaller the rise is in the price level.

Our final point: Globalization leads to greater specialization, which leads to greater increases in output, which in turn lead to smaller increases in the price level (for any given rise in the money supply). Globalization keeps the inflation rate lower than it would be if globalization did not exist.

Globalization →

Increased specialization →

Greater output →

Smaller rise in the price level for any given rise in the money supply

3. "Openness and Inflation," in Staff Papers of the Federal Reserve Bank of Dallas, No. 2, November 2007.

Specifically, continued increases in the money supply lead to continued increases in aggregate demand, which generate continued inflation.

Continued increases in the money supply → Continued increases in aggregate demand → Continued inflation

The money supply is the *only* factor that can continually increase without causing a reduction in one of the four components of total expenditures—consumption, investment, government purchases, or net exports. This point is important because someone might ask, can't government purchases continually increase and so cause continued inflation? This is unlikely to occur for two reasons:

- Government purchases cannot go beyond both real and political limits. The real upper limit is 100 percent of GDP. We do not know what the political upper limit is, but it is likely to be less than 100 percent of GDP. In either case, once the limit is reached, government purchases can no longer increase.
- Some economists argue that government purchases that are not financed with new money may crowd out one of the other expenditure components. (See the discussion of crowding out in Chapter 10.) Thus, increases in government purchases are not guaranteed to raise total expenditures because, if government purchases rise, consumption may fall to the degree that government purchases have increased. For example, for every additional dollar government spends on public education, households may spend $1 less on private education.

The emphasis on the money supply as the only factor that can continue to increase and thus cause continued inflation has led most economists to agree with Nobel Laureate Milton Friedman that "inflation is always and everywhere a monetary phenomenon."

SELF-TEST

1. The prices of houses, cars, and television sets have increased. Has there been inflation?
2. Is continued inflation likely to be supply side induced? Explain your answer.
3. What type of inflation is Milton Friedman referring to when he says that "inflation is always and everywhere a monetary phenomenon"?

MONEY AND INTEREST RATES

Let's review how changes in the money supply affect different economic variables.

What Economic Variables Are Affected by a Change in the Money Supply?

Throughout this text, we have talked about money and shown how changes in the money supply affect different economic variables. Specifically:

1. *Money and the supply of loans.* The last chapter discussed the actions of the Fed that change the money supply. For example, when the Fed undertakes an open market purchase, the money supply increases, as do reserves in the banking system. With greater reserves, banks can extend more loans. In other words, as a result of the Fed's conducting an open market purchase, the supply of loans rises. Similarly, when the Fed conducts an open market sale, the supply of loans decreases.
2. *Money and Real GDP.* This chapter shows how a change in the money supply can change aggregate demand and thereby change the price level and Real GDP in the short run. For example, look back at Exhibit 3(a). The economy starts at point 1, producing Q_N. An increase in the money supply shifts the AD curve rightward, from AD_1 to AD_2. In the short run, the economy moves to point 2 and produces a higher level of Real GDP (Q_1). Similarly, in the short run, a decrease in the money supply produces a lower level of Real GDP [see Exhibit 3(b)].
3. *Money and the price level.* This chapter also shows how a change in the money supply can change the price level. Again, look back at Exhibit 3(a). Initially, at point 1, the price level is P_1. An increase in the money supply shifts the AD curve rightward, from

AD_1 to AD_2. In the short run, the price level in the economy moves from P_1 to P_2. In the long run, the economy is at point 3 and the price level is P_3. Exhibit 3(b) shows how a decrease in the money supply affects the price level.

Thus, we know that changes in the money supply affect (1) the supply of loans, (2) Real GDP, and (3) the price level. Is there anything else the money supply can affect? Many economists say that, because the money supply affects the price level, it also affects the *expected inflation rate*, which is the inflation rate that you expect. For example, your expected inflation rate—the inflation rate you expect will be realized over the next year—may be 5 percent, 6 percent, or a different rate. Changes in the money supply affect the expected inflation rate, either directly or indirectly. We know from working with the equation of exchange that the greater the increase in the money supply is, the greater the rise in the price level will be. And we would expect that the greater the rise in the price level is, the higher the expected inflation rate will be, *ceteris paribus.* For example, we would predict that a money supply growth rate of, say, 10 percent a year generates a greater actual inflation rate and a larger expected inflation rate than a money supply growth rate of 2 percent a year.

So changes in the money supply (or changes in the rate of growth of the money supply) can affect:

1. the supply of loans,
2. Real GDP,
3. the price level, and
4. the expected inflation rate.

The Money Supply, the Loanable Funds Market, and Interest Rates

Exhibit 7(a) shows the loanable funds market. The demand for loanable funds is downward sloping, indicating that borrowers will borrow more funds as the interest rate declines. The supply of loanable funds is upward sloping, indicating that lenders will lend more funds as the interest rate rises. The equilibrium interest rate (i_1 percent) is determined through the forces of supply and demand. If there is a surplus of loanable funds, the interest rate falls; if there is a shortage of loanable funds, the interest rate rises.

Anything that affects either the supply of loanable funds or the demand for loanable funds will obviously affect the interest rate. All four of the factors that are affected by changes in the money supply—the supply of loans, Real GDP, the price level, and the expected inflation rate—affect either the supply of or demand for loanable funds.

THE SUPPLY OF LOANS A Fed open market purchase increases reserves in the banking system and therefore increases the supply of loanable funds. As a result, the interest rate declines [see Exhibit 7(b)]. This change in the interest rate due to a change in the supply of loanable funds is called the **liquidity effect**.

Liquidity Effect
The change in the interest rate due to a change in the supply of loanable funds.

REAL GDP A change in Real GDP affects both the supply of and demand for loanable funds. To understand this, you need to realize that there is (1) a link between supplying bonds and demanding loanable funds and (2) a link between demanding bonds and supplying loanable funds. In other words,

To *supply bonds* is to *demand loanable funds.*

To *demand bonds* is to *supply loanable funds.*

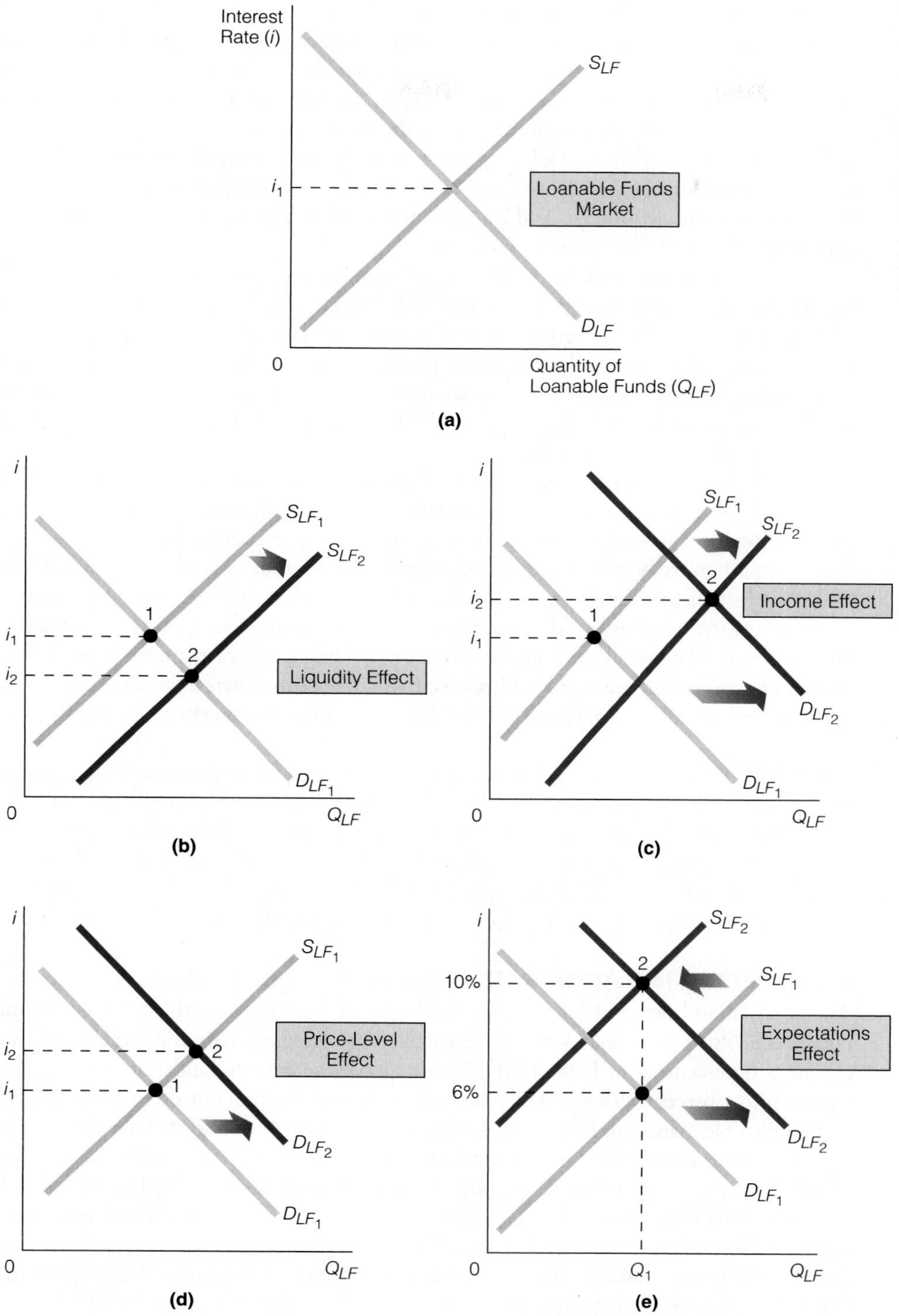

exhibit 7

The Interest Rate and the Loanable Funds Market

The loanable funds market is shown in part (a). The demand for loanable funds is downward sloping; the supply of loanable funds is upward sloping. Part (b) shows the liquidity effect, part (c) shows the income effect, part (d) shows the price-level effect, and part (e) shows the expectations effect.

To explain, suppose that corporations are the only economic actors who supply (sell) bonds and that people (like you) are the only economic actors who demand (buy) bonds. When a corporation supplies a bond, it is effectively seeking to borrow funds from you. It is saying, "If you will buy this bond from the corporation for, say, $10,000, the corporation promises to repay you $11,000 at a specified date in the future." Thus, by supplying bonds for sale, the corporation demands loanable funds from you, and you, if you buy or demand the bonds, supply loanable funds to the corporation.

Think of a simpler transaction to understand how you can supply one thing when you demand something else. When you *supply* the desk for sale that you produced, aren't you effectively *demanding* money? And isn't the person who buys, or *demands,* the desk from you effectively *supplying* money to you?

Given this background, let's ask two questions. First, how does Real GDP affect the supply of loanable funds? When Real GDP rises, people's wealth is greater. (Real GDP consists of goods, and goods are one component of wealth.) When people become wealthier, they often demand more bonds (in much the same way that they may demand more houses, cars, and jewelry). But, as we have just learned, to demand more bonds is to supply more loanable funds. So, when Real GDP rises, people (demand more bonds and thereby) supply more loanable funds.

Second, how does Real GDP affect the demand for loanable funds? When Real GDP rises, profitable business opportunities usually abound. Businesses decide to issue or supply more bonds to take advantage of these profitable opportunities. But, again, we know that to supply more bonds is to demand more loanable funds. So, when Real GDP rises, corporations issue, or supply, more bonds, and thereby demand more loanable funds.

In summary, when Real GDP increases, both the supply of and demand for loanable funds increase. The overall effect on the interest rate? Usually, the demand for loanable funds increases by more than the supply of loanable funds so that the interest rate rises. The change in the interest rate due to a change in Real GDP is called the **income effect**. See Exhibit 7(c).

Income Effect
The change in the interest rate due to a change in Real GDP.

THE PRICE LEVEL Chapter 7 discusses why the *AD* curve slopes downward. A downward-sloping *AD* curve is explained by (1) the real balance effect, (2) the interest rate effect, and (3) the international trade effect. With respect to the interest rate effect, when the price level rises, the purchasing power of money falls, and people may increase their demand for credit or loanable funds to borrow the funds necessary to buy a fixed bundle of goods. This change in the interest rate due to a change in the price level is called the **price-level effect**. See Exhibit 7(d).

Price-Level Effect
The change in the interest rate due to a change in the price level.

THE EXPECTED INFLATION RATE A change in the expected inflation rate affects both the supply of and demand for loanable funds. To see how, suppose the expected inflation rate is zero. Also assume that, when the expected inflation rate is zero, the equilibrium interest rate is 6 percent, as in Exhibit 7(e). Now suppose the expected inflation rate rises from 0 percent to 4 percent. What will this rise in the expected inflation rate do to the demand for and supply of loanable funds? Borrowers (demanders of loanable funds) will be willing to pay 4 percent more interest for their loans because they expect to be paying back the loans with dollars that have 4 percent less buying power than the dollars they are being lent. (Look at this in another way: If they wait to buy goods, the prices of the goods they want will have risen by 4 percent. To beat the price rise, they are willing to pay up to 4 percent more to borrow and purchase the goods now.) In effect, the demand for loanable funds curve shifts rightward so that at Q_1 borrowers are willing to pay a 4 percent higher interest rate. See Exhibit 7(e).

On the other side of the loanable funds market, the lenders (the suppliers of loanable funds) require a 4 percent higher interest rate to compensate them for the 4 percent less valuable dollars in which the loan will be repaid. In effect, the supply of loanable funds curve shifts leftward, so that at Q_1 lenders will receive an interest rate of 10 percent. See Exhibit 7(e).

Thus an expected inflation rate of 4 percent increases the demand for loanable funds and decreases the supply of loanable funds so that the interest rate is 4 percent higher than it was when the expected inflation rate was zero. A change in the interest rate due to a change in the expected inflation rate is referred to as the **expectations effect** (or *Fisher effect*, after economist Irving Fisher).

Exhibit 8 summarizes how a change in the money supply directly and indirectly affects the interest rate.

exhibit 8

How the Fed Affects the Interest Rate

This exhibit summarizes the way the Fed (through its monetary policy) affects the interest rate. For example, an open market operation (OMO) directly affects the supply of loanable funds and affects the interest rate. An OMO also affects Real GDP, the price level, and the expected inflation rate, and therefore indirectly affects either the supply of or demand for loanable funds, which in turn affects the interest rate.

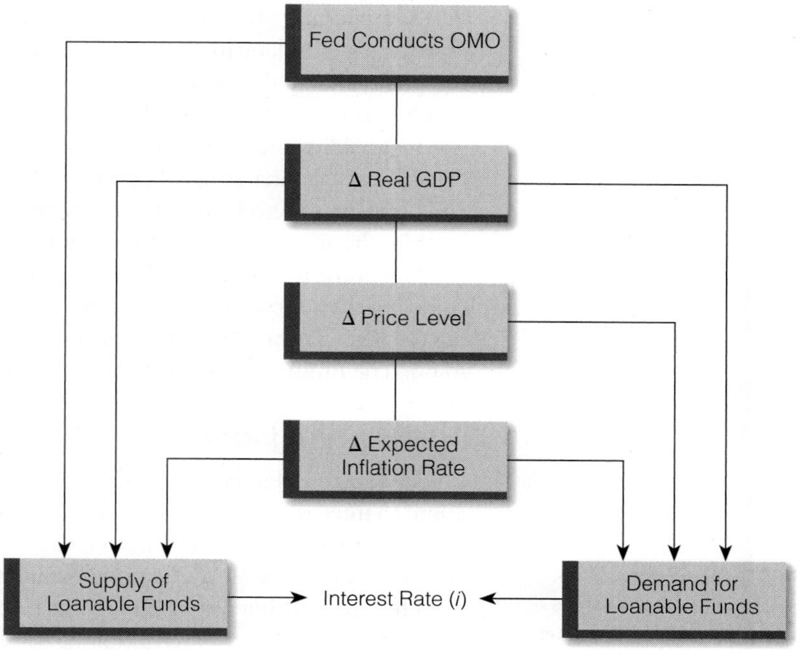

THE DIFFERENCE BETWEEN THE PRICE-LEVEL EFFECT AND THE EXPECTATIONS EFFECT To many people, the price-level effect sounds the same as the expectations effect. After all, both have something to do with the price level. But they are different. To illustrate the difference, consider a one-shot change in the money supply that ultimately moves the price level from a price index of 120 to a price index of 135. The price-level effect refers to the change in the interest rate that is related to the fact that the actual price level is rising. Think of the demand for loanable funds creeping up steadily as the price index rises from 120 to 121 to 122 to 123 and so on to 135. Once the price index hits 135, there is no further reason for the demand for loanable funds to rise because the price level isn't rising any more. Now, as the price level is rising, people's expected inflation rate is rising. They may feel they know where the price level is headed (from 120 to 135) and adjust accordingly. Once the price level hits 135 (and given the change in the money supply is one-shot), the expected inflation rate falls to zero. In other words, any change in the interest rate due to a rise in the expected inflation rate is now over, and therefore the expected inflation rate no longer has an effect on the interest rate. But certainly the price level still has an effect on the interest rate because the price level is higher than it was originally. In the end, the effect on the interest rate due to a rise in the price level remains, and the effect on the interest rate due to a rise in the expected inflation rate disappears.

Expectations Effect
The change in the interest rate due to a change in the expected inflation rate.

What Happens to the Interest Rate as the Money Supply Changes?

Suppose the Fed decides to raise the rate of growth of the money supply from, say, 3 percent to 5 percent a year. What effect does this have on the interest rate? Some people will quickly say that it will lower the interest rate, thinking perhaps that the only effect on the interest rate is the liquidity effect. In other words, as the Fed increases the rate of growth of the money supply, more reserves enter the banking system, more loans are extended, and the interest rate falls.

That would be the right answer if all an increase in the money supply growth rate did was to affect the supply of loanable funds. But, as explained, this isn't the only effect. Real

GDP changes, the price level changes, and the expected inflation rate changes, and changes in these factors affect the loanable funds market just as the Fed action did. Figuring out what happens to the interest rate is a matter of trying to figure out when each effect (liquidity, income, price-level, and expectations) occurs and how strong each effect is.

To illustrate, suppose everyone expects the Fed to continue to increase the money supply at a growth rate of 2 percent a year. Then, on January 1, the Fed announces that it will increase the rate of growth in the money supply to 4 percent and will begin open market purchases to effect this outcome immediately. One second after the announcement, people's expected inflation rate may rise. In other words, the expectations effect begins to affect interest rates immediately. On January 2, the interest rate is therefore higher than it was one day earlier. At this point, a natural conclusion would be that an increase in the rate of growth in the money supply *raises* the interest rate. The problem with this conclusion, though, is that not all the effects (liquidity, income, etc.) have occurred yet. In time, the liquidity effect puts downward pressure on the interest rate. Suppose this begins to happen on January 15, and the interest rate begins to fall from what it was on January 2. Then, someone on January 15 could say, "Obviously, an increase in the rate of growth of the money supply *lowers* interest rates."

The point is that a change in the money supply affects the economy in many ways—changing the supply of loanable funds directly, changing Real GDP and therefore changing the demand for and supply of loanable funds, changing the expected inflation rate, and so on. The timing and magnitude of these effects determine changes in the interest rate.

The Nominal and Real Interest Rates

If you were to call a bank and ask what it charges for a given type of loan, the bank would quote an interest rate. The quoted interest rate is the rate we have been discussing, the interest rate that comes about through the interaction of the demand for and supply of loanable funds. Sometimes, this interest rate is called the **nominal interest rate**, or market interest rate.

Nominal Interest Rate
The interest rate actually charged (or paid) in the market; the market interest rate. Nominal interest rate = Real interest rate + Expected inflation rate.

The nominal interest rate may not be the true cost of borrowing because part of the nominal interest rate is a reflection of the expected inflation rate. To illustrate, let's suppose the nominal interest rate is 9 percent, and the expected inflation rate is 2 percent. If you take out a loan for $10,000 at 9 percent, you will have to pay back the loan amount ($10,000) plus $900 in interest at the end of the year. In other words, for a $10,000 loan, you will have to repay $10,900.

Now let's suppose the expected inflation rate turns out to be the actual inflation rate. As an example, people expect the inflation rate to be 2 percent, and it turns out to be 2 percent. In this case, the dollars you pay back will be worth less than the dollars you borrowed—by 2 percent. In other words, you borrowed dollars that were worth 2 percent more in purchasing power than the dollars you repaid.

This fact should be taken into account in determining your real cost of borrowing. Economists would say that the real cost of borrowing was not 9 percent, but 7 percent. The real cost of borrowing is sometimes called the **real interest rate**, which is equal to the nominal interest rate minus the expected inflation rate.[4]

Real Interest Rate
The nominal interest rate minus the expected inflation rate. When the expected inflation rate is zero, the real interest rate equals the nominal interest rate.

$$\text{Real interest rate} = \text{Nominal interest rate} - \text{Expected inflation rate}$$

Given this equation, the nominal interest rate is therefore equal to the real interest rate plus the expected inflation rate.

$$\text{Nominal interest rate} = \text{Real interest rate} + \text{Expected inflation rate}$$

4. A broader definition is Real interest rate = Nominal interest rate − Expected rate of change in the price level. This definition is useful because we will not always be dealing with an expected inflation rate; we could be dealing with an expected deflation rate.

office hours

"DO CHANGES IN THE MONEY SUPPLY AFFECT REAL GDP?"

Student:
Do changes in the money supply affect Real GDP?

Instructor:
Let's go over what we have learned in this chapter. Take another look at Exhibit 2(c), which illustrates the simple quantity of money in terms of the *AD-AS* framework. Notice in particular that the *AS* curve is vertical; in other words, changes in the money supply, which then lead to a change in aggregate demand, do not change Real GDP. Changes in the money supply change only the price level. You can see this if you compare AD_1 in the exhibit with either AD_2 or AD_3.

Student:
So according to the simple quantity theory of money, changes in the money supply affect only the price level and not Real GDP.

Instructor:
That's correct. But now let's turn to Exhibit 3(a). In that exhibit, notice the two aggregate supply curves: *SRAS* and *LRAS*. Notice that the *SRAS* curve is upward sloping and the *LRAS* curve is vertical. Now let's shift the *AD* curve from AD_1 to AD_2 as a result of an increase in the money supply. Real GDP rises as a result of an increase in the money supply, but only in the short run. In the long run, Real GDP returns to the level we started at, Q_N.

Student:
This is the monetarist model, right? So what do we conclude?

Instructor:
Yes it is. We conclude that, using the monetarist model, changes in the money supply do affect Real GDP in the short run, but not in the long run. We can also say that the monetarist model, like the simple quantity theory of money, shows that changes in the money supply do affect the price level.

Student:
It seems to me that, in the long run, monetarism and the simple quantity theory of money are consistent. In other words, both say that money supply changes affect the price level but not Real GDP. Am I correct?

Instructor:
Yes, you're correct. Monetarism in the long run and the simple quantity theory of money hold the same position. It is only in the short run that monetarism differs from the simple quantity theory of money.

Student:
What specifically is the difference between monetarism in the short run and the simple quantity theory of money?

Instructor:
It is the aggregate supply (*AS*) curve. According to the simply quantity theory of money, the *AS* curve is vertical. Any change in aggregate demand therefore affects only the price level. But according to monetarism, the aggregate supply curve is *upward sloping* in the short run. Because of this upward-sloping short-run aggregate supply (*SRAS*) curve, a change in aggregate demand will bring about a change not only in the price level but also in Real GDP.

Student:
So economists should try to figure out whether the aggregate supply curve is or is not upward sloping in the short run. Do they do this kind of thing?

Instructor:
Yes they do.

Points to Remember

1. In both the simple quantity theory of money and in monetarism, changes in the money supply affect the price level.
2. In the simple quantity theory of money, changes in the money supply do not affect Real GDP. In monetarism, changes in the money supply affect Real GDP in the short run, but not in the long run.

SELF-TEST

1. If the expected inflation rate is 4 percent and the nominal interest rate is 7 percent, what is the real interest rate?
2. Is it possible for the nominal interest rate to immediately rise following an increase in the money supply? Explain your answer.
3. The Fed affects only the interest rate via the liquidity effect. Do you agree or disagree? Explain your answer.

a reader asks — How Do We Know the Expected Inflation Rate?

Is there some way to figure out the expected inflation rate at any given time?

One way to find out the expected inflation rate is to look at the spread—the difference—between the yield on conventional bonds and the yield on indexed bonds with the same maturity. For example, we can look at the spread between the yield on a 10-year Treasury bond and the yield on an inflation-indexed 10-year Treasury bond.

Before we do this, let's look at the difference between a conventional bond and an inflation-indexed bond. An inflation-indexed bond guarantees the purchaser a certain real rate of return, but a conventional, or nonindexed, bond does not. For example, suppose you purchase an inflation-indexed, 10-year, $1,000 security that pays 4 percent interest. If there is no inflation, the annual interest payment is $40. But if the inflation rate is 3 percent, the bond issuer marks up the value of your security by 3 percent—from $1,000 to $1,030. Your annual interest payment is then 4 percent of this new higher amount; that is, it is 4 percent of $1,030, or $41.20.

Investors are willing to accept a lower yield on inflation-indexed bonds because they get something that they don't get with conventional bonds: protection against inflation. So while a conventional bond may yield, say, 6 percent, an inflation-indexed bond may yield 4 percent. The spread is the difference between the two rates.

The difference, or spread, is a measure of the inflation rate that investors expect will exist over the life of the bond. To illustrate with real numbers, let's say that http://www.bloomberg.com/ reports that an inflation-indexed 10-year Treasury bond has a yield of 1.72 percent and that a conventional 10-year Treasury bond has a yield of 4.02. The difference, or spread, is therefore 2.3 percent. In other words, on this day, investors (or the market) expected that the inflation rate is going to be 2.3 percent.

So, by checking the spread between yields on conventional and inflation-indexed bonds of the same maturity, you can see what the market expects the inflation rate will be. As the spread widens, the market expects a higher inflation rate; as it narrows, the market expects a lower inflation rate.

Once again, here is the procedure:

1. Go to http://www.bloomberg.com.
2. Under Market Data, click Rates & Bonds.
3. Write down the yield on conventional 10-year Treasury bonds.
4. Write down the yield on inflation-indexed 10-year Treasury bonds.
5. Find the spread between the yields (the market's expected inflation rate).
6. By doing this daily, you can see whether the market's perception of inflation is changing. For example, if the spread is widening, the market believes inflation will be increasing. If the spread is narrowing, the market believes inflation will be decreasing.

Chapter Summary

THE EQUATION OF EXCHANGE

- The equation of exchange is an identity: $MV \equiv PQ$. The equation of exchange can be interpreted in different ways: (1) The money supply multiplied by velocity must equal the price level times Real GDP: $M \times V \equiv P \times Q$. (2) The money supply multiplied by velocity must equal GDP: $M \times V \equiv$ GDP. (3) Total expenditures (measured by MV) must equal the total sales revenues of business firms (measured by PQ): $MV \equiv PQ$.

- The equation of exchange is not a theory of the economy. However, the equation of exchange can be turned into a theory by making assumptions about some of the variables. For example, if we assume that both V and Q are constant, then we have the simple quantity theory of money, which predicts that changes in the money supply cause *strictly proportional* changes in the price level.
- A change in the money supply or a change in velocity will change aggregate demand and therefore lead to a shift in the AD curve. Specifically, either an increase in the money supply or an increase in velocity will increase aggregate demand and therefore shift the AD curve to the right. A decrease in the money supply or a decrease in velocity will decrease aggregate demand and therefore shift the AD curve to the left.
- In the simple quantity theory of money, Real GDP is assumed to be constant in the short run. This means the AS curve is vertical. Also, velocity is assumed to be constant so that only a change in money supply can change aggregate demand. In the face of a vertical AS curve, any change in the money supply shifts the AD curve and changes only the price level, not Real GDP.

MONETARISM

- According to monetarists, if the economy is initially in long-run equilibrium, (1) an increase in the money supply will raise the price level and Real GDP in the short run and will raise only the price level in the long run; (2) a decrease in the money supply will lower the price level and Real GDP in the short run and will lower only the price level in the long run; (3) an increase in velocity will raise the price level and Real GDP in the short run and will raise only the price level in the long run; (4) a decrease in velocity will lower the price level and Real GDP in the short run and will lower only the price level in the long run.

ONE-SHOT INFLATION AND CONTINUED INFLATION

- One-shot inflation can result from an increase in aggregate demand or a decrease in short-run aggregate supply.
- For one-shot inflation to change to continued inflation, a continued increase in aggregate demand is necessary and sufficient. Continued increases in the money supply cause continued increases in aggregate demand and continued inflation.

THE MONEY SUPPLY AND INTEREST RATES

- Changes in the money supply can affect the interest rate by means of the liquidity, income, price-level, and expectations effects.
- The change in the interest rate due to a change in the supply of loanable funds is called the liquidity effect. The change in the interest rate due to a change in Real GDP is called the income effect. The change in the interest rate due to a change in the price level is called the price-level effect. The change in the interest rate due to a change in the expected inflation rate is called the expectations effect (or Fisher effect).

NOMINAL AND REAL INTEREST RATES

- Real interest rate = Nominal interest rate − Expected inflation rate
- Nominal interest rate = Real interest rate + Expected inflation rate

Key Terms and Concepts

Equation of Exchange
Velocity
Simple Quantity Theory of Money
One-Shot Inflation
Continued Inflation
Liquidity Effect
Income Effect
Price-Level Effect
Expectations Effect
Nominal Interest Rate
Real Interest Rate

Questions and Problems

1 What are the assumptions and predictions of the simple quantity theory of money? Does the simple quantity theory of money predict well?

2 Can the money supply support a GDP level greater than itself? Explain your answer.

3 In the simple quantity theory of money, the AS curve is vertical. Explain why.

4 In the simple quantity theory of money, what will lead to an increase in aggregate demand? In monetarism, what will lead to an increase in aggregate demand?

5 According to the simple quantity of money, what will happen to Real GDP and the price level as the money supply rises. Explain your answer.

6 In monetarism, how will each of the following affect the price level in the short run?

a. An increase in velocity.

b. A decrease in velocity.

c. An increase in the money supply.

d. A decrease in the money supply.

7 According to monetarism, an increase in the money supply will lead to a rise in Real GDP in the long run. Do you agree or disagree with this statement? Explain your answer.

8 Suppose the objective of the Fed is to increase Real GDP. To this end, it increases the money supply. Can anything offset the increase in the money supply so that Real GDP does not rise? Explain your answer.

9 "A loaf of bread, a computer, and automobile tires have gone up in price; therefore, we are experiencing inflation." Do you agree or disagree with this statement? Explain your answer.

10 What is the difference in the long run between a one-shot increase in aggregate demand and a one-shot decrease in short-run aggregate supply?

11 "One-shot inflation may be a demand-side (of the economy) or a supply-side phenomenon, but continued inflation is likely to be a demand-side phenomenon." Do you agree or disagree with this statement? Explain your answer.

12 Explain how demand-induced one-shot inflation may seem like supply-induced one-shot inflation.

13 In recent years, economists have argued about the true value of the real interest rate at any one time and over time. Given that the Nominal interest rate = Real interest rate + Expected inflation rate, then Real interest rate = Nominal interest rate − Expected inflation rate. Why do you think there is so much disagreement over the true value of the real interest rate?

14 With respect to the interest rate, what is the liquidity effect? What is the price-level effect? What is the expectations effect?

15 The money supply rises. Is the interest rate guaranteed to decline initially? Why or why not?

16 To a potential borrower, which would be more important: the nominal interest rate or the real interest rate? Explain your answer.

17 The money supply rises on Tuesday and by Thursday the interest rate has risen. Is the rise more likely the result of the income effect or of the expectations effect? Explain your answer.

18 Suppose the money supply increased 30 days ago. Whether the nominal interest rate is higher, lower, or the same today as it was 30 days ago depends on what? Explain your answer.

19 John's brother Bill is looking for a job. John tells his brother that if the Fed "stimulates the economy," he will have an easier time finding a job. Is there any economics in this statement? How does John's assertion relate to the shape of the aggregate supply curve?

Working with Numbers and Graphs

1 How will things change in the *AD-AS* framework if a change in the money supply is completely offset by a change in velocity?

2 Graphically show each of the following:

a. Continued inflation due to supply-side factors.

b. One-shot demand-induced inflation.

c. One-shot supply-induced inflation.

3 Use the figure to answer the following questions.

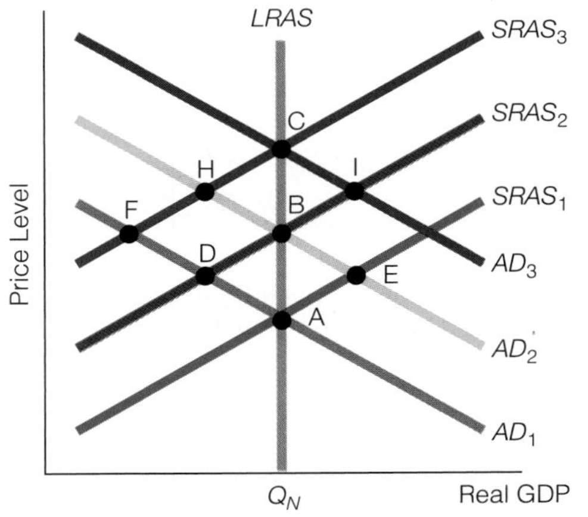

a. The economy is at point A when there is a one-shot, demand-induced inflation. Assuming no other changes in the economy, at what point will the economy settle (assuming the economy is self-regulating)?

b. The economy is at point A when it is faced with two adverse supply-side shocks. The Fed tries to counter these shocks by increasing aggregate demand. What path will the economy follow?

CHAPTER 14

MONETARY POLICY

Introduction When it comes to monetary policy, most economists agree that the goals of monetary policy are to stabilize the price level, to achieve low unemployment, and to promote economic growth, among other things. What they sometimes disagree about is the degree to which, and under what conditions, monetary policy achieves these goals. In this chapter we discuss monetary policy, beginning with the details of the money market. Then we discuss how changes in the money market—brought about by changes in the money supply—can affect the economy.

THE MONEY MARKET

We discuss the money market for two reasons. First, we want to show how changes in the money market can affect the interest rate. The last chapter showed how changes in the demand for and supply of loanable funds can affect the interest rate. In this chapter, we show how changes in the demand for and supply of money can affect the interest rate. (Often, there is more than one way to discuss the determination of interest rates.) Second, we want to show how changes in the money market can ripple outward and bring about changes in the goods and services market.

The Demand for Money

Like all markets, the money market has two sides: a demand side and a supply side.[1] An illustration of the demand for a good puts the price of the good on the vertical axis and the quantity of the good on the horizontal axis. Accordingly, an illustration of the **demand for money (balances)** puts the price of holding money balances on the vertical axis and

Demand for Money (Balances)
Represents the inverse relationship between the quantity demanded of money balances and the price of holding money balances.

1. In everyday language, the term *money market* is often used to refer to the market for short-term securities, where there is a demand for and supply of short-term securities. This is not the money market discussed here. In this money market, there is a demand for and supply of money.

exhibit 1

The Demand for and Supply of Money

(a) The demand curve for money is downward sloping. (b) The supply curve of money is a vertical line at the quantity of money, which is largely, but not exclusively, determined by the Fed.

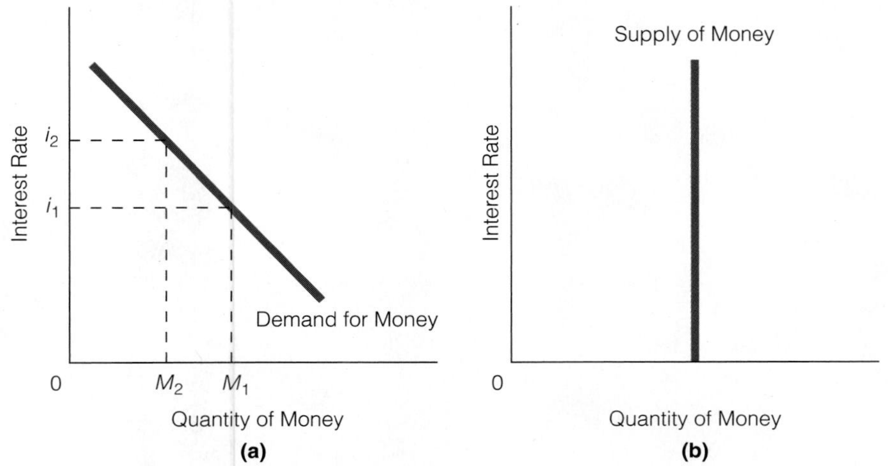

the quantity of money on the horizontal axis. What is the price of holding money balances? The price of holding money balances—specifically, the opportunity cost of holding money—is the interest rate. Money is one of many forms in which individuals may hold their wealth. By holding money, individuals forfeit the opportunity to hold that portion of their wealth in other forms. For example, the person who holds $1,000 in cash gives up the opportunity to purchase a $1,000 asset that yields interest (e.g., a bond). Thus the interest rate is the opportunity cost of holding money. One pays the price of forfeited interest by holding money.

Exhibit 1(a) illustrates the demand for money (balances). As the interest rate increases, the opportunity cost of holding money increases, and individuals choose to hold less money. As the interest rate decreases, the opportunity cost of holding money decreases, and individuals choose to hold more money.

exhibit 2

Equilibrium in the Money Market

At an interest rate of i_1, the money market is in equilibrium: There is neither an excess supply of money nor an excess demand for money.

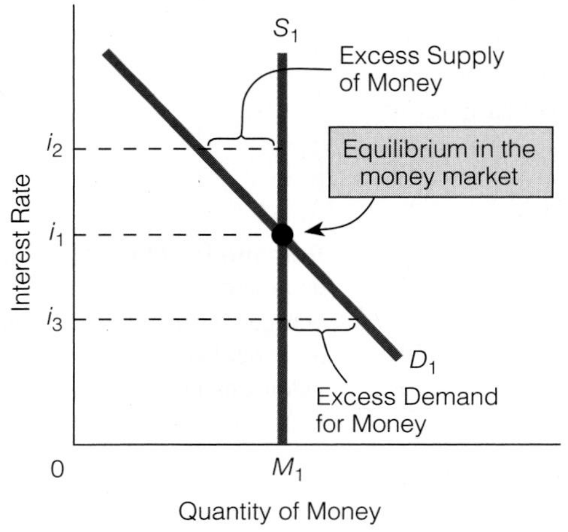

The Supply of Money

Exhibit 1(b) shows the supply of money as a vertical line at the quantity of money, which is largely determined by the Fed. The money supply is not exclusively determined by the Fed because both banks and the public are important players in the money supply process, as explained in earlier chapters. For example, when banks do not lend their entire excess reserves, the money supply is not as large as it is when they do.

Equilibrium in the Money Market

The money market is in equilibrium when the quantity demanded of money equals the quantity supplied. In Exhibit 2, equilibrium exists at the interest rate i_1. At a higher interest rate, i_2, the quantity supplied of money is greater than the quantity demanded, and there is an excess supply of money ("too much" money). At a lower interest rate, i_3, the quantity demanded of money is greater than the quantity supplied, and there is an excess demand for money ("too little" money). Only at i_1 are the quantity demanded and the quantity supplied of money equal. At i_1, there are no shortages or surpluses of money and no excess demands or excess supplies. Individuals are holding the amounts of money they want to hold.

Common MISCONCEPTIONS

About Having Too Much Money?

At the interest rate i_2 in Exhibit 2, the quantity supplied of money is greater than the quantity demanded, and there is an excess supply of money; in simple terms, individuals have "too much" money. Some people doubt that it is ever possible to have too much money, but this is a myth. It certainly is possible to have too much money *relative to other things.* For example, suppose you have $100,000 and nothing else—no food, no car, no television set. In this case, you might think that you have too much money and too few other things. In other words, you might be willing to trade some of your money for, say, food, a car, and a TV set.

TRANSMISSION MECHANISMS

Consider two markets: the money market and the goods and services market. Changes in the money market can ripple outward and affect the goods and services market. The routes, or channels, that these ripple effects travel are known as the **transmission mechanism**. Economists have different ideas about (1) how changes in the money market affect the goods and services market and (2) whether the transmission mechanism is direct or indirect. We discuss two major transmission mechanisms: the Keynesian and the monetarist.

Transmission Mechanism
The routes, or channels, traveled by the ripple effects that the money market creates and that affect the goods and services market (represented by the aggregate demand and aggregate supply curves in the *AD-AS* framework).

macro*theme* ➜ In Chapter 8, we said that not all economists agree as to how the economy works. Coming up are two different views on how changes in the money market eventually affect the goods and services market.

The Keynesian Transmission Mechanism: Indirect

The Keynesian route between the money market and the goods and services market is an indirect one. Refer to Exhibit 3 for a market-by-market depiction of the Keynesian transmission mechanism.

1. *The money market.* Suppose the money market is in equilibrium at interest rate i_1 in part (a). Then, the Fed increases the reserves of the banking system through an open market purchase, resulting in an increase in the money supply. The money supply curve shifts rightward from S_1 to S_2. The process increases the reserves of the banking system and therefore results in more loans being made. A greater supply of loans puts downward pressure on the interest rate, as reflected in the movement from i_1 to i_2.
2. *The investment goods market.* A fall in the interest rate stimulates investment. In the investment goods market in part (b), investment rises from I_1 to I_2.
3. *The goods and services market (AD-AS framework).* Recall that the Keynesian model has a horizontal aggregate supply curve in the goods and services market until full employment or Natural Real GDP is reached. The decline in the interest rate has brought about an increase in investment, as shown in part (b). Rising investment increases

exhibit 3

The Keynesian Transmission Mechanism

The exhibit shows how the Keynesian transmission mechanism operates given an increase in the money supply. (a) An increase in the money supply brings on a lower interest rate. (b) As a result, investment increases. (c) As investment increases, total expenditures rise and the aggregate demand curve shifts rightward. Real GDP rises from Q_1 to Q_2.

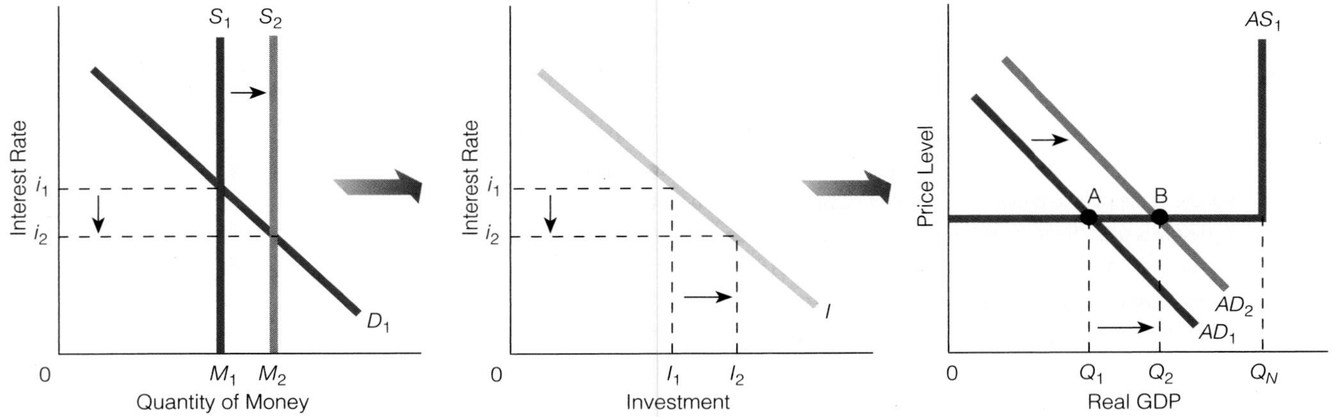

(a) Money Market

(b) Investment Goods Market

(c) Goods and Services Market (*AD–AS* framework)

total spending in the economy and shifts the *AD* curve to the right in part (c). As a result, Real GDP rises from Q_1 to Q_2, and the price level does not change. Due to the increase in Real GDP, the unemployment rate (*U*) drops.

In summary, when the money supply increases, the Keynesian transmission mechanism works as follows: An increase in the money supply lowers the interest rate, which causes investment to rise and the *AD* curve to shift rightward. As a result, Real GDP increases. The process works in reverse for a decrease in the money supply.

$$\text{Money supply} \uparrow \rightarrow i \downarrow \rightarrow I \uparrow \rightarrow AD \uparrow \rightarrow Q \uparrow, \bar{P}, U \downarrow$$
$$\text{Money supply} \downarrow \rightarrow i \uparrow \rightarrow I \downarrow \rightarrow AD \downarrow \rightarrow Q \downarrow, \bar{P}, U \uparrow$$

The Keynesian Mechanism May Get Blocked

The Keynesian transmission mechanism is *indirect.* Changes in the money market *do not directly affect* the goods and services market (and thus Real GDP) because the investment goods market stands between the two markets. It is possible (although not likely) that the link between the money market and the goods and services market could be broken in the investment goods market. We explain.

INTEREST-INSENSITIVE INVESTMENT Some Keynesian economists believe that investment is not always responsive to interest rates. For example, when business firms are pessimistic about future economic activity, a decrease in interest rates will do little, if anything, to increase investment. When investment is completely insensitive to changes in interest rates, the investment demand curve is vertical, as in Exhibit 4(a).

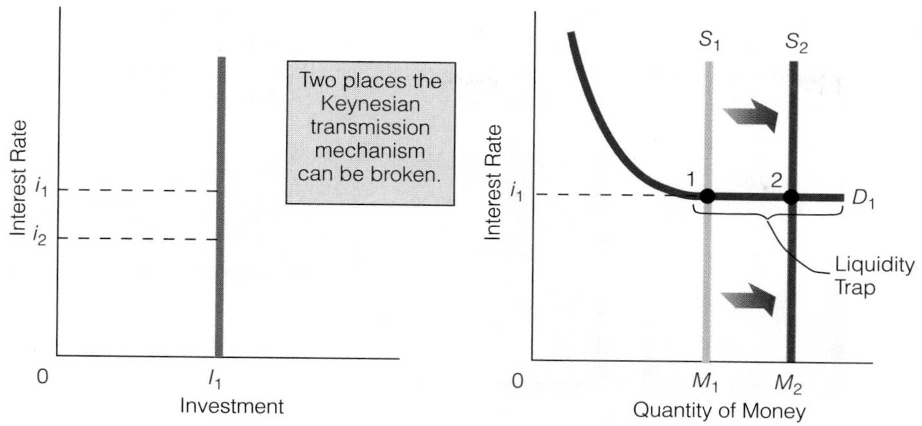

(a)
Interest-Insensitive Investment

(b)
Liquidity Trap

exhibit 4

Breaking the Link Between the Money Market and the Goods and Services Market: Interest-Insensitive Investment and the Liquidity Trap

The Keynesian transmission mechanism allows the link between the money market and the goods and services market to be broken in two places. (a) If investment is totally interest sensitive, a change in the interest rate will not change investment; therefore, aggregate demand and Real GDP will not change. (b) If the money market is in the liquidity trap, an increase in the money supply will not lower the interest rate. It follows that there will be no change in investment, aggregate demand or Real GDP.

Consider what happens to the Keynesian transmission mechanism described in Exhibit 3. If the investment demand curve is vertical (instead of downward sloping), a fall in interest rates will not increase investment; and if investment does not increase, neither will aggregate demand or Real GDP. In addition, unemployment won't fall. Thus, the Keynesian transmission mechanism would be short-circuited in the investment goods market, and the link between the money market in part (a) of Exhibit 3 and the goods and services market in part (c) would be broken.

$$\text{Money supply} \uparrow \rightarrow i \downarrow$$
$$\text{Investment insensitive to changes in } i \rightarrow \overline{I} \rightarrow \overline{AD} \rightarrow \overline{Q} \rightarrow, \overline{P}, \overline{U}$$

THE LIQUIDITY TRAP Keynesians have sometimes argued that the demand curve for money could become horizontal at some low interest rate. Before we discuss why this might occur, let's look at the consequences. Notice that in Exhibit 4(b), the demand curve for money becomes horizontal at i_1. This horizontal section of the demand curve for money is referred to as the **liquidity trap**.

Liquidity Trap
The horizontal portion of the demand curve for money.

What happens if the money supply is increased (e.g., from S_1 to S_2) when the money market is in the liquidity trap? The money market moves from point 1 to point 2, and individuals are willing to hold all the additional money supply at the given interest rate. What happens to the Keynesian transmission mechanism illustrated in Exhibit 3? Obviously, if an increase in the money supply does not lower the interest rate, then there will be no change in investment, aggregate demand, or Real GDP. The liquidity trap can break the link between the money market and the goods and services market.

$$\text{Money supply} \uparrow$$
$$\text{Liquidity trap} \rightarrow \overline{i} \rightarrow \overline{I} \rightarrow \overline{AD} \rightarrow \overline{Q}, \overline{P}, \overline{U}$$

exhibit 5

The Keynesian View of Monetary Policy

According to the Keynesian transmission mechanism, if the Fed increases reserves in the banking system and therefore raises the money supply, the interest rate will drop, stimulating investment and aggregate demand. Consequently, Real GDP will rise, and the unemployment rate will drop. However, things may not work out this way if there is a liquidity trap or if investment is insensitive to changes in the interest rate.

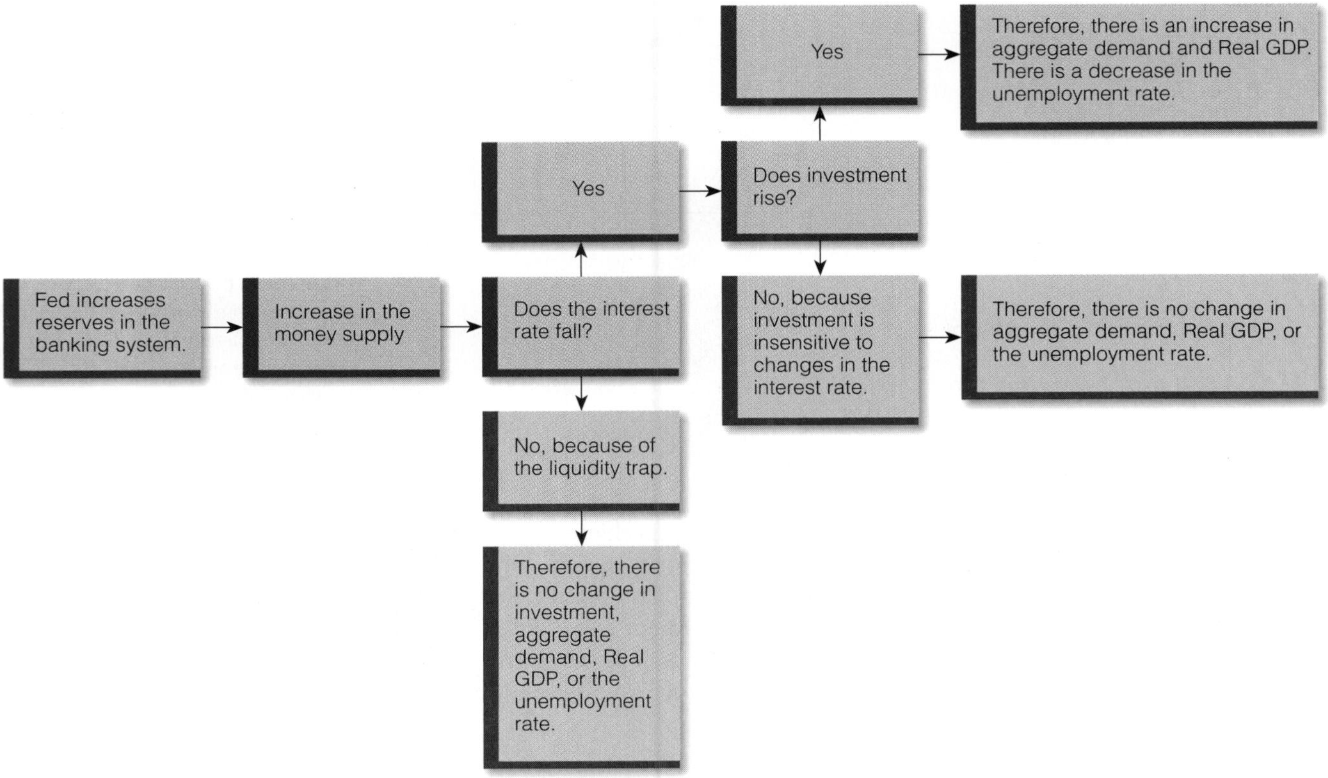

Because the Keynesian transmission mechanism is indirect, both *interest-insensitive investment demand* and the *liquidity trap* may occur. Therefore, Keynesians conclude, at times monetary policy will be unable to increase Real GDP and decrease unemployment. Viewing the money supply as a string, some economists have argued that you can't push on a string. In other words, you can't always force Real GDP up by increasing (pushing up) the money supply.

See Exhibit 5 for a review of the Keynesian transmission mechanism and how it may get blocked.

BOND PRICES, INTEREST RATES, AND THE LIQUIDITY TRAP The liquidity trap, or the horizontal section of the demand curve for money, seems to come out of the clear blue sky. Why might the demand curve for money become horizontal at some low interest rate? To understand an explanation of the liquidity trap, you must first understand the relationship between bond prices and interest rates.

Consider Jessica Howard, who buys good X for $100 today and sells it one year later for $110. Her actual rate of return is 10 percent because the difference between the selling price and buying price ($10) divided by the buying price ($100) is 10 percent.

Now suppose good X is a bond. Jessica buys the bond for $100 and sells it one year later for $110. This time the question is what is her actual interest rate return, or what interest rate did Jessica earn? The answer is the same: 10 percent.

Further suppose that Jessica buys the bond for $90 instead of $100 but still sells it for $110. Her interest rate return is 22 percent ($20 ÷ $90 = 22 percent). The point is simple: *As the price of a bond decreases, the actual interest rate return, or simply the interest rate, increases.*

Let's look at a slightly more complicated example that illustrates the inverse relationship between bond prices and interest rates. Suppose last year Rob Lewis bought a bond for $1,000 that promises to pay him $100 a year in interest. The annual interest rate return is 10 percent ($100 ÷ $1,000 = 10 percent). Suppose, however, that the market or nominal interest rate is higher now than last year when Rob bought his bond. Now bond suppliers have to promise to pay $120 a year to someone who buys a $1,000 bond.

What effect does this change have on the price Rob can get in the market for the $1,000 bond he bought last year, assuming he wants to sell it? If someone can buy a new $1,000 bond that pays $120 a year, why pay Rob $1,000 for an (old) bond that pays only $100? Rob has to lower the price of his bond below $1,000, but the question is by how much? The price has to be far enough below $1,000 so that the interest rate return on his old bond will be competitive with (i.e., equal to) the interest rate return on new bonds.

Rob's bond will sell for $833. At a price of $833, a buyer of his bond will receive $100 a year and an interest rate of 12 percent, which is the same interest rate offered by a new $1,000 bond paying $120 a year. Thus, $100 is the same percentage of $833 as $120 is of $1,000: 12 percent. We conclude that *the market interest rate is inversely related to the price of old or existing bonds.*

Keeping this in mind, consider the liquidity trap again. An increase in the money supply does not result in an excess supply of money at a low interest rate because individuals believe that bond prices are so high (because low interest rates mean high bond prices) that an investment in bonds is likely to turn out to be a bad deal. Individuals would rather hold all the additional money supply than use it to buy bonds, which, as they believe, are priced so high that they have no place to go but down.

Finding ECONOMICS

In Rising Demand for Bonds

Kenneth reads in the newspaper that the demand for bonds is rising. Is there any information here that relates to the interest rate? Yes; if the demand for bonds rises, it follows that the price of bonds will rise too. Because we know that the price of bonds and the interest rate are inversely related, the interest rate is about to decline.

The Monetarist Transmission Mechanism: Direct

In monetarist theory, there is a direct link between the money market and the goods and services market. The monetarist transmission mechanism is short. Changes in the money market have a direct impact on aggregate demand, as illustrated in Exhibit 6. An increase in the money supply from S_1 to S_2 in part (a) leaves individuals with an excess supply of money. As a result, they increase their spending on a wide variety of goods. Households buy more refrigerators, personal computers, television sets, clothes, and vacations. Businesses purchase additional machinery. The aggregate demand curve in part (b)

economics 24/7

IF YOU'RE SO SMART, THEN WHY AREN'T YOU RICH?

Upon meeting a professional economist, the general member of the public often asks some economics-related question, such as: "What stocks should I buy?" "Is this a good time to buy bonds?" "Are interest rates going up?" "Where do you think the economy is headed?" The professional economist will often answer the question, usually explaining things well enough that the general member of the public thinks, "Yes, but if you're so smart [about the economy], then why aren't you rich?" Some economists are, in fact, rich, but many are not. Still, the question is a good one, and it helps us to understand the public's perception of economists and the science of economics.

How can someone be smart about the economy and still not be rich? The inverse relationship between bond prices and interest rates helps us understand how this can be true. To become rich using the bond market, the rule to follow is simple: Buy bonds when you think interest rates are as high as they will go (because then bond prices will be low), and sell bonds when you think interest rates are as low as they will go (because then bond prices will be high). Buy low, sell high—the road to riches! To take the road to riches, all you have to do is predict interest rates. Now you may think it should be easy for economists to predict interest rates, but it isn't. We illustrate just how difficult it is to predict interest rates by structuring our arguments in terms of the bond market.

We begin with the fundamentals. There is a demand for and supply of bonds in the bond market. The demand curve for bonds slopes downward: Buyers of bonds will buy more bonds at lower prices than at higher prices. The supply curve of bonds slopes upward: Suppliers of bonds will offer to sell more bonds at higher prices than at lower prices. In this regard, the demand for and supply of bonds is no different from the demand for and supply of any good (cars, computers, DVD players, etc.). Buyers will buy more bonds at lower prices, and suppliers will offer to sell more bonds at higher prices.

Thus, we know that the demand for and supply of bonds must work together to determine the price of bonds. A rise in the demand for bonds will raise the price of bonds, *ceteris paribus*, in the same way that a rise in the demand for television sets will raise the price of television sets. Similarly, an increase in the supply of bonds will lower the price of bonds in the same way that an increase in the supply of houses will lower the price of houses.

exhibit 6

The Monetarist Transmission Mechanism

The monetarist transmission mechanism is short and direct. Changes in the money market directly affect aggregate demand in the goods and services market. For example, an increase in the money supply leaves individuals with an excess supply of money that they spend on a wide variety of goods.

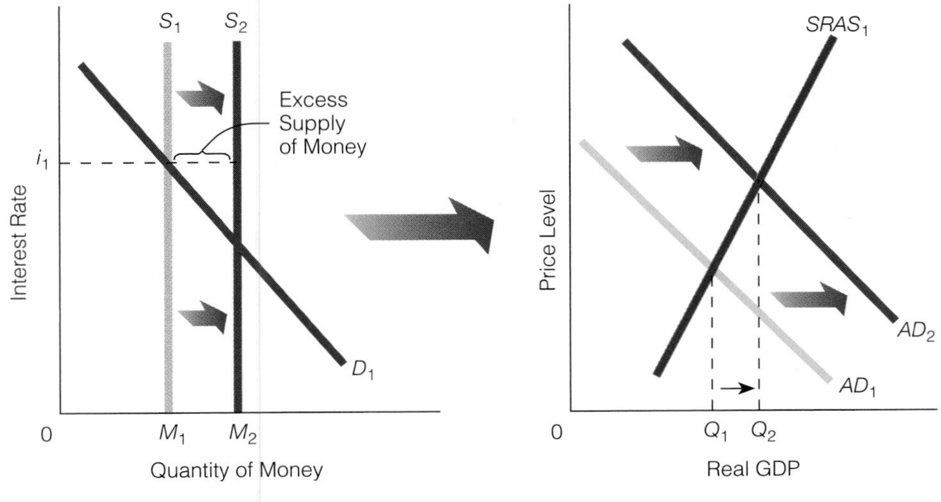

(a)
Money Market

(b)
Goods and Services Market
(*AD–AS* framework)

Recall that certain factors that will change demand and supply. For example, a change in income, preferences, prices of substitutes, and so on will change demand; a change in resource prices, (certain) taxes, and so on will change supply. The same holds for the demand and supply of bonds. Describing the details of all the factors affecting the demand for and supply of bonds isn't necessary. Let's just say that factors A–F can change the demand for bonds and that factors G–L can change the supply of bonds; that is, the demand for bonds depends on factors A, B, C, D, E, and F, and the supply of bonds depends on factors G, H, I, J, K, and L.

We can now enumerate the reasons predicting interest rates is difficult:

1. *We have to know how each of the factors A–F affects the demand for bonds.* For example, does an increase in factor B increase or decrease the demand for bonds?
2. *We have to know how each of the factors G–L affects the supply of bonds.* Does a rise in factor K increase or decrease the supply of bonds?
3. *If any of the factors A–L change, we need to know immediately which are changing.* For example, a change in factor C changes the demand for bonds, in turn changing the price of bonds. If bond prices change, so do interest rates. So if factor C changes and we are unaware of the change, there is no way to predict the change in interest rates.
4. *Even if we know which factors are changing, we still have to determine the impact of each relevant factor on the demand for and supply of bonds.* Suppose a rise in factor A increases the demand for bonds, and a rise in factor J increases the supply of bonds. If A and J both rise, we can predict that the demand for bonds will rise and that the supply of bonds will rise, but we don't know how much each will rise relative to the other.

On top of knowing about and understanding the effect of all these possible changes and interactions, the economist must then make predictions based on several cause-and-effect conditions:

- If the demand for bonds rises by more than the supply of bonds, then the price of bonds will rise. (Can you show this graphically?) And if bond prices rise, interest rates fall.
- But if the supply of bonds rises by more than the demand for bonds, the price of bonds will fall. (Can you show this graphically?) And if bond prices fall, interest rates rise.
- Finally, if the supply of bonds rises by the same amount as the demand for bonds rises, the price of bonds will not change. And if bond prices don't change, neither do interest rates.

We conclude that, to predict interest rates accurately, we need to know:

1. *What factors affect the demand for and supply of bonds.* Is it A, B, and C, or A, B, D, and E?
2. *How those factors affect the demand for and supply of bonds.* Does a rise in A increase or decrease the demand for bonds?
3. *Which factors are changing.* Did B just change?
4. *How much bond demand and supply change given that some factors are changing.* Did demand rise by more than supply, or did supply rise by more than demand?

Now do you see why not all economists are rich?

is directly affected. In the short run, Real GDP rises from Q_1 to Q_2. The process works in reverse for a decrease in the money supply.

$$\text{Money supply} \uparrow \rightarrow AD\uparrow \rightarrow Q\uparrow, P\uparrow, U\downarrow$$
$$\text{Money supply} \downarrow \rightarrow AD\downarrow \rightarrow Q\downarrow, P\downarrow, U\uparrow$$

The Keynesian transmission mechanism from the money market to the goods and services market is indirect; the monetarist transmission mechanism is direct.

SELF-TEST

(Answers to Self-Test questions are in the Self-Test Appendix.)

1. Explain the inverse relationship between bond prices and interest rates.
2. "According to the Keynesian transmission mechanism, as the money supply rises, there is a direct impact on the goods and services market." Do you agree or disagree with this statement? Explain your answer.
3. Explain how the monetarist transmission mechanism works when the money supply rises.

exhibit 7

Monetary Policy and a Recessionary Gap

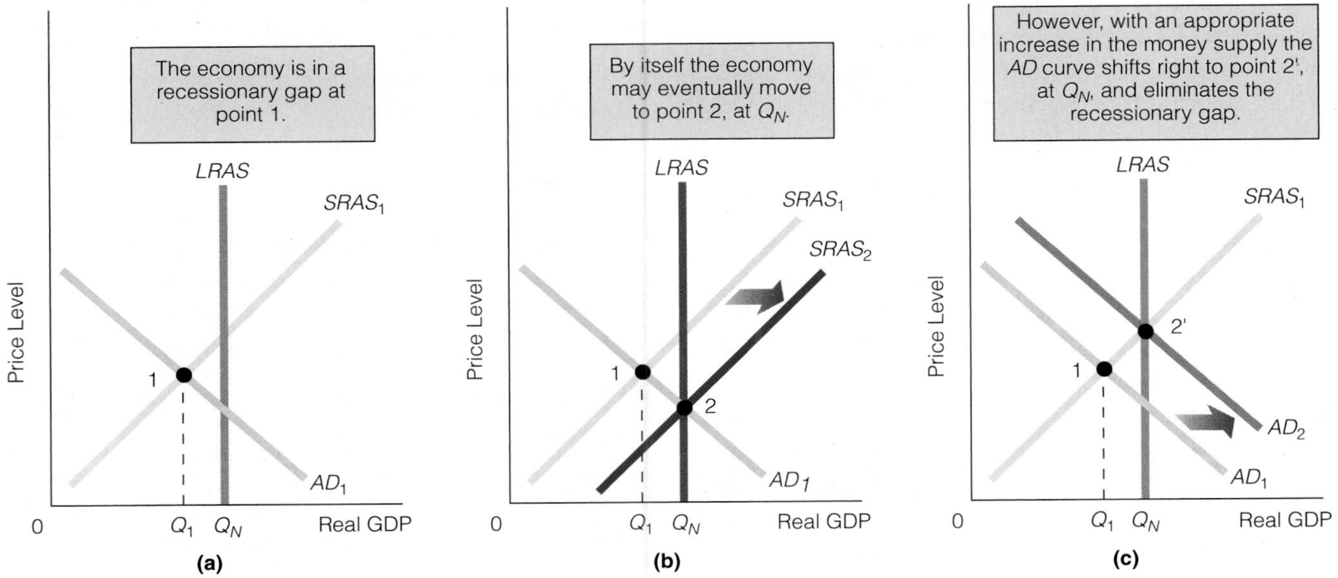
The economy is in a recessionary gap at point 1.
LRAS
$SRAS_1$
Price Level
1
AD_1
0
Q_1 Q_N
Real GDP
(a)
By itself the economy may eventually move to point 2, at Q_N.
LRAS
$SRAS_1$
$SRAS_2$
Price Level
1
2
AD_1
0
Q_1 Q_N
Real GDP
(b)
However, with an appropriate increase in the money supply the AD curve shifts right to point 2', at Q_N, and eliminates the recessionary gap.
LRAS
$SRAS_1$
Price Level
2'
1
AD_2
AD_1
0
Q_1 Q_N
Real GDP
(c)

MONETARY POLICY AND THE PROBLEM OF INFLATIONARY AND RECESSIONARY GAPS

In Chapter 10, we explained how expansionary and contractionary fiscal policies might be used to rid the economy of recessionary and inflationary gaps, respectively, and questioned the effectiveness of fiscal policy. In this section, we discuss how monetary policy might be used to eliminate both recessionary and inflationary gaps.

In Exhibit 7(a), the economy is in a recessionary gap at point 1; aggregate demand is too low to bring the economy into equilibrium at its natural level of Real GDP. Economist A argues that, in time, the short-run aggregate supply curve will shift rightward to point 2 [see Exhibit 7(b)]; so it is best to leave things alone.

Economist B says that the economy will take too long to get to point 2 on its own and that in the interim the economy is suffering the high cost of unemployment and a lower level of output.

Expansionary Monetary Policy
The policy by which the Fed increases the money supply.

Economist C maintains that the economy is stuck in the recessionary gap. Economists B and C propose **expansionary monetary policy** to move the economy to its Natural Real GDP level. An appropriate increase in the money supply will shift the aggregate demand curve rightward to AD_2, and the economy will be in long-run equilibrium at point 2′ [see Exhibit 7(c)]. The recessionary gap is eliminated through the use of expansionary monetary policy.[2]

2. In a static framework, expansionary monetary policy refers to an increase in the money supply, and contractionary monetary policy refers to a decrease in the money supply. In a dynamic framework, expansionary monetary policy refers to an increase in the rate of growth of the money supply, and contractionary monetary policy refers to a decrease in the growth rate of the money supply. In the real world, where things are constantly changing, the growth rate of the money supply is more indicative of the direction of monetary policy.

exhibit 8

Monetary Policy and an Inflationary Gap

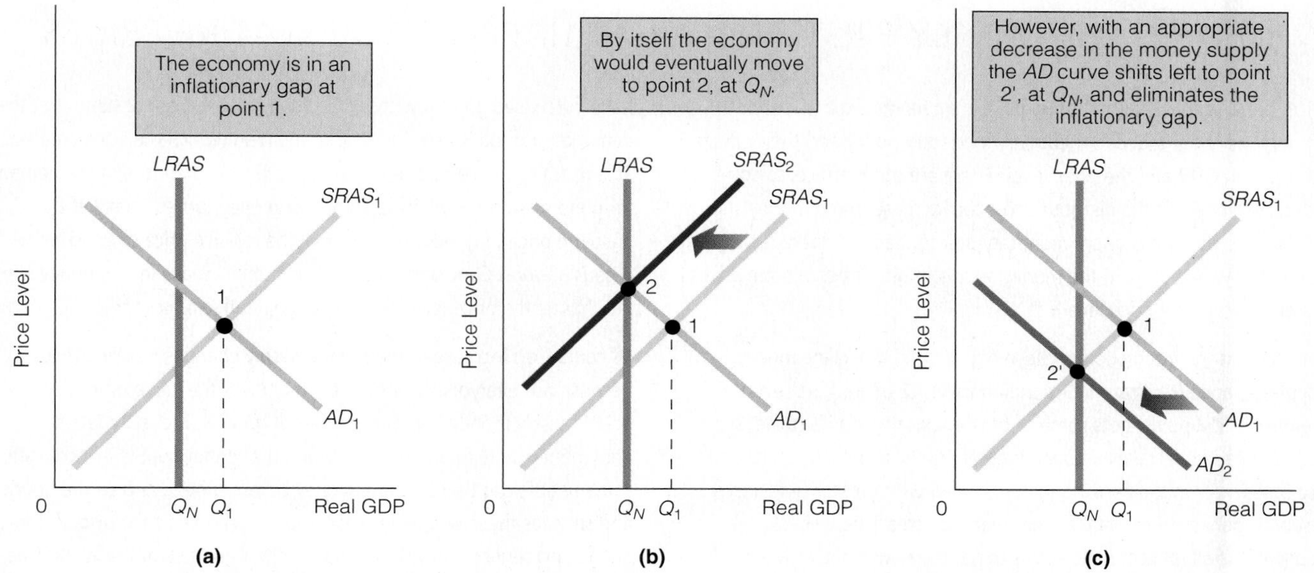
The economy is in an inflationary gap at point 1.
LRAS
SRAS1
AD1
1
Price Level
0
QN Q1
Real GDP
(a)
By itself the economy would eventually move to point 2, at QN.
LRAS
SRAS2
SRAS1
2
1
AD1
Price Level
0
QN Q1
Real GDP
(b)
However, with an appropriate decrease in the money supply the AD curve shifts left to point 2', at QN, and eliminates the inflationary gap.
LRAS
SRAS1
1
2'
AD1
AD2
Price Level
0
QN Q1
Real GDP
(c)

In Exhibit 8(a), the economy is in an inflationary gap at point 1. Economist A argues that, in time, the economy will move to point 2 [see Exhibit 8(b)]; so it is best to leave things alone.

Economist B argues that it would be better to decrease the money supply (**contractionary monetary policy**) so that aggregate demand shifts leftward to AD_2 and the economy moves to point 2′ [see Exhibit 8(c)].

Contractionary Monetary Policy
The policy by which the Fed decreases the money supply.

Economist C agrees with economist B and points out that the price level is lower at point 2′ than at point 2, although Real GDP is the same at both points.

Most Keynesians believe that the natural forces of the market economy work much faster and more assuredly in eliminating an inflationary gap than in eliminating a recessionary gap. In terms of Exhibits 7 and 8, they argue that it is much more likely that the short-run aggregate supply curve in Exhibit 8(b) will shift leftward to point 2, eliminating the inflationary gap, than that the short-run aggregate supply curve in Exhibit 7(b) will shift rightward to point 2, eliminating the recessionary gap. The reason is that wages and prices rise more quickly than they fall. (Recall that many Keynesians believe wages are inflexible in a downward direction.) Consequently, Keynesians are more likely to advocate expansionary monetary policy to eliminate a stubborn recessionary gap than contractionary monetary policy to eliminate a not so stubborn inflationary gap.

macro*theme* → Notice the link between how economists believe the economy works and the type of policy they propose. For instance, suppose the economy is in a recessionary gap. We saw economist A, who believes the economy is self-regulating, propose that nothing should be done. In time, the economy will remove itself from the recessionary gap. But economist C, who believes the economy is stuck in a recessionary gap, proposed government action—specifically, expansionary monetary policy to shift the *AD* curve rightward and thus get the economy out of the recessionary gap.

economics 24/7

WHO GETS THE MONEY FIRST AND WHAT HAPPENS TO RELATIVE PRICES?

In our discussion of monetary policy, we have talked about both expansionary and contractionary monetary policy and their effects on Real GDP and the price level. There are other effects to consider. First, there is the distribution of the increase in the money supply (in the case of expansionary monetary policy). Second, there is the issue of how a change in the money supply might affect relative prices (as opposed to the price level).

Let's look at the interaction of these two effects. When the money supply expands (say from $1.41 trillion to $1.42 trillion), not every member of the public gets some of the new money. To illustrate, suppose the Fed undertakes an open market purchase, which results in a rise in reserves in the banking system. Faced with greater (and excess) reserves, banks start to make more loans (or create new checkable deposits). The first economic actors to get the new money (as a result of the open market purchase) are the banks; the second economic actors are the individuals and firms who take out loans. Now let's say that one of the second economic actors is Caroline, who spends the money from her new loan to buy good X from Richard. If Caroline would not have purchased good X without the loan, then we can assume that the demand for good X rises because of the loan (which the bank created as a result of the Fed's open market purchase). Therefore, if the demand for good X rises, so will its absolute (or money) price. Finally, if the absolute price of good X rises, so will the relative price of good X rise, *ceteris paribus*. Conclusion: Not only can an increase in the money supply change the price level, it can change relative prices too.

Of course, an increase in the money supply changes relative prices because not everyone gets the new money at the same time. Caroline gets the new money before the seller of good X (Richard) gets the new money, and so on. In short, when the money supply is increased, some people get that the new money before others, and so the goods and services these people buy rise in price relative to the prices of the goods and services they do not buy. If the Carolines of the world (the ones to get the new money first) buy good X and not good Y, whereas the non-Carolines of the world (the ones to get the new money farther down the road) buy good Y, we can expect that initially the price of good X will rise relative to good Y.

MONETARY POLICY AND THE ACTIVIST-NONACTIVIST DEBATE

Recall that some economists argue that fiscal policy is ineffective (owing to crowding out) or works in unintended and undesirable ways (owing to lags). Other economists, notably Keynesians, believe that neither is the case and that fiscal policy not only can, but also should be, used to smooth out the business cycle. This point of contention is part of the activist-nonactivist debate, which encompasses both fiscal and monetary policy. This section addresses *monetary policy* within the activist-nonactivist debate.

Activists argue that monetary policy should be deliberately used to smooth out the business cycle. They are in favor of economic **fine-tuning**, which is the (usually frequent) use of monetary policy to counteract even small undesirable movements in economic activity. Sometimes, the monetary policy they advocate is called either *activist* or *discretionary monetary policy.*

Nonactivists argue *against* the use of activist or discretionary monetary policy. Instead, they propose a rules-based monetary policy. Sometimes, the monetary policy they propose is called either *nonactivist* or *rules-based monetary policy.* An example of a rules-based monetary policy is one based on a predetermined steady growth rate in the money supply, such as allowing the money supply to grow 3 percent a year, no matter what is happening in the economy.

Activists
Persons who argue that monetary and fiscal policies should be deliberately used to smooth out the business cycle.

Fine-Tuning
The (usually frequent) use of monetary and fiscal policies to counteract even small undesirable movements in economic activity.

Nonactivists
Persons who argue against the deliberate use of discretionary fiscal and monetary policies. They believe in a permanent, stable, rule-oriented monetary and fiscal framework.

economics 24/7

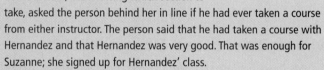

MONETARY POLICY AND BLUE EYES

Two days before the beginning of the fall semester at a college in the Midwest, Suzanne, a student at the college, was waiting in line to register for classes. As she waited, she looked through the fall schedule. She had to take an economics principles course at 10 a.m., and two sections were listed for that time. The instructor for one section was Hernandez; Jones was the instructor for the other section. Suzanne, not knowing which section to take, asked the person behind her in line if he had ever taken a course from either instructor. The person said that he had taken a course with Hernandez and that Hernandez was very good. That was enough for Suzanne; she signed up for Hernandez' class.

© PHOTODISC GREEN/GETTY IMAGES

While a student in Hernandez' class, Suzanne met the person whom she ended up marrying. His name is Bob. Suzanne often says to Bob, "You know, if that guy behind me in line that day had said that Hernandez wasn't a good teacher or hadn't said anything at all, I might never have taken Professor Hernandez' class. I might have taken Jones's class instead, and I would never have met you. I'd probably be married to someone else right now." This (untrue) story is representative of the many little things that happen every day. Little things can make big differences.

With this in mind, consider another story (this one about monetary policy) that is also not true but that is still representative of something that, if it hasn't happened, certainly can.

A few years ago, Real GDP was far below its natural level, and the Fed decided to increase the money supply. As a result, the *AD* curve in the economy shifted to the right. One of the first places to feel the new demand in the economy was Denver, where economic activity increased. Jake, who lived in Austin at the time, was out of work and looking for a job. He heard about the job prospects in Denver, and so one day he got into his car and headed for Denver. Luckily for him, a few days after arriving in Denver, he got a job and rented an apartment near his workplace. He became a friend of Nick, who lived in the apartment across the hall.

Nick, knowing that Jake was new in town, asked Jake if he wanted a date with his girlfriend's friend, Melanie, and Jake said yes. Jake and Melanie ended up dating for two years, and they've been married now for ten years. They have three children, all of whom have blue eyes.

One day, the youngest child asked her mother why she had blue eyes. Her mother told her it's because both she and her daddy have blue eyes. And that's not an incorrect explanation, as far as it goes. But we can't help wondering if the youngest child has blue eyes because of an event that took place years ago, an event that has to do with the Fed and the money supply. After all, if the Fed hadn't increased the money supply when it did, maybe Denver's job prospects wouldn't have been so healthy, and maybe Jake wouldn't have left Austin. But then, if Jake had not left Austin, he wouldn't have married Melanie and had three children, each with blue eyes. We're just speculating, of course.

The Case for Activist (or Discretionary) Monetary Policy

The case for activist (or discretionary) monetary policy rests on three major claims:

1. *The economy does not always equilibrate quickly enough at Natural Real GDP.* Consider the economy at point 1 in Exhibit 7(a). Some economists maintain that, left on its own, the economy will eventually move to point 2 in part (b). Activists often argue that the economy takes too long to move from point 1 to point 2 and that too much lost output and too high an unemployment rate must be tolerated in the interim. They believe that an activist monetary policy speeds things along so that higher output and a lower unemployment rate can be achieved more quickly.

2. *Activist monetary policy works; it is effective at smoothing out the business cycle.* Activists are quick to point to the undesirable consequences of the constant monetary policy of the mid-1970s. In 1973, 1974, and 1975, the money supply growth rates were 5.5 percent, 4.3 percent, and 4.7 percent, respectively. These percentages represent a nearly constant growth rate in the money supply. The economy, however, went through a recession during this time (Real GDP fell between 1973 and 1974 and between 1974 and 1975). Activists argue that an activist and flexible monetary policy would have reduced the high cost the economy had to pay in terms of lost output and high unemployment.
3. *Activist monetary policy is flexible; nonactivist (rules-based) monetary policy is not.* Activists argue that flexibility is a desirable quality in monetary policy; inflexibility is not. The implicit judgment of activists is that the more closely monetary policy can be designed to meet the particulars of a given economic environment, the better. For example, at certain times the economy requires a sharp increase in the money supply and at other times, a sharp decrease; at still other times, only a slight increase or decrease is needed. Activists argue that activist (discretionary) monetary policy can change as the monetary needs of the economy change; nonactivist, rules-based, or "the-same-for-all-seasons" monetary policy cannot.

The Case for Nonactivist (or Rules-Based) Monetary Policy

The case for nonactivist (or rules-based) monetary policy also rests on three major claims:

1. *In modern economies, wages and prices are sufficiently flexible to allow the economy to equilibrate at reasonable speed at Natural Real GDP.* For example, nonactivists point to the sharp drop in union wages in 1982 in response to high unemployment. In addition, they argue that government policies largely determine the flexibility of wages and prices. For example, when government decides to cushion people's unemployment (e.g., through unemployment compensation), wages will not fall as quickly as when government does nothing. Nonactivists believe that a laissez-faire, hands-off approach by government promotes speedy wage and price adjustments and therefore a quick return to Natural Real GDP.
2. *Activist monetary policies may not work.* Some economists argue that there are really two types of monetary policy: (1) monetary policy that is anticipated by the public and (2) monetary policy that is unanticipated. Anticipated monetary policy may not be effective at changing Real GDP or the unemployment rate. We discuss this subject in detail in the next chapter, but here is a brief explanation. Suppose the public correctly anticipates that the Fed will soon increase the money supply by 10 percent. Consequently, the public reasons that aggregate demand will increase from AD_1 to AD_2, as shown in Exhibit 9, and prices will rise.

   Workers are particularly concerned about the expected higher price level because they know higher prices decrease the buying power of their wages. In an attempt to maintain their real wages, workers bargain for and receive higher money wage rates, thereby shifting the short-run aggregate supply curve from $SRAS_1$ to $SRAS_2$ in Exhibit 9.

   Now, if the *SRAS* curve shifts leftward (owing to higher wage rates) to the same degree as the *AD* curve shifts rightward (owing to the increased money supply), Real GDP does not change, but stays constant at Q_1. Thus, *a correctly anticipated increase in the money supply will be ineffective at raising Real GDP.*
3. *Activist monetary policies are likely to be destabilizing rather than stabilizing; they are likely to make matters worse rather than better.* Nonactivists point to *lags* as the main

exhibit 9

Expansionary Monetary Policy and No Change in Real GDP

If expansionary monetary policy is anticipated (thus, a higher price level is anticipated), workers may bargain for and receive higher wage rates. It is possible that the *SRAS* curve will shift leftward to the same degree that expansionary monetary policy shifts the *AD* curve rightward. Result: No change in Real GDP.

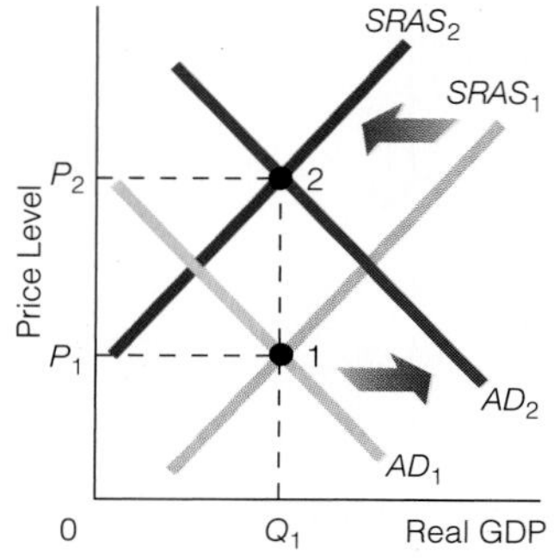

reason that activist (or discretionary) monetary policies are likely to be destabilizing. (The total lag consists of the data, wait-and-see, legislative, transmission, and effectiveness lags discussed in Chapter 10.) Nonactivists argue that a long lag (e.g., 12 to 20 months) makes it almost impossible to conduct effective activist monetary policy. By the time the Fed's monetary stimulus arrives on the scene, the economy may not need any stimulus, and thus it will likely destabilize the economy. In this instance, the stimulus makes things worse rather than better.

Exhibit 10 illustrates the last point. Suppose the economy is currently in a recessionary gap at point 1. The recession is under way before Fed officials recognize it. After they are aware of the recession, however, the officials consider expanding the money supply in the hopes of shifting the *AD* curve from AD_1 to AD_2 so that it will intersect the *SRAS* curve at point 1′, at Natural Real GDP.

In the interim, however, unknown to everybody, the economy is regulating itself: The *SRAS* curve is shifting to the right. Fed officials don't realize this shift is occurring because it takes time to collect and analyze data about the economy. Thinking that the economy is not regulating itself, or not regulating itself quickly enough, Fed officials implement expansionary monetary policy, and the *AD* curve shifts rightward. By the time the increased money supply is felt in the goods and services market, the *AD* curve intersects the *SRAS* curve at point 2. In short, the Fed has moved the economy from point 1 to point 2 and not, as it had hoped, from point 1 to point 1′. The Fed has moved the economy into an inflationary gap. Instead of stabilizing and moderating the business cycle, the Fed has intensified it.

exhibit 10

Monetary Policy May Destabilize the Economy

In this scenario, the *SRAS* curve is shifting rightward (ridding the economy of its recessionary gap), but Fed officials do not realize this is happening. They implement expansionary monetary policy, and the *AD* curve ends up intersecting $SRAS_2$ at point 2 instead of intersecting $SRAS_1$ at point 1′. Fed officials end up moving the economy into an inflationary gap and thus destabilizing the economy.

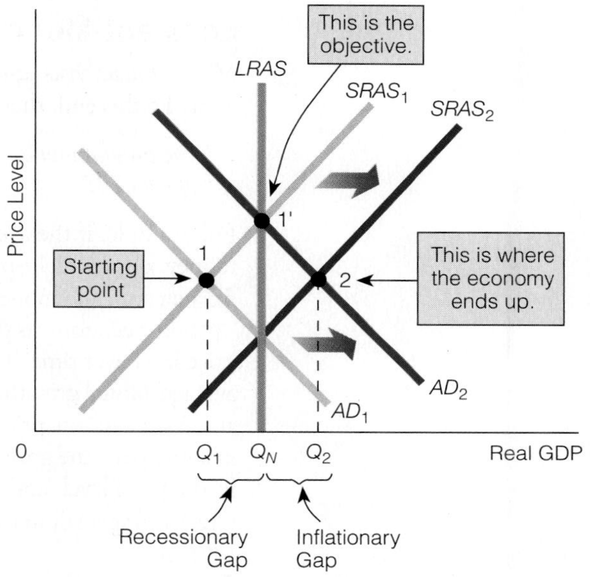

Thinking like AN ECONOMIST

Specifying the Conditions

Ask an economist a question, and you are likely to get a conditional answer. For example, asked whether monetary policy stabilizes or destabilizes the economy, an economist may answer that it can do either—depending on conditions. For instance, starting in a recessionary gap, if expansionary monetary policy shifts the *AD* curve rightward by just the right amount to intersect the *SRAS* curve and the *LRAS* curve at Natural Real GDP, then monetary policy stabilizes the economy. But if the monetary policy shifts the *AD* curve rightward by more than this amount, it may move the economy into an inflationary gap, thereby destabilizing the economy. If-then thinking is common in economics, as are if-then statements.

SELF-TEST

1. Why are Keynesians more likely to advocate expansionary monetary policy to eliminate a recessionary gap than to advocate contractionary monetary policy to eliminate an inflationary gap?
2. How might monetary policy destabilize the economy?
3. If the economy is stuck in a recessionary gap, does this make the case for activist (expansionary) monetary policy stronger or weaker? Explain your answer.

NONACTIVIST MONETARY PROPOSALS

In this section, we outline the following four nonactivist (or rules-based) monetary proposals:

1. Constant-money-growth-rate rule.
2. Predetermined-money-growth-rate rule.
3. The Taylor rule.
4. Inflation targeting.

Constant-Money-Growth-Rate Rule

Many nonactivists argue that the sole objective of monetary policy is to stabilize the price level. To this end, they propose a *constant-money-growth-rate rule.* One version of the rule is:

> *The annual money supply growth rate will be constant at the average annual growth rate of Real GDP.*

For example, if the average annual Real GDP growth rate is approximately 3.3 percent, the money supply will be put on automatic pilot and will be permitted to grow at an annual rate of 3.3 percent. The money supply will grow at this rate regardless of the state of the economy.

Some economists predict that a constant-money-growth-rate rule will bring about a stable price level over time. This prediction is based on the equation of exchange ($MV \equiv PQ$). If the average annual growth rate in Real GDP (Q) is 3.3 percent and the money supply (M) grows at 3.3 percent, the price level should remain stable over time. Advocates of this rule argue that in some years the growth rate in Real GDP will be below its average rate, causing an increase in the price level, and in other years the growth rate in Real GDP will be above its average rate, causing a fall in the price level, but over time the price level will be stable.

Predetermined-Money-Growth-Rate Rule

Critics of the constant-money-growth-rate rule point out that it makes two assumptions: (1) Velocity is constant. (2) The money supply is defined correctly. Critics argue that velocity has not been constant in some periods. Also, not yet clear is which definition of the money supply (M1, M2, or some broader monetary measure) is the proper one and therefore which money supply growth rate should be fixed.

Largely in response to the charge that velocity is not always constant, some nonactivists prefer the following rule:

> *The annual growth rate in the money supply will be equal to the average annual growth rate in Real GDP minus the growth rate in velocity.*

In other words,

$$\%\Delta M = \%\Delta Q - \%\Delta V$$

With this rule, the growth rate of the money supply is not fixed. It can vary from year to year, but it is predetermined in that it is dependent on the growth rates of Real GDP and velocity. For this reason, we call it the *predetermined-money-growth-rate rule.* To illustrate the workings of this rule, consider the following extended version of the equation of exchange:

$$\%\Delta M + \%\Delta V = \%\Delta P + \%\Delta Q$$

Suppose $\%\Delta Q$ is 3 percent and $\%\Delta V$ is 1 percent. The rule specifies that the growth rate in the money supply should be 2 percent. This growth rate would keep the price level

economics 24/7

ASSET-PRICE INFLATION

During the years 1999–2004, the price level in the United States grew at a fairly modest annual average rate of 2.4 percent. But during those same years, asset prices (especially house prices) grew rapidly. In some cities, house prices increased by 10 to 15 percent per year. If the rapid rise in house prices had occurred in consumer prices, there is no doubt the Fed would have acted quickly to slow the pace. In short, the Fed would have likely reduced the money supply.

© BRAND X PICTURES/JUPITER IMAGES

Why doesn't the Fed act the same way when the rise in prices is in assets? Some economists have argued that it should. They argue that the Fed should target a broadly defined price level that includes both consumer prices and asset prices (e.g., house and stock prices). A few central banks—namely the European Central Bank, the Bank of England, and the Reserve Bank of Australia—have recently given some support to the view that monetary policy should sometimes consider the growth in asset prices (even when consumer price inflation is low). For example, in 2004, both the Bank of England and the Reserve Bank of Australia began to adjust their respective monetary policies based on the rapid rise in asset prices in Great Britain and Australia.

In an article in *The Wall Street Journal* on February 18, 2004, Otmar Issing, the chief economist for the European Central Bank (ECB), discussed the role of a central bank in a world where consumer price inflation is low but asset price inflation is high. He states, "Just as consumer-price inflation is often described as a situation of 'too much money chasing too few goods,' asset-price inflation could similarly be characterized as 'too much money chasing too few assets.'" He goes on to say that all central banks face a challenge in the future: how to deal with asset-price inflation in a way that is not harmful to the overall economy. He states, "As societies accumulate wealth, asset prices will have a growing influence on economic developments. The problem of how to design monetary policy under such circumstances is probably the biggest challenge for central banks in our times."[3]

3. Otmar Issing, "Money and Credit," *The Wall Street Journal*, February 18, 2004.

stable; there would be a 0 percent change in P:

$$\%\Delta M + \%\Delta V = \%\Delta P + \%\Delta Q$$
$$2\% + 1\% = 0\% + 3\%$$

The Fed and the Taylor Rule

Economist John Taylor has argued for a middle ground, of sorts, between activist and nonactivist monetary policy. He has proposed that monetary authorities use a rule to guide them in making their discretionary decisions.

The rule that John Taylor has proposed has come to be known as the *Taylor rule*, which specifies how policy makers should set the target for the (nominal) federal funds rate. (Recall from an earlier chapter that the federal funds rate is the interest rate banks charge one another for reserves.) The economic thinking implicit in the Taylor rule is that there is some federal funds rate target that is consistent with (1) stabilizing inflation around a rather low inflation rate and (2) stabilizing Real GDP around its full-employment level. The aim is to find this federal funds rate target and then to use the Fed's tools to hit the target.

The Taylor rule, which, according to Taylor, will find the right federal funds rate target, is:

$$\text{Federal funds rate target} = \text{Inflation} + \text{Equilibrium real federal funds rate} + \tfrac{1}{2}\,\text{Inflation gap} + \tfrac{1}{2}\,\text{Output gap}$$

Let's briefly discuss the four components of the rule:

1. *Inflation.* This is the current inflation rate.
2. *Equilibrium real federal funds rate.* The real federal funds rate is simply the nominal federal funds rate adjusted for inflation. Taylor assumes the equilibrium real federal funds rate is 2 percent.
3. *½ inflation gap.* The inflation gap is the difference between the actual inflation rate and the target for inflation. Taylor assumes that an appropriate target for inflation is about 2 percent. If this target were accepted by policy makers, they would effectively be saying that they would not want an inflation rate higher than 2 percent.
4. *½ output gap.* The output gap is the percentage difference between actual Real GDP and its full-employment or natural level.

For example, suppose the current inflation rate is 1 percent, the equilibrium real federal funds rate is 2 percent, the inflation gap is 1 percent, and the output gap is 2 percent. The federal funds rate target can be calculated with the formula:

$$\begin{aligned}\text{Federal funds rate target} &= \text{Inflation} + \text{Equilibrium real federal funds rate} \\ &\quad + \tfrac{1}{2}\text{ Inflation gap} + \tfrac{1}{2}\text{ Output gap} \\ &= 1\% + 2\% + \tfrac{1}{2}(1\%) + \tfrac{1}{2}(2\%) \\ &= 4.5\%\end{aligned}$$

Inflation Targeting

Inflation Targeting
Targeting that requires the Fed to keep the inflation rate near a predetermined level.

Many economists today argue that the Fed should practice **inflation targeting**, which requires the Fed try to keep the inflation rate near a predetermined level. Three major issues surround inflation targeting. The first deals with whether the inflation rate target should be a specific percentage rate (e.g., 2.5 percent) or a narrow range (e.g., 1.0–2.5 percent). Second, whether it is a specific percentage rate or range, what should the rate or range be? For example, if it is specific percentage rate, should it be, say, 2.0 percent or 3.5 percent? The last issue deals with whether the inflation rate target should be announced or not. In other words, if the Fed adopts an inflation rate target of, say, 2.5 percent, should it disclose the rate to the public?

Numerous central banks in the world practice inflation targeting, and they do announce their targets. For example, the Bank of Canada has set a target of 2 percent (inflation), and it has been announcing its inflation target since 1991. Other central banks that practice inflation targeting include the Bank of England, the Central Bank of Brazil, the Bank of Israel, and the Reserve Bank of New Zealand.

For an inflation rate target approach, the Fed would simply undertake monetary policy actions to keep the actual inflation rate near or at its target. For example, if its target rate is 2 percent and the actual inflation rate is, say, 5 percent, it would cut back the growth rate in the money supply (or the absolute money supply) to bring the actual inflation rate nearer to the target rate.

The proponents of inflation targeting argue that such a policy is more in line with the Fed's objective of maintaining near price stability. The critics of inflation targeting often argue that such a policy will constrain the Fed at times, such as when it might need to overlook the target to deal with a financial crisis.

SELF-TEST

1. Would a rules-based monetary policy produce price stability?
2. What is the inflationary gap? The output gap?

office hours

"DOES MONETARY POLICY ALWAYS HAVE THE SAME EFFECTS?"

Student:
Does monetary policy always have the same effects?

Instructor:
Instead of my giving you the answer, think back to the Keynesian transmission mechanism and try to answer your question.

Student:
In the transmission mechanism, an increase in the money supply lowers the interest rate. The lower interest rate then increases investment. And the increased investment raises aggregate demand.

Instructor:
Ask yourself if the lower interest rate always raises investment.

Student:
No, it doesn't always raise investment. If investment is interest insensitive, the lower interest rate will leave investment unchanged.

Instructor:
There is something else, too. Suppose investment is responsive to changes in the interest rate. In other words, if the interest rate falls, investment will rise. But the question is whether investment always rises by the same amount. For example, if in year 1 the interest rate falls from 6 percent to 5 percent and investment rises from $300 billion to $400 billion, does it follow that every time the interest rate falls from 6 percent to 5 percent, investment will rise by $100 billion?

Student:
I see your point. You're saying that, although investment might always rise as the interest rate falls, it does not necessarily rise by the same amount every time. And, of course, if it does not rise by the same amount every time, then there is no guarantee that aggregate demand will rise by the same amount every time (because increases in investment lead to increases in aggregate demand).

Instructor:
That's correct. We'd now have to conclude that expansionary monetary policy won't always increase aggregate demand by the same amount. In other words, at one time a money supply expansion of $30 billion might raise aggregate demand more at one time than at some other time.

Student:
So one answer to my question—whether monetary policy always has the same effects—is, no, monetary policy doesn't always change aggregate demand by the same amount.

Instructor:
That's correct. This discussion also helps us to understand why economists—even those of the same school of thought—might disagree with each other. For example, suppose Smith and Jones both believe that monetary policy affects the economy through the Keynesian transmission. Just because both accept the Keynesian transmission mechanism, they don't both necessarily think that a given increase in the money supply is going to affect aggregate demand to the same degree. Although both might agree that an expansion in the money supply will increase aggregate demand, they might disagree as to how much aggregate demand will increase. Smith might think aggregate demand will rise only a little because investment will not rise much when the interest rate drops. Jones might think aggregate demand will rise a lot because investment will rise a lot when the interest rate drops.

Points to Remember

1. Monetary policy doesn't always have the same effects. With reference to the Keynesian transmission mechanism, expansionary monetary policy might lead to a large change in investment at some times (when investment is highly responsive to changes in the interest rate) and only a small change in investment at other times (when investment is somewhat insensitive to changes in the interest rate). Expansionary monetary policy therefore might not always change aggregate demand to the same degree.
2. Even economists of the same school of thought can disagree with each other at times. For example, although two economists might agree that a rise in the money supply will change investment (or aggregate demand), they might disagree as to *how much* investment (or aggregate demand) will change.

a reader asks — Are There More Than Two Transmission Mechanisms?

A transmission mechanism describes the routes, or channels, traveled by the ripples that the money market creates and that affect the goods and services market. We learned about the Keynesian and monetarist transmission mechanisms in this chapter. Are there other transmission mechanisms?

Yes, economists have put forth quite a few transmission mechanisms. We'll talk about a few.

One transmission mechanism focuses on monetary policy and stock prices. It says that when monetary policy is expansionary, individuals find themselves with excess money and use the excess to buy stocks. Greater demand for stocks drives up their price and increases the market value of firms. (The market value of a firm is the value investors believe a firm is worth; it is calculated by multiplying the number of shares outstanding by the current price per share.) As the market value of a firm rises, the firm decides to increase its investment spending. Higher investment, in turn, leads to greater aggregate demand and, in the short run, to greater Real GDP.

Another, similar transmission mechanism focuses on consumption spending instead of investment spending. Again, with an increase in the money supply, initially individuals find themselves with excess money and use it to buy stocks, and so the demand for and prices of stocks rise. Because stocks make up a part of a person's financial wealth, higher stock prices mean greater financial wealth for some people. They spend some fraction of the increase in financial wealth on consumer goods. As consumption rises, so does aggregate demand, and in the short run Real GDP rises.

Another transmission mechanism looks at the effect of monetary policy on the exchange rate. An expansion in the money supply puts downward pressure on the interest rate (at least initially). As domestic interest rates fall, domestic dollar deposits become less attractive relative to deposits denominated in foreign currencies. As people move out of dollar-denominated deposits, the exchange-rate value of the dollar falls. In other words, the dollar depreciates relative to other currencies. Dollar depreciation and foreign currency appreciation make U.S. exports less expensive for foreigners and foreign imports more expensive for Americans. Exports rise and imports fall; so net exports rise. As a result of net exports rising, aggregate demand rises, and, at least in the short run, so does Real GDP.

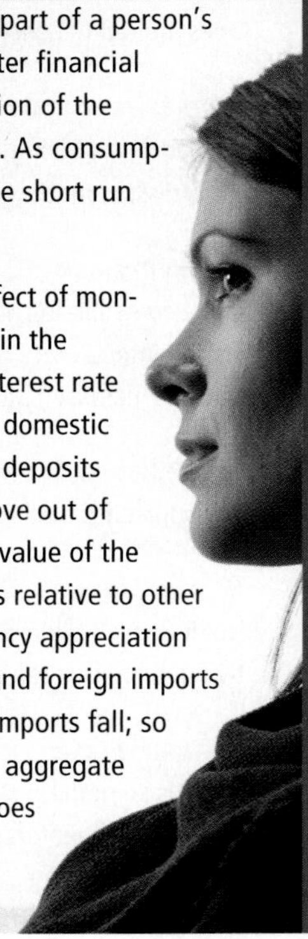

Chapter Summary

THE KEYNESIAN TRANSMISSION MECHANISM

- The Keynesian route between the money market and the goods and services market is indirect. Changes in the money market must affect the investment goods market before the goods and services market is affected. Assuming that no liquidity trap exists and investment is not interest insensitive, the transmission mechanism works as follows for an increase in the money supply: An increase in the money supply lowers the interest rate and increases investment. This increases aggregate demand and thus shifts the *AD* curve rightward. Consequently, Real GDP rises, and the unemployment rate falls. Under the same assumptions, the transmission mechanism works as follows for a decrease in the money supply: A decrease in the money supply raises the interest rate and decreases investment. This decreases aggregate demand and thus shifts the *AD* curve leftward. As a result, Real GDP falls, and the unemployment rate rises.
- The Keynesian transmission mechanism may be short-circuited either by the liquidity trap or by interest-insensitive investment. Both are Keynesian notions. If either is present, Keynesians predict that expansionary monetary policy will be unable to change Real GDP or unemployment.

THE MONETARIST TRANSMISSION MECHANISM

- The monetarist route between the money market and the goods and services market is direct. Changes in the money supply affect aggregate demand. An increase in the money supply causes individuals to increase their spending on a wide variety of goods.

BOND PRICES AND INTEREST RATES

- Interest rates and the price of old or existing bonds are inversely related.

THE ACTIVIST-NONACTIVIST DEBATE

- Activists argue that monetary policy should be deliberately used to smooth out the business cycle; they favor using activist, or discretionary, monetary policy to fine-tune the economy. Nonactivists argue against the use of discretionary monetary policy; they propose nonactivist, or rules-based, monetary policy.
- The case for discretionary monetary policy rests on three major claims: (1) The economy does not always equilibrate quickly enough at Natural Real GDP. (2) Activist monetary policy works. (3) Activist monetary policy is flexible, and flexibility is a desirable quality in monetary policy.
- The case for nonactivist monetary policy rests on three major claims: (1) There is sufficient flexibility in wages and prices in modern economies to allow the economy to equilibrate at reasonable speed at Natural Real GDP. (2) Activist monetary policies may not work. (3) Activist monetary policies are likely to make matters worse rather than better.

NONACTIVIST (OR RULES-BASED) MONETARY PROPOSALS

- The constant-money-growth-rate rule states that the annual money supply growth rate will be constant at the average annual growth rate of Real GDP.
- The predetermined-money-growth-rate rule states that the annual growth rate in the money supply will be equal to the average annual growth rate in Real GDP minus the growth rate in velocity.
- The Taylor rule holds that the federal funds rate should be targeted according to the following: Federal funds rate target = Inflation + Equilibrium real federal funds rate + ½ Inflation gap + ½ Output gap.
- Inflation targeting requires the Fed to keep the inflation rate near a predetermined level.

Key Terms and Concepts

Demand for Money (Balances)
Transmission Mechanism
Liquidity Trap
Expansionary Monetary Policy
Contractionary Monetary Policy
Activists
Fine-Tuning
Nonactivists
Inflation Targeting

Questions and Problems

1. Consider the following: Two researchers, A and B, are trying to determine whether eating fatty foods leads to heart attacks. The researchers proceed differently. Researcher A builds a model in which fatty foods may first affect X in one's body, and, if X is affected, then Y may be affected, and, if Y is affected, then Z may be affected. Finally, if Z is affected, the heart is affected, and the individual has an increased probability of suffering a heart attack. Researcher B doesn't proceed in this step-by-step fashion. She conducts an experiment to see whether people who eat many fatty foods have more, fewer, or the same number of heart attacks as people who eat few fatty foods. Which researcher's methods have more in common with the research methodology implicit in the Keynesian transmission mechanism? Which researcher's methods have more in common with the research methodology implicit in the monetarist transmission mechanism? Explain your answer.
2. If bond prices fall, will individuals want to hold more or less money? Explain your answer.
3. Why is the demand curve for money downward sloping?
4. Explain how it is possible to have too much money.
5. Explain how the Keynesian transmission mechanism works.
6. Explain how the monetarist transmission mechanism works.
7. It has been suggested that nonactivists are not concerned with the level of Real GDP and unemployment because most (if not all) nonactivist monetary proposals set as their immediate objective the stabilization of the price level. Discuss.
8. Suppose the combination of more accurate data and better forecasting techniques made it easy for the Fed to predict a recession 10 to 16 months in advance. Would this strengthen the case for activism or nonactivism? Explain your answer.
9. Suppose it were proved that there is no such thing as a liquidity trap and investment is not interest insensitive. Would this be enough to disprove the Keynesian claim that expansionary monetary policy is not always effective at changing Real GDP? Why or why not?
10. Both activists and nonactivists make good points for their respective positions. Do you think there is anything activists could say to nonactivists to convince them to accept the activist position, and vice versa? If so, what is it? If not, why not?
11. The discussion of supply and demand in Chapter 3 noted that if two goods are substitutes, the price of one and the demand for the other are directly related. For example, if Pepsi-Cola and Coca-Cola are substitutes, an increase in the price of Pepsi-Cola will increase the demand for Coca-Cola. Suppose that bonds and stocks are substitutes. We know that interest rates and bond prices are inversely related. What do you predict is the relationship between stock prices and interest rates? Explain your answer.
12. Argue the case for and against a monetary rule.
13. How does inflation targeting work?
14. Monetary policy can affect relative prices. Do you agree or disagree with this statement? Explain your answer.

Working with Numbers and Graphs

1 Manuel bought a bond last year for $10,000 that promises to pay him $900 a year. This year, he can buy a bond for $10,000 that promises to pay $1,000 a year. If Manuel wants to sell his old bond, what is its price likely to be?

2 Charu bought a bond last year for $10,000 that promises to pay her $1,000 a year. This year, it is possible to buy a bond for $10,000 that promises to pay $800 a year. If Charu wants to sell her old bond, what is its price likely to be?

3 Suppose the annual average percentage change in Real GDP is 2.3 percent, and the annual average percentage change in velocity is 1.1 percent. Using the monetary rule discussed in the text, what percentage change in the money supply will keep prices stable (on average)?

4 Graphically show that the more interest insensitive the investment demand curve is, the less likely it is that monetary policy will be effective at changing Real GDP.

5 Which panel in the figure best describes the situation in each of parts (a)–(d)?

a. Expansionary monetary policy that effectively removes the economy from a recessionary gap.

b. Expansionary monetary policy that is destabilizing.

c. Contractionary monetary policy that effectively removes the economy from an inflationary gap.

d. Monetary policy that is ineffective at changing Real GDP.

6 Graphically portray the Keynesian transmission mechanism under the following conditions:

a. A decrease in the money supply.

b. No liquidity trap.

c. Downward-sloping investment demand.

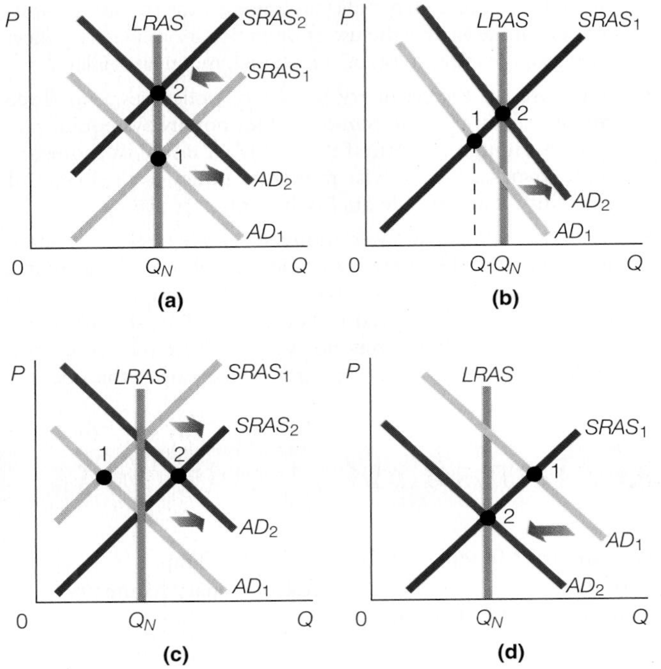

7 Graphically portray the monetarist transmission mechanism when the money supply declines.

8 According to the Taylor rule, if inflation is 5 percent, the inflation gap is 3 percent, and the output gap is 2 percent, what does the federal funds rate target equal?

©AP PHOTO/PETAR PETROV

CHAPTER 15

EXPECTATIONS THEORY AND THE ECONOMY

Introduction Until now, we have not discussed the role of expectations in the economy. In this chapter, we discuss two expectations theories: adaptive and rational. We begin our discussion of expectations theory and the economy with a debate that raged within the economic profession years ago over the shape of the Phillips curve.

PHILLIPS CURVE ANALYSIS

The **Phillips curve** is used to analyze the relationship between inflation and unemployment. We begin the discussion of the Phillips curve by focusing on the work of three economists: A. W. Phillips, Paul Samuelson, and Robert Solow.

Phillips Curve
A curve that originally showed the relationship between wage inflation and unemployment and that now more often shows the relationship between price inflation and unemployment.

The Phillips Curve

In 1958, A. W. Phillips of the London School of Economics published a paper in the economics journal, *Economica.* The paper was titled "The Relation Between Unemployment and the Rate of Change of Money Wages in the United Kingdom, 1861–1957." As the title suggests, Phillips collected data about the rate of change in money wages, sometimes referred to as *wage inflation,* and *unemployment rates* in the United Kingdom over almost a century. He then plotted the rate of change in money wages against the unemployment rate for each year. Finally, he fit a curve to the data points (Exhibit 1).

AN INVERSE RELATIONSHIP The curve, which came to be known as the Phillips curve, is downward sloping, suggesting that the rate of change of money wage rates (wage inflation) and unemployment rates are *inversely related.*[1] This inverse relationship suggests

1. Why is there an inverse relationship between wage inflation and unemployment? Early explanations focused on the state of the labor market, given changes in aggregate demand. When aggregate demand is increasing, businesses expand production and hire more employees. As the unemployment rate falls, the labor market becomes tighter, and employers find it increasingly difficult to hire workers at old wages. Businesses must offer higher wages to obtain additional workers. Unemployment and money wage rates move in opposite directions.

a trade-off between wage inflation and unemployment. Higher wage inflation means lower unemployment; lower wage inflation means higher unemployment.

Policy makers concluded from the Phillips curve that lowering both wage inflation and unemployment was impossible; they could do one or the other. So the combination of low wage inflation and low unemployment was unlikely. This was the bad news.

The good news was that rising unemployment and rising wage inflation did not go together either. Thus, the combination of high unemployment and high wage inflation was unlikely.

exhibit 1

The Original Phillips Curve

This curve was constructed by A. W. Phillips, using data for the United Kingdom from 1861 to 1913. (The relationship here is also representative of the experience of the United Kingdom through 1957.) The original Phillips curve suggests an inverse relationship between wage inflation and unemployment; it represents a wage inflation–unemployment trade-off. (Note: Each dot represents a single year.)

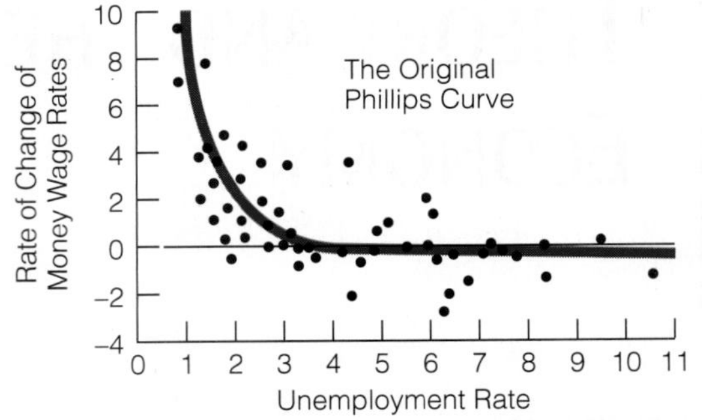

Samuelson and Solow: The Americanization of the Phillips Curve

In 1960, two American economists, Paul Samuelson and Robert Solow, published an article in the *American Economic Review* in which they fit a Phillips curve to the U.S. economy from 1935 to 1959. In addition to using American data instead of British data, they measured *price inflation rates* (instead of wage inflation rates) against unemployment rates. They found an inverse relationship between (price) inflation and unemployment (see Exhibit 2).[2]

Economists concluded from the Phillips curve that **stagflation**, or high inflation together with high unemployment, was extremely unlikely. The economy could register (1) high unemployment and low inflation or (2) low unemployment and high inflation. Also, economists noticed that the Phillips curve presented policy makers with a *menu of choices.* For example, policy makers could choose to move the economy to any of the points on the Phillips curve in Exhibit 2. If they decided that a point like A, with high unemployment and low inflation, was preferable to a point like D, with low unemployment and high inflation, then so be it. It was simply a matter of reaching the right level of aggregate demand. To Keynesian economists, who were gaining a reputation for advocating fine-tuning the economy (i.e., using small-scale measures to counterbalance undesirable economic trends), this conclusion seemed consistent with their theories and policy proposals.

Stagflation
The simultaneous occurrence of high rates of inflation and unemployment.

exhibit 2

The Phillips Curve and a Menu of Choices

Samuelson and Solow's early work using American data showed that the Phillips curve was downward sloping. Economists reasoned that stagflation was extremely unlikely and that the Phillips curve presented policy makers with a menu of choices—point A, B, C, or D.

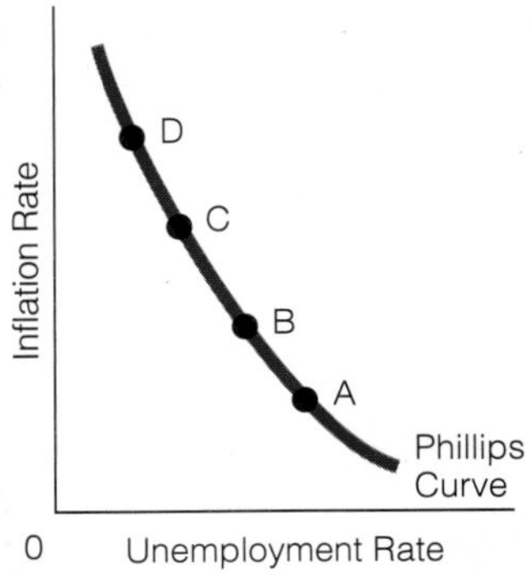

THE CONTROVERSY BEGINS: ARE THERE REALLY TWO PHILLIPS CURVES?

This section discusses the work of Milton Friedman and the hypothesis that there are two, not one, Phillips curves.

Things Aren't Always as We Thought

In the 1970s and early 1980s, economists began to question many of the conclusions about the Phillips curve. Their questions were largely prompted by events after 1969. Consider Exhibit 3, which shows U.S. inflation and unemployment rates for the years 1961–2003. The 1961–1969 period, which is shaded, depicts the original Phillips curve trade-off between inflation and unemployment. The remaining period, 1970–2003, as a whole does not, although some subperiods, such as 1976–1979, do.

2. Today, when economists speak of the Phillips curve, they are usually referring to the relationship between price inflation rates and unemployment rates instead of the relationship between wage inflation rates and unemployment rates.

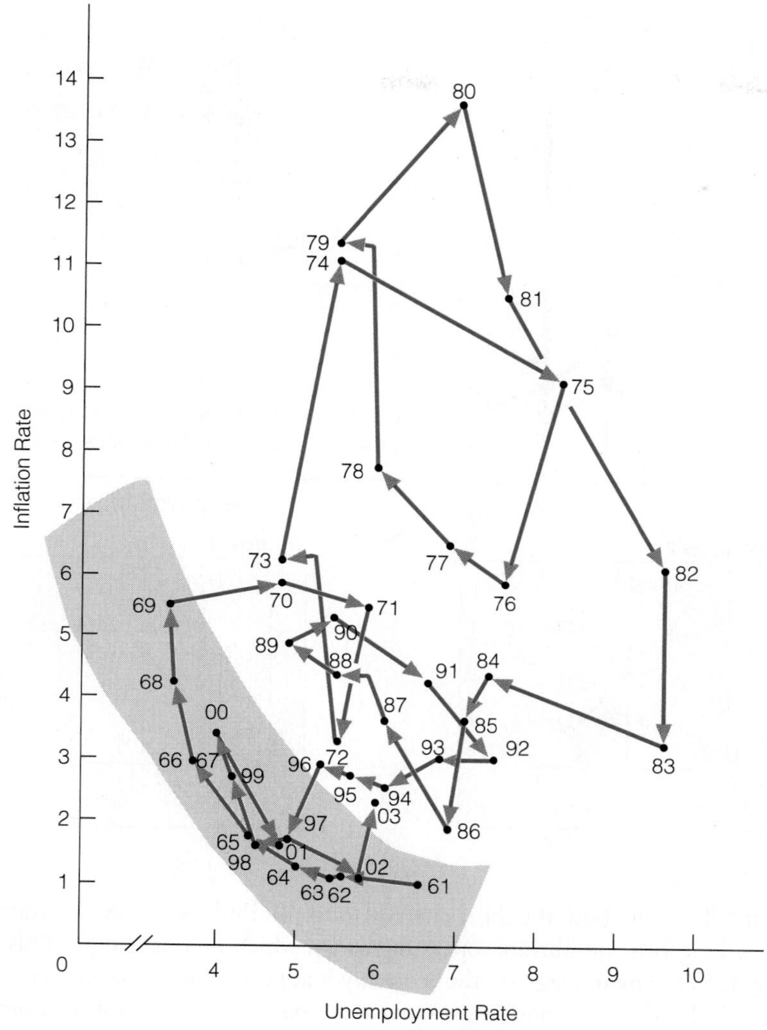

exhibit 3

The Diagram That Raises Questions: Inflation and Unemployment, 1961–2003

The period 1961–1969 clearly depicts the original Phillips curve trade-off between inflation and unemployment. The later period, 1970–2003, as a whole, does not. However, some subperiods do, such as 1976–1979. The diagram presents empirical evidence that stagflation may exist; an inflation-unemployment trade-off may not always hold.

Focusing on the period 1970–2003, we note that stagflation—high unemployment and high inflation—is possible. For example, 1975, 1981, and 1982 are definitely years of stagflation. The existence of stagflation implies that a trade-off between inflation and unemployment may not always exist.

Friedman and the Natural Rate Theory

Milton Friedman, in his presidential address to the American Economic Association in 1967 (published in the *American Economic Review*), attacked the idea of a *permanent* downward-sloping Phillips curve. Friedman's key point was that there are two, not one, Phillips curves: a short-run Phillips curve and a long-run Phillips curve. Friedman said, "There is always a temporary tradeoff between inflation and unemployment; there is no permanent tradeoff." In other words, *there is a trade-off in the short run but not in the long run.* Friedman's discussion not only introduced two types of Phillips curves but also opened the macroeconomics door wide, once and for all, to expectations theory—that is, to the idea that people's expectations about economic events affect economic outcomes.

exhibit 4

Short-Run and Long-Run Phillips Curves

Starting at point 1 in the main diagram, and assuming that the expected inflation rate stays constant as aggregate demand increases, the economy moves to point 2. As the expected inflation rate changes and comes to equal the actual inflation rate, the economy moves to point 3. Points 1 and 2 lie on a short-run Phillips curve. Points 1 and 3 lie on a long-run Phillips curve. (Note: The percentages in parentheses following the *SRAS* curves in the windows refer to the expected inflation rates.)

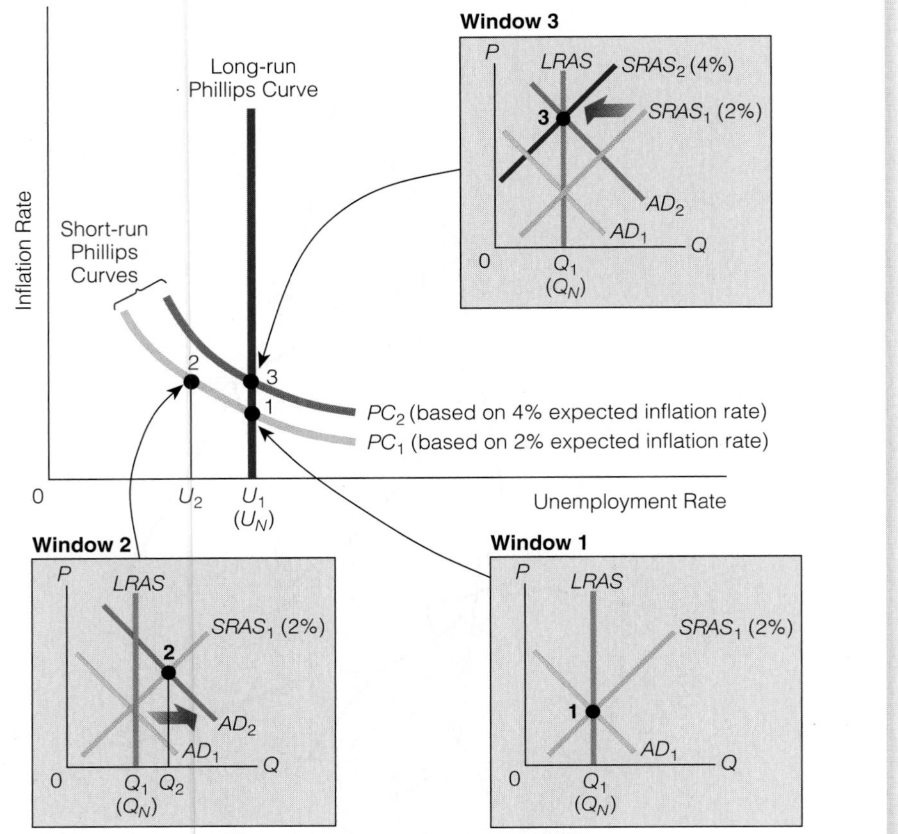

Exhibit 4 illustrates both the short-run and long-run Phillips curves. We start with the economy in long-run equilibrium, operating at Q_1, which is equal to Q_N. This is shown in window 1. In the main diagram, the economy is at point 1 at the natural rate of unemployment, U_N. Further and most important, *we assume that the expected inflation rate and the actual inflation rate are the same* at 2 percent.

Now suppose government *unexpectedly* increases aggregate demand from AD_1 to AD_2, as shown in window 2. As a result, the *actual* inflation rate increases (say, to 4 percent), but in the short run (immediately after the increase in aggregate demand), individual decision makers do not know this. Consequently, the *expected* inflation rate remains at 2 percent. In short, aggregate demand increases at the same time that people's expected inflation rate remains constant. Because of this combination of events, certain things happen. The higher aggregate demand causes temporary shortages and higher prices. Businesses then respond to higher prices and higher profits by increasing output. Higher output requires more employees, and so businesses start hiring more workers. As job vacancies increase, many currently unemployed individuals find work. Furthermore, many of these newly employed persons accept the prevailing wage rate because they think the wages will have greater purchasing power (recall that they expect the inflation rate to be 2 percent) than, in fact, those wages will turn out to have.

So far, the results of an increase in aggregate demand with no change in the expected inflation rate are (1) an increase in Real GDP from Q_1 to Q_2 (see window 2) and (2) a corresponding decrease in the unemployment rate from U_1 to U_2 (see the main diagram). Thus, the economy has moved from point 1 to point 2 in the main diagram.

This raises a question: Is point 2 a stable equilibrium? Friedman answered that it is not. He argued that, *as long as the expected inflation rate is not equal to the actual inflation rate, the economy is not in long-run equilibrium.*

For Friedman, as for most economists today, the movement from point 1 to point 2 on PC_1 is a short-run movement. Economists refer to PC_1, along which short-run movements occur, as a *short-run Phillips curve.*

In time, inflation expectations begin to change. As prices continue to climb, wage earners realize that their real (inflation-adjusted) wages have fallen. In hindsight, they realize that they accepted nominal (money) wages based on an expected inflation rate (2 percent) that was too low. So they revise their inflation expectations upward.

At the same time, some wage earners quit their jobs because they choose not to continue working at such low *real wages.* Eventually, the combination of some workers quitting their jobs and most (if not all) workers revising their inflation expectations upward causes wage rates to move upward.

Higher wage rates shift the short-run aggregate supply curve from $SRAS_1$ to $SRAS_2$ (see window 3), ultimately moving the economy back to Natural Real GDP and to the natural rate of unemployment at point 3 (see the main diagram). The curve that connects point 1, where the economy started, and point 3, where it ended, is called the *long-run Phillips curve.*

Thus, the short-run Phillips curve exhibits a trade-off between inflation and unemployment, whereas the long-run Phillips curve does not. This idea is implicit in what has come to be called the **Friedman natural rate theory** (or the *Friedman fooling theory*). According to this theory, in the long run, the economy returns to its natural rate of unemployment, and it moved away from the natural unemployment rate in the first place only because workers were fooled (in the short run) into thinking the inflation rate was lower than it was.

Friedman Natural Rate Theory
The idea that, in the long run, unemployment is at its natural rate. Within the Phillips curve framework, the natural rate theory specifies that there is a long-run Phillips curve, which is vertical at the natural rate of unemployment.

How, specifically, do people's expectations relate to the discussion of the short- and long-run Phillips curves? Look at Exhibit 4 again. The economy starts out at point 1 in the main diagram, and then something happens: Aggregate demand increases. This increase raises the inflation rate, *but workers don't become aware of the change in the inflation rate for a while.* In the interim, their expected inflation rate is too low, and, as a result, they are willing to work at jobs (and produce output) that they wouldn't work at if they perceived the inflation rate realistically.

In time, workers perceive the inflation rate realistically. In other words, the expected inflation rate is no longer too low; it has risen to equal the actual inflation rate. There is a predicted response in the unemployment rate and output as a result: The unemployment rate rises and output falls.

To summarize, because workers' expectations (of inflation) are, in the short run, inconsistent with reality, workers produce more output than they would have produced if their expectations were consistent with reality. This is how people's expectations can affect such real economic variables as Real GDP and the unemployment rate.

Exhibit 5 may also help explain the Friedman natural rate theory.

Thinking like AN ECONOMIST

Perceptions of Reality Matter

A person says she bases her actions on reality. When it rains, she pulls out an umbrella; when she has a hard time seeing, she gets her eyes checked. People also base their actions on their *perceptions* of reality, as workers do in the Friedman natural rate theory. Although the inflation rate has actually increased, workers don't perceive the change. Thus, in the short run (during the time period in which they misperceive reality), workers base their actions not on reality, but on their perception of it.

exhibit 5

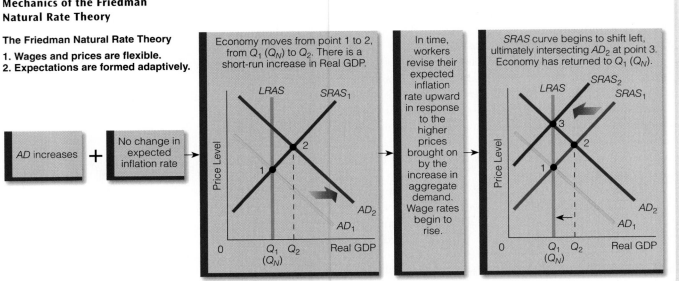

Mechanics of the Friedman Natural Rate Theory

The Friedman Natural Rate Theory

1. **Wages and prices are flexible.**
2. **Expectations are formed adaptively.**

AD increases + No change in expected inflation rate →

Economy moves from point 1 to 2, from Q_1 (Q_N) to Q_2. There is a short-run increase in Real GDP.

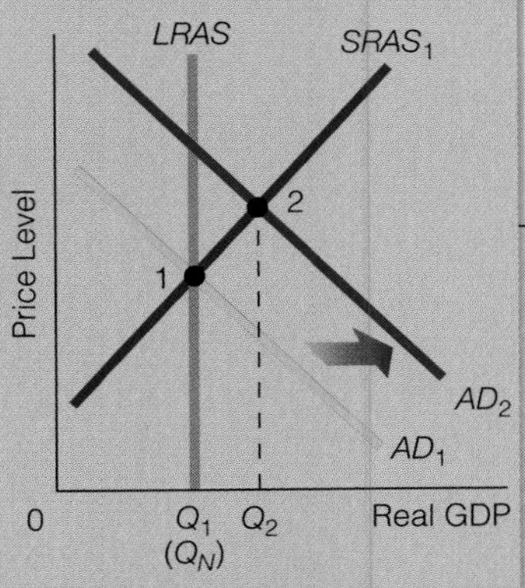

→ In time, workers revise their expected inflation rate upward in response to the higher prices brought on by the increase in aggregate demand. Wage rates begin to rise. →

SRAS curve begins to shift left, ultimately intersecting AD_2 at point 3. Economy has returned to Q_1 (Q_N).

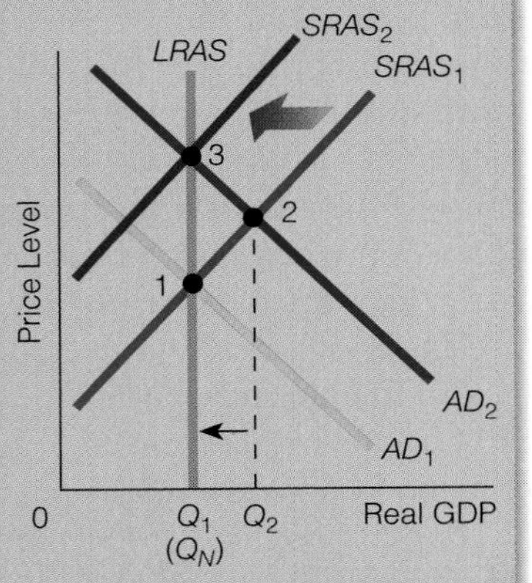

macro*theme* → One of the biggest questions in macroeconomics is how does the economy work? More specifically, how do we explain what happens in the economy? With the inclusion of expectations in our macroeconomic discussion, some economists are telling us that what happens in the economy has much to do with people's expectations. In other words, what happens in an economy depends not only on real factors—such as the amount of resources, the current state of monetary policy, and so on—but also on what people think affects what happens in an economy.

How Do People Form Their Expectations?

Implicit in the Friedman natural rate theory is an assumption about how individuals form their expectations. Essentially, the theory holds that individuals form their expected inflation rate by looking at past inflation rates. To illustrate, suppose that the actual inflation rates in years 1–4 are as shown in the following table. What do you think the inflation rate will be in year 5? Friedman assumes that people weight past inflation rates to come up with their expected inflation rate. For example, John may assign the following weights to the inflation rates in the past four years:

Year	Inflation Rate	Weight
1	5 percent	10%
2	3 percent	20%
3	2 percent	30%
4	2 percent	40%

In other words, as year 5 approaches, the weight assigned to the present year's inflation rate rises. Based on these weights, John forms his expected inflation rate (his best guess of the inflation rate in the upcoming year) by finding the weighted average of the inflation rates in the past 4 years.

$$\text{Expected inflation rate} = 0.10(5\text{ percent}) + 0.20(3\text{ percent}) + 0.30(2\text{ percent}) + 0.40(2\text{ percent}) = 2.5\text{ percent}$$

John's expected inflation rate is 2.5 percent.

Notice that, in forming an expected inflation rate this way, John is always looking to the past. He is, in a sense, looking over his shoulder to see what has happened and then, based on what has happened, figuring out what he thinks *will happen*. In economics, a person who forms an expected inflation rate this way is said to have **adaptive expectations.** In short, the Friedman natural rate theory implicitly assumes that people have adaptive expectations.

Adaptive Expectations
Expectations that individuals form from past experience and modify slowly as the present and the future become the past (as time passes).

Some economists have argued this point. They believe that people form their expected inflation rate not by using adaptive expectations, but instead by holding *rational expectations.* We discuss this view in the next section.

Finding ECONOMICS

At the Bargaining Table

Suppose you read the following report in the newspaper: "Recent wage negotiations between management and labor unions in the city have come to a halt. The two sides in the negotiations are unable so far to come to an agreement on annual wage rate increases for the duration of the four-year contract. . . ." Where is the economics? First, if the so-called two sides are negotiating an annual wage rate increase, then each side is probably basing the increase on their expected inflation rate. Management might be saying, "We believe that the average annual inflation rate over the next four years will be 2 percent; so we are willing to agree to an annual wage rate increase of 2 percent each year for the next four years." The labor unions might be saying, "Since we expect the average annual inflation rate over the next four years to be 3.5 percent, we believe that 3.5 percent is the right annual wage rate increase for us."

SELF-TEST

(Answers to Self-Test questions are in the Self-Test Appendix.)

1. What condition must exist for the Phillips curve to present policy makers with a permanent menu of choices (between inflation and unemployment)?
2. Is there a trade-off between inflation and unemployment? Explain your answer.
3. The Friedman natural rate theory is sometimes called the fooling theory. Who is being fooled, and what are they being fooled about?

RATIONAL EXPECTATIONS AND NEW CLASSICAL THEORY

Rational expectations have played a major role in the Phillips curve controversy. The work of economists Robert Lucas, Robert Barro, Thomas Sargent, and Neil Wallace is relevant to this discussion. (In this text, the natural rate theory built on adaptive expectations is called the Friedman natural rate theory; the natural rate theory built on rational expectations is called the new classical theory.)

Rational Expectations

In the early 1970s, a few economists, including Robert Lucas of the University of Chicago (winner of the 1995 Nobel Prize in Economics), began to question the short-run tradeoff between inflation and unemployment. Essentially, Lucas combined the natural rate theory with rational expectations.[3]

Rational Expectations
Expectations that individuals form based on past experience and on their predictions about the effects of present and future policy actions and events.

Rational expectations holds that individuals form the expected inflation rate not only on the basis of their past experience with inflation (looking over their shoulders), but also on their predictions about the effects of present and future policy actions and events. In short, the expected inflation rate is formed by looking at the past, present, and future. To illustrate, suppose the inflation rate has been 2 percent for the past seven years. Then, the chairman of the Fed's Board of Governors speaks about "sharply stimulating the economy." Rational expectationists argue that the expected inflation rate might immediately jump upward based on the current announcement by the chairman.

A major difference between adaptive and rational expectations is the *speed* at which the expected inflation rate changes. If the expected inflation rate is formed adaptively, then it is slow to change. Because it is based only on the past, individuals wait until the present and the future become the past before changing their expectations. If the expected inflation rate is formed rationally, it changes quickly because it is based on the past, present, and future.

Do People Really Anticipate Policy?

One implication of rational expectations is that people anticipate policy. Suppose you chose people at random on the street and asked them this question: What do you think the Fed will do in the next few months? Do you think you would be more likely to receive an intelligent answer or the response, "What's the Fed?" Most readers of this text would probably expect the second answer. In fact, there is a general feeling that the person on the street knows little about economics or economic institutions. So the answer to our question seems to be no, people don't really anticipate policy. But suppose you chose people at random on Wall Street and asked the same question. In this case, the answer to our question is likely to be yes, at least *these* people anticipate policy.

We suggest that not all persons need to anticipate policy. *As long as some do*, the consequences may be the same *as if* all persons do. For example, Juanita Estevez is anticipating policy if she decides to buy 100 shares of SKA because her best friend, Tammy Higgins, heard from her friend, Kenny Urich, that his broker, Roberta Gunter, told him that SKA's stock is expected to go up. Juanita is anticipating policy because it is likely that Roberta Gunter obtained her information from a researcher in the brokerage firm who makes it his business to watch the Fed and to anticipate its next move.

Of course, anticipating policy is not done just for the purpose of buying and selling stocks. Labor unions hire professional forecasters (Fed watchers) to predict future inflation rates, which is important information to have during wage contract negotiations. Banks hire forecasters to predict inflation rates, which they incorporate into the interest rate they charge. Export businesses hire forecasters to predict the future exchange-rate value of the dollar. The average investor may subscribe to a business or investment newsletter for information on which to base predictions of interest rates, the price of gold, or next year's

3. Rational expectations appeared on the economic scene in 1961, when John Muth published "Rational Expectations and the Theory of Price Movements" in *Econometrica*. For about ten years, the article received little attention from the economics profession. Then, in the early 1970s, with the work of Robert Lucas, Thomas Sargent, Neil Wallace, Robert Barro, and others, the article began to be noticed.

inflation rate more accurately. The person thinking of refinancing a mortgage watches one of the many financial news shows on television to find out about the government's most recent move and how it will affect interest rates in, say, the next three months.

Finding ECONOMICS

While Playing a Game of Chess

Where is the economics in a game of chess? Chess players often anticipate each other's moves. Player 1 might be thinking that if she moves from e4 to e5, player 2 will move from b5 to c3. But then, the first player asks herself, what comes next? Will player 2 then be likely to move from c3 to d6?

What people do in a game of chess and what they do when predicting government policy actions might not be all that different. In a game of chess you are playing to win, and whether you win depends on how well you can anticipate your opponent's moves. Anticipating policy actions is not much different, as you will shortly see. How well you do in the economy also has a lot to do on how well you anticipate government policy actions.

New Classical Theory: The Effects of Unanticipated and Anticipated Policy

New classical theory makes two major assumptions: (1) Expectations are formed rationally; (2) wages and prices are flexible. With these assumptions in mind, we discuss new classical theory in two settings: when policy is unanticipated and when policy is anticipated.

UNANTICIPATED POLICY Consider Exhibit 6(a). The economy starts at point 1, where $Q_1 = Q_N$. Unexpectedly, the Fed begins to buy government securities, and the money supply and aggregate demand increase. The aggregate demand curve shifts rightward from AD_1 to AD_2. Because the policy action was unanticipated, individuals are caught off guard; so the anticipated price level (P_1), on which the short-run aggregate supply curve is based, is not likely to change immediately. (This is similar to saying, as we did in the discussion of the Friedman natural rate theory, that individuals' expected inflation rate is less than the actual inflation rate.)

In the short run, the economy moves from point 1 to point 2, from Q_1 to Q_2. (The economy has moved up the short-run Phillips curve to a higher inflation rate and lower unemployment rate.) In the long run, workers correctly anticipate the higher price level and increase their wage demands accordingly. The short-run aggregate supply curve shifts leftward from $SRAS_1$ to $SRAS_2$, and the economy moves to point 3.

ANTICIPATED POLICY Now consider what happens when policy is anticipated, particularly when it is *correctly* anticipated. When individuals anticipate that the Fed will buy government securities and that the money supply, aggregate demand, and prices will increase, they adjust their present actions accordingly. For example, workers bargain for higher wages so that their real wages will not fall when the price level rises. As a result, the short-run aggregate supply curve will shift leftward from $SRAS_1$ to $SRAS_2$ *at the same time* that the aggregate demand curve shifts rightward from AD_1 to AD_2 [see Exhibit 6(b)].The economy moves directly from point 1 to point 2. Real GDP does not change, remaining at its natural level throughout the adjustment period; so the unemployment rate does not change either. There is no short-run trade-off between inflation and unemployment. The short-run Phillips curve and the long-run Phillips curve are the same; the curve is vertical.

exhibit 6

Rational Expectations in an *AD-AS* Framework

The economy is in long-run equilibrium at point 1 in both (a) and (b). In (a), there is an unanticipated increase in aggregate demand. In the short run, the economy moves to point 2. In the long run, it moves to point 3. In (b), the increase in aggregate demand is correctly anticipated. Because the increase is anticipated, the short-run aggregate supply curve shifts from $SRAS_1$ to $SRAS_2$ at the same time the aggregate demand curve shifts from AD_1 to AD_2. The economy moves directly to point 2, which is comparable to point 3 in (a).

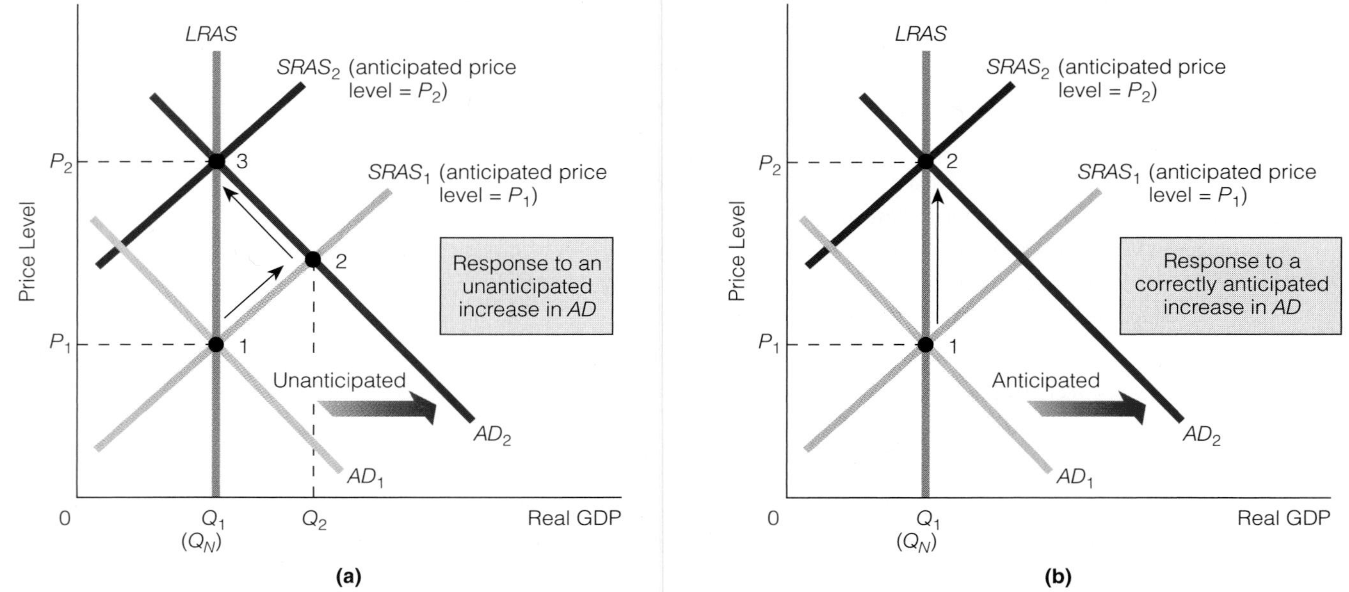

Policy Ineffectiveness Proposition (PIP)

Using rational expectations, we showed (in Exhibit 6) that if the rise in aggregate demand is unanticipated, there is a short-run increase in Real GDP, but if the rise in aggregate demand is correctly anticipated, there is no change in Real GDP.

To understand the implications of these results, consider the two types of macroeconomic policies: fiscal and monetary. Both types of policies can theoretically increase aggregate demand. For example, assuming no crowding out or incomplete crowding out, expansionary fiscal policy shifts the *AD* curve rightward, and expansionary monetary policy does the same. In both cases, expansionary policy is effective at increasing Real GDP and lowering the unemployment rate in the short run.

New classical economists question this scenario. They argue that (1) if the expansionary policy change is correctly anticipated, (2) if individuals form their expectations rationally, and (3) if wages and prices are flexible, then neither expansionary fiscal policy nor expansionary monetary policy can increase Real GDP and lower the unemployment rate in the short run. This argument is called the **policy ineffectiveness proposition (PIP)**.

Policy Ineffectiveness Proposition (PIP)
If (1) a policy change is correctly anticipated, (2) individuals form their expectations rationally, and (3) wages and prices are flexible, then neither fiscal policy nor monetary policy is effective at meeting macroeconomic goals.

New classical economists are not saying that monetary and fiscal policies are never effective. Instead, they are saying that monetary and fiscal policies are not effective under certain conditions, specifically, when (1) policy is correctly anticipated, (2) when people form their expectations rationally, and (3) when wages and prices are flexible.

Think about what this means. If, under certain conditions, expansionary monetary and fiscal policy are not effective at increasing Real GDP and lowering the unemployment rate, the case for government fine-tuning the economy is questionable.

Thinking like AN ECONOMIST

If-Then Thinking

There is a lot of if-then thinking in economics. For example, *if* the price of a good falls and nothing else changes, *then* the quantity demanded of a good will rise. That is the kind of thinking we have here. New classical economists are saying that *if* people anticipate policy correctly, and *if* people form their expectations rationally, and *if* wages and prices are flexible, *then* monetary and fiscal policies are not effective at changing Real GDP. Of course, the logic begs the question of whether the conditional statements (the if statements) actually hold in the real world.

Rational Expectations and Incorrectly Anticipated Policy

Now suppose that wages and prices are flexible, that people form their expectations rationally, and that they anticipate policy—but this time they anticipate policy *incorrectly.* What happens?

To illustrate, consider Exhibit 7. The economy is in long-run equilibrium at point 1, where $Q_1 = Q_N$. People believe the Fed will increase aggregate demand by increasing the money supply, but they *incorrectly anticipate* the degree to which aggregate demand will be increased. Thinking that aggregate demand will increase from AD_1 to AD_2, they immediately revise their anticipated price level to P_2 (the long-run equilibrium position of the AD_2 curve and the *LRAS* curve). As a result, the short-run aggregate supply curve shifts leftward from $SRAS_1$ to $SRAS_2$.

However, the actual increase in aggregate demand is less than anticipated, and the aggregate demand curve shifts rightward only from AD_1 to AD'_2. As a result, the economy moves to point 2′, to a lower Real GDP and a higher unemployment rate. We conclude that a policy designed to increase Real GDP and lower unemployment can do just the opposite if the policy is less expansionary than anticipated.

In this example, people incorrectly anticipated policy in a particular direction; that is, they mistakenly believed that the aggregate demand curve was going to shift to the right more than it actually did. They *overestimated the increase in aggregate demand.* If people can overestimate the increase in aggregate demand, then they can probably *underestimate* it too. In short, when discussing rational expectations, we get different outcomes in the short run depending on whether policy is (1) unanticipated, (2) anticipated correctly, (3) anticipated incorrectly in one direction, or (4) anticipated incorrectly in the other direction.

exhibit 7

The Short-Run Response to an Aggregate Demand–Increasing Policy That Is Less Expansionary Than Anticipated (in the New Classical Theory)

Starting at point 1, people anticipate an increase in aggregate demand from AD_1 to AD_2. Based on this, the short-run aggregate supply curve shifts leftward from $SRAS_1$ to $SRAS_2$. It turns out, however, that the aggregate demand curve shifts rightward only to AD'_2 (less than anticipated). As a result, the economy moves to point 2′, to a lower Real GDP and a higher unemployment rate.

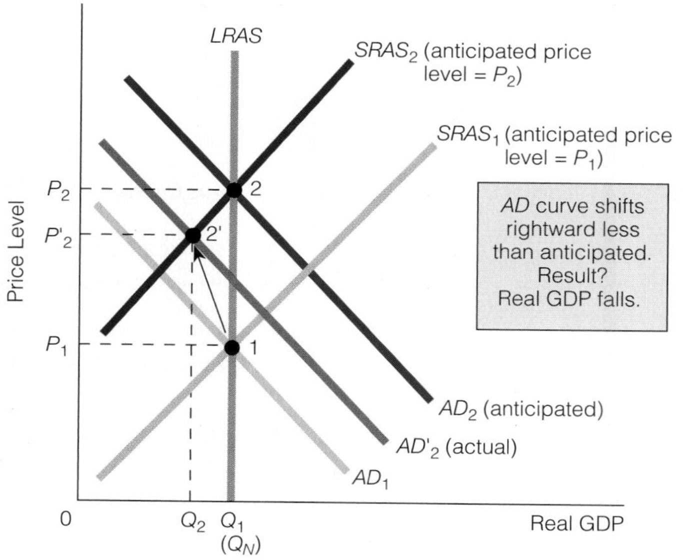

economics 24/7

RATIONAL EXPECTATIONS IN THE COLLEGE CLASSROOM

If people hold rational expectations, the outcome of a policy will be different if the policy is unanticipated than if it is anticipated. Specifically, unanticipated policy changes can move the economy away from the natural unemployment rate, but correctly anticipated policy changes cannot. Does something similar happen in a college classroom?

© BANANA STOCK/JUPITER IMAGES

Suppose Ana's history class starts at 9:00 a.m., and she "naturally" arrives 1 minute before class starts. In other words, her so-called natural waiting time is 1 minute.

The first day of class, Ana arrives at 8:59, her instructor arrives at 8:59:30, and she starts class promptly at 9:00 a.m.

The second day of class, Ana arrives at 8:59, her instructor arrives at 9:01:30, and she starts class at 9:02 a.m. On this day, Ana has waited 3 minutes, which is more than her natural waiting time of 1 minute.

The third, fourth, and fifth days of class are the same as the second. So for the second through fifth days, Ana is operating at more than her natural waiting time. Rational expectations hold that people will not continue to make the same mistake. In this case, Ana will take her professor's recent arrival time into account and adjust accordingly. On the sixth day of class, instead of arriving at 8:59, Ana arrives at 9:01. This day, the instructor again arrives at 9:01:30 and begins class at 9:02 a.m., and Ana has moved back to her natural waiting time of 1 minute.

So far, Ana's natural waiting time was met on the first day of class. On the second through fifth days of class, the professor obviously had a change of policy as to her arrival time. Ana didn't anticipate this change of policy; so she was fooled into waiting more than her natural waiting time. But Ana did not continue to make the same mistake. She adjusted to her professor's policy change and went back to her 1-minute natural waiting time.

Now let's change things a bit. Suppose at the end of the first day of class, the professor says, "I know I arrived at class at 8:59:30 today, but I won't do this again. From now on, I will arrive at 9:01:30."

In this situation, the professor has announced her policy change. Ana hears the announcement and therefore correctly anticipates the professor's arrival time from now on. With this information, she adjusts her behavior. Instead of arriving at class at 8:59, she arrives at 9:01. Thus, she has correctly anticipated her professor's policy change, and she will remain at her natural waiting time (she will not move from it, even temporarily).

Common MISCONCEPTIONS

About Changes in the Money Supply and Real GDP

Until we introduced new classical theory, we always held that an increase in the money supply either raised Real GDP or at least left it unchanged.

- In the simple quantity theory of money in terms of the *AD-AS* framework, the aggregate supply curve was vertical. Increases in *AD* brought about by increases in the money supply simply increased the price level and left the Real GDP level unchanged.
- In the simple Keynesian theory, an increase in *AD* brought about by an increase in the money supply led to an increase in Real GDP if the increase came within the horizontal section of the Keynesian *AS* curve. If the increase in *AD* came within the vertical section of the Keynesian *AS* curve, Real GDP did not change.

(continued)

Common Misconceptions (continued)

- In the monetarist theory, an increase in *AD* brought about by an increase in the money supply led to an increase in Real GDP in the short run. (Remember that the *SRAS* curve in the model is upward sloping.)

Having looked at these theories, we might conclude that, given an increase in the money supply, Real GDP may remain unchanged or increase, but never decrease. Along comes the new classical theory and labels this conclusion a myth. According to this theory, an increase in the money supply may lead to a decrease in Real GDP in the short run (as just discussed). Specifically, when policy is anticipated incorrectly (for example, when *AD* increases less than individuals' expectations), we can get a rise in the money supply, leading to a decline in Real GDP in the short run.

How to Fall into a Recession Without Really Trying

Suppose the public witnesses the following series of events in three consecutive years.

1. The federal government runs a budget deficit and finances the deficit by borrowing from the public (issuing Treasury bills, notes, and bonds).
2. The Fed conducts open market operations and buys many of the government securities.
3. Aggregate demand increases and the price level rises.
4. At the same time, Congress says it will do whatever is necessary to bring inflation under control. The chairman of the Fed says the Fed will soon move against inflation.
5. Congress, the president, and the Fed do *not* move against inflation.

According to some economists, if the government says it will do X but continues to do Y, then people will see through the charade. They will equate saying X with doing Y. In other words, the equation in their heads will read Say X = Do Y. They will also always base their behavior on what they expect the government to do, not on what it says it will do.[4]

Now suppose the government says it will do X and actually does it. People will not know the government is telling the truth this time, and they will continue to think that saying X really means doing Y.

Some new classical economists say this is what happened in the early 1980s and that it goes a long way to explaining the 1981–1982 recession. They tell this story:

1. President Reagan proposed and Congress approved tax cuts in 1981.
2. Although some economists insisted the tax cuts would stimulate so much economic activity that tax revenues would increase, the public believed the tax cuts would decrease tax revenues and increase the size of the budget deficit (that existed at the time).
3. People translated larger budget deficits into more government borrowing.
4. They anticipated greater money supply growth connected with the larger deficits because they had seen this happen before.
5. Greater money supply growth would mean an increase in aggregate demand and in the price level.
6. The Fed said it would not increase the money supply, but it had said this before and acted contrarily; so few people believed the Fed this time.

4. Rational expectations have sometimes been reduced to the adage, "Fool me once, shame on you; fool me twice, shame on me."

economics 24/7

RATIONAL EXPECTATIONS AND THE BOY WHO CRIED WOLF

You may know the fable about the boy and the wolf: A young boy liked to play tricks on people. One day, the boy's father (a shepherd) had to go out of town, and he asked his son to take care of the sheep while he was gone. As the boy was watching the sheep, he suddenly began yelling, "Wolf, wolf, wolf!" The townspeople came running because they thought the boy needed help protecting the sheep from the wolf. When they arrived, they found the boy laughing at the trick he had played on them. The same thing happened two or three more times. Finally, one day, a real wolf appeared. The boy called, "Wolf, wolf, wolf!" but no one came. The townspeople were not going to be fooled again. And so the wolf ate the sheep.

©BRAND X PICTURES/JUPITER IMAGES

The fable about the boy and the wolf has something in common with a concept explained in this chapter: the unintended consequences of saying one thing and doing another. In the new classical economic story of the 1981–1982 recession, the public incorrectly anticipated Fed policy, and as a result the economy fell into a recession. But the public incorrectly anticipated Fed policy because in the past the Fed had said one thing and done another. It had said X but done Y.

It's the same with the boy and the wolf. The first few times the boy cried wolf, the townspeople were fooled; the boy was simply playing a trick on them. In their minds, crying wolf came to equal no wolf. When the boy cried wolf the last time and actually meant it, no one came to help him, and the wolf ate the sheep. Just as the Fed might have learned that saying one thing and doing another can result in a recession, the boy learned that saying one thing and meaning another can result in sheep being killed. The moral of our story is that, if you tell a lie again and again, people will no longer believe you when you tell the truth.

7. The Fed actually did not increase the money supply as much as individuals thought it would.
8. Monetary policy was therefore not as expansionary as individuals had anticipated.
9. As a result, the economy moved to a point like 2′ in Exhibit 7. Real GDP fell, unemployment increased, and a recession ensued.

The moral of the story, according to new classical economists, is that if the Fed says it is going to do X, then it had better do X. If it doesn't, the next time the Fed says it is going to do X, no one will believe it, and the economy may fall into a recession. The recession will be an unintended effect of the Fed's having said one thing and doing another in the past.

Thinking like AN ECONOMIST

What People Think Can Matter to Outcomes

Think of how economics might differ from chemistry. In chemistry, if you add 2 molecules of hydrogen to 1 molecule of oxygen, you always get water. But in economics, if you add expansionary monetary policy to an economy, you don't always get a rise in short-run Real GDP. Sometimes you get a rise (when policy is unanticipated), sometimes no change (when policy is correctly anticipated), and other times a decline (when policy is incorrectly anticipated in a particular direction).

(continued)

Thinking Like An Economist (continued)

What is often frustrating to economists is that sometimes the layperson thinks that economics works the same way as chemistry: X plus Y should always give us Z. Sadly, that is not how economics works. The factor affecting economics that does not affect chemistry is the human factor. What new classical economists teach us about human beings is that their perceptions of things (vis-à-vis reality) have a large part to play in determining outcomes.

SELF-TEST

1. Does the policy ineffectiveness proposition (PIP) always hold?
2. When policy is unanticipated, what difference is there between the natural rate theory built on adaptive expectations and the natural rate theory built on rational expectations?
3. If expectations are formed rationally, does it matter whether policy is unanticipated, anticipated correctly, or anticipated incorrectly? Explain your answer.

NEW KEYNESIANS AND RATIONAL EXPECTATIONS

The new classical theory assumes that wages and prices are completely flexible. In this theory, an increase in the anticipated price level results in an immediate and equal rise in wages and prices, and the aggregate supply curve immediately shifts to the long-run equilibrium position.

In response to the assumption of flexible wages and prices, a few economists began to develop what has come to be known as the *New Keynesian rational expectations theory.* This theory assumes that rational expectations are a reasonable characterization of how expectations are formed, but it drops the new classical assumption of complete wage and price flexibility. Economists who propose this theory argue that long-term labor contracts often prevent wages and prices from fully adjusting to changes in the anticipated price level. (In other words, prices and wages are somewhat sticky, rigid, or inflexible.)

Consider the possible situation at the end of the first year of a three-year wage contract. Workers may realize that the price level is higher than they expected when they negotiated the contract, but they are unable to do much about it because their wages are locked in for the next two years. Price rigidity might also come into play because firms often engage in fixed-price contracts with their suppliers. As discussed in Chapter 9, Keynesian economists today assert that, for microeconomic-based reasons, long-term labor contracts and above-market wages are sometimes in the best interest of both employers and employees (efficiency wage theory).

To see what the theory predicts, look at Exhibit 8. The economy is initially in long-run equilibrium at point 1. The public anticipates an increase in aggregate demand from AD_1 to AD_2, and, as a result, the anticipated price level changes. Because of some wage and price rigidities, however, the short-run aggregate supply curve does not shift all the way from $SRAS_1$ to $SRAS_2$, and the economy does not move from point 1 to point 2 (as in new classical theory). The short-run aggregate supply curve shifts instead to $SRAS'_2$ because rigidities prevent complete wage and price adjustments. In the short run, the economy moves from point 1 to point 2′, from Q_N to Q_A. Had the policy been unanticipated, Real GDP would have increased from Q_N to Q_{UA} in the short run.

exhibit 8

The Short-Run Response to Aggregate Demand–Increasing Policy (in the New Keynesian Theory)

Starting at point 1, an increase in aggregate demand is anticipated. As a result, this short-run aggregate supply curve shifts leftward, but not all the way to $SRAS_2$ (as would be the case in the new classical model). Instead it shifts only to $SRAS'_2$ because of some wage and price rigidities; the economy moves to point 2′ (in the short run), and Real GDP increases from Q_N to Q_A. If the policy had been unanticipated, Real GDP would have increased from Q_N to Q_{UA}.

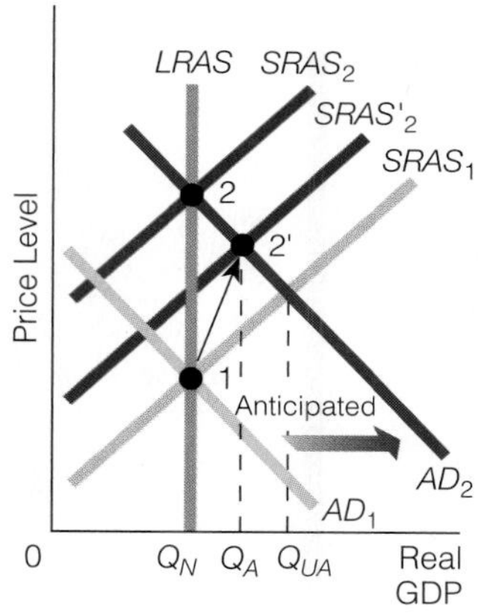

Thinking like AN ECONOMIST

Predictions Matter

Suppose someone says that the assumptions of the New Keynesian theory (rational expectations and some price and wage rigidities) seem more reasonable than the assumptions of the Friedman natural rate theory and new classical theory. Would it naturally follow that the New Keynesian theory is right and the others are wrong?

According to economists, the answer is no. We have all encountered theories with reasonable sounding assumptions that ended up being wrong. (As just one example, at one time in the world's history, it seemed reasonable to assume that the earth was flat.) Instead, economists judge a theory by how well it predicts and explains real-world events, not by how reasonable its assumptions might sound to someone.

LOOKING AT THINGS FROM THE SUPPLY SIDE: REAL BUSINESS CYCLE THEORISTS

Throughout this chapter, changes in Real GDP have originated on the demand side of the economy. When discussing the Friedman natural rate theory, the new classical theory, and the New Keynesian theory, we begin our analysis by shifting the *AD* curve to the right. Then we explain what happens in the economy as a result. Given the presentation in this chapter, someone might believe that all changes in Real GDP originate on the demand side of the economy. In fact, some economists believe this to be true.

Other economists do not. One group of such economists—called *real business cycle theorists*—believe that changes on the supply side of the economy can lead to changes in Real GDP and unemployment. Real business cycle theorists argue that a decrease in Real GDP (which refers to the recessionary or contractionary part of a business cycle) can be brought about by a major supply-side change that reduces the capacity of the economy to produce. Moreover, they argue that what looks like a contraction in Real GDP originating on the demand side of the economy can be, in essence, the effect of what has happened on the supply side.

Exhibit 9 helps illustrate the process. We start with an adverse supply shock that reduces the capacity of the economy to produce. This effect is represented by a shift inward in the economy's production possibilities frontier or a leftward shift in the long-run aggregate supply curve from $LRAS_1$ to $LRAS_2$, which moves the economy from point A to point B. As shown in Exhibit 9, a leftward shift in the long-run aggregate supply curve means that Natural Real GDP has fallen.

As a result of the leftward shift in the *LRAS* curve and the decline in Real GDP, firms reduce their demand for labor and scale back employment. Due to the lower demand for labor (which puts downward pressure on money wages) and the higher price level, real wages fall.

As real wages fall, workers choose to work less, and unemployed persons choose to extend the length of their unemployment. Due to less work and lower real wages, workers have less income. Lower incomes soon lead workers to reduce consumption.

Because consumption has fallen, or because businesses have become pessimistic (prompted by the decline in the productive potential of the economy), or because of both reasons, businesses have less reason to invest. As a result, firms borrow less from banks, the volume of outstanding loans falls, and therefore the money supply falls. A decrease in

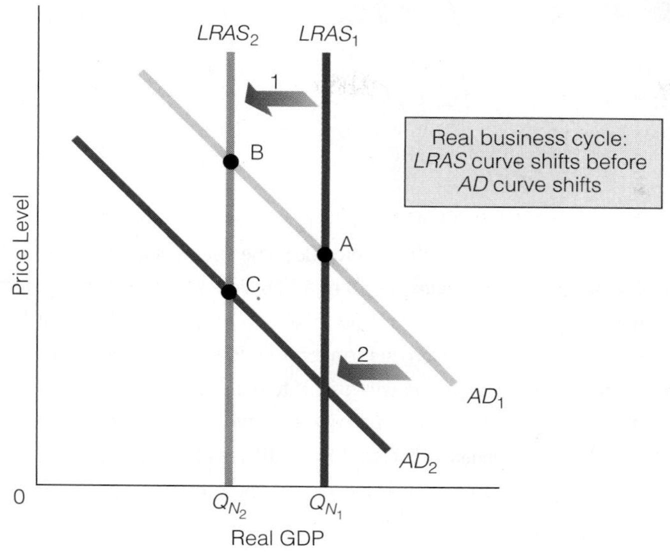

exhibit 9

Real Business Cycle Theory

We start with a supply-side change capable of reducing the capacity of the economy to produce. This is manifested by a leftward shift of the long-run aggregate supply curve from $LRAS_1$ to $LRAS_2$ and a fall in the Natural Real GDP level from Q_{N1} to Q_{N2}. A reduction in the productive capacity of the economy filters to the demand side of the economy and, in our example, reduces consumption, investment, and the money supply. The aggregate demand curve shifts leftward from AD_1 to AD_2.

the money supply causes the aggregate demand curve to shift leftward, from AD_1 to AD_2 in Exhibit 9, and the economy moves to point C.

Real business cycle theorists sometimes point out how easy it is to confuse a demand-induced decline in Real GDP with a supply-induced decline. In our example, both the aggregate supply side and the aggregate demand side of the economy change, but the aggregate supply side changes first. If the change in aggregate supply is overlooked, and only the changes in aggregate demand are observed (or specifically, a change in one of the variables that can change aggregate demand, such as the money supply), then the contraction in Real GDP will appear to be demand induced. In terms of Exhibit 9, the leftward shift in the *LRAS* curve would be overlooked, but the leftward shift in the *AD* curve would be observed, giving the impression that the contraction is demand induced.

If real business cycle theorists are correct, the cause-effect analysis of a contraction in Real GDP would be turned upside down. As just one example, changes in the money supply may be an effect of a contraction in Real GDP (which originates on the supply side of the economy), not its cause.

SELF-TEST

1. *The Wall Street Journal* reports that the money supply has recently declined. Is this consistent with a demand-induced business cycle, with a supply-induced business cycle, or with both? Explain your answer.
2. How are New Keynesians who believe people hold rational expectations different from new classical economists who believe people hold rational expectations?

office hours

"DOES NEW CLASSICAL THEORY CALL THE EFFECTS OF FISCAL AND MONETARY POLICY INTO QUESTION?"

Student:

When I started this course in macroeconomics, I was hoping to learn the unequivocal answers to some simple questions, such as what effect does fiscal policy have on the economy? What effect does monetary policy have on the economy? I don't think I am learning this. For example, it seems that fiscal and monetary policy can have different effects on Real GDP in the short depending on whether policy is unanticipated, anticipated incorrectly, or anticipated correctly. Am I right about this?

Instructor:

You're right. A given policy action (such as expansionary monetary policy) can have different effects on Real GDP (in the short run) depending on whether the policy is unancipated, anticipated correctly, and so on.

Student:

What am I supposed to learn from this?

Instructor:

The obvious point, which you have identified, is that policy actions have different effects depending on the degree to which individuals anticipate the policy correctly. The not so obvious point is that it might not be wise to use government policy actions to stabilize the economy.

Student:

How do you come to that point? What are the details?

Instructor:

Let's say that the economy is currently in a recessionary gap and Real GDP is $11 trillion. Policy makers want to raise the GDP level to Natural Real GDP at, say, $11.2 trillion. To achieve this goal, either expansionary fiscal or monetary policy is implemented. Are we guaranteed to raise Real GDP from $11 trillion to $11.2 trillion?

Student:

No.

Instructor:

Why is that?

Student:

Well, according to new classical economists, it's because individuals may incorrectly anticipate the policy in such as way as to reduce Real GDP instead of raise it.

Instructor:

That's right. To provide some details, suppose the Fed plans to raise the money supply by $40 billion and the public incorrectly anticipates the Fed's planning to raise the money supply by much more than $40 billion. In the short run, the *AD* curve will shift to the right and the *SRAS* curve will to shift to the left, but the *SRAS* curve will be shifting left *by more than* the *AD* curve will be shifting to the right. (This happened in Exhibit 7.) And the result will be a decline, not an increase, in Real GDP—at least in the short run.

Student:

So the monetary policy action can end up doing the very opposite of what it was intended to do. It was intended to raise Real GDP but it lowered it instead.

Instructor:

That's correct. What the new classical economists are really pointing out is that we can't always be sure of a discretionary policy action's effect on Real GDP. In turn, this should make economists less sure, or a little more humble, when it comes to advocating certain economic policy actions for government to implement.

Points to Remember

1. According to new classical economists, economic policy actions may not always have the same effect on Real GDP in the short run.
2. Economic policy actions may accomplish the opposite of what they were intended to accomplish.

a reader asks | Do Expectations Matter?

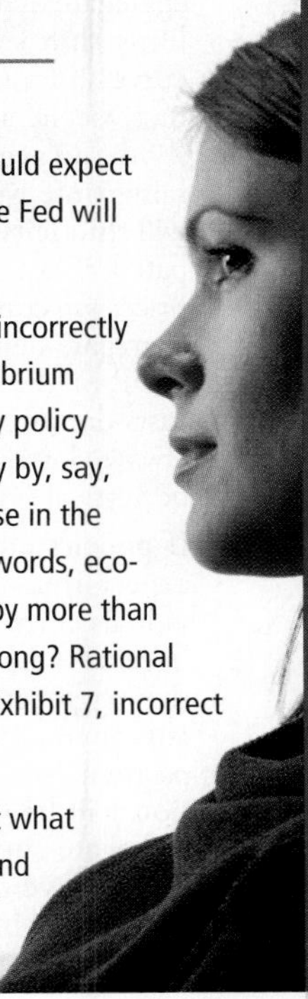

What insights, if any, does the introduction of expectations into macroeconomics provide?

You know that changes in such things as taxes, government purchases, interest rates, the money supply, and other factors can change Real GDP, the price level, and the unemployment rate. For example, starting from a state of long-run equilibrium, a rise in the money supply will raise Real GDP and lower the unemployment rate in the short run and raise the price level in the long run. Or consider that an increase in productivity can shift the *SRAS* curve to the right and thus bring about a change in Real GDP and the price level. In short, most of this text discusses how changes in real variables can affect the economy.

With the introduction of expectations theory, we move to a different level of analysis. Now we learn that what people think can also affect the economy. In other words, not only can a change in the world's oil supply affect the economy—almost everyone would expect that—but so can whether someone believes that the Fed will increase the money supply.

Recall our explanation of rational expectations and incorrectly anticipated policy. The economy is in long-run equilibrium when the Fed undertakes an expansionary monetary policy move. The Fed expects to increase the money supply by, say, $10 billion, and economic agents believe the increase in the money supply will be closer to $20 billion. In other words, economic agents think that the money supply will rise by more than it will rise. Does it matter that their thoughts are wrong? Rational expectations theory says that it does. As shown in Exhibit 7, incorrect thoughts can lead to Real GDP declining.

The insight that expectations theory provides is that what people think can affect Real GDP, unemployment, and prices. Who would have thought it?

Chapter Summary

THE PHILLIPS CURVE

- A. W. Phillips plotted a curve to a set of data points that exhibited an inverse relationship between wage inflation and unemployment. This curve came to be known as the Phillips curve. From the Phillips curve relationship, economists concluded that neither the combination of low inflation and low unemployment nor the combination of high inflation and high unemployment was likely.
- Economists Paul Samuelson and Robert Solow fit a Phillips curve to the U.S. economy. Instead of measuring wage inflation against unemployment rates (as Phillips did), they measured price inflation against unemployment rates. They found an inverse relationship between inflation and unemployment rates.
- Based on the findings of Phillips and Samuelson and Solow, economists concluded the following: (1) Stagflation, or high inflation and high unemployment, is extremely unlikely. (2) The Phillips curve presents policy makers with a menu of different combinations of inflation and unemployment rates.

FRIEDMAN NATURAL RATE THEORY

- Milton Friedman pointed out that there are two types of Phillips curves: a short-run Phillips curve and a long run Phillips curve. The short-run Phillips curve exhibits the inflation-unemployment trade-off; the long-run Phillips curve does not. Consideration of both short- and long-run Phillips curves opened macroeconomics to expectations theory.
- The Friedman natural rate theory holds that in the short run, a decrease (increase) in inflation is linked to an increase (decrease) in unemployment, but in the long run, the economy returns to its natural rate of unemployment. In other words, there is a trade-off between inflation and unemployment in the short run but not in the long run.
- The Friedman natural rate theory was expressed in terms of adaptive expectations. Individuals formed their inflation expectations by considering past inflation rates. Later, some economists expressed the theory in terms of rational expectations. Rational expectations theory holds that individuals form their expected inflation rate by considering present and past inflation rates, as well as all other available and relevant information—in particular, the effects of present and future policy actions.

NEW CLASSICAL THEORY

- Implicit in the new classical theory are two assumptions: (1) Individuals form their expectations rationally. (2) Wages and prices are completely flexible.

- In the new classical theory, policy has different effects (1) when it is unanticipated and (2) when it is anticipated. For example, if the public correctly anticipates an increase in aggregate demand, the short-run aggregate supply curve will likely shift leftward at the same time the aggregate demand curve shifts rightward. If the public does not anticipate an increase in aggregate demand (but one occurs), then the short-run aggregate supply curve will not shift leftward at the same time the aggregate demand curve shifts rightward; it will shift leftward sometime later. If policy is correctly anticipated, if expectations are formed rationally, and if wages and prices are completely flexible, then an increase or decrease in aggregate demand will change only the price level, not Real GDP or the unemployment rate. The new classical theory casts doubt on the belief that the short-run Phillips curve is always downward sloping. Under certain conditions, it may be vertical (as is the long-run Phillips curve).
- If policies are anticipated but not credible, and if rational expectations are a reasonable characterization of how individuals form their expectations, then certain policies may have unintended effects. For example, if the public believes that aggregate demand will increase by more than it (actually) increases (because policy makers have not done in the past what they said they would do), then anticipated inflation will be higher than it would have been, the short-run aggregate supply curve will shift leftward by more than it would have otherwise, and the (short-run) outcomes of a policy that increases aggregate demand will be lower Real GDP and higher unemployment.

NEW KEYNESIAN THEORY

- Implicit in the New Keynesian theory are two assumptions: (1) Individuals form their expectations rationally. (2) Wages and prices are not completely flexible (in the short run).
- If policy is anticipated, the economic effects predicted by the new classical theory and the New Keynesian theory are not the same (in the short run). Because the New Keynesian theory assumes that wages and prices are not completely flexible in the short run, given an anticipated change in aggregate demand, the short-run aggregate supply curve cannot immediately shift to its long-run equilibrium position. The New Keynesian theory predicts a short-run trade off between inflation and unemployment (in the Phillips curve framework).

REAL BUSINESS CYCLE THEORY

- Real business cycle contractions (in Real GDP) originate on the supply side of the economy. A contraction in Real GDP might follow this pattern: (1) An adverse supply shock reduces the economy's ability to produce. (2) The *LRAS* curve shifts leftward. (3) As a result, Real GDP declines and the price level rises. (4) The number of persons employed falls, as do real wages, owing to a decrease in the demand for labor (which lowers money wages) and a higher price level. (5) Incomes decline. (6) Consumption and investment decline. (7) The volume of outstanding loans declines. (8) The money supply falls. (9) The *AD* curve shifts leftward.

Key Terms and Concepts

Phillips Curve
Stagflation
Friedman Natural Rate Theory
Adaptive Expectations
Rational Expectations
Policy Ineffectiveness Proposition (PIP)

Questions and Problems

1. What does it mean to say that the Phillips curve presents policy makers with a menu of choices?
2. According to Friedman, how do we know when the economy is in long-run equilibrium?
3. What is a major difference between adaptive and rational expectations? Give an example of each.
4. "The policy ineffectiveness proposition (connected with new classical theory) does not eliminate policy makers' ability to reduce unemployment through aggregate demand–increasing policies because they can always increase aggregate demand by more than the public expects." What might be the weak point in this argument?
5. Why is the new classical theory associated with the word *classical*? Why has it been said that the classical theory failed where the new classical theory succeeds, because the former could not explain the business cycle (the ups and downs of the economy), but the latter can?
6. Suppose a permanent downward-sloping Phillips curve existed and offered a menu of choices of different combinations of inflation and unemployment rates to policy makers. How do you think society would go about deciding which point on the Phillips curve it wanted to occupy?
7. Assume a current short-run trade-off between inflation and unemployment and a change in technology that permits the wider dispersion of economic policy news. How would the change affect the trade-off? Explain your answer.
8. New Keynesian theory holds that wages are not completely flexible because of such things as long-term labor contracts. New classical economists often respond that experience teaches labor leaders to develop and bargain for contracts that allow for wage adjustments. Do you think the new classical economists have a good point? Why or why not?

9 What evidence can you point to that suggests individuals form their expectations adaptively? What evidence can you point to that suggests individuals form their expectations rationally?

10 Explain both the short-run and long-run movements of the Friedman natural rate theory, assuming expectations are formed adaptively.

11 Explain both the short-run and long-run movements of the new classical theory, assuming expectations are formed rationally and policy is unanticipated.

12 "Even if some people do not form their expectations rationally, the new classical theory is not necessarily of no value." Discuss.

13 In the real business cycle theory, why can't the change in the money supply prompted by a series of events catalyzed by an adverse supply shock be considered the cause of the business cycle?

14 The expected inflation rate is 5 percent, and the actual inflation rate is 7 percent. According to Friedman, is the economy in long-run equilibrium? Explain your answer.

Working with Numbers and Graphs

1 Illustrate graphically what would happen in the short run and in the long run if individuals hold rational expectations, prices and wages are flexible, and individuals underestimate the decrease in aggregate demand.

2 In each of the following figures, the starting point is 1. Which part illustrates each of the following?

a. Friedman natural rate theory (short run).

b. New classical theory (unanticipated policy, short run).

c. Real business cycle theory.

d. New classical theory (incorrectly anticipated policy, overestimating increase in aggregate demand, short run).

e. Policy ineffectiveness proposition (PIP).

3 Illustrate graphically what would happen in the short run and in the long run if individuals hold adaptive expectations, if prices and wages are flexible, and if there is a decrease in aggregate demand.

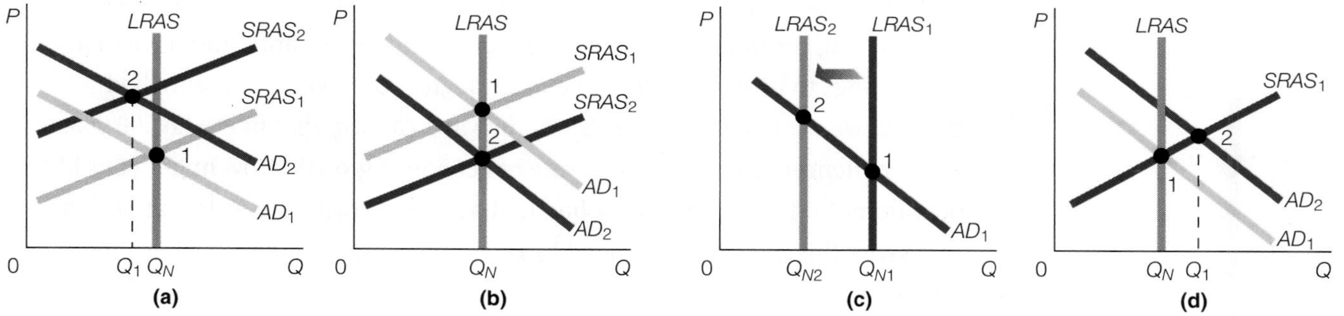

© COMSTOCK IMAGES/JUPITER IMAGES

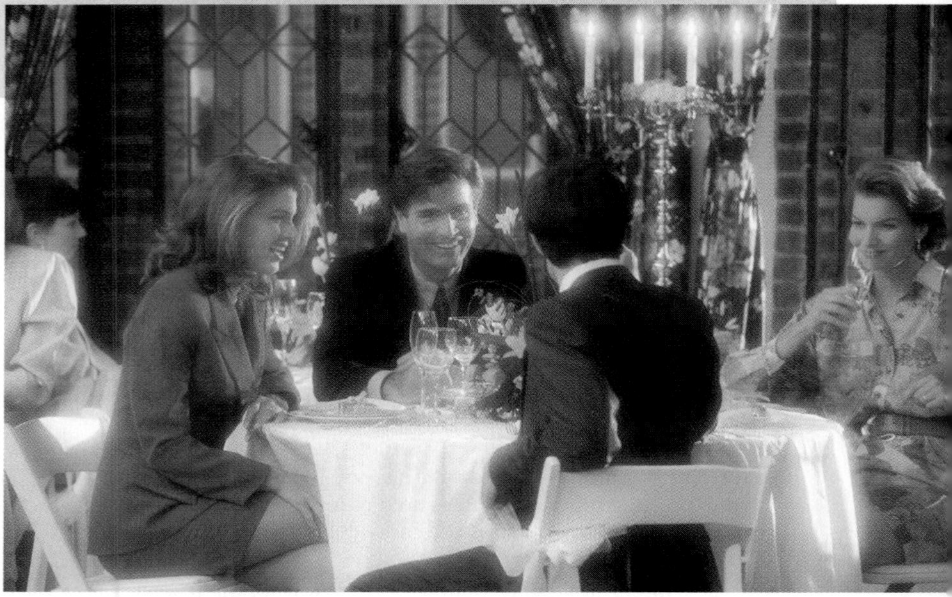

CHAPTER 16

ECONOMIC GROWTH

Introduction Rarely do we think of how we came to have the standard of living we enjoy. Most of us live in comfortable houses, drive nice cars, work on fast computers, enjoy exciting sporting events, attend lively jazz concerts, visit relaxing vacation spots, go to the movies and restaurants, and have many other things to be grateful for. To a large degree, our lives are so enriched because we were born to parents who live in a country that in the last 60 years has experienced a relatively high rate of economic growth. How might your life be different if the U.S. economy had had a lower growth rate over that period? To answer this question, you need to know the causes and effects of economic growth.

A FEW BASICS ABOUT ECONOMIC GROWTH

Absolute Real Economic Growth
An increase in Real GDP from one period to the next.

Per Capita Real Economic Growth
An increase from one period to the next in per capita Real GDP, which is Real GDP divided by population.

The term *economic growth* refers either to absolute real economic growth or to per capita real economic growth. **Absolute real economic growth** is an increase in Real GDP from one period to the next. Exhibit 1 shows absolute real economic growth (or the percentage change in Real GDP) for the United States for the period 1993–2006.

Per capita real economic growth is an increase from one period to the next in per capita Real GDP, which is Real GDP divided by population.

$$\text{Per capita Real GDP} = \frac{\text{Real GDP}}{\text{Population}}$$

> **macro*theme*** ➔ In Chapter 5, we said that one of the two variables that macroeconomists are concerned with learning about is Real GDP, Q. Economic growth, the topic of this chapter, deals with factors that cause an increase in Q.

exhibit 1

Absolute Real Economic Growth Rates for the United States, 1995–2006

This exhibit shows the absolute real economic growth rates (or percentage change in Real GDP) in the United States for the period 1995–2006.

Source: *Economic Report of the President*, 2007.

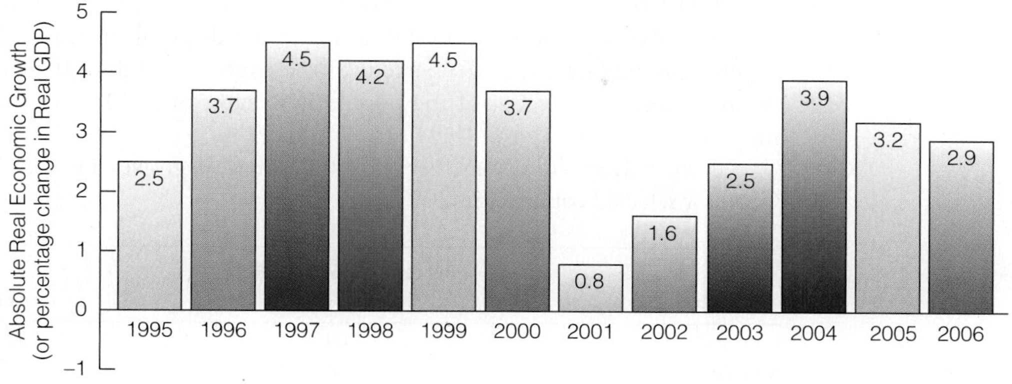

Do Economic Growth Rates Matter?

Suppose the absolute real economic growth rate is 4 percent in one country and 3 percent in another country. The difference in these growth rates may not seem very significant. But if they are sustained over a long period of time, the people who live in the two countries will see a real difference between their standards of living. If a country's economic growth rate is 4 percent each year, its Real GDP will double in 18 years. If a country has a 3 percent annual growth rate, its Real GDP will double in 24 years. In other words, a country with a 4 percent growth rate can double its Real GDP in 6 fewer years than a country with a 3 percent growth rate. (To calculate the time required for any variable to double, simply divide its percentage growth rate into 72. This is called the *rule of 72.*)

To look at economic growth rates in another way, suppose two countries have the same population. Real GDP is $300 billion in country A and $100 billion in country B. Country A is therefore 3 times richer than country B. Now suppose the annual economic growth rate is 3 percent in country A and 6 percent in country B. In just 15 years, country B will be the richer country.

As a real-world example of how a difference in growth rates matters, in 1960 Bolivia and Malaysia had approximately the same per capita Real GDP. Over the next 40 years, Malaysia grew at an average annual growth rate of 9 percent, whereas Bolivia grew at an average annual growth rate of 0.5 percent. The result in 2000 was that per capita Real GDP in Malaysia was 3.5 times higher than it was in Bolivia.

Growth Rates in Selected Countries

Suppose in a given year, country A has an economic growth rate of 7 percent, and country B has an economic growth rate of 1 percent. Is the material standard of living in country A necessarily higher than in country B? Not at all. A snapshot (in time) of the growth rate in two countries doesn't tell us anything about growth rates in previous years, nor does it speak to per capita Real GDP. For example, did country A have the same 7 percent growth rate last year and the year before? Does country A have a higher per capita Real GDP?

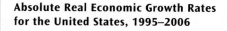

Now suppose that the per capita Real GDP in country C is $30,000 and that the per capita Real GDP in country D is $2,000. Must the material standard of living in country C be higher than in country D? Probably so, but not necessarily. We say "not necessarily" because we do not know the *income distribution* in either country. All a per capita Real GDP figure tells us is that *if* we were to divide a country's entire Real GDP *equally* among all the people in the country, each person would have a certain dollar amount of Real GDP at his or her disposal. In reality, 2 percent of the population may have, say, 70 percent of the country's Real GDP as income, whereas the remaining 98 percent of the population shares only 30 percent of Real GDP as income.

Given such qualifications, here are the economic growth rates and per capita Real GDP for selected countries in 2007.[1]

Country	Percentage Growth Rate in Real GDP (%)	Per Capita Real GDP
Australia	3.9	$34,154
Austria	3.4	36,065
Belgium	2.7	33,607
Canada	2.7	36,243
Denmark	1.8	35,213
France	1.9	30,724
Germany	2.5	32,228
Italy	1.5	28,434
Japan	2.1	31,696
Netherlands	3.5	36,783
Sweden	2.6	34,457
United States	2.2	43,267

Finding Economics

In a Restaurant

It is 6 p.m. and Xavier drives his new $45,000 car to a restaurant, where he and a friend have dinner. The bill comes to $86.75. After dinner, Xavier and his friend attend a play and later return to Xavier's 3,500-square-foot house. They sit out by the swimming pool and talk about everything and nothing. Where is the economics? Is economic growth relevant to the evening?

Economic growth is the silent actor of the evening. Xavier and his friend can enjoy such a comfortable and satisfying evening because they live in a country that has experienced economic growth over the years.

Or look at it this way. Although there are people like Xavier and his friend all over the world, not all of them *can* have the same evening. Individuals living in countries that have experienced much less economic growth over the years are not as likely to experience the same kind of evening.

Here are a few startling facts: About 24,000 people die every day from hunger or hunger-related causes, and three-fourths of the deaths are of children under the age of 5. The vast majority of people who die of hunger live in countries of the world that have experienced relatively little economic growth.

1. The sources for the data include the Bureau of Labor Statistics and the *CIA World Factbook*, 2008.

Common MISCONCEPTIONS

About a Rising Standard of Living

Most of us have lived in a country and during a time when standards of living have increased. However, standards of living have not always increased, nor must they always increase. If you had lived during the 1700s in Western Europe, your standard of living would *not* have been much different from what it would have been had you lived in the year 1000. Most people living at these times did not live long enough to notice any economic growth. The world they were born into, and died in, was much the same decade after decade. Their parents, grandparents, and great grandparents lived much the same lives. A rising standard of living within a generation or two is a relatively new phenomenon.

Thinking like AN ECONOMIST

The Importance of Economic Growth

Economic growth has been a major topic of discussion for economists for over two centuries. Adam Smith, the founder of modern economics, wrote a book on the subject that was published in 1776: *An Inquiry into the Nature and Causes of the Wealth of Nations.* In the book, Smith set out to answer the question of why some countries are rich and others are poor. Today, we'd ask why is the per capita Real GDP high in some countries and low in others? For economists, getting the right answer to this question is of major importance to millions—if not billions—of people.

Two Types of Economic Growth

Economic growth can be shown in two of the frameworks of analysis used so far in this book: the production possibilities frontier (PPF) framework and the *AD-AS* framework. Within these two frameworks, we consider two types of economic growth: (1) economic growth that occurs from an inefficient level of production and (2) economic growth that occurs from an efficient level of production.

ECONOMIC GROWTH FROM AN INEFFICIENT LEVEL OF PRODUCTION

A production possibilities frontier is shown in Exhibit 2(a). If the economy is currently operating at point A, below the PPF, obviously it is not operating at its Natural Real GDP

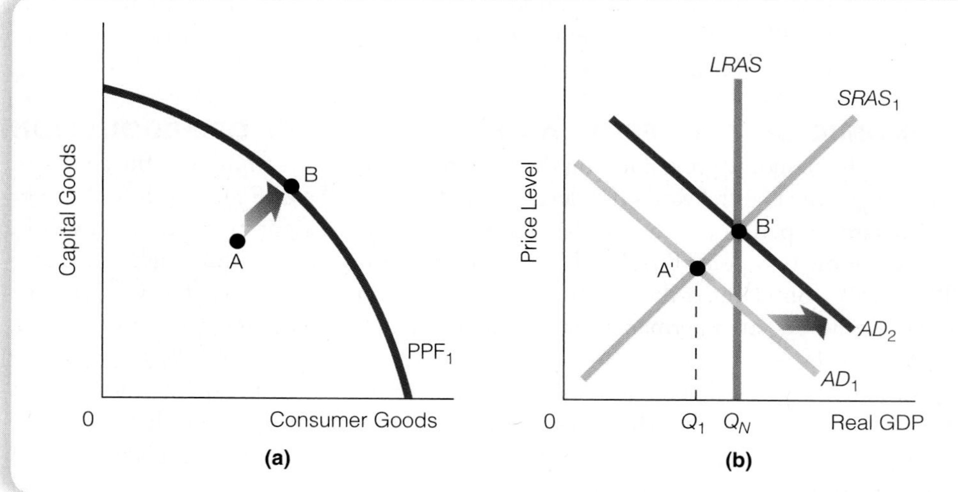

exhibit 2

Economic Growth from an Inefficient Level of Production

The economy is at point A in (a) and at point A′ in (b). Currently, the economy is at an inefficient point, or below Natural Real GDP. Economic growth is evidenced as a movement from point A to B in (a), and as a movement from A′ to B′ in (b).

economics 24/7

HOW ECONOMIZING ON TIME CAN PROMOTE ECONOMIC GROWTH

If a society obtains more resources, its production possibilities frontier (PPF) will shift to the right, and economic growth is therefore possible. One way to obtain more resources is by means of a technological change or innovation that makes it possible to use fewer resources to produce a particular good. To illustrate, suppose 100 units of a given resource are available. Currently, 10 units of the resource are needed to produce 20 units of good X, and 90 units of the resource are used to produce 900 units of other goods.

Now suppose a technological change or innovation makes it possible to produce 20 units of good X with only 5 units of the resource. This means 95 units of the resource can be used to produce other goods. With more resources going to produce other goods, more other goods can be produced. Perhaps with 95 units of the resource going to produce other goods, 950 units of other goods can be produced. In short, a technological advance or innovation that saves resources in the production of one good makes growth possible.

With this in mind, consider the resource of time. Usually, when people think of resources, they think of labor, capital, and natural resources. But time is a resource too because it takes time (in much the same way that it takes labor or capital) to produce goods. Any technological advance that economizes on time frees up time that can be used to produce other goods.

To illustrate, consider a simple everyday example. With today's computers, people can make calculations, write books, key reports, design buildings, and do many other things in less time than in the past. Thus, more time is available to do other things. Having more time to produce other things promotes economic growth.

Another example is money. Before money was available, people made barter trades. In a barter economy, finding people to trade with takes time, and money saves this time. Because everyone accepts money, it is easier for people to acquire the goods and services they want. Money makes trading easier and quicker. In other words, it saves time. Money is a kind of technology that saves time and promotes economic growth.

level. If it were, the economy would be located on the PPF instead of below it. Instead, the economy is at an inefficient point or at an inefficient level of production.

Point A in Exhibit 2(a) corresponds to point A′ in Exhibit 2(b). At point A′, the economy is in a recessionary gap, operating below Natural Real GDP. Suppose that, through expansionary monetary or fiscal policy, the aggregate demand curve shifts rightward from AD_1 to AD_2. The economy is pulled out of its recessionary gap and is now producing Natural Real GDP at point B′ in Exhibit 2(b).

What does the situation look like now in Exhibit 2(a)? Obviously, if the economy is producing at its Natural Real GDP level, it is operating at full employment or at the natural unemployment rate. The economy has moved from point A (below the PPF) to point B (on the PPF). The economy has moved from operating at an inefficient level of production to operating at an efficient level.

ECONOMIC GROWTH FROM AN EFFICIENT LEVEL OF PRODUCTION

How can the economy grow if it is on the PPF in Exhibit 2(a)—exhibiting efficiency—or producing at the Natural Real GDP level in Exhibit 2(b)? The PPF must shift to the right (or outward) in part (a), or the *LRAS* curve must shift to the right in (b). In other words, if the economy is at point B in Exhibit 3(a), it can grow if the PPF shifts rightward from PPF_1 to PPF_2. Similarly, if the economy is at point B′ in Exhibit 3(b), Real GDP can be raised beyond Q_{N1} on a permanent basis only if the *LRAS* curve shifts to the right from $LRAS_1$ to $LRAS_2$.

Although we have described economic growth from both an inefficient and efficient level of production, usually when economists speak of economic growth, they are speaking about it from an efficient level of production. That is, they are talking about a shift rightward in the PPF or in the *LRAS* curve.

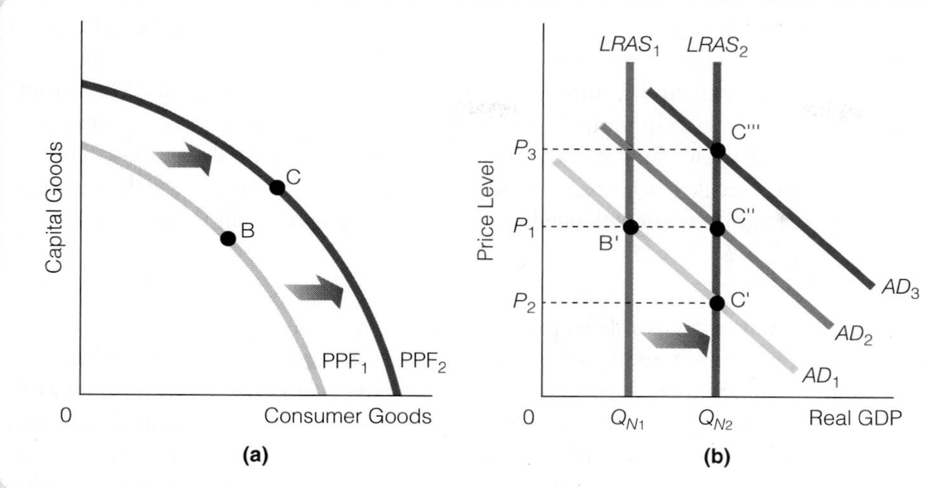

exhibit 3

Economic Growth from an Efficient Level of Production

The economy is at point B in (a) and at point B′ in (b). Economic growth can only occur in (a) if the PPF shifts rightward from PPF_1 to PPF_2. It can only occur in (b) if the *LRAS* curve shifts from $LRAS_1$ to $LRAS_2$.

Economic Growth and the Price Level

Economic growth can occur with a falling price level, a rising price level, or a stable price level. To see this, look again at Exhibit 3(b). The *LRAS* curve shifts from $LRAS_1$ to $LRAS_2$. Three possible aggregate demand curves may be consistent with this new *LRAS* curve: AD_1, AD_2, or AD_3.

- If AD_1 is the relevant *AD* curve, economic growth occurs with a declining price level. Before the *LRAS* curve shifts to the right, the price level is P_1; after the shift, it is lower, at P_2.
- If AD_2 is the relevant *AD* curve, economic growth occurs with a stable price level. Before the *LRAS* curve shifts to the right, the price level is P_1; after the shift, it is the same, at P_1.
- If AD_3 is the relevant *AD* curve, economic growth occurs with a rising price level. Before the *LRAS* curve shifts to the right, the price level is P_1; after the shift, it is higher, at P_3.

In recent decades, the U.S. economy has witnessed economic growth with a rising price level. In other words, the *AD* curve has been shifting to the right at a faster rate than the *LRAS* curve has been shifting to the right.

What Causes Economic Growth?

This section looks at some of the determinants of economic growth—that is, the factors that can shift the PPF or the *LRAS* curve to the right. These factors include natural resources, labor, capital, technological advances, free trade as technology, the property rights structure, and economic freedom. We then discuss some of the policies that promote economic growth.

Natural Resources

People often think that countries with a plentiful supply of natural resources experience economic growth, whereas countries short of natural resources do not. In fact, some countries with an abundant supply of natural resources have experienced rapid growth in the past (e.g., the United States), and others have experienced no growth or only slow growth (e.g., Ghana, in certain years). Also, some countries that are short of natural resources, such as Singapore, have grown very fast. Natural resources don't seem to be either a sufficient or a necessary factor for growth: Countries rich in natural resources are not guaranteed economic growth, and countries poor in natural resources may grow economically. Nevertheless, a nation rich in natural resources is likely to experience growth, *ceteris paribus.* For example, if a place such as Hong Kong, which has few natural resources, had been blessed with much fertile soil, instead of only a little, and many raw materials, instead of almost none, it might have experienced more economic growth than it has.

Labor

Increased labor makes it possible to produce more output (more Real GDP). However, whether the average productivity of labor rises, falls, or stays constant (as additional workers are added to the production process) depends on how productive the additional workers are relative to existing ones. (Average labor productivity is total output divided by total labor hours. For example, if $6 trillion of output is produced in 200 billion labor hours, then average labor productivity is $30 per hour.) If the additional workers are less productive, labor productivity will decline. If they are more productive, labor productivity will rise. And if they are equally as productive, labor productivity will stay the same.

Either an increase in the labor force or an increase in labor productivity leads to increases in Real GDP, but only an increase in labor productivity tends to lead to an increase in per capita Real GDP.

How then do we achieve an increase in labor productivity? One way is through increased education, training, and experience, which are increases in what economists call *human capital.* Another way is through (physical) capital investment. Combining workers with more capital goods tends to increase their productivity. For example, a farmer with a tractor is more productive than a farmer without one.

Capital

As just mentioned, capital investment can lead to increases in labor productivity and therefore to increases not only in Real GDP, but also in per capita Real GDP. But capital goods do not fall from the sky. Getting more of one thing often means forfeiting something else. To produce more capital goods that are not directly consumable, present consumption must be reduced. For example, Robinson Crusoe, alone on an island and fishing with a spear, must give up some of the time he would have spent catching fish to weave a net (a physical capital good), with which he hopes to catch more fish. If Crusoe gives up some of his present consumption—if he chooses not to consume now—he is, in fact, saving. There is a link between nonconsumption, or saving, and capital formation. As the saving rate increases, capital formation increases and so does economic growth.

Exhibit 4 shows that for the period 1970–1990, countries with higher investment rates largely tended to have higher per capita Real GDP growth rates. For example, investment was a higher percentage of GDP in Austria, Norway, and Japan than it was in the United States. And these countries experienced a higher per capita Real GDP growth rate than the United States did.

Technological Advances

Technological advances make it possible to obtain more output from the same amount of resources. Compare the amount of work done by a business that uses computers with the amount accomplished by a business without them.

Technological advances may be the result of new capital goods or of new ways of producing goods. The use of computers is an example of a technological advance that is the

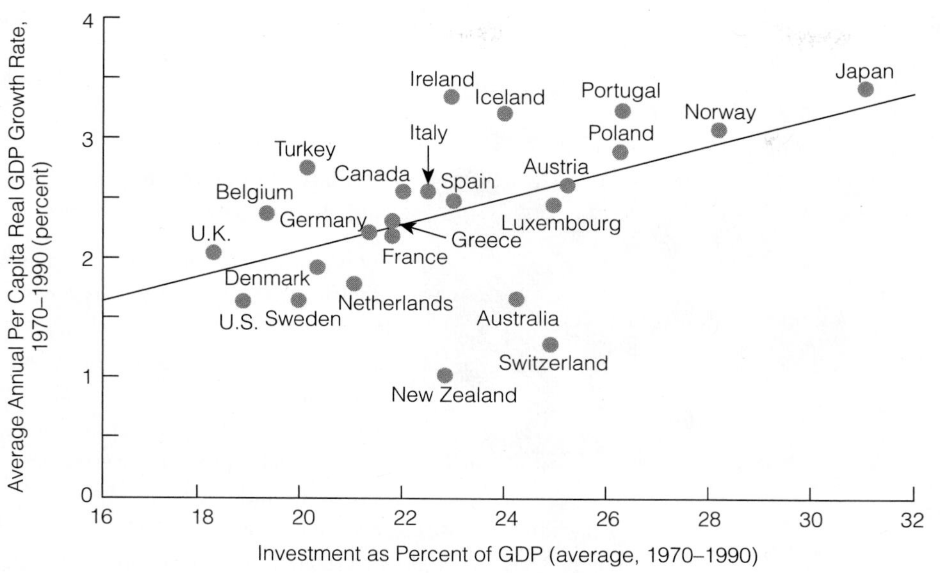

exhibit 4

Investment and Per Capita Real Economic Growth for Selected Countries, 1970–1990

Generally, but not always, countries in which investment is a larger percentage of GDP have higher per capita Real GDP growth rates.

Source: Council of Economic Advisors, *Economic Report of the President*, 1997 (Washington, DC: U.S. Government Printing Office, 1997).

result of a new capital good. New and improved management techniques are an example of a new way of producing goods.

Technological advances usually come as the result of companies, and of a country, investing in research and development (R&D). Research and development, in general terms, encompasses such things as scientists working in a lab to develop a new product and managers figuring out, through experience, how to motivate workers to work to their potential.

Free Trade as Technology

Suppose that someone in the United States has invented a machine that can turn wheat into cars[2] and that the only problem with the machine is that it works only in Japan. So people in the United States grow wheat and ship it to Japan. There, the machine turns the wheat into cars. The cars are then loaded on ships and brought to the United States. Many economists say there is really no difference between a machine that can turn wheat into cars and free trade between countries. Enabled by free trade, people in the United States grow wheat and ship it to Japan; after a while the ships come back loaded with cars. This is exactly what happens with our make-believe machine. There is really no discernible difference between a machine turning wheat into cars and trading wheat for cars. In both cases, wheat is given up to get cars.

If the machine is a technological advancement, then so is free trade, as many economists point out. In that technological advancements can promote economic growth, so can free trade.

Property Rights Structure

Some economists have argued that per capita real economic growth first appeared in areas with a system of institutions and property rights that encouraged individuals to direct

2. The essence of this example comes from David Friedman, *Hidden Order* (New York: HarperCollins, 1996), p. 70.

economics 24/7

ECONOMIC FREEDOM AND GROWTH RATES

There is some evidence that economic freedom matters to a country's economic growth rate. Consider when there were two Germanies: East Germany and West Germany. The two Germanies were much the same in terms of culture, people, climate, language, and so on, but West Germans enjoyed more economic freedom than East Germans. Did this major difference matter to economic growth? Most economists answer yes. Between 1950 and 1991, the average annual growth rate in East Germany was 1.3 percent; in West Germany it was 4.4 percent.

© AP PHOTO/JOCKEL FINCK

The same sort of difference holds between North Korea and South Korea. There is much more economic freedom in South Korea than in North Korea. During the second half of the twentieth century, the average annual growth rate in South Korea was more than three times higher than the average annual growth rate in North Korea.

The evidence from the two Koreas and two Germanies tells us that economic freedom *does* matter to economic growth, especially when other factors (that matter to growth) are much the same between the countries.

But when other factors aren't the same, problems arise. Suppose country A has less economic freedom than country B. Country A will not necessarily grow less than country B over the next five or ten years. The economic growth rate in a country could depend on the economic base from which the growth emanates. To illustrate, suppose country A has a Real GDP of $10 billion, and country B has a Real GDP of $100 billion. Suppose now that Real GDP grows by $2 billion in both countries. The economic growth rate in country A (the country with less economic freedom) is 20 percent, but the economic growth rate in country B (the country with more economic freedom) is only 2 percent. This does not mean that economic freedom is a hindrance to economic growth. Not at all. It may simply look that way because something different between the two countries—in this case, the economic base—isn't being considered.

their energies to effective economic projects. Property rights consist of the range of laws, rules, and regulations that define rights for the use and transfer of resources.

Consider two property rights structures. In one structure, people are allowed to keep the full monetary rewards of their labor. In the other, people are allowed to keep only half. Many economists would predict that the first property rights structure would stimulate more economic activity than the second, *ceteris paribus.* Individuals will invest more, take more risks, and work harder when the property rights structure allows them to keep more of the monetary rewards of their investing, risk taking, and labor.

Economic Freedom

Some economists believe that economic freedom leads to economic growth. Countries whose people enjoy a large degree of economic freedom develop and grow more quickly than countries whose people have little economic freedom. The Heritage Foundation and *The Wall Street Journal* have joined to produce an "index of economic freedom." This index is based on 50 independent variables divided into 10 broad categories of economic freedom, such as trade policy, monetary policy, property rights structure, regulation, fiscal burden of government, and so on. For example, a country with few tariffs and quotas (trade policy variables) is considered to have more economic freedom than a country with many tariffs and quotas.

The index is a number between 1 and 5. A country with a great deal of economic freedom has a low index, and a country with little economic freedom has a high index. Thus, free countries have an index between 1.00 and 1.95; mostly free countries, between 2.00 and 2.95; mostly unfree countries, between 3.00 and 3.95; and repressed countries, between 4.00 and 5.00.

The data show that economic freedom and Real GDP per capita are correlated. For the most part, the more economic freedom that a country's people have, the higher the Real GDP per capita will be. Some economists believe there is a cause-and-effect relationship: Greater economic freedom causes greater economic wealth.

Thinking like AN ECONOMIST

Both Tangibles and Intangibles Matter

When looking at the causes of economic growth, economists think in terms of both tangibles and intangibles. Tangibles include natural resources, labor, capital, and technological advances. Intangibles include the property rights structure, which directly affects individuals' incentives to apply the tangibles to the production of goods and services. No amount of natural resources, labor, capital, and technological advances can do it alone. People must be motivated to put them all together. In addition, the degree of motivation affects the result. In a world where it is easy to think that only the things that occupy physical space matter, the economist reminds us that we often need to keep looking.

Policies to Promote Economic Growth

As explained, economic growth can occur from either (1) an inefficient level of production or (2) an efficient level of production. When the economy is operating below its PPF, demand-inducing expansionary monetary or fiscal policy is often advocated. The policy's objective is to increase aggregate demand enough to raise Real GDP (and to lower the unemployment rate). We refer to such policies as *demand-side policies.*

Supply-side policies are designed to shift the PPF and the *LRAS* curve to the right. To understand the intent of these policies, recall the factors that cause economic growth: natural resources, labor, increases in human capital, increases in (physical) capital investment, technological advances, free trade as technology, property rights structure, and economic freedom. Any policies that promote these factors tend to promote economic growth. Two supply-side policies that do this are lowering taxes and reducing regulation.

TAX POLICY Some economists propose cutting taxes on such activities as working and saving to increase the productive capacity of the economy. For example, the line of thinking is that, if the marginal income tax rate is cut, workers will work more and that, as they work more, output will increase.

Other economists argue that if the tax is lowered on income placed in saving accounts, the return from saving will increase and thus the amount of saving will rise. In turn, this will make more funds available for investment, which will lead to greater capital goods growth and higher labor productivity. Ultimately, per capita Real GDP will increase.

REGULATORY POLICY Some economists say that government regulations may increase the cost of production for business and consequently reduce output. These economists are mainly referring to the costs of regulation, which may take the form of spending hours on required paperwork, adding safety features to a factory, or buying expensive equipment to reduce pollution emissions. Netted out, the benefits of these policies may

economics 24/7

RELIGIOUS BELIEFS AND ECONOMIC GROWTH

For given religious beliefs, increases in church attendance tend to reduce economic growth. In contrast, for given church attendance, increases in some religious beliefs—notably heaven, hell, and an afterlife—tend to increase economic growth.[3]

—Robert Barro and Rachel McCleary

Economists have been studying economic growth for more than 200 years. Some of the questions they have asked and tried to answer are why are some nations rich and others poor? What causes economic growth? Why do some nations grow faster than other nations?

In this chapter, we identify and discuss a few of the causes of economic growth but do not include any cultural determinants. Some economic researchers, however, argue that explanations for economic growth should be broadened to include such determinants. They argue that culture may influence personal traits, which may in turn affect economic growth. For example, personal traits such as honesty, thriftiness, the willingness to work hard, and openness to strangers may be related to economic growth.

Two Harvard economists, Robert Barro and Rachel McCleary, have analyzed one such cultural determinant: the role of religion in economic growth. Their work was based partly on the World Values Survey, which looked at a representative sample of people in 66 countries on all six inhabited continents between 1981 and 1997. The survey asked at least 1,000 people in each country about their basic values and beliefs: What is their religious affiliation? How often do they attend a religious service? Were they raised religiously or not?

Barro and McCleary found that economic growth responds negatively to church attendance (nations with a high rate of attendance at religious services grow more slowly than those with lower rates of attendance) but positively with religious beliefs in heaven, hell, and an afterlife. Specifically, in countries where the belief in heaven, hell, and an afterlife is strong, the growth of gross domestic product runs about 0.5 percent higher than average. (This result takes into account other factors, such as education, that influence growth rates.) Perhaps more telling, the belief in hell matters more to economic growth than the belief in heaven. Barro and McCleary suggest that religious beliefs stimulate growth because they help to sustain aspects of individual behavior that enhance productivity.

3. Robert Barro and Rachel McCleary, "Religion and Economic Growth" (NBER Working Paper No. 9682).

be greater than, less than, or equal to the costs, but certainly sometimes the costs lead to lowered output.

Economists who believe that the benefits do not warrant the costs often argue for some form of deregulation. In addition, some economists are trying to make the costs of regulation more visible to policy makers so that regulatory policy will take into account all the benefits and all the costs.

Industrial Policy
A deliberate policy by which government aids industries that are the most likely to be successful in the world marketplace—that is, waters the green spots.

WHAT ABOUT INDUSTRIAL POLICY? **Industrial policy** is a deliberate government policy of aiding industries that are the most likely to be successful in the world marketplace—watering the green spots.

The proponents of industrial policy argue that government needs to work with business firms in the private sector to help them compete in the world marketplace. In particular, they argue that government needs to identify the industries of the future—biotechnology, telecommunications, robotics, and computers and software—and help these industries grow and develop now. The United States will be disadvantaged in a relative sense, they argue, if governments of other countries aid some of their industries and the United States does not select some of its own industries for special assistance.

Critics maintain that, however good the intentions, industrial policy does not always turn out the way its proponents would like, for three reasons. First, in deciding which industries to help, government may favor the industries with the most political influence, not those that make the best economic sense in the long run. Critics argue that elected government officials are not beyond rewarding people who have helped them win elections. Thus, industrial policy may turn out to be a way to reward friends and injure enemies rather than to pursue good economic policy.

Second, critics argue that the government officials who design and implement industrial policy aren't really smart enough to identify the industries of the future. Thus, they shouldn't try to impose their uninformed guesses about the future on the economy.

Finally, critics argue that government officials who design and implement industrial policy are likely to hamper economic growth if they provide protection to some industries. For example, suppose the United States institutes an industrial policy. Government officials decide that the U.S. computer industry needs to be protected from foreign competition. In their effort to aid the computer industry, they impose tariffs and quotas on foreign competitors, prompting foreign nations to retaliate by placing tariffs and quotas on U.S. computers. In the end, we might simply have less free trade in the world, thereby hurting consumers because they would have to pay higher prices. A decrease in free trade would also hurt the people who work for export companies because many of them would lose their jobs, and it would prevent the U.S. computer industry from selling in the world marketplace. The end result would be the opposite of the purpose of the policy.

Economic Growth and Special Interest Groups

Although certain economic policies can promote economic growth, they may not necessarily be chosen. In fact, non–growth-promoting policies may be chosen.

To illustrate, consider two types of economic policies: growth-promoting policies and transfer-promoting policies. A growth-promoting policy increases Real GDP; it enlarges the size of the economic pie. A transfer-promoting policy leaves the size of the economic pie unchanged, but it increases the size of the slice that one group gets relative to another group.

For example, suppose group A, a special interest group, currently gets 1/1,000 of the economic pie, and the economic pie is \$1,000. It follows that the group gets a \$1 slice. Group A wants to get more than a \$1 slice, and it can do so in one of two ways. The first is to lobby for a policy that increases the size of its slice of the economic pie. In other words, group A gets a larger slice (say, a \$2 slice) at the expense of someone else's getting a smaller slice. Alternatively, group A can lobby for a policy that increases the size of the pie—say, from \$1,000 to \$1,500. In this case, group A gets not the full increase of \$500, but 1/1,000 of the increase, or 50 cents. So group A has to decide whether it is better to lobby for a growth-promoting policy (where it gets 1/1,000 of any increase in Real GDP) or to lobby for a transfer-promoting policy (where it gets 100 percent of any transfer).

According to Mancur Olson, in *The Rise and Decline of Nations,* special interest groups are more likely to argue for transfer-promoting policies than growth-promoting policies, and the cost-benefit calculation of each policy makes it so.[4] This behavior affects economic growth in that, the more special interest groups there are in a country, the more likely it is that transfer-promoting policies will be lobbied for instead of growth-promoting policies. Individuals will try to get a larger slice of a constant-sized economic pie rather than trying to increase the size of the pie. In short, numerous and politically strong special interest groups are detrimental to economic growth.

4. Mancur Olson, *The Rise and Decline of Nations* (New Haven, CT, and London: Yale University Press, 1982).

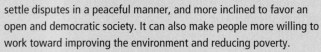

economics 24/7

GROWTH AND MORALITY[5]

There is more to life, liberty, and the pursuit of happiness than a faster car and an iPod nano.

—The Economist

© AP PHOTO/PORCHE AG

Almost everyone agrees that economic growth, especially sustained economic growth, can produce more, better, and newer goods and services. However, according to economist Benjamin Friedman, economic growth can make people happier, more tolerant, more willing to settle disputes in a peaceful manner, and more inclined to favor an open and democratic society. It can also make people more willing to work toward improving the environment and reducing poverty.

The thought that economic growth can do more than give us increased goods and services goes back to Adam Smith. According to Smith, when a nation is acquiring more—when it is getting richer—most of the people are happy and comfortable. When a nation is only maintaining its wealth or when its wealth is declining, its people are not as happy or as comfortable.

Essentially, Friedman argues that economists have looked at the benefits of economic growth too narrowly, stressing the rising material standard of living that comes with economic growth. But this emphasis, says Friedman, ignores the political, social, and moral aspects of economic growth. In his book, *The Moral Consequences of Economic Growth,* he says that "a rising standard of living lies not just in the concrete improvements it brings to how individuals live but in how it shapes the social, political, and ultimately the moral character of a people."

If Friedman is correct that economic growth affects not only the economic life of people but their political, social, and moral life too, then we need to ask why. Friedman says it is because people's estimate of how well off they are is made relative to their own past. People feel the happiest and the most tolerant of others when they believe that their own standard of living is rising—in other words, if they are better off this year than last year. When they are, people care less about how they stand relative to others. But if they do not see an increase in their standard of living relative to their past, they begin to care more about how they are doing relative to others. This comparison with others usually results in frustration and possibly social friction.

Friedman does not argue that there are absolutely no costs to growth. Instead, he simply makes the point that the benefits that come from growth may be greater and more far-reaching than we ever thought.

5. This feature is based on "Why the Rich Must Get Richer," *The Economist,* November 10, 2005.

Worries over Economic Growth

Several worries commonly come up in discussions of economic growth. One concerns the costs of growth. Some individuals argue that increased economic growth brings more pollution, more factories (and thus fewer open spaces), more crowded cities, more emphasis on material goods and getting ahead, more rushing around, more psychological problems, more people using drugs, more suicides, and the like. They argue for less growth instead of more.

Others maintain that there is no evidence of economic growth (or faster as opposed to slower economic growth) causing any or all of these problems. They argue that growth brings many positive things: more wealth and therefore less poverty, a society that is better able to support art projects and museums, less worry in people's lives (not having enough security is a huge worry), and so on. As for pollution and the like, such undesirable by-products would be diminished if the courts were to establish and strictly enforce property rights, particularly with respect to the rivers and the air (which are often the first to become polluted).

Another concern (of economic growth) concerns the relationship between economic growth and the future availability of resources. Some people believe that continued economic and population growth threaten the very survival of the human race because sooner or later the world will run out of resources: no more natural resources, no more clean air, no more pure water, and no more land for people to live on comfortably. They urge social policies that will slow down growth and preserve what we have.

Critics of this position often charge that such so-called doomsday forecasts are based on unrealistic assumptions, oversights, and flimsy evidence. For example, economist Julian Simon pointed out that, contrary to the doomsday forecasts, the quantity of arable land has increased owing to swamp drainage and land improvements, that there is not an inverse relationship between population growth and per capita income growth, that the incidence of famine is decreasing, that we are not running out of natural resources, and that, if or when scarcity of natural resources becomes a problem, rising relative prices of the resources will cause individuals to conserve them and stimulate economic activities to find substitutes.

SELF-TEST

(Answers to Self-Test questions are in the Self-Test Appendix.)

1. "Economic growth refers to an increase in GDP." Comment.
2. Country A has witnessed both economic growth and a rising price level during the past two decades. What does this imply about the *LRAS* and *AD* curves?
3. How can capital investment promote economic growth?
4. What are two worries about economic growth?

NEW GROWTH THEORY

Beginning in the 1980s, economists began discussing economic growth differently than they did in previous decades. They placed more attention on technology, ideas, and education. The discussion takes place under the rubric new growth theory.

What's New About New Growth Theory?

To talk about *new growth theory* assumes that a theory of economic growth came before it. Before new growth theory, there was *neoclassical growth theory.* Some economists believe that new growth theory came to exist to answer some of the questions that neoclassical growth theory could not, in much the same way that a new medical theory may arise to answer questions that an old medical theory can't answer.

Neoclassical growth theory emphasized two resources: labor and capital. Technology was discussed but only in a very shallow way. Technology was said to be exogenous; that is, it came from outside the economic system—it fell out of the sky, it was outside our control. We simply accepted this assumption as a given.

New growth theory holds that technology is endogenous; it is a central part of the economic system. More important, the amount and the quality of technology that is developed depends on the amount of resources we devote to it: The more resources that go to develop technology, the more and better technology is developed.

Paul Romer, whose name is synonymous with new growth theory, asks us to think about technology as we would about prospecting for gold. For one individual, the chances of finding gold are so small that, if one did find gold, the discovery would be viewed as nothing more than good luck. However, if 10,000 individuals mined for gold across a wide geographical area, the chances of finding gold would greatly improve. As with gold, so it is with technological advances. If one person is trying to advance technology, the chances of success are much smaller than if hundreds or thousands of persons are trying.

New growth theory also emphasizes the process of discovering and formulating ideas. According to Romer, discovering and implementing new ideas are what causes economic growth. Consider the difference between *objects* and *ideas.* Objects are material, tangible things—such as natural resources and capital goods. One explanation why some countries are poor is that they lack objects (natural resources and capital goods). The retort to this argument is that some countries with very few objects have still been able to grow economically. For example, in the 1950s, Japan had few natural resources and capital goods (and still doesn't have an abundance of natural resources), but it grew economically. Some economists believe that Japan grew because it had access to ideas or knowledge.

Discovery, Ideas, and Institutions

If the process of discovering ideas is important to economic growth, then it behooves us to figure out ways to promote the discovery process. One way is for business firms not to get locked into doing things one way and one way only. They must let their employees—from the inventor in the lab to the worker on the assembly line—try new ways of doing things. Some would carry this further: Businesses need to create an environment that is receptive to new ideas. They need to encourage their employees to try new ways of doing things.

Employee flexibility, which is a part of the discovery process, is becoming a larger part of the U.S. economy. To some degree, this trend is seen in the amount of time and effort firms devote to discovery in contrast to the amount of time they devote to actually manufacturing goods. Consider the computer software business. Millions of dollars and hundreds of thousands of work hours are devoted to coming up with new and useful software, whereas only a tiny fraction of the work effort and hours go into making, copying, and shipping the disks or CDs containing the software.

Expanding Our Horizons

Romer has said that "economic growth occurs whenever people take resources and rearrange them in ways that are more valuable." The word *rearrange* can be taken in a number of ways. We can think of it as in rearranging the pieces of a puzzle, as in changing the ingredients in a recipe, or as in rearranging how workers go about their daily work. When we rearrange anything, we do it differently. Sometimes, the rearrangement is better, and sometimes it is worse.

The point is that we don't know beforehand whether the change will be for better or worse. Think of how you study for a test. Perhaps you read the book first, then go back and underline, then study the book, and then finally study your lecture notes. Would it be better to study differently? Often, you won't know until you try. As with studying for a test, so it is with producing a car, computer software, or a shopping mall. We do not find better ways of doing things unless we experiment. And with repeated experiments, we often do discover new and better ideas, ideas that ultimately lead to economic growth.

We also don't know beforehand how great or small a change is needed. Small changes—changes perhaps no one would ever think would matter—can make a large difference. As an example, consider the research and development of new medicines. Sometimes, a change in only one or two molecules transforms a mildly effective medicine into a very effective one.

The policy prescription is that we should think of ways to make the process of discovering ideas, experimenting with different ways of doing things, and developing new technology more likely. Without such policy, we are likely to diminish our growth potential. If we believe that ideas are important to economic growth, then we need to have ideas about how to generate more of them. Paul Romer calls these meta-ideas: ideas about how to support the production and transmission of other ideas.

Some ways have been proposed. Perhaps we need to invest more funds in education or research and development. Or perhaps we need to find ways to better protect people's ideas (few people will invest the time, money, and effort to discover better ideas if the ideas can easily be stolen).

In the twenty-first century, countries with the most natural resources and capital goods aren't likely to be the ones that grow the fastest. If new growth theory is correct, the countries that have discovered how to encourage and develop the most and best ideas will be the leaders.

SELF-TEST

1. If technology is endogenous, what are the implications for economic growth?
2. According to new growth theory, what countries will grow the fastest in this century?
3. What does new growth theory have to do with prospecting for gold?

SHIFTS IN THREE CURVES AT ONCE: *AD, SRAS,* AND *LRAS*

In Chapter 7 we developed the basic *AD-AS* model, identified the factors that can shift both the *AD* and *SRAS* curves, and explained how short-run equilibrium in the economy is achieved (at the intersection of the *AD* and *SRAS* curves). In Chapter 8, we discussed how a self-regulating economy removes itself from a recessionary gap and from an inflationary gap. In the other macroeconomic chapters, when we were discussing the *AD-AS* model, we shifted the *AD* and *SRAS* curves and usually left the *LRAS* curve unchanged. Shifting the *LRAS* curve had to wait until this chapter, when our topic was economic growth.

We conclude a few things about the three main curves we have used to conduct most of our analysis: *AD, SRAS,* and *LRAS.* In particular, we know:

- Why the *AD* curve is downward sloping.
- Why the *SRAS* curve is usually upward sloping.
- Why the *LRAS* curve is vertical at Natural Real GDP.
- The factors that shift the *AD* curve.
- The factors that shift the *SRAS* curve.
- The factors that shift the *LRAS* curve.

Given this knowledge, we now assert that all three curves (*AD, SRAS,* and *LRAS*) can shift at the same time. Suppose the following events occur. An increase in the money supply shifts the *AD* curve to the right. At the same time, the *LRAS* curve shifts to the right because of an increase in labor and capital being utilized in the economy. The *SRAS* curve can certainly also shift to the right at the same time as the *LRAS* curve shifts to the right. After all, the ability to produce more output (at each and every price level) does not operate solely in the long run; that is, when the *LRAS* curve shifts to the right, the *SRAS* curve shifts to the right too.

But the *SRAS* curve does not always shift (on net) *to the same degree* as the *LRAS* curve does because some factors that can shift the *SRAS* curve do not shift the *LRAS* curve. For example, in Chapter 15, we saw that the expected price level (or expected inflation rate) could shift the *SRAS* curve. It does not, however, shift the *LRAS* curve (as discussed in this chapter).

So let's say that the *AD* curve and the *LRAS* curve shift to the right and that, although the *SRAS* curve can shift to the same degree as the *LRAS* curve, in this case it does not. In other words, some factor affects only the *SRAS* curve, and this factor *partially offsets*

exhibit 5

Shifts in Three Curves at Once

In this exhibit, all three curves (*ADS, SRAS, LRAS*) shift rightward. The *SRAS* curve in the exhibits shifts right by less than the *LRAS* curve. The economy is initially at point 1 and then moves to point 2. Notice that two things have occurred: (1) the price level has risen and (2) economic growth has occurred. However, since the *LRAS* has also shifted rightward, the economy at point 2 is in a recessionary gap. In other words, Q_2 is less than Q_{N2}. Eventually, $SRAS_2$ will shift to the right (we have not shown this) and bring the economy into its new long-run equilibrium position. One of the things this exhibits points out is that an economy can experience a higher price level and be in a recessionary gap too. This is different than what we have seen in earlier chapters.

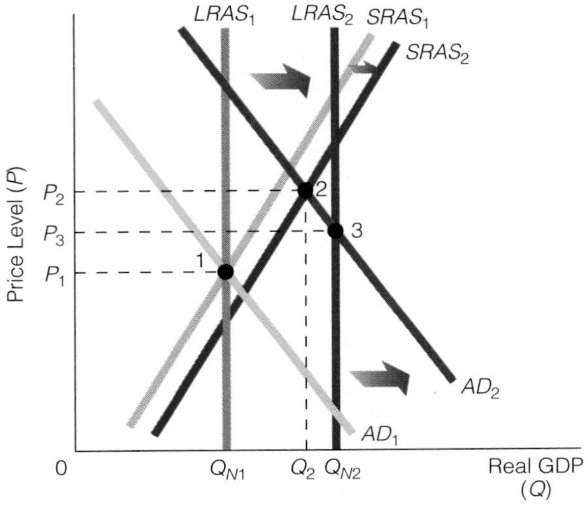

the *SRAS* shifting to the right to the same degree as the *LRAS* curve shifts to the right. We have illustrated this set of events in Exhibit 5. In the exhibit, the *AD* curve has shifted from AD_1 to AD_2, the *SRAS* curve (on net) has shifted from $SRAS_1$ to $SRAS_2$, and the *LRAS* curve has shifted from $LRAS_1$ to $LRAS_2$. Notice that the economy starts at point 1, with a price level of P_1 and a Natural Real GDP level of Q_{N1}. If the economy is at its Natural Real GDP level, the unemployment rate that exists is the natural unemployment rate (U_N). Assuming that the U_N is 4.5 percent, at point 1 we have a price level of P_1, a Natural Real GDP level of Q_{N1}, and a natural unemployment rate of 4.5 percent.

So all three curves (*AD, SRAS, LRAS*) have shifted rightward, but *SRAS* has shifted less than the *LRAS* curve. Where does the economy move? In the short run, the economy moves from point 1 to point 2. Examining this movement, two things have occurred: (1) The price level has risen from P_1 to P_2, and (2) Real GDP has risen from Q_{N1} to Q_2. In other words, the economy has simultaneously experienced both (1) inflation and (2) economic growth.

Now let's compare the unemployment rate at point 1 (or at Q_{N1}) with the unemployment rate at point 2 (or at Q_2). Normally, we would expect the unemployment rate at point 2 to be lower than at point 1 because Real GDP is higher at point 2 than at point 1. In other words, normally we think Real GDP and the unemployment rate are inversely related. But that is not the case this time because the *LRAS* curve has shifted to the right from $LRAS_1$ to $LRAS_2$, giving us a *new* Natural Real GDP level, Q_{N2}. Certainly it is possible for the *LRAS* curve to shift right, bringing about a new and higher Natural Real GDP level, and maintaining the old natural unemployment rate (which we set at 4.5 percent). In other words, the unemployment rates that correspond to Q_{N1} and Q_{N2} can both be 4.5 percent.

But if the unemployment rate at Q_{N2} is 4.5 percent and if Q_2 is lower than Q_{N2} (look at the horizontal axis in Exhibit 5), then the unemployment rate that corresponds to Q_2 is higher than 4.5 percent. Looked at differently, given the new *LRAS* curve of $LRAS_2$, the economy at point 2 is in a recessionary gap with its Real GDP level of Q_2 below the new Natural Real GDP level of Q_{N2}.

If the economy is self-regulating, we would expect the $SRAS_2$ curve in Exhibit 5 eventually to shift rightward until it intersects the $LRAS_2$ curve at point 3 (not shown). In other words, eventually the economy will be in long-run equilibrium at point 3.

This exhibit illustrates that three things are consistent with each other: inflation, economic growth, and a recessionary gap.

1. Inflation (an increase in the price level) occurs between points 1 and 2.
2. Economic growth (an increase in Real GDP) occurs between points 1 and 2.
3. A recessionary gap is made evident by comparing the Real GDP level at point 2 with the Natural Real GDP level at point 3.

One last point: Contrary to what we have seen in earlier chapters, we now see that a higher price level (P_2) can go along with an economy that is in a recessionary gap.

office hours

"WHAT IS THE DIFFERENCE BETWEEN BUSINESS CYCLE MACROECONOMICS AND ECONOMIC GROWTH MACROECONOMICS?"

Student:
I am searching for a way to put the macroeconomics in this chapter in perspective with the macroeconomics in the other chapters. Can you help?

Instructor:
In previous chapters the *LRAS* curve did not move. It was fixed at some Natural Real GDP level. In this chapter we discussed the factors that can shift the *LRAS* curve; we discussed how the economy can move from one Natural Real GDP level to a higher Natural Real GDP level.

Also, in previous chapters we mainly discussed business cycle macroeconomics. In this chapter we discussed economic growth macroeconomics.

Student:
Specifically, what does business cycle macroeconomics deal with?

Instructor:
It deals with two things: (a) differences between Real GDP and Natural Real GDP and (b) ways of moving the economy to its Natural Real GDP level. To illustrate, suppose that Natural Real GDP is $11 trillion and that the current Real GDP in the economy is $10 trillion. Obviously, because Real GDP is lower than Natural Real GDP, the economy is in a recessionary gap. If the economy is self-regulating, it will eventually move to its Natural Real GDP level. If it is not self-regulating, then perhaps monetary or fiscal policy can be used to move the economy to its Natural Real GDP level.

Student:
How does business cycle macroeconomics differ from what was discussed in this chapter?

Instructor:
In this chapter, we mainly discussed economic growth (occurring from an efficient level of production). Economic growth deals with the economy's moving from one Natural Real GDP level to a higher one—specifically, how the economy might move from a Natural Real GDP level of, say, $11 trillion to a higher Natural Real GDP level of, say, $11.7 trillion.

Student:
Does it follow that when we are discussing how the economy moves from one Natural Real GDP level to a higher one that we are simultaneously discussing rightward shifts in the *LRAS* curve?

Instructor:
Yes, that's correct. In fact, we can roughly define both business cycle macroeconomics and economic growth macroeconomics with respect to the *LRAS* curve. Business cycle macroeconomics deals with economic activity occurring around a single *LRAS* curve. Economic growth macroeconomics (starting from an efficient level of production) deals with rightward shifts in the *LRAS* curve.

Points to Remember

1. Business cycle macroeconomics deals with economic activity occurring around a single *LRAS* curve (or around a specific Natural Real GDP level).
2. Economic growth macroeconomics (starting from an efficient level production) deals with rightward shifts in the *LRAS* curve (or moving from a lower to a higher level of Natural Real GDP).

a reader asks — Can an Understanding of How Economies Grow Help Me?

This chapter explains that economic growth is largely a function of, or dependent on, such things as the amount of labor and capital that an economy employs, technological advancements, the property rights structure, and other factors. Can these factors translate into personal income growth? For example, if my objective is to grow my income over time, will knowing how economies grow help me achieve that goal?

Let's recall the factors that are important to economic growth: (1) natural resources, (2) labor, (3) capital, (4) technological advances, (5) free trade as technology, (6) the property rights structure, and (7) economic freedom. In terms of personal income growth, counterparts exist for some of these factors. For example, an individual's natural talent might be the counterpart of a country's natural resources. Just as a country might happen to have plentiful natural resources, so might an individual be lucky to be born with a natural talent, especially a talent that others value highly.

Two factors directly relevant to your income growth are labor and (human) capital. We know that more labor and greater labor productivity promote economic growth. Similarly, for an individual, more labor expended and greater labor productivity often lead to income growth. How can you individually expend more labor? The answer is to work more hours. How can you increase your labor productivity? As explained in the chapter, one way is through increased education, training, and experience. In other words, acquire more *human capital.* Simply put, one way to increase your income is to work more; another is to work better.

Finally, consider the roles of the property rights structure and economic freedom. We often observe people migrating to places where the property rights structure and level of economic freedom are conducive to their personal income growth. For example, very few people in the world migrate to North Korea, but many migrate to the United States.

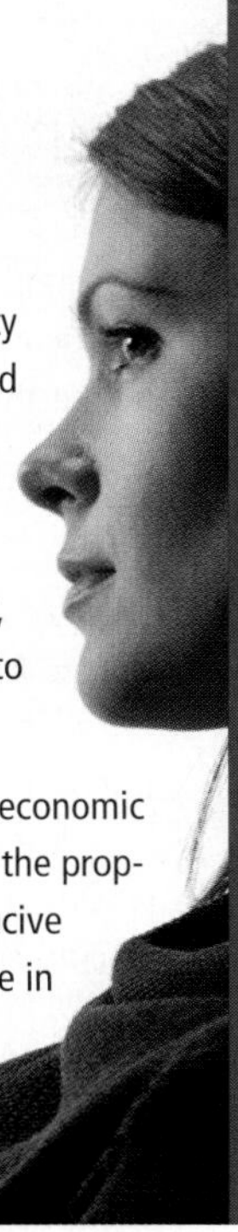

Chapter Summary

ECONOMIC GROWTH

- Absolute real economic growth is an increase in Real GDP from one period to the next.
- Per capita real economic growth refers to an increase from one period to the next in per capita Real GDP, which is Real GDP divided by population.
- Economic growth can occur starting from an inefficient level of production or from an efficient level of production.

ECONOMIC GROWTH AND THE PRICE LEVEL

- Usually, economists talk about economic growth as a result of a shift rightward in the PPF or in the *LRAS* curve.
- Economic growth can occur along with (1) an increase in the price level, (2) a decrease in the price level, or (3) no change in the price level.

CAUSES OF ECONOMIC GROWTH

- Factors related to economic growth include natural resources, labor, capital, technological advances, free trade as technology, the property rights structure, and economic freedom.
- Countries rich in natural resources are not guaranteed economic growth, and countries poor in natural resources may grow economically. Nevertheless, a country with more natural resources can evidence more economic growth, *ceteris paribus*, than those without.
- An increase in the amount of labor or in the quality of labor (as measured by increases in labor productivity) can lead to economic growth.
- More capital goods can lead to increases in economic growth. Capital formation, however, is related to saving: As the saving rate increases, capital formation increases.
- Technological advances may be the result of new capital goods or of new ways of producing goods. In either case, technological advances lead to economic growth.
- Economic growth is related to a country's property rights structure. Individuals will invest more, take more risks, and work harder; greater economic growth is likely when the property rights structure allows people to keep more of the fruits of their investing, risk taking, and labor, *ceteris paribus*.
- For the most part, the more economic freedom there is in a country, the higher the Real GDP per capita will be.

POLICIES TO PROMOTE ECONOMIC GROWTH

- Both demand-side and supply-side policies can be used to promote economic growth. Demand-side policies focus on shifting the *AD* curve to the right. Supply-side policies focus on shifting the *LRAS* curve to the right.
- Some economists propose cutting taxes on such activities as saving and working to increase the productive capacity of the economy. Other economists argue that regulations on business should be relaxed to increase the productive capacity of the economy.
- Industrial policy is a deliberate government policy of aiding industries that are the most likely to be successful in the world marketplace—that is, watering the green spots.
- Industrial policy has both proponents and opponents. The proponents argue that the government needs to identify the industries of the future and help them grow and develop now. The United States will fall behind, they argue, if it does not adopt an industrial policy while other countries do. The opponents of industrial policy argue that the government doesn't know which industries it makes economic sense to help and that industrial policy is likely to become protectionist and politically motivated.

ECONOMIC GROWTH AND SPECIAL INTEREST GROUPS

- According to Mancur Olson, the more special interest groups there are in a country, the more likely it is that transfer-promoting policies will be lobbied for instead of growth-promoting policies because individuals will try to get a larger slice of a constant-size economic pie rather than trying to increase the size of the pie.

NEW GROWTH THEORY

- New growth theory holds that technology is endogenous; neoclassical growth theory holds that technology is exogenous. When something is endogenous, it is part of the economic system, under our control or influence. When something is exogenous, it is not part of the system; it is assumed to be given to us, often mysteriously through a process that we do not understand.
- According to Paul Romer, discovering and implementing new ideas are what cause economic growth.
- Certain institutions can promote the discovery of new ideas and therefore promote economic growth.

CHANGES IN *AD*, *SRAS*, AND *LRAS* CURVES

- An economy can experience a rise in the price level and be in a recessionary gap too. See Exhibit 5.

Key Terms and Concepts

Absolute Real Economic Growth

Per Capita Real Economic Growth

Industrial Policy

Questions and Problems

1 Why might per capita real economic growth be a more useful measurement than absolute real economic growth?

2 Identify and explain the two types of economic growth.

3 Is it possible for economic growth to occur and for the price level to rise too? Explain your answer.

4 "Natural resources are neither a sufficient nor a necessary factor for growth." What does the statement mean?

5 How do we compute (average) labor productivity?

6 Is it possible to have more workers working, producing a higher Real GDP, at the same time that labor productivity is declining? Explain your answer.

7 How does an increased saving rate relate to increased labor productivity?

8 "Economic growth doesn't simply depend on having more natural resources, more or higher-quality labor, more capital, and so on; it depends on people's incentives to put these resources together to produce goods and services." Do you agree or disagree? Explain your answer.

9 "Economic growth can be promoted from either the demand side or the supply side." Do you agree or disagree? Explain your answer.

10 What is new about new growth theory?

11 How does discovering and implementing new ideas cause economic growth?

12 Explain how each of the following relates to economic growth:

a. Technological advance.

b. Labor productivity.

c. Natural resources.

d. Education.

e. Special interest groups.

13 Explain how free trade is a form of technology.

14 What is the difference between business cycle macroeconomics and economic growth macroeconomics?

15 The *AD* curve shifts to the right by more than the *SRAS* and *LRAS* curves (and the *SRAS* and *LRAS* curves shift to the right by the same amount). What happens to the price level and to Real GDP?

16 Can an economy experience a higher price level and a recessionary gap simultaneously? Explain your answer.

Working with Numbers and Graphs

1 The economy of country X is currently growing at 2 percent a year. How many years will it take to double the Real GDP of country X?

2 Diagrammatically represent each of the following:

a. Economic growth from an inefficient level of production.

b. Economic growth from an efficient level of production.

3 Diagrammatically represent each of the following:

a. Economic growth with a stable price level.

b. Economic growth with a rising price level.

c. Economic growth with a falling price level.

© BILLY E. BARNES/PHOTOEDIT

CHAPTER 17

INTERNATIONAL TRADE

Introduction Economics is about trade, and trade crosses boundaries. People trade not only with people who live in their city, state, or country, but also with people in other countries. Many of the goods you consume are undoubtedly produced in other countries. This chapter examines international trade and the prohibitions sometimes placed on it.

INTERNATIONAL TRADE THEORY

International trade takes place for the same reasons that trade at any level exists. Individuals trade to make themselves better off. Pat and Zach, both of whom live in Cincinnati, Ohio, trade because they both value something the other has more than they value some of their own possessions. On an international scale, Elaine in the United States trades with Cho in China because Cho has something that Elaine wants and Elaine has something that Cho wants.

Obviously, the countries of the world have different terrains, climates, resources, worker skills, and so on. Therefore, some countries will be able to produce goods that other countries cannot produce or can produce only at extremely high costs. For example, Hong Kong has no oil, and Saudi Arabia has a large supply of it. Bananas do not grow easily in the United States, but they flourish in Honduras. Americans could grow bananas if they used hothouses, but it is cheaper for Americans to buy bananas from Hondurans than to produce bananas themselves.

Major U.S. exports include automobiles, computers, aircraft, corn, wheat, soybeans, scientific instruments, coal, and plastic materials. Major imports include petroleum, automobiles, clothing, iron and steel, office machines, footwear, fish, coffee, and diamonds. Some of the countries of the world that are major exporters are the United States, Germany, Japan, France, and the United Kingdom. These same countries are also some of the major importers in the world.

How Countries Know What to Trade

Recall the concept of *comparative advantage,* an economic concept first discussed in Chapter 2. In this section, we discuss comparative advantage in terms of countries rather than in terms of individuals.

COMPARATIVE ADVANTAGE Assume a two-country–two-good world. The countries are the United States and Japan, and the goods are food and clothing. Both countries can produce the two goods in the four different combinations listed in Exhibit 1. For example, the United States can produce 90 units of food and 0 units of clothing, 60 units of food and 10 units of clothing, or other combinations. Japan can produce 15 units of food and 0 units of clothing, 10 units of food and 5 units of clothing, or other combinations.

Suppose the United States is producing and consuming the two goods in the combination represented by point B on its production possibilities frontier, and Japan is producing and consuming the combination of the two goods represented by point F on its production possibilities frontier. In this case, neither of the two countries is specializing in the production of one of the two goods, nor are the two countries trading with each other. We call this the *no specialization–no trade (NS-NT) case* (see column 1 in Exhibit 2).

Now suppose the United States and Japan decide to specialize in the production of a specific good and to trade with each other, in what is called the *specialization-trade (S-T) case.* Whether the two countries will be better off through specialization and trade is best explained by means of a numerical example, but first we need to find the answers to two other questions: What good should the United States specialize in producing? What good should Japan specialize in producing? The general answer to both questions is the same:

exhibit 1

Production Possibilities in Two Countries

The United States and Japan can produce the two goods in the combinations shown. Initially, the United States is at point B on its PPF and Japan is at point F on its PPF. Both countries can be made better off by specializing in and trading the good in which each has a comparative advantage.

United States			Japan		
Points on Production Possibilities Frontier	Food	Clothing	Points on Production Possibilities Frontier	Food	Clothing
A	90	0	E	15	0
B	60	10	F	10	5
C	30	20	G	5	10
D	0	30	H	0	15

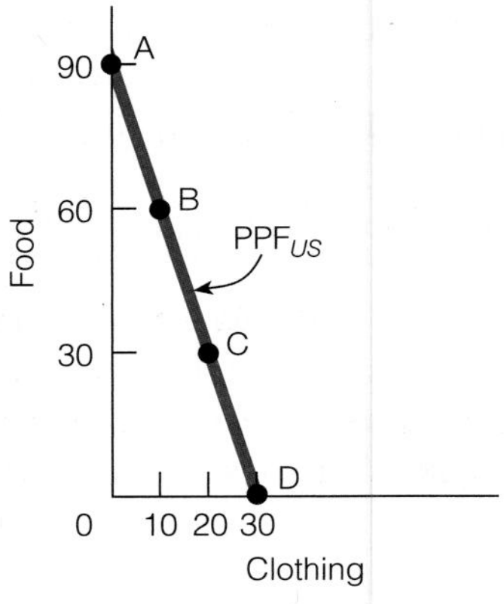

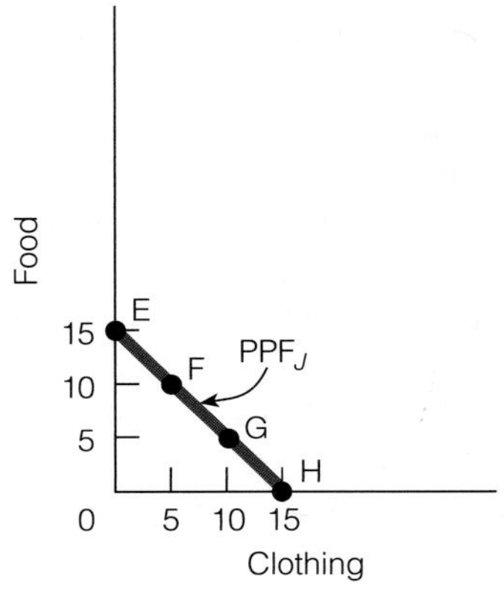

exhibit 2

Both Countries Gain from Specialization and Trade

Column 1: Both the United States and Japan operate independently of each other. The United States produces and consumes 60 units of food and 10 units of clothing. Japan produces and consumes 10 units of food and 5 units of clothing. Column 2: The United States specializes in the production of food; Japan specializes in the production of clothing. Column 3: The United States and Japan agree to the terms of trade of 2 units of food for 1 unit of clothing. They actually trade 20 units of food for 10 units of clothing. Column 4: Overall, the United States consumes 70 units of food and 10 units of clothing. Japan consumes 20 units of food and 5 units of clothing. Column 5: Consumption levels are higher for both the United States and Japan in the S-T case than in the NS-NT case.

	No Specialization-No Trade (NS-NT) Case		Specialization-Trade (S-T) Case			
Country	**(1) Production and Consumption in the NS-NT Case**		**(2) Production in the S-T Case**	**(3) Exports (−) Imports (+) Terms of Trade Are 2F = 1C**	**(4) Consumption in the S-T Case (2) + (3)**	**(5) Gains from Specialization and Trade (4) − (1)**
United States						
Food	60	Point B in Exhibit 1	90 Point A in Exhibit 1	−20	70	10
Clothing	10		0	+10	10	0
Japan						
Food	10	Point F in Exhibit 1	0 Point H in Exhibit 1	+20	20	10
Clothing	5		15	−10	5	0

Countries specialize in the production of the good in which they have a comparative advantage. A country has a **comparative advantage** in the production of a good when it can produce the good at lower opportunity cost than another country can.

Comparative Advantage
The situation when a country can produce a good at lower opportunity cost than another country can.

For example, in the United States, the opportunity cost of producing 1 unit of clothing (C) is 3 units of food (F); for every 10 units of clothing it produces, it forfeits 30 units of food. So the opportunity cost of producing 1 unit of food is 1/3 unit of clothing. In Japan, the opportunity cost of producing 1 unit of clothing is 1 unit of food (for every 5 units of clothing it produces, it forfeits 5 units of food). To recap, in the United States, the situation is 1 C = 3 F, or 1 F = 1/3 C; in Japan the situation is 1 C = 1 F, or 1 F = 1 C. The United States can produce food at a lower opportunity cost (1/3 C, as opposed to 1 C in Japan), whereas Japan can produce clothing at a lower opportunity cost (1 F, as opposed to 3 F in the United States). Thus, the United States has a comparative advantage in food, and Japan has a comparative advantage in clothing.

Suppose the two countries specialize in the production of the goods in which they have a comparative advantage. That is, the United States specializes in the production of food (producing 90 units), and Japan specializes in the production of clothing (producing 15 units). In Exhibit 1, the United States locates at point A on its PPF, and Japan locates at point H on its PPF (see column 2 in Exhibit 2).

SETTLING ON THE TERMS OF TRADE After they have determined the goods to specialize in producing, the two countries must settle on the terms of trade—that is, how much food to trade for how much clothing. The United States faces the following situation: For every 30 units of food it does not produce, it can produce 10 units of clothing, as shown in Exhibit 1. Thus, 3 units of food have an opportunity cost of 1 unit of clothing (3 F = 1 C), or 1 unit of food has a cost of 1/3 unit of clothing (1 F = 1/3 C). Japan faces the following situation: For every 5 units of food it does not produce, it can produce 5 units of clothing. Thus, 1 unit of food has an opportunity cost of 1 unit of clothing (1 F = 1 C). For the United States, 3 F = 1 C, and for Japan, 1 F = 1 C.

With these cost ratios, both countries should be able to agree on terms of trade that specify 2 F = 1 C. The United States would benefit by giving up 2 units of food instead of 3 units for 1 unit of clothing, whereas Japan would benefit by getting 2 units of food instead of only 1 unit for 1 unit of clothing. Suppose the two countries agree to the terms of trade of 2 F = 1 C and trade, in absolute amounts, 20 units of food for 10 units of clothing (see column 3 in Exhibit 2). Will they make themselves better off? We'll soon see that they do.

RESULTS OF THE SPECIALIZATION-TRADE (S-T) CASE Now the United States produces 90 units of food and trades 20 units to Japan, receiving 10 units of clothing in exchange. It consumes 70 units of food and 10 units of clothing. Japan produces 15 units of clothing and trades 10 to the United States, receiving 20 units of food in exchange. It consumes 5 units of clothing and 20 units of food (see column 4 in Exhibit 2).

Comparing the consumption levels in both countries in the two cases, the United States and Japan each consume 10 more units of food and no less clothing in the specialization-trade case than in the no specialization–no trade case (column 5 in Exhibit 2). We conclude that a country gains by specializing in producing and trading the good in which it has a comparative advantage.

Common MISCONCEPTIONS

About How Much We Can Consume

No country can consume beyond its PPF if it doesn't specialize and trade with other countries. But, as we have just seen, it can do so when there is specialization and trade. Look at the PPF for the United States in Exhibit 1. In the NS-NT case, the United States consumes 60 units of food and 10 units of clothing; that is, the United States consumes at point B on its PPF. In the S-T case, however, it consumes 70 units of food and 10 units of clothing. A point that represents this combination of the two goods is beyond the country's PPF.

How Countries Know when They Have a Comparative Advantage

Government officials of a country do not analyze pages of cost data to determine what their country should specialize in producing and then trade. Bureaucrats do not plot production possibilities frontiers on graph paper or calculate opportunity costs. Instead, the individual's desire to earn a dollar, a peso, or a euro determines the pattern of international trade. The desire to earn a profit determines what a country specializes in and trades.

To illustrate, Henri, an enterprising Frenchman, visits the United States and observes that beef is relatively cheap (compared with the price in France) and that perfume is relatively expensive. Noticing the price differences for beef and perfume between his country and the United States, he decides to buy some perfume in France, bring it to the United States, and sell it for the relatively higher U.S. price. With his profits from the perfume transaction, he buys beef in the United States, ships it to France, and sells it for the relatively higher French price. Obviously, Henri is buying low and selling high. He buys a good in the country where it is cheap and sells it in the country where it is expensive.

Henri's activities have a couple of consequences. First, he is earning a profit. The larger the price differences are between the two countries and the more he shuffles goods between countries, the more profit Henri earns.

Second, Henri's activities are moving each country toward its comparative advantage. The United States ends up exporting beef to France, and France ends up

economics 24/7

DIVIDING THE WORK

John and Veronica, husband and wife, have divided their household tasks: John usually does all the lawn work, fixes the cars, and does the dinner dishes, and Veronica cleans the house, cooks the meals, and does the laundry. Some sociologists might suggest that John and Veronica divided the household tasks along gender lines: Men have for years done the lawn work, fixed the cars, and so on, and women have for years cleaned the house, cooked the meals, and so on. In other words, John is doing man's work, and Veronica is doing woman's work.

© COMSTOCK IMAGES/JUPITER IMAGES

Maybe they have followed gender lines, but the question remains why certain tasks became man's work and others became woman's work. Moreover, their arrangement doesn't explain why John and Veronica don't split every task evenly. In other words, why doesn't John clean half the house and Veronica clean half the house? Why doesn't Veronica mow the lawn on the second and fourth week of every month and John mow the lawn every first and third week of the month?

The law of comparative advantage may be the answer to all these questions. Consider two tasks: cleaning the house and mowing the lawn. The following table shows how long John and Veronica take to complete the two tasks individually.

	Time to Clean the House	Time to Mow the Lawn
John	120 minutes	50 minutes
Veronica	60 minutes	100 minutes

Here is the opportunity cost of each task for each person.

	Opportunity Cost of Cleaning the House	Opportunity Cost of Mowing the Lawn
John	2.40 mowed lawns	0.42 clean houses
Veronica	0.60 mowed lawns	1.67 clean houses

In other words, John has a comparative advantage in mowing the lawn, and Veronica has a comparative advantage in cleaning the house.

Now let's compare two settings. In setting 1, John and Veronica each do half of each task. In setting 2, John only mows the lawn and Veronica only cleans the house.

In setting 1, John spends 60 minutes cleaning half of the house and 25 minutes mowing half of the lawn, for a total of 85 minutes; Veronica spends 30 minutes cleaning half of the house and 50 minutes mowing half of the lawn, for a total of 80 minutes. The total time spent by Veronica and John cleaning the house and mowing the lawn is 165 minutes.

In setting 2, John spends 50 minutes mowing the lawn, and Veronica spends 60 minutes cleaning the house. The total time spent by Veronica and John cleaning the house and mowing the lawn is 110 minutes.

In which setting are Veronica and John better off? John works 85 minutes in setting 1 and 50 minutes in setting 2; so he is better off in setting 2. Veronica works 80 minutes in setting 1 and 60 minutes in setting 2; so Veronica is also better off in setting 2. Together, John and Veronica spend 55 fewer minutes in setting 2 than in setting 1. Getting the job done in 55 fewer minutes is the benefit of specializing in various duties around the house. Given our numbers, we would expect that John will mow the lawn (and do nothing else) and Veronica will clean the house (and do nothing else).

exporting perfume to the United States. Just as the pure theory predicts, individuals in the two countries specialize in and trade the good in which they have a comparative advantage. The outcome is brought about spontaneously through the actions of individuals trying to make themselves better off; they are simply trying to gain through trade.

Thinking like AN ECONOMIST

The Benefits of Searching for Profit

Is the desire to earn profit useful to society at large? Henri's desire for profit ended up moving both the United States and France toward specializing in and trading the good in which they had a comparative advantage. As we showed earlier in the chapter, when countries specialize and trade, they are better off than when they do neither.

SELF-TEST

(Answers to Self-Test questions are in the Self-Test Appendix.)

1. Suppose the United States can produce 120 units of X at an opportunity cost of 20 units of Y, and Great Britain can produce 40 units of X at an opportunity cost of 80 units of Y. Identify favorable terms of trade for the two countries.
2. If a country can produce more of all goods than any other country, would it benefit from specializing and trading? Explain your answer.
3. Do government officials analyze data to determine what their country can produce at a comparative advantage?

TRADE RESTRICTIONS

International trade theory shows that countries gain from free international trade, that is, from specializing in the production of the goods in which they have a comparative advantage and trading those goods for other goods. In the real world, however, the numerous types of trade restrictions give rise to the question: If countries gain from international trade, why are there trade restrictions? The answer requires an analysis of costs and benefits; specifically, we need to determine who benefits and who loses when trade is restricted. But first, we need to explain some pertinent background information.

The Distributional Effects of International Trade

The previous section explained that specialization and international trade benefit individuals in different countries, but this benefit occurs on net. Not every individual person may gain.

To illustrate, Pam Dickson lives and works in the United States making clock radios. She produces and sells 12,000 clock radios per year at a price of $40 each. As the situation stands, there is no international trade. Individuals in other countries who make clock radios do not sell them in the United States.

Then one day, the U.S. market is opened to clock radios from China. Chinese manufacturers seem to have a comparative advantage in the production of clock radios because they sell their clock radios in the United States for $25 each. Pam realizes that she cannot compete at this price. Her sales drop to such a degree that she goes out of business. Thus, the introduction of international trade in this instance has harmed Pam personally.

Consumers' and Producers' Surpluses

The preceding example raises the issue of the distributional effects of free trade. The benefits of international trade are not equally distributed to all individuals in the

economics 24/7

YOU'RE GETTING BETTER BECAUSE OTHERS ARE GETTING BETTER

Smith can produce X in 30 minutes, and Y in 60 minutes. Jones can produce X in 2 hours and Y in 3 hours. Initially:

- Smith can produce X in 30 minutes and Y in 60 minutes.
- Jones can produce X in 2 hours and Y in 3 hours.

Smith is better at producing X and Y than Jones. Suppose that Smith gets even better at producing X. He can produce X in 15 minutes as opposed to 30 minutes.

- Smith can produce X in 15 minutes and Y in 60 minutes.
- Jones can produce X in 2 hours and Y in 3 hours.

Will Smith's getting better at producing X cause Jones to get better at producing Y? The quick and obvious answer is no. Smith's ability to produce X in 15 minutes instead of 30 minutes doesn't change the time it takes Jones to produce X and Y. It still takes Jones 2 hours to produce X and 3 hours to produce Y.

But look at things in terms of opportunity cost. Initially the opportunity cost for Smith of producing 1 X is ½ Y and the opportunity cost of producing 1 Y is 2 X. For Jones, the opportunity cost of producing 1 X is ⅔ Y and the opportunity cost of producing 1 Y is 1½ X. Given these opportunity costs, Smith has a comparative advantage in producing X, and Jones has a comparative advantage in producing Y.

When Smith gets better at doing X, his opportunity cost of producing 1 X now *falls* to ¼ Y and his opportunity cost of doing 1 Y *rises* to 4 Y. In other words, Smith's becoming better at producing X makes him relatively worse at producing Y.

As for Jones, because Smith has become relatively better at producing X, Jones has becoming relatively better at producing Y. We reach this conclusion by comparing Jones's opportunity cost of producing Y *before* and *after* Smith gets better at producing X. Before Smith gets better at producing X, Jones gives up 1½ X to get 1 Y whereas Smith has to give up 2 X to get 1 Y.

- Jones gives up 1½ X to get 1 Y.
- Smith gives up 2 X to get 1 Y.

We might say that Jones has only a *slight* comparative advantage over Smith when it comes to producing Y. But after Smith gets better at producing X, Jones gives up 1½ X to get 1 Y, whereas Smith gives up 4 X to get 1 Y.

- Jones gives up 1½ X to get 1 Y.
- Smith gives up 4 X to get 1 Y.

Jones now has a *substantial* comparative advantage over Smith when it comes to producing Y.

Suppose X is being a lawyer and Y is being a farmer. When Smith becomes better as a lawyer, Jones automatically becomes a better farmer (or a relatively lower low-cost farmer). If we change things and say that X is being an accountant and Y is driving a truck, then as Smith becomes a better accountant, Jones automatically becomes a better trucker.

Looking at things in terms of opportunity cost provides us with an insight into our world. Namely, as some people become better at what they do, they naturally make other people better at what they do. Become a better mathematician, singer, or teacher, and you naturally make others better (a lower low-cost producer) at what they do.

population. Therefore relevant to our discussion are the topics of consumers' and producers' surpluses, which were first discussed in Chapter 3.

Consumers' surplus is the difference between the maximum price a buyer is willing and able to pay for a good or service and the price actually paid.

Consumers' surplus = Maximum buying price − Price paid

Consumers' surplus is a dollar measure of the benefit gained by being able to purchase a unit of a good for less than one is willing to pay for it. For example, if Yakov would have paid $10 to see the movie at the Cinemax but paid only $4, his consumer surplus is $6. Consumers' surplus is the consumers' net gain from trade.

Producers' surplus (or sellers' surplus) is the difference between the price sellers receive for a good and the minimum or lowest price for which they would have sold the good.

Producers' surplus = Price received − Minimum selling price

Producers' surplus is a dollar measure of the benefit gained by being able to sell a unit of output for more than one is willing to sell it. For example, if Joan sold her knit sweaters for $24 each but would have sold them for as low as (but no lower than) $14 each, her producer surplus is $10 per sweater. Producers' surplus is the producers' net gain from trade.

Both consumers' and producers' surplus are represented in Exhibit 3. In part (a), the shaded triangle represents consumers' surplus. This triangle includes the area under the demand curve and above the equilibrium price. In part (b), the shaded triangle represents producers' surplus. This triangle includes the area above the supply curve and under the equilibrium price.

Finding ECONOMICS

While Negotiating the Price of a House

Robin is negotiating the price of the house she wants to buy from Yakov. Her last offer for the house was $478,000 and he countered with $485,000. She is thinking about offering $481,000. Where is the economics?

Obviously, in this negotiation each person is trying to increase his or her surplus at the expense of the other. Specifically, the lower the price Robin pays, the higher her consumers' surplus will be and the lower Yakov's producers' surplus. Alternatively, the higher the price Yakov receives, the higher his producers' surplus will be and the lower Robin's consumers' surplus.

exhibit 3

Consumers' and Producers' Surplus

(a) Consumers' surplus. As the shaded area indicates, the difference between the maximum or highest amount consumers would be willing to pay and the price they actually pay is consumers' surplus. (b) Producers' surplus. As the shaded area indicates, the difference between the price sellers receive for the good and the minimum or lowest price they would be willing to sell the good for is producers' surplus.

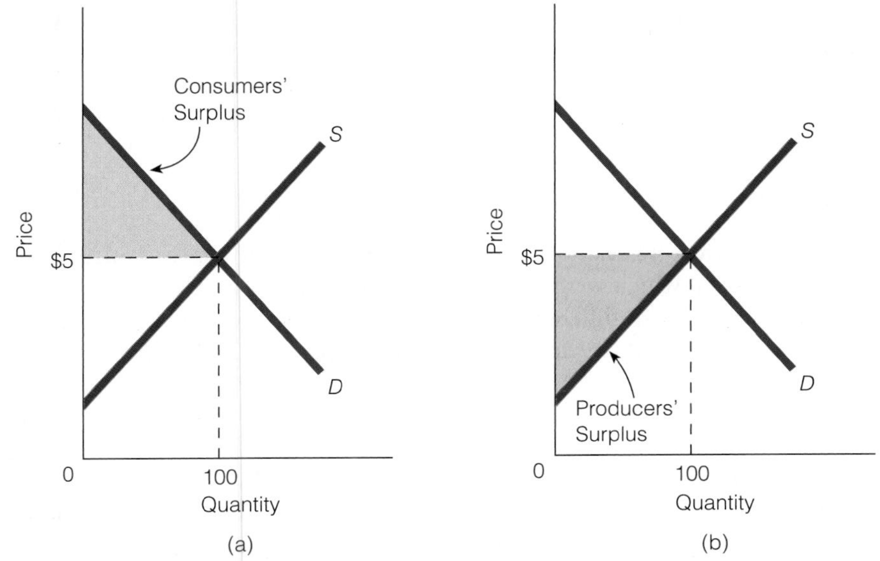

	Consumers' Surplus	Producers' Surplus	Government Tariff Revenue
Free trade (No tariff)	1 + 2 + 3 + 4 + 5 + 6	7	None
Tariff	1 + 2	3 + 7	5
Loss or Gain	− (3 + 4 + 5 + 6)	+3	+5

Result of Tariff = Loss to consumers + Gain to producers + Tariff revenue

= − (3 + 4 + 5 + 6) +3 +5

= − (4 + 6)

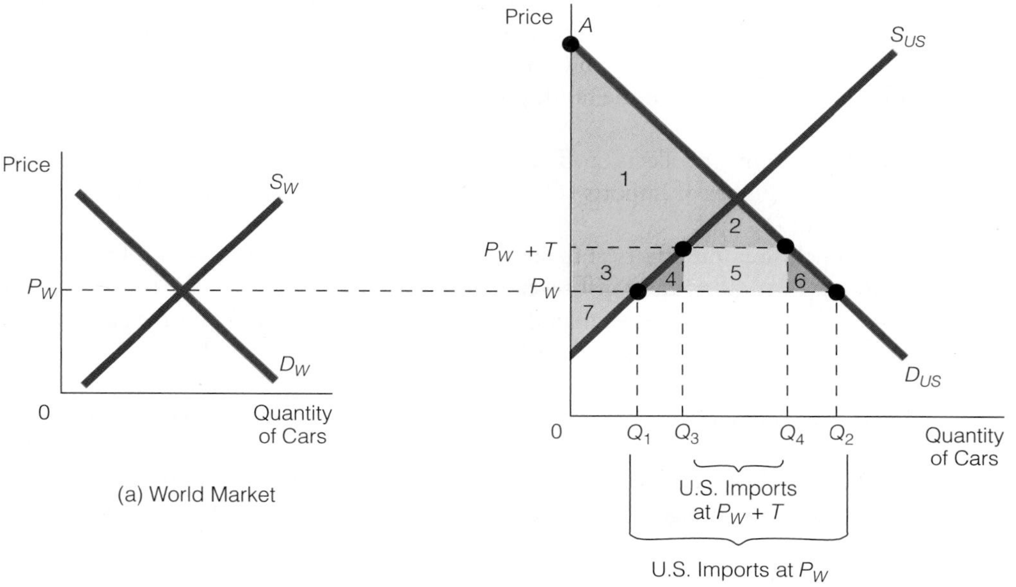

(a) World Market

(b) Domestic (U.S.) Market

exhibit 4

The Effects of a Tariff

A tariff raises the price of cars from P_W to $P_W + T$, decreases consumers' surplus, increases producers' surplus, and generates tariff revenue. Because consumers lose more than producers and government gain, there is a net loss due to the tariff.

The Benefits and Costs of Trade Restrictions

Of the numerous ways to restrict international trade, tariffs and quotas are two of the more common. We discuss these two methods using the tools of supply and demand concentrating on two groups: U.S. consumers and U.S. producers.

TARIFFS A **tariff** is a tax on imports. The primary effect of a tariff is to raise the price of the imported good for the domestic consumer. Exhibit 4 illustrates the effects of a tariff on cars imported into the United States. The world price for cars is P_W, as shown in Exhibit 4(a). At this price in the domestic U.S. market, U.S. consumers buy Q_2 cars, as shown in part (b). They buy Q_1 from U.S. producers and the difference between Q_2 and Q_1 ($Q_2 - Q_1$) from foreign producers. In other words, U.S. imports at P_W are $Q_2 - Q_1$.

Tariff
A tax on imports.

In this situation, consumers' surplus is the area under the demand curve and above the world price, P_W. This is the sum of the areas 1, 2, 3, 4, 5, and 6 [see Exhibit 4(b)]. Producers' surplus is the area above the supply curve and below the world price, P_W. This is area 7.

Now suppose a tariff is imposed. The price for imported cars in the U.S. market rises to $P_W + T$ (the world price plus the tariff). At this price, U.S. consumers buy Q_4 cars: Q_3 from U.S. producers and $Q_4 - Q_3$ from foreign producers. U.S. imports are $Q_4 - Q_3$, which is a smaller number of imports than at the pretariff price. An effect of tariffs, then, is to reduce imports. After the tariff has been imposed, at price $P_W + T$, consumers' surplus consists of areas 1 and 2, and producers' surplus consists of areas 3 and 7.

Thus consumers receive more consumers' surplus when tariffs do not exist and less when they do exist. In our example, consumers received areas 1 through 6 in consumers' surplus when the tariff did not exist but only areas 1 and 2 when the tariff did exist. Because of the tariff, consumers' surplus was reduced by an amount equal to areas 3, 4, 5, and 6.

Producers, though, receive less producers' surplus when tariffs do not exist and more when they do exist. In our example, producers received producers' surplus equal to area 7 when the tariff did not exist, but they received producers' surplus equal to areas 3 and 7 with the tariff. Because of the tariff, producers' surplus increased by an amount equal to area 3.

The government collects tariff revenue equal to area 5. This area is obtained by multiplying the number of imports ($Q_4 - Q_3$) by the tariff, which is the difference between $P_W + T$ and P_W.[1]

In conclusion, the effects of the tariff are a decrease in consumers' surplus, an increase in producers' surplus, and tariff revenue for government. Because the loss to consumers (areas 3, 4, 5, and 6) is greater than the gain to producers (area 3) plus the gain to government (area 5), *a tariff results in a net loss.* The net loss is areas 4 and 6.

Quota
A legal limit on the amount of a good that may be imported.

QUOTAS A **quota** is a legal limit on the amount of a good that may be imported. For example, the government may decide to allow no more than 100,000 foreign cars to be imported, or 10 million barrels of OPEC oil, or 30,000 Japanese television sets. A quota reduces the supply of a good and raises the price of imported goods for domestic consumers (Exhibit 5).

Once again, we consider the situation in the U.S. car market. At a price of P_W (established in the world market for cars), U.S. consumers buy Q_1 cars from U.S. producers and $Q_2 - Q_1$ cars from foreign producers. Consumers' surplus is equal to areas 1, 2, 3, 4, 5, and 6. Producers' surplus is equal to area 7.

Suppose now that the U.S. government sets a quota equal to $Q_4 - Q_3$. Because this is the number of foreign cars U.S. consumers imported when the tariff was imposed (see Exhibit 4), the price of cars rises to P_Q in Exhibit 5 (which is equal to $P_W + T$ in Exhibit 4). At P_Q, consumers' surplus is equal to areas 1 and 2, and producers' surplus consists of areas 3 and 7. The decrease in consumers' surplus due to the quota is equal to areas 3, 4, 5, and 6; the increase in producers' surplus is equal to area 3.

But what about area 5? This area is not transferred to government, as was the case when a tariff was imposed. Rather, it represents the additional revenue earned by the importers (and sellers) of $Q_4 - Q_3$. Before the quota, importers were importing $Q_2 - Q_1$, but only part of this total amount ($Q_4 - Q_3$) is relevant because this is the amount of imports now that the quota has been established. Before the quota was established, the dollar amount that the importers received for $Q_4 - Q_3$ was $P_W \times (Q_4 - Q_3)$, or area 8. Because of the quota, the price rises to P_Q, and they now receive $P_Q \times (Q_4 - Q_3)$, or areas 5 and 8. The difference between the total revenues on $Q_4 - Q_3$ with a quota and without a quota is area 5.

1. For example, if the tariff is $100 and the number of imports is 50,000, then the tariff is $5 million.

exhibit 5

The Effects of a Quota

A quota that sets the legal limit of imports at $Q_4 - Q_3$ causes the price of cars to increase from P_W to P_Q. A quota raises price, decreases consumers' surplus, increases producers' surplus, and increases the total revenue importers earn. Because consumers lose more than producers and importers gain, there is a net loss due to the quota.

	Consumers' Surplus	Producers' Surplus	Revenue of Importers
Free trade (No quota)	1 + 2 + 3 + 4 + 5 + 6	7	8
Quota	1 + 2	3 + 7	5 + 8
Loss or Gain	− (3 + 4 + 5 + 6)	+3	+5

Result of Quota = Loss to consumers + Gain to producers + Gain to importers
= − (3 + 4 + 5 + 6) +3 +5
= − (4 + 6)

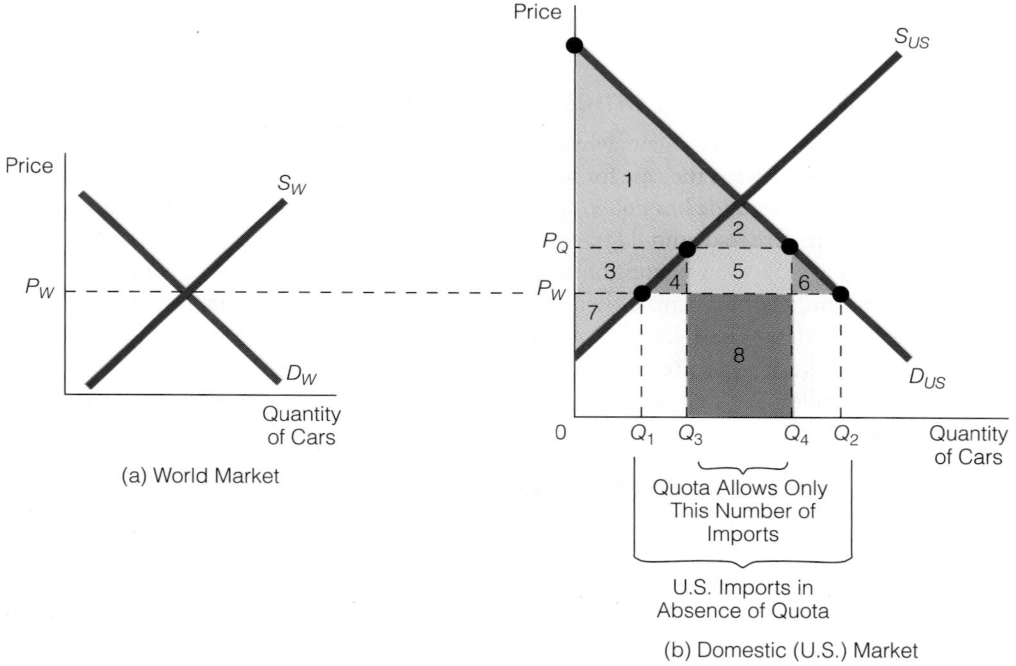

In conclusion, the effects of a quota are a decrease in consumers' surplus, an increase in producers' surplus, and an increase in total revenue for the importers who sell the allowed number of imported units. Because the loss to consumers (areas 3, 4, 5, and 6) is greater than the increase in producers' surplus (area 3) plus the gain to importers (area 5), there is a *net loss as a result of the quota.* The net loss is equal to areas 4 and 6.[2]

2. It is perhaps incorrect to imply that government receives nothing from a quota. Although it receives nothing directly, it may gain indirectly. Economists generally argue that because government officials are likely to be the persons who decide which importers will get to satisfy the quota, importers will naturally lobby them. Thus, government officials will likely receive something, if only dinner at an expensive restaurant while the lobbyist makes his or her pitch. In short, in the course of the lobbying, resources will be spent by lobbyists as they curry favor with government officials or politicians who have the power to decide who gets to sell the limited number of imported goods. In economics, lobbyists' activities geared toward obtaining special privileges are referred to as rent seeking.

Finding Economics

In a Policy Debate

There is a debate tonight at the college Irina attends. There will be four people on either side of the issue: Should the United States practice free trade? Irina attends the debate and comes away thinking that both sides made good points during the debate. The no-free-trade side argued that because other countries do not always practice free trade, neither should the United States. The pro-free-trade side argued that free trade leads to lower prices for U.S. consumers. Where is the economics?

Most of the debate, we believe, will fit into our discussion of Exhibits 4 and 5. These two exhibits show what happens to consumers and producers, and to society as a whole, as the result of both free and prohibited trade. The diagrams show (1) the benefits of prohibited free trade to domestic producers, (2) the costs of prohibited trade to domestic consumers, (3) tariff revenue to government, if it exists, and (4) the overall net costs to prohibited trade.

Why Nations Sometimes Restrict Trade

If free trade results in net gain, why do nations sometimes restrict trade? Based on the analysis in this chapter so far, the case for free trade (no tariffs or quotas) appears to be a strong one. The case for free trade has not gone unchallenged, however. Some persons maintain that at certain times free trade should be restricted or suspended. In almost all cases, they argue that doing so is in the best interest of the public or country as a whole. In a word, they advance a public interest argument. Other persons contend that the public interest argument is only superficial; down deep, they say, it is a special interest argument clothed in pretty words. As you might guess, the debate between the two groups is often heated.

The following sections describe some arguments that have been advanced for trade restrictions.

THE NATIONAL DEFENSE ARGUMENT It is often stated that certain industries—such as aircraft, petroleum, chemicals, and weapons—are necessary to the national defense. Suppose the United States has a comparative advantage in the production of wheat and country X has a comparative advantage in the production of weapons. Many Americans feel that the United States should not specialize in the production of wheat and then trade wheat to country X in exchange for weapons. Leaving weapons production to another country, they maintain, is too dangerous.

The national defense argument may have some validity, but even valid arguments may be abused. Industries that are not really necessary to the national defense may maintain otherwise. In the past, the national defense argument has been used by some firms in the following industries: pens, pottery, peanuts, papers, candles, thumbtacks, tuna fishing, and pencils.

THE INFANT INDUSTRY ARGUMENT Alexander Hamilton, the first U.S. secretary of the treasury, argued that so-called infant, or new, industries often need protection from older, established foreign competitors until they are mature enough to compete on an equal basis. Today, some persons voice the same argument. The infant industry argument is clearly an argument for temporary protection. Critics charge, however, that after an industry is protected from foreign competition, removing the protection is almost impossible; the once infant industry will continue to maintain that it isn't old enough to go it alone. Critics of the infant industry argument say that political realities make it unlikely that a benefit, once bestowed, will be removed.

Finally, the infant industry argument, like the national defense argument, may be abused. All new industries, whether they could currently compete successfully with foreign producers or not, would argue for protection on infant industry grounds.

economics 24/7

OFFSHORE OUTSOURCING, OR OFFSHORING

Outsourcing is the term used to describe work done for a company by another company or by people other than the original company's employees. It entails purchasing a product or process from an outside supplier rather than producing it in house. To illustrate, suppose company X has, in the past, hired employees for personnel, accounting, and payroll services. Currently, though, these duties are performed by a company in another state. Company X has outsourced these work activities.

©AFP/GETTY IMAGES

When a company outsources certain work activities to individuals in another country, it is said to be engaged in offshore outsourcing, or offshoring. Consider a few examples. A New York securities firm replaces 800 software engineering employees with a team of software engineers in India. A computer company replaces 200 on-call technicians in its headquarters in Texas with 150 on-call technicians in India.

The benefits of offshoring for a U.S. firm are obvious; it pays lower wages to individuals in other countries for the same work that U.S. employees do for higher wages. Benefits also flow to the employees hired in the foreign countries. The costs of offshoring are said to fall on persons who lose their jobs as a result, such as the software engineer in New York or the on-call computer technician in Texas. Some have argued that offshoring will soon become a major political issue and that it could bring with it a wave of protectionism.

There will undoubtedly be both proponents of and opponents to offshoring. On net, however, are there more benefits than costs or more costs than benefits? Consider a U.S. company that currently employs Jones as a software engineer, paying her $\$x$ a year. Then, one day, the company tells Jones that it has to let her go; it is replacing her with a software engineer in India who will work for $\$z$ a year (where $\$z$ is less than $\$x$).

Some have asked why Jones doesn't simply agree to work for $\$z$, the same wage as that agreed to by the Indian software engineer? Obviously, Jones can work elsewhere for some wage between $\$x$ and $\$z$. Assume this wage is $\$y$. Thus, even though offshoring has moved Jones from earning $\$x$ to earning $\$y$, $\$y$ is still more than $\$z$.

In short, the U.S. company is able to lower its costs from $\$x$ to $\$z$, and Jones's income falls from $\$x$ to $\$y$. The U.S. company lowers its costs more than Jones's income falls because the difference between $\$x$ and $\$z$ is greater than the difference between $\$x$ and $\$y$.

If the U.S. company operates within a competitive environment, its lower costs will shift its supply curve to the right and end up lowering prices. In other words, offshoring can end up reducing prices for U.S. consumers. The political fallout from offshoring might, in the end, depend on how visible, to the average American, the employment effects of offshoring are relative to the price reduction effect.

THE ANTIDUMPING ARGUMENT **Dumping** is the sale of goods abroad at a price below their cost and below the price charged in the domestic market. If a French firm sells wine in the United States for a price below the cost of producing the wine and below the price charged in France, it is dumping wine in the United States. Critics of dumping maintain that it is an unfair trade practice that puts domestic producers of substitute goods at a disadvantage.

Dumping
The sale of goods abroad at a price below their cost and below the price charged in the domestic market.

In addition, critics charge that dumpers seek only to penetrate a market and drive out domestic competitors, only to raise prices. However, some economists point to the infeasibility of this strategy. After the dumpers have driven out their competition and raised prices, their competition is likely to return. For their efforts, the dumpers, in turn, would have incurred only a string of losses (owing to their selling below cost). Opponents of the antidumping argument also point out that domestic consumers benefit from dumping because they pay lower prices.

THE FOREIGN EXPORT SUBSIDIES ARGUMENT Some governments subsidize firms that export goods. If a country offers a below-market (interest rate) loan to a company, it is often argued, the government subsidizes the production of the good the firm produces. If, in turn, the firm exports the good to a foreign country, that country's producers of substitute goods call foul. They complain that the foreign firm has been given an unfair advantage that they should be protected against.[3]

Others say that consumers should not turn their backs on a gift (in the form of lower prices). If foreign governments want to subsidize their exports and thus give a gift to foreign consumers at the expense of their own taxpayers, then the recipients should not complain. Of course, the recipients are usually not the ones who are complaining. Usually, the one's complaining are the domestic producers who can't sell their goods at as high a price because of the gift domestic consumers are receiving from foreign governments.

THE LOW FOREIGN WAGES ARGUMENT It is sometimes argued that American producers can't compete with foreign producers because American producers pay high wages to their workers and foreign producers pay low wages to their workers. The American producers insist that international trade must be restricted, or they will be ruined. However, the argument overlooks why American wages are high and foreign wages are low in the first place: productivity. High productivity and high wages are usually linked, as are low productivity and low wages. If an American worker, who receives $20 per hour, can produce (on average) 100 units of X per hour, working with numerous capital goods, then the cost per unit may be lower than when a foreign worker, who receives $2 per hour, produces (on average) 5 units of X per hour, working by hand. In short, a country's high-wage disadvantage may be offset by its productivity advantage, and a country's low-wage advantage may be offset by its productivity disadvantage. High wages do not necessarily mean high costs when productivity and the costs of nonlabor resources are included.

THE SAVING DOMESTIC JOBS ARGUMENT Sometimes, the argument against completely free trade is made in terms of saving domestic jobs. Actually, we have already discussed this argument in its different guises. For example, the low foreign wages argument is one form of it: If domestic producers cannot compete with foreign producers because foreign producers pay low wages and domestic producers pay high wages, domestic producers will go out of business and domestic jobs will be lost. The foreign export subsidies argument is another form of this argument: If foreign government subsidies give a competitive edge to foreign producers, not only will domestic producers fail, but as a result of their failure, domestic jobs will be lost. Critics of the saving domestic jobs argument (in all its guises) often assert that if a domestic producer is being outcompeted by foreign producers and if domestic jobs in an industry are being lost as a result, the world market is signaling that those labor resources could be put to better use in an industry in which the country holds a comparative advantage.

Thinking like AN ECONOMIST

Economics Versus Politics

International trade often becomes a battleground between economics and politics. The simple tools of supply and demand and consumers' and producers' surpluses show that free trade leads to net gains. On the whole, tariffs and quotas make living standards lower than they would be if free trade were permitted.

(continued)

3. Words are important in this debate. For example, domestic producers who claim that foreign governments have subsidized foreign firms say that they are not asking for economic protectionism, but only retaliation, or reciprocity, or simply tit for tat—words that have less negative connotation than those their opponents use.

Thinking Like An Economist (continued)

On the other side, though, are the realities of business and politics. Domestic producers may advocate quotas and tariffs to make themselves better off, giving little thought to the negative effects felt by foreign producers or domestic consumers.

Perhaps the battle over international trade comes down to this: Policies are largely advocated, argued, and lobbied for based more on their distributional effects than on their aggregate or overall effects. On an aggregate level, free trade produces a net gain for society, whereas restricted trade produces a net loss. But economists understand that even if free trade in the aggregate produces a net gain, not every single person will benefit more from free trade than from restricted trade. We have just shown how a subset of the population (producers) gains more, in a particular instance, from restricted trade than from free trade. In short, economists realize that the crucial question in determining real-world policies is more often, "How does it affect me?" than "How does it affect us?"

WORLD TRADE ORGANIZATION (WTO)

The international trade organization, the *World Trade Organization (WTO),* came into existence on January 1, 1995. It is the successor to the General Agreement on Tariffs and Trade (GATT), which was set up in 1947. Today, 151 countries in the world are members of the WTO.

According to the WTO, its "overriding objective is to help trade flow smoothly, freely, fairly, and predictably." It does this by administering trade agreements, acting as a forum for trade negotiations, settling trade disputes, reviewing national trade policies, assisting developing countries in trade policy issues, and cooperating with other international organizations. Perhaps its most useful and controversial role is adjudicating trade disputes. For example, suppose the United States claims that the Canadian government is preventing U.S. producers from openly selling their goods in Canada. The WTO will look at the matter, consult with trade experts, and then decide the issue. A country that is found engaging in unfair trade can either desist from this practice or face appropriate retaliation from the injured country.

In theory, at least, the WTO is supposed to lead to freer international trade, and there is some evidence that it has done so. The critics of the WTO often say that it has achieved this objective at some cost to a nation's sovereignty. For example, in some past trade disputes between the United States and other countries, the WTO has decided against the United States.

Also, some critics of the WTO often argue that the member countries often put trade issues above environmental issues and do not do enough to help the poor in the world. In the past, some of the critics of the WTO have taken to the streets to demonstrate against it. In a few cases, riots have broken out.

SELF-TEST

1. Who benefits and who loses from tariffs? Explain your answer.
2. Identify the directional change in consumers' surplus and producers' surplus when we move from free trade to tariffs. Is the change in consumers' surplus greater than, less than, or equal to the change in producers' surplus?
3. What is a major difference between the effects of a quota and the effects of a tariff?
4. Outline the details of the infant industry argument for trade restriction.

"SHOULD WE IMPOSE TARIFFS IF THEY IMPOSE TARIFFS?"

Student:

Here is a problem I have with our discussion of free and prohibited trade. Essentially, I am in favor of free international trade, but I think the United States should have free trade with those countries that practice free trade with it. In other words, if country X practices free trade with the United States, then the United States should practice free trade with it. But if country Y places tariffs on U.S. goods entering the country, then the United States ought to place tariffs on country Y's goods entering this country.

Instructor:

Many people feel the same way you do, but this opinion overlooks something that we showed in both Exhibits 4 and 5: the losses of moving from free trade to prohibited trade (where either tariffs or quotas exist) are greater than the gains. Remember? There is a net loss to society.

Student:

I just think it is only fair that other countries get what they give. If they give free trade to us, then we ought to give free trade back to them. If they place tariffs and quotas on our goods, then we ought to do the same to their goods.

Instructor:

You need to keep in mind the price the United States has to pay for this policy of tit for tat.

Student:

What do you mean? What price does the United States have to pay?

Instructor:

It has to incur the net loss illustrated in Exhibits 4 and 5. If you look back at Exhibit 4, for example, you will notice that moving from free trade to prohibited trade does the following: (1) decreases consumers' surplus, (2) increases producers' surplus, and (3) raises tariff revenue. But when we count up all the gains of prohibited trade and compare them with all the losses, we conclude that the losses are greater than the gains. In other words, there is a net loss to prohibited trade.

Student:

But suppose our practicing tit for tat (giving free trade for free trade and prohibited trade for prohibited trade) forces other countries to move away from prohibited trade. In other words, what I am saying is this: We need to look at this issue of free versus prohibited trade over time. Maybe the United States has to practice prohibited trade today (with those countries that impose tariffs on quotas on the United States) in order to force those countries to practice free trade tomorrow. Couldn't it work out that way?

Instructor:

It could work out that way. Or, then, things could escalate toward greater prohibited trade. In other words, country A imposes tariffs and quotas on country B, and then country B raises its tariffs and quotas even higher on country A; so country A retaliates and raises its tariffs and quotas on country B, and so on.

Student:

So what is your point? Is it that free trade is the best policy to practice no matter what other countries do?

Instuctor:

That is what many economists would say, but that is not really the point I am making here. I am simply making two points with respect to the discussion. First, in response to your position that that United States ought to practice tit for tat (give free trade for free trade, tariffs for tariffs, quotas for quotas), I am simply drawing your attention to the net loss Americans incur if they practice prohibited trade—no matter what other countries are doing. In other words, there is a net loss for Americans even if other countries are practicing free trade or prohibited trade. Second, with respect to your second point, about prohibited trade leading to free trade tomorrow, I am saying that we can't be sure that prohibited trade today won't lead to greater prohibitions on trade tomorrow. This is not to say you can't be right: It is possible for prohibited trade today to lead to less prohibited trade tomorrow.

Points to Remember

1. There is a net loss to a country that imposes tariffs or quotas on imported goods. This net loss exists no matter what another country is doing—whether it is practicing free or prohibited trade.
2. We cannot easily predict the outcome of the United States practicing tit for tat in international trade.

a reader asks | Why Does the Government Impose Tariffs and Quotas?

If tariffs and quotas result in higher prices for U.S. consumers, then why does the government impose them?

The answer is that government is sometimes more responsive to producer interests than to consumer interests. But then we have to wonder why. To explain, consider the following example.

Suppose there are 100 U.S. producers of good X and 20 million U.S. consumers of it. The producers want to protect themselves from foreign competition; so they lobby for and receive a quota on foreign goods that compete with good X. As a result, consumers must pay higher prices. For simplicity's sake, let's say that consumers must pay $40 million more. Thus, producers receive $40 million more for good X than they would have if the quota had not been imposed. If the $40 million received is divided equally among the 100 producers, each producer receives $400,000 more as a result of the quota. If the additional $40 million paid is divided equally among the 20 million consumers, each customer pays $2 more as a result of the quota.

A producer is likely to think, "I should lobby for the quota because if I'm effective, I'll receive $400,000." A consumer is likely to think, "Why should I lobby against the quota? If I'm effective, I'll save only $2. Saving $2 isn't worth the time and trouble my lobbying would take."

In short, the benefits of quotas are concentrated on relatively few producers, and the costs of quotas are spread out over relatively many consumers. Thus, each producer's gain is relatively large compared with each consumer's loss. We predict that producers will lobby government to obtain the relatively large gains from quotas but that consumers will not lobby government to keep from paying the small additional cost due to quotas.

Politicians are in the awkward position of hearing from people who want the quotas but not hearing from people who are against them. It is likely politicians will respond to the vocal interests. Politicians may mistakenly assume that consumers' silence means that they accept the quota policy, when in fact they may not. Consumers may simply not find it worthwhile to do anything to fight the policy.

Chapter Summary

SPECIALIZATION AND TRADE

- A country has a comparative advantage in the production of a good if it can produce the good at a lower opportunity cost than another country can.
- Individuals in countries that specialize and trade have a higher standard of living than would be the case if their countries did not specialize and trade.
- Government officials do not analyze cost data to determine what their country should specialize in and trade. Instead, the desire to earn a dollar, peso, or euro guides individuals' actions and produces the unintended consequence that countries specialize in and trade the good(s) in which they have a comparative advantage. However, trade restrictions can change this outcome.

TARIFFS AND QUOTAS

- A tariff is a tax on imports. A quota is a legal limit on the amount of a good that may be imported.
- Both tariffs and quotas raise the price of imports.
- Tariffs lead to a decrease in consumers' surplus, an increase in producers' surplus, and tariff revenue for the government. Consumers lose more through tariffs than producers and government (together) gain.
- Quotas lead to a decrease in consumers' surplus, an increase in producers' surplus, and additional revenue for the importers who sell the amount specified by the quota. Consumers lose more through quotas than producers and importers (together) gain.

ARGUMENTS FOR TRADE RESTRICTIONS

- The national defense argument states that certain goods—such as aircraft, petroleum, chemicals, and weapons—are necessary to the national defense and should be produced domestically whether the country has a comparative advantage in their production or not.

- The infant industry argument states that infant, or new, industries should be protected from free (foreign) trade so that they have time to develop and compete on an equal basis with older, more established foreign industries.
- The antidumping argument states that domestic producers should not have to compete (on an unequal basis) with foreign producers that sell products below cost and below the prices they charge in their domestic markets.
- The foreign export subsidies argument states that domestic producers should not have to compete (on an unequal basis) with foreign producers that have been subsidized by their governments.
- The low foreign wages argument states that domestic producers cannot compete with foreign producers that pay low wages to their employees when domestic producers pay high wages to their employees. For high-paying domestic firms to survive, limits on free trade are proposed.
- The saving domestic jobs argument states that through low foreign wages or government subsidies (or dumping, etc.), foreign producers will be able to outcompete domestic producers and that therefore domestic jobs will be lost. For domestic firms to survive and domestic jobs not to be lost, limits on free trade are proposed.
- Everyone does not accept the arguments for trade restrictions as valid. Critics often maintain that the arguments can be and are abused and that in most cases they are motivated by self-interest.

Key Terms and Concepts

Comparative Advantage

Tariff

Quota

Dumping

Questions and Problems

1 Although a production possibilities frontier is usually drawn for a country, one could be drawn for the world. Picture the world's production possibilities frontier. Is the world positioned at a point on the PPF or below it? Give a reason for your answer.

2 If country A is better than country B at producing all goods, will country A still be made better off by specializing and trading? Explain your answer. (Hint: Look at Exhibit 1.)

3 The desire for profit can end up pushing countries toward producing goods in which they have a comparative advantage. Do you agree or disagree? Explain your answer.

4 "Whatever can be done by a tariff can be done by a quota." Discuss.

5 Neither free trade nor prohibited trade comes with just benefits. Both come with benefits and costs. Therefore, free trade is neither better nor worse than prohibited trade. Comment.

6 Consider two groups of domestic producers: those that compete with imports and those that export goods. Suppose the domestic producers that compete with imports convince the legislature to impose a high tariff on imports—so high, in fact, that almost all imports are eliminated. Does this policy in any way adversely affect domestic producers that export goods? If so, how?

7 Suppose the U.S. government wants to curtail imports. Would it be likely to favor a tariff or a quota to accomplish its objective? Why?

8 Suppose the landmass known to you as the United States of America had been composed, since the nation's founding, of separate countries instead of separate states. Would you expect the standard of living of the people who inhabit this landmass to be higher, lower, or equal to what it is today? Why?

9 Even though Jeremy is a better gardener and novelist than Bill is, Jeremy still hires Bill as his gardener. Why?

10 Suppose that a constitutional convention is called tomorrow and that you are chosen as one of the delegates from your state. You and the other delegates must decide whether it will be constitutional or unconstitutional for the federal government to impose tariffs and quotas or to restrict international trade in any way. What would be your position?

11 Some economists have argued that because domestic consumers gain more from free trade than domestic producers gain from (import) tariffs and quotas, consumers should buy out domestic producers and rid themselves of costly tariffs and quotas. For example, if consumers save $400 million from free trade (through paying lower prices) and producers gain $100 million from tariffs and quotas, consumers can pay producers something more than $100 million but less than $400 million and get producers to favor free trade too. Assuming this scheme were feasible, what do you think of it?

12 If there is a net loss to society from tariffs, why do tariffs exist?

Working with Numbers and Graphs

1 Using the data in the table, answer the following questions:

a. For which good does Canada have a comparative advantage?

b. For which good does Italy have a comparative advantage?

c. What might be a set of favorable terms of trade for the two countries?

d. Prove that both countries would be better off in the specialization-trade case than in the no-specialization–no-trade case.

Points on Production Possibilities Frontier	Canada		Italy	
	Good X	Good Y	Good X	Good Y
A	150	0	90	0
B	100	25	60	60
C	50	50	30	120
D	0	75	0	180

2 In the following figure, P_W is the world price and $P_W + T$ is the world price plus a tariff. Identify the following:

a. The level of imports at P_W.

b. The level of imports at $P_W + T$.

c. The loss in consumers' surplus as a result of a tariff.

d. The gain in producers' surplus as a result of a tariff.

e. The tariff revenue as the result of a tariff.

f. The net loss to society as a result of a tariff.

g. The net benefit to society of moving from a tariff situation to a no-tariff situation.

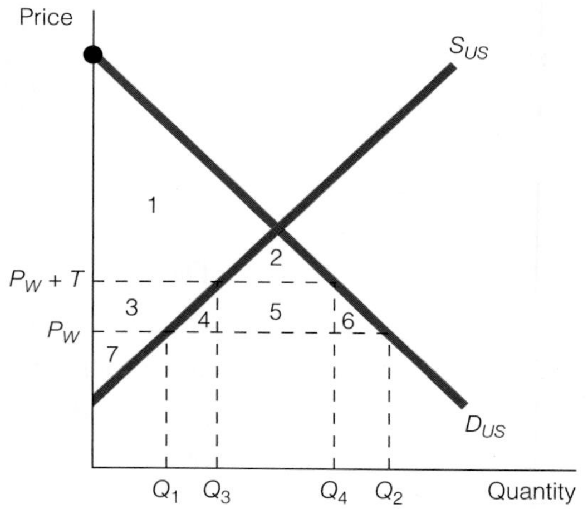

CHAPTER 18

INTERNATIONAL FINANCE

© PETER MENZEL/PHOTO RESEARCHERS

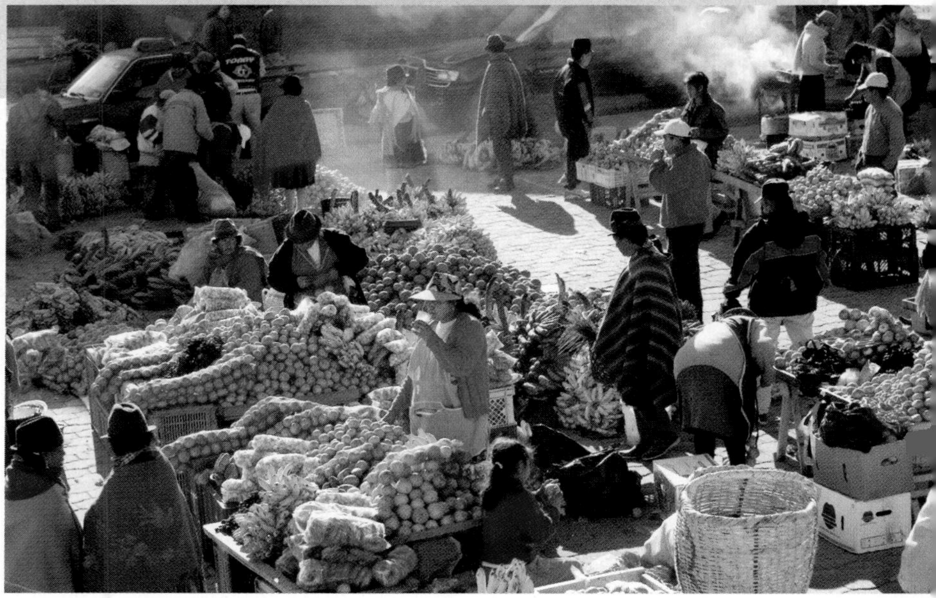

Introduction When people travel to a foreign country, they buy goods and services in the country, whose prices are quoted in yen, pounds, euros, pesos, or some other currency. For example, a U.S. tourist in Mexico might want to buy a good priced in pesos and to know what the good costs in dollars and cents. The answer depends on the current exchange rate between the dollar and the peso, but what determines the exchange rate? This is just one of the many questions answered in this chapter.

THE BALANCE OF PAYMENTS

Countries keep track of their domestic level of production by calculating their gross domestic product (GDP). Similarly, they keep track of the flow of their international trade (receipts and expenditures) by calculating their balance of payments. The **balance of payments** is a periodic (usually annual) statement of the money value of all transactions between residents of one country and residents of all other countries. The balance of payments provides information about a nation's imports and exports, domestic residents' earnings on assets located abroad, foreign earnings on domestic assets, gifts to and from foreign countries (including foreign aid), exchange of assets, and official transactions by governments and central banks.

Balance of Payments
A periodic (usually annual) statement of the money value of all transactions between residents of one country and the residents of all other countries.

Debit
In the balance of payments, any transaction that supplies the country's currency in the foreign exchange market.

Foreign Exchange Market
The market in which currencies of different countries are exchanged.

Balance of payments accounts record both debits and credits. A debit is indicated by a minus (−) sign, and a credit is indicated by a plus (+) sign. *Any transaction that supplies the country's currency in the foreign exchange market is recorded as a* **debit**. (The **foreign exchange market** is the market in which currencies of different countries are exchanged.) For example, a U.S. retailer wants to buy Japanese television sets so that he can sell them in his stores in the United States. To buy the TV sets from the Japanese, the retailer first has to supply U.S. dollars (in the foreign exchange market) in return for Japanese yen. Then he will turn over the yen to the Japanese in exchange for the television sets.

exhibit 1

Debits and Credits

Item	Definition	Example
Debit (−)	Any transaction that supplies the country's currency.	Jim, an American, supplies dollars in exchange for yen so that he can use the yen to buy Japanese goods.
Credit (+)	Any transaction that creates a demand for the country's currency.	Svetlana, who is Russian and living in Russia, supplies rubles in order to demand dollars so that she can use the dollars to buy U.S. goods.

Any transaction that creates a demand for the country's currency in the foreign exchange market is recorded as a **credit**. For example, a Russian retailer wants to buy computers from U.S. computer producers. To pay the U.S. producers, who want U.S. dollars, the Russian retailer must supply rubles (in the foreign exchange market) in return for dollars. Then she will turn over the dollars to the U.S. producers in exchange for the computers. Exhibit 1 presents a summary of debits and credits.

Credit
In the balance of payments, any transaction that creates a demand for the country's currency in the foreign exchange market.

The international transactions that are summarized in the balance of payments can be grouped into three categories, or three accounts—the current account, the capital account, and the official reserve account—and a statistical discrepancy. Exhibit 2 illustrates a U.S. balance of payments account for year Z. The data in the exhibit are hypothetical (to make the calculations simpler) but not unrealistic. In this section, we describe and explain each of the items in the balance of payments using the data in Exhibit 2 for our calculations.

Current Account

The **current account** includes all payments related to the purchase and sale of goods and services. The current account has three major components: exports of goods and services, imports of goods and services, and net unilateral transfers abroad.

Current Account
The account in the balance of payments that includes all payments related to the purchase and sale of goods and services. Components of the account include exports, imports, and net unilateral transfers abroad.

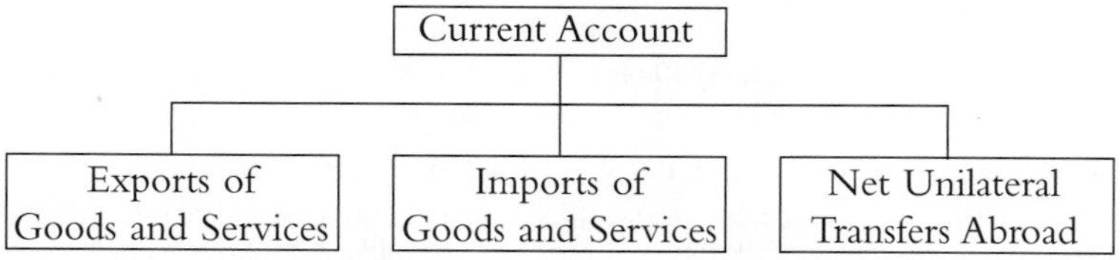

EXPORTS OF GOODS AND SERVICES Americans export goods (e.g., cars), they export services (e.g., insurance, banking, transportation, and tourism), and they receive income on assets they own abroad. All three activities increase the demand for U.S. dollars while increasing the supply of foreign currencies in the foreign exchange market; thus, they are recorded as credits (+). For example, if a foreigner buys a U.S. computer, payment must ultimately be made in U.S. dollars. Thus, she is required to supply her country's currency when she demands U.S. dollars. (We use *foreigner* in this chapter to refer to a resident of a foreign country.)

IMPORTS OF GOODS AND SERVICES Americans import goods and services, and foreigners receive income on assets they own in the United States. These activities increase the demand for foreign currencies while increasing the supply of U.S. dollars to the foreign exchange market; thus, they are recorded as debits (−). For example, if an

exhibit 2

U.S. Balance of Payments, Year Z

The data in this exhibit are hypothetical, but not unrealistic. All numbers are in billions of dollars. The plus and minus signs in the exhibit should be viewed as operational signs.

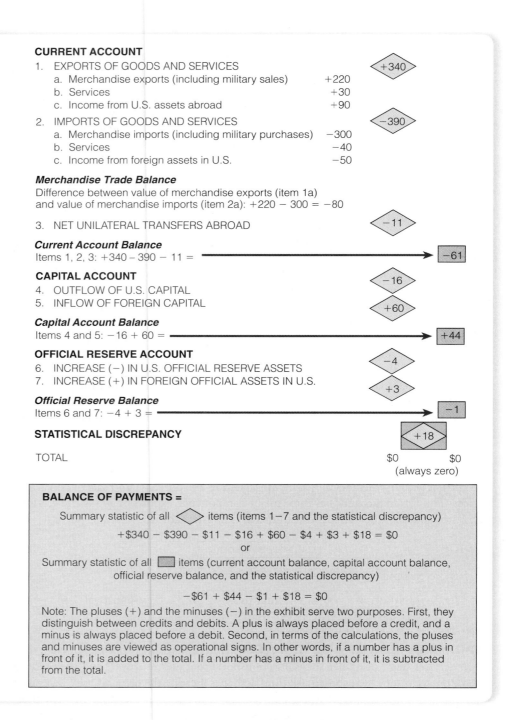

		Diamond items	Box items
CURRENT ACCOUNT			
1. EXPORTS OF GOODS AND SERVICES		+340	
a. Merchandise exports (including military sales)	+220		
b. Services	+30		
c. Income from U.S. assets abroad	+90		
2. IMPORTS OF GOODS AND SERVICES		−390	
a. Merchandise imports (including military purchases)	−300		
b. Services	−40		
c. Income from foreign assets in U.S.	−50		
Merchandise Trade Balance Difference between value of merchandise exports (item 1a) and value of merchandise imports (item 2a): +220 − 300 = −80			
3. NET UNILATERAL TRANSFERS ABROAD		−11	
Current Account Balance Items 1, 2, 3: +340 − 390 − 11 =			−61
CAPITAL ACCOUNT			
4. OUTFLOW OF U.S. CAPITAL		−16	
5. INFLOW OF FOREIGN CAPITAL		+60	
Capital Account Balance Items 4 and 5: −16 + 60 =			+44
OFFICIAL RESERVE ACCOUNT			
6. INCREASE (−) IN U.S. OFFICIAL RESERVE ASSETS		−4	
7. INCREASE (+) IN FOREIGN OFFICIAL ASSETS IN U.S.		+3	
Official Reserve Balance Items 6 and 7: −4 + 3 =			−1
STATISTICAL DISCREPANCY		+18	+18
TOTAL		$0	$0 (always zero)

BALANCE OF PAYMENTS =

Summary statistic of all ◇ items (items 1–7 and the statistical discrepancy)

+\$340 − \$390 − \$11 − \$16 + \$60 − \$4 + \$3 + \$18 = \$0

or

Summary statistic of all ▭ items (current account balance, capital account balance, official reserve balance, and the statistical discrepancy)

−\$61 + \$44 − \$1 + \$18 = \$0

Note: The pluses (+) and the minuses (−) in the exhibit serve two purposes. First, they distinguish between credits and debits. A plus is always placed before a credit, and a minus is always placed before a debit. Second, in terms of the calculations, the pluses and minuses are viewed as operational signs. In other words, if a number has a plus in front of it, it is added to the total. If a number has a minus in front of it, it is subtracted from the total.

American buys a Japanese car, payment must ultimately be made in Japanese yen. Thus, he is required to supply U.S. dollars when he demands Japanese yen.

In Exhibit 2, exports of goods and services total +\$340 billion in year Z, and imports of goods and services total −\$390 billion.[1] Before discussing the third component of the

1. In everyday language, people do not say, "Exports are a positive \$X billion and imports are a negative \$Y billion." Placing a plus sign (+) in front of exports and a minus sign (−) in front of imports simply reinforces the essential point that exports are credits and imports are debits. This will be useful later when we calculate certain account balances.

current account—net unilateral transfers abroad—we define some important relationships between exports and imports.

Look at the difference between the *value of merchandise exports* (1a in Exhibit 2) and the *value of merchandise imports* (2a in the exhibit). This difference is the merchandise trade balance or the balance of trade. Specifically, the **merchandise trade balance** is the difference between the value of merchandise exports and the value of merchandise imports. In year Z, the merchandise trade balance is \$220 billion − \$300 billion = −\$80 billion.

Merchandise Trade Balance
The difference between the value of merchandise exports and the value of merchandise imports.

Merchandise trade balance = Value of merchandise exports
− Value of merchandise imports

If the value of a country's merchandise exports is less than the value of its merchandise imports, it is said to have a **merchandise trade deficit**.

Merchandise Trade Deficit
The situation when the value of merchandise exports is less than the value of merchandise imports.

Merchandise trade deficit = Value of merchandise exports
< Value of merchandise imports

If the value of a country's merchandise exports is greater than the value of its merchandise imports, it is said to have a **merchandise trade surplus**.

Merchandise Trade Surplus
The situation when the value of merchandise exports is greater than the value of merchandise imports.

Merchandise trade surplus = Value of merchandise exports
> Value of merchandise imports

Exhibit 3 shows the U.S. merchandise trade balance from 1995 to 2007. Notice that there has been a merchandise trade deficit in each of these years.

NET UNILATERAL TRANSFERS ABROAD Unilateral transfers are one-way money payments. They can go from Americans or the U.S. government to foreigners or foreign governments. If an American sends money to a relative in a foreign country, if the U.S. government gives money to a foreign country as a gift or grant, or if an American retires in a foreign country and receives a Social Security check there, all these transactions are referred to as unilateral transfers. If an American or the U.S. government makes a unilateral transfer abroad, this gives rise to a demand for foreign currency and a supply of U.S. dollars; thus, it is entered as a debit item in the U.S. balance of payments accounts.

Unilateral transfers can also go from foreigners or foreign governments to Americans or to the U.S. government. If a foreign citizen sends money to a relative living in the United States, this is a unilateral transfer. If a foreigner makes a unilateral transfer to an American, this gives rise to a supply of foreign currency and a demand for U.S. dollars; thus, it is entered as a credit item in the U.S. balance of payments accounts.

Net unilateral transfers abroad include both types of transfers—from the United States to foreign countries and from foreign countries to the United States. The dollar amount of net unilateral transfers is negative if U.S. transfers are greater than foreign transfers. It is positive if foreign transfers are greater than U.S. transfers.

For year Z in Exhibit 2, we have assumed that unilateral transfers made by Americans to foreign citizens are greater than unilateral transfers made by foreign citizens to Americans. Thus, there is a *negative* net dollar amount, −\$11 billion.

Items 1, 2, and 3 in Exhibit 2—exports of goods and services, imports of goods and services, and net unilateral transfers abroad—comprise the current account. The **current account balance** is the summary statistic for these three items. In year Z, it is −\$61 billion. The news media sometimes call the current account balance the balance of payments. To an economist, this reference is incorrect; the balance of payments includes several more items.

Current Account Balance
In the balance of payments, the summary statistic for exports of goods and services, imports of goods and services, and net unilateral transfers abroad.

exhibit 3

U.S. Merchandise Trade Balance

In each of the years shown, 1995–2007, a merchandise trade deficit has existed.

Source: U.S. Department of Commerce, Bureau of Economic Analysis.

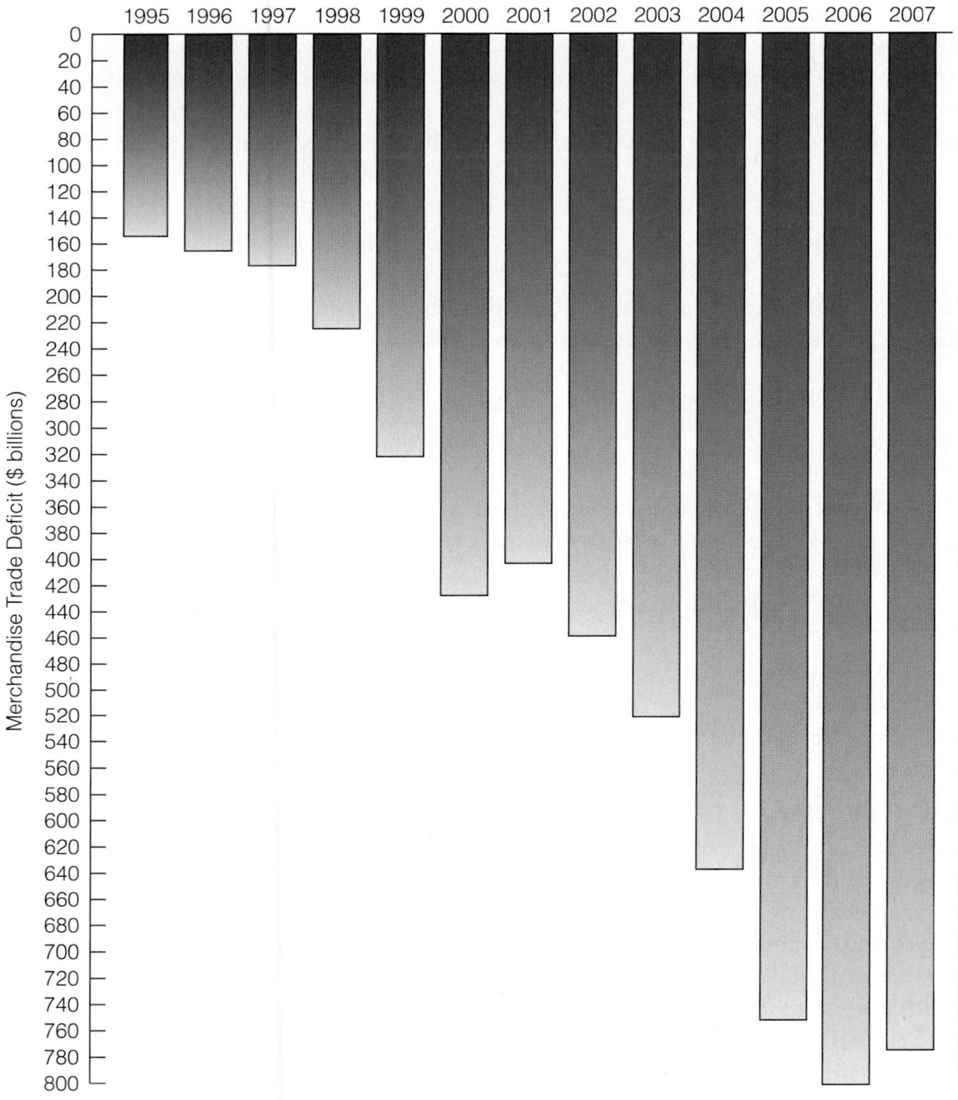

Capital Account

Capital Account
The account in the balance of payments that includes all payments related to the purchase and sale of assets and to borrowing and lending activities. Components include outflow of U.S. capital and inflow of foreign capital.

The **capital account** includes all payments related to the purchase and sale of assets and to borrowing and lending activities. Its major components are outflow of U.S. capital and inflow of foreign capital.

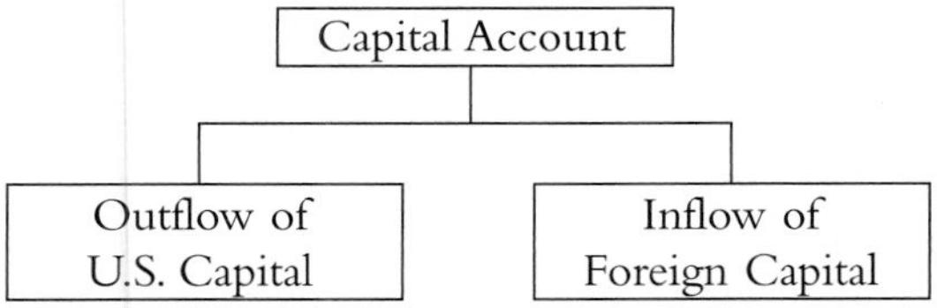

OUTFLOW OF U.S. CAPITAL American purchases of foreign assets and U.S. loans to foreigners are outflows of U.S. capital. As such, they give rise to a demand for foreign currency and a supply of U.S. dollars on the foreign exchange market. Hence, they are considered a debit. For example, if an American wants to buy land in Japan, U.S. dollars must be supplied to purchase (demand) Japanese yen.

INFLOW OF FOREIGN CAPITAL Foreign purchases of U.S. assets and foreign loans to Americans are inflows of foreign capital. As such, they give rise to a demand for U.S. dollars and to a supply of foreign currency on the foreign exchange market. Hence, they are considered a credit. For example, if a Japanese citizen buys a U.S. Treasury bill, Japanese yen must be supplied to purchase (demand) U.S. dollars.

Items 4 and 5 in Exhibit 2—outflow of U.S. capital and inflow of foreign capital—comprise the capital account. The **capital account balance** is the summary statistic for these two items. It is equal to the difference between the outflow of U.S. capital and the inflow of foreign capital. In year Z, it is $44 billion.

Capital Account Balance
The summary statistic for the outflow of U.S. capital equal to the difference between the outflow of U.S. capital and the inflow of foreign capital.

Official Reserve Account

A government possesses official reserve balances in the form of foreign currencies, gold, its reserve position in the **International Monetary Fund (IMF)**, and **special drawing rights (SDRs)**. Countries that have a deficit in their combined current and capital accounts can draw on their reserves. For example, if the United States has a deficit in its combined current and capital accounts of $5 billion, it can draw down its official reserves to meet this deficit.

Item 6 in Exhibit 2 shows that the United States increased its reserve assets by $4 billion in year Z. This is a debit item because if the United States acquires official reserves (say, through the purchase of a foreign currency), it has increased the demand for the foreign currency and supplied dollars. Thus, an increase in official reserves is like an outflow of capital in the capital account and appears as a payment with a negative sign. Therefore, an increase in foreign official assets in the United States is a credit item.

International Monetary Fund (IMF)
An international organization created to oversee the international monetary system. The IMF does not control the world's money supply, but it does hold currency reserves for member nations and make loans to central banks.

Special Drawing Right (SDR)
An international money, created by the IMF, in the form of bookkeeping entries; like gold and currencies, it can be used by nations to settle international accounts.

Statistical Discrepancy

If someone buys a U.S. dollar with, say, Japanese yen, someone must sell a U.S. dollar. Thus, dollars purchased equal dollars sold.

In all the transactions discussed so far—exporting goods, importing goods, sending money to relatives in foreign countries, buying land in foreign countries—dollars were bought and sold. The total number of dollars sold must always equal the total number of dollars purchased. However, balance of payments accountants do not have complete information; they can record only the credits and debits they observe. There may be more debits or credits than those observed in a given year.

Suppose in year Z, all debits are observed and recorded, but not all credits—perhaps because of smuggling activities, secret bank accounts, people living in more than one country, and so on. To adjust for this lack of information, balance of payments accountants use the *statistical discrepancy,* which is the part of the balance of payments that adjusts for missing information. In Exhibit 2, the statistical discrepancy is +$18 billion. This means that $18 billion worth of credits (+) went unobserved in year Z. There may have been some hidden exports and unrecorded capital inflows that year.

What the Balance of Payments Equals

The balance of payments is the summary statistic for:

- Exports of goods and services (item 1 in Exhibit 2).
- Imports of goods and services (item 2).

economics 24/7

MERCHANDISE TRADE DEFICIT, WE THOUGHT WE KNEW THEE

You read in the newspaper that the United States has a merchandise trade deficit; that is, the value of merchandise exports for the United States is *less than* the value of merchandise imports. In terms of Exhibit 2, 1a is less than 2a. For example, Americans exported $600 billion worth of goods and imported $800 billion worth of goods. The merchandise trade deficit is $200 billion.

The word *deficit* has a negative connotation to many people, who think of a trade deficit as something bad. It's bad, some people say, "Because it means Americans owe money to foreigners. Specifically, Americans are 'in debt' to foreigners to the tune of $200 billion."

Other people say that, because Americans are increasing demand for foreign-produced goods by more ($200 billion more, to be exact) than foreigners are increasing demand for U.S.-produced goods, demand is "leaving the country."

However, neither sentiment is correct. Americans do not owe foreigners anything and demand is not leaving the country.

The reason is obvious: Americans have already paid this $200 billion to foreigners. The $200 billion is part of the overall $800 billion that Americans spent on imported goods.

Still, even if Americans don't owe $200 billion to foreigners, isn't the $200 billion gone forever, never to return to the United States? That's not true either. Foreigners may have those dollars, but they're not going to burn them. They're not going to eat them. They're not going to give them away. What they are going to do with those dollars—in fact, the only thing they can do with those dollars—is use them to buy "something American."[2]

They could buy real estate in the United States. For example, a Brazilian man with dollars might end up buying an apartment in downtown Manhattan. In other words, the dollars that we thought would leave the country for good are coming back home.

A foreign firm with U.S. dollars could hire a construction company to build a factory in the United States—Tennessee, Virginia, or South Dakota—so that it can produce some of its goods in the United States and thus lower its transportation costs. An American might end up working at that factory and thus be paid with some of the dollars that once were held by foreigners. (And the American worker is likely to spend those dollars to buy U.S. goods and services.)

The main point is simple: The dollars that foreigners initially hold because of the merchandise trade deficit will begin to return to the United States. They're not gone forever.

2. If you are thinking that the foreigners who have the $200 billion can trade those dollars for other currencies, you are right. A Frenchman might trade some of his dollars for pesos, euros, or yen, but now someone else has the dollars the Frenchman once had, and we then have to ask what this new person will do with the dollars.

- Net unilateral transfers abroad (item 3).
- Outflow of U.S. capital (item 4).
- Inflow of foreign capital (item 5).
- Increase in U.S. official reserve assets (item 6).
- Increase in foreign official assets in the United States (item 7).
- Statistical discrepancy.

Calculating the balance of payments in year Z using these items, we have (in billions of dollars) $+340 - 390 - 11 - 16 + 60 - 4 + 3 + 18 = 0$.

Alternatively, the balance of payments is the summary statistic for:

- Current account balance.
- Capital account balance.
- Official reserve balance.
- Statistical discrepancy.

Calculating the balance of payments in year Z using these items, we have (in billions of dollars) $-61 + 44 - 1 + 18 = 0$. The balance of payments for the United States in year Z equals zero.

Common Misconceptions

About the Balance of Payments

There is a tendency to think that the balance of payments can be in deficit or surplus, but it is neither. The balance of payments always equals zero because the three accounts that comprise the balance of payments, taken together, plus the statistical discrepancy, include all of the sources and all of the uses of dollars in international transactions. Also, every dollar used must have a source, adding the sources (+) to the uses (−) necessarily gives us zero.

SELF-TEST

(Answers to Self-Test questions are in the Self-Test Appendix.)

1. If an American retailer buys Japanese cars from a Japanese manufacturer, is this transaction recorded as a debit or a credit? Explain your answer.
2. Exports of goods and services equal $200 billion and imports of goods and services equal $300 billion. What is the merchandise trade balance?
3. What is the difference between the merchandise trade balance and the current account balance?

THE FOREIGN EXCHANGE MARKET

If a U.S. buyer wants to purchase a good from a U.S. seller, the buyer simply gives the required number of U.S. dollars to the seller. If, however, a U.S. buyer wants to purchase a good from a seller in Mexico, the U.S. buyer must first exchange her U.S. dollars for Mexican pesos. Then, with the pesos, she buys the good from the Mexican seller. As explained, currencies of different countries are exchanged in the foreign exchange market. In this market, currencies are bought and sold for a price—the **exchange rate**. For instance, it might take $1.23 to buy a euro, 10 cents to buy a Mexican peso, and 13 cents to buy a Danish krone.

Exchange Rate
The price of one currency in terms of another currency.

In this section, we explain why currencies are demanded and supplied in the foreign exchange market. Then we discuss how the exchange rate expresses the relationship between the demand for and the supply of currencies.

The Demand for Goods

To simplify our analysis, we assume that there are only two countries in the world: the United States and Mexico. Thus there are only two currencies in the world: the U.S. dollar (USD) and the Mexican peso (MXN).We want to answer the following two questions:

1. What creates the demand for and the supply of dollars on the foreign exchange market?
2. What creates the demand for and the supply of pesos on the foreign exchange market?

Suppose an American wants to buy a couch from a Mexican producer. Before he can purchase the couch, the American must buy Mexican pesos; hence, Mexican pesos

exhibit 4

The Demand for Goods and the Supply of Currencies

are demanded. The American buys Mexican pesos with U.S. dollars; that is, he supplies U.S. dollars to the foreign exchange market to demand Mexican pesos. We conclude that *the U.S. demand for Mexican goods leads to (1) a demand for Mexican pesos and (2) a supply of U.S. dollars on the foreign exchange market* [see Exhibit 4(a)]. Thus, the demand for pesos and the supply of dollars are linked:

Demand for pesos ↔ Supply of dollars

The result is similar for a Mexican who wants to buy a computer from a U.S. producer. Before she can purchase the computer, the Mexican must buy U.S. dollars; hence, U.S. dollars are demanded. The Mexican buys the U.S. dollars with Mexican pesos. We conclude that *the Mexican demand for U.S. goods leads to (1) a demand for U.S. dollars and (2) a supply of Mexican pesos on the foreign exchange market* [see Exhibit 4(b)]. Thus, the demand for dollars and the supply of pesos are linked:

Demand for dollars ↔ Supply of pesos

Finding ECONOMICS

In a Trip to Ireland

Billy has just graduated from college and is planning a trip to Ireland. Where is the economics here? Obviously Billy cannot use dollars to buy goods and services in Ireland. He must use euros. He will have to buy euros with his dollars, and, in so doing, he supplies U.S. dollars.

The Demand for and Supply of Currencies

Exhibit 5 shows the markets for pesos and dollars. Part (a) shows the market for Mexican pesos. The quantity of pesos is on the horizontal axis, and the exchange rate—stated in terms of the dollar price per peso—is on the vertical axis. Exhibit 5(b) shows the market for U.S. dollars, which mirrors what is happening in the market for Mexican pesos. Notice that the exchange rates in (a) and (b) are reciprocals of each other. If 0.10 USD = 1 MXN, then 10 MXN = 1 USD.

exhibit 5

Translating U.S. Demand for Pesos into U.S. Supply of Dollars and Mexican Demand for Dollars into Mexican Supply of Pesos

(a) The market for pesos. (b) The market for dollars. The demand for pesos in (a) is linked to the supply of dollars in (b): When Americans demand pesos, they supply dollars. The supply of pesos in (a) is linked to the demand for dollars in (b): When Mexicans demand dollars, they supply pesos. In (a), the exchange rate is 0.10 USD = 1 MXN, which is equal to 10 MXN = 1 USD in (b). Exchange rates are reciprocals of each other.

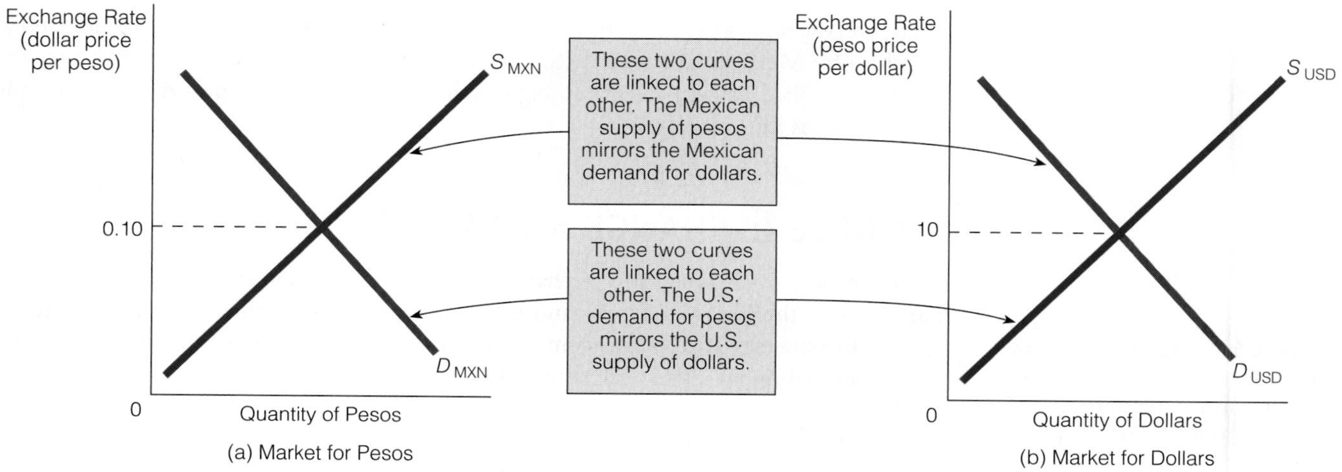

In Exhibit 5(a), the demand curve for pesos is downward sloping, indicating that, as the dollar price per peso increases, Americans buy fewer pesos and that, as the dollar price per peso decreases, Americans buy more pesos.

Dollar price per peso ↑	Americans buy fewer pesos.
Dollar price per peso ↓	Americans buy more pesos.

For example, if it takes $0.10 to buy a peso, Americans will buy more pesos than they would if it takes $0.20 to buy a peso. (It is analogous to buyers purchasing more soft drinks at $3 a six-pack than at $5 a six-pack.) Simply put, the higher the dollar price per peso, the more expensive Mexican goods are for Americans and the fewer Mexican goods Americans will buy. Thus, a smaller quantity of pesos is demanded.

The supply curve for pesos in Exhibit 5(a) is upward sloping. It is easy to understand why when we recall that the supply of Mexican pesos is linked to the Mexican demand for U.S. goods and U.S. dollars. Consider a price of $0.20 for 1 peso compared with a price of $0.10 for 1 peso. At 0.10 USD = 1 MXN, a Mexican buyer gives up 1 peso and receives 10 cents in return. But at 0.20 USD = 1 MXN, a Mexican buyer gives up 1 peso and receives 20 cents in return. Thus, U.S. goods are cheaper for Mexicans at the exchange rate of 0.20 USD = 1 MXN.

To illustrate, suppose a U.S. computer has a price tag of $1,000. At an exchange rate of 0.20 USD = 1 MXN, a Mexican will have to pay 5,000 pesos to buy the American computer; but at an exchange rate of 0.10 USD = 1 MXN, a Mexican will have to pay 10,000 pesos for the computer:

0.20 USD = 1 MXN	0.10 USD = 1 MXN
1 USD = (1 ÷ 0.20) MXN	1 USD = (1 ÷ 0.10) MXN
1,000 USD = (1,000 ÷ 0.20) MXN	1,000 USD = (1,000 ÷ 0.10) MXN
= 5,000 MXN	= 10,000 MXN

To a Mexican buyer, the American computer is cheaper at the exchange rate of \$0.20 per peso than at \$0.10 per peso.

Exchange Rate	Dollar Price	Peso Price
0.20 USD = 1 MXN	1,000 USD	5,000 MXN [(1,000 ÷ 0.20) MXN]
0.10 USD = 1 MXN	1,000 USD	10,000 MXN [(1,000 ÷ 0.10) MXN]

Therefore, the higher the dollar price is per peso, the greater will be the quantity demanded of dollars by Mexicans (because U.S. goods will be cheaper) and hence the greater the quantity supplied of pesos to the foreign exchange market. The upward-sloping supply curve for pesos illustrates this.

Flexible Exchange Rates

In this section, we discuss how exchange rates are determined in the foreign exchange market when the forces of supply and demand are allowed to rule. Economists refer to this as a **flexible exchange rate system**. In the next section, we discuss how exchange rates are determined under a fixed exchange rate system.

Flexible Exchange Rate System
The system whereby exchange rates are determined by the forces of supply and demand for a currency.

The Equilibrium Exchange Rate

In a completely flexible exchange rate system, the forces of supply and demand determine the exchange rate. In our two-country–two-currency world, suppose the equilibrium exchange rate (dollar price per peso) is 0.10 USD = 1 MXN, as shown in Exhibit 6. At this dollar price per peso, the quantity demanded of pesos equals the quantity supplied of pesos. There are no shortages or surpluses of pesos. At any other exchange rate, however, either an excess demand for pesos or an excess supply of pesos exists.

At the exchange rate of 0.12 USD = 1 MXN, a surplus of pesos exists. As a result, downward pressure will be placed on the dollar price of a peso (just as downward pressure will be placed on the dollar price of an apple if there is a surplus of apples). At the exchange rate of 0.08 USD = 1 MXN, there is a shortage of pesos, and upward pressure will be placed on the dollar price of a peso.

exhibit 6

A Flexible Exchange Rate System

The demand curve for pesos is downward sloping. The higher the dollar price for pesos, the fewer pesos will be demanded; the lower the dollar price for pesos, the more pesos will be demanded. At 0.12 USD = 1 MXN, there is a surplus of pesos, placing downward pressure on the exchange rate. At 0.08 USD = 1 MXN, there is a shortage of pesos, placing upward pressure on the exchange rate. At the equilibrium exchange rate, 0.10 USD = 1 MXN, the quantity demanded of pesos equals the quantity supplied of pesos.

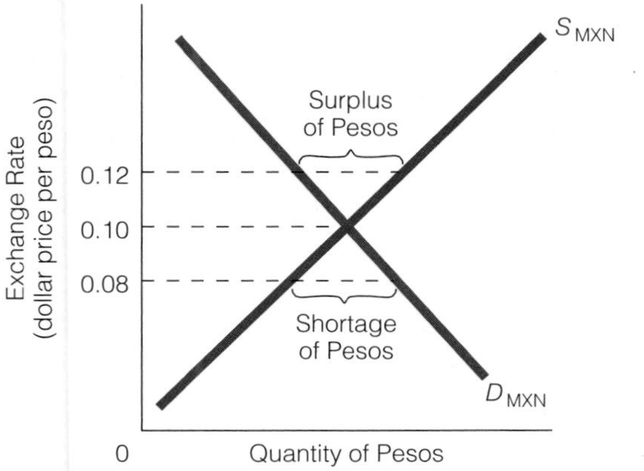

Thinking like AN ECONOMIST

Linkages

The demand for dollars is linked to the supply of pesos, and the demand for pesos is linked to the supply of dollars. Economists often think in terms of one activity being linked to another because economics, after all, is about exchange. In an exchange, one gives (supply) and one gets (demand): John supplies $25 to demand the new book from the shopkeeper; the shopkeeper supplies the new book so that he may demand the $25. The diagram for such a transaction usually represents the demand for and supply of the new book, but it could also represent the demand for and supply of the money. Of course, in international exchange, where monies are bought and sold before goods are bought and sold, the diagrams reflect both.

Changes in the Equilibrium Exchange Rate

Chapter 3 explains that a change in the demand for a good, in the supply of a good, or in both will change the good's equilibrium price. The same holds true for the price of currencies. A change in the demand for pesos, in the supply of pesos, or in both will change the equilibrium dollar price per peso. If the dollar price per peso rises—say, from 0.10 USD = 1 MXN to 0.12 USD = 1 MXN—the peso is said to have **appreciated** and the dollar to have **depreciated**. A currency has appreciated in value if it takes more of a foreign currency to buy it. A currency has depreciated in value if it takes more of it to buy a foreign currency.

Appreciation
An increase in the value of one currency relative to other currencies.

Depreciation
A decrease in the value of one currency relative to other currencies.

For example, a movement in the exchange rate from 0.10 USD = 1 MXN to 0.12 USD = 1 MXN means that it now takes 12 cents instead of 10 cents to buy a peso, so the dollar has depreciated. The other side of the coin, so to speak, is that it takes fewer pesos to buy a dollar; so the peso has appreciated. That is, at an exchange rate of 0.10 USD = 1 MXN, it takes 10 pesos to buy $1, but at an exchange rate of 0.12 USD = 1 MXN, it takes only 8.33 pesos to buy $1.

Factors That Affect the Equilibrium Exchange Rate

If the equilibrium exchange rate can change owing to a change in the demand for and supply of a currency, then it is important to understand what factors can change demand and supply. This section presents three.

A DIFFERENCE IN INCOME GROWTH RATES An increase in a nation's income will usually cause the nation's residents to buy more of both domestic and foreign goods. The increased demand for imports will result in an increased demand for foreign currency.

Suppose U.S. residents experience an increase in income, but Mexican residents do not. As a result, the demand curve for pesos shifts rightward, as illustrated in Exhibit 7. This causes the equilibrium exchange rate to rise from 0.10 USD = 1 MXN to 0.12 USD = 1 MXN. *Ceteris paribus,* if one nation's income grows and another's lags behind, the currency of the higher-growth-rate country *depreciates,* and the currency of the lower-growth-rate country *appreciates.* To many persons, this seems paradoxical; nevertheless, it is true.

exhibit 7

The Growth Rate of Income and the Exchange Rate

If U.S. residents experience a growth in income but Mexican residents do not, U.S. demand for Mexican goods will increase, and with it, the demand for pesos. As a result, the exchange rate will change; the dollar price of pesos will rise. The dollar depreciates, the peso appreciates.

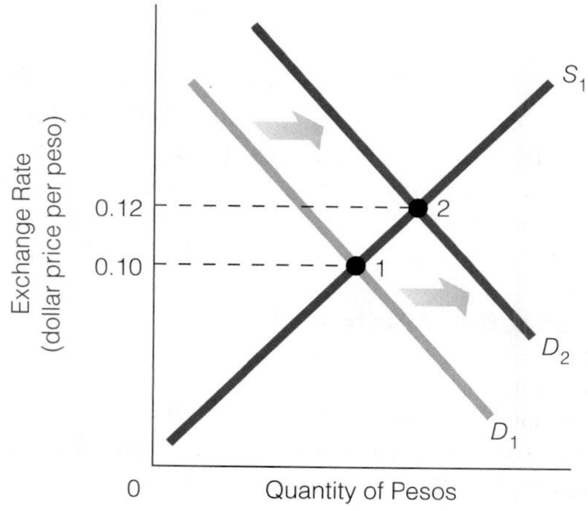

economics 24/7

BACK TO THE FUTURES

Meet (the fictional) Bill Whatley, owner of a Toyota dealership in Tulsa, Oklahoma. It is May, and Bill is thinking about a shipment of Toyotas he plans to buy in August. He knows that he must buy the Toyotas from Japan with yen, but he has a problem. The current price of ¥1 is $0.008. Bill wonders what the dollar price of a yen will be in August when he plans to make his purchase. If the price of ¥1 rises to $0.010, then, instead of paying $20,000 for a Toyota priced at ¥2.5 million, he will have to pay $25,000.[3] This difference of $5,000 may be enough to erase his profit on the sale of the Toyotas.

Bill can, however, purchase a futures contract today for the needed quantity of yen in August. A futures contract is a contract in which the seller agrees to provide a good (in this example, a currency) to the buyer on a specified future date at an agreed-on price. In short, Bill can buy yen today at a specified dollar price and take delivery of the yen at a later date (in August). Problem solved.

But if the price of ¥1 falls to $0.007 in August, Bill would have to pay only $17,500 (instead of $20,000) for a Toyota priced at ¥2.5 million. Although he could increase his profit in this case, Bill, like other car dealers, might not be interested in assuming the risk associated with changes in exchange rates. He may prefer to lock in a sure thing.

Who would sell yen to Bill? The answer is someone who is willing to assume the risk of changes in the value of currencies. For example, Julie Jackson thinks that the dollar price of a yen will go down between now and August. Therefore, she'll enter into a contract with Bill requiring her to give him ¥2.5 million in August for $20,000—the exchange rate specified in the contract being 1 JPY = 0.008 USD. If she's right and the actual exchange rate in August is 1 JPY = 0.007 USD, then she can purchase the ¥2.5 million for $17,500 and fulfill the contract with Bill by turning the yen over to him for $20,000. She walks away with $2,500 in profit.

Many economists argue that futures contracts offer people a way of dealing with the risk associated with a flexible exchange rate system. If a person doesn't know what next month's exchange rate will be and doesn't want to take the risk of waiting to see, then he can enter into a futures contract and effectively shift the risk to someone who voluntarily assumes it.

3. If ¥1 equals $0.008, then a Toyota with a price of ¥2.5 million costs $20,000 because ¥2.5 million × $0.008 = $20,000. If ¥1 equals $0.010, then a Toyota with a price of ¥2.5 million costs $25,000 dollars because ¥2.5 million × $0.010 equals $25,000.

DIFFERENCES IN RELATIVE INFLATION RATES Suppose the U.S. price level rises 10 percent at a time when Mexico experiences stable prices. An increase in the U.S. price level will make Mexican goods relatively less expensive for Americans and U.S. goods relatively more expensive for Mexicans. As a result, the U.S. demand for Mexican goods will increase, and the Mexican demand for U.S. goods will decrease.

In turn, the demand for and the supply of Mexican pesos are affected. As shown in Exhibit 8, the demand for Mexican pesos will increase; Mexican goods are relatively cheaper than they were before the U.S. price level rose. The supply of Mexican pesos will decrease; American goods are relatively more expensive, and so Mexicans will buy fewer American goods; thus, they demand fewer U.S. dollars and supply fewer Mexican pesos.

As Exhibit 8 shows, the result of an increase in the demand for Mexican pesos and a decrease in their supply constitutes an *appreciation* in the peso and a *depreciation* in the dollar. It takes 11 cents instead of 10 cents to buy 1 peso (dollar depreciation); it takes 9.09 pesos instead of 10 pesos to buy $1 (peso appreciation).

Purchasing Power Parity (PPP) Theory
Theory stating that exchange rates between any two currencies will adjust to reflect changes in the relative price levels of the two countries.

An important question is how much will the U.S. dollar depreciate as a result of the rise in the U.S. price level? (Recall that there is no change in Mexico's price level.) The **purchasing power parity (PPP) theory** predicts that the U.S. dollar will depreciate by 10 percent as a result of the 10 percent rise in the U.S. price level. This requires the dollar price of a peso to rise to 11 cents (10 percent of 10 cents is 1 cent, and 10 cents plus 1 cent

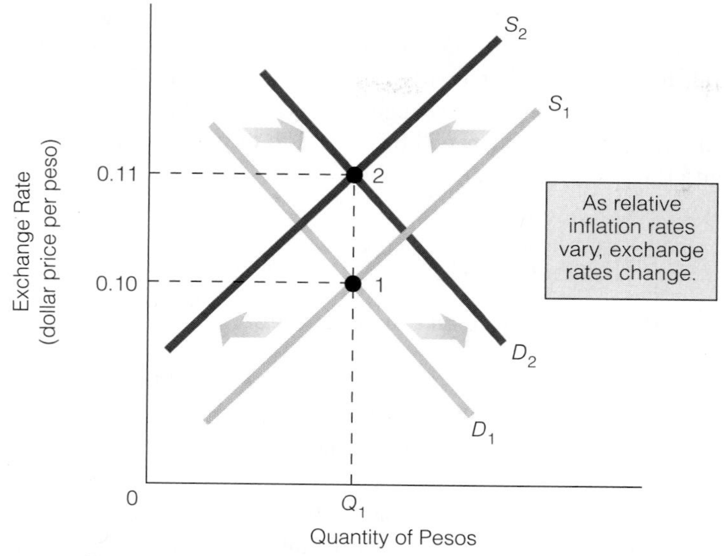

exhibit 8

Inflation, Exchange Rates, and Purchasing Power Parity (PPP)

If the price level in the United States increases by 10 percent while the price level in Mexico remains constant, then the U.S. demand for Mexican goods (and therefore pesos) will increase and the supply of pesos will decrease. As a result, the exchange rate will change; the dollar price of pesos will rise. The dollar depreciates, and the peso appreciates. PPP theory predicts that the dollar will depreciate in the foreign exchange market until the original price (in pesos) of American goods to Mexican customers is restored. In this example, this requires the dollar to depreciate 10 percent.

equals 11 cents). A 10 percent depreciation in the dollar restores the *original relative prices of American goods to Mexican customers.*

Consider a U.S. car with a price tag of $20,000. If the exchange rate is 0.10 USD = 1 MXN, a Mexican buyer of the car will pay 200,000 pesos. If the car price increases by 10 percent to $22,000 and the dollar depreciates 10 percent (to 0.11 USD = 1 MXN), the Mexican buyer of the car will still pay only 200,000 pesos.

Exchange Rate	Dollar Price	Peso Price
0.10 USD = 1 MXN	20,000 USD	200,000 MXN [(20,000/0.10) MXN]
0.11 USD = 1 MXN	22,000 USD	200,000 MXN [(22,000/0.11) MXN]

In short, the PPP theory predicts that *changes in the relative price levels of two countries will affect the exchange rate in such a way that 1 unit of a country's currency will continue to buy the same amount of foreign goods* as it did before the change in the relative price levels. In our example, the higher U.S. inflation rate causes a change in the equilibrium exchange rate and leads to a depreciated dollar, but 1 peso continues to have the same purchasing power it previously did.

On some occasions, the PPP theory of exchange rates has predicted accurately, but not on others. Many economists suggest that the theory does not always predict accurately because the demand for and the supply of a currency are affected *by more than the difference in inflation rates between countries.* For example, as noted, different income growth rates affect the demand for a currency and therefore the exchange rate. In the *long run,* however, and particularly when there is a *large difference in inflation rates across countries,* the PPP theory does predict exchange rates accurately.

CHANGES IN REAL INTEREST RATES As shown in the U.S. balance of payments in Exhibit 2, more than goods flow between countries. Financial capital also moves between countries. The flow of financial capital depends on different countries' *real interest rates*—interest rates adjusted for inflation.

To illustrate, suppose initially that the real interest rate is 3 percent in both the United States and Mexico. Then the real interest rate in the United States increases to 4.5 percent. As a result, Mexicans will want to purchase financial assets in the United States that pay a higher real interest rate than do financial assets in Mexico. The Mexican demand for dollars will increase, and therefore Mexicans will supply more pesos. As the supply of pesos increases on the foreign exchange market, the exchange rate (the dollar price per peso) will change; fewer dollars will be needed to buy pesos. In short, the dollar will appreciate, and the peso will depreciate.

Finding ECONOMICS

In the President Speaking to an Economic Advisor

The president of the United States is speaking to an economic advisor. The president asks, "What are the effects of the rather large budget deficits?" In response, the advisor might say that large budget deficits can affect interest rates, the value of the dollar, exports and imports, and the merchandise trade balance. "How so?" the president asks. Big deficits, the advisor says, mean that the federal government will have to borrow funds, which will increase the demand for credit. This will push up the interest rate. As the U.S. interest rate rises relative to interest rates in other countries, foreigners will want to purchase financial assets in the United States that pay a higher return. This will increase the demand for dollars, the dollar will appreciate, and foreign currencies will depreciate. In turn, this will affect both import and export spending, and thus it will affect the merchandise trade balance.

SELF-TEST

1. In the foreign exchange market, how is the demand for dollars linked to the supply of pesos?
2. What could cause the U.S. dollar to appreciate against the Mexican peso on the foreign exchange market?
3. Suppose that the U.S. economy grows and that the Swiss economy does not. How will this affect the exchange rate between the dollar and the Swiss franc? Why?
4. What does the purchasing power parity theory say? Give an example to illustrate your answer.

FIXED EXCHANGE RATES

Fixed Exchange Rate System
The system whereby a nation's currency is set at a fixed rate relative to all other currencies, and central banks intervene in the foreign exchange market to maintain the fixed rate.

The major alternative to the flexible exchange rate system is the **fixed exchange rate system**, which works the way it sounds. Exchange rates are fixed; they are not allowed to fluctuate freely in response to the forces of supply and demand. Central banks buy and sell currencies to maintain agreed-on exchange rates. The workings of the fixed exchange rate system are described in this section.

Fixed Exchange Rates and Overvalued/Undervalued Currency

Once again, we assume a two-country–two-currency world, but this time the United States and Mexico agree to fix the exchange rate of their currencies. Instead of letting the dollar depreciate or appreciate relative to the peso, the two countries agree to set the price of 1 peso at \$0.12; that is, they agree to the exchange rate of 0.12 USD = 1 MXN. Generally, we call this the fixed exchange rate or the *official price* of a peso.[4] We will deal

4. If the price of 1 peso is \$0.12, the price of \$1 is approximately 8.33 pesos. Thus, setting the official price of a peso in terms of dollars automatically sets the official price of a dollar in terms of pesos.

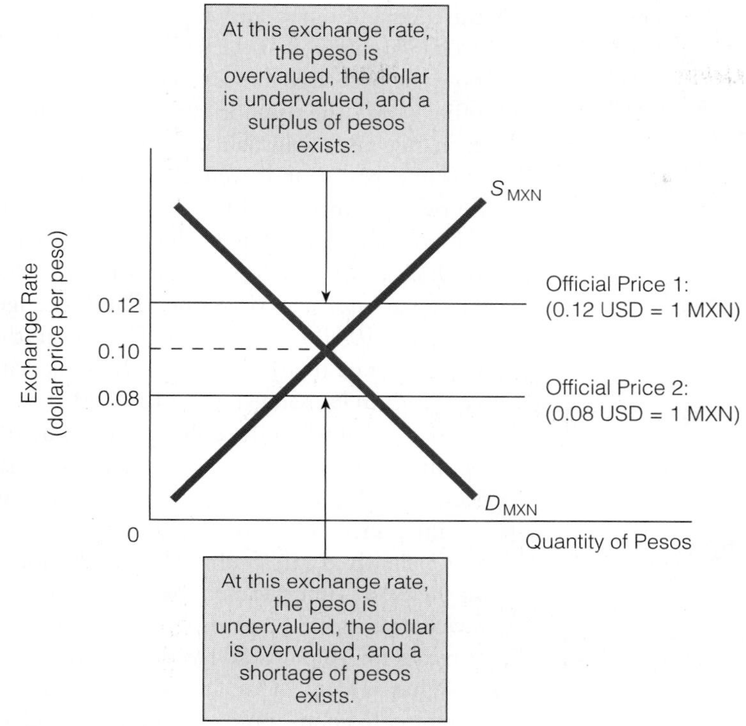

exhibit 9

A Fixed Exchange Rate System

In a fixed exchange rate system, the exchange rate is fixed—and it may not be fixed at the equilibrium exchange rate. The exhibit shows two cases. (1) If the exchange rate is fixed at official price 1, the peso is overvalued, the dollar is undervalued, and a surplus of pesos exists. (2) If the exchange rate is fixed at official price 2, the peso is undervalued, the dollar is overvalued, and a shortage of pesos exists.

with more than one official price in our discussion; so we refer to 0.12 USD = 1 MXN as official price 1 (Exhibit 9).

If the dollar price of pesos is above its equilibrium level (which is the case at official price 1), a surplus of pesos exists, and the peso is said to be **overvalued**. In other words, the peso is fetching more dollars than it would at equilibrium. For example, if in equilibrium, 1 peso trades for $0.10, but at the official exchange rate 1 peso trades for $0.12, then the peso is said to be overvalued.

Overvalued
A currency is overvalued if its price in terms of other currencies is above the equilibrium price.

Therefore, if the peso is overvalued, the dollar is undervalued; that is, it is fetching fewer pesos than it would at equilibrium. For example, if in equilibrium, $1 trades for 10 pesos, but at the official exchange rate, $1 trades for 8.33 pesos, then the dollar is undervalued.

Similarly, if the dollar price of pesos is below its equilibrium level (which is the case at official price 2 in Exhibit 9), a shortage of pesos exists, and the peso is **undervalued**; the peso is not fetching as many dollars as it would at equilibrium. Therefore, if the peso is undervalued, the dollar must be overvalued.

Undervalued
A currency is undervalued if its price in terms of other currencies is below the equilibrium price.

Overvalued peso ↔ Undervalued dollar
Undervalued peso ↔ Overvalued dollar

What Is So Bad About an Overvalued Dollar?

You read in the newspaper that the dollar is overvalued and that economists are concerned about the overvalued dollar. Why would economists be concerned?

Economists are concerned because the exchange rate—and hence the value of the dollar in terms of other currencies—affects the amount of U.S. exports and imports. Because it affects exports and imports, it naturally affects the merchandise trade balance.

exhibit 10

Fixed Exchange Rates and an Overvalued Dollar

Initially, the demand for and supply of pesos are represented by D_1 and S_1, respectively. The equilibrium exchange rate is 0.10 USD = 1 MXN, which also happens to be the official (fixed) exchange rate.

In time, the demand for pesos rises to D_2, and the equilibrium exchange rate rises to 0.12 USD = 1 MXN. The official exchange rate is fixed, however, so the dollar will be overvalued. As explained in the text, this can lead to a trade deficit.

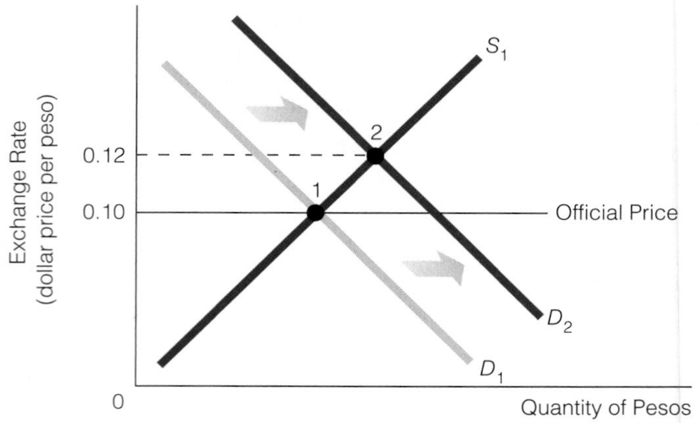

To illustrate, suppose the demand for and supply of pesos are represented by D_1 and S_1 in Exhibit 10. With this demand curve and supply curve, the equilibrium exchange rate is 0.10 USD = 1 MXN. Let's also suppose the exchange rate is fixed at this exchange rate. In other words, the equilibrium exchange rate and the fixed exchange rate are initially the same.

Time passes and eventually the demand curve for pesos shifts to the right, from D_1 to D_2. Under a flexible exchange rate system, the exchange rate would rise to 0.12 USD = 1 MXN. But a fixed exchange rate is in effect—not a flexible one. The exchange rate stays fixed at 0.10 USD = 1 MXN. This means that the fixed exchange rate (0.10 USD = 1 MXN) is below the new equilibrium exchange rate (0.12 USD = 1 MXN).

Recall that when the dollar price per peso is below its equilibrium level (which is the case), the peso is undervalued and the dollar is overvalued. At equilibrium (point 2 in Exhibit 10), 1 peso would trade for $0.12, but at its fixed rate (point 1), it trades for only $0.10; so the peso is undervalued. At equilibrium (point 2), $1 would trade for 8.33 pesos, but at its fixed rate (point 1), it trades for 10 pesos; so the dollar is overvalued.

What is bad about an overvalued dollar is that it makes U.S. goods more expensive for foreigners to buy, possibly affecting the U.S. merchandise trade balance. For example, suppose a U.S. good costs $100. At the equilibrium exchange rate (0.12 USD = 1 MXN), a Mexican would pay 833 pesos for the good, but at the fixed exchange rate (0.10 USD = 1 MXN), he will pay 1,000 pesos.

Exchange Rate	Dollar Price	Peso Price
0.12 USD = 1 MXN (equilibrium)	100 USD	833 MXN [(100 ÷ 0.12) MXN]
0.10 USD = 1 MXN (fixed)	100 USD	1,000 MXN [(100 ÷ 0.10) MXN]

The higher the prices are of U.S. goods (exports), the fewer of those goods Mexicans will buy, and, as just shown, an overvalued dollar makes U.S. export goods higher in price.

Ultimately, an overvalued dollar can affect the U.S. merchandise trade balance. As U.S. exports become more expensive for Mexicans, they buy fewer U.S. exports. If exports fall below imports, the result is a U.S. trade deficit.[5]

Government Involvement in a Fixed Exchange Rate System

In Exhibit 9, suppose the governments of Mexico and the United States agree to fix the exchange rate at 0.12 USD = 1 MXN. At this exchange rate, a surplus of pesos exists. To maintain the exchange rate at 0.12 USD = 1 MXN, the Federal Reserve System (the Fed) could buy the surplus of pesos with dollars. Consequently, the demand for pesos

5. The other side of the coin, so to speak, is that if the dollar is overvalued, the peso must be undervalued. An undervalued peso makes Mexican goods cheaper for Americans. So while the overvalued dollar is causing Mexicans to buy fewer U.S. exports, the undervalued peso is causing Americans to import more goods from Mexico. In conclusion, U.S. exports fall, U.S. imports rise, and we move closer to a trade deficit, or, if one already exists, it becomes larger.

economics 24/7

BIG MAC ECONOMICS

In an earlier chapter, we explained why goods that can be easily transported from one location to another usually sell for the same price in all locations. For example, if a candy bar can be moved from Atlanta to Seattle, we would expect the candy bar to sell for the same price in both locations. The reason is that, if the candy bar is priced higher in Seattle than Atlanta, people will move candy bars from Atlanta (where the price is relatively low) to Seattle to fetch the higher price. In other words, the supply of candy bars will rise in Seattle and fall in Atlanta. These changes in supply in the two locations affect the price of the candy bars in the two locations. In Seattle the price will fall, and in Atlanta the price will rise. This price movement will stop when the price of a candy bar is the same in the two locations.

© CHARLES PERTWEE/BLOOMBERG NEWS/LANDOV

Now consider a good that is sold all over the world: McDonald's Big Mac. Suppose the exchange rate between the dollar and the yen is $1 = ¥100 and the price of a Big Mac in New York City is $3 and ¥400 in Tokyo. Given the exchange rate, a Big Mac is not selling for the same price in the two cities. In New York, it is $3, but in Tokyo it is $4 (the price in Tokyo is ¥400, and $1 = ¥100). Stated differently, in New York, $1 buys one-third of a Big Mac, but in Tokyo, $1 buys only one-fourth of a Big Mac.

However, Big Macs won't be shipped from New York to Tokyo to fetch the higher price. Instead, the exchange rate is likely to adjust in such a way that the price of a Big Mac is the same in both cities.

Now ask yourself what the exchange rate has to be between the dollar and yen before the Big Mac is the same dollar price in New York and Tokyo. Of the three following exchange rates, pick the correct one:

1. $1 = ¥133.33
2. $1 = ¥150.00
3. $1 = ¥89.00

The answer is the first one: $1 = ¥133.33. At this exchange rate, a Big Mac in New York is $3, and a Big Mac in Tokyo that is ¥400 is $3 (once we have computed its price in dollars). At the exchange rate of $1 = ¥133.33, ¥1 equals $0.0075, and $0.0075 times ¥400 is $3.

The *purchasing power parity theory* in economics predicts that the exchange rate between two currencies will adjust so that, in the end, $1 buys the same amount of a given good in all places around the world. Thus, if the exchange rate is initially $1 = ¥100 when a Big Mac is $3 in New York and ¥400 in Tokyo, it will change to become $1 = ¥133.33. That is, the dollar will soon appreciate relative to the yen.

The Economist, a well-known economics magazine, publishes what it calls the Big Mac index each year. It shows current exchange rates and the cost of a Big Mac in different countries (just as we did here). Then it predicts which currencies will appreciate and depreciate based on this information. *The Economist* does not always predict accurately, but it does do so in many cases.

If you want to predict whether the euro, pound, or peso is going to appreciate or depreciate in the next few months, looking at exchange rates in terms of the price of a Big Mac will be a useful approach.

will increase, and the demand curve will shift to the right, ideally, by enough to raise the equilibrium rate to the current fixed exchange rate.

Alternatively, instead of the Fed's buying pesos (to mop up the excess supply of pesos), the Banco de Mexico (the central bank of Mexico) could buy pesos with some of its reserve dollars. (It doesn't buy pesos with pesos because using pesos would not reduce the surplus of pesos on the market.) This action by the Banco de Mexico will also increase the demand for pesos and raise the equilibrium rate.

Finally, the two actions could be combined; that is, both the Fed and the Banco de Mexico could buy pesos.

Options Under a Fixed Exchange Rate System

Suppose there is a surplus of pesos in the foreign exchange market, indicating that the peso is overvalued and the dollar is undervalued. Suppose also that, although the Fed and the Banco de Mexico each attempt to rectify this situation by buying pesos, this combined action is not successful. The surplus of pesos persists for weeks, along with an overvalued peso and an undervalued dollar. A few options are available to pursue.

Devaluation
A government action that changes the exchange rate by lowering the official price of a currency.

Revaluation
A government action that changes the exchange rate by raising the official price of a currency.

DEVALUATION AND REVALUATION Mexico and the United States could agree to reset the official price of the dollar and the peso. Doing so entails *devaluation* and *revaluation.* A **devaluation** occurs when the official price of a currency is lowered. A **revaluation** occurs when the official price of a currency is raised.

For example, suppose the first official price of a peso is 0.10 USD = 1 MXN, and the first official price of $1 is 10 pesos. Mexico and the United States agree to change the official price of their currencies. The second official price is 0.12 USD = 1 MXN, and the second official price of $1 is 8.33 pesos.

Moving from the first official price to the second, the peso has been revalued because it takes *more dollars to buy a peso* (12 cents instead of 10). Of course, moving from the first official price to the second means the dollar has been devalued because it takes *fewer pesos to buy a dollar* (8.33 pesos instead of 10).

One country might want to devalue its currency, but another country might not want to revalue its currency. For example, if Mexico wants to devalue its currency relative to the U.S. dollar, U.S. authorities might not always willingly comply. To see why, we have to understand that the United States will not sell as many goods to Mexico if the dollar is revalued. As explained earlier, revaluing the dollar means Mexicans have to pay more for it; instead of paying, say, 8.33 pesos for $1, Mexicans might have to pay 10 pesos. At a revalued dollar (a higher peso price for a dollar), Mexicans will find U.S. goods more expensive and not want to buy as many. Americans who produce goods to sell to Mexico may see that a revalued dollar will hurt their pocketbooks, and so they will argue against it.

PROTECTIONIST TRADE POLICY (QUOTAS AND TARIFFS) Recall that an overvalued dollar can bring on or widen a trade deficit. To deal with both the trade deficit and the overvalued dollar at the same time, some say a country can impose quotas and tariffs to reduce domestic consumption of foreign goods. (Chapter 17 explains how both tariffs and quotas meet this objective.) A drop in the domestic consumption of foreign goods goes hand in hand with a decrease in the demand for foreign currencies. In turn, this decrease can affect the value of the country's currency on the foreign exchange market. In this case, it can get rid of an overvalued dollar.

Economists are quick to point out, though, that trade deficits and overvalued currencies are sometimes used as an excuse to promote trade restrictions, many of which simply benefit special interests (e.g., U.S. producers that compete for sales with foreign producers in the U.S. market).

CHANGES IN MONETARY POLICY Sometimes, a nation can use monetary policy to support the exchange rate or the official price of its currency. Suppose the United States is continually running a merchandise trade deficit; year after year, imports are outstripping exports. To remedy this, the United States might enact a tight monetary policy to retard inflation and drive up interest rates (at least in the short run). The tight monetary policy will reduce the U.S. rate of inflation and thereby lower U.S. prices relative to prices in other nations. This effect will make U.S. goods relatively cheaper than they were before (assuming other nations don't also enact a tight monetary policy) and promote U.S. exports and discourage foreign imports. It will also generate a flow of investment funds into the United States in search of higher real interest rates.

Some economists argue against fixed exchange rates because they think it unwise for a nation to adopt a particular monetary policy simply to maintain an international exchange rate. Instead, they believe domestic monetary policies should be used to meet domestic economic goals, such as price stability, low unemployment, low and stable interest rates, and so forth.

The Gold Standard

If nations adopt the gold standard, they *automatically fix* their exchange rates. Suppose the United States defines a dollar as equal to 1/10 of an ounce of gold and Mexico defines a peso as equal to 1/100 of an ounce of gold. Therefore, 1 ounce of gold could be bought with either 10 dollars or 100 pesos. The fixed exchange rate between dollars and pesos is 10 MXN = 1 USD or 0.10 USD = 1 MXN.

To have an international gold standard, countries must do the following:

1. Define their currencies in terms of gold.
2. Stand ready and willing to convert gold into paper money and paper money into gold at the rate specified (e.g., the United States would buy and sell gold at $10 an ounce).
3. Link their money supplies to their holdings of gold.

With this last point in mind, consider how a gold standard would work. Initially assume that the gold standard (fixed) exchange rate of 0.10 USD = 1 MXN is the equilibrium exchange rate. Then a change occurs: Inflation in Mexico raises prices there by 100 percent. A Mexican table that was priced at 2,000 pesos before the inflation is now priced at 4,000 pesos. At the gold standard (fixed) exchange rate, Americans now have to pay $400 (4,000 pesos ÷ 10 pesos per dollar) to buy the table, whereas before the inflation Americans had to pay only $200 (2,000 pesos ÷ 10 pesos per dollar) for the table. As a result, Americans buy fewer Mexican tables; Americans import less from Mexico.

At the same time, Mexicans import more from the United States because American prices are now relatively lower than before inflation hit Mexico. As a quick example, suppose that before inflation hit Mexico, an American pair of shoes cost $200 and that, as before, a Mexican table cost 2,000 pesos. At 0.10 USD = 1 MXN, the $200 American shoes cost 2,000 pesos and the 2,000-peso Mexican table cost $200. In other words, 1 pair of American shoes traded for (or equaled) 1 Mexican table.

Then inflation raised the price of the Mexican table to 4,000 pesos, or $400. Because the American shoes are still $200 (there has been no inflation in the United States) and the exchange rate is still fixed at 0.10 USD = 1 MXN, 1 pair of American shoes no longer equals 1 Mexican table; instead, it equals 1/2 of a Mexican table. In short, the inflation in Mexico has made U.S. goods *relatively cheaper* for Mexicans. As a result, Mexicans buy more U.S. goods; they import more from the United States.

To summarize, the inflation in Mexico has caused Americans to buy fewer goods from Mexico and Mexicans to buy more goods from the United States. In terms of the merchandise trade balance for each country, in the United States, imports decline (Americans are buying less from Mexico) and exports rise (Mexicans are buying more from the United States); so the U.S. trade balance is likely to move into surplus. Contrarily, in Mexico, exports decline (Americans are buying less from Mexico) and imports rise (Mexicans are buying more from the United States); so Mexico's trade balance is likely to move into deficit.

On a gold standard, Mexicans have to pay for the difference between their imports and exports with gold. Gold is therefore shipped to the United States. An increase in the supply of gold in the United States expands the U.S. money supply. A decrease in the supply of gold in Mexico contracts the Mexican money supply. Prices are affected in both countries. In the United States, prices begin to rise; in Mexico, they begin to fall.

As U.S. prices go up and Mexican prices go down, the earlier situation begins to reverse itself. American goods look more expensive to Mexicans, and they begin to buy less, whereas Mexican goods look cheaper to Americans, and they begin to buy more. Consequently, American imports begin to rise and exports begin to fall; Mexican imports begin to fall and exports begin to rise. Thus, by changing domestic money supplies and price levels, the gold standard begins to correct the initial trade balance disequilibrium.

The change in the money supply that the gold standard sometimes requires has prompted some economists to voice the same charge against the gold standard that is often heard against the fixed exchange rate system: It subjects domestic monetary policy to international instead of domestic considerations. In fact, many economists cite this as part of the reason many nations abandoned the gold standard in the 1930s. At a time when unemployment was unusually high, many nations with trade deficits felt that matters would only get worse if they contracted their money supplies to live by the edicts of the gold standard.

SELF-TEST

1. Under a fixed exchange rate system, if one currency is overvalued, then another currency must be undervalued. Explain why this statement is true.
2. How does an overvalued dollar affect U.S. exports and imports?
3. In each of the following cases, identify whether the U.S. dollar is overvalued or undervalued:
   a. The fixed exchange rate is \$2 = £1, and the equilibrium exchange rate is \$3 = £1.
   b. The fixed exchange rate is \$1.25 = €1, and the equilibrium exchange rate is \$1.10 = €1.
   c. The fixed exchange rate is \$1 = 10 pesos, and the equilibrium exchange rate is \$1 = 14 pesos.
4. Under a fixed exchange rate system, why might the United States want to devalue its currency?

Fixed Exchange Rates Versus Flexible Exchange Rates

As in many economic situations, any exchange rate system has both its costs and its benefits. This section discusses some of the arguments and issues surrounding fixed exchange rates and flexible exchange rates.

Promoting International Trade

Which are better at promoting international trade: fixed or flexible exchange rates? This section presents the case for each.

THE CASE FOR FIXED EXCHANGE RATES Proponents of a fixed exchange rate system often argue that fixed exchange rates promote international trade, whereas flexible exchange rates stifle it. A major advantage of fixed exchange rates is certainty. Individuals in different countries know from day to day the value of their nation's currency. With flexible exchange rates, individuals are less likely to engage in international trade because of the added risk of not knowing from one day to the next how many dollars, euros, or yen they will have to trade for other currencies. Certainty is a necessary ingredient in international trade; flexible exchange rates promote uncertainty, which hampers international trade.

Economist Charles Kindleberger, a proponent of fixed exchange rates, believes that having fixed exchange rates is analogous to having a single currency for the entire United States instead of having a different currency for each of the 50 states. One currency in the United States promotes trade, whereas 50 different currencies would hamper it. In Kindleberger's view:

> *The main case against flexible exchange rates is that they break up the world market. . . . Imagine trying to conduct interstate trade in the USA if there were fifty different state monies, none of which was dominant. This is akin to barter, the inefficiency of which is explained time and again by textbooks.*[6]

THE CASE FOR FLEXIBLE EXCHANGE RATES Advocates of flexible exchange rates, as noted, maintain that it is better for a nation to adopt policies to meet domestic economic goals than to sacrifice domestic economic goals to maintain an exchange rate. Also, the chance is too great that the fixed exchange rate will diverge greatly from the equilibrium exchange rate, creating persistent balance of trade problems leading deficit nations to impose trade restrictions (tariffs and quotas) that hinder international trade.

Optimal Currency Areas

As of 2008, the European Union (EU) consists of 27 member states. According to the European Union, its ultimate goal is "an ever closer union among the peoples of Europe, in which decisions are taken as closely as possible to the citizen." As part of meeting this goal, the EU established its own currency—the euro—on January 1, 1999.[7] Although euro notes and coins were not issued until January 1, 2002, certain business transactions were made in euros beginning January 1, 1999.

The European Union and the euro are relevant to a discussion of an *optimal currency area.* An **optimal currency area** is a geographic area in which exchange rates can be fixed or a *common currency* used without sacrificing domestic economic goals, such as low unemployment. The concept of an optimal currency area originated in the debate over whether fixed or flexible exchange rates are better. Most of the pioneering work on optimal currency areas was done by Robert Mundell, the winner of the 1999 Nobel Prize in Economics.

Optimal Currency Area
A geographic area in which exchange rates can be fixed or a common currency used without sacrificing domestic economic goals, such as low unemployment.

Before discussing an optimal currency area, we need to look at the relationships among labor mobility, trade, and exchange rates. *Labor mobility* means that it is easy for the residents of one country to move to another country.

TRADE AND LABOR MOBILITY Suppose there are only two countries: the United States and Canada. The United States produces calculators and soft drinks, and Canada produces bread and muffins. Currently, the two countries trade with each other, and there is complete labor mobility between them.

One day, the residents of both countries reduce their demand for bread and muffins and increase their demand for calculators and soft drinks. In other words, relative demand changes. Demand increases for U.S. goods and falls for Canadian goods. Business firms in Canada lay off employees because their sales have plummeted. Incomes in Canada begin to fall, and the unemployment rate begins to rise. In the United States, prices initially rise because of the increased demand for calculators and soft drinks. In response to the higher demand for their products, U.S. business firms begin to hire more workers and increase their production. Their efforts to hire more workers drive wages up and reduce the unemployment rate.

Because labor is mobile, some of the newly unemployed Canadian workers move to the United States to find work, easing the economic situation in both countries. The

6. Charles Kindleberger, *International Money* (London: Allen and Unwin, 1981), p. 174.

7. So far, 15 of the 27 member states have adopted the euro as their official currency.

movement of labor will reduce some of the unemployment problems in Canada, and, with more workers in the United States, more output will be produced, thus dampening upward price pressures on calculators and soft drinks. Thus, changes in relative demand pose no major economic problems for either country if labor is mobile.

TRADE AND LABOR IMMOBILITY Now let's suppose that relative demand has changed but that labor is *not* mobile between the United States and Canada. We assume labor immobility, perhaps due to either political or cultural barriers to people moving between the two countries. If people cannot move, what happens in the economies of the two countries depends largely on whether exchange rates are fixed or flexible.

If exchange rates are flexible, the value of U.S. currency changes vis-à-vis Canadian currency. If Canadians want to buy more U.S. goods, they will have to exchange their domestic currency for U.S. currency. This increases the demand for U.S. currency on the foreign exchange market at the same time that it increases the supply of Canadian currency. Consequently, U.S. currency appreciates and Canadian currency depreciates. Because Canadian currency depreciates, U.S. goods become relatively more expensive for Canadians; so they buy fewer. And because U.S. currency appreciates, Canadian goods become relatively cheaper for Americans; so they buy more. Canadian business firms begin to sell more goods; so they hire more workers, the unemployment rate drops, and the bad economic times in Canada begin to disappear.

If exchange rates are fixed, however, U.S. goods will not become relatively more expensive for Canadians, and Canadian goods will not become relatively cheaper for Americans. Consequently, the bad economic times in Canada (high unemployment) might last for a long time indeed instead of beginning to reverse. Thus, if labor is immobile, changes in relative demand may pose major economic problems when exchange rates are fixed but not when they are flexible.

COSTS, BENEFITS, AND OPTIMAL CURRENCY AREAS Flexible exchange rates have both benefits (just discussed) and costs. The costs include the cost of exchanging one currency for another (there is a charge to exchange, say, U.S. dollars for Canadian dollars or U.S. dollars for Japanese yen) and the added risk of not knowing what the value of one's currency will be on the foreign exchange market on any given day. For many countries, the benefits outweigh the costs, and so they have flexible exchange rate systems.

Suppose some of the costs of flexible exchange rates could be eliminated, while maintaining the benefits. Two countries could have a fixed exchange rate or adopt a common currency and retain the benefits of flexible exchange rates when labor is mobile between the two countries. Then there is no reason to have separate currencies that float against each other because resources (labor) can move easily and quickly in response to changes in relative demand. The two countries can either fix exchange rates or adopt the same currency.

When labor in countries within a certain geographic area is mobile enough to move easily and quickly in response to changes in relative demand, the countries are said to constitute an *optimal currency area.* Countries in such an area can either fix their currencies or adopt the same currency and thus keep all the benefits of flexible exchange rates without any of the costs.

It is commonly argued that the states within the United States constitute an optimal currency area. Labor can move easily and quickly between, say, North Carolina and South Carolina in response to relative demand changes. Some economists argue that the countries that compose the European Union are within an optimal currency area and that adopting a common currency—the euro—will benefit these countries. Other economists disagree. They argue that, although labor is somewhat more mobile in Europe today than in the past, certain language and cultural differences make labor mobility less than sufficient to truly constitute an optimal currency area.

THE CURRENT INTERNATIONAL MONETARY SYSTEM

Today's international monetary system is best described as a managed flexible exchange rate system, sometimes referred to more casually as a **managed float**. In a way, this system is a rough compromise between the fixed and flexible exchange rate systems. The current system operates under flexible exchange rates, but not completely. Nations now and then intervene to adjust their official reserve holdings to moderate major swings in exchange rates.

Managed Float
A managed flexible exchange rate system, under which nations now and then intervene to adjust their official reserve holdings to moderate major swings in exchange rates.

Proponents of the managed float system stress the following advantages:

1. *It allows nations to pursue independent monetary policies.* Under a (strictly) fixed exchange rate system, fixed either by agreement or by gold, a nation with a merchandise trade deficit might have to enact a tight monetary policy to retard inflation and to promote its exports. This type of action is not needed with the managed float, whose proponents argue that solving trade imbalances by adjusting one price—the exchange rate—is better than adjusting the price level.
2. *It solves trade problems without trade restrictions.* As stated earlier, under a fixed exchange rate system, nations sometimes impose tariffs and quotas to solve trade imbalances. For example, a deficit nation might impose import quotas so that exports and imports of goods will be more in line. Under the current system, trade imbalances are usually solved through changes in exchange rates.
3. *It is flexible and therefore can easily adjust to shocks.* In 1973–1974, the OPEC nations dramatically raised the price of oil, resulting in trade deficits for many oil-importing nations. A fixed exchange rate system would have had a hard time accommodating such a major change in oil prices, but the current system had little trouble. Exchange rates took much of the shock (there were large changes in exchange rates), thus allowing most nations' economies to weather the storm with a minimum of difficulty.

Opponents of the current international monetary system stress the following disadvantages:

1. *It promotes exchange rate volatility and uncertainty and results in less international trade than would be the case under fixed exchange rates.* Under a flexible exchange rate system, volatile exchange rates make conducting business riskier for importers and exporters. As a result, there is less international trade than there would be under a fixed exchange rate system. Proponents respond that the futures market in currencies allows importers and exporters to shift the risk of fluctuations in exchange rates to others. For example, if an American company wants to buy a quantity of a good from a Japanese company three months from today, it can contract today for the desired quantity of yen that it will need at a specified price. It will not have to worry about a change in the dollar price of yen during the next three months. Purchasing a futures contract has a cost, but it is usually modest.
2. *It promotes inflation.* As we have seen, the monetary policies of different nations are not independent of one another under a fixed exchange rate system. For example, a nation with a merchandise trade deficit is somewhat restrained from inflating its currency because this will worsen the deficit problem. The deficit will make the nation's goods more expensive relative to foreign goods and promote the purchase of imports. In its attempt to maintain the exchange rate, a nation with a merchandise trade deficit would have to enact a tight monetary policy. Under the current system, a nation with a merchandise trade deficit does not have to maintain exchange rates or try to solve its deficit problem through changes in its money supply. Opponents of the current system argue that this frees nations to inflate, predicting that more inflation will result than would occur under a fixed exchange rate system.

3. *Changes in exchange rates alter trade balances in the desired direction only after a long time; in the short run, a depreciation in a currency can make the situation worse instead of better.* It is often argued that soon after a depreciation in a trade-deficit nation's currency, the trade deficit will increase (not decrease, as hoped). The reason is that import demand is inelastic in the short run: Imports are not very responsive to a change in price. For example, suppose Mexico is running a trade deficit with the United States at the present exchange rate of 0.12 USD = 1 MXN. At this exchange rate, the peso is overvalued. Mexico buys 2,000 television sets from the United States, each with a price tag of $500. Assume Mexico therefore spends 8.33 million pesos on imports of American television sets. Now suppose that the overvalued peso begins to depreciate, say, to 0.11 USD = 1 MXN and that, in the short run, Mexican customers buy only 100 fewer American television sets; that is, they import 1,900 television sets. At a price of $500 each and an exchange rate of 0.11 USD = 1 MXN, Mexicans now spend 8.63 million pesos on imports of American television sets. In the short run, then, a depreciation in the peso has widened the trade deficit because imports fell by only 5 percent, whereas the price of imports (in terms of pesos) increased by 9.09 percent. As time passes, imports will fall off more (it takes time for Mexican buyers to shift from higher-priced American goods to lower-priced Mexican goods), and the deficit will shrink.

SELF-TEST

1. What is an optimal currency area?
2. Country 1 produces good X, and country 2 produces good Y. People in both countries begin to demand more of good X and less of good Y. Assume that there is no labor mobility between the two countries and that a flexible exchange rate system exists. What will happen to the unemployment rate in country 2? Explain your answer.
3. How important is labor mobility in determining whether an area is an optimal currency area?

office hours

"WHY IS THE DEPRECIATION OF ONE CURRENCY TIED TO THE APPRECIATION OF ANOTHER CURRENCY?"

Student:

I know that when the dollar depreciates, some other currency appreciates. Is this just the way it is? For example, if $1 equals €1, and then $1.25 equals €1, the arithmetic of exchange rates tells me that now $1 will only fetch €0.8. Is that all there is to it?

Instructor:

Not exactly. You are focusing on the arithmetic (of exchange rates) to the exclusion of the economics. There is an economic reason why dollar appreciation is linked to euro appreciation.

Student:

What is that economic reason?

Instructor:

Think of what can lead to the dollar's depreciating. Let's suppose that you want to travel to Germany where the euro is used. You take your dollars and buy euros with them. In other words, you do two things: You (1) buy euros by (2) supplying dollars.

Now think of how you are affecting the market for euros and the market for dollars. You are increasing the *demand for euros* in the market for euros, and you are increasing the *supply of dollars* in the market for dollars. Remember in Exhibit 5 how we linked the demand for one currency with the supply of another? That is happening here: Your demand for euros is linked to your supply of dollars. So, if you increase the demand for euros, you are automatically increasing the supply of dollars.

Student:

I'm used to thinking that my action of buying something affects only one market. For instance, when I buy more books, this action affects only the market for books. You seem to be telling me that this is not the case when I buy a currency, such as the euro. To buy euros is to supply dollars.

Instructor:

That's right. So when you increase the demand for euros, you automatically increase the supply of dollars. And then we have to ask ourselves, what happens in each of the two markets—the market for euros and the market for dollars?

Student:

Well, if I increase the demand for euros, the price of a euro in terms of dollars will rise. Also, if I increase the supply of dollars, the price of a dollar in terms of euros will fall.

Instructor:

And what do you call it when the price of a euro has risen in terms of dollars?

Student:

We say the dollar has depreciated because it now takes more dollars and cents to buy a euro.

Instructor:

And what do you call it when the price of a dollar has fallen in terms of euros?

Student:

We say the euro has appreciated because it now takes fewer euros to buy a dollar.

Instructor:

So let's go back to your original query. You wondered whether the dollar's depreciating and the euro's appreciating were just matters of arithmetic. Now we know that they aren't. They are a matter of curves shifting in different markets.

Points to Remember

1. To buy a currency is to affect two markets, not just one. If you buy euros, you affect the euro market. But by selling dollars to buy euros, you also affect the dollar market.
2. The fact that when one currency depreciates another appreciates is a matter of curves shifting in two currency markets.

a reader asks | How Do I Convert Currencies?

I plan to travel to several different countries during the summer. How do I convert prices of products in other countries into dollars?

Here is the general formula to use:

Price of the product in dollars =
Price of the product in foreign currency
× Price of the foreign currency in dollars

For example, suppose you travel to Mexico and see something priced at 100 pesos. You'd change the general formula into a specific one:

Price of the product in dollars =
Price of the product in pesos
× Price of a peso in dollars

If the dollar price of a peso is, say, \$0.12, then the dollar price of the product is \$12. Here is the calculation:

$$\text{Price of the product in dollars} = 100 \times 0.12 = 12$$

Or suppose you are in Tokyo and you see a product for ¥10,000. What is the price in dollars? At the exchange rate of 0.008 USD = 1 JPY, it is \$80.

$$\text{Price of the product in dollars} = 10{,}000 \times 0.008 = 80$$

Now let's suppose you are in Russia and you don't know the exchange rate between dollars and rubles. You pick up a newspaper to find out (often, exchange rates are quoted in the newspaper). But instead of finding the exchange rate quoted in terms of the dollar price of a ruble (e.g., \$0.0318 for 1 ruble), you find the ruble price of a dollar (31.4190 rubles for \$1). What do you do now?

Perhaps the easiest thing to do is first convert rubles per dollar into dollars per ruble and then use the earlier formula to find the price of the Russian product in dollars. Recall that exchange rates are reciprocals, so:

$$\text{Dollars per ruble} = \frac{1}{\text{Rubles per dollar}}$$

To illustrate, if it takes 31.4190 rubles to purchase \$1, then it takes 0.0318 dollars to buy 1 ruble. Here is the computation:

$$\text{Dollars per ruble} = \frac{1}{31.41990} = 0.0318$$

Now, because you know that \$0.0318 = 1 ruble, then if, say, a Russian coat costs 10,000 rubles, it costs \$318:

$$\text{Price of the product in dollars} = 10{,}000 \times 0.0318 = 318$$

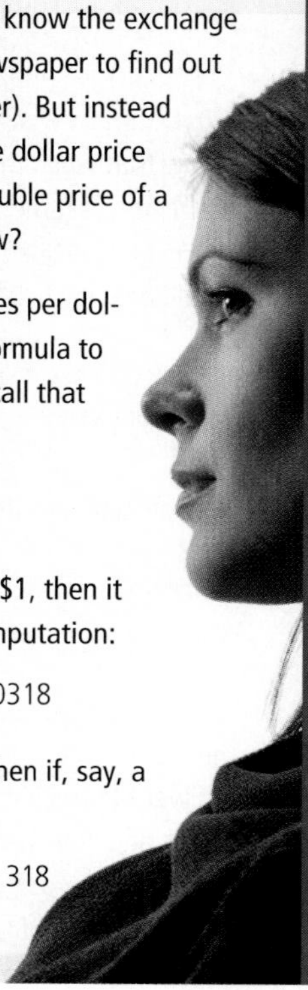

Chapter Summary

BALANCE OF PAYMENTS

- The balance of payments provides information about a nation's imports and exports, domestic residents' earnings on assets located abroad, foreign earnings on domestic assets, gifts to and from foreign countries, and official transactions by governments and central banks.
- In a nation's balance of payments, any transaction that supplies the country's currency in the foreign exchange market is recorded as a debit (−). Any transaction that creates a demand for the country's currency is recorded as a credit (+).
- The three main accounts of the balance of payments are the current account, the capital account, and the official reserve account.
- The current account includes all payments related to the purchase and sale of goods and services. The three major components of the account are exports of goods and services, imports of goods and services, and net unilateral transfers abroad.
- The capital account includes all payments related to the purchase and sale of assets and to borrowing and lending activities. The major components are outflow of U.S. capital and inflow of foreign capital.
- The official reserve account includes transactions by the central banks of various countries.
- The merchandise trade balance is the difference between the value of merchandise exports and the value of merchandise imports. If exports are greater than imports, a nation has a trade surplus; if imports are greater than exports, a nation has a trade deficit.
- The balance of payments equals Current account balance + Capital account balance + Official reserve balance + Statistical discrepancy.

THE FOREIGN EXCHANGE MARKET

- The market in which currencies of different countries are exchanged is called the foreign exchange market. In this market, currencies are bought and sold for a price: the exchange rate.
- When the residents of a nation demand a foreign currency, they must supply their own currency. For example, if Americans demand Mexican goods, they also demand Mexican pesos and supply U.S. dollars. If Mexicans demand American goods, they also demand U.S. dollars and supply Mexican pesos.

FLEXIBLE EXCHANGE RATES

- Under flexible exchange rates, the foreign exchange market will equilibrate at the exchange rate where the quantity demanded of a currency equals the quantity supplied of the currency; for example, the quantity demanded of U.S. dollars equals the quantity supplied of U.S. dollars.
- If the price of a nation's currency increases relative to a foreign currency, the nation's currency is said to have appreciated. For example, if the price of a peso rises from 0.10 USD = 1 MXN to 0.15 USD = 1 MXN, the peso has appreciated. If the price of a nation's currency decreases relative to a foreign currency, the nation's currency is said to have depreciated. For example, if the price of a dollar falls from 10 MXN = 1 USD to 8 MXN = 1 USD, the dollar has depreciated.
- Under a flexible exchange rate system, the equilibrium exchange rate is affected by a difference in income growth rates between countries, a difference in inflation rates between countries, and a change in (real) interest rates between countries.

FIXED EXCHANGE RATES

- Under a fixed exchange rate system, countries agree to fix the price of their currencies. The central banks of the countries must then buy and sell currencies to maintain the agreed-on exchange rate.
- If a persistent deficit or surplus in a nation's combined current and capital account exists at a fixed exchange rate, the nation has a few options to deal with the problem: devalue or revalue its currency, enact protectionist trade policies (in the case of a deficit), or change its monetary policy.
- A gold standard automatically fixes exchange rates. To have an international gold standard, nations must do the following: (1) define their currencies in terms of gold, (2) stand ready and willing to convert gold into paper money and paper money into gold at a specified rate, and (3) link their money supplies to their holdings of gold. The change in the money supply that the gold standard sometimes requires has prompted some economists to voice the same charge against the gold standard that is often heard against the fixed exchange rate system: It subjects domestic monetary policy to international instead of domestic considerations.

THE CURRENT INTERNATIONAL MONETARY SYSTEM

- Today's international monetary system is described as a managed flexible exchange rate system, or managed float. For the most part, the exchange rate system is flexible, although nations periodically intervene in the foreign exchange market to adjust rates. Because it is a managed float system, it is difficult to tell whether nations will emphasize the float part or the managed part in the future.
- Proponents of the managed flexible exchange rate system believe it offers several advantages: (1) It allows nations to pursue independent monetary policies. (2) It solves trade problems without trade restrictions. (3) It is flexible and therefore can easily adjust to shocks.
- Opponents of the managed flexible exchange rate system believe it has several disadvantages: (1) It promotes exchange rate volatility and uncertainty and results in less international trade than would be the case under fixed exchange rates. (2) It promotes inflation. (3) It corrects trade deficits only a long time after a depreciation in the currency; in the interim, it can make matters worse.

Key Terms and Concepts

Balance of Payments
Debit
Foreign Exchange Market
Credit
Current Account
Merchandise Trade Balance
Merchandise Trade Deficit
Merchandise Trade Surplus
Current Account Balance
Capital Account
Capital Account Balance
International Monetary Fund (IMF)
Special Drawing Right (SDR)
Exchange Rate
Flexible Exchange Rate System
Appreciation
Depreciation
Purchasing Power Parity (PPP) Theory
Fixed Exchange Rate System
Overvalued
Undervalued
Devaluation
Revaluation
Optimal Currency Area
Managed Float

Questions and Problems

1 Suppose the United States and Japan have a flexible exchange rate system. Explain whether each of the following events will lead to an appreciation or depreciation in the U.S. dollar and Japanese yen.

a. U.S. real interest rates rise above Japanese real interest rates.

b. The Japanese inflation rate rises relative to the U.S. inflation rate.

c. Japan imposes a quota on imports of American radios.

2 Give an example that illustrates how a change in the exchange rate changes the relative price of domestic goods in terms of foreign goods.

3 Suppose the media report that the United States has a deficit in its current account. What does this imply about the U.S. capital account balance and official reserve account balance?

4 Suppose Canada has a merchandise trade deficit and Mexico has a merchandise trade surplus. The two countries have a flexible exchange rate system; so the Mexican peso appreciates and the Canadian dollar depreciates. However, soon after the depreciation of the Canadian dollar, Canada's trade deficit grows instead of shrinks. Why might this occur?

5 What are the strong and weak points of the flexible exchange rate system? What are the strong and weak points of the fixed exchange rate system?

6 Individuals do not keep a written account of their balance of trade with other individuals. For example, John doesn't keep an account of how much he sells to Alice and how much he buys from her. In addition, neither cities nor any of the 50 states calculate their balance of trade with all other cities and states. However, nations do calculate their merchandise trade balance with other nations. If nations do it, should individuals, cities, and states do it? Why or why not?

7 Every nation's balance of payments equals zero. Therefore, is each nation on an equal footing in international trade and finance with every other nation? Explain your answer.

8 Suppose your objective is to predict whether the euro (the currency of the European Union) and the U.S. dollar will appreciate or depreciate on the foreign exchange market in the next two months. What information would you need to help make your prediction? Specifically, how would this information help you predict the direction of the foreign exchange value of the euro and dollar? Next, explain how a person who could accurately predict exchange rates could become extremely rich in a short time.

9 Suppose the price of a Big Mac always rises by the percentage rise in the price level of the country in which it is sold. According to the purchasing power parity (PPP) theory, we would expect the price of a Big Mac to be the same everywhere in the world. Why?

10 If everyone in the world spoke the same language, would the world be closer to or further from being an optimal currency area? Explain your answer.

Working with Numbers and Graphs

1 The following foreign exchange information appeared in a newspaper:

	U.S. Dollar Equivalent		Currency per U.S. Dollar	
	Thurs.	**Fri.**	**Thurs.**	**Fri.**
Russia (ruble)	0.0318	0.0317	31.4190	31.5290
Brazil (real)	0.3569	0.3623	2.8020	2.7601
India (rupee)	0.0204	0.0208	48.9100	47.8521

a. Between Thursday and Friday, did the U.S. dollar appreciate or depreciate against the Russian ruble?

b. Between Thursday and Friday, did the U.S. dollar appreciate or depreciate against the Brazilian real?

c. Between Thursday and Friday, did the U.S. dollar appreciate or depreciate against the Indian rupee?

2 If $1 equals ¥0.0093, what does ¥1 equal?

3 If $1 equals 7.7 krone (Danish), what does 1 krone equal?

4 If $1 equals 31 rubles, what does 1 ruble equal?

5 If the current account is −$45 billion, the capital account is +$55 billion, and the official reserve balance is −$1 billion, what does the statistical discrepancy equal?

6 Why does the balance of payments always equal zero?

© JOAO VIRISSIMO/SHUTTERSTOCK

CHAPTER 19

GLOBALIZATION AND INTERNATIONAL IMPACTS ON THE ECONOMY

Introduction In the world in which we live, we hear much of *globalization*. In this chapter we discuss what globalization is, the causes of it, the costs and benefits of it, and its future. We then return to a framework of analysis we first used in the macroeconomics part of this text—aggregate demand and aggregate supply (*AD-AS*)—and we use *AD-AS* to discuss some of the effects of globalization on a national economy.

WHAT IS GLOBALIZATION?

Many economists define **globalization** as one of two things:

1. A phenomenon by which individuals and businesses in any part of the world are much more affected by events elsewhere in the world than before.
2. The growing integration of the national economies of the world to the degree that we may be witnessing the emergence and operation of a single worldwide economy.

These factors—people and businesses across the world having greater impact on each other, creating a smaller world, and the movement toward a worldwide economy—are repeated in the many different definitions of globalization. Let's take a closer look at these key features.

Globalization
A phenomenon by which economic agents in any given part of the world are more affected by events elsewhere in the world than before; the growing integration of the national economies of the world to the degree that we may be witnessing the emergence and operation of a single worldwide economy.

A Smaller World

The first definition emphasizes that economic agents in any given part of the world are affected by events elsewhere in the world. If you live in the United States, you are not affected only by what happens in the United States but also by what happens in Brazil, Russia, and China. For example, in recent years, the Chinese government was taking much of the money it earned in trade with the United States and buying bonds issued by the U.S. government. As a result of the Chinese purchases of U.S. bonds, interest rates in the United States ended up being lower than they would have been. Because of lower interest rates, some people were able to take out mortgage loans to buy houses that they would not be eligible for otherwise. Some people took out car loans to buy cars that they otherwise would not have been able to buy.

But can you see how, in a sense, globalization makes the world smaller? China hasn't moved physically; it isn't any closer to the United States (in terms of distance) than it was 100 years ago. Still, because of globalization, what happens in distant China today has an effect on you, just as, in the past, what happened in locations only 10 miles or 100 miles away would affect you. For all practical purposes, we live in a smaller world today than people did 100 years ago.

Finding ECONOMICS

In a Clothing Store

Brandon is at a clothing store buying a number of items—shirts, sweaters, trousers, etc. He doesn't check to see in which country each of these items was produced. Instead, he just checks out the item and its price, and he decides whether to buy it. Where is the economics?

Many of the items Brandon buys were very likely produced in other countries. To Brandon, buying an item of clothing produced in China, Brazil, or India is really no different from buying an item of clothing in a factory 10 miles away. For Brandon, China, Brazil, or India might as well be down the street. In some ways, the world Brandon lives in is a small world, one in which distance doesn't matter as much as it used to; it is one in which trades between people living in different countries are becoming increasingly more common.

A World Economy

Globalization is closely aligned with a movement toward more free enterprise, freer markets, and more freedom of movement for people and goods. Thomas Friedman, author of several books on globalization, states that "globalization means the spread of free-market capitalism in the world." Economic globalization is essentially a free enterprise activity, and to the degree that many countries are globalizing, they are moving toward greater free enterprise practices. Much of this globalization and much of the movement toward freer markets are occurring in the world today.

With globalization, the world is moving from hundreds of national economies toward *one large world economy.* In this world economy, speaking about *different* economic systems does not make as much sense as it once did. Speaking about *the* economic system for that one world economy does make sense. And, as explained, the economic system that best describes what is happening in the world economy is free enterprise or capitalism.

Finding ECONOMICS

***In* The Economist**

"Mr. Bhattacharjee is not the first leader to preach socialism while practising capitalism." Mr. Bhattacharjee is the chief minister of the Indian state, West Bengal. The statement about him was made in *The Economist* (a news magazine that covers economic issues in particular) in November 2007. Where is the economics? The statement gives us a glimpse into the what is happening in the world today with respect to the adoption of economic systems—specifically, the movement is toward capitalism.

economics 24/7

SHOULD YOU LEAVE A TIP?

In the United States, tipping in restaurants is common, amounting to $16 billion a year. Yet 24 percent of the individuals in one study said that they thought tipping was unfair to customers. In the past, some states prohibited tipping. For example, in the early 1900s, Arkansas, Mississippi, Iowa, South Carolina, Tennessee, and Washington passed laws to prohibit tipping.

© MOODBOARD/ALAMY

Of all the people in the rest of the world, some have the same tipping practices as Americans, but certainly not all. For example, adding an automatic service charge to a restaurant bill is increasingly customary in European restaurants, rather than tipping the server. Little tipping of any sort goes on in Argentina and Vietnam. Much less tipping occurs (i.e., fewer service providers expect tips) in Australia, New Zealand, and Italy than in the United States, and more tipping goes on in Mexico and Egypt than in the United States.

In several studies, researchers looked at the number of different service providers (out of a total of 33) for which tipping is customary in a given country. The more service providers it was customary to tip in a country, the higher the country's so-called prevalence of tipping. For example, if it was customary to tip 31 different service providers in country A but only 15 in country B, then country A would have a higher prevalence of tipping than country B.

The conclusion of these studies is that countries where success and materialism were highly valued had a higher prevalence of tipping than countries where caring and personal relationships were highly valued. In addition, the prevalence of tipping increased as the national need for achievement and recognition rose. In one study, tipping was more prevalent in countries with lower taxes than in countries with higher taxes.

If it becomes increasingly relevant to speak of a world economy instead of hundreds of national economies, will tipping practices around the world become more common? If they do become more common, toward what degree of tipping will they gravitate? Because we do not know the answer to these questions, why ask? The answer is twofold: First, the questions get us to think about what changes we are likely to see in our everyday lives and, as globalization continues, whether the changes will be only in the economic realm (e.g., we can buy more clothes from China), or whether they will disperse outward into the social and cultural realms. Second, the questions force us to separate into categories things that are so deeply embedded in the character of a people (and therefore unlikely to change) from things that are somewhat superficial (and therefore more likely to change). Which is a rock (incapable of absorbing), and which is a sponge (capable of absorbing)?

Two Ways to See Globalization

Sometimes, a definition is not as good a description or explanation as a picture. Let's create two mental pictures that should give you a good idea of what globalization is about. The first picture is of a world without any barriers to trade, where the cost of dealing with anyone in the world is essentially the same.

No Barriers

Suppose land was not divided into nation states—no United States, no China, no Russia. Also suppose physical, economic, or political barriers to trade did not exist. Essentially, then, you could trade with anyone, no matter where in the world this person lived. You could trade with a person living 5,000 miles away as easily as you could trade with your next-door neighbor.

In this pretend world, businesses could hire workers and set up factories anywhere in the world. People could open savings accounts in banks 7,000 miles away or buy stock in companies located on the other side of the globe.

Now, in a sense, our world—the world that we live in today—is moving in this direction. As this movement proceeds, a nation's economy (e.g., the U.S. economy) becomes more and more a part of the world economy. As this process continues, speaking about a world or global economy, rather than about the Russian, U.S., or Chinese economy, becomes increasingly relevant.

A Union of States

The second way to see globalization is familiar to people who reside in the United States, made up as it is of 50 states. Today, moving goods and services among these states is easy. A person can produce goods in, say, North Carolina and then transport them (with only a few exceptions) for sale to every state in the country. In addition, a person living anywhere in the United States can move to any state and work, save, purchase, sell, and so on. In other words, within the United States, free movement of people and goods is possible.

Some people will argue today that economic globalization is, in a way, similar to changing countries (of the world) into states of one country. It is similar to making independent countries such as the United States, Russia, China, Brazil, and Japan into the United States of the World.

GLOBALIZATION FACTS

How do you know globalization is occurring? You need to see certain things happening in the world before you can say that globalization is taking place.

You need to see:

- Countries in the world opening up to more trade with each other.
- People in one country investing some of their money in other countries.
- Companies in one country hiring people in other countries.

Essentially, you need to see people in the world acting more like they once acted only within their individual countries. Some evidence suggests that all these things are happening.

International Trade

Tariff
A tax on imports.

The average **tariff** rate in the United States was 40 percent in 1946. The average tariff today is today is about 1.6 percent. Also, federal government revenue from tariffs in the early 1900s accounted for half of all federal government revenues, whereas today tariffs account for less than 2 percent. Exhibit 1 presents average tariff rates in the United States during the period 1930–2007.

The decline in tariff rates in the United States has also been accompanied by similar declines in countries such as India, China, Brazil, and many others. For example, in 2000, the average tariff rate in China was 18.7 percent; one year later, it was 12.8 percent. In 2000, the average tariff rate in India was 30.2 percent; one year later, it was 21 percent. Furthermore, both India and China are trading more with other countries. For example, 15 years ago, China did not trade much with the countries of Europe. Today, for most European countries, China is one of their top five trading partners.

exhibit 1

Average U.S. Tariff Rates, 1930–2007

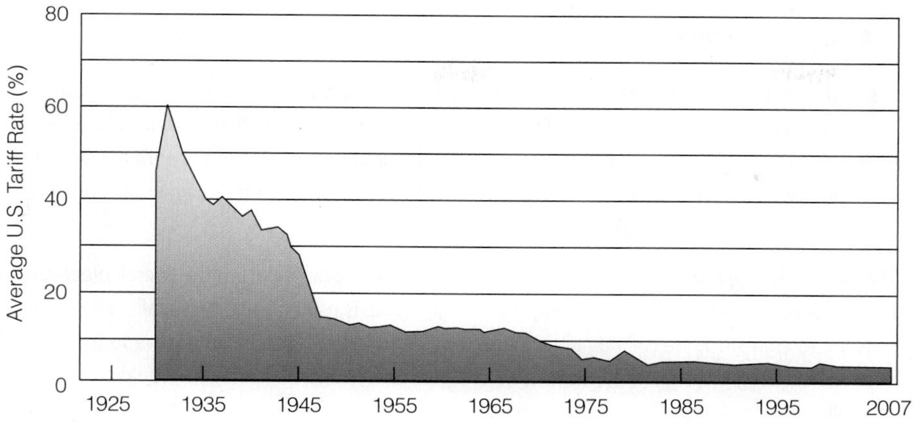

As further evidence of globalization, between 1973 and 2007, countries exported and imported more goods. Exports became a larger percentage of a country's total output. To explain these changes, think of an analogy. Suppose you produce computers. Last year, all the computers you produced were purchased by residents of the country in which you live. This year, residents of your country purchase half the computers you produced, and persons who live in foreign countries purchased the other half. In 2007, U.S. exports and imports were more like the second scenario; in 1973, things were closer to the first scenario.

Foreign Exchange Trading

When people of one country want to trade with people of another country or invest in a foreign company, they have to buy the currency used in the other country. So if globalization occurs, we would expect a lot more currency exchanges to take place. In economics, *foreign exchange trading* is a term that means buying and selling foreign currencies. In 1995, daily foreign exchange trading was 60 times higher than it was in 1977. In 1992, daily foreign exchange trading amounted to $820 billion. In 1998, this amount had risen to $1.5 trillion, close to doubling in just 6 years. In 2007, foreign exchange trading had risen to over $3 trillion.

Foreign Direct Investment

If a U.S. company wants to invest in a company in, say, Russia, it undertakes what is called *foreign direct investment.* The more foreign direct investment there is, the more likely the process of globalization is at work. In 1975, foreign direct investment amounted to $23 billion. In 1997, it had risen to $644 billion, a 30-fold increase. Between 1984 and 2003, U.S. investment holdings in foreign companies tripled, and foreign investment in the U.S. increased six-fold.

Personal Investments

Many people in the United States own stocks. If you own a number of stocks, you are said to have a stock portfolio. In 1980, these stock portfolios were comprised of no more than 2 percent of foreign stocks. Today, it is 14 percent. Thus, Americans are increasingly buying stock in foreign companies.

Finding ECONOMICS

In a Foreign Stock Transaction

Two years ago Jake bought a few foreign stocks. Specifically, he bought 1,000 shares of an Irish firm's stock and 400 shares of a French firm's stock. In both Ireland and France the currency used is the euro. In recent months, the value of the dollar in relationship to the euro has been falling. In other words, it now takes more dollars and cents to buy a euro than it did when Jake bought the stock. Where is the economics?

The economics appears in two places. First, buying foreign stocks is part of the overall globalization picture. Second, Jake's return for buying the foreign stocks is rising as the dollar falls. When Jake sells the foreign stock, he will be paid in euros, and euros are rising in value relative to the dollar. So, when he exchanges the euros for dollars, he will get more dollars now than he would have before the dollar fell in value (in relation to the euro).

The World Trade Organization

The World Trade Organization (WTO) is an international organization whose mission is to promote international free trade (trade between countries). In 1948, only 23 countries of the world chose to be members of the precursor to the WTO, GATT (General Agreement on Tariffs and Trade); in mid-2008, that number had risen to 151 countries.

Business Practices

More and more, Americans are working for foreign companies that have offices in the United States. For example, the number of Americans working for foreign companies (with offices in the United States) grew from 4.9 million in 1991 to 6.5 million in 2001, an increase of 1.6 million.

MOVEMENT TOWARD GLOBALIZATION

How did we come to live in a global economy? Did someone push a button years ago to start the process? Globalization has been on the world stage for longer than the past two decades. In fact, the world has gone through different globalization periods. For example, globalization was occurring during the period from the mid-1800s to the late 1920s. Some people today refer to it as the First Era of Globalization. In some ways, when it came to the movement of people, the world then was freer than the world today, as evidenced by the fact that many people moved from country to country without a passport, which was not required.

The First Era of Globalization was largely ended by World Wars I and II and the Great Depression. Even though the Great Depression and the world wars were over by 1945, globalization did not start anew. The Cold War essentially divided the world into different camps (free versus unfree, capitalist versus communist), which led to relatively high political and economic barriers. The visible symbol of these barriers—the Berlin Wall—separated not only East from West Germany but one group of countries living under one political and economic system from another group of countries living under a different political and economic system.

The more recent period of globalization of today has several causal factors. Not everyone agrees as to what all the factors are, and not everyone agrees on the weight one assigns to each of the factors. For example, some people will argue that one factor means more

economics 24/7

PROPER BUSINESS ETIQUETTE AROUND THE WORLD

Customs and traditions differ among countries, sometimes when it comes to conducting business. Not knowing how business is done in a country can act as a stumbling block to getting business done. What follows is a list of countries and certain rules of business etiquette in the different countries.[1]

Beijing, China

- If someone offers you his or her business card, accept with both hands, read it immediately, and then present your business card to the person.
- In business, men normally wear a suit and tie.

Berlin, Germany

- When out with German business associates, try not to talk about sports. Many businesspeople believe that sports talk is the domain of the uneducated.
- Drinking before all have raised their glasses together is considered impolite.

Dubai, United Arab Emirates

- Do not arrange appointments on Friday because it is Dubai's day of prayer and rest.
- Business slows down during the month of Ramadan (when Muslims fast). Foreign businesspeople are expected to observe the slower pace.

Hong Kong

- Running out of business cards is considered impolite.

Mexico City

- Having business cards printed in English on one side and in Spanish on the other is considered good form.
- Business clothing is fairly formal.

Sydney, Australia

- Knowing about the latest sports matches is important.
- Don't take yourself too seriously.

Tokyo, Japan

- Remove your shoes when entering a Japanese home.

Zurich, Switzerland

- People often greet each other when entering an office or shop. Try to do the same, even if your greeting is in your own language.
- Talking about money or personal wealth is frowned upon.

1. The reference guide is *The Economist*'s City Guide.

to globalization than another factor. Still, it is important that you are aware of the causal factors of globalization most often mentioned.

The End of the Cold War

The Cold War intensified after World War II and, most agree, ended with the visible fall of the Berlin Wall in 1989. This event, although historic in and of itself, occurred at the time when the Soviet empire was beginning to crumble, and many of the communist East European countries were breaking away from the Soviet Union. As some explain the event, the end of the Cold War resulted in turning two different worlds (the capitalist and communist worlds) into one. It resulted in a thawing of not only political but economic relations between former enemies. You might not trade with your enemy, but once that person or country is no longer your enemy, you don't feel the same need to exclude him or it from your political and economic life.

At the beginning of this section, we asked you to imagine a world where no barriers affected your trading with anyone in the world. The barriers might be distance, culture, politics, or anything else. The Cold War acted as a political barrier between certain groups of countries; once it ended, one barrier standing in the way of trade disappeared.

One way to view the current period of economic liberalization (freer markets, lower tariffs) and globalization is to ask whether it would be occurring as it is today if the United States and the Soviet Union were still engaged in the Cold War. This is doubtful. Even though the end of the Cold War might not be the full and only cause for the current period of globalization, if the Cold War had not ended, globalization would probably not be accelerating at the pace it is today.

Advancing Technology

In the past, innovations such as the internal combustion engine, steamship, telephone, and telegraph led to increased trade between people in different countries. All of these inventions led to lower transportation or communication costs, and lower costs mean fewer barriers to trade. What technology often does is lower the hindrances (of physical distance) that act as stumbling blocks to trade. For example, the cost of a 3-minute telephone call from New York to London in 1930 was $250. In 1960, it was $60.42; in 1980, it was $6.32; and in 2000, it was 40 cents. Today, the cost is even less. As the costs of communicating continue to fall, in some sense, the hindrance of physical distance (to trade) is overcome. Businesspeople in the United States, for example, can more cheaply talk with businesspeople in China.

Now consider the price of a computer over the years. The cost of a computer in 1960—one comparable to the desktop computer that many people today have on their desks at home—was $1.8 million. That computer was $199,983 in 1970, $27,938 in 1980, $7,275 in 1990, and only $1,000 in 2000. People today not only use computers for their work, but they communicate with others via the Internet. The personal computer and Internet technology make it possible for people to communicate with others over long distances, thus increasing the probability that they will trade with each other, such as on eBay or craigslist.

Today, even farmers in poor developing countries can have access to people and information that they didn't have access to only a few years ago. A farmer in the Ivory Coast can check agricultural prices in the world with a cell phone—something that was unheard of a decade ago. Or consider such innovations as online banking. Years ago, it was common to have your bank just down the road from you. Today, it is possible to open up an account with an online bank, many of which are located nowhere near you.

Policy Changes

Governments have the power to slow down the process of globalization if they want. Suppose two countries, A and B, have free economic relations with each other. Neither country imposes tariffs on the goods of the other. Neither country prevents its citizens from going to the other country to live and work. Neither country hampers its citizens from investing in the other country. Then, one day, for whatever reason, the government of country A decides to impose tariffs on the goods of country B and limit its citizens from traveling to and investing in country B. In other words, the government of country A decides to close its political and economic doors. Just as a government of one country can close the door on another, it can open the door too, and it can do so a little, more than a little, or a lot. In recent decades, governments of many countries have been opening their doors to other countries. China has opened its door, India has opened its door, and Russia has opened its door.

The driving forces of this most recent period of globalization have been (1) the end of the Cold War, (2) technological changes that lower the costs of transporting goods and communicating with people, and (3) government policy changes that express an openness toward freer markets and long-distance trade.

SELF-TEST

(Answers to Self-Test questions are in the Self-Test Appendix.)

1. Some have said that the end of the Cold War has led to greater globalization. Explain the reasoning.
2. What is globalization?
3. How might advancing technology lead to increased globalization?

BENEFITS AND COSTS OF GLOBALIZATION

Some people believe that globalization is, in general, a good thing and that its benefits outweigh its costs. Other people take the opposite view that the costs of globalization are greater than the benefits. Let's look at what those who favor globalization say are its benefits and what those who oppose it say are its costs. As you read, you will probably begin to form your own opinion.

The Benefits

TRADE To say that the world is undergoing globalization is really no more than saying that people are trading with more people, at greater distances, than they once did. They are trading different things: money for goods, their labor services for money, their savings for expected returns, and so on. Expanding trade—which is what globalization is about—is no more than extending the benefits of trading to people you might not have traded with earlier.

Economist David Friedman compared free international trade to a technology. He says that you can produce, say, cars in two ways. You can set up factories in Detroit, Michigan, and produce cars. Or you can harvest wheat in the Midwest, load it on ships and send it to Japan, and then wait for the ships to return with cars.

Looking at things the second way sometimes brings out the magic of trade. After all, with free trade across countries, wheat gets turned into cars, an accomplishment that really is magical. The lesson Friedman is trying to communicate is that we all think a technological improvement is a good thing because it often leads to a higher standard of living. So trading with people across the world really is nothing more than a technology of sorts; it is a way to turn wheat into cars. The more we trade with others, the more magic we witness.

INCOME PER PERSON Now let's consider the benefits of globalization in a slightly more concrete way. As both India and China opened up their economies to globalization in recent decades, they experienced increases in income per person. For example, between 1980 and 2000, income per person doubled in India. Between 1940 and 2000, income per person increased by 400 percent in China, much of this increase coming in recent years. According to the International Monetary Fund, these dramatic increases in income per person accompanied the expansion of free international trade (which is a key component of globalization).

PRICES Numerous studies have established a link between lower prices and the degree of international trade and globalization. Simply put, international trade (a key component of globalization) lowers prices. For example, Exhibit 2 shows the CPI (consumer price index) and an import price index for the period 1990–2004. The CPI (which contains domestic goods and imported goods) rose faster than the import price index (which contains only imported goods). Also, between 1977 and 2004, the inflation-adjusted prices for an array of goods traded between countries fell, while the inflation-adjusted prices for an array of goods not traded between countries actually increased. Some of the traded

exhibit 2

CPI and Import Price Index, 1990–2004

The CPI increased at a faster rate during the period 1990–2004 than the import price index (which both increased and decreased during the period).

Source: Bureau of Labor Statistics.

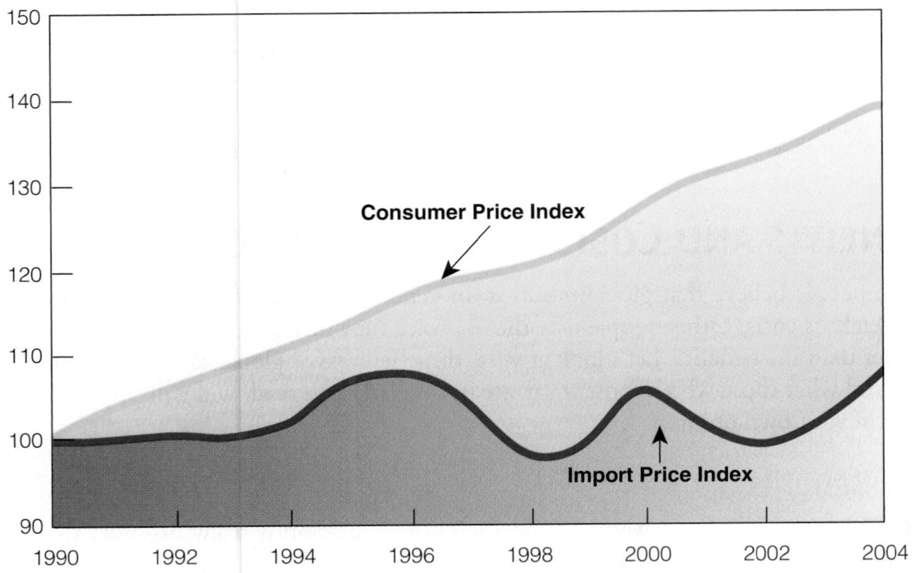

goods whose prices fell include audio equipment (26 percent), TV sets (51 percent), toys (34 percent), and clothing (9 percent); some of the nontraded goods whose prices increased include whole milk (28 percent), butter (23 percent), ice cream (18 percent), and peanut butter (9 percent).

PRODUCTIVITY AND INNOVATION Firms that face global competition are often pushed to increase their productivity and to innovate more. According to the 2006 *Economic Report of the President,* "Studies show that firms exposed to the world's best practices demonstrate higher productivity through many channels, such as learning from these best practices, and also creating new products and processes in response to this exposure." For example, one study from the United Kingdom showed that almost 3 times as many firms that faced global competition reported product or process innovations than firms that did not face global competition.

Or consider the extreme case of North and South Korea. The two countries share a people and a culture, but North Korea avoided the process of globalization during the period in which South Korea embraced it. What we observe is that South Koreans enjoy a much higher standard of living than North Koreans.

The Costs

INCREASED INCOME INEQUALITY Globalization's critics often point out that globalization seems to go hand in hand with increased income inequality between rich and poor countries in the world. In fact, income inequality has increased. For example, 100 years ago, people in rich countries had about 10 times more income than people in poor countries. Today, they have about 75 times more income. Without a doubt, globalization and income inequality are strongly correlated. The question, though, is whether globalization causes the inequality. The critics of globalization say it does, whereas the supporters say it does not.

The supporters of globalization argue that it is much like a train. Economic systems that get on the train will benefit (and reach their economic destinies faster), but those that don't will get left increasingly farther behind. In other words, it may not be globalization that delivers greater income inequality but rather a combination of some countries globalizing while others are not. (If everyone is walking, some faster than others, then some will always be in front of others. If those who are walking fast start to run while the others continue their slow walking pace, the gap between the ones in front and the ones in back will grow.)

Of course, getting on the globalization train is not always a matter of choice. Sometimes, a conductor on the train doesn't let some people on. Some rich countries work against some poor countries when it comes to the poor countries' globalization efforts. For example, tariffs on goods imported from the poor, developing world are 30 percent above the global average for all tariffs.

LOSING AMERICAN JOBS Many critics of globalization argue that globalization can result in Americans losing certain jobs. Suppose a U.S. company hires engineers in India to do jobs once done by Americans. This practice of hiring people in other countries is often called **offshoring**.

Offshoring
Work done for a company by persons other than the original company's employees in a country other than the one in which the company is located.

Some Americans may lose their jobs to workers in other countries due to globalization. It has already happened. Over the past few years, a major New York securities firm replaced its team of 800 American software engineers, who earned about $150,000 per year, with an equally competent team in India earning an average of about $20,000 a year. Additionally, the number of radiologists in the United States is expected to fall significantly because it is now possible to send the data (that U.S. radiologists analyze) over the Internet to Asian radiologists, who can analyze the data at a fraction of the cost.

Keep in mind, though, that offshoring is a two-way street: The United States might offshore certain jobs to, say, India or China, but foreign countries around the world offshore jobs to the United States too. Although some Americans lose jobs due to globalization efforts, jobs are always being lost (and found) in a dynamic economy that is responding to market changes. Even if the degree of offshoring in the United States were zero, people would still be losing old jobs and getting new jobs every day.

MORE POWER TO BIG CORPORATIONS Many critics of globalization argue that the process will simply hand over the world (and especially the developing countries) to large Western corporations (headquartered in the United States, the United Kingdom, Canada, etc.). In fact, in the minds of many people, globalization is not defined as in this chapter, but rather as the process of *corporatizing* the world. Instead of governments deciding what will and will not be done, large corporations will assume the responsibility.

The proponents of globalization often point out a major difference between a corporation and a government. First, a government can force people to do certain things (such as pay taxes or join the military). No corporation can do the same; instead, corporations can simply produce goods that they hope customers will buy. Additionally, the proponents of globalization often argue that the critics overestimate the influence and reach of large transnational companies. For example, in 2000, the top 100 transnational companies produced only 4.3 percent of the entire world's output, which is about as much as what one country, the United Kingdom, produced in 2000.

Common MISCONCEPTIONS

About Offshoring

Some people talk as if globalization is only about offshoring. In other words, with globalization, jobs leave the United States for other countries. However, globalization involves not only offshoring, but *inshoring* too. As an example, a foreign country sets up an operation in the United States and employs Americans. By one estimate, in 2004, the United States had outsourced 10 million jobs, but it had insourced 6.5 million jobs.

economics 24/7

WILL GLOBALIZATION CHANGE THE SOUND OF MUSIC?

Suppose you had only 100 people to whom you could sell a good. Given this small number, you had better sell something that some of the 100 people want to buy. For example, if the 100 people don't like fruit salad, then you better not produce and offer to sell fruit salad; if some of them like bread, then perhaps you should produce and offer to sell bread.

Now increase the number of people from 100 to 1 million. A group of 1 million is much more likely than a group of 100 to contain people who like fruit salad. In other words, as the size of the potential customer base increases, the number of things you can sell increases too. In a world of 100 people, you can sell only bread, but in a world of 1 million people, you can sell fruit salad or bread.

The point is simple: The larger the size of the potential customer base (the more people you can possibly sell to), the greater the variety of goods is likely to be. Globalization is, to a large degree, expanding everyone's ability to potentially sell to more people. American companies aren't limited to selling only to Americans; they can sell to others in the world too. Chinese firms aren't limited to selling only to Chinese; they can sell to others in the world too.

As a musician, you can play different styles of music: jazz, pop, classical, hard rock, metal, hip-hop, and so on. If you are limited to selling your music to the people of a single state of the United States, you can offer to sell fewer styles of music than if you could sell your music to the people who reside throughout the United States.

More specifically, consider the musician in the United States who is experimenting with a new style of music. With a population (305 million) of only the United States as a potential customer base, the musician might not yet have enough actual customers to make it worth producing and offering to sell this particular, unique, and narrowly defined music. However, if the musician can draw on the population of the world (6.6 billion), then she might be able to find enough people who are willing to buy her new type of music.

As we move toward a world economy, we see a greater variety within almost every category of goods: a greater variety of music to listen to, books to read, types of television shows to watch, and so on. Today, the greater variety of goods you see in your world is an effect of globalization.

The Continuing Globalization Debate

Many (but certainly not all) economists argue that the worldwide benefits of globalization are likely to be greater than the worldwide costs. Of course, not everyone is going to see the beneficial side of globalization. To a large degree, whether people support or criticize globalization seems to depend on where they are sitting. Globalization doesn't affect everyone in the same way, and often *how* it affects *you* determines how you feel about it. For example, suppose Sanders, an American worker residing in New York, loses his job to an Indian worker in New Delhi, India, who will do Sanders' job for less pay. In this case, Sanders incurs real costs, but for Sanders' company, the change means lower costs and higher profits. For the company's customers, the change might mean lower prices. So in this case, Sanders is probably a strong opponent of offshoring, but his company and its customers are probably supporters.

Seeing the benefits of globalization is often much more difficult than seeing its costs. For example, the supporters of globalization argue that it brings greater economic wealth, lower prices (than would otherwise exist), more innovation, less poverty, and so on. Yet seeing all these benefits is sometimes difficult. When you buy cheaper goods or different goods because of globalization, you probably never say, "Wow, I can't believe all the benefits I get from globalization!" In fact, you might not even connect the lower-priced goods with globalization at all. The benefits of globalization tend to be difficult to perceive, partly because they are so widely dispersed.

The costs of globalization, in contrast, are more visible, often because they are so concentrated. A person who loses a job because of freer international trade in the world knows exactly what is to blame for his predicament. He surely could receive some benefits from globalization (in the role of a consumer), but he also could, for a time, incur some rather high costs (in the role of an unemployed worker). This person is likely to know of the costs but be unaware of the benefits.

In the end, the people who receive only benefits from globalization might not be able to see the benefits or to connect them with globalization. The people who receive benefits and costs from globalization may be aware only of the costs. This one-sided view could create strong antiglobalization sentiment in a country.

More or Less Globalization: A Tug of War?

Is increased globalization inevitable? Will the day come when all countries in the world are similar to the 50 states in the United States—part of one global economy with easy movement of people, resources, financial capital, goods, and services among the countries? Or will the conditions that prevented globalization reappear and reverse the recent trend?

Think of this struggle as a tug of war. The forces of globalization pull in one direction, and the forces of antiglobalization pull in the other. As of today, the forces of globalization are moving things in their direction. The trend may not continue uninterrupted. Surely, at any time, the forces of antiglobalization could put on a burst of energy and make an extra strong tug on the rope.

To help answer the question about the future of globalization, recall what we said about the driving forces of the most recent era of globalization: the end of the Cold War, changes in technology (which lowered the costs of transportation and communication), and policy changes that opened up countries' economies to each other.

Less Globalization

INCREASED POLITICAL TENSION The end of the Cold War is a historical fact that we cannot undo, but we could enter a period when political tensions among countries or among groups of countries emerge. We are not suggesting that such a period of tension will happen, only that it could. If it did, it could slow down globalization or, depending on the severity of the tension, even reverse it.

Terrorism Another inhibiting factor to globalization is global terrorism. Global terrorism tends to motivate certain countries into closing borders and into being much more careful about the people and goods crossing their borders.

Technology We cannot undo our technology. We cannot go from a world with the Internet to one without it. So it is unlikely that anything on the technological front will slow down or reverse globalization.

Government Policies Policy changes can slow down or reverse globalization. Governments of countries that opened up their economies to others could reverse their course; doors that opened to others can be closed. We cannot say whether this sort of isolationism will happen in the future.

More Globalization

Some still argue that, even with the forces of antiglobalization looming on the horizon, the forces of globalization are stronger. In the end, these individuals say, the forces of globalization will win the tug of war. They believe that in the long run, economics influences politics, not the other way around. As some proof of that assertion, they often point to the former Soviet Union and to China. Both were strongly communist countries. Both countries saw, in the end, that they were worse off by holding themselves outside the orbit of free market forces. You might say that they found themselves out of step with the economic forces that were loudly playing on the world stage.

Many economists argue that globalization is not just a passing trend. They argue that the basic globalization force that will probably not be overcome—no matter how strong the political forces may be against it—is the human inclination that the founder of modern economics, Adam Smith, noticed more than 200 years ago. Smith said that human beings want to trade with each other. In fact, the desire to trade separates us from all other species, he says. In his words, "Man is an animal that makes bargains: no other animal does this—no dog exchanges bones with another."

We want to trade with people: our next-door neighbor, the person down the street, the person on the other side of town, the person in the next state, the person on the other side of the country, and ultimately the person on the other side of the world. Some economists go on to suggest that our trading inclination is a good thing in that, when we trade with people, we not only tolerate them but we have much less reason to fight with them. Robert Wright, a visiting scholar at the University of Pennsylvania, argues that it is not a coincidence that religious toleration is high in the United States, a country that is open to trade and globalization. We often see, he argues, that people who live in countries that trade with other people—people who live in countries that are open to other people—are people who tolerate others.

In a similar vein, Thomas Friedman advanced his "Golden Arches theory of conflict prevention," which says that "no two countries that both had McDonald's had fought a war against each other since each got its McDonald's." The United States will not fight Germany because both countries have McDonald's. France won't fight Mexico because both countries have McDonald's. Certainly, it is not the sheer presence of a McDonald's that prevents people from fighting with other people. McDonald's is symbolic of certain things being present in the country. For Friedman, the franchise is a symbol for a certain degree of economic globalization and a level of economic development sufficient enough to support a large middle class.

SELF-TEST

1. Identify some of the benefits of globalization.
2. Identify some of the costs of globalization.

INTERNATIONAL FACTORS AND AGGREGATE DEMAND

In a world that is undergoing globalization, what happens in one country can affect events in another country. Simply put, changes in other countries can influence the U.S. economy. In this first section we discuss two international factors that can affect the U.S. economy by first affecting U.S. aggregate demand: net exports and the J-curve.

Net Exports

In an earlier chapter, net exports are defined as the difference between exports (*EX*) and imports (*IM*). For example, if exports are $80 billion and imports are $60 billion, then net exports are $20 billion. Also, recall that if net exports rise, the *AD* curve shifts to the right; if net exports fall, the *AD* curve shifts to the left.

Now we discuss two factors that can change net exports: (1) foreign Real GDP and (2) the exchange rate. To simplify matters, we assume there are only two countries in the world: the United States and Japan. With respect to these two countries, let's consider the two factors.

FOREIGN REAL GDP (OR FOREIGN REAL NATIONAL INCOME) As Japan's Real GDP (or real national income) rises, the Japanese buy more U.S. goods; so U.S. exports rise. As a result, U.S. net exports rise, and the *AD* curve shifts to the right. As Japan's Real GDP falls, the Japanese buy fewer U.S. goods; so U.S. exports fall. As a result, U.S. net exports fall, and the *AD* curve shifts to the left.

This is how economic expansions and contractions in other countries are felt in the United States. Given a contraction in Japan, with a lower Real GDP in Japan, the Japanese buy fewer U.S. goods. U.S. exports fall, and so do net exports. As a result, the *AD* curve in the United States shifts to the left. Because the *AD* curve shifts to the left, Real GDP in the United States falls.

EXCHANGE RATE Recall that the exchange rate is the price of one country's currency in terms of another country's currency. If a country's currency *appreciates*, it takes less of that country's currency to buy the other currency. On the other hand, if a country's currency *depreciates*, it takes more of that country's country to buy the other currency.

Appreciation and depreciation affect the prices of a country's goods. If, say, the U.S. dollar depreciates relative to the Japanese yen, U.S. residents have to pay more dollars to buy Japanese goods. To illustrate, suppose the dollar price of a yen is $0.012 and that a Toyota is priced at ¥2 million. At this exchange rate, a U.S. resident pays $24,000 for a Toyota ($0.012 × ¥20 million = $24,000). If the dollar depreciates to $0.018 for ¥1, then the U.S. resident will have to pay $36,000 for a Toyota.

As the dollar depreciates, Japanese goods become more expensive for U.S. residents; so they buy fewer Japanese goods. Thus, U.S. imports decline.[2] The other side of the coin is that, as the dollar depreciates relative to the yen, the yen appreciates relative to the dollar. Thus U.S. goods become less expensive for the Japanese, and they buy more U.S. goods; so U.S. exports rise.

In summary, a depreciation in the dollar and an appreciation in the yen will raise U.S. exports, lower U.S. imports, and therefore raise U.S. net exports. This shifts the U.S. *AD* curve to the right, leading to a rise in the U.S. Real GDP level.

The series of events are symmetrical if the U.S. dollar appreciates relative to the Japanese yen. In this case, U.S. goods become more expensive for the Japanese, causing them to buy fewer U.S. goods; so U.S. exports fall. And Japanese goods become cheaper for U.S. residents, causing them to buy more Japanese goods; so U.S. imports rise. A decline in U.S. exports, along with a rise in U.S. imports, will cause U.S. net exports to fall. The U.S. *AD* curve shifts to the left, leading to a decline in U.S. Real GDP.

For a quick review of the international factors that can shift the U.S. *AD* curve, see Exhibit 3.

The J-Curve

So far, we have assumed that if the dollar depreciates relative to the Japanese yen, U.S. residents and the Japanese will buy more U.S. goods and fewer Japanese goods. Thus, U.S. exports rise, U.S. imports fall, and therefore U.S. net exports rise.

2. Throughout this chapter, unless otherwise explicitly stated, we assume that if the physical quantity of exports rises (falls), the total spending on exports rises (falls). Also, if the physical quantity of imports rises (falls), the total spending on imports rises (falls). Because of this assumption, it is not necessary to differentiate constantly between the physical quantity of imports and the total spending on imports. Given our assumption, they go up and down together. One place we explicitly drop this assumption is in the discussion of the J-curve.

economics 24/7

HOW HARD WILL IT BE TO GET INTO HARVARD IN 2025?

The Indian Institute of Technology (in India) is one of the hardest universities in the world to be admitted to, largely because of its reputation. It has been compared to putting Harvard, MIT (Massachusetts Institute of Technology), and Princeton together.

© INDEX STOCK IMAGERY/JUPITER IMAGES

In an average year, about 178,000 high school seniors in India take the exam necessary to apply to the Indian Institute of Technology. Just over 3,500 students (only 1.96 percent of all applicants) are admitted. In comparison, the admission rate of Harvard University is nearly 10 percent. Often, students from India who are admitted to MIT, Princeton, and Cal Tech (all of which are listed in the top 10 of U.S. colleges and universities) cannot gain admission to the Indian Institute of Technology.

Other highly prestigious U.S. universities and colleges—such as Brown, Columbia, Cornell, Dartmouth, Harvard, the University of Pennsylvania, Princeton, Yale, Stanford, Northwestern, and Duke—have some of the most selective admission criteria of all colleges and universities in the country. Each year, students who have the grade point average and standardized test scores to be considered for admission are turned away.

This phenomenon has been occurring at the same time that college tuition in this country has been increasing rapidly. For example, during the period 1990–2003, college tuition went up by 130 percent, considerably more than medical care costs, the price of housing, food, gasoline, cars, and so on.

If we look around the world at other prestigious institutions of higher learning, we see the same theme: The admission rate is usually low, and the cost is usually high.

Consider how grades (one major criterion) and money actually function in admissions: They are rationing devices. We know that because of scarcity, some mechanism has to ration the available resources, goods, and services. Still we have to ask why these two rationing devices—grades and money—have become stiffer when it comes to being admitted to the top universities in the world. Why must grades be ever higher and ever more money required?

The answer is twofold. First, the population of the world increased while the number of Harvards did not. Harvard cannot clone itself; nor can Yale, the Indian Institute of Technology, or MIT. To a large degree, the world has only one Harvard, Oxford (in the United Kingdom), and Indian Institute of Technology. We can produce more computers, houses, and dining room chairs as the population of the world increases, but producing more Harvards seems to be much more difficult. So, over time, top-notch, one-of-a-kind educational institutions become scarce. As a result, the rationing devices for such institutions must do more work to ration, and it will become harder and more expensive to get admitted to such places.

The second reason involves globalization. One of things that pays a high dividend in a global economy is education. Brains seem to matter more than brawn, increasing the overall demand for a college education—not just at Harvard but at all levels of higher education (from community colleges to four-year state and private universities). So, will the premium placed on education in a global economy cause the demand at the most prestigious educational establishments to rise at a faster rate than at other colleges? That question is like asking, if the premium for playing music were to rise, would the demand to be at Juilliard (one of the premier music institutions in the world) rise faster than the demand to study with the local piano teacher down the street? The likely answer is yes. With a growing world population, and with the global economy paying a high premium to those who are educated (compared to those who are not), we can expect it to get increasingly difficult and more expensive to be admitted to the world's best institutions of higher learning.

But this scenario may not happen initially. There may be a difference between what *initially* happens and what *ultimately* happens. To illustrate, suppose U.S. residents are currently buying 100,000 cars from the Japanese, the average Japanese car sells for ¥2 million, and the exchange rate is currently \$0.012 per yen. This means U.S. residents are

exhibit 3

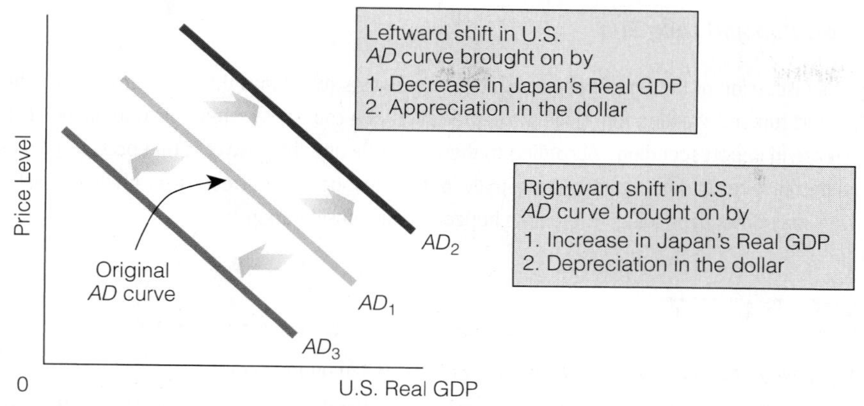

International Impacts on the U.S. *AD* Curve

Anything that increases U.S. net exports shifts the U.S. *AD* curve to the right. This includes an increase in Japan's Real GDP (in a two-country world, where the two countries are Japan and the United States) and a depreciation in the dollar. Anything that decreases U.S. net exports shifts the U.S. *AD* curve to the left. This includes a decrease in Japan's Real GDP and an appreciation in the dollar.

spending an average of $24,000 a car for 100,000 cars. Thus, a total of $2.4 billion is spent on imported Japanese cars.

Now suppose the exchange rate changes, and the dollar depreciates to $0.018 per yen, causing the average price of a Japanese car to be $36,000. At this higher price, U.S. residents buy fewer Japanese cars, but they don't buy that many fewer initially. Instead of buying 100,000 cars, they initially buy 90,000 cars. Now a total of $3.24 billion is spent on imported Japanese cars. Instead of declining after a depreciation in the dollar, U.S. spending on imports has initially risen. If we assume U.S. exports have not changed yet, a rise in U.S. imports will lead to a fall in U.S. net exports and cause the U.S. *AD* curve to shift to the left.

But this situation is not likely to last. In time, U.S. residents will switch from the higher-priced Japanese goods to lower-priced U.S. goods. For example, in time, U.S. residents purchase only 60,000 Japanese cars. At this number, with the exchange rate of $0.018 per yen, U.S. spending on imported Japanese cars is $2.16 billion. In time, too, U.S. exports will rise, and the combination of rising exports and falling imports will lead to an increase in net exports. The U.S. *AD* curve will shift to the right.

exhibit 4

The J-Curve

The United States starts with net exports of –$40 billion. As the dollar depreciates, net exports increase to –$60 billion. With time, net exports become $0. If we follow the course of net exports, we map out a J. This is called the J-curve.

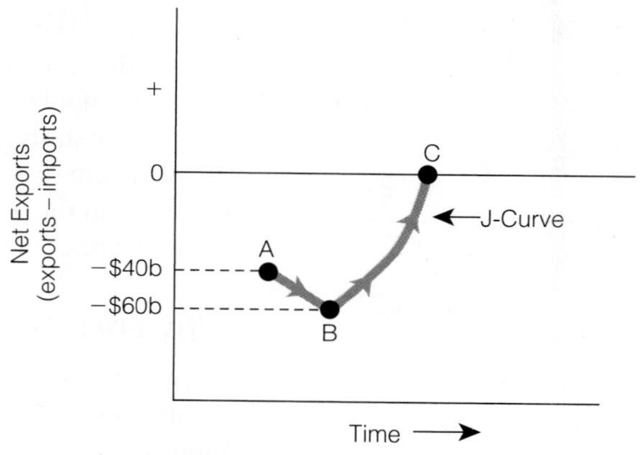

This phenomenon in which import spending initially rises after a depreciation and then later falls is summarized in the **J-curve**, so-called because a curve showing the change in net exports due to a currency depreciation has the shape of a J. In Exhibit 4, the United States initially has negative net exports of –$40 billion (its imports of $130 billion are greater than its exports of $90 billion). This position is represented by point A in the exhibit.

J-Curve
The curve that shows a short-run worsening in net exports after a currency depreciation, followed by an improvement.

Next, the dollar depreciates relative to the yen. Total spending on imports rises to, say, $150 billion; so net exports rise to –$60 billion. This is represented by point B. In time, though, exports rise to, say, $100 billion and imports fall to, say, $100 billion, making net exports equal to zero. This is represented by point C.

If we start at point A and draw a line to point B and then to point C, we have a J-curve. This is the route that net exports may take after a depreciation in a country's currency.

Thinking like AN ECONOMIST

Short Run and Long Run

The discussion of the J-curve points out that economists sometimes think in terms of both the short run and the long run. Does the depreciation of a country's currency lead to an increase or a decrease in import spending? According to the J-curve theory, the answer is that both an increase and a decrease result. Imports increase initially, but in the long run they decrease. An economist's answers may differ depending on the time horizon under consideration.

SELF-TEST

1. Explain how an economic boom in one country can be felt in another country.
2. Predict and explain what will happen to U.S. Real GDP if the dollar appreciates relative to the Japanese yen.

INTERNATIONAL FACTORS AND AGGREGATE SUPPLY

Just as international factors can affect the demand side of the U.S. economy, certain international factors can affect the supply side. This section discusses a few international factors that can shift the U.S. aggregate supply curve.

Foreign Input Prices

In an earlier chapter, we stated that a change in the price of inputs will shift the short-run aggregate supply (*SRAS*) curve. For example, if the price of labor (wage rate) rises, the *SRAS* curve shifts leftward.

American producers buy inputs not only from other Americans but also from foreigners. A rise in the price of foreign inputs leads to a leftward shift in the U.S. *SRAS* curve. A fall in the price of foreign inputs leads to a rightward shift in the U.S. *SRAS* curve.

Why Foreign Input Prices Change

Supply and demand in the input market in the foreign country could change, possibly causing a rise in the price of foreign inputs. For example, suppose U.S. producers buy input X from Japan. The supply of X in Japan could fall, or the demand for X in Japan could rise. Either or both changes would increase the price of X for U.S. producers.

THE EXCHANGE RATE A change in the exchange rate between the dollar and the yen could change the price for a foreign input. For example, a depreciation in the dollar relative to the yen would make input X more expensive for U.S. producers. An appreciation in the dollar would make input X less expensive for U.S. producers. Exhibit 5 presents a summary of the points in this section.

FACTORS THAT AFFECT BOTH AGGREGATE DEMAND AND AGGREGATE SUPPLY

Changes in some international factors can affect both aggregate demand and short-run aggregate supply in the United States. Two of these factors are the exchange rate and relative interest rates.

exhibit 5

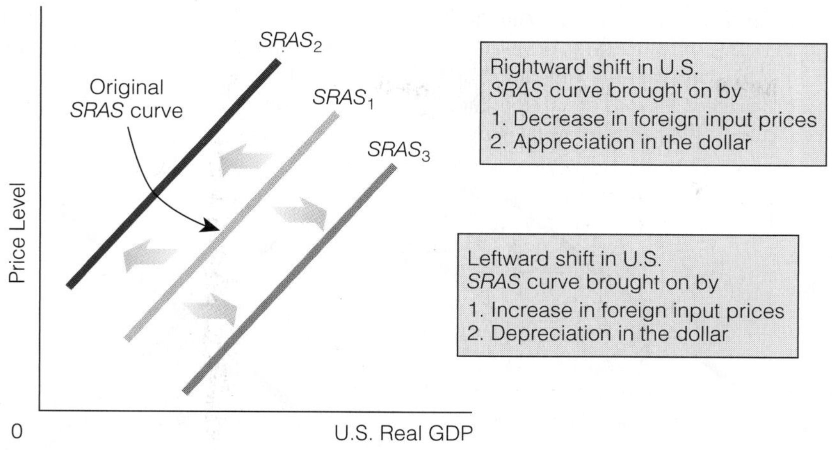

International Impacts on the U.S. *SRAS* Curve

The U.S. *SRAS* curve shifts if foreign input prices change. If foreign input prices rise, the U.S. *SRAS* curve shifts leftward; if foreign input prices fall, the *SRAS* curve shifts rightward. Similarly, if the dollar depreciates, foreign inputs become more expensive and the *SRAS* curve shifts leftward. If the dollar appreciates, foreign inputs become cheaper and the *SRAS* curve shifts rightward.

The Exchange Rate

As discussed, changes in exchange rates affect both the *AD* and *SRAS* curves. The overall, or net, effect on Real GDP depends on how much the *AD* curve shifts relative to the shift in the *SRAS* curve. We consider two cases: dollar depreciation and dollar appreciation.

DOLLAR DEPRECIATION As the dollar depreciates, the *AD* curve shifts rightward and the *SRAS* curve leftward. If the *AD* curve shifts rightward by more than the *SRAS* curve shifts leftward, Real GDP rises [see Exhibit 6(a)]. If the *AD* curve shifts rightward by less than the SRAS curve shifts leftward, Real GDP falls [see Exhibit 6(b)]. If the *AD* curve shifts rightward by the same amount that the *SRAS* curve shifts leftward, Real GDP does not change [see Exhibit 6(c)]. In each of these three cases, the price level rises. In summary, dollar depreciation raises the price level and may accompany an increasing, decreasing, or constant Real GDP.

DOLLAR APPRECIATION As the dollar appreciates, the *AD* curve shifts leftward and the *SRAS* curve rightward. Once again, what happens to Real GDP depends on the relative shifts of the two curves. If the *AD* curve shifts leftward by more than the *SRAS* curve shifts rightward, Real GDP falls. If the *AD* curve shifts leftward by less than the *SRAS* curve shifts rightward, Real GDP rises. If the *AD* curve shifts leftward by the same amount that the *SRAS* curve shifts rightward, Real GDP does not change. In each case, though, the price level falls. In summary, dollar appreciation lowers the price level and may accompany an increasing, decreasing, or constant Real GDP.

The Role That Interest Rates Play

In a two-country world with only the United States and Japan, real interest rates rise in the United States and remain constant in Japan. The higher real interest rates in the United States will attract foreign capital (in search of the highest return possible). Because foreigners will be interested in dollar-denominated assets that pay interest, they will have to exchange their country's currency for U.S. dollars. This will increase the demand for U.S. dollars and lead to an appreciation in the dollar.

Then, if the dollar appreciates, we know that both the U.S. *AD* and *SRAS* curves are affected. The *AD* curve shifts leftward and the *SRAS* curve shifts rightward. As explained earlier, the effect on Real GDP depends on the relative shifts in the two curves. Many

exhibit 6

Depreciation in the Dollar: Effects on the Price Level and Real GDP

A change in exchange rates affects both aggregate demand and short-run aggregate supply. If the dollar depreciates, the *AD* curve shifts rightward and the *SRAS* curve shifts leftward. The overall impact on Real GDP—up, down, or unchanged—depends on whether the *AD* curve shifts rightward by (a) more, (b) less, or (c) an amount equal to the leftward shift in the *SRAS* curve. In all three cases, dollar depreciation leads to a higher price level.

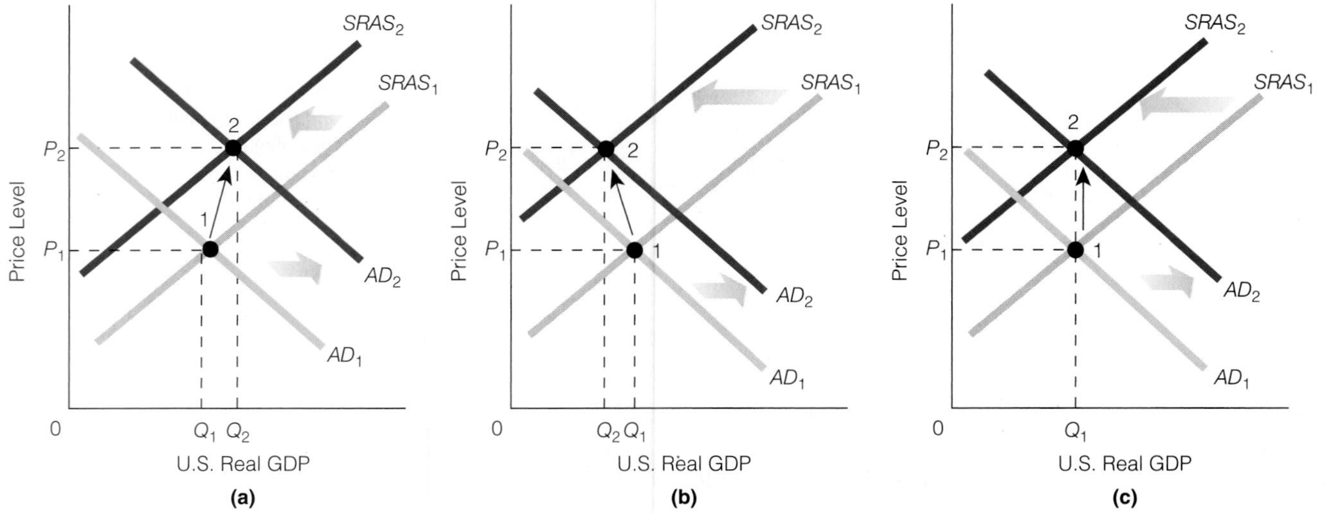

economists argue, however, that given the interest rate differential, the *AD* curve typically tends to shift leftward by more than the *SRAS* curve shifts rightward, and thus Real GDP falls [see Exhibit 7(a)]. In summary, typically, a rise in real interest rates in the United States relative to foreign interest rates tends to decrease U.S. Real GDP.

Now suppose real interest rates fall in the United States relative to interest rates in Japan. The higher real interest rate in Japan attracts capital to Japan. The demand for yen rises, and as a result the yen appreciates and the dollar depreciates. A depreciated dollar shifts the U.S. *AD* curve rightward and the *SRAS* curve leftward [see Exhibit 7(b)]. Many economists argue that given the interest rate differential discussed here, the *AD* curve typically tends to shift rightward by more than the *SRAS* curve shifts leftward, and thus Real GDP rises. In summary, typically a fall in real interest rates in the United States relative to foreign interest rates tends to increase U.S. Real GDP.

SELF-TEST

1. How do foreign input prices affect the U.S. *SRAS* curve?
2. What is the effect on the U.S. price level of lower real interest rates in Japan than in the United States? Explain your answer.

Deficits: International Effects and Domestic Feedback

Deficits in the United States—both budget and trade deficits—affect the U.S. economy. Earlier chapters explored how the budget deficit can directly affect the U.S. economy. However, the budget deficit can also have international effects, and these international effects can have domestic feedback that also affects the U.S. economy. This section looks

exhibit 7

International Interest Rates, Exchange Rates, and Real GDP

(a) If the U.S. real interest rate is higher than the Japanese real interest rate, capital will flow from Japan to the United States. In the process, the demand for the dollar rises, and the dollar appreciates. Dollar appreciation causes the *AD* curve to shift leftward by more than the *SRAS* curve shifts rightward, which is typical given the initial event. As a result, U.S. Real GDP falls. (b) If the U.S. real interest rate is lower than the Japanese real interest rate, capital will flow from the United States to Japan. In the process, the demand for yen rises, the supply of dollars rises, and the yen appreciates and the dollar depreciates. Dollar depreciation causes the *AD* curve to shift rightward and the *SRAS* curve to shift leftward. We have drawn the *AD* curve shifting rightward by more than the *SRAS* curve shifts leftward, which is typical given the initial event. As a result, U.S. Real GDP rises.

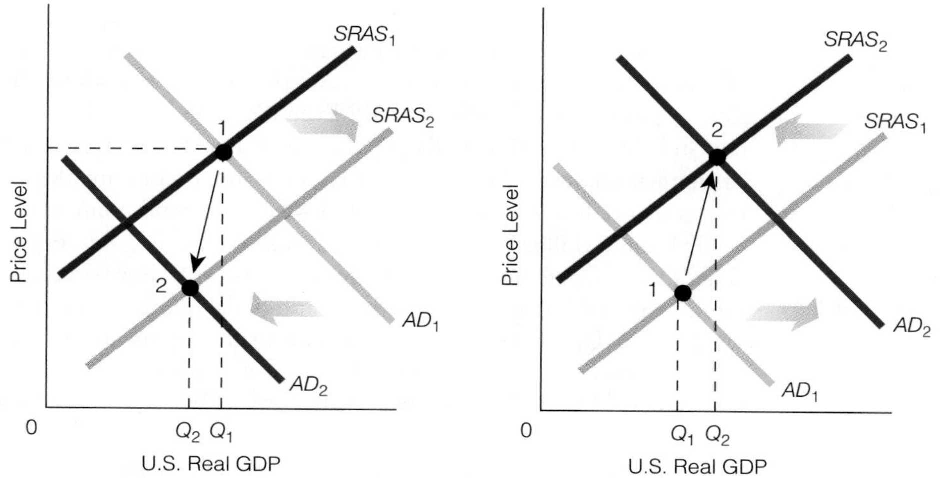

(a)
Higher Real Interest Rates in the United States

(b)
Lower Real Interest Rates in the United States

at the possibilities of international feedback effects and the relationship between the budget deficit and the trade deficit.

The Budget Deficit and Expansionary Fiscal Policy

Suppose North Dakotans want their elected representatives in Congress to push for a particular spending program that will assist them and no one else—and their elected representatives oblige them. Congress passes the spending program but does not raise the taxes necessary to pay for it. This domestic action can affect the international economic scene, and here is a scenario to show how.

Even with a budget deficit, Congress passes the spending program to help North Dakotans but neither raises taxes to finance the program nor cuts any other spending programs on the books. As a result of these actions—one more spending program, no fewer spending programs, and no more taxes—the budget deficit grows. To finance the growing budget deficit, the U.S. Treasury borrows more funds in the credit (or loanable funds) market than it would have borrowed if the latest spending program had not been passed. The increased demand for credit raises the real interest rate. The higher U.S. interest rate attracts foreign capital. The demand for dollars in the foreign exchange market rises, and the dollar appreciates.

As this happens, the U.S. *AD* curve shifts leftward, and the *SRAS* curve shifts rightward. The *AD* curve shifts leftward by more than the *SRAS* shifts rightward, putting downward pressure on Real GDP.

But Real GDP might not *actually* decrease. We have discussed only how a rising budget deficit affects the exchange rate (via the interest rate) and feeds back in the domestic economy. The direct effect of the rising budget deficit on the domestic economy also needs to be considered. Under certain conditions (e.g., zero crowding out), expansionary fiscal policy can raise aggregate demand and is effective at raising Real GDP. So:

1. The rising budget deficit affects the domestic economy directly and pushes *Real GDP upward.*
2. But increased deficit financing raises U.S. interest rates and prompts increased foreign capital inflows, an increased demand for dollars, and dollar appreciation. Under typical conditions, an appreciated dollar feeds back into the domestic economy and pushes *Real GDP downward.*

Obviously, what happens *on net* depends on how strong the international feedback effects are on the domestic economy. Are they strong enough to offset the initial expansionary push (upward) in Real GDP? Even if not, and Real GDP rises on net, we can still conclude that expansionary fiscal policy raises Real GDP more in a **closed economy** than in an **open economy**. The reason is that, in a closed economy, the international feedback effects that reduce Real GDP are absent (see the second point in the preceding list).

Closed Economy
An economy that does not trade goods and services with other countries.

Open Economy
An economy that trades goods and services with other countries.

Exhibit 8(a) illustrates the point. With zero crowding out, expansionary fiscal policy shifts the aggregate demand curve from AD_1 to AD_2. But because of the higher interest rates, increased foreign capital inflows, and dollar appreciation, the *AD* curve shifts leftward from AD_2 to AD_3, and the *SRAS* curve shifts rightward from $SRAS_1$ to $SRAS_2$.

In a closed economy, Real GDP rises from Q_1 to Q_2. In an open economy, where international feedback effects play a role, Real GDP ends up at a lower level, Q_3.

The Budget Deficit and Contractionary Fiscal Policy

If expansionary fiscal policy raises Real GDP more in a closed economy than in an open economy, what are the effects of contractionary fiscal policy in a closed or open economy? Suppose reduced government spending decreases the budget deficit. With a diminished budget deficit, the U.S. Treasury borrows fewer funds in the credit market than it would have borrowed if government spending had not been reduced. The decreased demand for loanable funds lowers the real interest rate (relative to foreign interest rates), making foreign assets seem more desirable. The demand for foreign currencies increases, and the dollar depreciates in value.

As this happens, the U.S. *AD* curve shifts to the right, and the *SRAS* curve shifts to the left. The *AD* curve shifts rightward by more than the *SRAS* curve shifts leftward, putting upward pressure on Real GDP. However, Real GDP might not *actually* increase because we haven't yet considered the effect of the lower budget deficit (due to the reduction in government spending) on the domestic economy. Under certain conditions, a cut in government spending reduces aggregate demand and therefore reduces Real GDP. So:

1. The cut in government spending reduces the budget deficit and affects the domestic economy directly, pushing *Real GDP downward.*
2. But reduced deficit financing lowers U.S. interest rates and prompts increased capital outflows, increased demand for foreign currencies, and dollar depreciation. Under typical conditions, a depreciated dollar feeds back into the domestic economy and pushes *Real GDP upward.*

What happens *on net* depends on whether the international feedback effects on the domestic economy are strong enough to offset the initial contractionary push in Real GDP.

Even if the international feedback effects on the domestic economy do not outweigh the initial contractionary push (downward) in Real GDP, and Real GDP falls on net, we can still conclude that contractionary fiscal policy lowers Real GDP more in a closed economy than in an open economy.

exhibit 8

Expansionary and Contractionary Fiscal Policy in Open and Closed Economies

(a) The consequences of expansionary fiscal policy for both open and closed economies. Congress passes a spending program without raising taxes, and the *AD* curve shifts from AD_1 to AD_2. To finance the growing budget deficit, the Treasury borrows more funds in the loanable funds market, and the interest rate rises. The higher interest rate attracts foreign capital and causes the dollar to appreciate. As the dollar appreciates, the *AD* curve shifts from AD_2 to AD_3, and the *SRAS* curve shifts from $SRAS_1$ to $SRAS_2$. Real GDP goes from Q_1 to Q_2 in a closed economy, and from Q_1 to Q_3 in an open economy. Expansionary fiscal policy raises Real GDP more in a closed economy than in an open economy. (b) Contractionary fiscal policy lowers Real GDP more in a closed economy than in an open economy.

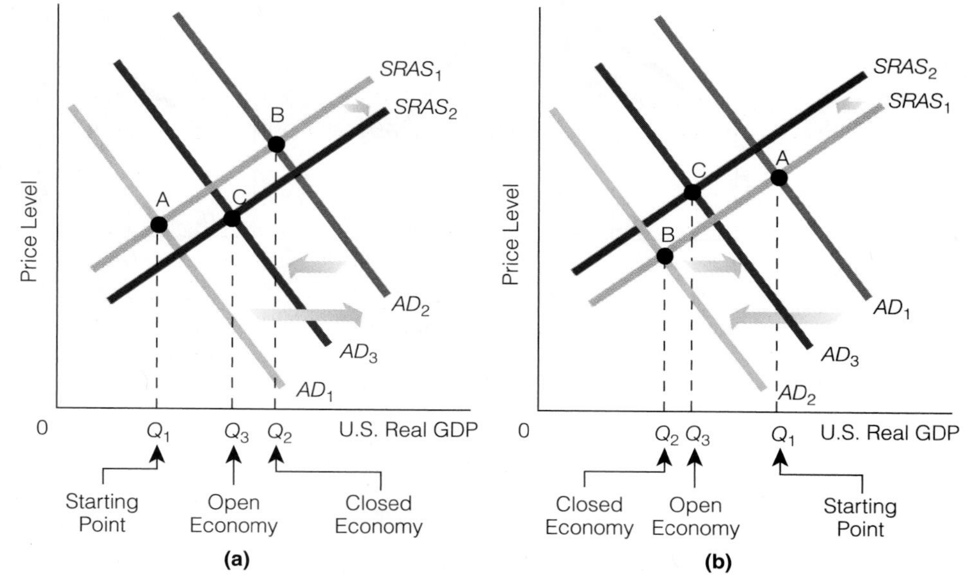

Exhibit 8(b) illustrates our point. The cut in government spending shifts the *AD* curve from AD_1 to AD_2. But because of the lower interest rates, increased capital outflows, and dollar depreciation, the *AD* curve shifts rightward from AD_2 to AD_3, and the *SRAS* curve shifts leftward from $SRAS_1$ to $SRAS_2$.

In a closed economy, Real GDP falls from Q_1 to Q_2. In an open economy, where international feedback effects play a role, Real GDP ends up at a higher level, Q_3.

The Effects of Monetary Policy

Monetary policy certainly affects international economic factors that feed back to the United States. Here we consider both expansionary and contractionary monetary policy.

EXPANSIONARY MONETARY POLICY Suppose the Federal Reserve increases the money supply. In Exhibit 9(a), the increase causes the *AD* curve to shift rightward from AD_1 to AD_2 and Real GDP to rise from Q_1 to Q_2.

An increase in the money supply also has international effects. Expansionary monetary policy causes interest rates to fall in the short run (the liquidity effect), leading to an outflow of capital from the United States. Americans begin to supply more dollars on the foreign exchange market so that they can purchase foreign assets. As the supply of dollars rises, the dollar depreciates.

Dollar depreciation affects both U.S. aggregate demand and U.S. short-run aggregate supply. As noted, it shifts the *AD* curve to the right and the *SRAS* curve to the left. In

exhibit 9

Expansionary and Contractionary Monetary Policy in Open and Closed Economies

(a) The consequences of expansionary monetary policy for both open and closed economies. The Fed increases the money supply, and the *AD* curve shifts from AD_1 to AD_2. Real GDP rises from Q_1 to Q_2. The increased money supply leads to lower interest rates in the short run, promoting U.S. capital outflow and a depreciated dollar, which raises U.S. exports, lowers U.S. imports, and raises U.S. net exports. Higher net exports shift the *AD* curve rightward from AD_2 to AD_3. The depreciated dollar shifts the *SRAS* curve leftward from $SRAS_1$ to $SRAS_2$. Real GDP ends up at Q_3. Expansionary monetary policy raises Real GDP more in an open economy than in a closed economy. (b) Contractionary monetary policy lowers Real GDP more in an open economy than in a closed economy.

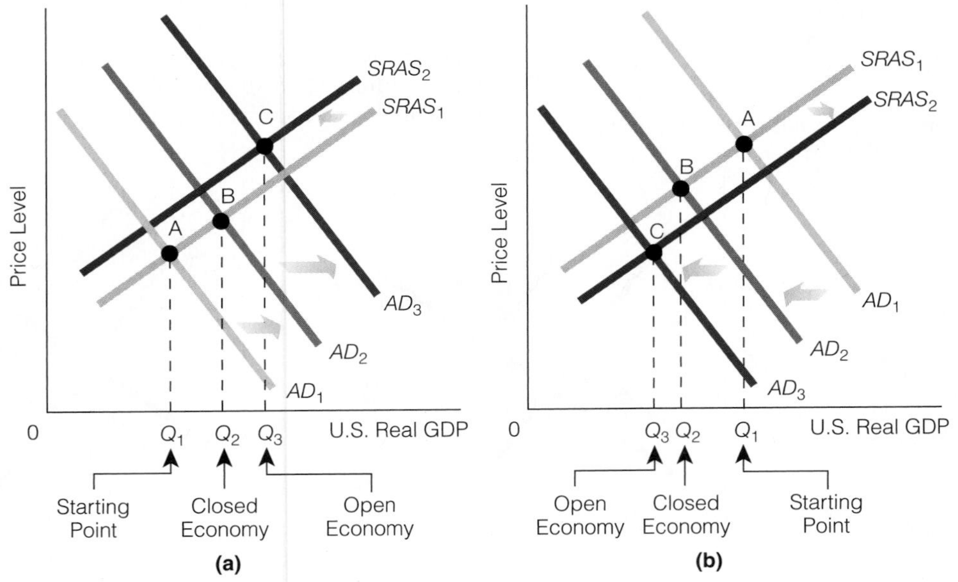

Exhibit 9(a), the *AD* curve shifts to the right (from AD_2 to AD_3) and the *SRAS* curve shifts to the left (from $SRAS_1$ to $SRAS_2$). Consequently, Real GDP rises from Q_2 to Q_3.

Therefore, expansionary monetary policy raises Real GDP more in an open economy than in a closed economy.

CONTRACTIONARY MONETARY POLICY If the Federal Reserve contracts the money supply, in the *AD-AS* framework, the *AD* curve shifts leftward from AD_1 to AD_2, and Real GDP falls from Q_1 to Q_2 [see Exhibit 9(b)].

There are also international effects of a decrease in the money supply. Contractionary monetary policy causes interest rates to rise, leading to an inflow of foreign capital into the United States. The demand for dollars rises on the foreign exchange market, and the dollar appreciates. Dollar appreciation affects both U.S. aggregate demand and U.S. short-run aggregate supply. As we know, dollar appreciation shifts the *AD* curve to the left and the *SRAS* curve to the right. In Exhibit 9(b), the *AD* curve shifts from AD_2 to AD_3, and the *SRAS* curve shifts from $SRAS_1$ to $SRAS_2$. Consequently, Real GDP falls from Q_2 to Q_3.

Therefore, contractionary monetary policy lowers Real GDP more in an open economy than in a closed economy.

SELF-TEST

1. Explain how expansionary monetary policy works in an open economy.
2. Explain how expansionary fiscal policy works in an open economy.

office hours

"WHY DO SOME PEOPLE FAVOR GLOBALIZATION AND OTHERS DO NOT?"

Student:
One of the things I have noticed about globalization is that some people in the United States seem to be in favor of it and others seem to be against it. Why is this?

Instructor:
It probably has much to do with how the benefits and costs of globalization are distributed across the population. People in one location might receive mainly the benefits, and people in some other location might incur mostly the costs.

Student:
Do any real world examples illustrate your point?

Instructor:
A while back *The New York Times* reported about two cities in Michigan: Holland and Greenville.[3] In Holland, a factory was losing business and firing workers. Then a German company bought it. Today the factory is shipping wastewater treatment equipment to countries in the Middle East and in Asia. Also, it is operating with twice as many workers as it did before the German company bought it. The people in Holland, Michigan, see this as a benefit of globalization.

But only 60 miles away from Holland, in Greenville, Michigan, the story is different. In Greenville, a Swedish company shut down what had been the largest refrigerator factory in the country and eliminated about 2,700 jobs in the town. For the people of Greenville, globalization seemed to come with costs.

Student:
What do most economists say about globalization? Do think that for the country as a whole globalization comes with net benefits (more benefits than costs) or net costs (more costs than benefits)?

Instructor:
Most economists seem to think that globalization comes with net benefits.

Student:
But economic policy isn't always determined by what economists think, is it?

Instructor:
You're right about that. Economic policy does not get made in a political vacuum. Politics plays a role in deciding which economic policies get adopted and implemented. Think about this in terms of our Michigan cities example. Suppose we went to Greenville, where jobs had been lost, and tell the residents of the city that globalization, on net, is good for the country. Suppose we said that, for the country as a whole, there are more benefits from globalization than costs. What would the residents of Greenville say? They might say that is all well and good, but globalization hasn't been that good to them and that is what matters. As a result, their vote, to the extent that they have one on the issue, is *against* globalization.

Student:
I see. In other words, sometimes what might be beneficial for the country (as a whole) is not beneficial for some part of the country.

Instructor:
That is the way some things turn out.

Points to Remember

1. Globalization can come with net benefits for a country, but not everyone in the country necessarily benefits from globalization.
2. The benefits and costs of globalization are not evenly spread throughout a country. The benefits may fall on some people and the costs on others.

3. See Peter S. Goodman, "2 Outcomes when Foreigners Buy Factories," *New York Times*, April 7, 2008.

a reader asks | Will My Job Be Sent Overseas?

One hears much these days about outsourcing or offshoring jobs. Are some jobs more likely to be sent overseas than others?

When it comes to some jobs, location matters. With others, location doesn't seem to matter. First, let's look at some jobs where location matters.

If you are sick and need a doctor, you prefer to have a doctor close to you. If you live in Ithaca, New York, you will probably want a doctor who works in Ithaca, New York, not in Bangkok, 8,553 miles away.

If you need a plumber, you will probably want a plumber close by, not one on the other side of the world. If you want to go out to eat, you will most likely go to a restaurant near where you live, not one on the other side of the world.

Now when it comes to buying a book, location may not matter. Where the bookseller resides may not matter, as long as you can get the book fairly quickly. When it comes to someone answering your technical computer questions, it may not matter where the technician is situated. As long as the technician speaks your language, listens well, and gives clear and concise instructions, you probably don't care where he or she is located.

In short, when a provider's (supplier's, worker's) location is important to you, the job that the provider performs will probably not be offshored to another country. When a provider's location is not important to you, the probability of the provider's job being offshored rises.

In 2004, *Forbes* magazine ran a story titled "Ten Professions Not Likely to Be Outsourced." Here is the list:

- Chief executive officer
- Physician and surgeon
- Pilot, copilot, and flight engineer
- Lawyer
- Computer and information systems manager
- Sales manager
- Pharmacist
- Chiropractor
- Physician's assistant
- Education administrator, elementary and secondary school

Chapter Summary

WHAT IS GLOBALIZATION?

- Globalization is a phenomenon by which individuals and businesses in any part of the world are much more affected by events elsewhere in the world than before; it is the growing integration of national economies of the world to the degree that we may be witnessing the emergence and operation of a single worldwide economy.
- Certain facts provide evidence that globalization is occurring. Some of these facts are (1) lower tariff rates in many countries, (2) many countries exporting and importing more goods than in the past, (3) greater foreign exchange trading, (4) more foreign direct investment, (5) many more people owning foreign stocks, (6) many more countries having joined the WTO in recent years, and (7) a greater number of Americans working for foreign companies that have offices in the United States.

MOVEMENT TOWARD GLOBALIZATION

- What has caused this most recent push toward globalization? In the chapter we identified (1) the end of the Cold War, (2) advancing technology, and (3) policy changes as causal factors.

BENEFITS AND COSTS OF GLOBALIZATION

- Some of the benefits of globalization include (1) benefits from increased international trade, (2) greater income per person, (3) lower prices for goods, (4) greater product variety, and (5) increased productivity and innovation.
- Some of the costs of globalization include (1) increased income inequality (although there is some debate), (2) offshoring, and (3) increased economic power for

large corporations (although there is some debate here too).

- When it comes to globalization, it is often much more difficult to see the benefits than the costs. The benefits are largely dispersed over a large population, but the costs (e.g., offshoring) might be concentrated on relatively few.

THE FUTURE OF GLOBALIZATION

- The future of globalization is under debate. Some persons argue that globalization will continue; others say it will stall and (perhaps) backtrack.

NET EXPORTS AND AGGREGATE DEMAND

- An increase in net exports will shift the *AD* curve to the right. A decrease in net exports will shift the *AD* curve to the left.
- Two factors can change net exports: foreign Real GDP (or real national income) and exchange rates. For example, in a two-country world (Japan and the United States), an increase in Japan's Real GDP and a depreciation in the dollar will increase U.S. net exports and shift the U.S. *AD* curve to the right. Alternatively, a decrease in Japan's Real GDP and an appreciation in the dollar will decrease U.S. net exports and shift the U.S. *AD* curve to the left.

THE AGGREGATE SUPPLY CURVE AND INTERNATIONAL FACTORS

- A change in foreign input prices will impact the U.S. *SRAS* curve. For example, an increase in foreign input prices will shift the U.S. *SRAS* curve to the left. A decrease in foreign input prices will shift the U.S. *SRAS* curve to the right.
- A change in foreign input prices can be the result of changes in the input market in the foreign country.
- A change in foreign input prices (paid by U.S. producers) can be the result of a change in the exchange rate. For example, if the dollar depreciates, U.S. producers will pay higher prices for foreign inputs. If the dollar appreciates, U.S. producers will pay lower prices for foreign inputs.

INTERNATIONAL FACTORS AND AGGREGATE DEMAND AND SHORT-RUN AGGREGATE SUPPLY

- A change in the exchange rate will affect both the U.S. *AD* curve and the U.S. *SRAS* curve. For example, if the dollar depreciates, the *AD* curve will shift to the right, and the *SRAS* curve will shift to the left.
- A change in real interest rates will affect both the U.S. *AD* curve and the U.S. *SRAS* curve. To illustrate, suppose the U.S. real interest rate rises relative to the Japanese interest rate. Higher real interest rates in the United States will attract foreign capital. Foreigners, in search of U.S. assets that pay interest, will bid up the price of a dollar; thus, the dollar appreciates. If the dollar appreciates, the *AD* curve will shift to the left, and the *SRAS* curve will shift to the right. The U.S. price level will fall. What happens to the U.S. Real GDP depends on the relative shifts in the *AD* and *SRAS* curves. Typically, the *AD* curve shifts leftward by more than the *SRAS* curve shifts rightward, and so Real GDP falls.

FISCAL AND MONETARY POLICY IN CLOSED AND OPEN ECONOMIES

- Expansionary fiscal policy raises Real GDP more in a closed economy than in an open economy.
- Contractionary fiscal policy lowers Real GDP more in a closed economy than in an open economy.
- Expansionary monetary policy raises Real GDP more in an open economy than in a closed economy.
- Contractionary monetary policy lowers Real GDP more in an open economy than in a closed economy.

Key Terms and Concepts

Globalization	Offshoring	Closed Economy	Open Economy
Tariff	J-Curve		

Questions and Problems

1 Why might it be easier to recognize the costs of globalization than the benefits?

2 If globalization continues over the next few decades, how might your life be different?

3 How might governments impact globalization?

4 Identify and explain two of the benefits and two of the costs of globalization.

5 What effect might advancing technology have on globalization?

6 Some have argued that the end of the Cold War acted as a catalyst toward greater globalization. How so?

7 What is Thomas Friedman's "Golden Arches theory of conflict prevention"?

8 David Friedman said that free (international) trade is a technology. Explain what he means.

9 Will globalization lead to some people losing jobs? Explain your answer.

10 How do tariff rates in the United States today compare with 1946?

11 Assume a two-country world where the two countries are the United States and Japan. Note the impact on U.S. Real GDP of each of the following:

   a. A fall in the real interest rate in the United States relative to the real interest rate in Japan.

   b. An economic expansion in Japan.

12 Give a numerical example to illustrate what the depreciation of a country's currency does to the prices of its imports.

13 If Americans buy fewer units of good X, which is produced in Japan, will they necessarily spend less money overall on good X? Explain your answer.

14 "The discussion of the J-curve points out that economists sometimes think in terms of both the short run and the long run." Do you agree or disagree? Explain your answer.

15 Explain how a change in the exchange rate can change both the U.S. *AD* and *SRAS* curves.

16 Suppose country A undertakes a policy mix of contractionary fiscal policy and expansionary monetary policy. What do you predict would happen to real interest rates, the value of country A's currency, and net exports? Explain your answer.

17 Why might import spending rise in a country soon after a depreciation of its currency? Is import spending likely to fall over time? Explain your answers.

18 Explain why expansionary monetary policy is more likely to increase Real GDP in an open economy than in a closed economy.

19 Explain why contractionary fiscal policy is more likely to decrease Real GDP in a closed economy than in an open economy.

20 Explain why contractionary monetary policy lowers Real GDP more in an open economy than in a closed economy.

Working with Numbers and Graphs

1 Starting with an exchange rate of $1 = ¥114 and a price tag of ¥10,000 for a Japanese item, show what happens to the price of the Japanese item if the yen depreciates by 5 percent.

2 Graphically show and explain the domestic and feedback effects on Real GDP in the United States as a result of contractionary fiscal policy.

3 Graphically show and explain the domestic and feedback effects on Real GDP in the United States as a result of contractionary monetary policy.

© IOANA DRUTU/SHUTTERSTOCK

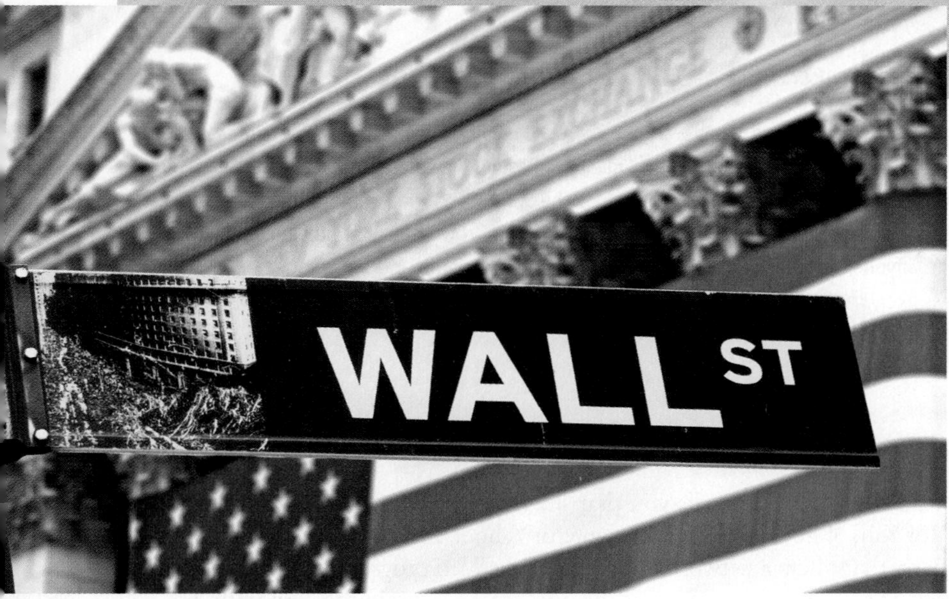

CHAPTER 20

STOCKS, BONDS, FUTURES, AND OPTIONS

Introduction Economic and financial news is all around us. "The economy is headed toward recession." "The value of the dollar is falling." "The budget deficit is growing" "The stock market took a loss today." "Bonds are strong."

In much of this book we have talked about various economic news items. In this chapter we turn to the part of economics that deals with financial matters. In this chapter we discuss stocks, bonds, futures, and options.

FINANCIAL MARKETS

Everyone has heard of stocks and bonds, and everyone knows that stocks and bonds can be sold and purchased. But not everyone knows the economic purpose served by stocks and bonds.

Buying and selling stocks and bonds take place in financial markets, which serve the purpose of channeling money from some people to other people. To illustrate, Jones has saved $10,000 over two years, and Smith is just starting a new company. Smith needs money to get the new company up and running. On the other hand, Jones would like to invest the savings and receive a return. Jones and Smith may not know each other; in fact, they may live on opposite ends of the country. A financial market, however, can bring these two people together. It allows Jones either to invest in Smith's company or to lend Smith some money. For example, Jones might either buy stock in Smith's company or buy a bond that Smith's company is issuing. In this chapter, we discuss more about how people like Smith and Jones help each other through a financial market. Specifically, in this section, we discuss stocks, and in the next section, bonds.

Common MISCONCEPTIONS

About Financial Brokers

Smith has $10,000 to lend, and Jones wants to borrow $10,000. The problem is that Smith and Jones do not know each other. Enter the middleman, Brown, who stands between the Smiths and Joneses of the world. He is the person who brings the Smiths and Joneses together. For his services rendered, he is paid a fee. Some people will argue that Brown does not provide any worthwhile service to anyone, but they're wrong. His service is to bring Smith and Jones together. Without Brown, it is less likely that Smith will lend and Jones will borrow—that is, less likely that Smith and Jones will enter into a mutually advantageous trade.

STOCKS

Stock
A claim on the assets of a corporation that gives the purchaser a share of the corporation.

What does it mean when someone tells you that she owns 100 shares of a stock? If Jane owns 100 shares of Yahoo! stock, she is a part owner in Yahoo!, Inc., which is a global Internet media company that offers a network of World Wide Web programming. A **stock** is a claim on the assets of a corporation that gives the purchaser a share in the corporation.

In our example, Jane is not an owner in the sense that she can walk into Yahoo! headquarters (in Santa Clara, California) and start issuing orders. She cannot hire or fire anyone, and she cannot decide what the company will or will not do over the next few months or years. But still she is an owner, and as an owner she can, if she wants, sell her ownership rights in Yahoo!. All she has to do is find a buyer for her 100 shares of stock. Most likely, she could do so in a matter of minutes, if not seconds.

Finding ECONOMICS

At an Online Brokerage Website

Frank has an account with TD Ameritrade. He goes online one morning to see what price Yahoo! stock (symbol YHOO) is selling at. At 10:45 A.M. EDT, the stock is selling at $29.74 a share. One minute later it is selling for one cent less at $29.73. Where is the economics? Supply and demand are at work with respect to Yahoo! stock. The equilibrium price is changing fairly fast in this market. At 10:45 A.M. EDT the equilibrium price is $29.74. One minute later it has fallen to $29.73. Ten minutes later it has risen to $27.99. Think of how fast the market for Yahoo! stock equilibrates compared to some other markets (such as the housing market).

Where Are Stocks Bought and Sold?

Groceries are bought and sold at the grocery store. Clothes are bought and sold at the clothing store. But where are stocks bought and sold?

To answer that question, let's go back to 1792, when 24 men met under a buttonwood tree on what is now Wall Street in New York City. These men essentially bought and sold stock (for themselves and their customers) at this location. Someone might have said, "I want to sell 20 shares in company X. Are you willing to buy them for $2 a share?"

From this humble beginning came the New York Stock Exchange (NYSE). Every weekday (excluding holidays), men and women meet at the NYSE in New York City and buy and sell stock. For example, suppose you own 100 shares of a stock that is listed on the NYSE. You do not have to go to the NYSE in New York to sell it. You simply contact a stockbroker (either over the phone, in person, or online), who conveys your wishes to sell the stock to a person at the NYSE itself. That person at the NYSE then executes your order.

The NYSE is not the only exchange where stocks are bought and sold. For example, there are the American Stock Exchange (AMEX) and the NASDAQ stock market (NASDAQ is pronounced "NAS-dak" and stands for National Association of Securities Dealers Automated Quotations). Buying and selling stock on the NASDAQ do not take place in the same way as on the NYSE. Instead of the buying and selling taking place in a central location, the NASDAQ is an electronic stock market with trades executed through a sophisticated computer and telecommunications network. The NYSE might in fact change to this kind of market in the near future; instead of people meeting in one location to buy and sell stock, they could do it electronically.

Increasingly, Americans are not only buying and selling stocks on the U.S. stock exchanges and markets, but in foreign stock exchanges and markets too. For example, an American might buy a stock listed on the German Stock Exchange, the Montreal Stock Exchange, or the Swiss Exchange.

The Dow Jones Industrial Average (DJIA)

You may have heard news commentators say, "The Dow fell 302 points on heavy trading." They are talking about the **Dow Jones Industrial Average (DJIA)**, which first appeared on the scene more than 100 years ago, on May 26, 1896, and was devised by Charles H. Dow. Dow took 11 stocks, summed their prices on a particular day, and then divided by 11. The average price was the DJIA. (Some of the original companies included American Cotton Oil, Chicago Gas, National Lead, and U.S. Rubber.)

Dow Jones Industrial Average (DJIA)
The most popular, widely cited indicator of day-to-day stock market activity. The DJIA is a weighted average of 30 widely traded stocks on the New York Stock Exchange.

When Charles Dow first computed the DJIA, the stock market was not highly regarded in the United States. Prudent investors bought bonds, not stocks. Stocks were thought to be the arena for speculators and conniving Wall Street operators. It was thought back then that Wall Streeters managed stock prices to make themselves better off at the expense of others. There was a lot of gossip about what was and was not happening in the stock market.

Dow devised the DJIA to convey information about what was happening in the stock market. Before the DJIA, people had a hard time figuring out whether the stock market, on average, was rising or falling. Instead, they knew only that a particular stock went up or down by so many cents or dollars. The average price of a certain number of stocks, he thought, would largely mirror what was happening in the stock market as a whole. With this number, people could then have some sense of what the stock market was doing on any given day.

Today, the DJIA consists of 30 stocks that are widely held by individuals and institutional investors (see Exhibit 1, which shows the 30 stocks in the Dow Industrial Average as of February 19, 2008). The list can and does change from time to

exhibit 1

The 30 Stocks of the Dow Jones Industrial Average (DJIA)

Here are the 30 stocks that comprise the Dow Jones Industrial Average.

3M Co.	Home Depot Inc.
Alcoa Inc.	Intel Corp.
American Express Co.	International Business Machines Corp.
AT&T Inc.	Johnson & Johnson
Bank of America	JPMorgan Chase & Co.
Boeing Co.	Kraft Foods, Inc.
Caterpillar Inc.	McDonald's Corp.
Chevron	Merck & Co. Inc.
Citigroup Inc.	Microsoft Corp.
Coca-Cola Co.	Pfizer Inc.
E.I. DuPont de Nemours & Co.	Procter & Gamble Co.
ExxonMobil Corp.	United Technologies Corp.
General Electric Co.	Verizon Communications Inc.
General Motors Corp.	Wal-Mart Stores Inc.
Hewlett-Packard Co.	Walt Disney Co.

exhibit 2

DJIA, January 1, 2004–October 13, 2008

Here we show the ups and downs of the DJIA from January 1, 2004, to October 13, 2008.

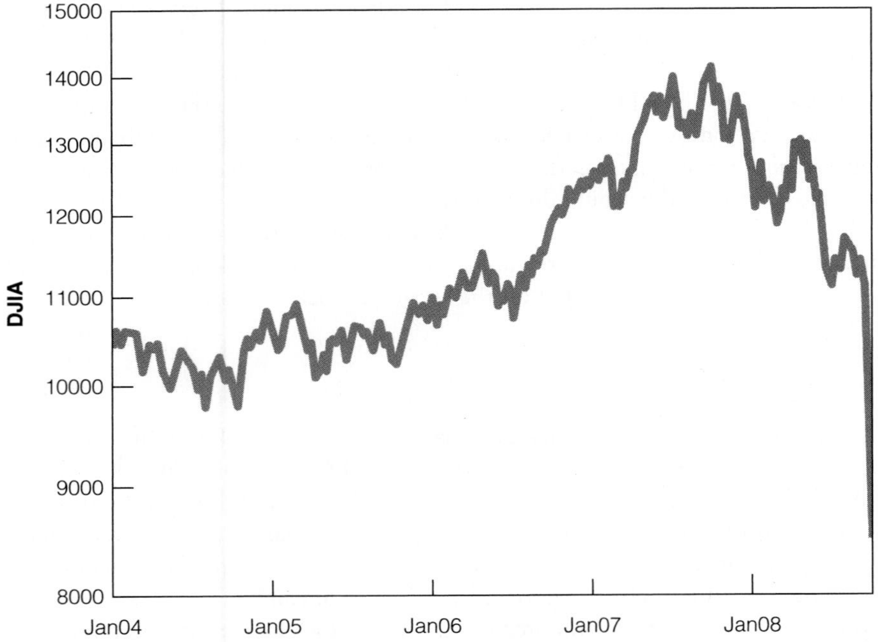

time, as determined by the editors of *The Wall Street Journal.* And the DJIA is no longer computed simply by summing the prices of stocks and dividing by 30. A special divisor is used to avoid distortions that can occur, such as companies splitting their stock shares. Exhibit 2 shows the Dow Jones Industrial Average during the period of January 1, 2004–October 13, 2008.

In addition to the DJIA, other prominent stock indexes are cited in the United States. A few include the NASDAQ Composite, the Standard & Poor's 500, the Russell 2000, and the Wilshire 5000. There are also prominent stock indexes around the world, such as the Hang Seng (in Hong Kong), the Bovespa (Brazil), IPC (Mexico), BSE 30 (India), CAC 40 (France), and others.

What causes the DJIA to go up? What causes it to go down? Economic consulting firms have attempted to find out what influences the Dow. According to many economists, the Dow is closely connected to changes in such things as consumer credit, business expectations, exports and imports, personal income, and the money supply. For example, increases in consumer credit are expected to push up the Dow, the thought being that when consumer credit rises, people will buy more goods and services, and this is good for the companies that sell goods and services. When consumer credit falls, the opposite effect occurs.

How the Stock Market Works

To raise money for investment in a new product or a new manufacturing technique, a company can do one of three things. First, it can go to a bank and borrow the money. Second, it can borrow the money by issuing a bond (a promise to repay the borrowed money with interest; you will learn more about bonds later in the chapter). Third, it can sell or issue stock in the company or, put another way, sell part of the company. Stocks are also called *equity* because the buyer of the stock has part ownership of the company.

economics 24/7

ARE SOME ECONOMISTS POOR INVESTORS?

You might think that economists would do pretty well in the stock market compared to the average person. After all, the job of economists is to understand how markets work and to study key economic indicators.

So how do you explain a May 11, 2005, article in the *Los Angeles Times* titled "Experts Are at a Loss on Investing"? The article looked at the investments of four economists—all Nobel Prize winners in economics. Not one of them said that he invests the way he should invest, and none of them seemed to be getting rich through their investments. Often, there seems to be a big difference between knowing what to do and doing it.

Harry M. Markowitz won the Nobel Prize in Economics in 1990 for his work in financial economics. He is known as the father of modern portfolio theory, the main idea being that people should diversify their investments.

Markowitz, however, did not follow his own advice. Most of his life, he put half of his money in a stock fund and the other half in a conservative, low-interest investment. Markowitz, age 77 at the time, says, "In retrospect, it would have been better to have been more in stocks when I was younger."

George Akerlof, who won the Nobel Prize in Economics in 2001, had invested most of his money in money market accounts, which tend to have relatively low interest rate returns but are safe. Akerlof, when confronted with this fact, said, "I know it's utterly stupid."

Clive Granger, who won the Nobel Prize in Economics in 2003, was asked about his investments. He said, "I would rather spend my time enjoying my income than bothering about investments."

Daniel Kahneman, who won the Nobel Prize in Economics in 2002, had this to say about his investments: "I think very little about my retirement savings, because I know that thinking could make me poorer or more miserable or both."

Almost every activity comes with both benefits and costs. There are certainly benefits to investing wisely, but there are costs too. It takes time to find out about various investments, to research them, and to keep informed on how they are doing.

The actions of our four Nobel Prize winners also point out something else. Many people think that economics is simply about money and money matters, but it is not. It is about utility and happiness and making oneself better off. Each of our four Nobel Prize winners might not have been doing the best thing for his wallet, but certainly each knew this and continued on the same path anyway. Each was willing to sacrifice some money to live a preferred lifestyle.

What is the lesson for you? Should you care nothing about your investments and hope that your financial future will take care of itself? Or should you spend all your time regularly watching, researching, and evaluating various investments that either you have made or plan to make? Neither extreme is sensible. You can learn enough about investments to protect yourself from the financial uncertainties of the future but not spend so much time worrying about the future that you don't enjoy the present.

When a company is initially formed, the owners set up a certain amount of stock, which is worth very little. The owners of the company try to find people (usually friends and associates) who would be willing to buy the stock (in the hopes that one day it will be worth something). In these early days of the company, anyone who owned stock would find it nearly impossible to sell it. For example, if Jones owned 100 shares of some new company that almost no one had heard of, hardly anyone would be willing to pay any money to buy the stock.

As the company grows and needs more money, it may decide to offer its stock on the open market. In other words, it offers its stock to anyone who wants to buy it. By this time, the company may be known well enough that some people are willing to buy it. The company makes what is called an **initial public offering (IPO)** of its stock. The process is quite simple. Usually, an **investment bank** sells the stock for the company for an initial

Initial Public Offering (IPO)
A company's first offering of stock to the public.

Investment Bank
A firm that acts as an intermediary between the company that issues the stock and the public that wishes to buy the stock.

price—say, $10 a share. How do you find out about an IPO? They are announced in *The Wall Street Journal.*

For example, suppose that William Welch started a company in 1895 and that, through the years, the company was passed down to family members. In 2009, the family members running the company want to expand it to two, three, or four times its current size. To get the money to do this, one way is to sell shares in the company—that is, by issuing stock. Once they have issued shares in the company to the public, the company is no longer solely family owned. Now many of the public own part of it too.

Once there is an IPO, the stock is usually traded on a stock exchange or in an electronic stock market. Sometimes, the stock that initially sold for $10 will rise in price, and sometimes it will fall like a rock. Its success or failure all depends on what people in the stock market think the issuing company will do in the future. If they think the company is destined for big earnings, the stock will likely rise in price. If they think the company is destined for losses, or only marginal earnings, the stock will likely fall in price.

In a way, you can think of trading stock in much the same way as trading baseball cards, paintings, or anything else. The price depends on the forces of supply and demand. If demand rises and supply is constant, then the price of the stock will rise. If demand falls and supply is constant, then the price of the stock will fall.

Why Do People Buy Stock?

Millions of people in the United States, and in countries all over the world, buy stock every day. Sometimes, people buy a stock because they hear that others are buying it and because they think the stock is hot. In other words, the stock is very popular and everyone wants it. In the 1990s, some of the Internet stocks fit this description. People bought stocks such as Yahoo!, Amazon.com, and eBay just because they thought the Internet was the wave of the future and almost anything connected with the Internet was destined for great profit.

More often, though, people buy a stock because they think the earnings of the company that initially issued the stock are likely to rise. (Remember that a share of stock represents ownership in a company.) The more profitable that company is expected to be, the more likely people are going to want to own that company, and therefore the greater the demand for the company's stock.

Dividend
A share of the profits of a corporation distributed to stockholders.

Most people therefore buy stock for a couple of typical reasons. Some people buy stocks for the **dividends**, which are payments made to stockholders based on a company's profits. For example, suppose company X has issued one million shares of stock that are owned by investors. Each year, the company tabulates its profit and loss, and, if there is a profit, it distributes some of the profit among the owners of the company as dividends. This year's dividend might be $1 for each share of stock a person owns. So if Jones owns 50,000 shares of stock, she will receive a dividend check for $50,000.

The other reason to buy stock is for the expected gain in its price. Stockholders can make money if they buy shares at a lower price and sell at a higher price. For example, Smith buys 100 shares of Microsoft stock today. He thinks that the company is going to do well and that a year from now he can sell it for as much as $50 more a share than he purchased it. In other words, he hopes to earn $5,000 on his stock purchase.

People also sell stock for many reasons. Smith might sell his 100 shares of IBM because he needs the money, perhaps to help his son pay for college or to put together a down payment for a house. Another common reason for selling stock is that the stockholder thinks the stock is likely to go down in price soon. It is better today to sell at $25 a share than to sell one week from now at $18 a share.

Common MISCONCEPTIONS

About Stocks

Someone buys a stock at $100 a share, and five weeks later the stock is selling for $86 a share. The person decides not to sell the stock because, he says, "I can't take the loss." That response signifies that the person thinks the share price of the stock will rise. ("I can't sell today because I can't take the loss. I have to wait until the price rises so that I won't have to take a loss.") But the price that has gone down is not guaranteed to go up. In fact, a misconception is that a stock's price has gone so low that it has nowhere to go but up. The share price of a stock can start at, say, $500, and continue to go down until no one is willing to pay anything for the stock. In other words, the share price of a stock can fall to zero.

How to Buy and Sell Stock

Buying and selling stock are relatively easy. You can buy or sell stock through a full-service stockbrokerage firm, a discount broker, or an online broker. With all varieties of brokers, you usually open an account by depositing a certain dollar amount, commonly between $1,000 and $2,500. Once you have opened an account, you can begin to trade (buy and sell stock).

With a full-service broker, you may call up on the phone and ask your broker to recommend a good stock. Your broker, usually called an *account representative,* might say that you should buy X, Y, or Z stock. When you ask why these are good stocks to buy, the representative may say that the firm's research department has looked closely at them and believes they are headed for good times based on the current economic situation in the country, the level of exports, the new technology that is coming to market, and other factors.

If you do not require help selecting stocks, you can go either to a discount broker or to an online broker. You can call up a discount broker, as you did a full-service broker, and say you want to buy or sell so many shares of a given stock. The broker will execute the trade for you but not offer any advice.

You can do the same thing online. You go to your broker's website, log in, enter your username and password, and then buy or sell stock. You may, for example, submit an order to buy 100 shares of stock X. Your online broker will register your buy request and then advise you when it has been executed. Your account, easily visible online, will show how much cash you have in it, how many shares of a stock you hold, and so on.

Buying Stocks or Buying the Market

You can use various methods to decide which stocks to purchase. The first way is to buy shares of stock that you think are going to rise in price. So you might buy 50 shares of Microsoft, 100 shares of General Electric, and 500 shares of Amazon.com.

Another way is to invest in a stock mutual fund, which is a collection of stocks that is managed by a fund manager who works for a mutual fund company. For example, Smith may operate Mutual Fund Z at Mutual Fund Company Z. If you put, say, $10,000 into Mutual Fund Z, you are in effect buying stocks in that fund. If the fund consists of stocks A, B, C, W, and X, the fund manager may, on any given day, buy more of A and sell some of B or sell all of C and add stock D to the fund portfolio. Thus, as a buyer of the fund, you put your money into the manager's hands, and the fund manager does what he or she thinks is best to maximize the overall returns from the fund.

Mutual fund companies often advertise the records of their fund managers. They might say, "Our fund managers have the best record on Wall Street. Invest with us and get the highest returns you can." You may be prompted to put your money in the hands of the experts because you feel they know better than you which stocks to buy and sell and when to do each.

You could use another strategy, though, and buy the stocks that make up a stock index. For example, the DJIA, a stock index, gives us information on the performance of the 30 stocks that make up the Dow. Other indexes are made up differently. The Standard & Poor's 500 index is a broad index of stock market activity because it is made up of 500 of the largest U.S. companies. Another broad-based stock index is the Wilshire 5000, which consists of the stocks of about 6,500 firms. (Yes, even though it consists of more than 5,000 firms, it is still called the Wilshire 5000.) So, instead of buying a mutual fund that consists of various stocks picked by the so-called experts, you can buy a mutual fund that consists of the stocks that make up a particular index.

An easy way to do this is to buy what are called Spyders. The term *Spyders* comes from SPDRs, which stands for Standard & Poor's Depository Receipts. Spyders are securities that represent ownership in the SPDR Trust, which buys the stocks that make up the Standard & Poor's (S&P) 500 index, and that are traded under the symbol SPY. Spyders cost one-tenth of the S&P index (the total of the share prices of the stocks in the S&P). For example, if the S&P index is 1,350, then a Spyder will sell for $135.

When you buy Spyders, you are buying the stock of 500 companies. Because you are buying the stock of so many companies, you are said to be buying the market. For example, suppose Jack decides to buy the market instead of buying a few individual stocks. He opens an account with an online broker; that is, he goes online, opens an account, and sends the broker a check so that he can start trading (buying and selling stock). He then checks (at the online broker website) on the current price of Spyders, which is, say, $135 per share. He decides to buy 100 shares, for a total price of $13,500. (His online broker charges him a small commission for this stock purchase.) In a minute or less, he sees that he has purchased the 100 shares of Spyders. That's all there is to it.

How to Read the Stock Market Page

Once you have purchased some stock, you will want to find out how it is doing. Is it rising or falling in price? Is it paying a dividend? How many shares were traded today?

One of the places you can go to find the answers to these questions, as well as other information, is the newspaper. On the stock market page (keep in mind that many newspapers are online), you will see something similar to what you see in Exhibit 3. Let's look at each item in each column of the bottom line.

exhibit 3

How to Read the Stock Market Page of a Newspaper

We show here part of the stock market page of a newspaper. We explain how to read the page in the text.

(1)	(2)	(3)	(4)	(5)	(6)	(7)	(8)	(9)	(10)	(11)	(12)
52W high	**52W low**	**Stock**	**Ticker**	**Div**	**Yield %**	**P/E**	**Vol 00s**	**High**	**Low**	**Close**	**Net chg**
45.39	19.75	ResMed	RMD			57.5	3831	42.00	39.51	41.50	-1.90
11.63	3.55	Revlon A	REV				162	6.09	5.90	6.09	+0.12
77.25	55.13	RioTinto	RTP	2.30	3.2		168	72.75	71.84	72.74	+0.03
31.31	16.63	RitchieBr	RBA			20.9	15	24.49	24.29	24.49	-0.01
8.44	1.75	RiteAid	RAD				31028	4.50	4.20	4.31	+0.21
38.63	18.81	RobtHall	RHI			26.5	6517	27.15	26.50	26.50	+0.14
51.25	**27.69**	**Rockwell**	**ROK**	**1.02**	**2.1**	**14.5**	**6412**	**47.99**	**47.00**	**47.54**	**+0.24**

52W High This stands for the high price of the stock over the past 52 weeks. For this stock, you see the number 51.25, which is $51.25.

52W Low This stands for the low price of the stock over the past 52 weeks. For this stock, you see the number 27.69, which is $27.69.

Stock In this column, you see Rockwell. This is either an abbreviation of the name or the full name of the company whose stock we are investigating. The company here is Rockwell Automation Incorporated.

Ticker ROK is the stock or ticker symbol for Rockwell Automation Incorporated.

Div This stands for dividend. You see the number 1.02 on the bottom line, which means that the last annual dividend per share of stock was $1.02. For example, a person who owned 5,000 shares of Rockwell Automation stock would have received $1.02 per share or $5,100 in dividends. (A blank means the company does not currently pay out dividends.)

Yield % The yield of a stock is the dividend divided by the closing price.

$$\text{Yield} = \frac{\text{Dividend per share}}{\text{Closing price per share}}$$

The closing price of the stock (shown in the one of the later columns) is 47.54 ($47.54). If we divide the dividend ($1.02) by the closing price ($47.54), we get a yield of 2.1 percent. The higher the yield, the better the prospects are for the stock, *ceteris paribus.* For example, a stock that yields 5 percent is better than a stock that yields 3 percent, if all other things between the two stocks are the same.

P/E This stands for P/E ratio, or price-earnings ratio. The number here, 14.5, is obtained by taking the latest closing price per share and dividing it by the latest available net earnings per share.

$$\text{P/E} = \frac{\text{Closing price per share}}{\text{Net earnings per share}}$$

A stock with a P/E ratio of 14.5 means that the stock is selling for a share price that is 14.5 times its earnings per share.

A high P/E ratio usually indicates that people believe there will be higher-than-average growth in earnings. Suppose that most stocks have a P/E ratio of 14.5, that is, they sell for a share price that is 14.5 times their earnings per share. Also suppose that stock X has a P/E ratio of, say, 50. What would make stock X have a P/E ratio so much higher than most stocks? Obviously, the people buying stock X expect that its future earnings will somehow warrant the higher prices they are paying for the stock today. Whether or not they are right remains to be seen.

Vol 00s This stands for volume in the hundreds. The number 6412 translates to 641,200. It means that 641,200 shares of this stock were traded (bought and sold) on this day.

High This stands for the high price the stock traded for on this day. The number is 47.99 ($47.99).

Low This stands for the low price the stock traded for on this particular day. The number is 47.00 ($47.00).

Close This is the share price of the stock when trading stopped on this day: 47.54 ($47.54).

Net Chg. This stands for net change: +0.24 (+$0.24). The price of the stock on this particular day closed 24 cents higher than it did the day before.

Common MISCONCEPTIONS

About the DJIA

Some people seem to think that if they don't own any of the stocks making up the DJIA, the ups and downs in the index don't affect them. But this is not exactly true. Many economists say that what happens in the stock market—or to the DJIA—is a forerunner of future economic events. So if the DJIA goes down over time, it is indicating that the economic future is somewhat depressed; if it goes up over time, it is indicating that the economic future looks good. The economic future—good or bad—is something that does affect you. It affects what prices you pay, how easy or hard it is to get a job, how large or small an increase in income you get, and so on.

SELF-TEST

(Answers to Self-Test questions are in the Self-Test Appendix.)

1. How many stocks does the DJIA consist of?
2. Why do people buy stocks?
3. What does the yield of a stock equal?
4. What does a P/E ratio of 23 mean?

BONDS

Bond
An IOU, or promise to pay.

If a company in St. Louis wants to build a new factory, how can it get the necessary money? Recall that companies use three principal ways to raise money. First, they can go to banks and take out loans. Second, they can issue stock, or sell ownership rights in the company. Third, they can issue bonds. A **bond** is simply an IOU, or a promise to pay. Typically, companies, governments, or government agencies issue bonds. In each case, the purpose of issuing a bond is to borrow money. The issuer of a bond is a borrower, and the person who buys the bond is a lender.

The Components of a Bond

There are three major components of a bond: face (par) value, maturity date, and coupon rate.

Face Value (Par Value)
Dollar amount specified on a bond, the total amount the issuer of the bond will repay to the buyer of the bond.

FACE VALUE The **face value**, or **par value**, of a bond is the total amount the issuer of the bond will repay to the buyer of the bond. For example, suppose Smith buys a bond from Company Z, and the face value of the bond is $1,000. Company Z promises to pay Smith $1,000 at some point in the future.

economics 24/7

$1.3 QUADRILLION

At the close of the 20th century, the editors of the financial magazine *The Economist* identified the highest-returning investments for each year, beginning in 1900 and ending in 1999. For example, the highest returning investment in 1974 was gold, in 1902 it was U.S. Treasury bills, and in 1979 it was silver.

© NONSTOCK/JUPITER IMAGES

The editors then asked how much income a person would have earned at the end of 1999, if she had invested $1 in the highest-returning investment in 1900, and then taken the returns from that investment and invested it in the highest-returning investment in 1901, and so on for each year during the century. After taxes and dealer costs, she would have earned $1.3 quadrillion. (Quadrillion comes after trillion. In 2008, Warren Buffet, the richest person in the world, had $62 billion; so $1.3 quadrillion is 20,967 times what Warren Buffet had at the time.) So, with perfect foresight (or with a crystal ball that always correctly tells you what the highest-returning investment of the year will be), you could be rich beyond your imagination.

After the editors ran their experiment, they changed it. They went back and asked themselves what one would have earned over the 20th century if, instead of investing in the highest returning investment in a given year, she invested in it one year late. That is, if X is the best investment in 1956, then invest in it in 1957.

The editors made this change in the belief that many people invest in a hot investment only when it is too late. By the time they hear about it, investing in it at that point is usually too late. (Think of an investment as a mountain: Going up the mountain is comparable to increasing returns on the investment, and going down the mountain is comparable to decreasing returns. It's only when the investment is near its peak that many people hear about it. But then it's too late. There is no place to go but down.)

To put this into context, the person with the crystal ball or with perfect foresight would have invested in the Polish stock market in 1993, when no one was talking about it, and he would have reaped a 754 percent gain. The typical investor would have invested in it one year later, in 1994, when everyone was talking about it. The problem is that the Polish stock market fell by 55 percent in 1994.

So the person who invested always one year late over the 20th century would have earned, after taxes and dealer costs, $290.

What are the economic lessons? First, the best investments are often the ones that you don't hear about until it is too late. Second, ignoring the first lesson—thinking that a popular investment is necessarily a good investment—is often the way to low returns.

MATURITY DATE The maturity date is the day that the issuer of the bond must pay the buyer the face value; it is the date the bond is said to come due. For example, suppose Smith buys a bond with a face value of $1,000 that matures on December 31, 2015. On December 31, 2015, he receives $1,000 from the issuer of the bond.

COUPON RATE The coupon rate is the percentage of the face value that the bondholder receives each year until the bond matures. For example, suppose Smith buys a bond with a face value of $1,000 that matures in 5 years and has a coupon rate of 10 percent. He receives a coupon payment of $100 each year for 5 years.

To illustrate, Jorge buys a bond with a face value of $1,000 and a coupon rate of 7 percent. The maturity date of the bond is 10 years from today. Each year, for the next 10 years, Jorge receives 7 percent of $1,000 from the issuer, which amounts to $70 a year for each of 10 years. In the 10th year, he also receives $1,000 from the bond issuer. This bond has a maturity date in 10 years, a coupon rate of 7 percent, and a face value of $1,000.

Bond Ratings

Bonds are rated or evaluated. The more likely it is that the bond issuer will pay the face value of the bond at maturity and meet all scheduled coupon payments, the higher the bond's rating will be. Two of the best-known ratings are Standard & Poor's and Moody's. If a bond gets a rating of AAA from Standard & Poor's or a rating of Aaa from Moody's, it has received the highest rating possible. You can be sure that it is one of the securest bonds you can buy; there is little doubt that the bond issuer will pay the face value of the bond at maturity and meet all scheduled coupon payments.

Bonds rated in the B to D category are of lower quality than those in the A category. A bond in the C category may be in default (the issuer of the bond cannot pay off the bond), and those in the D category are definitely in default.

Bond Prices and Yields (or Interest Rates)

The price that a person pays for a bond depends on market conditions. The greater the demand is for the bond relative to the supply, the higher the price will be. The price is important because it determines the yield, or interest rate, that the bondholder receives on the bond. (In everyday language, the yield is referred to as the interest rate on the bond. For example, someone might ask what interest rate is that bond paying? We could easily substitute the term *yield* for the term *interest rate* and give an answer of something like "5.26 percent.")

Let's suppose that Gupta is the owner of a bond with a face value of $1,000 and a coupon rate of 5 percent. He decides to sell this bond to Jones for $950. Now we know that the coupon payment on this bond will be 5 percent of $1,000 each year, or $50; so Jones can expect to receive $50 each year. But the **yield** on the bond is the coupon payment divided by the price paid for the bond.

Yield
Equal to the annual coupon payment divided by the price paid for the bond.

$$\text{Yield (or interest rate)} = \frac{\text{Annual coupon payment}}{\text{Price paid for the bond}}$$

In this example, it is $50 ÷ $950 = 5.26 percent. For the bond buyer, the higher the yield is, the better the deal is.

As another example, suppose Robin buys a bond with the face value of $1,000 for $900. The coupon rate on the bond is 4 percent. Because the coupon rate is 4 percent, Robin receives 4 percent of $1,000 (the face value of the bond) each year through the time the bond matures: $40 a year. Because Robin bought the bond for a price lower than the face value, her yield will be higher than the coupon rate. To find the yield, divide the annual coupon payment of $40 by the price of the bond ($900). This gives Robin a yield of 4.4 percent.

Now suppose Robin had paid $1,100 for the bond instead of $900. In this case, the yield would be 3.6 percent, which is lower than the coupon rate. In other words, as the price paid for the bond rises, the yield declines.

Finally, the coupon rate and the yield are the same when the price paid for the bond equals the face value. For example, a bond with a face value of $1,000 and a coupon rate of 5 percent is purchased for $1,000. The yield ($50 ÷ $1,000) is 5 percent, which is equal to the coupon rate.

Common MISCONCEPTIONS

About the Coupon Rate and Yield (Interest Rate)

Many people seem to think that the coupon rate of a bond is the yield that the bond earns. This is not true. The yield (or interest rate) and the coupon rate are two different things. Only when the price of the bond equals the face value of the bond does the yield (interest rate) equal the coupon rate. When the price of the bond is lower the face value of the bond, the yield will be greater than the coupon rate; when the price of the bond is greater than the face of the bond, the yield will be less than the coupon rate.

Types of Bonds

This section briefly describes some of the many types of bonds issued by companies, governments, and government agencies.

CORPORATE BONDS A corporate bond is issued by a private corporation. Corporate bonds may sell for a price above or below face value depending on current supply-and-demand conditions. The interest that corporate bonds pay is fully taxable.

MUNICIPAL BONDS Municipal bonds are issued by state and local governments. States may issue bonds to help pay for a new highway. Local governments may issue bonds to finance a civic auditorium or a sports stadium. Many people purchase municipal bonds because the interest paid on the bonds is not subject to federal taxes.

TREASURY BILLS, NOTES, AND BONDS When the federal government wants to borrow funds, it can issue Treasury bills (T-bills), notes, or bonds. These securities differ only in their time to maturity. Although called by different names, all are bonds. Treasury bills mature in 13, 26, or 52 weeks. Treasury notes mature in 2 to 10 years, and Treasury bonds mature in more than 10 to 30 years. Treasury bills, notes, and bonds are considered very safe investments because it is unlikely the federal government will default on its bond obligations. After all, the federal government has the power to tax to pay off bondholders.

INFLATION-INDEXED TREASURY BONDS In 1997, the federal government began to issue inflation-indexed bonds. The first indexed Treasury bonds that were issued matured in 10 years and were available at face values as small as $1,000.

What is the difference between an inflation-indexed Treasury bond and a Treasury bond that is not indexed? An inflation-indexed Treasury bond guarantees the purchaser a certain real rate of return, but a nonindexed Treasury bond does not. For example, suppose you purchase an inflation-indexed, 10-year, $1,000 bond that pays a 4 percent coupon rate. If there is no inflation, the annual interest payment will be $40. But if the inflation rate is, say, 3 percent, the government will mark up the value of the bond by 3 percent—from $1,000 to $1,030. Then it will pay 4 percent on this higher dollar amount. So instead of paying $40 each year, it pays $41.20. By increasing the monetary value of the security by the rate of inflation, the government guarantees the bondholder a real return of 4 percent.

How to Read the Bond Market Page

On the bond market page of the newspaper, you can find information about the different types of bonds. Here we discuss how to read the information that relates to both corporate bonds and Treasury bonds. First, let's look at corporate bonds.

CORPORATE BONDS Not all publications will present corporate bond information in exactly the same format. The format we show you here is common, though.

(1) Bonds	(2) Cur Yld	(3) Vol	(4) Close	(5) Net Chg
AT&T 6 5/8 34	6.7	115	99 1/2	−3/4

Bonds This column presents three pieces of information: (1) the abbreviation for the company that issued the bond—AT&T, a telecommunications company; (2) the coupon rate of the bond, 6 5/8; and (3) the year the bond matures, 2034.

Cur Yld In this column, you find the current yield. (We showed how to compute the yield on a bond.) If the bond is purchased today (hence the word *current*), it will provide a yield of 6.7 percent.

Vol. In this column is the volume, 115. The dollar volume today is $115,000.

Close In this column, you find the closing price for the bond on this day, 99 1/2. Bond prices are quoted in points and fractions, and each point is $10. Thus, 99 1/2 is $999.50: $99.5 \times 10 = \$999.50$.

Net Chg. In this column, you find the net change for the day. Here, it is −3/4, which means the price on this day was $7.50 lower than it was the previous day.

TREASURY BONDS Not all publications will present Treasury bond information in exactly the same format. The format we show you here is common, though.

(1) Rate	(2) Maturity	(3) Bid	(4) Ask	(5) Chg	(6) Yield
7 3/4	Feb. 09	105:12	105:14	−1	5.50

Rate In this column, you find the coupon rate of the bond. This Treasury bond pays 7 3/4 percent of the face value of the bond in annual interest payments.

Maturity In this column, you find when the bond matures. This Treasury bond matures in February 2009.

Bid In this column, you find how much the buyer is willing to pay for the bond (or the price you will receive if you sell the bond): 105:12. The number after the colon stands for 32nds of $10. Therefore, 105:12 is $1,053.75. First, multiply $105 \times \$10 = \$1,050$. Second, turn 12/32 into 0.375, and multiply by $10, giving you $3.75. Then add $3.75 to $1,050 to get $1,053.75.

Ask In this column, you find how much the seller is asking for to sell the bond. This is the price you will pay if you buy the bond: $1,054.37.

Chg. In this column, you find the change in the price of the bond from the previous trading day, expressed in 32nds. Therefore, −1 means that the price of the bond fell by 1/32nd of $10, or approximately 32 cents from the previous day.

Yield In this column, you find the yield, which is based on the ask price. Someone who buys the bond today (at the ask price) and holds it to maturity will reap a return of 5.50 percent.

Risk and Return

Whether buying stocks or bonds, the common denominator is that people buy them for the return. Simply stated, they hope to make money. How much money people can hope to make is tied directly to the different risk and return factors of stocks and bonds. For example, buying stock in a new company might be much riskier than buying a Treasury bond issued by the U.S. Treasury. You can be fairly sure that the U.S. Treasury is going to pay off that bond because the U.S. government has the ability to tax people. But you can't be so sure of a positive return on the stock you buy in the new company. You might buy the stock for $10 one day, and three days later it falls to $1 and stays at that price (or thereabouts) for 10 years.

In Chapter 1, we said there was a well-known principle in economics: There is no such thing as a free lunch. Applied to stocks and bonds (or any investment), that principle means you never get something for nothing. In short, higher returns come with higher risks, and lower returns come with lower risks. Treasury bonds, for example, will often pay (relatively) low returns because they are so safe (risk-free).

SELF-TEST

1. What is a bond?
2. If the coupon payment on a bond is $400 a year and the coupon rate is 7 percent, then what is the face value?
3. If the annual coupon payment for a bond is $1,000 and the price paid for the bond was $9,500, then what is the yield or interest rate?
4. What is the difference between a municipal bond and a Treasury bond?

FUTURES AND OPTIONS

In this section, we discuss both futures and options.

Futures

Myers is a miller. He buys wheat from the wheat farmer, turns the wheat into flour, and then sells the flour to the baker. Obviously, he wants to earn a profit for what he does. How much, if any, profit he earns depends on the price at which he can buy the wheat and the price at which he can sell the flour.

Myers decides to buy a futures contract in wheat. A **futures contract** is a contract in which the seller agrees to provide a good (in this case, wheat) to the buyer on a specified future date at an agreed-on price. For example, Myers might buy bushels of wheat now, for a price of $3 a bushel, to be delivered to him in six months.

Futures Contract
An agreement to buy or sell a specific amount of something (commodity, currency, financial instrument) at an agreed-on price on a stipulated future date.

But who would sell him the futures contract? A likely possibility is a speculator, someone who buys and sells commodities to profit from changes in the market. A speculator assumes risk in the hope of making a gain.

Suppose Smith, a speculator, believes that the price of wheat six months from now is going to be lower than it is today. She may look at things this way: "The price of wheat today is $3 a bushel. I think the price of wheat in six months will be close to $2 a bushel. Why not promise the miller that I will deliver him as much wheat as he wants in six months if, in return, he agrees today to pay me $3 a bushel for it. Then, in six months, I will buy the wheat for $2 a bushel, sell it to the miller for $3 a bushel, and earn myself $1 profit per bushel." So Myers, the miller, and Smith, the speculator, enter into a futures contract. Myers buys 200 bushels of wheat for delivery in six months; Smith sells 200 bushels of wheat for delivery in six months.

Each party gets something out of the deal. Myers, the miller, gets peace of mind. He knows that he will be able to buy the wheat at a price that will let him earn a profit on his deal with the baker. Smith takes a chance, which she is willing to take, for the chance of earning a profit.

As another example, Wilson is a farmer who grows primarily corn. The current price of corn is $3.34 a bushel. Wilson doesn't have any corn to sell right now, but he will in two months. He hopes that between now and two months, the price of corn won't fall to, say, something under $3. He decides to enter into a futures contract in corn. He promises to deliver 5,000 bushels of corn two months from now for $3.34 a bushel. Leung, a speculator in corn, decides that this is a good deal for him because he believes that in two months the price of a bushel of corn will have risen to $3.94. So Wilson and Leung enter into a futures contract. Two months pass and the price of corn has dropped to $3.10. Leung turned out to be wrong about the price rising. So farmer Wilson delivers 5,000 bushels of corn to speculator Leung, for which Leung pays Wilson $3.34 a bushel (for a total of $16,700), as agreed. Then Leung turns around and sells the corn for $3.10 a bushel (receiving $15,500), losing $1,200 on the deal.

CURRENCY FUTURES A futures contract can be written for wheat, as we have seen, or for a currency, a stock index, or even bonds. Here is how a currency futures contract works.

You check the dollar price of a euro today and find that it is $1.20. Thus, for every $1.20, you get 1 euro in return. You expect that, in three months, you will have to pay $1.50 to buy a euro. With this in mind, you enter into a futures contract. Essentially, you say that you are willing to buy $10 million worth of euros three months from now for $1.20 a euro. Who might be willing to enter into this contract with you? Anyone who thinks the dollar price of a euro will be lower (not higher) in three months. Suppose you and Werner enter a contract. You promise to buy $10 million worth of euros in three months (at $1.20 a euro), and Werner promises to sell you $10 million worth of euros in three months (at $1.20 a euro).

Three months pass, and it now takes $1.30 to buy a euro. Werner has to buy $10 million worth of euros at an exchange rate of $1.30 per euro. For $10 million, he gets 7,692,307 euros, which he turns over to you for $1.20 each, leaving him with $9,230,768. Obviously, Werner has taken a loss; he spent $10 million to get $9,230,768 in return, for a loss of $769,232.

On the other side of the deal, you now have 7,692,307 euros, for which you paid $9,230,768. If you sell them all, because you get $1.30 for every euro, you will get approximately $10 million. You are better off by $769,232.

Option
A contract that gives the owner the right, but not the obligation, to buy or sell shares of a stock at a specified price on or before a specified date.

Options

An **option** is a contract that gives the owner of the option the right, but not the obligation, to buy or sell shares of a stock at a specified price on or before a specified date. There are two types of options: calls and puts.

CALL OPTION Call options give the owner of the option the right to *buy* shares of a stock at a specified price within the time limits of the contract. The specified price at which the buyer can buy shares of a stock is called the *strike price*. For example, Brown buys a call option for $20. The call option specifies that he can buy 100 shares of IBM stock at a strike price of $150 within the next month. If the price of IBM stocks falls below $150, Brown doesn't exercise his call option. He simply tears it up and accepts the fact that he has lost $20. If he still wants to buy IBM stock, he can do so through his stockbroker as he normally does and pay the going price, which is lower than $150. But if the price rises above $150, he exercises his call option, buys the stock at $150 a share, and then sells it for the higher market price. He has made a profit.

If Brown buys a call option, then there has to be someone who sells it to him. Anyone who would sell Brown a call option is a person who thought the option wouldn't be exercised. For example, if Jones believed that the price of IBM was going to fall below $150, then he would gladly sell a call option to Brown for $20, thinking that the option would never be exercised. That's $20 in his pocket.

PUT OPTIONS Put options give the owner the right, but not the obligation, to *sell* (rather than buy, as in a call option) shares of a stock at a strike price during some period of time. For example, suppose Martin buys a put option to sell 100 shares of IBM stock at $130 during the next month. If the share price rises above $130, Martin will not exercise his put option. He will simply tear it up and sell the stock for more than $130. On the other hand, if the price drops below $130, then he will exercise his option to sell the stock for $130 a share.

People who think the price of the stock is going to decline buy put options. Obviously, the people who think the price of the stock is going to rise sell put options. Why not sell a put option for, say, $20, if you expect the price of the stock to rise? The buyer is not going to exercise the option.

HOW YOU CAN USE CALL AND PUT OPTIONS You can use call and put options in a number of ways. Suppose you think a stock, currently selling for $250 a share, is going to rise in price during the next few months. You don't have enough money to buy many shares of stock, but you would like to benefit from the rise in the price of the stock. In such a case, you can buy a call option, which will sell for a fraction of the cost of the stock. So with limited resources, you decide to buy the call option, which gives you the right to buy, say, 100 shares of the stock at $250 anytime during the next three months.

A natural question is, if you don't have the money to buy the stock at $250 a share now, how are you going to buy it at $250 in a few months? You don't have to buy the stock. If you are right that the price of the stock will rise, then your call option will become worth more to people. In other words, if you bought the option when the price of the stock was $250 and the stock rises to $300, then your call option has become more valuable. You can sell it and benefit from the uptick in the price of the stock.

Alternatively, let's say you expect the price of the stock to fall. Then you can buy a put option. In other words, you buy the right to sell the stock for $250 any time during the next three months. If the price does fall, your option becomes more valuable. In fact, the farther the price falls, the more valuable your put option becomes. People who have the stock and want to sell it for a price higher than it currently fetches on the market will be willing to buy your put option from you for some price higher than the price you paid.

As an example, the current price of a call option for AT&T stock is $10, and the current price of the AT&T stock is $100. Ginny decides to buy a call option for $10, giving her the right to buy AT&T at a price of $100. Five months pass, and the price of AT&T shares has risen to $150. If Ginny wants, she can exercise her call option to buy AT&T stock at $100 (which is $50 less than the current price of $150). In other words, she can spend $100 to buy a share of stock, which she can turn around and immediately sell for $150, making a profit of $50 per share.

SELF-TEST

1. What is a futures contract?
2. You expect that a stock will rise in the next few months, but you do not have enough money to buy many shares of the stock. What can you do instead?
3. What is a put option?

office hours

"I HAVE THREE QUESTIONS."

Student:

Can a firm that issues a bond set the coupon rate at any rate it wants?

Instructor:

No. To illustrate, suppose company A needs to borrow $10 million and decides to issue $1,000 bonds. The only way anyone would be willing to buy one of these bonds (lend the company $10,000) is if the company promised the buyers a rate of return comparable to the interest rate they could get if they simply put the money in a savings account. The company has to set the coupon rate in such a way that it attracts people to its bonds. If people are earning, say, 5 percent on their savings accounts, they will not lend money to the company unless the company pays a coupon rate of at least 5 percent. In short, the coupon rate is set at a competitive level—not just any level the company wants to set it at.

Student:

Is it a good idea to buy stock?

Instructor:

A lot depends on such factors as your age (are you at the beginning of your work career or near the end), your income, and how much you can afford to invest in the stock market. There is no guarantee that the stock you buy will go up in price. For example, consider what happened to the DJIA over the 1930s. At the beginning of 1930, the Dow stood around 250, but at the end of 1939, it was around 150. Over the decade of the 1930s, the Dow went down by 40 percent.

However, having said this, stock prices have gone up over the long run. For example, suppose we look at the S&P Index during the period 1926–2004. The data show that you would have had a 70 percent likelihood of earning a positive investment return over a 1-year period, but that would have risen to 86.5 percent chance of a positive investment return if you had held the stocks in the index over a 5-year period. The probability of a positive return goes up to 97.1 percent if you had held the stocks for 10 years.

Student:

Last question: Suppose I buy 100 shares of stock at a price of $40 a share. The stock goes down in price to $32. Shouldn't I wait until the share price rises to $40 or higher before I sell it?

Instructor:

When it comes to stock, what goes down is not guaranteed to go up. Even if the stock's price has gone down by $8, it might go down more. You want always to look forward, to the future (not backward, to the past), when deciding whether to sell a stock. if you think there is a reason for the price to fall even farther, it is better to sell at $32 (and take an $8 per share loss) than to sell at $25 and take a bigger loss. If you think there is a reason for the price to rise, then hold on to the stock.

Points to Remember

1. A company that issues bonds cannot set the coupon rate at whatever rate it wants.
2. Based on the period 1926–2004, the longer a person would have held stocks, the higher the probability he or she would have received a positive return.
3. Stocks that go down in price are not guaranteed to go up in price.

a reader asks | Is There a Financial Language All Its Own?

Sometimes, when I watch the financial news, I hear people using unfamiliar terms. Some of the terms they use seem to be peculiar to their field of financial expertise. What are some of these terms and what do they mean?

Here are some of the terms, followed by what they mean:

After the Bell
After the close of the stock market.

Air Pocket Stock
A stock that plunges fast and furiously, much like an airplane that hits an air pocket.

Big Board
A nickname for the New York Stock Exchange.

Bo Derek
A perfect stock or investment, named after the movie actress who starred in the 1979 movie *10*.

Bear Market
A market in which prices are expected to fall.

Bull Market
A market in which prices are expected to rise. The terms *bull* and *bear* come from how these animals attack their opponents. The bull puts its horns up in the air, and a bear moves its paws down (across its opponent).

Casino Finance
An investment strategy that is considered extremely risky.

Deer Market
A flat market in which not much is happening and investors are usually timid; neither a bull nor a bear market.

Eat Well, Sleep Well
A phrase that expresses the idea that, when it comes to investing, no one gets anything for nothing. If you want a high return, you usually have to assume some risk. If you don't want to take on much risk, then you will likely have a low return. In short, high risk comes with high return, and low risk comes with low return. Do you want a risky investment that may end up feeding you well, or do you want a safe investment that lets you sleep at night?

Falling Knife
A stock whose price has fallen significantly in a short time—"Don't try to catch a falling knife" (you can hurt yourself).

Goldilocks Economy
An economy that is not too hot or too cold but just right. People often referred to the economy in the mid- to late 1990s in the United States as the Goldilocks economy.

Lemon
A disappointing investment.

Love Money
Money given by family or friends to a person to start a business.

Nervous Nellie
An investor who isn't comfortable with investing, mainly because of the risks.

Sandwich Generation
People, usually of middle age, who are sandwiched, in a sense, between their children and their parents. They are said to have to take care of two groups of people, one on either side of them.

Santa Claus Rally
A jump in the price of stocks that often occurs the week between Christmas and New Year.

Short Selling
A technique used by investors who are trying to benefit from a falling stock price. To illustrate, Brian, who believes that stock X will soon fall in price, borrows the stock from someone who currently owns it and promises to return it later. He then sells the stock, hoping to buy it back later at a lower price.

War Babies
The name given to stocks issued by companies that produce military hardware (e.g., tanks, airplanes, etc.).

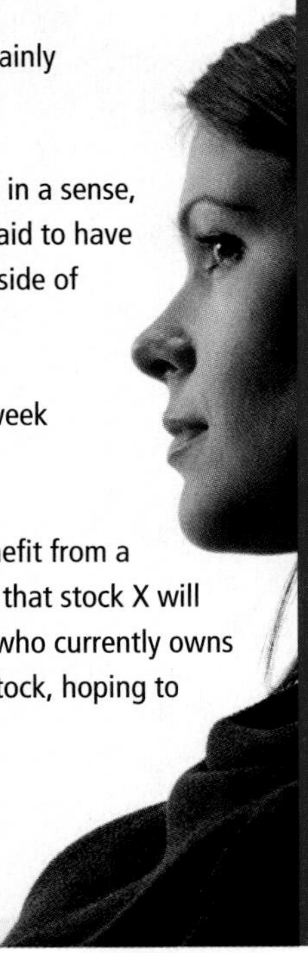

Chapter Summary

STOCKS

- A stock is a claim on the assets of a corporation that gives the purchaser a share (ownership) in the corporation. Stocks are sometimes called equity because the buyer of the stock has part ownership of the company that initially issued the stock.
- Stocks are bought and sold on exchanges and markets such as the New York Stock Exchange.
- Some people buy stocks for the dividends, which are payments made to stockholders based on a company's profits; others attempt to make money by buying shares at a lower price and selling at a higher price.

- Today, 30 stocks make up the Dow Jones Industrial Average (DJIA). The DJIA was devised by Charles Dow to convey information about what was happening in the stock market.
- A stock index fund consists of the stocks that make up an index.
- The yield (or interest rate) of a stock is equal to the dividend divided by the closing price of the stock.
- The P/E ratio for a stock is equal to the closing price per share (of the stock) divided by the net earnings per share. A stock with a P/E ratio of, say, 15 means that the stock is selling for a share price that is 15 times its earnings per share.

BONDS

- A bond is an IOU, or a promise to pay, typically issued by companies, governments, or government agencies.
- The three major components of a bond are face or par value, maturity date, and coupon rate.
- The price that a person pays for a bond depends on market conditions: The greater the demand is for the bond relative to the supply, the higher the price will be.
- The yield on the bond is the coupon payment divided by the price paid for the bond.
- Bonds are rated or evaluated. The more likely it is that the bond issuer will pay the face value of the bond at maturity and meet all scheduled coupon payments, the higher the bond's rating will be.
- The price of a bond and its yield (or interest rate) are inversely related.

FUTURES AND OPTIONS

- In a futures contract, a seller agrees to provide a good to the buyer on a specified future date at an agreed-on price.
- An option is a contract giving the owner the right, but not the obligation, to buy or sell a particular good at a specified price on or before a specified date.

Key Terms and Concepts

Stock	Initial Public Offering (IPO)	Dividend	Yield
Dow Jones Industrial Average (DJIA)	Investment Bank	Bond	Futures Contract
		Face Value (Par Value)	Option

Questions and Problems

1 What is the purpose of financial markets?

2 What does it mean if the Dow Jones Industrial Average rises by, say, 100 points in a day?

3 What does it mean to buy the market?

4 What does it mean if someone invests in a mutual fund? in a stock market fund?

5 If the share price of each of 500 stocks rises on Monday, does everyone in the stock market believe that stocks are headed even higher? (No one will buy a stock if he or she thought share prices were headed lower.)

6 Which of the two stocks has a bigger gap between its closing price and net earnings per share: Stock A with a P/E ratio of 15 or Stock B with a P/E ratio of 44? Explain your answer.

7 "An issuer of a bond is a borrower." Do you agree or disagree? Explain your answer.

8 If the face value of a bond is $10,900 and the annual coupon payment is $600, what is the coupon rate?

9 Why might a person purchase an inflation-indexed Treasury bond?

10 "If you can predict interest rates, then you can earn a fortune buying and selling bonds." Do you agree or disagree? Explain your answer.

11 Why might a person buy a futures contract?

12 Why might a person buy a call option?

13 "The currency speculator who sells futures contracts assumes the risk that someone else doesn't want to assume." Do you agree or disagree? Explain your answer.

14 If you thought the share price of a stock was going to fall, would you buy a call option or a put option?

Working with Numbers and Graphs

1 You own 1,250 shares of stock X, and you read in the newspaper that the dividend for the stock is 3.88. What did you earn in dividends?

2 The closing price of a stock is 90.25, and the dividend is 3.50. What is the yield of the stock?

3 The closing price of the stock is $66.40, and the net earnings per share are $2.50. What is the stock's P/E ratio?

4 The face value of a bond is $10,000, and the annual coupon payment is $850. What is the coupon rate?

5 A person buys a bond that matures in 10 years and pays a coupon rate of 10 percent. The face value of the bond is $10,000. How much money will the bondholder receive in the tenth year?

Self-Test Appendix

Chapter 1

CHAPTER 1, PAGE 5

1 False. It takes two things for scarcity to exist: finite resources and infinite wants. If people's wants were equal to or less than the finite resources available to satisfy their wants, there would be no scarcity. Scarcity exists only because people's wants are greater than the resources available to satisfy their wants. Scarcity is the condition of infinite wants clashing with finite resources.

2 Because of scarcity, there is a need for a rationing device. People will compete for the rationing device. For example, if dollar price is the rationing device, people will compete for dollars.

3 Because our unlimited wants are greater than our limited resources—that is, because scarcity exists—some wants must go unsatisfied. We must choose which wants we will satisfy and which we will not.

CHAPTER 1, PAGE 13

1 Every time a person is late to history class, the instructor subtracts one-tenth of a point from the person's final grade. If the instructor raised the opportunity cost of being late to class—by subtracting one point from the person's final grade—economists predict there would be fewer persons late to class. In summary, the higher the opportunity cost of being late to class, the less likely people will be late to class.

2 Yes. To illustrate, suppose the marginal benefits and marginal costs (in dollars) are as follows for various hours of studying.

Hour	Marginal Benefits	Marginal Costs
First hour	$20.00	$10.00
Second hour	$14.00	$11.00
Third hour	$13.00	$12.00
Fourth hour	$12.10	$12.09
Fifth hour	$11.00	$13.00

Clearly, you will study the first hour because the marginal benefits are greater than the marginal costs. Stated differently, there is a net benefit of $10 (the difference between the marginal benefits of $20 and the marginal costs of $10) for studying the first hour. If you stop studying after the first hour and do not proceed to the second, then you will forfeit the net benefit of $3 for the second hour. To maximize your net benefits of studying, you must proceed until the marginal benefits and the marginal costs are as close to equal as possible. (In the extreme, this is an epsilon away from equality. However, economists simply speak of "equality" between the two for convenience.) In this case, you will study through the fourth hour. You will not study the fifth hour because it is not worth it; the marginal benefits of studying the fifth hour are less than the marginal costs. In short, there is a net cost to studying the fifth hour.

3 You might feel sleepy the next day, you might be less alert while driving, and so on.

Chapter 2

CHAPTER 2, PAGE 39

1 A straight-line PPF represents constant opportunity costs between two goods. For example, for every unit of X produced, one unit of Y is forfeited. A bowed-outward PPF represents increasing opportunity costs. For example, we may have to forfeit one unit of X to produce the eleventh unit of Y, but we have to forfeit two units of X to produce the one hundredth unit of Y.

2 A bowed-outward PPF is representative of increasing costs. In short, the PPF would not be bowed outward if increasing costs did not exist. To prove this, look back at Exhibits 1 and 2. In Exhibit 1, costs are constant (not increasing), and the PPF is a straight line. In Exhibit 2, costs are increasing, and the PPF is bowed outward.

3 The first condition is that the economy is currently operating *below* its PPF. It is possible to move from a point below the PPF to a point on the PPF and get more of all goods. The second condition is that the economy's PPF shifts outward.

4 False. Take a look at Exhibit 5. There are numerous productive efficient points, all of which lie on the PPF.

CHAPTER 2, PAGE 44

1 Transaction costs are the costs associated with the time and effort needed to search out, negotiate, and consummate a trade. The transaction costs are likely to be higher for buying a house than for buying a car because buying a house is a more detailed and complex process.

2 Under certain conditions, Smith will buy good X from Jones. For example, suppose Smith and Jones agree on a price of, say, $260, and neither person incurs transaction costs greater than $40. If transaction costs are zero for each person, then each person benefits $40 from the trade. Specifically, Smith buys the good for $40 less than his maximum price, and Jones sells the good for $40 more than his minimum price. But suppose each person incurs a transaction cost of, say, $50. Smith would be unwilling to pay $260 to Jones and $50 in transaction costs (for a total of $310) when he is only willing to pay a maximum price of $300 for good X. Similarly, Jones would be unwilling to sell good X for $260 and incur $50 in transaction costs (leaving him with only $210, or $10 less than his minimum selling price).

3 Answers will vary. Sample answer: John buys a magazine and reads it. There is no third-party effect. Sally asks a rock band to play at a party. Sally's next-door neighbor (a third party) is disturbed by the loud music.

CHAPTER 2, PAGE 48

1 If George goes from producing 5X to 10X, he gives up 5Y. This means the opportunity cost of 5 more X is 5 fewer Y. It follows that the opportunity cost of 1X is 1Y. Conclusion: The opportunity cost of 1X is 1Y.

2 If Harriet produces 10 more X she gives up 15Y. It follows that the opportunity cost of 1X is 1.5Y, and the opportunity cost of 1Y is 0.67X. If Bill produces 10 more X, he gives up 20Y. It follows that the opportunity cost of 1X is 2Y, and the opportunity cost of 1Y is 0.5X. Harriet is the lower cost producer of X, and Bill is the lower cost producer of Y. In short, Harriet has the comparative advantage in the production of X; Bill has the comparative advantage in the production of Y.

Chapter 3

CHAPTER 3, PAGE 66

1 Popcorn is a normal good for Sandi. Prepaid telephone cards are an inferior good for Mark.

2 Asking why demand curves are downward sloping is the same as asking why price and quantity demanded are inversely related (as one rises, the other falls). There are two reasons mentioned in this section: (1) as price rises, people substitute lower priced goods for higher priced goods, and (2) because individuals receive less utility from an additional unit of a good they consume, they are only willing to pay less for the additional unit. The second reason is a reflection of the law of diminishing marginal utility.

3 Suppose only two people, Bob and Alice, have a demand for good X. At a price of $7, Bob buys 10 units and Alice buys 3 units; at a price of $6, Bob buys 12 units and Alice buys 5 units. One point on the market demand curve represents a price of $7 and a quantity demanded of 13 units; another point represents $6 and 17 units. A market demand curve is derived by adding the quantities demanded at each price.

4 A change in income, preferences, prices of related goods, number of buyers, and expectations of future price can change demand. A change in the price of the good changes the quantity demanded of the good. For example, a change in *income* can change the *demand* for oranges, but only a change in the *price* of oranges can directly change the *quantity demanded* of oranges.

CHAPTER 3, PAGE 71

1 It would be difficult to increase the quantity supplied of houses over the next ten hours, so the supply curve in (a) is vertical, as in Exhibit 8. It is possible to increase the quantity supplied of houses over the next three months, however, so the supply curve in (b) is upward sloping.

2 a. The supply curve shifts to the left.

b. The supply curve shifts to the left.

c. The supply curve shifts to the right.

3 False. If the price of apples rises, the *quantity supplied* of apples will rise—not the *supply* of apples. We are talking about a *movement* from one point on a supply curve to a point higher up on the supply curve and not about a shift in the supply curve.

CHAPTER 3, PAGE 82

1 Disagree. In the text, we plainly saw how supply and demand work at an auction. Supply and demand are at work in the grocery store, too, although no auctioneer is present. The essence of the auction example is the auctioneer raising the price when there was a shortage and lowering the price when there was a surplus. The same thing happens at the grocery store. For example, if there is a surplus of corn flakes, the manager of the store is likely to have a sale (lower prices) on corn flakes. Many markets without auctioneers act *as if* there are auctioneers raising and lowering prices in response to shortages and surpluses.

2 No. It could be the result of a higher supply of computers. Either a decrease in demand or an increase in supply will lower price.

3 a. Lower price and quantity

b. Lower price and higher quantity

c. Higher price and lower quantity

d. Lower price and quantity

4 At equilibrium quantity, the maximum buying price and the minimum selling price are the same. For example, in Exhibit 15, both prices are $40 at the equilibrium quantity 4. Equilibrium quantity is the only quantity at which the maximum buying price and the minimum selling price are the same.

5 $44; $34.

CHAPTER 3, PAGE 85

1 Yes, if nothing else changes—that is, yes, *ceteris paribus*. If some other things change, though, they may not. For example, if the government imposes an effective price ceiling on gasoline, Jamie may pay lower gas prices at the pump but have to wait in line to buy the gas (due to first come, first served trying to ration the shortage). It is not clear if Jamie is better off paying a higher price and not waiting in line or paying a lower price and waiting in line. The point, however, is that buyers don't necessarily prefer lower prices to higher prices unless everything else (quality, wait, service, etc.) stays the same.

2 Disagree. Both long-lasting shortages and long lines are caused by price ceilings. First, the price ceiling is imposed, creating the shortage; then, the rationing device first come, first served emerges because price isn't permitted to fully ration the good. There are shortages every day that don't cause long lines to form. Instead, buyers bid up price, output and price move to equilibrium, and there is no shortage.

3 Buyers might argue for price ceilings on the goods they buy—especially if they don't know that price ceilings have some effects they may not like (e.g., fewer exchanges, FCFS used as a rationing device). Sellers might argue for price floors on the goods they sell—especially if they expect their profits to rise. Employees might argue for a wage floor on the labor services they sell—especially if they don't know that they may lose their jobs or have their hours cut back as a result.

Chapter 4

CHAPTER 4, PAGE 94

1 The price of food will rise along with the premium for food insurance.

2 The new demand curve would be between D_1 and D_2.

CHAPTER 4, PAGE 95

1 City 2

2 City 2

CHAPTER 4, PAGE 96

1 If supply and tuition are constant and demand rises, the shortage of openings at the university will become greater. The university will continue to use its nonprice rationing devices (GPA, SAT scores, ACT scores) but will have to raise the standards of admission. Instead of requiring a GPA of, say, 3.5 for admission, it may raise the requirement to 3.8.

2 Not likely. A university that didn't make admission easier in the face of a surplus of openings might not be around much longer. When tuition cannot be adjusted directly—in other words, when the rationing device of price cannot be adjusted—it is likely that the nonprice rationing device (standards) will be.

CHAPTER 4, PAGE 97

1 Any price above 70 cents.

2 Assuming that tolls are not used, freeway congestion will worsen. An increase in driving population simply shifts the demand curve for driving to the right.

CHAPTER 4, PAGE 99

1 Agree. At any price below equilibrium price, a shortage exists: The quantity demanded of kidneys is greater than the quantity supplied of kidneys. As price rises toward its equilibrium level, quantity supplied rises and quantity demanded falls until the two are equal.

2 It depends on whether or not $0 is the equilibrium price of kidneys. If it is—that is, if the kidney demand and supply curves intersect at $0—then there is no shortage of kidneys. But if, at $0, the quantity demanded of kidneys is greater than the quantity supplied, then a shortage exists.

CHAPTER 4, PAGE 101

1 Yes. At the equilibrium wage rate, the quantity demanded of labor equals the quantity supplied. At a higher wage (the minimum wage), the quantity supplied stays constant (given the vertical supply curve), but the quantity demanded falls. Thus, a surplus results.

2 The person is assuming that the labor demand curve is vertical (no matter what the wage rate is the quantity demanded of labor is always the same).

CHAPTER 4, PAGE 102

1 Look at the demand curve and the supply curve between Q_2 and Q_1. Notice that the demand curve lies *above* the supply curve in this area. This means that buyers are willing to pay more for each of the units between Q_2 and Q_2 (more, say, for the $Q_2 + 1$ unit) than sellers need to receive for them to place these units on the market. In short, moving from an equilibrium price to a price floor lowers the number of mutually beneficial trades that will be made. As discussed in Chapter 3, price floors lead to fewer exchanges.

2 It is likely that producers care more about how a change affects them than how it affects society. At the price floor, they receive more producers' surplus than they receive at the equilibrium price, even though consumers lose, in terms of consumers' surplus, more than producers gain. Look at it like this: Producers gain $10 and consumers lose $12. The sum of positive $10 and negative $12 is negative $2. Producers may not care about the sum (−$2); they care about their $10 gain.

CHAPTER 4, PAGE 104

1 Moving from a system where patients cannot sue their HMOs to one where they can gives patients something they didn't have before (the right to sue) at a higher price (higher charges for health care coverage). The "free lunch"—the right to sue—isn't free after all.

2 If the students get the extra week and nothing else changes, then the students will probably say they are better off. In other words, more of one thing (time) and no less of anything else makes one better off. But if because of the extra week, the professor grades their papers harder than she would have otherwise, then some or all of the students may say that they weren't made better off by the extra week.

CHAPTER 4, PAGE 105

1 One possible answer is: There are two cities, one with clean air and the other with dirty air. The demand to live in the clean-air city is higher than the demand to live in the dirty-air city. As a result, housing prices are higher in the clean-air city than in the dirty-air city.

2 Ultimately, the person who owns the land in the good-weather city receives the payment. Look at it this way: People have a higher demand for houses in good-weather cities than they do for houses in bad-weather cities. As a result, house builders receive higher prices for houses built and sold in good-weather cities. Because of the higher house prices in good-weather cities, house builders have a higher demand for land in good-weather cities. In the end, higher demand for land translates into higher land prices or land rents for landowners.

CHAPTER 4, PAGE 107

1 Suppose University X gives a full scholarship to every one of its football players (all of whom are superathletes). In addition, suppose that the full scholarship (translated into wages) is far below the equilibrium wage of each of the football players. (Think of it this way: Each football player gets a wage, or full scholarship, of $10,000 a year, when his equilibrium wage is $40,000 a year.) Paying lower than the equilibrium wage will end up transferring dollars and other benefits from the football players to the university to the

new field house and track and perhaps to you if you use the track for exercise.

2 If paying student athletes (a wage above the full scholarship) lowers consumers' demand for college athletics, then the equilibrium wage for college athletes is not as high as shown in Exhibit 10.

CHAPTER 4, PAGE 108

1 Answers will vary. Students sometimes say that it is "fairer" if everyone is charged the same price. Is it unfair then that movie goers pay less if they go to the 2 p.m. movie than if they go to the 8 p.m. movie?

2 In the application dealing with the kidney market, there was a price ceiling that resulted in a shortage of kidneys. In the application dealing with the 10 a.m. class, the university charged a below-equilibrium price for the 10 a.m. class, leading to a shortage of such classes.

Chapter 5

CHAPTER 5, PAGE 124

1 The CPI is calculated as follows: (1) define a market basket, (2) determine how much it would cost to purchase the market basket in the current year and in the base year, (3) divide the dollar cost of purchasing the market basket in the current year by the dollar cost of purchasing the market basket in the base year, and (4) multiply the quotient by 100. For a review of this process, see Exhibit 2.

2 It is a year that is used for comparison purposes with other years.

3 Annual (nominal) income has risen by 13.85 percent while prices have risen by 4.94 percent. We conclude that because (nominal) income has risen more than prices, real income has increased. Alternatively, you can look at it this way: Real income in year 1 is $31,337, and real income in year 2 is $33,996.

CHAPTER 5, PAGE 128

1 The frictionally unemployed person has readily transferable skills, and the structurally unemployed person does not.

2 It implies that the (actual, measured) unemployment rate in the economy is greater than the natural unemployment rate. For example, if the unemployment rate is 8 percent and the natural unemployment rate is 6 percent, the cyclical unemployment rate is 2 percent.

Chapter 6

CHAPTER 6, PAGE 138

1 The three approaches are expenditure, income, and value-added. In the expenditure approach, we add the amount of money spent by buyers on final goods and services. In the income approach, we sum the payments to the resources of production. In our example in the text, income consisted of the returns to labor (wages) and entrepreneurship (profits). In the value-added approach, we sum the dollar value contribution over all stages of production.

2 No. GDP doesn't account for all productive activity (e.g., it omits the production of nonmarket goods and services). Even if GDP is $0, it doesn't necessarily follow that there was no production in the country.

CHAPTER 6, PAGE 147

1 In the expenditure approach, GDP is computed by finding the sum of consumption, investment, government purchases, and net exports. (Net exports are equal to exports minus imports.)

2 Yes. To illustrate, suppose consumption is $200, investment is $80, and government purchases are $70. The sum of these three spending components of GDP is $350. Now suppose exports are $0 but imports are $100, which means that net exports are −$100. Since GDP = $C + I + G + (EX - IM)$, it follows that GDP is $250.

3 No. Each individual would have $40,000 worth of goods and services only if the entire GDP were equally distributed across the country. There is no indication that this is the case. The $40,000 (per capita GDP) says that the "average" person in the country has access to $40,000 worth of goods and services, but in reality, there may not be any "average" person. For example, if Smith earns $10,000 and Jones earns $20,000, then the average person earns $15,000. But neither Smith nor Jones earns $15,000, so neither is average.

CHAPTER 6, PAGE 151

1 We can't know for sure; we can say what might have caused the rise in GDP. It could be (a) a rise in prices, no change in output; (b) a rise in output, no change in prices; (c) rises in both prices and output; or (d) a percentage increase in prices that is greater than the percentage decrease in output, or some other situation.

2 More output was produced in year 2 than in year 1.

3 Yes. Business cycles—ups and downs in Real GDP—don't prevent Real GDP from growing over time. Exhibit 9 shows Real GDP higher at the second peak than at the first even though there is a business cycle between the peaks.

Chapter 7

CHAPTER 7, PAGE 167

1 Real balance effect: a rise (fall) in the price level causes purchasing power to fall (rise), which decreases (increases) a person's monetary wealth. As people become less (more) wealthy, the quantity demanded of Real GDP falls (rises).

2 If the dollar appreciates, it takes more foreign currency to buy a dollar and fewer dollars to buy foreign currency. This makes U.S. goods (denominated in dollars) more expensive for foreigners and foreign goods cheaper for Americans. In turn, foreigners buy fewer U.S. exports, and Americans buy more foreign imports. As exports fall and imports rise, net exports fall. If net exports fall, total expenditures fall, *ceteris paribus.* As total expenditures fall, the *AD* curve shifts to the left.

3 If personal income taxes decline, disposable incomes rise. As disposable incomes rise, consumption rises. As consumption rises, total expenditures rise, *ceteris paribus.* As total expenditures rise, the *AD* curve shifts to the right.

CHAPTER 7, PAGE 171

1 As wage rates decline, the cost per unit of production falls. In the short run (assuming prices are constant), profit per unit rises. Higher profit causes producers to produce more units of their goods and services. In short, the *SRAS* curve shifts to the right.

2 Last year, 10 workers produced 100 units of good X in 1 hour. This year, 10 workers produced 120 units of good X in 1 hour.

3 Workers initially misperceive the change in their real wage due to a change in the price level. For example, suppose the nominal wage is $30 and the price level is 1.50; it follows that the real wage is $20. Now suppose the nominal wage falls to $25 and the price level falls to 1.10. The real wage is now $22.72. But suppose workers misperceive the decline in the price level and mistakenly believe it has fallen to 1.40.They will now perceive their real wage as $17.85 ($25/1.40). In other words, they will misperceive their real wage as falling when it has actually increased. How will workers react if they believe their real wage has fallen? They will cut back on the quantity supplied of labor, which will end up reducing output (or Real GDP). This process is consistent with an upward-sloping *SRAS* curve: A decline in the price level leads to a reduction in output.

CHAPTER 7, PAGE 178

1 In long-run equilibrium, the economy is producing Natural Real GDP. In short-run equilibrium, the economy is not producing Natural Real GDP, although the quantity demanded of Real GDP equals the quantity supplied of Real GDP.

2 The diagram should show the price level in the economy at P_1 and Real GDP at Q_1 but the intersection of the *AD* curve and the *SRAS* curve at some point other than (P_1, Q_1). In addition, the *LRAS* curve should not be at Q_1 or at the intersection of the *AD* and *SRAS* curves.

Chapter 8

CHAPTER 8, PAGE 187

1 Say's law states that supply creates its own demand. In a barter economy, Jones supplies good X only so that she can use it to demand some other good (e.g., good Y). The act of supplying is motivated by the desire to demand. Supply and demand are opposite sides of the same coin.

2 No, total spending will not decrease. For classical economists, an increase in saving (reflected in a decrease in consumption) will lower the interest rate and stimulate investment spending. So one spending component (consumption) goes down, and another spending component (investment) goes up. Moreover, according to classical economists, the decrease in one spending component will be completely offset by an increase in another spending component so that overall spending does not change.

3 Prices and wages are flexible; they move up and down in response to market conditions.

CHAPTER 8, PAGE 192

1 A recessionary gap exists if the economy is producing a Real GDP level that is less than Natural Real GDP. An inflationary gap exists if the economy is producing a Real GDP level that is more than Natural Real GDP.

2 When the economy is in a recessionary gap, the labor market has a surplus. When the economy is in an inflationary gap, there is a shortage in the labor market.

3 The economy is somewhere above the institutional PPF and below the physical PPF.

CHAPTER 8, PAGE 198

1 In a recessionary gap, the existing unemployment rate is greater than the natural unemployment rate, implying that unemployment is relatively high. As wage contracts expire, business firms will negotiate new ones that pay workers lower wage rates. As a result, the *SRAS* curve shifts rightward. As this happens, the price level begins to fall. The economy moves down the *AD* curve—eventually to the point where it intersects the *LRAS* curve. At this point, the economy is in long-run equilibrium.

2 In an inflationary gap, the existing unemployment rate is less than the natural unemployment rate, implying that unemployment is relatively low. As wage contracts expire, business firms will negotiate contracts that pay workers higher wage rates. As a result, the *SRAS* curve shifts leftward. As this happens, the price level begins to rise. The economy moves up the *AD* curve—eventually to the point where it intersects the *LRAS* curve. At this point, the economy is in long-run equilibrium.

3 Any changes in aggregate demand will affect—in the long run—only the price level, not the Real GDP level or the unemployment rate. Stated differently, changes in *AD* in an economy will have no long-run effect on the Real GDP that a country produces or on its unemployment rate; changes in *AD* will change only the price level in the long run.

Chapter 9

CHAPTER 9, PAGE 208

1 Keynesians mean that an economy may not self-regulate at Natural Real GDP (Q_N). Instead, an economy can get stuck in a recessionary gap.

2 To say that the economy is self-regulating is the same as saying that prices and wages are flexible and adjust quickly. They are just two ways of describing the same thing.

3 The main reason is that Say's law may not hold in a money economy. The question is why *doesn't* Say's law hold in a money economy? Keynes argued that an increase in saving (which leads to a decline in demand) does not necessarily bring about an equal amount of additional investment (which would lead to an increase in demand), because neither saving nor investment is exclusively affected by changes

in the interest rate. See Exhibit 1 for how Keynes might have used numbers to explain his position.

CHAPTER 9, PAGE 214

1 Autonomous consumption is one of the components of overall consumption. To illustrate, look at the consumption function: $C = C_0 + (MPC)(Y_d)$. The part of overall consumption (C) that is autonomous is C_0. This part of consumption does not depend on disposable income. The part of consumption that does depend on disposable income (i.e., the part that changes as disposable income changes) is the $(MPC)(Y_d)$ part. For example, assume the $MPC = 0.80$. If Y_d rises by $1,000, then consumption goes up by $800.

2 $1/1 - 0.70 = 1/0.30 = 3.33$.

3 The multiplier falls. For example, if $MPC = 0.20$, then the multiplier is 1.25, but if $MPC = 0.80$, then the multiplier is 5.

CHAPTER 9, PAGE 218

1 Keynes believed that the economy may not always self-regulate itself at Natural Real GDP. In other words, households and businesses (the private sector of the economy) are not always capable of generating enough aggregate demand in the economy so that the economy equilibrates at Natural Real GDP.

2 The increase in autonomous spending will lead to a greater increase in total spending and to a shift rightward in the *AD* curve. If the economy is operating in the horizontal section of the Keynesian *AS* curve, Real GDP will rise, and there will be no change in prices.

3 Agree. The economist who believes the economy is inherently unstable sees a role for government. Government is supposed to stabilize the economy at Natural Real GDP. The economist who believes the economy is self-regulating (capable of moving itself to Natural Real GDP) sees only a small, if any, role for government in the economy because the economy is already doing the job government would supposedly do.

CHAPTER 9, PAGE 224

1 When *TP* is greater than *TE*, firms are producing and offering for sale more units of goods and services than households and government want to buy. As a result, business inventories rise above optimal levels. In reaction, firms cut back on their production of goods and services. This leads to a decline in Real GDP, which stops falling when *TP* equals *TE*.

2 When *TE* is greater than *TP*, households and businesses want to buy more than firms are producing and offering for sale. As a result, business inventories fall below optimal levels. In reaction, firms increase their production of goods and services. This leads to a rise in Real GDP, which stops rising when *TP* equals *TE*.

Chapter 10

CHAPTER 10, PAGE 235

1 With a proportional income tax, the tax rate is constant as a taxpayer's income rises. With a progressive income tax, the tax rate rises as income rises (up to some point). With a regressive income tax, the tax rate falls as income rises.

2 In 2005, the top 5 percent of income earners received 35.75 percent of all income and paid 59.67 percent of all income taxes.

3 Individual income tax, corporate income tax, and Social Security taxes.

4 The cyclical budget deficit is that part of the budget deficit that is the result of a downturn in economic activity.

CHAPTER 10, PAGE 242

1 If there is no crowding out, expansionary fiscal policy is predicted to increase aggregate demand and, if the economy is in a recessionary gap, either reduce or eliminate the gap. However, if there is, say, complete crowding out, expansionary fiscal policy will not meet its objective. The following example illustrates complete crowding out: If government purchases rise by $100 million, private spending will decrease by $100 million so that there is no net effect on aggregate demand.

2 Suppose the economy is currently in a recessionary gap at time period 1. Expansionary fiscal policy is needed to remove the economy from its recessionary gap, but fiscal policy lags (data lag, wait-and-see lag, etc.) may be so long that, by the time the fiscal policy is implemented, the economy has moved itself out of the recessionary gap, making the expansionary fiscal policy not only unnecessary but potentially capable of moving the economy into an inflationary gap. Exhibit 5 illustrates the process.

3 The federal government spends more on a given program. As a result, the budget deficit grows, and the federal government increases its demand for loanable funds (or credit) to finance the larger deficit. Because of the greater demand for loanable funds, the interest rate rises, and business firms cut back on investment. An increase in government spending has indirectly led to a decline in investment spending.

CHAPTER 10, PAGE 245

1 Let's suppose that a person's taxable income rises by $1,000 to $45,000 and that her taxes rise from $10,000 to $10,390 as a result. Her marginal tax rate—the percentage of her additional taxable income she pays in taxes—is 39 percent. Her average tax rate—the percentage of her (total) income she pays in taxes—is 23 percent.

2 Not necessarily. It depends on whether the percentage rise in tax rates is greater or less than the percentage fall in the tax base. Here's a simple example: Suppose the average tax rate is 10 percent and the tax base is $100. Tax revenues then equal $10. If the tax rate rises to 12 percent (a 20 percent rise) and the tax base falls to $90 (a 10 percent fall), tax revenues rise to $10.80. In other words, if the tax rate rises by a greater percentage than the tax base falls, tax revenues rise. But then suppose that the tax base falls to $70 (a 30 percent fall) instead of to $90. Now tax revenues are $8.40. In other words, if the tax rate rises by a smaller percentage than the tax base falls, tax revenues fall.

Chapter 11

CHAPTER 11, PAGE 257

1 Money evolved because individuals wanted to make trading easier (i.e., less time-consuming). In a barter economy, this need motivated people to accept the good with relatively greater acceptability than all other goods. In time, the effect snowballed, and finally the good with initially relatively greater acceptability emerged into a good that was widely accepted for purposes of exchange. At this point, the good became money.

2 No. M1 will fall, but M2 will not rise; it will remain constant. To illustrate, suppose M1 is \$400 and M2 is \$600. If people remove \$100 from checkable deposits, M1 will decline to \$300. For purposes of illustration, think of M2 as equal to M1 + money market accounts. The M1 component of M2 falls by \$100, but the money market accounts component rises by \$100; so there is no net effect on M2. Thus M1 falls and M2 remains constant.

3 In a barter (moneyless) economy, a double coincidence of wants will not occur for every transaction. When it does not occur, the cost of the transaction increases because more time must be spent to complete the trade. In a money economy, money is acceptable for every transaction; so a double coincidence of wants is not necessary. All buyers offer money for what they want to buy, and all sellers accept money for what they want to sell.

CHAPTER 11, PAGE 267

1 \$55 million

2 \$6 billion

3 \$0. Bank A was required to hold only \$1 million in reserves but held \$1.2 million instead. Therefore, its loss of \$200,000 in reserves does not cause it to be reserve deficient.

Chapter 12

CHAPTER 12, PAGE 274

1 Federal Reserve Bank of New York.

2 The Fed controls the money supply.

3 Acting as the lender of last resort means the Fed stands ready to lend funds to banks that are suffering cash management, or liquidity, problems.

CHAPTER 12, PAGE 281

1 a. The money supply falls.
b. The money supply rises.
c. The money supply falls.

2 The federal funds rate is the interest rate that one bank charges another bank for a loan. The discount rate is the interest rate that the Fed charges a bank for a loan.

3 Reserves in bank A rise; reserves in the banking system remain the same (bank B lost the reserves that bank A borrowed).

4 Reserves in bank A rise; reserves in the banking system rise because there is no offset in reserves for any other bank.

Chapter 13

CHAPTER 13, PAGE 290

1 If M times V increases, total expenditures increase. In other words, people spend more. For example, instead of spending \$3 billion on goods and services, they spend \$4 billion. But if there is more spending (greater total expenditures), there must be greater total sales. P times Q represents this total dollar value of sales.

2 The equation of exchange is a truism: MV necessarily equals PQ. This is similar to saying that 2 + 2 necessarily equals 4. It cannot be otherwise. The simple quantity theory of money, which is built on the equation of exchange, can be tested against real-world events. That is, the simple quantity theory of money assumes that both velocity and Real GDP are constant and then, based on these assumptions, predicts that changes in the money supply will be strictly proportional to changes in the price level. Because this prediction can be measured against real-world data, the simple quantity theory of money may offer insights into the way the economy works. The equation of exchange does not do this.

3 a. *AD* curve shifts rightward.
b. *AD* curve shifts leftward.
c. *AD* curve shifts rightward.
d. *AD* curve shifts leftward.

CHAPTER 13, PAGE 294

1 a. As velocity rises, the *AD* curve shifts to the right. In the short run, P and Q rise. In the long run, Q will return to its original level, and P will be higher than it was in the short run.
b. As velocity falls, the *AD* curve shifts to the left. In the short run, P and Q fall. In the long run, Q will return to its original level, and P will be lower than it was in the short run.
c. As the money supply rises, the *AD* curve shifts to the right. In the short run, P and Q rise. In the long run, Q will return to its original level, and P will be higher than it was in the short run.
d. As the money supply falls, the *AD* curve shifts to the left. In the short run, P and Q fall. In the long run, Q will return to its original level, and P will be lower than it was in the short run.

2 Yes, a change in velocity can offset a change in the money supply (on aggregate demand). Suppose that the money supply rises and velocity falls. A rise in the money supply shifts the *AD* curve to the right, and a fall in velocity shifts the *AD* curve to the left. If the strength of each change is the same, there is no change in *AD*.

CHAPTER 13, PAGE 301

1 We cannot answer this question based on the information given. We know only that three prices have gone up; we don't know if other prices (in the economy) have gone up, if other prices have gone down, or if some have gone up and others have gone down. To determine whether inflation has occurred, we have to know what has happened to the price level, not simply to three prices.

2 No. For continued inflation (continued increases in the price level) to be the result of continued decreases in *SRAS,* workers would have to continually ask for and receive higher wages while output was dropping and the unemployment rate rising. This set of conditions is not likely.

3 Continued inflation.

CHAPTER 13, PAGE 308

1 Three percent.

2 Yes, it is possible if the expectations effect immediately sets in and outweighs the liquidity effect.

3 Certainly, the Fed directly affects the supply of loanable funds and the interest rate through an open market operation. But it works as a catalyst to indirectly affect the loanable funds market and the interest rate via the changes in Real GDP, the price level, and the expected inflation rate. We can say this: The Fed directly affects the interest rate by means of the liquidity effect, and it indirectly affects the interest rate by means of the income, price-level, and expectations effects.

Chapter 14

CHAPTER 14, PAGE 319

1 Kahn buys a bond for a face value of $10,000 that promises to pay a 10 percent interest rate each year for 10 years. In one year, though, bonds are offered for a face value of $10,000 that pay an 11 percent interest rate each year for 10 years. If Kahn wants to sell his bond, he won't be able to sell it for $10,000 because no one today will pay $10,000 for a bond that pays a 10 percent interest rate when a $10,000, 11 percent bond is available. Kahn has to lower the price of his bond if he wants to sell it. Thus, as interest rates rise, bond prices decrease (for old or existing bonds).

2 We disagree for two reasons. First, if the money market is in the liquidity trap, a rise in the money supply will not affect interest rates and therefore will not affect investment or the goods and services market. Second, even if the money market is not in the liquidity trap, a rise in the money supply affects the goods and services market not directly, but indirectly: The rise in the money supply lowers the interest rate, causing investment to rise (assuming investment is not interest insensitive). As investment rises, the *AD* curve shifts rightward, affecting the goods and services market. In other words, there is an important intermediate market between the money market and the goods and services market in the Keynesian transmission mechanism. Thus, the money market can affect the goods and services market only indirectly.

3 A rise in the money supply brings about an excess supply of money in the money market that flows to the goods and services market, stimulating aggregate demand.

CHAPTER 14, PAGE 325

1 Keynesians believe that prices and wages are inflexible downward but not upward. They believe it is more likely that natural forces will move an economy out of an inflationary gap than out of a recessionary gap.

2 Suppose the economy is regulating itself out of a recessionary gap, but this is not known to Fed officials. Thinking that the economy is stuck in a recessionary gap, the Fed increases the money supply. When the money supply is felt in the goods and services market, the *AD* curve intersects the *SRAS* curve (that has been moving rightward, unbeknownst to officials) at a point that represents an inflationary gap. In other words, the Fed has moved the economy from a recessionary gap to an inflationary gap instead of from a recessionary gap to long-run equilibrium at the Natural Real GDP level.

3 Being stuck in a recessionary gap makes the case stronger, *ceteris paribus.* If the economy can't get itself out of a recessionary gap, then the case is stronger for the Fed to take action. However, this is not to say that expansionary monetary policy will work ideally. There may still be problems with the correct implementation of the policy.

CHAPTER 14, PAGE 328

1 The answer to this open-ended question depends on many factors. First, the answer depends on what the rule specifies because not all rules are alike. Second, it depends on the stability and predictability of velocity. For example, suppose the rule specifies that each year the money supply will rise by the average annual growth rate in Real GDP. If velocity is constant, this kind of rise will produce price stability. But if velocity is extremely volatile, changes in it might offset changes in the money supply, leading to deflation instead of price stability. For example, suppose Real GDP rises by 3 percent and the money supply increases by 3 percent, but velocity decreases by 3 percent. The change in velocity offsets the change in the money supply, leaving a net effect of a 3 percent rise in Real GDP. This, then, would lead to a 3 percent decline in the price level.

2 The inflation gap is the difference between the actual inflation rate and the target for inflation. The output gap is the percentage difference between actual Real GDP and its full-employment or natural level.

Chapter 15

CHAPTER 15, PAGE 339

1 A given Phillips curve identifies different combinations of inflation and unemployment; for example, 4 percent inflation with 5 percent unemployment and 2 percent inflation with 7 percent unemployment. For these combinations of inflation and unemployment to be permanent, there must be only one (downward-sloping) Phillips curve that never changes.

2 Sometimes there is and sometimes there isn't. Look at Exhibit 3. Unemployment is higher and inflation is lower in 1964 than in 1965; so there is a trade-off between these two years. But both unemployment and inflation are higher in 1980 than in 1979; that is, between these two years, there is no trade-off between inflation and unemployment.

3 Workers are fooled into thinking that the inflation rate is lower than it is. In other words, they underestimate the inflation rate and therefore overestimate the purchasing power of their wages.

CHAPTER 15, PAGE 347

1 No. PIP says that, under certain conditions, neither expansionary fiscal policy nor expansionary monetary policy will be able to increase Real GDP and lower the unemployment rate in the short run. The conditions are that the policy change is anticipated correctly, that individuals form their expectations rationally, and that wages and prices are flexible.

2 There is no difference. Given an unanticipated increase in aggregate demand, the economy moves from point 1 to 2 [in Exhibit 6(a)] in the short run and then to point 3. This occurs whether people are holding rational or adaptive expectations.

3 Yes. To illustrate, suppose the economy is initially in long-run equilibrium at point 1 in Exhibit 6(a). As a result of an unanticipated rise in aggregate demand, the economy will move from point 1 to point 2 and then to point 3. If there is a correctly anticipated rise in aggregate demand, the economy will simply move from point 1 to point 2, as in Exhibit 6(b). If there is an incorrectly anticipated rise in aggregate demand—and furthermore, the anticipated rise overestimates the actual rise—then the economy will move from point 1 to point 2′ in Exhibit 7. In conclusion, Real GDP may initially increase, remain constant, or decline depending on whether the rise in aggregate demand is unanticipated, anticipated correctly, or anticipated incorrectly (overestimated in our example), respectively.

CHAPTER 15, PAGE 349

1 Both. The relevant question is was the decline in the money supply caused by a change on the supply side of the economy? If the answer is no, then the decline in the money supply is consistent with a demand-induced business cycle. If the answer is yes, then it is consistent with a supply-induced (real) business cycle.

2 New Keynesians believe that prices and wages are somewhat inflexible; new classical economists believe that prices and wages are flexible.

Chapter 16

CHAPTER 16, PAGE 367

1 An increase in GDP does not constitute economic growth because GDP can rise from one year to the next if prices rise and output stays constant. Economic growth refers to an increase either in Real GDP or in per capita Real GDP. The key word is "real," as opposed to nominal (or money) GDP.

2 If the *AD* curve remains constant, a shift rightward in the *LRAS* curve (which is indicative of economic growth) will bring about falling prices. If the *AD* curve shifts to the right by the same amount that the *LRAS* curve shifts rightward, prices will remain stable. Only if the *AD* curve shifts to the right by more than the *LRAS* curve shifts to the right could we witness economic growth and rising prices.

3 Labor is more productive when more capital goods are available. Furthermore, a rise in labor productivity promotes economic growth (an increase in labor productivity is defined as an increase in output relative to total labor hours). So increases in capital investment can lead to increases in labor productivity and therefore to economic growth.

4 One worry concerns the costs of economic growth. Some persons argue that economic growth brings related "bads": pollution, crowded cities, heightened emphasis on material goods, more psychological problems, and so on. The other worry concerns the relationship between economic growth and the future availability of resources. Specifically, some persons argue that continued economic (and population) growth threatens the survival of the human race because it brings us closer and closer to the time when the world runs out of resources. Both these worries (and the arguments put forth relevant to these worries) have their critics.

CHAPTER 16, PAGE 369

1 If technology is endogenous, then we can promote advances in technology. Technology does not simply fall out of the sky; we can promote it, not simply wait for it to rain down on us. Thus we can actively promote economic growth through technology.

2 In new growth theory, ideas are important to economic growth. Countries that discover how to encourage and develop new and better ideas will likely grow faster than those that do not. New growth theory, in essence, places greater emphasis on the intangibles (e.g., ideas) in the growth process than on the tangibles (e.g., natural resources, capital, etc.).

3 Technology is important to economic growth, but technology does not simply fall from the sky. We can improve our chances of obtaining growth-enhancing technology the more we search for it, in much the same way that our chances of finding gold increase with the number of people prospecting for it.

Chapter 17

CHAPTER 17, PAGE 380

1 For the United States, 1X = 1/6Y or 1Y = 6X. For England, 1X = 2Y or 1Y = 1/2X. Let's focus on the opportunity cost of 1X in each country. In the United States, 1X = 1/6Y, and in Great Britain, 1X = 2Y. Terms of trade that are between these two end points would be favorable for the two countries. For example, 1X = 1Y is good for the United States because it would prefer to give up 1X and get 1Y in trade than to give up 1X and only get 1/6Y (without trade). Similarly, Great Britain would prefer to give up 1Y and get 1X in trade than to give up 1Y and get only 1/2X (without trade). Any terms of trade between 1X = 1/6Y and 1X = 2Y will be favorable to the two countries.

2 Yes, this is what the theory of comparative advantage shows. Exhibit 1 shows that the United States could produce more of both food and clothing than Japan. Still, the United States benefits from specialization and trade, as shown in Exhibit 2. In column 5 of this exhibit, the United States can consume 10 more units of food by specializing and trading.

3 No. Individuals' desire to buy low and sell high (earn a profit) pushes countries into producing and trading at a comparative advantage. Government officials do not collect

cost data and then issue orders to firms in the country to produce X, Y, or Z. We have not drawn the PPFs in this chapter and identified the cost differences between countries to show what countries actually do in the real world. We described things technically to simply show how countries benefit from specialization and trade.

CHAPTER 17, PAGE 389

1 Domestic producers benefit from tariffs because producers' surplus rises; domestic consumers lose because consumers' surplus falls. Also, government benefits in that it receives the tariff revenue. Moreover, consumers lose more than producers and government gains, so that there is a net loss resulting from tariffs.

2 Consumers' surplus falls more than producers' surplus rises.

3 With a tariff, the government receives tariff revenue. With a quota, it does not. In the latter case, the revenue that would have gone to government goes instead to the importers who get to satisfy the quota.

4 Infant or new domestic industries need to be protected from older, more established competitors until they are mature enough to compete on an equal basis. Tariffs and quotas provide these infant industries the time they need.

Chapter 18

CHAPTER 18, PAGE 401

1 A debit. When an American enters into a transaction in which he has to supply U.S. dollars in the foreign exchange market (to demand a foreign currency), the transaction is recorded as a debit.

2 We do not have enough information to answer this question. The merchandise trade balance is the difference between the value of *merchandise* exports and *merchandise* imports. The question gives only the value of exports and imports. *Exports* is a more inclusive term than merchandise exports. Exports include (a) merchandise exports, (b) services, and (c) income from U.S. assets abroad (see Exhibit 2). Similarly, *imports* is a more inclusive term than merchandise imports. It includes (a) merchandise imports, (b) services, and (c) income from foreign assets in the United States.

3 The merchandise trade balance includes fewer transactions than are included in the current account balance. The merchandise trade balance is the summary statistic for merchandise exports and merchandise imports. The current account balance is the summary statistic for exports of goods and services (which include merchandise exports), imports of goods and services (which include merchandise imports), and net unilateral transfers abroad (see Exhibit 2).

CHAPTER 18, PAGE 408

1 As the demand for dollars increases, the supply of pesos increases. For example, suppose someone in Mexico wants to buy something produced in the United States. The American wants to be paid in dollars, but the Mexican doesn't have any dollars; she has pesos. So she has to buy dollars with pesos; in other words, she has to supply pesos to buy dollars. Thus, as she demands more dollars, she will necessarily have to supply more pesos.

2 The dollar is said to have appreciated (against the peso) when it takes more pesos to buy a dollar and fewer dollars to buy a peso. For this to occur, either the demand for dollars must increase (i.e., the supply of pesos increases) or the supply of dollars must decrease (i.e., the demand for pesos decreases). To see this graphically, look at Exhibit 5(b). The only way for the peso price per dollar to rise (on the vertical axis) is for either the demand curve for dollars to shift to the right or the supply curve of dollars to shift to the left. Each of these occurrences is mirrored in the market for pesos in part (a) of the exhibit.

3 *Ceteris paribus,* the dollar will depreciate relative to the franc. As incomes for Americans rise, the demand for Swiss goods rises. This increases the demand for francs and the supply of dollars on the foreign exchange market. In turn, this leads to a depreciated dollar and an appreciated franc.

4 The purchasing power parity (PPP) theory states that the exchange rate between any two currencies will adjust to reflect changes in the relative price levels of the two countries. For example, suppose the U.S. price level rises 5 percent and Mexico's price level remains constant. According to the PPP theory, the U.S. dollar will depreciate 5 percent relative to the Mexican peso.

CHAPTER 18, PAGE 414

1 The terms *overvalued* and *undervalued* refer to the equilibrium exchange rate: the exchange rate at which the quantity demanded and quantity supplied of a currency are the same in the foreign exchange market. Let's suppose the equilibrium exchange rate is 0.10 USD = 1 MXN. This is the same as saying that 10 pesos = \$1. If the exchange rate is fixed at 0.12 USD = 1 MXN (which is the same as 8.33 pesos = \$1), the peso is overvalued and the dollar is undervalued. Specifically, a currency is overvalued if 1 unit of it fetches more of another currency than it would in equilibrium; a currency is undervalued if 1 unit of it fetches less of another currency than it would in equilibrium. In equilibrium, 1 peso would fetch \$0.10, and at the current exchange rate it fetches 0.12 dollars; so the peso is overvalued. In equilibrium, \$1 would fetch 10 pesos, and at the current exchange rate, it fetches only 8.33 pesos; so the dollar is undervalued.

2 An overvalued dollar means some other currency, say the Japanese yen, is undervalued. An overvalued dollar makes U.S. goods more expensive for the Japanese; so they buy fewer U.S. goods, thus reducing U.S. exports. On the other hand, an undervalued yen makes Japanese goods cheaper for Americans; so they buy more Japanese goods, and the U.S. imports more. Thus, an overvalued dollar reduces U.S. exports and raises U.S. imports.

3 a. Dollar is overvalued.

b. Dollar is undervalued.

c. Dollar is undervalued.

4 The devaluation of a country's currency makes it cheaper for foreigners to buy the country's products.

CHAPTER 18, PAGE 418

1 An optimal currency area is a geographic area in which exchange rates can be fixed or a common currency used without sacrificing any domestic economic goals.

2 As the demand for good Y falls, the unemployment rate in country 2 will rise. This increase in the unemployment rate is likely to be temporary, though. The increased demand for good X (produced by country 1) will increase the demand for country 1's currency, leading to an appreciation in country 1's currency and a depreciation in country 2's currency. Country 1's good (good X) will become more expensive for the residents of country 2, and they will buy less. Country 2's good (good Y) will become less expensive for the residents of country 1, and they will buy more. As a result of the additional purchases of good Y, country 2's unemployment rate will begin to decline.

3 Labor mobility is very important to determining whether or not an area is an optimal currency area. If there is little or no labor mobility, an area is not likely to be an optimal currency area. If there is labor mobility, an area is likely to be an optimal currency area.

Chapter 19

CHAPTER 19, PAGE 431

1 As some explain it, the end of the Cold War resulted in turning two different worlds (the capitalist and communist worlds) into one. It resulted in a thawing of not only political but economic relations between former enemies. You might not trade with your enemy, but once that person or country is no longer your enemy, you don't feel the same need to exclude him or it from your political and economic life.

2 Globalization is the phenomenon by which individuals and businesses in any part of the world are much more affected than before by events elsewhere in the world; it is the growing integration of the national economies of the world to the degree that we may be witnessing the emergence and operation of a single worldwide economy.

3 Advancing technology can reduce both transportation and communication costs, making it less costly to trade with people around the world.

CHAPTER 19, PAGE 436

1 Benefits identified in the section include (a) benefits from increased international trade, (b) higher income per person, (c) lower prices for goods, (d) greater product variety, and (e) increased productivity and innovation.

2 Costs identified in the section include (a) increased income inequality, (b) offshoring, and (c) more power for big corporations.

CHAPTER 19, PAGE 440

1 In country A, there is an economic expansion, and real income in the country rises. As a result, residents of the country buy more imports from country B. In country B, exports rise relative to imports, thus increasing net exports. As net exports in country B rise, the *AD* curve for country B shifts to the right, increasing Real GDP.

2 If the dollar appreciates, the Japanese yen depreciates. U.S. products become more expensive for the Japanese, and Japanese products become cheaper for Americans. U.S. imports will rise, U.S. exports will fall, and consequently U.S. net exports will fall. As a result, the *AD* curve in the United States will shift leftward, pushing down Real GDP.

CHAPTER 19, PAGE 442

1 Foreign input prices can change directly as a result of supply conditions in the foreign country, or they can change indirectly as a result of a change in the exchange rate. In either case, as foreign input prices rise—either directly or as a result of a depreciated dollar—the U.S. *SRAS* curve shifts leftward. If foreign input prices fall—either directly or as a result of an appreciated dollar—the *SRAS* curve shifts rightward.

2 The higher real interest rates in the United States attract capital to the United States, increasing the demand for the dollar. As a result, the dollar appreciates and the yen depreciates. An appreciated dollar shifts the U.S. *AD* curve leftward and the U.S. *SRAS* curve rightward. The *AD* curve shifts leftward by more than the *SRAS* curve shifts rightward; so the price level falls.

CHAPTER 19, PAGE 446

1 When the money supply is raised, the *AD* curve shifts rightward, pushing up Real GDP. Also, as a result of the increased money supply, interest rates may decline in the short run. This promotes U.S. capital outflow and a depreciated dollar. As a result of the depreciated dollar, imports become more expensive for Americans, and U.S. exports become cheaper for foreigners. Imports fall and exports rise, thereby increasing net exports and *again* shifting the *AD* curve to the right. Real GDP rises.

2 Expansionary fiscal policy pushes the *AD* curve rightward and (under certain conditions) raises Real GDP. If the expansionary fiscal policy causes a deficit, then the government will have to borrow to finance the deficit, and interest rates will be pushed upward. As a result of the higher interest rates, foreign capital inflows and dollar appreciation increase, thus pushing the *AD* curve leftward and the *SRAS* curve rightward.

Chapter 20

CHAPTER 20, PAGE 460

1 30.

2 Stocks are purchased either for the dividends that the stocks may pay, the expected gain in price (of the stock), or both.

3 The yield of a stock is the dividend per share (of the stock) divided by the closing price per share.

4 A P/E ratio of 23 means that the stock is selling for a share price that is 23 times its earnings per share.

CHAPTER 20, PAGE 465

1 A bond is an IOU or a promise to pay. The issuer of a bond is borrowing funds and promising to pay back those funds (with interest) at a later date.

2 $0.07x = \$400$, so $x = \$400/0.07$, or $5,714.29.

3 $1,000/$9,500 = 10.53 percent.

4 Municipal bonds are issued by state and local governments, and a Treasury bond is issued by the federal government.

CHAPTER 20, PAGE 468

1 A futures contract is a contract in which the seller agrees to provide a good to the buyer on a specified future date at an agreed-on price.

2 You can buy a call option, which sells for a fraction of the cost of the stock. A call option gives the owner of the option the right to buy shares of a stock at a specified price within the time limits of the contract.

3 A put option gives the owner the right, but not the obligation, to *sell* (rather than buy, as in a call option) shares of a stock at a strike price during some period of time.

Web Chapter 21

CHAPTER 21, PAGE 476

1 A farmer protects herself through the futures market. Specifically, she enters into a futures contract with someone who will guarantee to take delivery of her foodstuff (in the future) for a stated price. Then, if the price goes up or down between the present and the future, the farmer does not have to worry. She has locked in the price of her foodstuff.

2 If the farmer faces an inelastic demand curve, the order of preference would be (b), (a), (c). That is, he prefers (b) to (a) and (a) to (c). In (b), if all farmers except himself have bad weather, then the market supply curve of the individual farmer's product shifts to the left, bringing about a higher price. But the individual farmer's supply curve doesn't shift to the left; it stays where it is. Thus, the individual farmer sells the same amount of output at the higher price. Consequently, his total revenue rises. In (a), both the market supply curve and the individual farmer's supply curve shift left; so the farmer has less to sell at a higher price. Again, if the demand is inelastic, the individual farmer will increase his total revenue but not as much as in (b), where the individual farmer's output did not fall. Finally, in (c), the market supply curve shifts to the right, lowering price. If demand is inelastic, this lowers total revenue.

3 Increased productivity will lead to higher total revenue when demand is elastic. To illustrate, increased productivity shifts the supply curve to the right. This lowers price. If demand is elastic, then the percentage rise in quantity sold is greater than the percentage fall in price; therefore, total revenue rises. In summary, increased productivity leads to higher total revenue when demand is elastic.

CHAPTER 21, PAGE 480

1 Because the deficiency payment is the difference between the target price and the market price, the answer depends on the market price. If the market price is, say, $4, and the target price is $7, then the deficiency payment is $3.

2 A farmer pledges a certain number of bushels of foodstuff to obtain a loan—say, 500 bushels. He receives a loan equal to the number of bushels times the designated loan rate per bushel. For example, if the loan rate is $2 per bushel and 500 bushels are pledged, then the loan is $1,000. The farmer either pays back the loan with interest or keeps the loan and forfeits the bushels. Which course of action the farmer takes depends on the market price of the crop. If the market price is higher than the loan rate, the farmer pays back the loan and sells the crop. If the market price is less than the loan rate, the farmer forfeits the crop. A nonrecourse loan guarantees that the farmer will not receive less than the loan rate for each bushel of the crop.

3 The effects of a price support are (a) a surplus, (b) fewer exchanges (less bought by private citizens), (c) higher prices paid by consumers of the crop (on which the support exists), and (d) government purchase and storage of the surplus crop (for which taxpayers pay).

GLOSSARY

Absolute (Money) Price The price of a good in money terms.

Absolute Real Economic Growth An increase in Real GDP from one period to the next.

Activists Persons who argue that monetary and fiscal policies should be deliberately used to smooth out the business cycle.

Adaptive Expectations Expectations that individuals form from past experience and modify slowly as the present and the future become the past (as time passes).

Aggregate Demand The quantity demanded of all goods and services (Real GDP) at different price levels, *ceteris paribus*. A curve that shows the quantity demanded of all goods and services (Real GDP) at different price levels, *ceteris paribus*.

Aggregate Supply The quantity supplied of all goods and services (Real GDP) at different price levels, *ceteris paribus*.

Appreciation An increase in the value of one currency relative to other currencies.

Automatic Fiscal Policy Changes in government expenditures and/or taxes that occur automatically without (additional) congressional action.

Autonomous Consumption The part of consumption that is independent of disposable income.

Bad Anything from which individuals receive disutility or dissatisfaction.

Balance of Payments A periodic (usually annual) statement of the money value of all transactions between residents of one country and the residents of all other countries.

Balanced Budget The budget when government expenditures equal tax revenues.

Barter Exchanging goods and services for other goods and services without the use of money.

Base Year The year chosen as a point of reference or basis of comparison for prices in other years; a benchmark year.

Board of Governors The governing body of the Federal Reserve System.

Bond An IOU, or promise to pay.

Budget Deficit The deficit when government expenditures are greater than tax revenues.

Budget Surplus The surplus when tax revenues are greater than government expenditures.

Capital Produced goods that can be used as inputs for further production, such as factories, machinery, tools, computers, and buildings.

Capital Account The account in the balance of payments that includes all payments related to the purchase and sale of assets and to borrowing and lending activities. Components include outflow of U.S. capital and inflow of foreign capital.

Capital Account Balance The summary statistic for the outflow of U.S. capital equal to the difference between the outflow of U.S. capital and the inflow of foreign capital.

Capital Consumption Allowance (Depreciation) The estimated amount of capital goods used up in production through natural wear, obsolescence, and accidental destruction.

Cash Leakage Occurs when funds are held as currency instead of deposited into a checking account.

Ceteris Paribus A Latin term meaning "all other things constant" or "nothing else changes."

Checkable Deposits Deposits on which checks can be written.

Closed Economy An economy that does not trade goods and services with other countries.

Comparative Advantage The situation where someone or a country can produce a good at lower opportunity cost than someone else or another country can.

Complements Two goods that are used jointly in consumption. If two goods are complements, the demand for one rises as the price of the other falls (or the demand for one falls as the price of the other rises).

Complete Crowding Out A decrease in one or more components of private spending that completely offsets the increase in government spending.

Consumer Price Index (CPI) A widely cited index number for the price level; the weighted average of prices of a specific set of goods and services purchased by a typical household.

Consumers' Surplus (CS) The difference between the maximum price a buyer is willing and able to pay for a good or service and the price actually paid. CS = Maximum buying price – Price paid

Consumption The sum of spending on durable goods, nondurable goods, and services.

Consumption Function The relationship between consumption and disposable income. In the consumption function used in this text, consumption is directly related to disposable income and is positive even at zero disposable income: $C = C_0 + (MPC)(Y_d)$.

Continued Inflation A continued increase in the price level.

Contractionary Fiscal Policy Decreases in government expenditures and/or increases in taxes to achieve economic goals.

Contractionary Monetary Policy The policy by which the Fed decreases the money supply.

Credit In the balance of payments, any transaction that creates a demand for the country's currency in the foreign exchange market.

Crowding Out The decrease in private expenditures that occurs as a consequence of increased government spending or the financing needs of a budget deficit.

Currency Coins and paper money.

Current Account The account in the balance of payments that includes all payments related to the purchase and sale of goods and services. Components of the account include exports, imports, and net unilateral transfers abroad.

Current Account Balance In the balance of payments, the summary statistic for exports of goods and services, imports of goods and services, and net unilateral transfers abroad.

Cyclical Deficit The part of the budget deficit that is a result of a downturn in economic activity.

Cyclical Unemployment Rate The difference between the unemployment rate and the natural unemployment rate.

Deadweight Loss The loss to society of not producing the competitive, or supply-and-demand-determined, level of output.

Debit In the balance of payments, any transaction that supplies the country's currency in the foreign exchange market.

Decisions at the Margin Decision making characterized by weighing the additional (marginal) benefits of a change against the additional (marginal) costs of a change with respect to current conditions.

Demand The willingness and ability of buyers to purchase different quantities of a good at different prices during a specific time period.

Demand Curve The graphical representation of the law of demand.

Demand for Money (Balances) Represents the inverse relationship between the quantity demanded of money balances and the price of holding money balances.

Demand Schedule The numerical tabulation of the quantity demanded of a good at different prices. A demand schedule is the numerical representation of the law of demand.

Depreciation A decrease in the value of one currency relative to other currencies.

Devaluation A government action that changes the exchange rate by lowering the official price of a currency.

Discount Rate The interest rate the Fed charges depository institutions that borrow reserves from it.

Discretionary Fiscal Policy Deliberate changes of government expenditures and/or taxes to achieve economic goals.

Disequilibrium A state of either surplus or shortage in a market.

Disequilibrium Price A price other than equilibrium price. A price at which quantity demanded does not equal quantity supplied.

Disposable Income The portion of personal income that can be used for consumption or saving. It is equal to personal income minus personal taxes (especially income taxes).

Disutility The dissatisfaction one receives from a bad.

Dividend A share of the profits of a corporation distributed to stockholders.

Double Coincidence of Wants In a barter economy, a requirement that must be met before a trade can be made. It specifies that a trader must find another trader who is willing to trade what the first trader wants and at the same time wants what the first trader has.

Double Counting Counting a good more than once when computing GDP.

Dow Jones Industrial Average (DJIA) The most popular, widely cited indicator of day-to-day stock market activity. The DJIA is a weighted average of 30 widely traded stocks on the New York Stock Exchange.

Dumping The sale of goods abroad at a price below their cost and below the price charged in the domestic market.

Economic Growth Increases in Real GDP.

Economics The science of scarcity; the science of how individuals and societies deal with the fact that wants are greater than the limited resources available to satisfy those wants.

Efficiency Exists when marginal benefits equal marginal costs.

Efficiency Wage Models These models hold that it is sometimes in the best interest of business firms to pay their employees higher-than-equilibrium wage rates.

Employment Rate The percentage of the civilian noninstitutional population that is employed: Employment rate = Number of employed persons/Civilian noninstitutional population.

Entrepreneurship The particular talent that some people have for organizing the resources of land, labor, and capital to produce goods, seek new business opportunities, and develop new ways of doing things.

Equation of Exchange An identity stating that the money supply times velocity must be equal to the price level times Real GDP.

Equilibrium Equilibrium means "at rest." Equilibrium in a market is the price quantity combination from which there is no tendency for buyers or sellers to move away. Graphically, equilibrium is the intersection point of the supply and demand curves.

Equilibrium Price (Market-Clearing Price) The price at which quantity demanded of the good equals quantity supplied.

Equilibrium Quantity The quantity that corresponds to equilibrium price. The quantity at which the amount of the good that buyers are willing and able to buy equals the amount that sellers are willing and able to sell, and both equal the amount actually bought and sold.

Ex Ante Phrase that means "before," as in before a trade.

Excess Reserves Any reserves held beyond the required amount. The difference between (total) reserves and required reserves.

Exchange (Trade) The process of giving up one thing for something else.

Exchange Rate The price of one currency in terms of another currency.

Expansionary Fiscal Policy Increases in government expenditures and/or decreases in taxes to achieve particular economic goals.

Expansionary Monetary Policy The policy by which the Fed increases the money supply.

Expectations Effect The change in the interest rate due to a change in the expected inflation rate.

Exports Total foreign spending on domestic (U.S.) goods.

Ex Post Phrase that means "after," as in after a trade.

Face Value (Par Value) Dollar amount specified on a bond, the total amount the issuer of the bond will repay to the buyer of the bond.

Federal Funds Market A market where banks lend reserves to one another, usually for short periods.

Federal Funds Rate The interest rate in the federal funds market; the interest rate banks charge one another to borrow reserves.

Federal Open Market Committee (FOMC) The 12-member policy-making group within the Fed. The committee has the authority to conduct open market operations.

Federal Reserve Notes Paper money issued by the Fed.

Federal Reserve System (the Fed) The central bank of the United States.

Final Good A good in the hands of its final user.

Fine-Tuning The (usually frequent) use of monetary and fiscal policies to counteract even small undesirable movements in economic activity.

Fiscal Policy Changes in government expenditures and/or taxes to achieve macroeconomic goals, such as low unemployment, stable prices, and economic growth.

Fixed Exchange Rate System The system whereby a nation's currency is set at a fixed rate relative to all other currencies, and central banks intervene in the foreign exchange market to maintain the fixed rate.

Fixed Investment Business purchases of capital goods, such as machinery and factories, and purchases of new residential housing.

Flexible Exchange Rate System The system whereby exchange rates are determined by the forces of supply and demand for a currency.

Foreign Exchange Market The market in which currencies of different countries are exchanged.

Fractional Reserve Banking A banking arrangement that allows banks to hold reserves equal to only a fraction of their deposit liabilities.

Frictional Unemployment Unemployment due to the natural "frictions" of the economy, which is caused by changing market conditions and is represented by qualified individuals with transferable skills who change jobs.

Friedman Natural Rate Theory The idea that, in the long run, unemployment is at its natural rate. Within the Phillips curve framework, the natural rate theory specifies that there is a long-run Phillips curve, which is vertical at the natural rate of unemployment.

Full Employment The condition that exists when the unemployment rate is equal to the natural unemployment rate.

Futures Contract An agreement to buy or sell a specific amount of something (commodity, currency, financial instrument) at an agreed-on price on a stipulated future date.

Globalization A phenomenon by which economic agents in any given part of the world are more affected by events elsewhere in the world than before; the growing integration of the national economies of the world to the degree that we may be witnessing the emergence and operation of a single worldwide economy.

Good Anything from which individuals receive utility or satisfaction.

Government Purchases Federal, state, and local government purchases of goods and services and gross investment in highways, bridges, and so on.

Government Transfer Payments Payments to persons that are not made in return for goods and services currently supplied.

Gross Domestic Product (GDP) The total market value of all final goods and services produced annually within a country's borders.

Imports Total domestic (U.S.) spending on foreign goods.

Income Effect The change in the interest rate due to a change in Real GDP.

Incomplete Crowding Out The decrease in one or more components of private spending that only partially offsets the increase in government spending.

Industrial Policy A deliberate policy by which government aids industries that are the most likely to be successful in the world marketplace—that is, waters the green spots.

Inferior Good A good the demand for which falls (rises) as income rises (falls).

Inflation An increase in the price level.

Inflationary Gap The condition in which the Real GDP that the economy is producing is greater than the Natural Real GDP and the unemployment rate is less than the natural unemployment rate.

Inflation Targeting Targeting that requires the Fed to keep the inflation rate near a predetermined level.

Initial Public Offering (IPO) A company's first offering of stock to the public.

Interest Rate Effect The changes in household and business buying as the interest rate changes (which, in turn, is a reflection of a change in the demand for or supply of credit brought on by price level changes).

Intermediate Good A good that is an input in the production of a final good.

International Monetary Fund (IMF) An international organization created to oversee the international monetary system. The IMF does not control the world's money supply, but it does hold currency reserves for member nations and make loans to central banks.

International Trade Effect The change in foreign sector spending as the price level changes.

Inventory Investment Changes in the stock of unsold goods.

Investment The sum of all purchases of newly produced capital goods, changes in business inventories, and purchases of new residential housing.

Investment Bank A firm that acts as an intermediary between the company that issues the stock and the public that wishes to buy the stock.

J-Curve The curve that shows a short-run worsening in net exports after a currency depreciation, followed by an improvement.

Labor The physical and mental talents people contribute to the production process.

Labor Force Participation Rate The percentage of the civilian noninstitutional population that is in the civilian labor force. Labor force participation rate = Civilian labor force/Civilian noninstitutional population.

Laffer Curve The curve, named after Arthur Laffer, that shows the relationship between tax rates and tax revenues. According to the Laffer curve, as tax rates rise from zero, tax revenues rise, reach a maximum at some point, and then fall with further increases in tax rates.

Laissez-Faire A public policy of not interfering with market activities in the economy.

Land All natural resources, such as minerals, forests, water, and unimproved land.

Law of Demand As the price of a good rises, the quantity demanded of the good falls, and as the price of a good falls, the quantity demanded of the good rises, *ceteris paribus.*

Law of Increasing Opportunity Costs As more of a good is produced, the opportunity costs of producing that good increase.

Law of Supply As the price of a good rises, the quantity supplied of the good rises, and as the price of a good falls, the quantity supplied of the good falls, *ceteris paribus.*

Liquidity Effect The change in the interest rate due to a change in the supply of loanable funds.

Liquidity Trap The horizontal portion of the demand curve for money.

Long-Run Aggregate Supply (*LRAS*) Curve The *LRAS* curve is a vertical line at the level of Natural Real GDP. It represents the output the economy produces when wages and prices have adjusted to their (final) equilibrium levels and neither producers nor workers have any relevant misperceptions.

Long-Run Equilibrium The condition that exists in the economy when wages and prices have adjusted to their (final) equilibrium levels and workers do not have any relevant misperceptions. Graphically, long-run equilibrium occurs at the intersection of the *AD* and *LRAS* curves.

M1 Currency held outside banks plus checkable deposits plus traveler's checks.

M2 M1 plus savings deposits (including money market deposit accounts) plus small-denomination time deposits plus (retail) money market mutual funds.

Macroeconomics The branch of economics that deals with human behavior and choices as they relate to highly aggregate markets (e.g., the goods and services market) or the entire economy.

Managed Float A managed flexible exchange rate system, under which nations now and then intervene to adjust their official reserve holdings to moderate major swings in exchange rates.

Marginal Benefits Additional benefits. The benefits connected to consuming an additional unit of a good or undertaking one more unit of an activity.

Marginal Costs Additional costs. The costs connected to consuming an additional unit of a good or undertaking one more unit of an activity.

Marginal (Income) Tax Rate The change in a person's tax payment divided by the change in his or her taxable income: ΔTax payment/ΔTaxable income.

Marginal Propensity to Consume (*MPC*) The ratio of the change in consumption to the change in disposable income: $MPC = \Delta C/\Delta Y_d$.

Marginal Propensity to Save (*MPS*) The ratio of the change in saving to the change in disposable income: $MPS = \Delta S/\Delta Y_d$.

Market Any place people come together to trade.

Medium of Exchange A function of money, anything that is generally acceptable in exchange for goods and services.

Merchandise Trade Balance The difference between the value of merchandise exports and the value of merchandise imports.

Merchandise Trade Deficit The situation when the value of merchandise exports is less than the value of merchandise imports.

Merchandise Trade Surplus The situation when the value of merchandise exports is greater than the value of merchandise imports.

Microeconomics The branch of economics that deals with human behavior and choices as they relate to relatively small units—an individual, a firm, an industry, a single market.

Monetary Policy Changes in the money supply, or in the rate of change of the money supply, to achieve particular macroeconomic goals.

Monetary Wealth The value of a person's monetary assets. Wealth, as distinguished from monetary wealth, refers to the value of all assets owned, both monetary and nonmonetary. In short, a person's wealth equals his or her monetary wealth (e.g., $1,000 cash) plus nonmonetary wealth (e.g., a car or a house).

Money Any good that is widely accepted for purposes of exchange and in the repayment of debt.

Money Market Deposit Account An interest-earning account at a bank or thrift institution. Usually, a minimum balance is required for an MMDA, and most offer limited check-writing privileges.

Money Market Mutual Fund An interest-earning account at a mutual fund company. Usually, a minimum balance is required for an MMMF account. Most MMMF accounts offer limited check-writing privileges. Only retail MMMFs are part of M2.

Multiplier The number that is multiplied by the change in autonomous spending to obtain the overall change in total spending. The multiplier (m) is equal to $1/(1 - MPC)$. If the economy is operating below Natural Real GDP, then the multiplier turns out to be the number that is multiplied by the change in autonomous spending to obtain the change in Real GDP.

National Income Total income earned by U.S. citizens and businesses, no matter where they reside or are located. National income is the sum of the payments to resources (land, labor, capital, and entrepreneurship). National income = Compensation of employees + Proprietors' income + Corporate profits + Rental income of persons + Net interest.

Natural Real GDP The Real GDP that is produced at the natural unemployment rate. The Real GDP that is produced when the economy is in long-run equilibrium.

Natural Unemployment Unemployment caused by frictional and structural factors in the economy. Natural unemployment rate = Frictional unemployment rate + Structural unemployment rate.

Net Domestic Product (NDP) GDP minus the capital consumption allowance.

Net Exports Exports minus imports.

Neutral Good A good the demand for which does not change as income rises or falls.

Nominal Income The current-dollar amount of a person's income.

Nonactivists Persons who argue against the deliberate use of discretionary fiscal and monetary policies. They believe in a permanent, stable, rule-oriented monetary and fiscal framework.

Normal Good A good the demand for which rises (falls) as income rises (falls).

Normative Economics The study of "what should be" in economic matters.

Offshoring Work done for a company by persons other than the original company's employees in a country other than the one in which the company is located.

One-Shot Inflation A one-time increase in the price level. An increase in the price level that does not continue.

Open Economy An economy that trades goods and services with other countries.

Open Market Operations The buying and selling of government securities by the Fed.

Open Market Purchase The buying of government securities by the Fed.

Open Market Sale The selling of government securities by the Fed.

Opportunity Cost The most highly valued opportunity or alternative forfeited when a choice is made.

Optimal Currency Area A geographic area in which exchange rates can be fixed or a common currency used without sacrificing domestic economic goals, such as low unemployment.

Option A contract that gives the owner the right, but not the obligation, to buy or sell shares of a stock at a specified price on or before a specified date.

Overvalued A currency is overvalued if its price in terms of other currencies is above the equilibrium price.

Own Price The price of a good. For example, if the price of oranges is $1, this is its own price.

Per Capita Real Economic Growth An increase from one period to the next in per capita Real GDP, which is Real GDP divided by population.

Personal Income The amount of income that individuals actually receive. It is equal to national income minus undistributed corporate profits, social insurance taxes, and corporate profits taxes, plus transfer payments.

Phillips Curve A curve that originally showed the relationship between wage inflation and unemployment and that now more often shows the relationship between price inflation and unemployment.

Policy Ineffectiveness Proposition (PIP) If (1) a policy change is correctly anticipated, (2) individuals form their expectations rationally, and (3) wages and prices are flexible, then neither fiscal policy nor monetary policy is effective at meeting macroeconomic goals.

Positive Economics The study of "what is" in economic matters.

Price Ceiling A government-mandated maximum price above which legal trades cannot be made.

Price Floor A government-mandated minimum price below which legal trades cannot be made.

Price Index A measure of the price level.

Price Level A weighted average of the prices of all good and services.

Price Support A government-mandated minimum price for agricultural products; an example of a price floor.

Price-Level Effect The change in the interest rate due to a change in the price level.

Producers' (Sellers') Surplus (PS) The difference between the price sellers receive for a good and the minimum or lowest price for which they would have sold the good. *PS* = Price received – Minimum selling price

Production Possibilities Frontier (PPF) Represents the possible combinations of two goods that can be produced in a certain period of time under the conditions of a given state of technology and fully employed resources.

Productive Inefficiency The condition where less than the maximum output is produced with given resources and technology. Productive inefficiency implies that more of one good can be produced without any less of another good being produced.

Progressive Income Tax An income tax system in which one's tax rate rises as one's taxable income rises (up to some point).

Proportional Income Tax An income tax system in which a person's tax rate is the same no matter what his or her taxable income is.

Public Debt The total amount that the federal government owes its creditors.

Purchasing Power The quantity of goods and services that can be purchased with a unit of money. Purchasing power and the price level are inversely related: As the price level goes up (down), purchasing power goes down (up).

Purchasing Power Parity (PPP) Theory Theory stating that exchange rates between any two currencies will adjust to reflect changes in the relative price levels of the two countries.

Quota A legal limit on the amount of a good that may be imported.

Rational Expectations Expectations that individuals form based on past experience and on their predictions about the effects of present and future policy actions and events.

Rationing Device A means for deciding who gets what of available resources and goods.

Real Balance Effect The change in the purchasing power of dollar-denominated assets that results from a change in the price level.

Real GDP The value of the entire output produced annually within a country's borders, adjusted for price changes.

Real Income Nominal income adjusted for price changes.

Recessionary Gap The condition in which the Real GDP that the economy is producing is less than the Natural Real GDP and the unemployment rate is greater than the natural unemployment rate.

Regressive Income Tax An income tax system in which a person's tax rate declines as his or her taxable income rises.

Relative Price The price of a good in terms of another good.

Required Reserve Ratio (*r*) A percentage of each dollar deposited that must be held on reserve (at the Fed or in the bank's vault).

Required Reserves The minimum amount of reserves a bank must hold against its checkable deposits as mandated by the Fed.

Reserve Requirement The rule that specifies the amount of reserves a bank must hold to back up deposits.

Reserves The sum of bank deposits at the Fed and vault cash.

Revaluation A government action that changes the exchange rate by raising the official price of a currency.

Savings Deposit An interest-earning account at a commercial bank or thrift institution. Normally, checks cannot be written on savings deposits, and the funds in a savings deposit can be withdrawn (at any time) without a penalty payment.

Say's Law Supply creates its own demand. Production creates demand sufficient to purchase all the goods and services produced.

Scarcity The condition in which our wants are greater than the limited resources available to satisfy those wants.

Shortage (Excess Demand) A condition in which quantity demanded is greater than quantity supplied. Shortages occur only at prices below equilibrium price.

Short-Run Aggregate Supply (*SRAS*) Curve A curve that shows the quantity supplied of all goods and services (Real GDP) at different price levels, *ceteris paribus.*

Short-Run Equilibrium The condition that exists in the economy when the quantity demanded of Real GDP equals the (short-run) quantity supplied of Real GDP. This condition is met where the aggregate demand curve intersects the short-run aggregate supply curve.

Simple Deposit Multiplier The reciprocal of the required reserve ratio, $1/r$.

Simple Quantity Theory of Money The theory assuming that velocity (V) and Real GDP (Q) are constant and predicting that changes in the money supply (M) lead to strictly proportional changes in the price level (P).

Special Drawing Right (SDR) An international money, created by the IMF, in the form of bookkeeping entries; like gold and currencies, it can be used by nations to settle international accounts.

Stagflation The simultaneous occurrence of high rates of inflation and unemployment.

Stock A claim on the assets of a corporation that gives the purchaser a share of the corporation.

Store of Value A function of money, the ability of an item to hold value over time.

Structural Deficit The part of the budget deficit that would exist even if the economy were operating at full employment.

Structural Unemployment Unemployment due to structural changes in the economy that eliminate some jobs and create other jobs for which the unemployed are unqualified.

Subsidy A monetary payment by government to a producer of a good or service.

Substitutes Two goods that satisfy similar needs or desires. If two goods are substitutes, the demand for one rises as the price of the other rises (or the demand for one falls as the price of the other falls).

Supply The willingness and ability of sellers to produce and offer to sell different quantities of a good at different prices during a specific time period.

Supply Curve The graphical representation of the law of supply.

Supply Schedule The numerical tabulation of the quantity supplied of a good at different prices. A supply schedule is the numerical representation of the law of supply.

Surplus (Excess Supply) A condition in which quantity supplied is greater than quantity demanded. Surpluses occur only at prices above equilibrium price.

T-Account A simplified balance sheet that shows the changes in a bank's assets and liabilities.

Target Price A guaranteed price; if the market price is below the target price, the farmer receives a deficiency payment equal to the difference between the market price and the target price.

Tariff A tax on imports.

Tax Base In terms of income taxes, the total amount of taxable income. Tax revenue = Tax base × (average) Tax rate.

Technology The body of skills and knowledge concerning the use of resources in production. An advance in technology commonly refers to the ability to produce more output with a fixed amount of resources or the ability to produce the same output with fewer resources.

Term Auction Facility (TAF) Program Under the Term Auction Facility (TAF) Program, the Federal Reserve auctions funds to depository institutions. Each TAF auction is for a fixed amount, with the TAF rate determined by the auction process (subject to a minimum bid rate).

Terms of Trade How much of one thing is given up for how much of something else.

Theory An abstract representation of the real world designed with the intent to better understand the world.

Tie-In Sale A sale whereby one good can be purchased only if another good is also purchased.

Time Deposit An interest-earning deposit with a specified maturity date. Time deposits are subject to penalties for early withdrawal. Small-denomination time deposits are deposits of less than $100,000.

Total Surplus (*TS*) The sum of consumers' surplus and producers' surplus: $TS = CS + PS$.

Transaction Costs The costs associated with the time and effort needed to search out, negotiate, and consummate an exchange.

Transmission Mechanism The routes, or channels, traveled by the ripple effects that the money market creates and that affect the goods and services market (represented by the aggregate demand and aggregate supply curves in the *AD-AS* framework).

U.S. Treasury Securities Bonds and bond-like securities issued by the U.S. Treasury when it borrows.

Undervalued A currency is undervalued if its price in terms of other currencies is below the equilibrium price.

Unemployment Rate The percentage of the civilian force that is unemployed: Unemployment rate = Number of unemployed persons/Civilian labor force.

Unit of Account A function of money, a common measure in which relative values are expressed.

Value Added The dollar value contributed to a final good at each stage of production.

Velocity The average number of times a dollar is spent to buy final goods and services in a year.

Wealth The value of all assets owned, both monetary and nonmonetary.

Yield Equal to the annual coupon payment divided by the price paid for the bond.

INDEX

D

E

N

O

P

T